AKEHURST'S MODERN INTRODUCTION TO INTERNATIONAL LAW

'Professor Malanczuk has written a new edition of Michael Akehurst's textbook which maintains its high traditions of clarity, precision and coherence. The new edition, more detailed and more widely referenced, will appeal to a wider audience of students than its predecessor, while still satisfying the needs of those seeking an accessible introduction to International Law, whether lawyers or not.'

Colin Warbrick, *University of Durham*

First published in 1970, *A Modern Introduction to International Law* rapidly established itself as the most widely used and successful textbook in its field. It covers a variety of topics from diplomatic immunity to human rights and from recognition of governments to war crimes. This new edition is now completely revised and updated to take account of many new developments and includes additional chapters on human rights, state responsibility, the environment and the economy.

Akehurst's Modern Introduction to International Law is ideal for students concerned with the relationship between international politics and international law and provides clear and authoritative guidance through a complex and ever changing field of study.

Peter Malanczuk is Professor of International Law at the Law Faculty of Erasmus University Rotterdam.

AKEHURST'S MODERN INTRODUCTION TO INTERNATIONAL LAW

Seventh revised edition

Peter Malanczuk

Assessor iur., Dr. iur.,
Professor of International Law, Law Faculty, Erasmus University
Rotterdam,
Former Legal Assistant to the President of the Iran–United States
Claims Tribunal,
Counsel, Lalive & Partners, Attorneys-at-Law, Geneva,
Member, Tianjin Board of Arbitration, China

Routledge
Taylor & Francis Group

LONDON AND NEW YORK

First published in 1970 by HarperCollins Academic
Second edition 1971
Third edition 1977
Fourth edition 1982
Fifth edition 1987
Sixth edition 1987

Simultaneously published in the USA and Canada
by Routledge
711 Third Avenue, New York, NY 10017 (8th Floor)

Seventh edition 1997

Routledge is an imprint of the Taylor & Francis Group, an informa business

© 1997 Routledge

Typeset in Ehrhardt by
RefineCatch Ltd, Bungay, Suffolk

British Library Cataloguing in Publication Data
A catalogue record for this book is available from the British Library

Library of Congress Cataloging in Publication Data
A catalog record for this book is available from the Library of Congress

ISBN10: 0-415-16553-9 (hbk)   ISBN13: 978-0-415-16553-2 (hbk)
ISBN10: 0-415-11120-X (pbk)   ISBN13: 978-0-415-11120-1 (pbk)

Contents

Preface

A Modern Introduction to International Law by the late Professor Michael Akehurst was first published in 1970. Passing through six editions, it became a classic among student textbooks within departments of law and political science alike and it has been translated into Spanish, Portuguese, Japanese and Chinese. Since the last edition in 1987, however, due to the author's death, the text has been merely reprinted without change and, in view of the manifold new developments in international law and international relations in the ten years that have passed since the sixth edition, especially after the end of the Cold War, it became outdated. While I have therefore sought to build upon the solid groundwork laid by Dr Akehurst (who, unfortunately, I did not know personally) and to retain his clarity of style and unique focus on the interrelationship between legal theory and political practice, I found it necessary to subject the contents and structure of the book to a thorough scrutiny, reorganization and some enlargement, including additional chapters on important new branches of international law. But I would like to record my deep respect to Michael Akehurst who contributed much to education and to the study of international law, also by means of many other masterly publications which he wrote, and who, in a collection of essays dedicated to his memory, has been described by his British colleagues as 'one of the most gifted international lawyers of his generation'.[1]

In preparing a revised and updated new version of the book, I have tried to produce an edition that will meet the needs of students and other readers for an introduction to international law, as well as providing a more comprehensive account than the previous edition of the general scope of the subject as it stands today, although I have become acutely aware of the difficulty of trying to achieve this within a single book that should not become too long. At the same time, by incorporating more systematic and extensive references, it has been designed to serve as a point of departure for more advanced study and for research. The revised text aims at a broader and somewhat more cosmopolitan audience by drawing upon a variety of legal systems, perspectives and also on literature in languages other than English. The conceptual approach is based upon a historical perspective of international law and emphasizes its dynamic nature as a process which evolved from its limited European origins to a universal system and is characterized by the strong impact of power relations, as well as by the diversity of the national legal systems, cultures, and political and economic structures with which it interacts.

Compared with the sixth edition, too many changes as regards

1 V. Lowe (ed.), *The United Nations and Principles of International Law: Essays in Memory of Michael Akehurst*, 1994.

arrangement and treatment have been made for these divergencies to be enumerated in all their detail. But there are a number of alterations concerning the structure and contents of the book which should be mentioned. In Chapter 1, I have included a discussion of the problem of defining international law, of the concepts of general and regional international law, of the special characteristics of international law as a decentralized legal system and have given an indication of the ever-increasing scope of international law with regard to the subject matters it covers. Chapter 2 has been rewritten and much expanded by giving a condensed systematic overview of the historical phases of the development of international law. Chapter 3 on the sources of international law now starts with an explanation of the concept of legal sources and it has been revised in many parts, taking into account the recent literature and decisions, such as the 1996 Advisory Opinion of the International Court of Justice on the legality of nuclear weapons. Sections have also been added addressing the concepts of 'soft law', obligations *erga omnes* and international crimes. In Chapter 4 on international law and municipal law, I have added a brief explanation of the relevant dualist and monist theories and reduced the previous emphasis on English law by referring also to other legal systems, including the United States, European continental legal systems and the constitutional reforms in Russia and Eastern Europe. Chapter 5 on states and governments explains the criteria of a state in more detail than the previous edition and includes a discussion of the experience of the break-up of Yugoslavia in connection with the problem of the recognition of states.

In Chapter 6, dealing with international organizations, individuals and companies, Michael Akehurst had also included human rights and the concept of nationality, and in the following Chapter 7 he had discussed the treatment of aliens, including expropriation, the nationality of claims, and other preliminary objections, such as the local remedies rule. In view of the development of international law, I decided to adopt a different approach. The increasing importance of the protection of human rights on the international level has made it imperative to add a separate and expanded chapter on the topic (Chapter 14). Nationality, the treatment of aliens (except for expropriation of foreign property) and preliminary objections are now dealt with in a new Chapter 17 on state responsibility for internationally wrongful acts within the framework of the International Law Commission's attempt to codify the law in this area. This rearrangement was also chosen because of the close connection of the topic to the methods of dispute settlement, which are treated in Chapter 18. Expropriation of foreign property, on the other hand, seemed to fit better into a new chapter on international economic law which I have also added (Chapter 15).

Chapter 6, therefore, is now limited to a discussion of the legal personality of entities other than states in international law. This provided room for a more detailed treatment of international organizations, individuals and companies and to include new parts on the role of non-governmental organizations, insurgents and national liberation movements, and ethnic minorities and indigenous peoples. In Chapter 7 on jurisdiction, I have submitted a more detailed discussion of the concept of universal criminal jurisdiction, and added new parts on universal jurisdiction of national courts over crimes against human rights (with special reference to recent US practice), on the illuminating case of 'Ivan the Terrible', and some more reference to the problem of the exercise of extraterritorial jurisdiction, as, for example, in the case of the 1996 US Helms-Burton Act. The general order and content of the following chapters on immunity from jurisdiction (Chapter 8), treaties (Chapter 9) and acquisition of territory (Chapter 10) have remained largely the same as that written by Michael Akehurst. In Chapter 11 on state succession, changes were made to give a more systematic overview of the complicated topic and by adding text on the principle of 'moving treaty boundaries', as well as on recent practice with regard to the secession of the Baltic States, the dismemberment of the Soviet Union, Yugoslavia and Czechoslovakia and the unification of Germany and Yemen. The main changes in Chapter 12, dealing with the law of the sea, reflect the entry into force of the 1982 Law of the Sea Convention and the modification of the controversial deep seabed mining regime in 1994. Chapter 13 on air law and the law governing outer space has been expanded to provide a more detailed account of these relatively young areas of international law and a concluding part on the legal significance of the so-called 'common heritage of mankind' principle has been added.

As mentioned above, this is followed by new separate chapters on human rights (Chapter 14), international economic law (Chapter 15), the international protection of the environment (Chapter 16) and on state responsibility (Chapter 17). The arrangement of the remaining chapters has also been altered for systematic reasons. In view of the importance of the topic for understanding the peculiar nature of international law, Chapter 18 on the peaceful settlement of disputes between states has been much expanded, taking into account also the experience of ICSID, the Iran–United States Claims Tribunal and the complex dispute settlement mechanism under the 1982 Law of the Sea Convention. Chapter 19 on international wars, civil wars and the right to self-determination concerns the legality of the use of force (*ius ad bellum*) and also discusses new developments with regard to the self-determination of ethnic, cultural and linguistic minorities and indigenous peoples. In Chapter 20, the laws of war (*ius in bello*), international humanitarian law and international criminal responsibility of individuals for war crimes are dealt with, including new parts on the International Criminal Tribunals for former Yugoslavia and Rwanda, and on the project to establish a Permanent International Criminal Court. Chapter 21 on the Charter and the organs of the United Nations now deals with certain matters which the previous edition covered in Chapter 15. I have added some new text on the problem of the UN membership of the Former Yugoslavia and some more details, *inter alia*, on the UN budgetary problems and the role of the UN Secretary-General. The final Chapter 22 on the role of the United Nations with regard to the maintenance of international peace and security contains new material on the practice of the UN Security Council under Chapter VII of the UN Charter after the end of the Cold War and includes detailed case studies of the invasion of Kuwait by Iraq in 1990, the Allied intervention in the Kurdish crisis in 1991, the humanitarian intervention in Somalia in 1992, the tragedy in Rwanda in 1994, the intervention in Haiti in 1994, and the break-up of Yugoslavia. I have also added a part on the new forms of UN peacekeeping and, finally, some critical reflections on the role of the Security Council after the end of the Cold War.

As regards more technical matters, the new edition has transferred references from the text to notes and provides for extensive cross-references in the notes (which is a more useful guide than only having to rely on the index). In addition to the index and the table of cases, a separate table of treaties and other relevant documents, as well as a table of abbreviations have been included. While I have attempted to provide enough details of leading cases and other documents to make discussion of them intelligible, to encourage the reading of source material I have often given references to *Cases and Materials on International Law* (4th edn 1991), by Professor D. J. Harris, and *Basic Documents in International Law*, by Professor I. Brownlie (4th edn 1995). Moreover, systematic use has been made for the purpose of further study in references to the magnificent *Encyclopedia of Public International Law*, edited by Professor R. Bernhardt, the *Restatement of the Law (Third): The Foreign Relations Law of the United States* (1987), prepared by the American Law Institute, and, where appropriate, to *The Charter of the United Nations – A Commentary* (1995), edited by Professor B. Simma, and to *United Nations – Law, Policies and Practice* (1995), edited by Professor R. Wolfrum. All of these excellent works provide good further explanation and well-selected bibliographies on the matters addressed in the various chapters of this book.

I am very grateful to Peter Morris (T.M.C. Asser Instituut, The Hague) who carefully read the whole manuscript and improved and enriched it with his experience as the Assistant General Editor of the *Netherlands Yearbook of International Law*. I am also indebted to the 'anonymous reviewer' who has studied the text on behalf of the publishers and who has made very valuable comments and suggestions. I owe thanks to my departmental colleague Olivier Ribbelink (University of Amsterdam) who has given helpful comments on a number of chapters. My thanks are further due to Bruno Simma (University of Munich) and Malgosia Fitzmaurice (Queen Mary and Westfield College, University of London) for sharing their thoughts with me at an early stage of the preparation of the manuscript. At a time when funds for university libraries are still being cut, I record that I could not have prepared this edition without access to the excellent facilities of the libraries of the Peace Palace in The Hague and of the Max Planck Institute in Heidelberg, whose staff have in every way been most helpful. In addition, I have received immense, untiring and very capable help in both research and secretarial services from Liu Jian. Finally, I would like to thank the publishers for their confidence, patience and impressive spirit of cooperation.

The final preparation of the manuscript for publication was completed during September 1996.

Peter Malanczuk
The Hague
November 1996

Abbreviations

AASL	*Annals of Air and Space Law*	AVR	*Archiv des Völkerrechts*
AC	*Appeal Cases* (UK)	AYIL	*Australian Yearbook of International Law*
AD	*Annual Digest and Reports of Public International Law Cases*		
		BayVBl.	*Bayerische Verwaltungsblätter*
AFDI	*Annuaire Français de Droit International*	BCICLR	*Boston College International and Comparative Law Review*
AFDMAS	*Annals Français Droit Maritime et Aéro-Spatial*	BENELUX	BENELUX Economic Union (Belgium, The Netherlands and Luxembourg)
AI	*Arbitration International*		
AJIA	*Australian Journal of International Affairs*	BPIL	*British Practice in International Law*
AJICL	*African Journal of International and Comparative Law*	Brooklyn JIL	*Brooklyn Journal of International Law*
AJIL	*American Journal of International Law*	Brownlie BDIL	I. Brownlie (ed.), *Basic Documents in International Law*, 4th edn, 1995
AJPIL	*Austrian Journal of Public and International Law*		
		BYIL	*British Year Book of International Law*
ALADI	Latin American Integration Association		
		CACM	Central American Common Market
All ER	*All England Law Reports*		
ANC	African National Congress	Cardoza LR	*Cardoza Law Review*
Ann. IDI	*Annuaire de l'Institut de Droit International*	CARICOM	Caribbean Community
		Cd., Cmd., Cmnd., Cm.	*Command Papers* (UK) 1900–1918, 1919–1956, 1956–1986, 1986– respectively
Anu. DI	*Anuario de Derecho Internacional*		
APEC	Asian-Pacific-Economic-Cooperation		
		CEFTA	Central European Free Trade Area
ARABSAT	Arab Satellite Organization		
Arizona JICL	*Arizona Journal of International and Comparative Law*	CENTO	Central Treaty Organization
		CFCs	chlorofluorocarbons
ASDI	*Annuaire Suisse de Droit International*	ChD	*Law Reports, Chancery Division* (UK)
ASEAN	Association of South East Asian Nations	CIA	Central Intelligence Agency
		CILSA	*The Comparative and International Law Journal of Southern Africa*
ASIL IELIGNewsl.	*ASIL International Environmental Law Interest Group Newsletter*	CJIELP	*Colorado Journal of International Environmental Law and Policy*
ASIL IELNews	*ASIL International Environmental Law News*		
		CJPS	*Canadian Journal of Political Science*
ASIL Proc.	*Proceedings of the American Society of International Law*		
		Cl. Ct.	*US Court of Claims Reports*
ASILS ICJ	*Association of Student International Law Societies International Law Journal*	CLB	*Commonwealth Law Bulletin*
		CLP	*Current Legal Problems*
		CLR	*Commonwealth Law Reports*
AsYIL	*Asian Yearbook of International Law*	CMLR	*Common Market Law Reports*
AUJILP	*American University Journal of International Law and Policy*	Colum. JTL	*Columbia Journal of Transnational Law*
AULR	*American University Law Review*	Colum. LR	*Columbia Law Review*

Colum. JIL	*Columbia Journal of International Law*	**EU**	European Union
Cong. Rec.	*Congressional Records* (US)	**Eur.-Asia Stud.**	*Europe-Asia Studies*
Conn. JIL	*Connecticut Journal of International Law*	**EURATOM**	European Atomic Energy Community
Cornell ILJ	*Cornell International Law Journal*	**EUTELSAT**	European Telecommunications Satellite Organization
CSCE	Conference on Security and Cooperation in Europe	**Ex. D.**	*Law Reports, Exchequer Division* (UK)
CTS	*Consolidated Treaty Series*	**F. 2d**	*Federal Reports* (Second Series) (US)
CWILJ	*California Western International Law Journal*	**F. (J.C.)**	*Fraser, Justiciary Cases* (Scotland)
CWRJIL	*Case Western Reserve Journal of International Law*	**F. Supp.**	*Federal Supplement* (US)
CYIL	*Canadian Yearbook of International Law*	**FA**	*Foreign Affairs*
		FAO	Food and Agriculture Organization
Dalhouse LJ	*Dalhouse Law Journal*	**FAZ**	*Frankfurter Allgemeine Zeitung*
Denning LJ	*Denning Law Journal*	**FCN**	Friendship, Commerce and Navigation Treaty
Denver JILP	*Denver Journal of International Law and Policy*	**Fla. JIL**	*Florida Journal of International Law*
Dept. State Bull.	*Department of State Bulletin* (US)		
DGVR	*Berichte der Deutschen Gesellschaft für Völkerrecht*	**Fordham ILJ**	*Fordham International Law Journal*
		FP	*Foreign Policy*
Dick. JIL	*Dickinson Journal of International Law*	**FS Bernhardt**	U. Beyerlin/M. Bothe/R. Hofmann/E.-U. Petersmann (eds), *Recht zwischen Umbruch und Bewahrung. Festschrift für Rudolf Bernhardt*, 1995
Doc.	Document(s)		
DOMREP	Mission of the Representative of the UN Secretary-General in the Dominican Republic		
		FSIA	Foreign Sovereign Immunity Act (US)
Droit et Soc.	*Droit et Société*	**FTA**	Canada-United States Free Trade Agreement
Duke JCIL	*Duke Journal of Comparative and International Law*	**FYIL**	*Finnish Yearbook of International Law*
EA	*Europa-Archiv*		
EC	European Community	**GA**	United Nations General Assembly
ECE	UN Economic Commission for Europe		
ECOSOC	United Nations Economic and Social Council	**Ga. JICL**	*Georgia Journal of International and Comparative Law*
ECOWAS	Economic Community of West African States	**GATS**	General Agreement on Trade in Services
ECSC	European Coal and Steel Community	**GATT**	General Agreement on Tariffs and Trade
EEA	European Economic Area	**GEF**	Global Environmental Facility (World Bank)
EEC	European Economic Community		
EFTA	European Free Trade Association	**Geo. LJ**	*Georgetown Law Journal*
EJIL	*European Journal of International Law*	**GNP**	Gross National Product
		Gov. & Oppos.	*Government and Opposition*
ELQ	*Ecology Law Quarterly*	**GYIL**	*German Yearbook of International Law*
Emory ILR	*Emory International Law Review*		
EPIL	*Encyclopedia of Public International Law* (R. Bernhardt, ed., EPIL 1 = EPIL, Instalment 1; EPIL I = EPIL, Volume I)	**Hague YIL**	*Hague Yearbook of International Law*
		Harris CMIL	D.J. Harris, *Cases and Materials on International Law*, 4th edn, 1991
EPL	*Environmental Policy and Law*	**Harvard ILJ**	*Harvard International Law Journal*
ER	*English Reports*	**Harvard LR**	*Harvard Law Review*
ESA	European Space Agency	**Hastings ICLR**	*Hastings International and Comparative Law Review*
ET	*European Taxation*		
ETS	European Treaty Series	**Hastings LJ**	*Hastings Law Journal*

High Tech. LJ	*High Technology Law Journal*	ILQ	*International Law Quarterly*
HM	*Helsinki Monitor*	ILR	*International Law Reports*
Houston JIL	*Houston Journal of International Law*	ILT	*The Irish Law Times and Solicitors' Journal*
HRLJ	*Human Rights Law Journal*	IMF	International Monetary Fund
HRQ	*Human Rights Quarterly*	IMO	International Maritime Organization
HV	*Humanitäres Völkerrecht*		
IA	*International Affairs*	Indian JIL	*Indian Journal of International Law*
IAEA	International Atomic Energy Agency	INMARSAT	International Maritime Satellite Organization
IATA	International Air Transport Association	INTELSAT	International Telecommunications Satellite Organization
IBRD	International Bank for Reconstruction and Development (World Bank)	IO	*International Organization*
		IP	*International Peacekeeping*
ICAO	International Civil Aviation Organization	IPTF	International Police Task Force
		IQ	*The Indonesian Quarterly*
ICC	International Chamber of Commerce	IR	*International Relations*
		Iran-US CTR	*Iran-United States Claims Tribunal Reports*
ICJ	International Court of Justice		
ICJ Rep.	*International Court of Justice Reports of Judgments, Advisory Opinions and Orders*	IRRC	*International Review of the Red Cross*
		Israel LR	*Israel Law Review*
ICJYb	*Yearbook of the International Court of Justice*	ITO	International Trade Organization
		ITU	International Telecommunication Union
ICLQ	*International and Comparative Law Quarterly*	IUCN	International Union for the Conservation of Nature
ICRC	International Committee of the Red Cross	IYIL	*Italian Yearbook of International Law*
ICSID	International Centre for the Settlement of Investment Disputes	Jap. Ann. IL	*The Japanese Annual of International Law*
ICSID Rev.	*ICSID Review—Foreign Investment Law Journal*	JDI	*Journal du droit international*
ICTY Bull.	*International Criminal Tribunal for the Former Yugoslavia Bulletin*	JIArb.	*Journal of International Arbitration*
IDA	International Development Association	JPR	*Journal of Peace Research*
		JSpaceL	*Journal of Space Law*
IFAD	International Fund for Agricultural Development	JTLP	*Journal of Transnational Law & Policy*
IFC	International Finance Corporation	JWTL	*Journal of World Trade Law*
		KB	*King's Bench* (UK)
IFOR	Implementation Force in (former) Yugoslavia	KCA	*Keesing's Contemporary Archives*
		LAS	League of Arab States
IHT	*International Herald Tribune*	Leg. Stud.	*Legal Studies*
IJ	*International Journal*	LJIL	*Leiden Journal of International Law*
IJECL	*International Journal of Estuarine and Coastal Law*		
		LNOJ	League of Nations Official Journal
IL	*The International Lawyer*	LNTS	League of Nations Treaty Series
ILA	International Law Association	LPIB	*Law and Policy of International Business*
ILA Rep.	*Report(s) of the Conference(s) of the International Law Association*		
		LOS Bull.	*Law of the Sea Bulletin*
ILC	International Law Commission	Loyola LAICLJ	*Loyola of Los Angeles International and Comparative Law Journal*
ILCYb	*Yearbook of the International Law Commission*		
		LQR	*Law Quarterly Review*
ILM	*International Legal Materials*	MERCOSUR	Mercado Comun del Sur (Treaty Establishing a Common Market between Argentina, Brazil, Paraguay and Uruguay)
ILO	International Labour Organization		
ILP	*International Law and Policy*		

MFN	most-favoured-nation clause
Mich. JIL	*Michigan Journal of International Law*
MIGA	Multilateral Investment Guarantee Agency
MINURSO	Mission des Nations Unies pour le Réferendum de la Sahara de l'Ouest (United Nations Mission for the Referendum in Western Sahara)
Mont. LR	*Montana Law Review*
MSF	Médecins Sans Frontières
NAFO	North Atlantic Fisheries Organization
NAFTA	North American Free Trade Agreement
NATO	North Atlantic Treaty Organization
NCJILCR	*North California Journal of International Law and Commercial Regulation*
NGOs	non-governmental organizations
NIEO	New International Economic Order
NILR	*Netherlands International Law Review*
NJILB	*Northwestern Journal of International Law and Business*
NLJ	*New Law Journal*
Nordic JIL	*Nordic Journal of International Law*
NQHR	*Netherlands Quarterly of Human Rights*
NULR	*Northwestern University Law Review*
NWICO	New World Information and Communication Order
NYIL	*Netherlands Yearbook of International Law*
NYL. Sch. ICL	*New York Law School Journal of International and Comparative Law*
NYUJILP	*New York University Journal of International Law and Politics*
NYULR	*New York University Law Review*
OAS	Organization of American States
OAU	Organization of African Unity
OCSE	Organization for Cooperation and Security in Europe
ODA	Official Development Aid
ODECA	Organization of Central American States
OECD	Organization for Economic Cooperation and Development
OIC	Organization of the Islamic Conference
Okla. CULR	*Oklahoma City University Law Review*
ONUC	Opérations des Nations Unies pour le Congo (United Nations Force in the Congo)
ONUCA	United Nations Observer Group in Central America
ONUMOZ	United Nations Operation in Mozambique
ONUSAL	United Nations Observer Mission in El Salvador
ONUVEH	UN Observer Group for the Verification of the Elections in Haiti
OPEC	Organization of Petroleum Exporting Countries
Osteur.-Recht	*Osteuropa-Recht*
Ottawa LR	*Ottawa Law Review*
Pace ILR	*Pace International Law Review*
Palestine YIL	*Palestine Yearbook of International Law*
PCA	Permanent Court of Arbitration
PCIJ	Permanent Court of International Justice
PCIJ Series A	Permanent Court of International Justice, Collection of Judgments (1922–1930)
PCIJ Series A/B	Permanent Court of International Justice, Collection of Judgments, Orders and Advisory Opinions (1931–1940)
PCIJ Series B	Permanent Court of International Justice, Collection of Advisory Opinions (1922–1930)
PD	*Law Reports, Probate, Divorce and Admiralty Division*, 1875–90 (UK)
Pepp. LR	*Pepperdine Law Review*
P.L.	*Public Law*
PLO	Palestine Liberation Organization
Proc. IISL	*Proceedings of the International Institute of Space Law*
PYIL	*Polish Yearbook of International Law*
QB	*Law Reports, Queen's Bench Division* (U.K.)
RBDI	*Revue Belge de Droit International*
RdC	*Recueil des Cours* (Hague Academy of International Law)
RDI	*Revue de Droit International, de Sciences Diplomatiques et Politiques*
REDI	*Revue Egyptienne de Droit International*
Restatement (Third)	American Law Institute, *Restatement (Third) of the Foreign Relations Law of the United States*, 2 vols, 1987
RFDAS	*Revue Française de Droit Aérien et Spatial*
RGDIP	*Revue Générale de Droit International Public*

RIA	*Review of International Affairs*
RIAA	*Reports of International Arbitral Awards* (United Nations)
RIS	*Review of International Studies*
RSDI	*Revue Suisse de Droit International*
RPF	Rwandese Patriotic Front
S. Ct.	*Supreme Court Reporter* (US)
San Diego LR	*San Diego Law Review*
Santa Clara LR	*Santa Clara Law Review*
SAYIL	*South African Yearbook of International Law*
SC	United Nations Security Council
SCHR.-REIHE DT. GRUPPE AAA	*Schriftenreihe der Deutschen Gruppe der AAA.* Association des Auditeurs et Anciens Auditeurs de l'Académie de Droit International de La Haye
SDR	special drawing rights
SELA	Sistema Económico Latinoamericano (Latin American Economic System)
SEW	*Sociaal-Economische Wetgeving. Tijdschrift voor Europees en Economisch Recht*
SIA	State Immunity Act (UK)
Simma CUNAC	B. Simma (ed.), *The Charter of the United Nations. A Commentary*, 1995
Sing. JLS	*Singapore Journal of Legal Studies*
SP	*Space Policy*
Space Comm.	*Space Communications*
Sri Lanka JIL	*Sri Lanka Journal of International Law*
St. Louis ULJ	*St. Louis University Law Journal*
Stanford JIL	*Stanford Journal of International Law*
Stat.	*United States Statutes at Large*
Suffolk TLJ	*Suffolk Transnational Law Journal*
SWAPO	South West African People's Organization
SWMTEP	System-Wide Medium-Term Environment Programme
TA	*Transnational Associations*
Temple ICLJ	*Temple International and Comparative Law Journal*
Texas ILJ	*Texas International Law Journal*
TNCs	transnational corporations
Trans. Grot. Soc.	*Transactions of the Grotius Society*
TRIMS	trade-related investment measures
TRIPS	trade-related intellectual property rights
TSJ	*Telecommunications & Space Journal*
UKTS	United Kingdom Treaties Series
UN	United Nations
UNAMIC	United Nations Advance Mission in Cambodia

UNAMIR	United Nations Assistance Mission for Rwanda
UNASOG	United Nations Aouzou Strip Observation Group
UNAVEM	United Nations Angola Verification Mission
UNCC	United Nations Compensation Commission
UNCED	United Nations Conference on Environment and Development
UNCHR	United Nations Centre for Human Rights
UNCITRAL	United Nations Commission on International Trade Law
UNCLOS	United Nations Conference on the Law of the Sea
UNCOPUOS	United Nations Committee on the Peaceful Uses of Outer Space
UNCRO	United Nations Confidence Restoration Operation in Croatia
UNCTAD	United Nations Conference on Trade and Development
UNDOF	United Nations Disengagement Observer Force (Golan Heights)
UNDP	United Nations Development Programme
UNEF	United Nations Emergency Force
UNEP	United Nations Environment Programme
UNESCO	United National Educational, Scientific and Cultural Organization
UNFICYP	United Nations Peacekeeping Force in Cyprus
UNGOMAP	United Nations Good Offices Mission in Afghanistan and Pakistan
UNIDO	United Nations Industrial Development Organization
UNIFIL	United Nations Interim Force in Lebanon
UNIIMOG	United Nations Iran-Iraq Military Observer Group
UNIKOM	United Nations Iraq-Kuwait Observation Mission
UNIPOM	United Nations India-Pakistan Observation Mission
UNISPACE	United Nations Conference on the Exploration and Peaceful Uses of Outer Space
UNITAF	Unified Task Force
UNMIH	United Nations Mission in Haiti
UNMOT	United Nations Mission of Observers in Tajikistan
UNOMIG	United Nations Observer Mission in Georgia
UNOMIL	United Nations Observer Mission in Liberia

UNOMUR	United Nations Observer Mission in Uganda-Rwanda	**Vand. JTL**	*Vanderbilt Journal of Transnational Law*
UNOSOM	United Nations Operation in Somalia	**Vand. LR**	*Vanderbilt Law Review*
UNPO	Unrepresented Nations and Peoples Organization	**Virginia JIL**	*Virginia Journal of International Law*
UNPREDEP	United Nations Preventive Deployment Force in the former Yugoslav Republic of Macedonia	**VN**	*Vereinte Nationen*
		VRÜ	*Verfassung und Recht in Übersee*
		WEU	Western European Union
		WHO	World Health Organization
UNPROFOR	United Nations Protection Force in (former) Yugoslavia	**WIPO**	World Intellectual Property Organization
UNSF	United Nations Security Force in West New Guinea (West Irian)	**Wis. ILJ**	*Wisconsin International Law Journal*
		WLR	*Weekly Law Reports* (UK)
UNTAC	United Nations Transitional Authority in Cambodia	**WMO**	World Meteorological Organization
UNTAG	United Nations Transitional Assistance Group in Namibia	**Wolfrum UNLPP**	R. Wolfrum (ed.), *United Nations: Law, Policies and Practice*, 2 vols, 1995 (*UNLPP I =* UNLPP Vol. 1; *UNLPP II =* UNLPP Vol. 2)
UNTS	United Nations Treaties Series		
UNYb	*United Nations Yearbook*		
UNYOM	United Nations Yemen Observation Mission		
		WTO	World Trade Organization
UPU	Universal Postal Union	**Yale JIL**	*Yale Journal of International Law*
US	*United States Reports* (Supreme Court)	**Yale LJ**	*Yale Law Journal*
		YIEL	*Yearbook of International Environmental Law*
US-Mexico LJ	*United States-Mexico Law Journal*	**ZaöRV**	*Zeitschrift für ausländisches öffentliches Recht und Völkerrecht*
USCMA	*United States Court Military Appeals*		
		ZLW	*Zeitschrift für Luft- und Weltraumrecht*
USTS	United States Treaty Series		

1   Introduction

The problem of defining international law

The term 'international law' was first used by Jeremy Bentham in 1780 in his *Introduction to the Principles of Morals and Legislation.* Since about 1840, in the English and Romance languages it has replaced the older terminology 'law of nations' or 'droit de gens' which can be traced back to the Roman concept of *ius gentium* and the writings of Cicero.[1] In the German, Dutch, Scandinavian and Slavic languages the older terminology is still in use ('Völkerrecht', 'Volkenrecht', etc.).

Until the period between the two World Wars, writers found no difficulty in defining (public) international law,[2] in one formulation or another, as the law that governs the relations between states amongst each other. The prevailing positivist doctrine[3] of the nineteenth century and first half of the twentieth century held that only states could be subjects of international law, in the sense of enjoying international legal personality[4] and being capable of possessing international rights and duties, including the right to bring international claims.[5]

However, this did not quite reflect reality even at that time. The Holy See,[6] although not a state, was recognized to have international legal personality, and so, for certain purposes, were insurgents[7] and some forerunners of modern international organizations.[8] Since the inter-war period, the matter has become more complicated due to both the expansion of the scope of international law into new areas and the emergence of actors other than states on the international plane, such as intergovernmental organizations established by states, non-governmental organizations created by private individuals, transnational companies, individuals and groups, including minorities and indigenous peoples.[9] Some of these new actors have also acquired international legal personality or, at least, certain rights under international law, even if only granted by treaties concluded between states.

This development is reflected, for example, in the change of the definition in the *Restatement (Third)* by the American Law Institute of the *Foreign Relations Law of the United States*, according to which international law

> consists of rules and principles of general application dealing with the conduct of states and of international organizations and with their relations *inter se*, as well as with some of their relations with persons, whether natural or juridical.[10]

Some recent textbooks refrain from any attempt to define international

1 See, for example, Cicero, *De officiis*, lib. III, 17, 69.
2 For the meaning of private international law see Chapter 4 below, 71–4.
3 See Chapter 2 below, 16–17.
4 See Chapter 6 below, 91–2.
5 See Chapters 17, 256–7 and 18, 262–9 below.
6 See Chapter 5 below, 76.
7 See Chapters 6, 104–5 and 19, 318–26 below.
8 See Chapters 2, 22 and 6, 92–6 below.
9 See Chapters 6, 105–8 and 19, 338–41 below.
10 *Restatement (Third)*, para. 101, 22–4. The previous *Restatement* only referred to 'those rules of law applicable to a state or international organization that cannot be modified unilaterally by it', *ibid.*, at 24. The concept of 'foreign relations law of the United States' is broader than 'international law as it applies to the United States'. It includes 'domestic law that has substantial significance for the foreign relations of the United States or has other substantial international consequences.', *ibid.*, para. 1, at 7.

11 See, for example, I. Brownlie, *Principles of Public International Law*, 4th edn 1990. On the sources of international law see Chapter 3 below, 33–62.

12 R.Y. Jennings, International Law, *EPIL* II (1995), 1159–78, at 1165.

13 See M. Koskenniemi, The Future of Statehood, *Harvard ILJ* 32 (1991), 397; C. Schreuer, The Waning of the Sovereign State: Towards a New Paradigm for International Law?, *EJIL* 4 (1993), 447–71; L.A. Khan, *The Extinction of Nation-States. A World Without Borders*, 1996 and Chapter 2 below, 17–18 on the doctrine of state sovereignty.

14 See Chapter 21 below, 369–73.

15 Article 35, UN Charter, text in *Brownlie BDIL*, 1. See Chapter 22 below, 385–430.

16 Article 34(1), Statute of the ICJ, *ibid.*, 438. See Chapter 18 below, 281–93.

17 See Chapter 17 below, 256–7.

18 See Chapter 5 below, 75–90.

19 See Chapter 3 below, 36–48.

20 See O. Schindler, Regional International Law, *EPIL* 7 (1984), 404–9 and Chapters 2, 14–15 and 3, 41 below.

21 See Chapter 3 below, 44.

22 See Chapter 2 below, 30–2.

23 See Chapter 2 below, 28–33.

24 See E. McWhinney, *United Nations Law Making: Cultural and Ideological Relativism and International Law Making for an Era of Transition*, 1984; R.-J. Dupuy (ed.), *The Future of International Law in a Multicultural World*, 1984; A. Cassese, *International Law in a Divided World*, 1986.

law and enter directly into the discussion of its 'sources'.[11] On a similar basis, Sir Robert Jennings, the distinguished writer and former President of the International Court of Justice, has even called into question the general need for an objective definition of international law with regard to actually using and applying it.[12] At any rate, in the exposition of the subject in a textbook, emphasis must be placed at the outset on the circumstance that, although increasing global interdependence and the emergence of new players on the international level have put into question the role of the state in international affairs,[13] international law is still *predominantly* made and implemented by states. International organizations are to a large extent dependent upon these territorial entities and the willingness of their governments to support them. Only states can be members of the United Nations,[14] only states are entitled to call upon the UN Security Council if there is a threat to international peace and security,[15] only states may appear in contentious proceedings before the International Court of Justice,[16] and only states can present a claim on behalf of a national who has been injured by another state,[17] if there is no treaty to the contrary. The individual has no individual rights in this respect under customary international law and is dependent on the political discretion of the home state as to whether or not to present the claim. In other words, the international legal system is still *primarily* geared towards the international community of states, represented by governments.[18]

General and regional international law

'General international law' refers to rules and principles that are applicable to a large number of states, on the basis of either customary international law or multilateral treaties.[19] If they become binding upon all states, they are often referred to as 'universal international law'. But there is also regional international law, which applies only to certain groups of states, such as, for example, certain rules on diplomatic asylum recognized only by South American states,[20] or the law of the European Union. Moreover, the term 'particular international law' is used to denote rules which are binding upon two or a few states only. Mere usage, in the sense of widespread practice observed between states without any sense of legal obligation, is often called international comity.[21]

Regionalism tends to undermine the universality of international law, but it is an important existing feature of the international system.[22] The universality of international law was at one stage challenged by the Communist theory of international law and at a later stage by the numerous new states emerging from the process of decolonization after the Second World War.[23] These challenges in principle no longer appear. But obviously the community of more than 185 states in existence today is rather heterogeneous in terms of military, political and economic power, territorial size and population, political structure, and cultural and ideological orientation. This diversity also affects the interpretation and operation of international law to a considerable extent.[24] Almost all of the existing states, however, are members of the United Nations and of regional organizations of various kinds and agree on certain fundamental principles of international law as laid down in the United Nations Charter and the Friendly Relations Declaration of 1970.[25]

Characteristics of international law

International law has a number of special characteristics making it completely different from highly developed national legal systems which are connected with the existence of the modern state and its apparatus. The modern state which emerged in Europe after the fourteenth century centralized the use of force by making it a state monopoly, developing a standing army and a more or less efficient bureaucracy.[26] It increasingly engaged in economic and social regulation, and created a sophisticated system of legal institutions, principles and rules regulating society.

The Western concept of law, with its national and philosophical variations, became a central instrument for the organization and development of both state and civil society. In a systematic sense, this is reflected in the distinction between the three functions, typically entrusted to central organs, of law-making (legislature), law determination (courts and tribunals), and law enforcement (administration, police, army). Domestic law is addressed to a large number of governmental bodies and private individuals and groups of individuals. International law, on the other hand, is primarily concerned with the legal regulation of the international intercourse of states which are organized as territorial entities, are limited in number and consider themselves, in spite of the obvious factual differences in reality, in formal terms as 'sovereign' and 'equal'.[27] Thus, international law is a horizontal legal system, lacking a supreme authority, the centralization of the use of force, and a differentiation of the three basic functions of law-making, law determination, and law enforcement typically entrusted to central organs. The United Nations General Assembly is not a world legislature,[28] the International Court of Justice in The Hague can operate only on the basis of the consent of states to its jurisdiction,[29] and the law–enforcement capacity of the United Nations Security Council is both legally and politically limited.[30]

Nevertheless, a state which violates an international obligation is responsible for the wrongful act towards the injured state, or, under certain circumstances, to the international community as a whole.[31] The injured state can raise an international claim which it may pursue on the basis of special remedies, if available, or by resorting to third-party mediation or conciliation, arbitration or judicial proceedings.[32] In the end, however, the role of self-help by states in cases of a violation of their rights is predominant in international law, as compared with the restricted admissibility of self-help of individuals in national legal systems.

If one state commits an illegal act against another state, and refuses to make reparation or to appear before an international tribunal, there is (or was until recently) only one sanction available to the injured state: self-help.[33] Self-help exists as a sanction in all legal systems. In earlier primitive legal systems, most sanctions involved the use of self-help in one form or another. Even in modern legal systems an individual may defend himself against assault, retake property which has been stolen from him, evict

25 Text in *Brownlie BDIL*, 36. See Chapter 2 below, 32.

26 For a recent study see H. Spruyt, *The Sovereign State and Its Competitors*, 1995. See also Chapter 2 below, 10, 17–18.

27 See B. Broms, *The Doctrine of Equality of States as Applied in International Organizations*, 1959; R.P. Anand, Sovereign Equality of States in International Law, *RdC* 197 (1986), 13–228; G. Jaenicke, States, Equal Treatment and Non-Discrimination, *EPIL* 10 (1987), 456–65; J.M. Castro Rial, States, Sovereign Equality, *ibid.*, 477–81.

28 See Chapters 3, 52–4 and 21, 377–9 below.

29 See Chapter 18 below, 281–93.

30 See Chapters 18, 292–3, 21, 373–7 and 22, 390–1, 425–9 below.

31 See Chapters 3, 58–60 and 17, 254–72 below.

32 See Chapter 18 below, 273–305.

33 B.-O. Bryde, Self-Help, *EPIL* 4 (1982), 215–17.

34 See Chapter 19 below, 306–18.
35 See Chapter 17 below, 271–2.
36 See Chapter 22 below, 387–415.
37 See Chapter 3 below, 52–4.
38 See Chapters 21, 373–9 and 22, 385–416, 425–30 below.
39 See Chapter 15 below, 225–7.

trespassers from his land and terminate a contract if the other party has broken a major term of that contract. But in modern societies self-help has become the exception rather than the rule, whereas in international law it has remained the rule.

At one time states might even go to war to enforce their legal rights. However, this is no longer lawful, with certain exceptions such as self-defence against armed attack.[34] The remaining forms of self-help are countermeasures, such as retorsion and reprisals.[35]

Retorsion is a lawful act which is designed to injure the wrongdoing state – for example, cutting off economic aid (this is lawful because there is no legal obligation to provide economic aid, apart from under special treaty provisions).

Reprisals are acts which would normally be illegal but which are rendered legal by a prior illegal act committed by the other state. For instance, if state A expropriates property belonging to state B's citizens without compensation, state B can retaliate by doing the same to the property of state A's citizens. Reprisals must be proportionate to the original wrong; for instance, state B could not expropriate property worth several times the value of the property which its citizens had lost; still less would it be entitled to kill or imprison state A's citizens.

One disadvantage of retorsion and reprisals is that the state imposing these measures may injure itself as much as the state against which they are directed; this is particularly so when one state cuts off trade with another state. A recent example has been the reluctance of the United States to use trade sanctions to enforce its criticism of human rights practices in China, in view of the huge Chinese market opportunities for American companies. A more serious disadvantage of self-help is that it works effectively only if the injured state is in some way more powerful or more determined than the wrongdoing state.

Not surprisingly, therefore, there has been a recent tendency for sanctions to be imposed by large groups of states, working through international organizations such as the United Nations.[36] But the United Nations Security Council can impose sanctions only in limited circumstances, and in the past was often paralysed by the power of veto possessed by each of its five permanent members. The United Nations General Assembly is not subject to the veto, but its resolutions are usually not legally binding (although they are an institutionalized form of public opinion and can be instruments of political pressure).[37] Both the Security Council and the General Assembly, being political rather than judicial bodies, base their decisions on political considerations and sometimes pay little attention to the legal rights and wrongs of a dispute.[38]

International organizations with more specialized functions may exercise a more effective control over their members, especially if, like the International Monetary Fund, they provide essential services.[39] A state which was excluded from membership of the Fund would be unable to borrow gold and foreign currency from the Fund to meet a balance of payments crisis. And regional organizations may exercise an even stricter discipline over their members; for instance, the Court of Justice of the

European Union has compulsory jurisdiction over member states which are accused of breaking the rules of Community law.[40]

However, it must be admitted that sanctions work less effectively in international law than in national law. States are few in number and unequal in strength, and there are always one or two states which are so strong that other states are usually too weak or too timid or too disunited to impose sanctions against them. But this does not mean that international law as a whole works less effectively than national law – only that it works in a different way.

In international law there is considered to be collective responsibility of the whole community of a state which has committed an internationally wrongful act. Thus, the civilian population of Iraq, in spite of some precautions taken, was in effect made to suffer under the sanctions adopted by the international community in response to the invasion and occupation of Kuwait by the Iraqi Government in the Second Gulf War.[41] International law has, therefore, often been described as a 'primitive legal system'. But this is a rather misleading characterization. It is true that the impact of power and politics is much more immediately recognizable and directly relevant in international law than in national law. It is also true that international law, due to the lack of central institutions, is heavily dependent on national legal systems (often called 'municipal law')[42] for its implementation. There are also other features which explain the comparison of the international legal system to the unsophisticated institutions, principles and rules of pre-modern societies. However, on the whole, this characterization fails to distinguish the different nature of international law (as a horizontal, decentralized legal system governing primarily the relations between states) and of developed (centralized and institutionalized) national legal systems. It also does not adequately reflect the relatively high degree of differentiation of international law with regard to the areas it now covers, the proliferation of multilateral and bilateral treaties, the considerable increase since 1945 of the main traditional subjects of international law and the emergence of new actors on the international level, in particular the large number of international organizations created by states for a broad variety of functions.

International law as 'law'

There is an old dispute going back to the early writings of Hobbes and Pufendorf, reinforced in the nineteenth century by Austin's influential legal theory, on the issue whether international law may be properly called 'law'.[43] The controversy has focused on the relevance of the lack of sanctions in cases of violation of international norms as compared to municipal law and it has often confused the question of whether international law is 'law' with the problem of the effectiveness and enforcement of international law.[44] In foreign policy thinking, the reductionist perception of international law is still prevalent in the 'realist' school which emphasizes the role of power and of national interest in international relations and is connected with names such as Morgenthau,[45] Kennan and is also reflected in the latest book by Henry Kissinger.[46]

40 Articles 169 and 170, EC Treaty.

41 See the report by C. Jochnick/R. Normand/S. Zaidi, *Unsanctioned Suffering – A Human Rights Assessment of United Nations Sanctions on Iraq*, Centre for Social and Economic Rights, 1996; R. Provost, Starvation as a Weapon: Legal Implications of the United Nations Food Blockade Against Iraq and Kuwait, *Colum. JTL* 30 (1992), 577–639; E.J. Garmise, The Iraqi Claims Process and the Ghost of Versailles, *NYULR* 67 (1992), 840–78; R. Normand/C. Jochnick, The Legitimation of Violence: A Critical Analysis of the Gulf War, *Harvard ILJ* 35 (1994), 387–416; B. Graefrath, Iraqi Reparations and the Security Council, *ZaöRV* 55 (1995), 1–68. See also Chapter 22 below, 396–9.

42 See Chapter 4 below, 63–71.

43 See *Harris CMIL*, 1–17.

44 On the problem of the enforcement of international obligations, see the Colloquium in Commemoration of the 600th Anniversary of the University of Heidelberg, 22 and 23 September 1986, *ZaöRV* 47 (1987), 1 *et seq.* (with contributions by R. Jennings, R. Bernhardt, K. Zemanek, K. Doehring, E. Stein, G.A. Frowein, G.K.A. Ofosu-Amaah, T. Stein, R. Dolzer and S. Rosenne); P. van Dijk, Normative Force and Effectiveness of International Norms, *GYIL* 30 (1987), 9; W.E. Butler (ed.), *Control Over Compliance with International Law*, 1991; J. Delbrück (ed.), *The Future of International Law Enforcement. New Scenarios–New Law?*, 1993; A.P. Rubin, Enforcing the Rules of International Law, *Harvard ILJ* 34 (1993), 149–61; J. Delbrück (ed.), *Allocation of Law Enforcement Authority in the International System*, 1994.

45 H.J. Morgenthau, *Politics Among Nations. The Struggle for Power and Peace*, 1948. See also the earlier work by E.H. Carr, *The Twenty Years Crisis 1919–1939. An Introduction to the Study of International Relations*, 1940.

46 H.A. Kissinger, *Diplomacy*, 1994. See also Chapter 2 below, 32–3.

47 R.St.J. Macdonald, Foreign Policy, Influence of Legal Considerations Upon, *EPIL* II (1995), 442–6; S.A. Watts, The International Rule of Law, *GYIL* 36 (1993), 15–45.

48 B. Simma, Reciprocity, *EPIL* 7 (1984), 400–4.

49 On the role of Legal Advisers and the impact of international law on foreign policy decision-making see the Symposium in *EJIL* 2 (1991), 132 *et seq.* (with contributions by S.M. Schwebel, G. Guillaume, M. Krafft and A.D. Watts); A. Cassese, The Role of Legal Advisers in Ensuring that Foreign Policy Conforms to International Legal Standards, *Mich. JIL* 14 (1992), 139; B. Mawhinney/K. Girtel, Fourth Legal Advisers' Meeting at UN Headquarters in New York, *AJIL* 88 (1994), 379–82; M.A.G. Félix, Fifth Legal Advisers' Meeting at UN Headquarters in New York, *AJIL* 89 (1995), 644–9.

50 See Chapter 3 below, 39–40.

51 See Chapter 3 below, 60–2.

52 See Chapter 4 below, 65–71.

53 See L. Henkin, *How Nations Behave*, 2nd edn 1979. For an instructive description of how governments, courts, international organizations and other bodies apply international legal norms in the course of their work see R. Higgins, *Problems and Process: International Law and How We Use It*, 1994.

54 See M. Fromont, *Les Grands Systèmes de droit contemporains*, 1987; K. Zweigert/H. Kötz, *Introduction to Comparative Law*, 2nd edn 1992; C. Varga, *Comparative Legal Culture*, 1992; *International Encyclopedia of Comparative Law*, Vol. II, Chapter 1: The Different Conceptions of the Law; J. Kropholler, Comparative Law, Function and Methods, *EPIL* I (1992), 702–7; W.E. Butler, Comparative Law and International Law, *ibid.*, 699–702; M. Hilf, Comparative Law and European Law, *ibid.*, 695–9; R.A. Danner/M.-L. Bernal (eds), *Introduction to Foreign Legal Systems*, 1994.

55 For an example of the differences in the area of constitutional law in two Western federal systems of government see W.J. Josef, The Role of Basic Values in the Constitutional Hermeneutics of Germany and the United States, *ZaöRV* 56 (1996), 178–204. See further S.P. Sinha, *Legal Polycentricity and International Law*, 1996; P. Legrand, European Legal Systems Are Not Converging, *ICLQ* 45 (1996), 52–81.

Certainly, the actual role and capability of international law in governing the relations between states must not be exaggerated, in view of the decisive significance of military, economic, political and ideological factors of power. In fact, the role of international law in international relations has always been limited, but it is rarely insignificant.[47] Its function in structuring the international system has been enhanced because of increasing global interdependence and the self-interest of states in regulating their intercourse rationally on the basis of reciprocity.[48] Therefore, disputes between states are usually accompanied by – in a given case naturally often conflicting – references to international law.

Foreign ministries do not unnecessarily employ a regular staff of legal advisors.[49] States continuously conclude and implement bilateral and international treaties and establish and operate international organizations. More and more compilations of state practice in international law have been appearing.[50] Serious efforts are being made to codify international law.[51] Modern national constitutions usually contain references to international law.[52] All of this corresponds to the empirical fact that most states are careful to observe most obligations of international law most of the time,[53] even in the absence of a compulsory dispute settlement procedure and centralized enforcement agency. Spectacular cases of violation of international law, which attract the attention of the media more than regular conduct, are exceptional and should not be confused with the ordinary course of business between states.

The old discussion on whether international law is true 'law' is therefore a moot point. First, it should be noted that the general concept of 'law' itself and its relative status in society is subject to quite divergent views throughout the world, as has been shown by the modern discipline of comparative legal studies.[54] It is based on different ideas, methods and traditions, as a consequence of historical and cultural diversity,[55] including the Anglo-Saxon common law tradition in England, the Commonwealth states and the United States, the European continental civil law tradition based on notions of Roman law, the Marxist conception of law as a product of class struggle and historical formations of society, the Islamic concept of law with no separation between state, society and religion, and special traditions in Asia and in Africa. This diversity is also relevant for proper understanding of the different national perceptions on the role and interpretation of international law itself.

Secondly, as regards international law as 'law', the arguments of the critics centred upon the absence of a legislature and, more recently, upon the topic of sanctions and compliance without recognizing the historical, structural and functional differences between legal systems within states and the international legal system as the necessary starting point of analysis. A horizontal system of law operates in a different manner from a centralized one and is based on principles of reciprocity and consensus rather than on command, obedience and enforcement. A system of law designed primarily for the external relations of states does not work like any internal legal system of a state. After all, there is no reason to assume that the international legal system must, or should, follow the historical models of centralized systems of national law. In effect, what distinguishes the rules and principles of international law from 'mere morality' is that they are accepted in practice as legally binding by states in their intercourse because they are useful to reduce complexity and uncertainty in international relations. While international law is clearly weaker than municipal law from the viewpoint of independent enforcement, it still provides the external relevant terms of legal reference for the conduct of states in their international relations, based on the fact that, in spite of all differences, they are members of an existing international community.[56]

The scope of international law

The process of change in international law from a system of coordination of the international intercourse of mainly European states in limited areas, such as diplomatic relations and war, to a universal system of cooperation in numerous fields between quite different entities reflects the advances of natural sciences and technology,[57] increasing global economic and political interdependence and the need to address problems which can no longer be properly dealt with within a national framework, such as in the fields of communications, international trade, economics and finance, environment and development, or the massive problem of refugee flows. The concept of 'sovereignty' of states, although particularly cherished due to their historical experience by the new states which have emerged from the process of decolonization since the 1960s, is becoming more and more antiquated in view of the globalization of the economy and increasing interdependence of states.[58]

International law now covers vast and complex areas of transnational concern, including traditional topics, such as the position of states,[59] state succession,[60] state responsibility,[61] peace and security,[62] the laws of war,[63] the law of treaties,[64] the law of the sea,[65] the law of international watercourses,[66] and the conduct of diplomatic relations,[67] as well as new topics, such as international organizations,[68] economy and development,[69] nuclear energy,[70] air law and outer space activities,[71] the use of the resources of the deep sea,[72] the environment,[73] communications,[74] and, last but not least, the international protection of human rights.[75] This development has resulted in increasing specialization in both academia and legal professions in practice. As noted by Oscar Schachter:

> It is no longer possible for a 'generalist' to cope with the volume and complexity of the various branches of international law. Increasingly, the professional international lawyer, whether practitioner or scholar, is a specialist in a particular branch of the law and each branch develops its own complicated and often arcane doctrine.[76]

This specialization reflects the fact that international law has 'through maturity, acquired complexity',[77] but the development also now poses problems with regard to the unity of the academic subject.[78] The literature on international law has indeed become an immense area of study. While the total production of books on international law had amounted to about

56 See R. Jennings/A. Watts (eds), *Oppenheim's International Law*, Vol. I, Part 1, 9th edn 1992, 8–14; H. Mosler, International Legal Community, *EPIL* II (1995), 1251–5.
57 M. Lachs, Thoughts on Science, Technology and World Law, *AJIL* 86 (1992), 673–97.
58 On the doctrine of sovereignty see Chapter 2 below, 17–18.
59 See Chapters 5, 75–90, 7, 109–17 and 8, 118–29 below.
60 See Chapter 11 below, 161–72.
61 See Chapter 17 below, 254–72.
62 See Chapter 22 below, 385–430.
63 See Chapters 19, 306–41 and 20, 342–63 below.
64 See Chapter 9 below, 130–46.
65 See Chapter 12 below, 173–97.
66 See Chapter 16 below, 242–3.
67 See Chapter 8 below, 123–7.
68 See Chapters 6, 91–6 and 21, 364–84 below.
69 See Chapter 15 below, 222–40.
70 See Chapter 16 below, 244.
71 See Chapter 13 below, 198–208.
72 See Chapter 12 below, 173–5, 193–5.
73 See Chapter 16 below, 241–53.
74 See Chapter 13 below, 201–3.
75 See Chapter 14 below, 209–21.
76 O. Schachter, *International Law in Theory and Practice*, 1991, 1.
77 T. M. Franck, *Fairness in International Law and Institutions*, 1995, 5.
78 See L.A.N.M. Barnhoorn/K.C. Wellens (eds), *Diversity in Secondary Rules and the Unity of International Law*, 1995.

79 J. Schwietzke, Review of: E. Beyerly, *Public International Law. A Guide to Information Sources, ZaöRV* 52 (1992), 1052–3.
80 See, for example, D. Wyatt/A. Dashwood, *European Community Law,* 3rd edn 1993; D.A.O. Edward/R.C. Lane, *European Community Law,* 2nd edn 1995; and the articles in *EPIL* II (1995), 127 *et seq.*
81 See Chapter 6 below, 95–6.

2,000 titles in 1785, by 1967 it had reached the figure of 80,000 books. Currently some 700 books and 3,000 articles on international law are published annually.[79]

The present book offers only a first introduction to fundamental elements and selected areas of international law. Furthermore, European Community law, which, although part of international law, has become a highly specialized area,[80] is outside the scope of this introduction, except for some reference to certain essential characteristics to describe the uniqueness of the 'supra-national' European Union as compared with other forms of international organizations.[81]

2 History and theory

The origin of international law is a matter of dispute among scholars.[1] Some authors start by examining the relations and treaties between political entities from ancient times (3000 BC), including pre-classical antiquity in the Near East, ancient Greece and Persia, and the Romano–Hellenistic period.[2] The prevailing view in the study of international law is that it emerged in Europe in the period after the Peace of Westphalia (1648), which concluded the Thirty Years War.

Again we find different opinions in the literature on the proper classification of the subsequent development. In his interesting book on the epochs of the history of international law, the German diplomat and historian Grewe argues that there were three distinct systems of international law after the sixteenth century, each of which was characterized by the interests, ideologies and policies of the power that was predominant in the relevant period: the international legal orders of the Spanish age (1494–1648), the French age (1648–1815) and of the English age (1815–1919)[3] (which the Scots and the Welsh, of course, in contrast to Grewe, would prefer to call 'British').[4] The *Encyclopedia of Public International Law*, edited by Rudolf Bernhardt, basically differentiates between the periods from 1648 to 1815, 1815 to the First World War, the inter-war period, and developments since the Second World War.[5] But it also has separate entries for regional developments in Africa, the Far East, the Islamic world, Latin America, and South and South-East Asia,[6] to avoid the impression of a Eurocentric approach and to clarify that the development of international rules and principles was not a European matter only. With regard to Asia, the work of C.H. Alexandrowicz especially has brought many new insights which had been lost in the course of European expansion.[7] As noted by R.P. Anand, it is incorrect

> to assume that international law has developed only during the last four or five hundred years and only in Europe, or that Christian civilization has enjoyed a monopoly in regard to prescription of rules to govern inter-state conduct. As Majid Khadduri points out: 'In each civilization the population tended to develop within itself a community of political entities – a family of nations – whose interrelationships were regulated by a set of customary rules and practices, rather than being a single nation governed by a single authority and a single system of law. Several families of nations existed or coexisted in areas such as the ancient Near East, Greece and Rome, China, Islam and Western Christendom, where at least one distinct civilization had developed in each of them. Within each civilization a body of principles and rules developed for regulating the conduct of states with one another in peace and war'.[8]

1 See W.G. Grewe, *Epochen der Völkerrechtsgeschichte*, 1984, 19–25; A. Cassese, *International Law in a Divided World*, 1986, 37–8; H. Steiger, Völkerrecht, in O. Brunner/W. Conze/R. Koselleck (eds), *Geschichtliche Grundbegriffe*, Vol. 7, 1992, 97–140. For a good collection of documents see W.G. Grewe (ed.), *Fontes Historiae Iuris Gentium: Sources Relating to the History of International Law*, Vol. I: 1380 BC–1493 (1985), Vol. II: 1493–1815 (1988), Vol. III ½: 1815–1945 (1992). See also A. Nussbaum, *A Concise History of the Law of Nations*, 1962; J.H.W. Verzijl, *International Law in Historical Perspective*, 11 vols, 1968–1991; P.S. Onuf/N. Onuf, *Federal Union, Modern World, The Law of Nations in an Age of Revolutions, 1776–1814*, 1993; H. Legohérel, *Histoire du droit international public*, 1996.
2 W. Preiser, History of the Law of Nations: Ancient Times to 1648, *EPIL* II (1995), 716–49.
3 Grewe (1984), *op. cit.*, 43. For an excellent analysis of the strategic–economic reasons for the changes in the international system see P. Kennedy, *The Rise and Fall of the Great Powers, Economic Change and Military Conflict from 1500 to 2000*, 1987. See also C.J. Barlett, *The Global Conflict. The International Rivalry of the Great Powers, 1880–1990*, 2nd edn 1994.
4 On the multinational nature of the British unitary state and regionalist tendencies, see P. Malanczuk, *Region und unitarische Struktur in Großbritannien*, 1984.
5 History of the Law of Nations, *EPIL* II (1995): S. Verosta, 1648 to 1815, 749–67; H.-U. Scupin, 1815 to the First World War, 767–93; W.G. Grewe, the First World War to the Second World War, 839–49; O. Kimminich, Since the Second World War, 849–61.
6 History of the Law of Nations – Regional Developments, *EPIL* II (1995): T.O. Elias, Africa, 793–802; S. Miyazaki, Far East, 802–9; A.S. El-Kosheri, Islam,

809–18; A.T.Y. Serra, Latin America, 818–24; N. Singh, South and South-East Asia, 824–39.

7 C.H. Alexandrowicz, *An Introduction to the History of the Law of Nations in the East Indies* (16th, 17th and 18th centuries), 1967; Treaty and Diplomatic Relations Between European and South Asian Powers in the Seventeenth and Eighteenth Centuries, *RdC* 123 (1968-I), 121 *et seq.* See also J.A. Thomas, History and International Law in Asia: A Time for Review, in R.St.J. Macdonald (ed.), *Essays in Honour of Wang Tieya*, 1994, 813–57.

8 R.P. Anand, The Influence of History on the Literature of International Law, in R.St.J. Macdonald/D.M. Johnston (eds), *The Structure and Process of International Law*, 1983, 342.

9 See Chapter 22 below, 395–415, 423–30.

10 See Grewe (1984), *op. cit.*; Anand, *op. cit.*, 344. On one aspect see also T. Meron, The Authority to Make Treaties in the Late Middle Ages, *AJIL* 89 (1995), 1–20.

11 See text below, 17–18.

The problem of periodization is well-known in historical studies in general. To a large extent the classification of history into periods is arbitrary and depends on the criteria applied. Therefore, not too much importance should be attached to it. For the purposes of this introduction it suffices to broadly distinguish between the 'classical' system of international law (1648–1918) and the development of 'modern' or 'new' international law since the First World War. The classical system was based on the recognition of the modern sovereign state as the only subject of international law. This system was composed of numerous sovereign states considered as legally equal and who accepted the unlimited right to wage war to enforce claims and protect national interests. In essence it reflected the interaction among European powers and the imposition of their international legal order upon the rest of the world in the three centuries following the Peace of Westphalia. From 1919 onwards a fundamental transformation of the international system took place with the attempt to organize the international community and to ban the use of force. The development of modern international law can conveniently be described in the stages from the First World War to the Second World War, including the split of the international community in the wake of the Russian Revolution and the creation of the League of Nations, from the establishment of the United Nations to decolonization (1945–60), and from the further expansion of the international community to the end of the Cold War marked by the dissolution of the Soviet empire (1960–89). The attempt to find a 'New World Order' after the end of the bipolar East–West conflict and the difficulties in the current phase of the development of international law will be addressed in the final chapter of this book.[9]

The formation of European international law

Even during the Middle Ages in Western Europe international law existed.[10] But medieval Europe was not very suitable for the development of international law, because it was not divided into states in the modern sense. Nowadays we think of states as having undisputed political control over their own territory, and as being independent of external political control. Medieval kings were not in this position; internally, they shared power with their barons, each of whom had a private army; externally, they acknowledged some sort of allegiance to the Pope and to the Holy Roman Emperor. When strong centralized states, such as England, Spain, France, the Netherlands and Sweden began to emerge, claiming unrestricted sovereignty and no longer submitting to a superior authority, new international standards evolved, also in relation to non-European powers like the Ottoman Empire, China and Japan. In the fifteenth and sixteenth centuries, with the discovery of the sea routes to the Far East and the rediscovery of America, the sea powers transcended the previous limits of the political world of Europe. This was followed by the development of the concept of the sovereign state, first in theory in the sixteenth century by Bodin,[11] then in reality in Spain and, in the transition to the seventeenth century, also in France.

Features of European international law in state practice after 1648

In state practice, the year 1648 marking the Peace of Westphalia[12] is considered as a watershed, at least in Europe where a new political order was created, to be replaced only after the defeat of Napoleon by the Vienna Congress of 1815. Within Europe the Peace of Westphalia ended the devastating religious wars between Catholic and Protestant countries and led to the recognition of Protestant powers and of the fact that the state is independent of the Church. Three hundred or so political entities, constituting the remains of the Holy Roman Empire, received the right to enter into alliances with foreign powers under certain restrictions. While Germany was divided into a number of comparatively small states, France, Sweden and the Netherlands were recognized as new big powers, and Switzerland and the Netherlands were accorded the position of neutral states. The Empire disintegrated and the decline of the power of the Church accelerated. As the Italian scholar Cassese notes with regard to the system set up by the Peace of Westphalia: 'by the same token it recorded the birth of an international system based on a plurality of independent states, recognizing no superior authority over them.'[13]

The Peace of Westphalia envisaged a collective security system which obliged parties to defend its provisions against all others. Disputes were to be referred to a peaceful settlement or a legal adjudication. If no solution was found on this basis within three years, all other parties were to come to the assistance of the injured party and allowed to use force. This system was never put into practice. Power politics and continuously shifting military alliances among European states overruled it, reflecting the attempt to maintain a balance of power[14] which was the prevailing political principle in their foreign policy. Friedrich Gentz, the collaborator of Metternich, was later (1806) to define the European balance of power accurately as 'an organization of separately existing states of which no single one has the ability to impair the independence or the basic rights of the others without meeting with effective resistance and thus having to risk danger for itself'.[15]

What became known as 'European public law' (*ius publicum europaeum*; *droit public de l'Europe*) evolved from the increased diplomatic and violent intercourse and ever-changing alliances among European powers on the basis of this principle, which was to be only temporarily abolished through the conquest of Europe by Napoleon. The French Revolution of 1789, however, had profoundly challenged the basis of the existing system by advocating the ideas of freedom and self-determination of people[16] which were meant to be implemented beyond the boundaries of France, and denied the rights of monarchs to dispose of state territory and population according to their own discretion.

With the restoration of the old order in Europe at the Vienna Congress of 1815,[17] the second attempt in history to create a collective security system was somewhat more successful, of course, under its own terms and historical conditions. The Treaties of Paris created the Holy Alliance of Christian nations between the monarchies of Austria, Russia and Prussia, and an anti-revolutionary military alliance between Austria, Prussia,

12 See A.-M. de Zayas, Westphalia, Peace of (1648), *EPIL* 7 (1984), 536–9.
13 Cassese, *op. cit.*, 37.
14 See A. Vagts/D. Vagts, Balance of Power, *EPIL* I (1992), 313–15.
15 Cited by Verosta, 1648 to 1815, *op. cit.*, at 751.
16 See Chapter 19 below, 326–40.
17 F. Münch, Vienna Congress (1815), *EPIL* 7 (1984), 522–5.

18 See S. Verosta, Aix-La-Chapelle, Congress of (1818), *EPIL* I (1992), 94–5; Verosta, Holy Alliance, *EPIL* II (1995), 861–3.
19 A. Randelzhofer, Great Powers, *EPIL* II (1995), 618–22.
20 T. Schieder, Crimean War, *EPIL* I (1992), 867–9.
21 Text in 114 CTS 409. See T. Schieder, Paris Peace Treaty (1856), *EPIL* 7 (1984), 376–8.
22 F. Münch, Berlin Congress (1878), *EPIL* I (1992), 387–9.
23 F. Münch, Balkan Wars (1912/1913), *EPIL* I (1992), 319–21.
24 On this period see S. Verosta, *Kollektivaktionen der Mächte des Europäischen Konzerts (1886-1914)*, 1988.
25 J. Fisch, *Die europäische Expansion und das Völkerrecht*, 1984; F. Ermarcora, Colonies and Colonial Régime, *EPIL* I (1992), 662–6.

Russia, and England, joined later also by France, to intervene against liberal and nationalist uprising threatening the established order.[18]

The era of cooperation between the Great Powers[19] in Europe came to an end with the dispute over the Balkans and their diverging strategic interests with regard to the declining Turkish empire. The Crimean War,[20] in which Russia was defeated by the alliance of France and Great Britain, supported by Piedmont-Sardinia and Turkey, ended with the Paris Peace Treaty of 1856.[21] But the Berlin Congress of 1878[22] failed to solve the Balkan problems and the struggle of European powers over the distribution of spoils emerging in the Orient from the disintegration of the Ottoman Empire culminated in the Balkan Wars of 1912/13,[23] bringing the Concert of Europe to its end.[24]

Colonization and the relation to non-European powers

One important aspect of the nature of international law in the age of European colonization of the world,[25] was the relationship of European states, unified by Christianity, to non-European powers. European expansion abroad in the interest of trade and commerce was promoted in England, the Netherlands and France by ruthless profit-making companies, such as the British East India Company, enjoying privileges which permitted them to perform state functions in overseas territories. On the inter-state level, at first Europeans were prepared to admit that non-European states had at least limited rights under the European system of international law. Non-European states were also often willing to concede that European states had at least limited rights under their various non-European systems of international law, and so legal relations, at the beginning on equal footing, between European and non-European states became possible. However, these relations did not constitute a true universal legal system based on common values or institutions, and states existed separately without any extensive cooperation.

The Europeans recognized the Mogul Empire in India, the Ottoman Empire, Persia, China, Japan, Burma, Siam (renamed Thailand in 1939) and Ethiopia as established political entities, but they were aware that these states did not play a major role in global affairs. By the Paris Peace Treaty of 1856 Turkey was even expressly admitted (as the first non-Christian nation) to the Concert of Europe. On the other hand, the Ottoman Empire, for example, had found it difficult to accept the Christian nations it was confronted with at its borders in Europe as equal and was insisting on its superiority. Similarly, China, 'the empire in the centre of the earth', preferred isolation to contact with foreigners, from whom nothing more than tribute was expected to be due. When a British delegation from King George III (1760–1821), backed by some handsome new technical gifts, requested in 1793 that China accept a British envoy, the Emperor responded:

> As to your entreaty to send one of your nationals to be accredited to my Celestial Court and to be in control of your country's trade with China, this request is contrary to all usage of my dynasty and cannot possibly be entertained . . . Our ceremonies and code of laws differ so completely from your own that, even if

your Envoy were able to acquire the rudiments of our civilization, you could not possibly transplant our manners and customs to your alien soil . . . Swaying the wide world, I have but one aim in view, namely, to maintain a perfect governance and to fulfill the duties of the state . . . I set no value on objects strange or ingenious, and have no use for your country's manufactures.[26]

Japan, after the ascent to power of the Shoguns, ended the infiltration by Christian missionaries and also cut itself off from all alien contact, the only exception being Dutch merchants who were permitted to continue business at a trading post at Nagasaki. It took until the nineteenth century for European powers to re-establish trade with China and Japan with the threat and use of force, invoking, *inter alia*, the alleged legal principle of 'freedom of trade'.

In sum, although legally all members of the international community were equal, in fact, the international system was dominated by the great powers of Britain, France, Spain, Portugal, the United States, Russia, Austria, Prussia and the Netherlands. Following the industrial revolution in Europe after the late eighteenth century, in the nineteenth century the international community to a large extent had virtually become a European one on the basis of either conquest or domination. By about 1880 Europeans had subdued most of the non-European states, which was interpreted in Europe as conclusive proof of the inherent superiority of the white man, and the international legal system became a white man's club, to which non-European states would be admitted only if they produced evidence that they were 'civilized'.

In the case of old powers, such as Turkey, Siam (Thailand), China and Japan, Western states basically relied on the so-called capitulation system, treaties which were designed to establish lasting privileges for European trade and commerce in those states and which exempted Europeans from local jurisdiction. In the case of communities without sufficient central authority, the method was simply conquest and appropriation. Conquest and appropriation became particularly apparent in the scramble for Africa,[27] the dividing up of the continent among European powers at the Berlin West Africa Conference 1884/5, which managed to settle the issues among colonial powers without provoking another European war.[28]

Only rarely were nations which had been selected for colonization able to offer effective resistance, as in the case of Ethiopia in 1896 when Emperor Menelik's forces humiliated the Italians in the battle of Adwa. The fate of China offers an illuminating example. After the Opium War of 1842, fought under the premise of securing the sale of the drug in China, the Treaty of Nanking compelled China to surrender the island of Hong Kong to Britain.[29] It was followed by other 'unequal treaties' imposing diplomatic relations and increasing the number of available trading ports.[30] The anti-foreign spirit in China in response to Western intervention in the distracted Empire resulted in the famous Boxer rebellion. The Boxers, known in China as 'Patriotic Harmonious Fists', found official support for their 'China for the Chinese' objective. But following attacks on Western legations in Beijing and the murder of Europeans, military intervention led

26 Emperor Ch'ieng-lung, cited by Verosta, 1648 to 1815, *op. cit.*, at 761.
27 See T. Pakenham, *The Scramble for Africa 1876–1912*, 1992.
28 F. Münch, Berlin West Africa Conference (1884/1885), *EPIL* I (1992), 389–91.
29 A.D. Hughes, Hong Kong, *EPIL* II (1995), 870–3. See also *Harris CMIL*, 235. On the agreement to return Hong Kong to China in 1997 see Chapter 10 below, 158.
30 See Wang Tieya, International Law in China: Historical and Contemporary Perspectives, *RdC* 221 (1990-II), 193–369; W. Morvay, Unequal Treaties, *EPIL* 7 (1984), 514–17. See also Chapters 9, 139–40 and 10, 158 below.

31 Hamsworth, *History of the World*, Vol. 2, 1908, 823.
32 See P. Malanczuk, Monroe Doctrine, *EPIL* 7 (1984), 339–44.
33 See text below, 30.
34 See Serra (1995), *op. cit.*; C. Gray, International Law 1908–1983, *Leg. Stud.* 3 (1983), 267–82, 269 *et seq.*; J.A. Barberis, Les Règles spécifiques du droit international en Amérique Latine, *RdC* 235 (1992–IV), 81–227.

by Admiral Sir Edward Seymour crushed the rebellion at Lang-Fang in June 1900. The Peace Commission of the victors sentenced Princes Tuan and Fukuo to death, which sentence, because of their imperial rank, was converted to penal servitude for life. Prince Chuang and the Presidents of the Board of Censors and Board of Punishment were forced to commit suicide; three other high officials were beheaded. In addition, a protocol, signed on 7 September 1901, fixed the indemnity to be paid by China at 450,000,000 taels, on which 4 per cent interest was to be charged until the capital was paid off at the end of 39 years.[31]

Japan was somewhat more fortunate because it had decided in the nineteenth century to adapt its feudal system to the more advanced foreign technology and organization of the West. This was a reaction to the opening of the country by the cannons of the American Commodore Perry, the subsequent conclusion of a trade and 'friendship' treaty in 1854, other treaties with European powers putting their nationals under the jurisdiction of their consuls, and the repeated bombardment of Japanese ports. The adaptation was one of the reasons which later enabled Japan to defeat Russia in the war of 1904/5, to occupy Korea and Manchuria, and gain recognition as a new major power in the Peace of Portsmouth (USA) of 1905. The end of white rule and the complex process of decolonization in Asia was then brought forward by Japanese aggression and initial victories in the Second World War, which helped to destroy the myth of the invincibility of the European colonial masters.

The Western hemisphere

European states, however, were also confronted with new problems in the wake of the American rebellion against Britain. The American Declaration of Independence of 1776, invoking the principle of self-determination, had led to the recognition after seven years of war of a new subject of international law by the mother country, followed at the beginning of the nineteenth century by the independence of Latin-American states from Spain and Portugal. The dissociation from Europe was expressed in the doctrine proclaimed by President Monroe in 1823 against European intervention in the Western hemisphere.[32] The Monroe doctrine, never accepted as a legal one in Europe, however, was to become the basis for numerous interventions by the United States in Latin America. Nevertheless, the United States and Latin American countries remained within the system of European international law and made significant contributions to its development. While the practice of the United States, to take one important example, furthered international arbitration to settle disputes,[33] South American states attempted to protect themselves against foreign intervention and European dominance by formulating a new regional American international law.[34] On the whole, the general American attitude towards international relations was more idealistic and law-orientated than the traditional realistic and power-motivated perspective of European states. But even the United States, although it cherished freedom from colonial domination in its own history, for example, was engaged in opening up China, and took the Philippines in 1898 after the war with Spain.

From what has been outlined above, it naturally follows that in the 'classical period' the use of force short of war was also covered by international law.[35] A famous example for the latter was the failure of the Argentinian Foreign Minister Luis Drago at the beginning of the twentieth century to change the practice of powerful European states using armed force to achieve payment from other states for damage caused to them or their nationals ('gun-boat diplomacy').[36] Venezuela demanded that the question of debts owed to Britain, Germany and Italy for civil-war damage, the seizure of ships by the Venezuelan government, and stemming from loans granted to Venezuela for railways, be settled by a Venezuelan commission. The commission refused to accept full compensation of the European claims and, after an ultimatum, in 1902 the European claimant states sank three Venezuelan ships, bombarded Puerto Cabello and imposed a naval blockade upon Venezuela. The reaction of the United States to a note of protest sent by Drago with reference to the Monroe doctrine was negative. In effect, the United States pointed out that foreign intervention would not occur if Latin-American countries respected their international obligations concerning the protection of foreign property.[37]

Theory: naturalists and positivists

Having outlined some important aspects of state practice, it is now appropriate to turn to doctrine, which has always had much less influence on the actual development of international law than many writers have been willing to admit.[38] The notion of European international law was prepared by academic writers who during the formative period of international law provided legal concepts and systematic arguments justifying the interests of the emerging powers, especially with regard to the ambitions of their own respective countries, as may be noted in the development of the law of the sea.[39] Since they have, to some extent, left a mark on the modern law, it is necessary to say something about them, and in particular to describe the two main schools of thought: naturalists and positivists, lines of thinking about international law which still belong to the mainstream of Western conceptions of international law today, although they have faced challenge.[40]

The leading naturalist writer was the Dutchman Hugo Grotius (1583–1645), who is often regarded as the founder of modern international law;[41] other important naturalist writers were the Spaniards Vitoria (1486–1546)[42] and Suarez (1548–1617), Gentili, an Italian Protestant who fled to England (1552–1608),[43] and the Englishman Zouche (1590–1661). Although disagreeing about many things, all these writers agreed that the basic principles of all law (national as well as international) were derived, not from any deliberate human choice or decision, but from principles of justice which had a universal and eternal validity and which could be discovered by pure reason; law was to be found, not made.

These basic principles of law were called natural law. But Vitoria's early attempt to establish *ius naturae* as the universal law of humanity to include the so-called 'Indian' nations in the Americas in its sphere of legal protection remained a vain theoretical suggestion.[44] Natural law was originally regarded as having a divine origin, but Grotius wrote that

35 See Chapter 19 below, 306–9.
36 W. Benedek, Drago-Porter Convention (1907), *EPIL* I (1992), 1102–3.
37 See Chapter 17 below, 260–1.
38 On the role of doctrine as a subsidiary source of contemporary international law see Chapter 3 below, 51–2.
39 See Grewe (1984), *op. cit.*, 300 *et seq.*, 471 *et seq.*, 647 *et seq.*
40 See J.P. Egido, Natural Law, *EPIL* 7 (1984), 344–9; R. Ago, Positivism, *ibid.*, 385–93; H.J. Steiner, International Law: Doctrine and Schools of Thought in the Twentieth Century, *EPIL* II (1995), 1216–27; see also A. Verdross/H.F. Koeck, Natural Law: The Tradition of Universal Reason and Authority, in Macdonald/Johnston (eds), 1983, *op. cit.*, 17–50; M. Bos, Will and Order in the Nation-State System: Observations on Positivism and International Law, *ibid.*, 51–78.
41 See T.M.C. Asser Instituut (ed.), *International Law and the Grotian Heritage*, 1983; P. Haggenmacher, *Grotius et la doctrine de la guerre juste*, 1983; A. Dufour/P. Haggenmacher/J. Toman (eds), *Grotius et l'ordre juridique international*, 1985; H. Bull/B. Kingsbury/A. Roberts (eds), *Hugo Grotius and International Relations*, 1990; C.G. Roelofsen, Grotius and the 'Grotian Heritage' in International Law and International Relations, The Quartercentenary and its Aftermath (ca. 1980–1990), *Grotiana* 11 (1990), 6–28; O. Yasuaki (ed.), *A Normative Approach to War. Peace, War, and Justice in Hugo Grotius*, 1993; P. Borschenberg, *Hugo Grotius 'Commentarius in theses XI': An Early Treatise on Sovereignty, the Just War, and the Legitimacy of the Dutch Revolt*, 1994.
42 A. Truyol Serra *et al.* (eds), *Actualité de la pensée juridique de Francisco de Vitoria*, 1988.
43 See T. Meron, Common Rights of Mankind in Gentili, Grotius and Suarez, *AJIL* 85 (1991), 110–17.
44 M.v. Gelderen, The Challenge of Colonialism: Grotius and Vitoria on Natural Law and International Relations, *Grotiana* 14/5 (1993/4), 3–37.

45 M.W. Janis (ed.), *The Influence of Religion on the Development of International Law*, 1991.

natural law would still have existed even if God had not existed; instead, Grotius considered that the existence of natural law was the automatic consequence of the fact that men lived together in society and were capable of understanding that certain rules were necessary for the preservation of society. According to this line of argument, the prohibition of murder, for instance, was a rule of natural law, independently of any legislation forbidding murder, because every intelligent man would realize that such a rule was just and necessary for the preservation of human society.

The theory of natural law has a long tradition, going back to Roman times, and is still the official philosophy of law accepted by the Roman Catholic Church. But nowadays it is not accepted by many people outside the Roman Catholic Church.[45] Having religious overtones and being incapable of verification, the theory is suspect in a scientific and secular age. The essence of the theory was that law was derived from justice, and, although lawyers and judges often appeal to justice in order to fill gaps or to resolve uncertainties in the law, the theory of natural law must logically lead to a much more radical conclusion, namely that an unjust rule is not law at all and can be disregarded by the judge; but this is a conclusion which no modern legal system would accept. Even the supporters of the theory have been unable to state principles of natural law with any precision; for instance, 'Thou shalt not kill' may be accepted as a universally valid rule, necessary for the maintenance of human society, but writers on natural law do not agree about the number of exceptions to the rule which ought to be recognized.

However, in the sixteenth and seventeenth centuries the theory was universally accepted, and it performed a very useful function by encouraging respect for justice at a time when the collapse of the feudal system and the division of Europe between Catholics and Protestants might otherwise have led to complete anarchy. It is hard to think of any other foundations on which a system of international law could have been built at that time. Even the vagueness of the natural law theory, which is nowadays such a defect, was less apparent in the time of Grotius, who illustrated his arguments with biblical quotations, references to Greek and Roman history and – above all – analogies drawn from Roman private law, which at that time was admired as a fairly accurate reflection of natural law and was therefore copied by many European countries.

After Grotius' death the intellectual climate became more sceptical, and international law would have lost respect if it had remained based on the theory of natural law. People were beginning to argue by 1700 that law was largely positive, that is, man-made; consequently, law and justice were not the same thing, and laws might vary from time to time and from place to place, according to the whim of the legislator. Applied to international law, positivism (as this new theory was called) regarded the actual behaviour of states as the basis of international law. The first great positivist writer on international law was another Dutchman, Cornelis van Bynkershoek (1673–1743), who was to some extent ahead of his time; positivism had its roots in the eighteenth century but was not fully accepted until the nineteenth century. Unfortunately, apart from collecting the texts of treaties, little attempt was made to study the practice of states scientifically until the twentieth century.

An attempt to combine naturalism and positivism was made by the Swiss writer Emerich von Vattel (1714–67).[46] He emphasized the inherent rights which states derived from natural law, but said that they were accountable only to their own consciences for the observance of the duties imposed by natural law, unless they had expressly agreed to treat those duties as part of positive law. Vattel exercised a strong and pernicious influence on many writers and states during the eighteenth, nineteenth and early twentieth centuries; even today his influence is still sometimes felt. An intellectual climate which encourages states to assert their rights and to ignore their duties is a sure recipe for disorder.

The theory of sovereignty

One word which recurs frequently in the writings of Vattel's followers is 'sovereignty', and it is doubtful whether any single word has ever caused so much intellectual confusion and international lawlessness.

The theory of sovereignty began as an attempt to analyse the internal structure of a state. Political philosophers taught that there must be, within each state, some entity which possessed supreme legislative power and/or supreme political power. The theory dates back to the sixteenth century and political scientists usually refer to the writings of Machiavelli (1469–1527), Jean Bodin (1530–1596) and Thomas Hobbes (1588–1679).[47] But its best-known exponent, as far as lawyers are concerned, was John Austin (1790–1859), who defined law as the general commands of a sovereign, supported by the threat of sanctions. Since international law did not fit his theory, he said that international law was not law. In fact, it is hard to find any legal system which does fit his theory. In federal states like the United States, legislative power is divided by the constitution between the federation and the member states, neither of which has supreme legislative power. Even in England, where the Queen in Parliament has supreme legislative power, legislation is not the only source of law, nor the oldest source of law.

It was easy to argue, as a corollary to this theory, that the sovereign, possessing supreme power, was not himself bound by the laws which he made. Then, by a shift of meaning, the word came to be used to describe, not only the relationship of a superior to his inferiors *within* a state (internal sovereignty), but also the relationship of the ruler or of the state itself towards *other* states (external sovereignty). But the word still carried its emotive overtones of unlimited power above the law, and this gave a totally misleading picture of international relations. The fact that a ruler can do what he likes to his own subjects does not mean that he can do what he likes – either as a matter of law or as a matter of power politics – to other states.

When international lawyers say that a state is sovereign, all that they really mean is that it is independent, that is, that it is not a dependency of some other state. They do not mean that it is in any way above the law. It would be far better if the word 'sovereignty' were replaced by the word 'independence'. In so far as 'sovereignty' means anything in addition to

46 N.G. Onuf, Civitas Maxima: Wolff, Vattel and the Fate of Republicanism, *AJIL* 88 (1994), 280–303.
47 See G.H. Sabine/T.L. Thorson, *A History of Political Theory*, 4th edn 1973, Part III: The Theory of the National State.

48 *Wimbledon* case, PCIJ, series A, no. 1, 25. In this case Germany had refused the British steamship *Wimbledon*, chartered by a French company, access to the Kiel Canal on the grounds that the vessel had on board a cargo of munitions and artillery stores consigned to the Polish naval base at Danzig. The refusal was based upon German Neutrality Orders issued in 1920 in connection with the war between Russia and Poland. The court held that Germany had acted in violation of Art. 380 of the Versailles Peace Treaty; see I.v. Münch, The Wimbledon, *EPIL 2* (1981), 293–6.
49 See Chapter 5 below, 80.
50 See L. Wildhaber, Sovereignty and International Law, in Macdonald/ Johnston (eds), 1983, *op. cit.*, 425–52; F.H. Hinsley, *Sovereignty*, 2nd edn 1986; A. James, *Sovereign Statehood*, 1986; H. Steinberger, Sovereignty, *EPIL* 10 (1987), 397–418; I.D. DeLupis, *International Law and the Independent State*, 1988; R.H. Jackson, *Quasi-States: Sovereignty, International Relations and the Third World*, 1990; J. Bartelson, *A Genealogy of Sovereignty*, 1993; G. Gottlieb, *Nation Against State. A New Approach to Ethnic Conflicts and the Decline of State Sovereignty*, 1993; O. Schachter, Sovereignty – Then and Now, in Macdonald (ed.), 1994, *op. cit.*, 671–88; L. Henkin, The Mythology of Sovereignty, *ibid.*, 351–8; N. Schrijver, The Dynamics of Sovereignty in a Changing World, in K. Ginther/E. Denters/P.J.I.M. de Waart (eds), *Sustainable Development and Good Governance*, 1995, 80–9; M.R. Fowler/ J.M. Bunck, *Law, Power and the Sovereign State. The Evolution and the Application of the Concept of Sovereignty*, 1995; A. Chayes/A.H. Chayes, *The New Sovereignty. Compliance with International Regulatory Agreements*, 1995; K.M. Meesen, Sovereignty, in *Wolfrum UNLPP II*, 1193–201; A. Bleckmann, Article 2(1), in *Simma CUNAC*, 77–87. See also the literature in Chapter 1 above, 3 and Chapter 5 below, 13–80.
51 See Chapter 12 below, 181–94.
52 See Chapter 8 below, 118–26.
53 See Chapter 8 below, 123–9.
54 See Chapter 9 below, 130–46.
55 See Chapter 17 below, 256–69.
56 See Chapter 20 below, 350–1.

'independence', it is not a legal term with any fixed meaning, but a wholly emotive term. Everyone knows that states are powerful, but the emphasis on sovereignty exaggerates their power and encourages them to abuse it; above all, it preserves the superstition that there is something in international cooperation as such which comes near to violating the intrinsic nature of a 'sovereign' state.

At the end of the nineteenth century, many international lawyers, particularly in Germany, developed the doctrine of sovereignty to the point where it threatened to destroy international law altogether. Since 1914 there has been a reaction. International lawyers in the Western world have rejected the old dogmas about sovereignty and the inherent rights of states; indeed, scientific examinations of the practice of states, which were carried out for the first time in the twentieth century, have shown that those dogmas were never taken half as seriously by states as they were by theorists. In 1923, in the *Wimbledon* case, the Permanent Court of International Justice said: 'The Court declines to see, in the conclusion of any treaty by which a state undertakes to perform or refrain from performing a particular act, an abandonment of its sovereignty ... [T]he right of entering into international engagements is an attribute of state sovereignty.'[48]

Of course, one can imagine treaties containing such far-reaching obligations as depriving a state of its independence – for instance, a treaty whereby one state becomes a protectorate of another state.[49] But there is no fixed dividing line between independence and loss of independence; it is a matter of degree and opinion; even 'independence' shares some of the emotive qualities of the word 'sovereignty'. For instance, the idea of joining a supranational organization like the European Union, which would have been regarded as an intolerable restriction upon independence a century ago, is nowadays discussed in the more realistic terms of economic advantages and disadvantages. While in the West the doctrine of sovereignty has been losing much ground in view of increasing international interdependence, developing countries still value it highly as a 'cornerstone of international relations' to protect their recently gained political independence.[50]

Legal results of the period up to the First World War

What were the main legal results of the development of this 'classical' and basically European international law, which seemed to view states as living more in a situation of anarchy than of law and order? In the first place, a number of basic rules and principles of international law emerged in this period, such as the principle of territorial sovereignty securing exclusive control and jurisdiction of states over their territory, the freedom of the high seas,[51] the law on state immunity from the jurisdiction of foreign courts,[52] the law on diplomatic and consular relations,[53] the principle of *pacta sunt servanda* (treaties must be kept) and the law of treaties,[54] rules on the diplomatic protection of foreigners and their property,[55] and on neutrality.[56]

The unlimited right to use force

A central feature of classical international law was that it did not place any restriction on the right of states to use force and to go to war which was considered to be an inherent attribute of the sovereignty and equality of states. Effective annexation of conquered foreign territory was a valid legal title to acquire sovereignty over it.[57] There is also no doubt that the concepts of international law prevailing at this time served to facilitate the process of colonization. Sovereignty could be acquired over *terrae nullius*, territory allegedly belonging to nobody, a notion applied to areas throughout the world lacking a strong central power able to resist conquest. If resistance happened to occur, either treaties with local rulers were available as legal instruments, or war could be used.

The unlimited right to use force was also reflected in the doctrine of intervention.[58] In the sixteenth century, when the fundament of the theory of the modern sovereign state was laid by Machiavelli[59] and Bodin,[60] the specific historical doctrine of intervention, also advocated by such authors as Vitoria, Gentili, and Grotius, was primarily motivated by religious considerations.[61] These were superseded after the Thirty Years War (1618–48) by the practice of more general political intervention. Grewe also refers to comments by Grotius, not usually cited, which seem to indicate that the great writer, in accordance with the spirit of his age, when addressing humanitarian intervention, in reality meant the right of religious intervention founded upon natural law to protect fellow Christians. It is notable that even much later there were still writers such as de Martens who in 1883 justified intervention by the 'civilized powers', but only in relation to 'non civilized nations', when 'the Christian population of those countries is exposed to persecutions or massacres' by 'common religious interests and humanitarian considerations'.[62]

In the nineteenth century, the principle of non-intervention, as formulated earlier by Wolff and Vattel, had by then acquired general recognition. Nevertheless, the international legal order of the nineteenth century was characterized by certain exceptions to this principle, namely the right of intervention based on treaties and on the principles of self-help and self-preservation. Attempts by the monarchies of Austria, Russia and Prussia after 1815 generally to establish a principle of military intervention on the basis of the Holy Alliance, and by Napoleon III to find recognition of a right of intervention in favour of national self-determination remained unsuccessful.

However, a new independent reason for intervention based on 'humanity' emerged in theory which was related to the ideas of political liberalism and the concept of fundamental human rights. State practice in the nineteenth century increasingly invoked humanitarian reasons to justify intervention – often, however, as a disguise for intervention made for political, economic or other reasons. The doctrine played a role in the intervention by European powers in 1827 in support of the Greek uprising against the Turks, the intervention by Britain and France in 1856 in Sicily, allegedly in view of political arrests and supposed cruel treatment of the prisoners, and the famous intervention of Britain, France, Austria, Prussia, and Russia in Syria in 1860–1 following the murder of thousands of Christian Maronites

57 See Chapter 10 below, 151–4.
58 For the following see P. Malanczuk, *Humanitarian Intervention and the Legitimacy of the Use of Force*, 1993, 7–11 with references.
59 *Il Principe*, written in 1513, published in 1531. Less attention has been paid to Machiavelli's other important work, the *Discorsi*.
60 *De Rei publica* (1576), published in French in 1579.
61 Grewe (1984), *op. cit.*, 211–16.
62 F. de Martens, *Traité de droit international*, 1883, 398.

63 Grewe (1984), *op. cit.*, at 578, relying on Martens, Rougier and Dupuis, records that the action, which aimed at a reform of the Turkish administration, was based upon the fiction of an invitation to intervene by the Sultan. The conclusions of the study of the case by I. Pogany, Humanitarian Intervention in International Law: The French Intervention in Syria Re-Examined, *ICLQ* 5 (1986), 182, are somewhat different.
64 See Grewe (1984), *op. cit.*, at 579, stressing that the list is by no means exhaustive.
65 Scupin, *op. cit.*, at 771.
66 T. Schieder, Crimean War, *EPIL* 7 (1984), 59, at 61.
67 See Chapter 18 below, 273–305.
68 Text in 52 CTS 243. See H.-J. Schlochauer, Jay Treaty, *EPIL* 1 (1981), 108–11.

by the Druse Muslims.[63] These acts were the prelude to repeated interventions by European powers into the Ottoman Empire in response to uprisings and killings on Crete in 1866, in Bosnia in 1875, Bulgaria in 1877 and Macedonia in 1887. Other instances – of diplomatic intercession – on humanitarian grounds include the protest by Britain, France and Austria, supported by Italy, Spain, Portugal and Sweden in 1863 against the methods used by Russia to suppress the Polish uprising and numerous protests by the Great Powers, including the United States, against the suppression of the Jews. At the turn of the century and later, the intervention by the United States in Cuba in 1898 or the pressure exercised by Britain and the United States on Belgium because of the misery of the indigenous population in the Congo, and in 1912/13 on Peru in view of the ruthless exploitation of the local rubber collectors, could also be mentioned.[64]

This practice revealed a new tendency in the official grounds advanced by states to justify intervention in that period, but not a new rule of customary international law. In reality, states were mostly pursuing their own ends when intervening in another state for alleged humanitarian purposes, and thus the institution of intervention, as Scupin notes, 'was unable to provide a complete justification for such action'.[65] Especially the frequent interventions in the Ottoman Empire to protect Christians must be seen in the light of the divergent interests of European powers at stake in the Middle East and the political order of European Turkey. Humanitarian intervention was a welcome pretext in their rivalry to establish influence in the declining Empire of the 'old man at the Bosporus'. The Crimean War of 1853, in which Russia went to war with Turkey officially on the grounds of securing stronger guarantees for the protection of Christians and was then confronted with the unexpected French–British military alliance and pressure from Austria, is instructive historical evidence for 'the rise of a new era of power-political *realpolitik*'.[66]

The peaceful settlement of disputes

At least as a normative concept, the idea of the peaceful settlement of disputes[67] through negotiations, conciliation, mediation or arbitration evolved since the Peace of Westphalia, although the origins are much older. Arbitration, in the sense of eliminating a dispute by binding third-party decision, however, was not accepted by absolute monarchs in practice. The development of the modern history of arbitration commenced with the 1794 Jay Treaty of Amity, Commerce and Navigation, in which Britain and the United States agreed to settle by an arbitration commission claims for damages by British and American nationals whose property had been confiscated or ships taken by the enemy government.[68] From 1798 to 1804 the commission rendered over 536 awards, some of which became important precedents for the subsequent development of the law. This successful experience was the starting-point for a series of treaties containing arbitration clauses in the nineteenth century, but the development remained basically limited to bilateral treaties and disputes of subordinate political interest.

Prohibition of the slave trade

One aspect that deserves to be mentioned separately is the prohibition of the slave trade in the name of humanity.[69] By the eighteenth century, the expansion of European trade had come to cover not only goods, but in an extensive manner also human beings. It was based on a lucrative triangular trade transporting goods from Europe to Africa, African slaves, mostly sold by Arab dealers, to the plantations in America, and finally products and raw materials from America to Europe. The slave trade started in the sixteenth century when Spain granted fixed-term monopoly licences (*asientos*) to private entrepreneurs to introduce African slaves to Spanish America and then later involved other European countries. After Britain had acquired the monopoly from Spain to supply slaves to the Spanish colonies in 1713, it transferred it to the South Sea Company; it is estimated that between the years 1680 and 1786 British dealers alone transported over two million African slaves to America. In total, at least fifteen million Africans were enslaved for shipment to the Americas.

Opposition to this practice, from both in and beyond the United Kingdom, gradually led to its prohibition in international law in the nineteenth century. Following national measures, the first treaty to condemn the slave trade was concluded between France and Britain in 1814.[70] This humanitarian principle was also adopted at the Vienna Congress of 1815 and in subsequent multilateral treaties leading to the comprehensive General Act of the Brussels Conference relative to the African Slave Trade of 1890. The Act was ratified by all European states, the United States, Persia, Turkey, the Congo and Zanzibar and provided effective military and legal measures to terminate the slave trade, although the status of domestic slavery remained unaffected. In the abolition of the slave trade, the British Royal Navy, ruling the seas, played a central role as a maritime enforcement agency controlling shipping. At the same time, as a side-effect, Britain was placed in the useful position of being able to monitor overseas trade by other states in goods in general.

Humanization of the law of warfare

Furthermore, the humanization of the international law of warfare commenced with agreements concluded by the military commanders of the belligerent parties concerning prisoners of war, the wounded and sick, and the protection of military hospitals already prior to the nineteenth century.[71] Some more relevant developments occurred after the experience of the Crimean War (1853–6) and the lessons of the first modern war, the American Civil War (1861–5), with its enormous casualties on both sides (Union forces: 359,528 dead and 275,175 wounded; Confederate forces: about 258,000 dead and 225,000 wounded),[72] and the example of the 1863 Instructions for United States Armies in the Field (Lieber Code). The Geneva Convention of 1864, initiated by Henry Dunant, gave some status to work assisting the wounded. It recognized functions in relation to the state parties to the Convention of the International Committee of the Red Cross, founded as a private law association under the laws of the Canton of Geneva in 1863. It was followed by the Petersburg Declaration of 1868

69 A.M. Trebilcock, Slavery, *EPIL* 8 (1985), 481–4; O.I. Tiunov, Pacta sunt servanda: The Principle of Observing International Treaties in the Epoch of the Slave-Owning Society, *St. Louis ULJ* 38 (1994), 929-45.
70 Additional Articles to the Paris Peace Treaty of 30 May 1814, 63 CTS 193.
71 For the earlier development see M. Keen, *The Laws of War in the Late Middle Ages*, 1993; T. Meron, *Henry's Wars and Shakespeare's Laws: Perspectives on the Law of War in the Later Middle Ages*, 1993.
72 See P. Malanczuk, American Civil War, *EPIL* I (1992), 129–31.

73 The Institute is a private association of scholars that was founded in 1873 at the same time as the International Law Association, which is larger and more open. See F. Münch, Institut de Droit International, *EPIL* II (1995), 997–1000; R. Stödter, International Law Association, *ibid.*, 1207–8.

74 See Chapter 20 below, 342–63.

75 See D.W. Bowett, *The Law of International Institutions*, 4th edn 1982, 1–13; D. Vignes, The Impact of International Organizations on the Development and Application of Public International Law, in Macdonald/Johnston (eds), 1983, *op. cit.*, 809–55; I. Seidl-Hohenveldern/G. Loibl, *Das Recht der Internationalen Organisationen*, 5th edn 1992, 12–19.

76 F. Meißner, Rhine River, *EPIL* 12 (1990), 310–6.

77 B. Vitányi, Scheldt River, *EPIL* 12 (1990), 341–3.

78 I. Seidl-Hohenveldern, Danube River, *EPIL* I (1992), 934–7.

79 A. Noll, International Telecommunication Union, *EPIL* II (1995), 1379–85.

80 L. Weber, Universal Postal Union, *EPIL* 5 (1983), 383–6.

81 K. Pfanner, Industrial Property, Protection of, *EPIL* II (1995), 964–76.

82 See P. Katzenberger, Literary and Artistic Works, International Protection, *EPIL* 5 (1983), 202–11.

83 J.M. Mössner, Hague Peace Conferences of 1899 and 1907, *EPIL* II (1995), 671–7.

84 See K.J. Partsch, Vital Interests, *EPIL* 10 (1987), 526–8.

85 See A. D'Amato, Domestic Jurisdiction, *EPIL* I (1992), 1090–6. See also Chapters 18, 285–6 and 21, 368–9 below.

86 Text in *AJIL* 10 (1916), Supp. See H.-J. Schlochauer, Bryan Treaties (1913/1914), *EPIL* I (1992), 509–11.

prohibiting the use of small exploding projectiles, which, however, remained insignificant in practice. A conference in Brussels in 1874 and proposals presented by the Institut de Droit International[73] in 1880 paved the way for the Hague Peace Conferences of 1899 and 1907 laying down the basis for the development of modern international humanitarian law.[74]

First forms of international organizations

In the nineteenth century also the first rudimentary forms of international cooperation emerged.[75] Commerce required the internationalization of rivers and the establishment of international river commissions, as in the case of the Rhine (1831/68),[76] the Scheldt (1839)[77] and the Danube (1856/65).[78] Furthermore, the development of technology, communications and commerce prepared the way for international administrative unions with legal personality limited to the discharge of particular functions. These included the Geodetic Union (1864), concerned with surveying the earth, the International Telegraph Union (1865) as the forerunner of the current International Telecommunication Union,[79] the Universal Postal Union (1874),[80] the Berne Bureau for the Protection of Industrial Property (1883),[81] the Berne Bureau for the Protection of Literary and Artistic Works (1886),[82] and the Union for the Publication of Customs Tariffs (1890).

The Hague Peace Conferences of 1899 and 1907

The period of 'classical' international law came to an end with the two Hague Peace Conferences of 1899 and 1907,[83] the first initiated by Tsar Nicholas II on the basis of his famous peace manifesto, the second by President Theodore Roosevelt. The Conference of 1899 resulted in three conventions and three declarations dealing with the law of land warfare, the law of sea warfare and the peaceful settlement of disputes, which led to the innovation of the establishment of the Permanent Court of Arbitration in The Hague. It also adopted a non-binding resolution on limiting the military expenditure of parties. The 1907 Conference accepted a number of further instruments which partly dealt with the same matters as the earlier Conference. The Conferences, however, failed to address the real issues of the major tensions in the world and were thus unable to prevent the outbreak of the First World War. In addition, important aspects, such as the problem of colonialism, were entirely excluded from the agenda. It was also characteristic that the compromise finally agreed upon with regard to the settlement of conflicts by compulsory arbitration, at the insistence of Britain and France, reserved to states the right to determine for themselves what affected their 'vital interests'[84] falling within the *domaine réservé* (the domestic jurisdiction of states).[85] As a consequence, what was in fact excluded from the obligation to arbitrate was left to the discretion of states.

The attempt to remedy the deficiencies of the 'vital interests' clause by the American Secretary of State W.J. Bryan was objected to by the United States Senate. The so-called Bryan Treaties of 1913/14[86] were actually concluded only with the Western and Eastern European powers, and only after the war had already broken out. The United States and Germany did not enter into such a treaty. The disaster of the First World War itself began formally in accordance with classical international law, as it stood at that time, with declarations of war.

What happened to the concept of 'European public law' during this process? Towards the end of the nineteenth century, colonialism and relations with territories outside Europe were gradually depriving it of its content. At the Berlin Congress of 1878 only the six major European powers and Turkey were present. At the 1884/5 Berlin Congress twelve states, including the United States, were already participating. The Hague Peace Conference of 1899 assembled twenty-seven states, including the United States and Mexico, as well as Japan, China, Persia and Siam. At the second Peace Conference in 1907, forty-three states took part, among which were seventeen American and four Asian states, but no country from Africa. International law, albeit European in origin, was thus gradually moving towards a universal system.

The watershed after the First World War

The end of the First World War heralded a number of basic changes in the international legal system, reflecting the war experience. Defeated Germany had to take sole responsibility for the war, under Article 231 of the Treaty of Versailles,[87] lost the few colonies it had managed to acquire as well as one-third of its territory in Europe, and was submitted by the victors to a ruinous system of reparations,[88] which was severely criticized by the distinguished economist John Maynard Keynes and which helped to sow the seeds for the following war. The relative decline of European powers as major actors on the world level and the rise of the United States to global power manifested itself in the transformation of the British Empire into the British Commonwealth.[89]

Moreover, the old international community was split by the emergence of a new and radically different state, following the Russian Revolution of 1917. The Soviet Union declared itself at odds with the existing system of international law, but eventually came to some form of accommodation in order to be able to maintain economic and political intercourse with the outside world. The revolutionary new state displayed an attitude towards international law which was quite distinct from the mainstream of thinking.[90] Based upon Marxism, as interpreted by Lenin and later by Stalin, it originally denied that there could be one system of international law that applied equally to capitalist and socialist states and rejected the validity of older customary law and of treaties concluded by the Tsarist government. The attitude changed later,[91] but the Soviet Union remained on the fringe of international affairs until it attained the status of a great power after the Second World War.

The League of Nations

On the institutional level, the creation of the League of Nations was a revolutionary step in inter-state relations.[92] It followed the call in the last of President Wilson's Fourteen Points[93] for the establishment of '[a] general association of nations ... under specific covenants for the purpose of affording mutual guarantees of political independence and territorial

87 Text in 225 CTS 188. See E.v. Puttkamer, Versailles Peace Treaty (1919), *EPIL* 4 (1982), 276–82.

88 I. Seidl-Hohenveldern, Reparations, *EPIL* 4 (1982), 178–80.

89 L.C. Green, British Commonwealth, *EPIL* I (1992), 495–9. See also W. Dale, The Making and Remaking of Commonwealth Constitutions, *ICLQ* 42 (1993), 67–83; W. Morvay, *Souveränitätsübergang und Rechtskontinuität im Britischen Commonwealth*, 1974.

90 See V. Kartashkin, The Marxist-Leninist Approach: The Theory of Class Struggle and Contemporary International Law, in Macdonald/Johnston (eds), 1983, *op. cit.*, 79–102; T. Schweisfurth, The Role of Political Revolution in the Theory of International Law, *ibid.*, 913–53; *idem*, Socialist Conceptions of International Law, *EPIL* 7 (1984), 417–24.

91 See the short summary in the sixth edition of this book, 7–19 and K. Grzybowski, Soviet Theory of International Law for the Seventies, *AJIL* 77 (1983), 862–72. See also text below, 33.

92 See C. Parry, League of Nations, *EPIL* 5 (1983), 192–201; *The League of Nations in Retrospect: Proceedings of the Symposium*. Organized by the United Nations Library and the Graduate Institute of International Studies, Geneva 6–9 November 1980, 1983 and the review by L. Gross, *AJIL* 80 (1986), 200–15; H. Weber, League of Nations, in *Wolfrum UNLPP II*, 848–53.

93 A. Rustemeyer, Wilson's Fourteen Points, *EPIL* 7 (1984), 539–42, at 540.

94 K.T. Samson, International Labour Organization, *EPIL* II (1995), 1150–6. For the text of the ILO Constitution, see *Brownlie BDIL*, 50.
95 1928 General Treaty for Renunciation of War as an Instrument of National Policy, 94 LNTS 57 (1929). See C.D. Wallace, Kellogg–Briand Pact (1928), *EPIL* 3 (1982), 236–9.
96 K. Zemanek, Treaties, Secret, *EPIL* 7 (1984), 505–6; G.E. do Nascimento Silva, Diplomacy, Secret, *EPIL* I (1992), 1033–4, noting that at Versailles, Wilson himself reverted to secret diplomacy and held more than 150 meetings behind closed doors with Lloyd George, Clemenceau and Orlando.
97 See D. Rauschning, Mandates, *EPIL* 10 (1987), 288–95.
98 See F. Capotorti, Minorities, *EPIL* 8 (1985), 385–95. On the limited judicial activity of the Permanent Court of International Justice in this respect, see C. Weil, Minorities in Upper Silesia Case (Minority Schools), *EPIL* 2 (1981), 189–91; K. Lamers, Prince von Pless Administration (Orders), *ibid.*, 236–7; C. Weil, Polish Agrarian Reform (Orders), *ibid.*, 230–1; M. Vierheilig, Minority Schools in Albania (Advisory Opinion), *ibid.*, 191–2; Weil, German Minorities in Poland, Cases Concerning the, *EPIL* II (1995), 553–5; W. Benedek, Exchange of Greek and Turkish Populations (Advisory Opinions), *ibid.*, 304–5; C.V. Katte, Greco-Bulgarian 'Communities' (Advisory Opinion), *ibid.*, 622–3. On the current status of the protection of minorities in international law, see Chapters 6, 105–8 and 19, 338–41 below.

integrity to great and small states alike'. The twenty-six articles constituting the League were entered into Part I of each of the European Peace Treaties, just as the constitution of the new International Labour Organization[94] became incorporated as Part XIII.

The attempt to restrict the use of force

The prime purpose of the League was the promotion of international cooperation and the achievement of peace and security by the acceptance on the part of the parties, in principle, of 'obligations not to resort to war'. The absolute right of states to go to war was not intended to be excluded altogether. Thus, members of the League were submitted to a cooling-off period of three months before going to war. If the League Council, the Permanent Court of International Justice or an arbitral tribunal were concerned with a dispute, war was only permitted three months after a decision by the Court or the tribunal or the submission of the Council report. Members disregarding such obligations under the Covenant were deemed to have committed an 'act of war', entitling, but not obliging, other member states to go to war with the state which had broken the Covenant. In Article 16 the Covenant provided for economic sanctions as an instrument of redress, but Article 10, stipulating that members should undertake 'to respect and preserve as against external aggression the territorial integrity and existing political independence of all Members', was not linked to the sanctions system. Rather, the Council of the League was entrusted with the task of 'advising' on the methods of complying with this obligation. The uncertainty on the precise implications of this provision was the main reason why the United States Senate refused to ratify the Covenant.

The Paris Pact of 1928 on the Banning of War (Kellogg–Briand Pact),[95] initiated by the United States and France, attempted to achieve a broader prohibition of war, but it also refrained from establishing an effective enforcement mechanism. The right of self-defence, interpreted in a rather wide sense, was not affected. Britain reserved its rights to defend its vital interests in protecting the British Empire, and the United States kept the application of the Monroe Doctrine to its own discretion. Neither the League system nor the Paris Pact were yet able to effectively replace the old customary rule on the right of states to use armed force.

Other functions of the League

The League was further engaged in trying to promote disarmament and open diplomacy to abolish the practice of secret treaties.[96] Other functions included the establishment of the mandates system, as 'a trust for civilization', under Article 22 which put under international tutelage the nascent nations in the former colonies of the defeated powers and of colonial territories similarly detached.[97] Moreover, responsibilities were assumed by the League in the field of the treaty-based protection of minorities in Europe[98] and in social matters, such as health and fair labour standards.

The Permanent Court of Justice

Some advance was made in the inter-war period not only with regard to international legislation dealing with social and economic affairs, but also in international adjudication with the creation in 1921 of the Permanent Court of International Justice (PCIJ) in The Hague,[99] the forerunner of the present International Court of Justice, which was later established under the United Nations Charter.[100] The Court handed down thirty-two judgments in contentious cases, mostly between European states, and twenty-seven advisory opinions which assisted in clarifying rules and principles of international law. Operating within a still limited and relatively homogeneous society of nations, it enjoyed considerable authority, more than was to be accorded later to the International Court of Justice. The activity of the Permanent Court of International Justice offers an explanation for why the Permanent Court of Arbitration (PCA), which was established earlier but did not really constitute a standing court, received only a small number of cases.[101]

Failure of the League system

In the field of peace and security, the refusal of a great power, such as the United States, to join the League naturally placed the novel organization into a difficult position to achieve its objectives. In effect, the League subsequently came to be controlled by the interests of France and Britain. Ratification was also denied by the Hejaz (Arabia) and Ecuador, but it is interesting to note that all other generally recognized states were at some time a member of the League. Originally, the membership of the League was limited to the twenty-seven victor states signing the Treaty of Versailles, plus 'the British Empire' (the United Kingdom, the Dominions of Canada, Australia, New Zealand, South Africa and the still-dependent India), plus thirteen listed neutral states. Later twenty-two new members were admitted, including the former enemy states Austria and Bulgaria (1920), Hungary (1922) and Germany (1926). The Soviet Union, originally excluded, was admitted in 1934. But in the course of time sixteen members also withdrew, including Costa Rica (1927), Brazil (1928), Germany and Japan (1935), Italy (1939) and Spain (1941).

The League system failed for a variety of institutional and political reasons. The most important aspect is perhaps the inherent contradiction in the concept itself of collective security[102] in the form of a mere association of self-interested and sovereign states. The concept assumes that all states have an equally strong interest in preventing aggression, and that all states are willing to take the same risk to achieve this. If a great power is involved in an act of aggression, the validity of this assumption may well be very much open to doubt.[103] At any rate, it soon became clear that the organs of the League could only function to the extent that the member states were able to agree.

The League remained incapable of dealing with the Japanese aggression against China in 1932 when it occupied Manchuria, and with the Italian aggression against Abyssinia in 1935-6. Limited economic sanctions adopted by some fifty members of the League against Italy failed. This was the first and last attempt to enforce the Covenant against a major power. In the Spanish Civil War (1936-9), which was viewed as a threat to world peace because of the direct and indirect intervention of many states, the League affirmed the principle of non-intervention (the obligation of states

99 See H.-J. Schlochauer, Permanent Court of International Justice, *EPIL* 1 (1981), 163-79; P. Haggenmacher/R. Perruchoud/H. Dipla (eds), *Cour permanente de justice internationale 1922-1945*, Vols 5-I and 5-II, 1989.
100 See Chapter 18 below, 281-93.
101 H.-J. Schlochauer, Permanent Court of Arbitration, *EPIL* 1 (1981), 157-63. On the reform of the PCA see Chapter 18 below, 294.
102 Generally on the concept see J. Delbrück, Collective Security, *EPIL* I (1992), 646-56; K. Doehring, Collective Security, in *Wolfrum UNLPP I*, 110-5; G. Bestermöller, *Die Völkerbundsidee – Leistungsfähigkeit und Grenzen der Kriegsächtung durch Staatensolidarität*, 1995. See also Chapter 22 below, 387-415.
103 See H.A. Kissinger, *Diplomacy*, 1994, Chapter 10. For another critical view see A. Eban, The U.N. Idea Revisited, *FA* 74 (1995), 39-55.

104 See A.-M. de Zayas, Spanish Civil War, *EPIL* 7 (1984), 434–8.
105 Parry, *op. cit.*, at 200.
106 On Germany's international relations from 1933 to 1945 and the attitude towards international law, see D.F. Vagts, International Law in the Third Reich, *AJIL* 84 (1990), 661–704; A. Carty, Interwar German Theories of International Law: The Psychoanalytical and Phenomenological Perspectives of Hans Kelsen and Carl Schmitt, *Cardozo LR* 16 (1995), 1235–92.
107 For a new analysis on the basis of declassified documents fifty years later, see B.J. Bernstein, The Atomic Bombings Reconsidered, *FA* 74 (1995), 135–52.
108 On the 1996 advisory opinion given by the ICJ, see Chapter 20 below, 346–50.
109 See Chapter 20 below, 354–5.

not to intervene in the internal affairs of other states), demanded the withdrawal of all foreign combatants and condemned the bombardment of open towns, but the League's resolutions had little effect.[104] Japan's renewed aggression against China in 1937 merely produced a condemnation by the League of the aerial bombardment of undefended towns. Germany's attack on Poland in 1939 and the outbreak of the Second World War resulted in nothing more than the postponement of already arranged Assembly and Council sessions. The last action of the League was to expel the Soviet Union in 1939 because it refused to accept mediation of its claim against Finland.

A fair assessment of the failure of the League, however, must take into account its confrontation with the ruthless totalitarian regimes of the period. As noted by Clive Parry:

> it was the destiny of the League to encounter a greater measure of deliberate aggression, attended by a wilful and deliberate disregard of all humanitarian considerations, than has ever been manifested – again either before or since – in any comparable span of years. For Japan, Italy and Germany in turn asserted during the life of the League an absolute right to go to war for any reason or no reason, and an indifference to the laws of either war or peace to which the only ultimate answer could be, as in fact it proved to be, likewise war unlimited in scale or method.[105]

Development after the Second World War

The international legal system had failed to prevent the outbreak of the Second World War, to constrain the aggression by Hitler and to stop the unspeakable atrocities committed by Nazi Germany throughout Europe.[106] Nor did it prevent, to take a quite different example, the calculated Allied destruction by saturation bombing of German and Japanese cities, causing immense casualties among the civilian population. Before the United Nations Charter, signed on 26 June 1945, entered into force on 24 October 1945, the United States ended the war in the Pacific by using the atomic bomb against Hiroshima and Nagasaki in August 1945. Whether this was necessary, to force Japan into capitulation and save the lives of many American soldiers and further Japanese military and civilian casualties which an invasion of Japan may have resulted in, or was at least equally meant as a warning to Stalin, is still a matter of dispute among historians,[107] as also is the issue of the legality of nuclear weapons under current international law among lawyers.[108] The Nuremberg and Tokyo Trials affirmed the individual responsibility of German and Japanese leaders for committing crimes against peace, war crimes and crimes against humanity, but were often seen as the victor's justice, although the procedures were fair.[109]

The prohibition of the use of force and collective security in the United Nations Charter

The decision to establish a new global organization of states to preserve peace after the war had already been prepared by the Atlantic Charter of 1941, in which Roosevelt and Churchill declared their hope 'after the final destruction of Nazi tyranny . . . to see established a peace which will afford to all nations the means of dwelling in safety within their own boundaries' and 'to bring about the fullest collaboration between all nations in the economic field with the object of securing, for all, improved labour standards, economic advancement and social security'.[110]

The United Nations Charter, sponsored by the United States, Britain, the Soviet Union and China, and originally signed by fifty-one states, was designed to introduce law and order and an effective collective security system into international relations. On the basis of preparatory work done at the 1944 Dumbarton Oaks Conference, the Charter of the United Nations was adopted at the 1945 San Francisco Conference and entered into force on 24 October 1945.[111] The main innovation was the attempt to introduce a comprehensive ban on the use of force in Article 2(4) of the Charter, with the exception of the right of states to collective and individual self-defence against an armed attack, in Article 51.[112] The preservation of peace was made the overriding goal of the United Nations. While the League of Nations had possessed no institutional machinery and executive power to enforce the Covenant and decisions of the League, the United Nations Charter established a collective security system in Chapter VII, giving the Security Council the authority to determine whether there is a threat to or breach of international peace and security and to adopt binding economic and military measures against an aggressor state.[113]

The UN collective system did not work, due to the antagonism that developed between the former allies after the war, and during the Cold War in the following four decades, the United Nations failed to achieve its prime objective. Thus, for example, the controversial military 'quarantine' imposed by the United States upon Cuba in 1962 in response to the build-up in Cuba of Soviet missiles with a capability of reaching targets in large parts of the Western Hemisphere, used the regional system of the Organization of American States (OAS) instead of the non-functioning UN collective security system for legitimization.[114] Another example of the non-functioning of the UN collective security mechanism during the East–West conflict is the fact that the Vietnam War never led to any decision by the Security Council.[115]

The recognition of the special military, economic and political status of great powers, however, was built in from the beginning in the regulation of the voting procedure of the Security Council, giving the United States, the Soviet Union, Britain, France and China (originally represented by the government of Taiwan) as 'permanent members' the right to veto any decision they disliked.[116] The statement in Article 2(1) of the Charter that the organization 'is based on the principle of the sovereign equality of all its Members' was thus qualified by the fact that the five permanent members of the Security Council were made more equal than the rest of the member states. Similarly, the five official nuclear powers retained a privileged legal position in the later Treaty on the Non-Proliferation of Nuclear Weapons.[117] The relative decline of Britain and France as Great Powers became most apparent in the 1956 Suez crisis when the United States and the USSR found a rare occasion to unite in the UN Security Council and forced them to withdraw from their military occupation of the Suez

110 Text in *AJIL* 35 (1941), 191. See H.-J. Schlochauer, Atlantic Charter (1941), *EPIL* I (1992), 288–9.

111 See H.-J. Schlochauer, Dumbarton Oaks Conference (1944), *EPIL* I (1992), 1115–17; W. Benediks, *The San Francisco Conference on International Organization: April–June 1945*, 1994; W.G. Grewe, The History of the United Nations, in *Simma CUNAC*, 1–23; H. Weber, History of the United Nations, in *Wolfrum UNLPP I*, 572–80; R.C. Hilderbrand, *Dumbarton Oaks. The Origins of the United Nations and the Search for Postwar Security*, 1990. See Chapters 21, 364–84 and 22, 385–430 below.

112 See Chapter 19 below, 309–18.

113 See Chapter 22 below, 387–415, 425–30.

114 L. Weber, Cuban Quarantine, *EPIL* I (1992), 882–5.

115 For a critical assessment see R.S. McNamara (with B. VanDeMark), *In Retrospect: The Tragedy and Lessons of Vietnam*, 1994. See also Chapter 19 below, 325.

116 See Chapters 21, 374–7 and 22, 391 below.

117 See Chapter 20 below, 349.

118 B. Broms, Suez Canal, *EPIL* 12 (1990), 360–5. See also G. Marston, Armed Intervention in the 1956 Suez Canal Crisis: The Legal Advice Tendered to the British Government, *ICLQ* 37 (1988), 773. SC Res. 118 of 13 October 1956, UN Doc. S/3675, laid down the requirements for a satisfactory settlement of the dispute and the future status of the Canal.

119 See H.-J. Uibopuu, Socialist Internationalism, *EPIL* 9 (1986), 347–50; S.v. Schorlemer, Blocs and Groups of States, in *Wolfrum UNLPP I*, 69–77.

120 See A. Bleckmann, Decolonization, *EPIL* I (1992), 972–6; W. Morvay, British Territories, *ibid.*, 976–83; A. Bleckmann, French Territories, *ibid*, 986–90; J.G.C. *v.* Aggelen, Dutch Territories, *ibid.*, 983–6; F. de Quadros, Decolonization: Portuguese Territories, *ibid.*, 990–3; M.A. Ajomo, International Law, The United Nations and Decolonization, in E.G. Bello/B.A. Ajibola (eds), *Essays in Honour of Judge Taslim Olawale Elias*, 1992, 77–92; P. Kunig, Decolonization, in *Wolfrum UNLPP I*, 390–7.

121 See Chapter 19 below, 326–40.

122 K. Ginther, Liberation Movements, *EPIL* 3 (1982), 245–9. See Chapters 3, 104–9, 19, 336–8 below.

123 GA Res. 1514 (XV) of 14 December 1960, text in *Brownlie BDIL*, 307. See Chapter 19 below, 327.

124 D. Bindschedler-Robert, Korea, *EPIL* 12 (1990), 202–8; S. Brammer, Conflicts, Korea, in *Wolfrum UNLPP I*, 278-85. See Chapter 22 below, 391–3.

125 See Chapter 21 below, 371–2.

126 On the 'Uniting for Peace' Resolution, see Chapter 22 below, 392–3.

127 See Chapter 15 below, 225–8.

128 For a critical analysis see, N. Harris, *The End of the Third World. Newly Industrializing Countries and the Decline of an Ideology*, 1986. See also M.S. Rajan/V.S. Mani/C.S.R. Murthy, *The Nonaligned and the United States*, 1987; A.A. Fatouros, Developing States, *EPIL* I (1992), 1017–24; R. Heuser, Bandung Conference (1955), *ibid.*, 340–2; J. Betz, Developing Countries, in *Wolfrum UNLPP I*, 398–406 and Chapter 15 below, 233–40.

Canal[118] area, which they had undertaken (with Israel's simultaneous occupation of the Sinai Peninsula) in response to the nationalization of the Suez Canal Company by the Egyptian Government.

Decolonization and change in the composition of the international community

The composition of the international community had already started to change immediately after the Second World War. The Soviet Union created the 'socialist bloc' with the German Democratic Republic, Poland, Bulgaria, Hungary, Romania and Czechoslovakia under its hegemony, joined by the more independent Yugoslavia.[119] But perhaps more important for the structural transition of the international legal system has been the process of decolonization,[120] based upon the principle of self-determination laid down in the UN Charter and in the common Article 1 of the two 1966 International Human Rights Covenants.[121] The colonial empires of Britain, France, Belgium, the Netherlands, Portugal and Italy, often confronted with liberation movements,[122] eroded with the political independence, for example, of Syria (1945), Lebanon (1946), India and Pakistan (1947), Israel and Burma (1948), Indonesia (1949), Libya (1951), Tunisia, Morocco, Sudan and Ghana (1956), Malaya (1957) and Guinea (1958). The decolonization process was basically completed by the 1960s, after the landmark of the adoption by the UN General Assembly in 1960 of the Declaration on the Granting of Independence to Colonial Countries and Peoples.[123] The increase in the number of states to about 130 by the end of the 1960s, almost half of which were newly independent states, had a profound impact on the international system in general and the operation of international organizations in particular.

At the beginning, the United Nations had remained under the control of the West, which still commanded a majority of the seats in the General Assembly. Thus, it was not difficult to make the Korean War,[124] the Soviet Union being temporarily absent in the Security Council because of the dispute on the representation of China,[125] at least pro forma a United Nations operation.[126] The independence of numerous new states in Asia and Africa changed the whole scenario and the majority in the General Assembly and the assemblies of other international organizations shifted to an alliance between the block of communist countries and the new states of the so-called Third World. However, Western states retained their dominant position in the Security Council and in the relevant international financial institutions, such as the World Bank and the International Monetary Fund, due to their economic power where weighted voting applied according to the share of financial contribution.[127] Under the leadership of the United States the Western states also remained dominant in the international system in military and political terms.

Attitudes of Third World states towards international law

It is still much less easy to generalize about the so-called Third World[128] states of Africa, Asia and Latin America than it once was to generalize about the former bloc of communist states controlled by the Soviet Union. The newly independent states, which organized themselves as non-aligned countries between East and West in the Group of 77 formed during

UNCTAD I in 1964, do not form a bloc in any real sense. They have no common ideology. Their governments vary from the far right to the far left of the political spectrum. There are also considerable cultural and economic differences. However, there are certain facts which are true of the vast majority of states in the South, and these facts tend to make most of those states adopt a distinctive attitude towards international law.

Most developing countries were under alien rule during the formative period of international law, and therefore played no part in shaping that law. Occasionally their leaders argue that they are not bound by rules which they did not help to create. However, this argument is used only in relation to rules which go against the interests of the new states, and the argument that those states played no part in shaping the rules is only a subsidiary argument designed to strengthen the main contention that the rules are outmoded. Developing states have never dreamt of rejecting *all* rules of international law which were laid down before they became independent; to do so would mean rejecting many rules which operate to their advantage. The necessity of international law itself as a legal system regulating intercourse between states was accepted.[129]

Most countries in the South are poor (with a few exceptions, such as some of the oil-exporting countries and the 'New Tigers' in the Far East) and are anxious to develop their economies. Those which wished to develop their economies along socialist lines were therefore in the past opposed to the traditional rule of international law which forbids expropriation of foreign-owned property without compensation; but other Third World countries showed themselves prepared to accept the traditional rule as a means of encouraging foreign private investment.[130] This once fervently argued issue in North–South relations has now lost much of its former significance. The economic interests of developing countries also affect their attitudes to other rules of international law; for instance, if their fishing fleets are dependent on local fisheries, this naturally influences their position on the law of the sea, and some of them have tried to gain exclusive rights to local fisheries by claiming a wide territorial sea, exclusive fishing zone, or exclusive economic zone.[131]

Since 1973 Third World states have confronted the richer states more pressingly with their problems of poverty and economic development. Not surprisingly, the UN General Assembly and other assemblies of international organizations became their main forums to ventilate claims for a 'New International Economic Order',[132] a 'New International Communication Order' (which was one of the reasons why the United States and the United Kingdom left UNESCO), the application of the so-called 'common heritage of mankind' principle to the benefits of deep-sea mining[133] and the use of outer space,[134] and other mechanisms and concepts to attempt to change international law and to effect the recognition of a legal obligation of industrialized states to transfer technology and financial resources to the South. On the whole, Western states have not accepted these demands; they have helped the economic development of poorer states in many ways, but are usually reluctant to recognize or undertake any legal obligation to help poorer states.[135]

Moreover, many developing states have a feeling of resentment about

129 See Wang Tieya, The Third World and International Law, in Macdonald/Johnston (eds), 1983, *op. cit.*, 955 *et seq.*; M. Schweitzer, New States and International Law, *EPIL* 7 (1984), 349–53; F.E. Synder/S. Sathirathai (eds), *Third World Attitudes Toward International Law: An Introduction*, 1987; *Harris CMIL*, 18–21; M. Kusuma-Atmadja, The Contribution of New States to the Development of International Law, *Santa Clara LR* 32 (1992), 889–910; M. Shahabuddeen, Developing Countries and the Idea of International Law, in Macdonald (ed.), 1994, *op. cit.*, 721–36; M. Bedjaoui, La visión de las culturas no occidentales sobre la legitimidad del derecho international contemporáneo, *Anu. DI* 11 (1995), 23–62.
130 See Chapter 15 below, 235–9.
131 See Chapter 12 below, 176–84.
132 See Chapter 15 below, 233–5.
133 See Chapter 12 below, 193–5.
134 See Chapter 13 below, 207–8.
135 See Chapter 15 below, 233–5, 239–40.

136 See Chapter 11 below, 164–5.

137 See Chapter 14 below, 220.

138 See Chapter 19 below, 326–340.

139 See Chapter 3 below, 39–48.

140 See Chapter 3 below, 60–2.

141 See Chapter 3 below, 52–4.

142 For example, concerning the continental shelf, see Chapter 12 below, 191–3.

143 A. Carty, *The Decay of International Law? A Reappraisal of the Limits of Legal Imagination in International Affairs,* 1986.

144 R. Wolfrum, International Law of Cooperation, *EPIL* II (1995), 1242–7.

145 See M. Lachs, Legal Framework of an International Community, *Emory ILR* 6 (1992), 329–37; H. Mosler, International Legal Community, *EPIL* II (1995), 1251–5.

past exploitation, real or imagined. That is one reason why they usually claim that they have not succeeded to obligations accepted on their behalf by the former colonial powers before they became independent.[136] Almost all of them showed themselves as strongly opposed to all remaining forms of colonialism and apartheid,[137] although their reactions to violations of the principle of self-determination in other contexts are much weaker.[138]

For the reasons stated above, developing countries often feel that international law sacrifices their interests to those of Western states. They therefore demand changes in the law. Unfortunately, if there is no consensus, it is often difficult to change international law without breaking it. States may refuse to alter a treaty unless they are forced to do so. States which are dissatisfied with an existing rule of customary law may start following a new custom, but, until the new custom is widely established, they may be denounced as law-breakers by states following the old custom.[139] One solution for this problem has been the multilateral treaty; conferences called to draw up a treaty codifying the existing law can slip imperceptibly into amending the law.[140] Another solution favoured by developing countries has been to try to use the United Nations General Assembly as if it were a legislature; but the General Assembly is not really a legislature, and it is doubtful if its resolutions can be used as evidence of international law against states which vote against them.[141]

Nevertheless, major changes in international law have occurred since 1945. Western states were anxious not to drive Third World states into the arms of communist states, and have therefore agreed to many of the alterations sought by the non-aligned countries. Most of the rules which developing countries used to regard as contrary to their interests have changed, or are in the process of being changed. Similarly, when the interests of Western states change, such states are often just as ready as other states to abandon the old rules and to replace them with new rules which are more in keeping with their own interests.[142] Modern international law is not static, but has a dynamic nature and is in a continuous process of change. The accusation that international law is biased against the interests of Third World states is, on the whole, no longer true.

Universality and the challenge to the unity of international law

In the historical process of the transition from the classical system to the modern system, international law definitely lost its European character and was extended from a limited club of nations to a global system now covering some 185 states which are very heterogeneous entities in cultural, economic and political terms. The basic question ever since has been whether a truly universal system of law is possible at all under the conditions of a divided world with such deep cleavages in values, interests, and perceptions. Writers have frequently found that international law is in a 'crisis', or has entered into 'decay'.[143]

At least with respect to the basic normative framework, after 1945 international law entered into a new phase aiming at restricting the unfettered right of states to go to war and, in addition, transforming the previous mere coordination of sovereign states into a system of cooperation and mutual benefit.[144] The concept of the 'international legal community'[145] emerged in connection with two other basic concepts of international law – *jus cogens*[146] and international public order[147] – both referring to principles and rules of international law with a higher legal status than the other parts of international law. There were other significant changes in the international legal system after 1945. The main feature mostly emphasized is the shift from coexistence to cooperation of states, not only to achieve international peace and security, but also to further social and economic goals. This is reflected in the proliferation of international organizations, both global and regional, now numbering about 500 and active in a broad variety of fields, which appeared within a relatively short time as a new category of international legal subjects.[148] It was primarily in the social and economic field in which the United Nations and its specialized agencies were able to make some progress. Connected with this extension of the scope of activity was the enhanced process of the codification of international law.[149]

Another new development after 1945, as compared with classical international law, has been a stronger recognition of the position of the individual. While previously the individual was considered a mere 'object' of international regulations adopted by sovereign states, more room has been given to the thought of upgrading the status of human beings in international law. This is reflected in the development of rules on the international protection of refugees, the codification of human rights on the global and regional level following the Universal Declaration of Human Rights, proclaimed by the UN General Assembly in 1948, and the advancement of international humanitarian law in armed conflict with the four Geneva Red Cross Conventions of 1949 and the two Additional Protocols of 1977.[150]

The end of the East–West conflict,[151] apart from moving North–South issues[152] more to the forefront, has led to the resurgence of nationalism, to the rise of ethnic conflict and civil wars in various parts of the world, and to the hitherto unknown activism of the UN Security Council.[153] In Western legal literature the end of the Cold War has provoked a controversy on the legality of 'democratic intervention',[154] intervention to support or establish a democratic system of government in another state against 'illegitimate regimes', in connection with the discussion on humanitarian intervention.[155] The general proposition of this intervention theory is that there is a necessary structural link between democracy,[156] as it developed in Western constitutional history, and the effective guarantee of human rights. The problem is, of course, whether Western concepts, including those on the market economy and on human rights, can prevail throughout the world in the face of Asian, African and Islamic perceptions which are different for reasons of history, society and culture.

Moreover, after the wall in Berlin fell, writers, such as Francis Fukuyama,[157] declared the 'end of history' and the victory of Western democracy and capitalism. But, from a different perspective, perhaps the USSR and the United States were and are only experimental states in the long course of the history of a rather mixed international community. Western civilization is certainly not the only form of civilization in the

146 See Chapter 3 below, 57–8.
147 See G. Jaenicke, International Public Order, *EPIL* II (1995), 1348-51.
148 See Chapter 6 below, 92–6.
149 See Chapter 3 below, 60–2.
150 See Chapters 6, 100–4, 14, 209–21 and 20, 342–63 below.
151 M. Münchau, International Relations, East-West, in *Wolfrum UNLPP II*, 771–7. See also W.M. Reisman, International Law after the Cold War, *AJIL* 84 (1990), 859–66; E. McWhinny et al. (eds), *From Coexistence to Cooperation: International Law and Organization in the Post-Cold War Era*, 1991; G. Abi-Saab, A 'New World Order'? Some Preliminary Reflections, *Hague YIL* 7 (1994), 87–94.
152 J. Betz, International Relations, North-South, in *Wolfrum UNLPP II*, 778–88.
153 See Chapter 22 below, 391, 395–415, 423–30.
154 Lukashuk, The United Nations and Illegitimate Regimes: When to Intervene to Protect Human Rights, in L.F. Damrosch/D.J. Scheffer (eds), *Law and Force in the New International Order*, 1992, 143; T.M. Franck, Intervention Against Illegitimate Regimes, *ibid.*, 159; A.-M. Burley, Commentary on Intervention Against Illegitimate Regimes, *ibid.*, 177; V. Nanda, Commentary on International Intervention to Promote the Legitimacy of Regimes, *ibid.*, 181. See in this connection also on the entitlement to democracy, to be increasingly promoted and protected by collective international processes, T.M. Franck, The Emerging Right to Democratic Governance, *AJIL* 86 (1992), 46 *et seq.*; J. Crawford, Democracy and International Law, *BYIL* 64 (1993), 113–34.
155 See Chapter 14 below, 220–1.
156 D. Copp/J. Hamption/J. Roemer (eds), *The Idea of Democracy*, 1995.
157 F. Fukuyama, The End of History?, *The National Interest*, 1989, no. 16, 3–18.

158 S.P. Huntington, The Clash of Civilizations?, *FA* 72 (1993), 22–49.
159 See E. Sakakibara, The End of Progressivism, *FA* 74 (1995), 8–14.
160 See *EPIL* 6 (1983), dedicated to Regional Cooperation, Organizations and Problems; S. González Gálvez, The Future of Regionalism in an Asymmetrical System, in Macdonald/Johnston (eds), 1983, *op. cit.*, 661–83; R. Wolfrum (ed.), *Strengthening the World Order, Universalism versus Regionalism, Risks and Opportunities of Regionalization*, 1990; J.I. Charney, Universal International Law, *AJIL* 87 (1993), 529–51; A. Hurrell, Explaining the Resurgence of Regionalism in World Politics, *RIS* 21 (1995), 331–58; C. Schreuer, Regionalization, in *Wolfrum UNLPP II*, 1059–67; Schreuer, Regionalism v. Universalism, *EJIL* 6 (1995), 477–99.
161 UNGA Res. 2625 (XXV) of 24 October 1970, text in *Brownlie BDIL*, 36; see V.S. Mani, *Basic Principles of Modern International Law. A Study of the United Nations Debates on the Principles of International Law Concerning Friendly Relations and Cooperation Among States*, 1993; V. Lowe/C. Warbrick (eds), *The United Nations and the Principles of International Law – Essays in Memory of Michael Akehurst*, 1994 (with contributions by I. Sinclair, Ch. Gray, J. Merrills, V. Lowe, D. McGoldrick, A. Boyle, D. Freestone, A. James, P. Thornberry, C. Warbrick and G. White); G. Arangio-Ruiz, Friendly Relations Resolution, *EPIL* II (1995), 485–90.
162 See B. Simma, Editorial, *EJIL* 3 (1992), 215; P. Allott et al., *Theory and International Law: An Introduction*, 1991.
163 See text above, 15–17. On A. Verdross, see the contributions by B. Simma, A. Truyol y Serra, B. Conforti, A. Carty and I. Seidl-Hohenveldern in *EJIL* 6 (1995), 32–115. On D. Anzilotti, see R. Ago, P.-M. Dupuy, G. Gaja, J.M. Ruda and A. Tanca in *EJIL* 3 (1992), 92 *et seq.* On G. Scelles, see H. Thierry, A. Cassese, L. Condorelli, R.J. Dupuy and A. Tanca in *EJIL* 1 (1990), 193 *et seq.*
164 See M.S. McDougal/W.M. Reisman, International Law in Policy-Oriented Perspective, in Macdonald/Johnston (eds), 1983, *op. cit.*, 103–29; M. McDougal and Associates, *Studies in World Public Order*, 1987; G.L. Dorsey, The McDougal-Laswell Proposal to Build a World Public Order, *AJIL* 82 (1988), 41–50; M.S. McDougal, The Dorsey Comment: A Modest Retrogression, *ibid.*, 51–7; H.D. Laswell/M.S. McDougal, *Jurisprudence for a Free Society*, 2 Vols, 1992.

world, and its values and regulatory systems, including its law, are not necessarily appropriate or acceptable in other parts of the globe. On the other hand, whether Samuel Huntington's prediction[158] that 'civilization identity will be increasingly important in the future, and the world will be shaped in large measure by the interaction among seven or eight civilizations' and will lead to a clash of civilizations in the next century, remains to be seen.[159] Such predictions are not new (and are often false) in history, as we know from Spengler's 'Untergang des Abendlandes'.

Nevertheless, also from a legal perspective, there is no doubt that the question of the universal nature of international law has been reinforced not only by theoretical debate but also by the actual strong tendencies towards economic and political regionalism in the international system.[160] The answer to this question is not easy and needs to take into acount the content of contemporary international law in its various fields and the characteristics of the international law-making process. As a starting-point, however, it may be observed that there is at least universal agreement on some basic principles of international law, as laid down in the Friendly Relations Declaration, which after a long process of attempting to clarify the meaning of the United Nations Charter was adopted by all states by consensus in 1970.[161] These principles include:

1   the prohibition of the threat or use of force by states against the territorial integrity or political independence of any state, or in any other manner inconsistent with the purposes of the Charter;
2   the peaceful settlement of disputes between states in such a manner that international peace and security and justice are not endangered;
3   the duty not to intervene in matters within the domestic jurisdiction of any state, in accordance with the Charter;
4   the duty of states to cooperate with one another in accordance with the Charter;
5   the principle of equal rights and self-determination of peoples;
6   the principle of sovereign equality of states; and
7   the principle that states shall fulfil in good faith the obligations assumed by them in accordance with the Charter.

New developments in theory

Finally, it should at least be briefly mentioned that there have been some interesting new developments in theory during the past decade.[162] The old schools of natural law and positivism[163] are still with us, and it seems that the latter today forms the basis of mainstream thinking in international law in one form or another. In addition, the 'policy-orientated' New Haven school founded by the Yale professor Myres S. McDougal[164] gained widespread influence at the height of the Cold War even outside the United States. This perspective regards international law as a constant flow of authoritative decision-making in which legal argument is only one factor among many others; therefore, it has been criticized by positivist views (especially in Europe) as abandoning the very concept of law and legal rules. Often, however, in deciding a practical case in international law, such theories are not much different in their results.

In the West, a new school of 'Critical Legal Studies', which started in the United States, has emerged, vigorously challenging traditional positivist perceptions of international law from a methodological point of view based on analytical language philosophy and a hermeneutical theory of law.[165] The 'deconstruction' of international legal argumentation by these critical legal scholars denies that, in view of its indeterminacy, inconsistency and lack of coherence, international law has a distinct existence of its own. Other modes of inquiry, inspired by the writings of Thomas M. Franck, address basic issues of the 'legitimacy' and 'fairness' of the international legal system from a different angle.[166] In addition, some more utopian theories have entered the market-place of ideas[167] and there is also now a claim to a 'feminist approach' to international law.[168] Another interesting development to be mentioned is the effort recently being made to attempt to bridge the gap between international law theory and international relations theory.[169]

At least for the time being, the Marxist–Leninist theory of international law[170] has vanished from the arena and has become of mere historical interest. After the end of the Cold War and the dissolution of the Soviet Empire, there has been a change in attitude in the former Communist states towards international law in general, the precise implications and durability of which, however, remain to be seen.[171] The same applies to the awakening of interest in international law in China.[172] To which extent Islamic perceptions of international law are developing into a separate direction is also an open and interesting question.[173]

The output of theory, on the abstract level, is certainly of academic interest for understanding the nature of the international legal system, but it has limited relevance for the actual practice of states and the problems that have to be solved in daily life. As the enlightened Dutch scholar Röling noted in 1960:

> In all positive law is hidden the element of power and the element of interest. Law is not the same as power, nor is it the same as interest, but it gives expression to the former power-relation. Law has the inclination to serve primarily the interests of the powerful. 'European' international law, the traditional law of nations, makes no exception to this rule. It served the interest of prosperous nations.[174]

The real question is, therefore, which interests does international law now serve in a much more expanded, diverse, but increasingly interdependent world, and the answer requires a closer look at various branches of the 'law in action' in international relations in the following chapters.

165 See D. Kennedy, A New Stream of International Law Scholarship, *Wis. ILJ* 7 (1988), 6 *et seq.*; M. Koskenniemi, *From Apology to Utopia: The Structure of International Legal Argument*, 1989; Koskenniemi, The Politics of International Law, *EJIL* 1 (1990), 4–32; A. Carty, Critical International Law: Recent Trends in the Theory of International Law, *EJIL* 2 (1991), 66 *et seq.*; O. de Schutter, Les critical legal studies au pays du droit international public, *Droit et Soc.* 22 (1992), 585–605; G. Dencho, Politics or Rule of Law: Deconstruction and Legitimacy in International Law, *EJIL* 4 (1993), 1–14.

166 See T.M. Franck, *The Power of Legitimacy Among Nations*, 1990; T.M. Franck/S.W. Hawkins, Justice in the International System, *Mich. JIL* 10 (1989), 127; J.E. Alvarez, The Quest for Legitimacy: An Examination of the Power of Legitimacy Among Nations, *NYUJILP* 24 (1991), 199–267; Franck, *Fairness in International Law and Institutions*, 1995. See also D.D. Caron, The Legitimacy of the Collective Authority of the Security Council, *AJIL* 87 (1993), 552–88; Caron, Governance and Collective Legitimization in the New World Order, *Hague YIL* 6 (1993), 29–44.

167 See the inspiring writings by P. Allott, *Eunomia. New Order for a New World*, 1990; Allott, Reconstituting Humanity – New International Law, *EJIL* 3 (1992), 219–52.

168 See, for example, H. Charlesworth/ C. Chinkin/S. Wright, Feminist Approaches to International Law, *AJIL* 85 (1991), 613–45; D.G. Dallmeyer (ed.), *Reconceiving Reality: Women and International Law*, 1993.

169 See G. Doeker, Internationale Beziehungen und Völkerrecht als Gegenstand der Forschung und Lehre, *AVR* 19 (1980–1), 401 *et seq.*, with references to the Anglo-American literature which is traditionally much more open to such questions; K.W. Abbott, Modern International Relations Theory: A Prospectus for International Lawyers, *Yale JIL* 14 (1989), 335–411; A.-M. Slaughter Burley, International Law and International Relations Theory: A Dual Agenda, *AJIL* 87 (1993), 205–39; S.V. Scott, International Law as Ideology: Theorizing the Relationship between International Law and International Politics, *EJIL* 5 (1994), 313–25; D. Frei, International Relations, *EPIL* II (1995), 1359–64; A.C. Arend/ R.J. Beck/R.D.V. Lugt (eds), *International Rules. Approaches from International Law and International*

Relations, 1996; V. Rittberger (ed.), Regime Theory and International Relations, 1993; C. Brown, International Relations Theory: New Normative Approaches, 1992. See further C.A. Kiss/D. Shelton, Systems Analysis of International Law: A Methodological Inquiry, NYIL 17 (1986), 45-74.
170 See text above, 23. For a recent analysis from a Marxist point of view see B.S. Chimni, International Law and World Order: A Critique of Contemporary Approaches, 1993.
171 See Harris CMIL, 21–2; J.W.E. Butler (ed.), International Law and the International System, 1987; T. Schweisfurth, Das Völkergewohnheitsrecht – verstärkt im Blickfeld der sowjetischen Völkerrechtslehre, GYIL 30 (1987), 36; Quigley, Perestroika and International Law, AJIL 82 (1988),

788–97; Agora: New Thinking by Soviet Scholars, AJIL 83 (1989), 494–518 (with contributions by R.A. Mullerson and I.I. Lukashuk); E. McWhinney, The 'New Thinking' in Soviet International Law: Soviet Doctrines and Practice in the Post-Tunkin Era, CYIL 28 (1990), 309–37; W.E. Butler (ed.), Perestroika and International Law, 1990; A. Carty/ G. Danilenko (eds), Perestroika and International Law: Current Anglo-Soviet Approaches to International Law, 1990.
172 See H. Chun, Chinese Attitudes Toward International Law in the Post-Mao Era, 1978–1987, IL 21 (1987), 1127–66; Wang Tieya (1990), op. cit.; R. Heuser, Völkerrechtswissenschaft und Völkerrechtstheorie in der Volksrepublik China (1979–88), ZaöRV 49 (1989), 301–34.

173 See, for example, A.A. Ana'im, Islamic Ambivalence to Political Violence: Islamic Law and International Terrorism, GYIL 31 (1988), 307; D.A. Westbrook, Islamic International Law and Public International Law: Separate Expressions of World Order, Virginia JIL 33 (1993), 819–97; F. Malekian, The Concept of Islamic International Criminal Law. A Comparative Study, 1994; M. Khadduri, International Law, Islamic, EPIL II (1995), 1236–42. In 1992 the International Law Association (ILA) established a Committee on Islamic Law within International Law.
174 B.V.A. Röling, International Law in an Expanded World, 1960, 15.

3   Sources of international law

The word 'source of law' ('source de droit', 'Rechtsquelle') has a variety of interpretations.[1] The English legal philosopher H.L.A. Hart distinguishes between its use in a 'material' or 'historical sense' and in a 'formal' or 'legal' sense.[2] In the first non-legal sense it refers to a causal or historical influence explaining the factual existence of a given rule of law at a given place and time, for example, to show that a certain contemporary rule of Dutch law may originate from Roman law, or to state that the development of labour law has resulted from the political action taken by trade unions. In the legal sense, the term means the criteria under which a rule is accepted as valid in the given legal system at issue. These criteria distinguish binding law from legally non-binding other social or moral norms and the law *de lege lata* (the law as it currently stands) from the law *de lege ferenda* (the law as it may be, or should be, in the future).[3] In this sense, the term 'source' has a technical meaning related to the law-making process and must not be confused with information sources, research sources or bibliographies on international law.[4]

In developed national legal systems there are definite methods of identifying the law, primarily by reference to the constitution, legislation (statutes) and judicial case law. In the decentralized international legal system, lacking a hierarchical structure,[5] the problem of finding the law is much more complicated. There is no authority to adopt universally binding legislation[6] and no compulsory jurisdiction of international courts and tribunals without the consent of states. In this system the same subjects of international law[7] that are bound by international rules and principles have created them themselves.

The most important source of international law for centuries was customary law, evolving from the practice of states.[8] The recent attempt to codify international law and the conclusion of multilateral treaties in many important areas, such as diplomatic and consular relations,[9] the law of war[10] or the law of the sea,[11] have sought to clarify the law and to establish universally accepted norms. But customary law has still retained its predominance over treaty law or other sources in many other areas, such as, for example, state immunity[12] or state responsibility.[13] The changes in international society since 1945 have led to basic disputes on the sources of international law and it must be noted at the outset that they have become an area of considerable theoretical controversy. In particular, the two main traditional elements, custom and treaties, are now often difficult to distinguish clearly. As R. Jennings put it in 1981:

1 *Harris CMIL*, 23–68; *Restatement (Third)*, Vol. 1, paras. 102–3, 24–39; C. Dominice, Methodology of International Law, *EPIL* 7 (1984), 334 *et seq.*; R. Monaco, Sources of International Law, *ibid.*, 424 *et seq.*; B. Simma/P. Alston, The Sources of Human Rights Law: Custom, Jus Cogens, and General Principles, *AYIL* 12 (1988/9), 82–108; C. Sepúlveda, Methods and Procedures for the Creation of Legal Norms in the International System of States: An Inquiry into the Progressive Development of International Law in the Present Era, *GYIL* 33 (1990), 432; O. Schachter, *International Law in Theory and Practice*, 1991, Chapter III; U. Fastenrath, *Lücken im Völkerrecht*, 1991; E. Riedel, Standards and Sources. Farewell to the Exclusivity of the Sources Triad in International Law?, *EJIL* 2 (1991), 58–84; E. Frangou-Ikonomidou (ed.), *Sources of International Law*, 1992; U. Fastenrath, Relative Normativity in International Law, *EJIL* 4 (1993), 305–40; G. Tunkin, Is General International Law Customary Law Only?, *ibid.*, 534–41; H.H.G. Post, Some Curiosities in the Sources of the Law of Armed Conflict Conceived in a General International Legal Perspective, *NYIL* 25 (1994), 83–118.

2 H.L.A. Hart, *The Concept of Law*, 1961, 246–7. On the meaning of 'sources' see also R.Y. Jennings, International Law, *EPIL* 7 (1984), 284; I. Brownlie, *Principles of Public International Law*, 4th edn 1990, 1–3, discussing the common distinction between 'formal' sources (legal procedures and methods for creating binding rules) and 'material' sources (providing evidence of the content of rules in the sense of substantive law) which is not clearly applicable in international law.

3 On the need to distinguish clearly between the *lex lata* and mere propositions on the *lex ferenda* see R.Y. Jennings, An International Lawyer Takes Stock, *ICLQ* 39 (1990), 513–29, 514.

4 An excellent guide to the literature in this respect is *Public International Law – A Current Bibliography of Books and Articles*, published regularly by the Max Planck Institute for Comparative Public Law and International Law in Heidelberg, which evaluates over 1400 journals, in addition to other collected works, and also lists newly published books on all areas of public international law.
5 See Chapter 1 above, 3–5.
6 See O. Schachter, The Nature and Process of Legal Development in International Society, in R.St.J. Macdonald/D.M. Johnston (eds), *The Structure and Process of International Law*, 1983, 745–808; G.M. Danilenko, *Law-Making in the International Community*, 1993; K. Skubiszewski, International Legislation, *EPIL* II (1995), 1255–62;.
7 See Chapters 5, 75–90 and 6, 91–108 below.
8 See R. Bernhardt, Customary International Law, *EPIL* I (1992), 898–905.
9 See Chapter 8 below, 123–9.
10 See Chapter 20, 342–63 below.
11 See Chapter 12 below, 173–5.
12 See Chapter 8 below, 118–23.
13 See Chapter 17 below, 254–72.
14 R.Y. Jennings, What is International Law and How Do We Tell When We See It?, *ASDI* 37 (1981), 59–88, at 60.
15 Text in *Brownlie BDIL*, 438.
16 On the practice of the ICJ see M. Mendelson, The International Court of Justice and the Sources of International Law, in V. Lowe/M. Fitzmaurice (eds), *Fifty Years of the International Court of Justice*, 1996, 63–89.
17 *Op. cit.* See R. Bernhardt, Treaties, *EPIL* 7 (1984), 459–64. Further literature is listed in Chapter 9 below, 130, which deals with the law of treaties.

I doubt whether anybody is going to dissent from the proposition that there has never been a time when there has been so much confusion and doubt about the tests of the validity – or sources – of international law, than the present.[14]

Article 38(1) of the Statute of the International Court of Justice[15] provides:

The Court, whose function is to decide in accordance with international law such disputes as are submitted to it, shall apply:

(a) international conventions, whether general or particular, establishing rules expressly recognized by the contesting States;
(b) international custom, as evidence of a general practice accepted as law;
(c) the general principles of law recognized by civilized nations;
(d) . . . judicial decisions and the teachings of the most highly qualified publicists of the various nations, as subsidiary means for the determination of rules of law.

This provision is usually accepted as constituting a list of the sources of international law.[16] Some writers have criticized it on the grounds that it does not list all the sources of international law, or that it includes aspects which are not genuine sources, but none of the alternative lists which have been suggested has won general approval. It is therefore proposed to examine the sources listed in the Court's Statute before considering other possible sources of international law.

Treaties

The Statute of the International Court of Justice speaks of 'international conventions, whether general or particular, establishing rules expressly recognized by the contesting states'.[17] The word 'convention' means a treaty, and that is the only meaning which the word possesses in international law, and in international relations generally. This is a point worth emphasizing, because students have been known to confuse conventions with conferences, or to mix up conventions in international law with conventions of the constitution in British constitutional law. Other terms used as a synonym for treaties, or for particular types of treaties, are agreement, pact, understanding, protocol, charter, statute, act, covenant, declaration, engagement, arrangement, accord, regulation and provision. Some of these words have alternative meanings (that is, they can also mean something other than treaties), which makes the problem of terminology even more confusing.

Treaties are of growing importance in international law. The practice of publishing collections of treaties concluded by a certain state or group of states commenced during the second half of the seventeenth century. The most important collection, under various titles, until the Second World War, was started by G.F. von Martens in 1771 with his '*Recueil des principaux traités*'. Since 1945, in accordance with Article 102 of the UN Charter, more than 33,000 treaties have been registered with the United

Nations, several thousand of which are multilateral.[18] As collectivism has replaced *laissez-faire*, a large number of questions have become subject to governmental regulation – and to intergovernmental regulation when they transcend national boundaries. Modern technology, communications and trade have made states more interdependent than ever before, and more willing to accept rules on a vast range of problems of common concern – extradition of criminals, safety regulations for ships and aircraft, economic aid, copyright, standardization of road signs, protection of foreign investment, environmental issues and so on. The rules in question are usually laid down in treaties, with the result that international law has expanded beyond all recognition in the last 140 years (although it must be pointed out that most of the rules are too specialized to be dealt with in ordinary textbooks on international law).

Treaties are the major instrument of cooperation in international relations, and cooperation often involves a change in the relative positions of the states involved (for example, rich countries give money to poor countries). Treaties, therefore, are often an instrument of change – a point which is forgotten by those who regard international law as an essentially conservative force. The general trend, particularly after the Second World War, has been to enhance the role of treaties in international law-making, partly in response to increasing interdependence, partly as a solution to the controversies that exist between diverse groups of states as to the content and validity of older customary rules.

To some extent treaties have begun to replace customary law. Where there is agreement about rules of customary law, they are codified by treaty; where there is disagreement or uncertainty, states tend to settle disputes by *ad hoc* compromises – which also take the form of treaties. For example, capital-exporting countries have concluded some 1000 bilateral treaties promoting and protecting foreign investment to clarify the relevant legal framework.[19]

Law-making treaties and 'contract treaties'

Treaties are the maids-of-all-work in international law. Very often they resemble contracts in national systems of law, but they can also perform functions which in national systems would be carried out by statutes, by conveyances, or by the memorandum of association of a company. In national legal systems, legislative acts of parliament are regarded as sources of law, but contracts are not; contracts are merely legal transactions. (Contracts create rights and duties only for the contracting parties, who are very few in number, and it is generally agreed that a 'source of law' means a source of rules which apply to a very large number of people.) Some writers have tried to argue that treaties should be regarded as sources of international law only if they resemble national statutes in content, that is, if they impose the same obligations on all the parties to the treaty and seek to regulate the parties' behaviour over a long period of time. Such treaties are called 'law-making treaties' (*traités-lois*) and their purpose is to conclude an agreement on universal substantive legal principles (i.e. human rights treaties, Genocide Convention).[20] According to this theory, 'contract-treaties' (*traités-contrat*), that is, treaties which resemble contracts (for instance, a

18 *United Nations Treaties Series (UNTS)*; for a good reference work see M.J. Bowman/D.J. Harris (eds), *Multilateral Treaties: Index and Current Status*, 1984 and 10th cumulative supplement, 1993, with regular cumulative supplements. See also L. Wildhaber, Treaties, Multilateral, *EPIL* 7 (1984), 480–4; C. Parry (ed.), *The Consolidated Treaty Series (CTS)*, 1648–1918 (annotated); Hudson, *International Legislation* (1931–1950); C. Parry (ed.), *Index to British Treaties* (1101–1918); *United Kingdom Treaties Series (UKTS)* (from 1892); *League of Nations Treaty Series (LNTS)*. International Legal Materials *(ILM)*, which regularly publishes not only treaties but also other important documents relating to international law, is also very useful.
19 See Chapter 15 below, 237.
20 See V. de Visscher, *Problèmes d'interpretation judiciare en droit international public*, 1963, 128 *et seq.*

21 See Chapter 9 below, 145–6.
Another aspect where the distinction
may be relevant is in the interpretation
and application of the particular treaty,
see Bernhardt (1984), *op. cit.*, 461. See
also E. Raftopoulos, *The Inadequacy of
the Contractual Analogy in the Law of
Treaties*, 1990.
22 See Chapters 5, 75–90 and 6,
91–108 below.
23 R. Jennings, State Contracts in
International Law, *BYIL* 32 (1961), 156
et seq.; K.-H. Böckstiegel, *Der Staat als
Vertragspartner ausländischer
Privatunternehmen*, 1971; D.W. Bowett,
State Contracts with Aliens:
Contemporary Developments on
Compensation for Termination or
Breach, *BYIL* 59 (1988), 49 *et seq.*; E.
Paasivirta, Internationalization and
Stabilization of Contracts versus State
Sovereignty, *BYIL* 60 (1989), 315 *et
seq.*; M. Sornarajah, *International
Commercial Arbitration: The Protection
of State Contracts*, 1990; G.v. Hecke,
Contracts Between States and Foreign
Private Law Persons, *EPIL* I (1992),
814–19; see also v. Hecke, Contracts
Between International Organizations
and Private Law Persons, *ibid.*, 812–
14; A.F.M. Maniruzzaman, State
Contracts with Aliens. The Question of
Unilateral Change by the State in
Contemporary International Law, *JIArb.*
9 (1992), 141–71; G.R. Delaume,
*Transnational Contracts – Applicable
Law and Settlement of Disputes*, 1992.
24 P. Fisher, Concessions, *EPIL* I
(1992), 715–21; A.Z.E. Chiali,
Protection of Investment in the Context
of Petroleum Agreements, *RdC* 204
(1987-IV), 13–169.
25 The most important arbitration
cases since 1929 are listed in v. Hecke,
op. cit.

treaty whereby one state agrees to lend a certain sum of money to another state) are not sources of law, but merely legal transactions.

However, the analogy between national statutes and law-making treaties is misleading for two reasons. First, in national systems of law anyone who is contractually competent (i.e. anyone who is sane and not a minor) can enter into a contract, but parliamentary legislation is passed by a small group of people. In international law, any state can enter into a treaty, including a law-making treaty. Secondly, in national systems of law contracts create rights and duties only for the contracting parties, who are very few in number, whereas statutes of national law apply to a very large number of people. In international law all treaties, including law-making treaties, apply only to states which agree to them. Normally the parties to a law-making treaty are more numerous than the parties to a 'contract-treaty', but there is no reason why this should always be so.

The only distinction between a 'law-making treaty' and a 'contract-treaty' is one of content. As a result, many treaties constitute borderline cases, which are hard to classify. A single treaty may contain some provisions which are 'contractual', and others which are 'law-making'. The distinction between 'law-making treaties' and 'contract-treaties' is not entirely useless; for instance, a 'contract-treaty' is more likely to be terminated by the outbreak of war between the parties than a law-making treaty.[21] But it is too vague and imprecise to justify regarding law-making treaties as the only treaties which are a source of international law. The better view is to regard all treaties as a source of law. At any rate, the law of treaties applies to both types of treaties.

Parties to international treaties and 'internationalized contracts'

Only the subjects of international law – states, international organizations, and the other traditionally recognized entities[22] – can conclude treaties under international law. An international business contract concluded between a company based in state A and another enterprise located in state B is subject to one or another national legal system, but it is not a treaty under international law. Similarly, private law contracts between states, i.e. for the sale and purchase of goods, are usually concluded under the national law of one of the parties.

Some interesting problems have arisen in connection with agreements made between states and foreign corporations,[23] especially in the field of oil concessions,[24] permitting a foreign company to explore and exploit oil resources on the territory of the state. Usually, the parties to such agreements consent to a certain national legal system governing the contract. But occasionally, in the case of powerful multinational companies, such contracts have not been, fully or partially, placed under a national law, but under international law, general principles of law or only under the provisions of the contract itself. The reason for concluding such so-called internationalized contracts is to establish a balance between the parties and prevent the state party from evading its obligations under the contract by changing its own internal law. This is mostly secured by an arbitration clause referring disputes under the agreement to an international body.[25] There have been various attempts to find a proper legal classification of these internationalized contracts, but the practical relevance of the issue has declined in recent years, as parties now mostly declare a certain national law to be applicable.

The law of treaties is dealt with in Chapter 9 below.[26]

Custom

The second source of international law listed in the Statute of the International Court of Justice is 'international custom, as evidence of a general practice accepted as law'.[27] As confirmed by the ICJ in the *Nicaragua* case,[28] custom is constituted by two elements, the objective one of 'a general practice', and the subjective one 'accepted as law', the so-called *opinio iuris*. In the *Continental Shelf (Libya v. Malta)* case, the Court stated that the substance of customary international law must be 'looked for primarily in the actual practice and *opinio juris* of States'.[29] The definition has given rise to some vexed theoretical questions, such as: How is it possible to make law by practice? And how can something be accepted as law before it has actually developed into law?[30] But it is nevertheless the established doctrine, accepted by states, international tribunals and most writers alike.

Where to look for evidence of customary law

The main evidence of customary law is to be found in the actual practice of states, and a rough idea of a state's practice can be gathered from published material – from newspaper reports of actions taken by states, and from statements made by government spokesmen to Parliament, to the press, at international conferences and at meetings of international organizations; and also from a state's laws and judicial decisions, because the legislature and the judiciary form part of a state just as much as the executive does. At times the Foreign Ministry of a state may publish extracts from its archives; for instance, when a state goes to war or becomes involved in a particular bitter dispute, it may publish documents to justify itself in the eyes of the world. But the vast majority of the material which would tend to throw light on a state's practice concerning questions of international law – correspondence with other states, and the advice which each state receives from its own legal advisers – is normally not published; or, to be more precise, it is only recently that efforts have been made to publish digests of the practice followed by different states.[31] As far as the latter are reliable as evidence of the law,[32] it must also be taken into consideration that such an expensive enterprise is mostly not undertaken in developing countries and that the empirical basis for analytical generalizations, therefore, is in fact rather limited to the practice of certain countries. Valuable evidence can also be found in the documentary sources produced by the United Nations.[33]

Evidence of customary law may sometimes also be found in the writings of international lawyers, and in judgments of national and international tribunals, which are mentioned as subsidiary means for the determination of rules of law in Article 38(1)(d) of the Statute of the International Court of Justice.[34]

26 See Chapter 9 below.

27 M. Akehurst, Custom as a Source of International Law, *BYIL* 47 (1974–5), 1 *et seq.*; G.M. Danilenko, The Theory of International Customary Law, *GYIL* 31 (1988), 9 et seq; M.H. Mendelson, The Formation of Rules of Customary (General) International Law, *ILA Rep.* 1988, 935–59; J.A. Barberis, Réflexions sur la coutume internationale, *AFDI* 36 (1990), 9–46; J. Kirchner, Thoughts about a Methodology of Customary International Law, *AJPIL* 43 (1992), 215–39; Bernhardt (1992), *op. cit.*, 898–905; K. Wolfke, Some Persistent Controversies regarding Customary International Law, *NYIL* 24 (1993), 1–16; Wolfke, *Custom in Present International Law*, 2nd edn 1993; O. Elias, The Nature of the Subjective Element in Customary International Law, *ICLQ* 44 (1995), 501–20; I. M. Lobo de Souza, The Role of State Consent in the Customary Process, *ibid.*, 521–39; Meron, The Continuing Role of Custom in the Formation of International Humanitarian Law, *AJIL* 90 (1996), 238–49.

28 *Nicaragua v. USA* (Merits), *ICJ Rep.* 1986, 14, at 97. See Chapters 18, 284, 289 and 19, 311, 317, 319–22 and text below, 41.

29 *ICJ Rep.* 1985, 29. See also Advisory Opinion on the Legality of the Threat or Use of Nuclear Weapons, *ILM* 35 (1996), 809, at 826, para. 64. On the case see Chapter 20 below, 347–9.

30 See *Restatement (Third)*, Vol. 1, Reporters' Note to para. 102, at 30.

31 For example, C. Parry/G. Fitzmaurice (eds), *British Digest of International Law*; British and Foreign State Papers (1812–1970). On United States practice see Moore (ed.), *Digest of International Law* (1906); Hackworth (ed.), *Digest of International Law* (1940–1944); M.M. Whiteman (ed.), *Digest of International Law* (1963–1973); State Department (ed.), *Annual Digests of United States Practice in International Law* (since 1973); M. Nash (Leich) (ed.), *Cumulative Digest of United States Practice in International Law 1981–1988*, Book II, 1994; *Foreign Relations of the United States, Diplomatic Papers, and Papers Relating to the Foreign Relations of the United States* (since 1861), and the *Restatement (Third)*. On the practice of France see A. Kiss, *Répertoire de la pratique française en matière de droit international public* (1962–1972). Furthermore, a number of periodicals provide regular repertories of national state practice, for example, *AFDI, AJIL, AYIL, AJPIL, ASDI, BYIL, CYIL, IYIL, NYIL, RBDI* and *ZaöRV*.

32 See H. Mosler, Repetorien der nationalen Praxis in Völkerrechtsfragen – Eine Quelle zur Erschließung des allgemeinen Völkerrechts?, *Receuil d'études de droit international en hommage à P. Guggenheim*, 1968, 460–89.

33 For example, *UN Juridical Yearbook; UN Legislative Series; List of Treaty Collections; Cumulative Index of the Treaty Series; Repertoire of the Practice of the Security Council* (1946–1951, with supplements until 1971); *Repertory of Practice of United Nations Organs; Report of International Arbitral Awards (RIAA)*.

34 See text below, 51–2 and cf. also *The Paquete Habana* (1900), 175 US 677, 700–1.

35 M.E. Villiger,*Customary International Law and Treaties*, 1985.

36 See Chapter 7 below, 117.

37 *Restatement (Third)*, Vol. 1, para. 102, 27; B. Kishoiyian, The Utility of Bilateral Investment Treaties in the Formulation of Customary International Law, *NJILB* 14 (1994), 327–75.

38 On ratification and entry into force of treaties generally, see Chapter 9 below, 131–6.

39 Text in *Brownlie BDIL*, 388. See Chapter 9 below, 130–46.

40 See Chapters 18, 284 and 19, 311, 317, 319–22 below.

41 For the opposite case see D.W. Bowett, Treaty Revision in the Light of the Evolution of Customary International Law, *AJICL* 5 (1993), 84–96 and text below, 56–7.

42 See Chapter 2 above, 21–2.

Similarly, treaties can be evidence of customary law;[35] but great care must be taken when inferring rules of customary law from treaties, especially bilateral ones. For instance, treaties dealing with a particular subject matter may habitually contain a certain provision; thus, extradition treaties almost always provide that political offenders shall not be extradited.[36] It has sometimes been argued that a standard provision of this type has become so habitual that it should be regarded as a rule of customary law, to be inferred even when a treaty is silent on that particular point. On the other hand, why would states bother to insert such standard provisions in their treaties, if the rule existed already as a rule of customary law? The problem is a difficult one, and one needs to know more about the intentions of the parties to the treaties in question before one is safe in invoking a standard treaty provision as evidence of customary law. Even so, the mere existence of identical bilateral treaties does not generally support a corresponding norm of customary law. At least the network of bilateral treaties must be widespread before it can amount to state practice resulting in customary law.[37]

The case of multilateral treaties is different and may definitely constitute evidence of customary law. If the treaty claims to be declaratory of customary law, or is intended to codify customary law, it can be quoted as evidence of customary law even against a state which is not a party to the treaty. This is so even if the treaty has not received enough ratifications to come into force.[38] It may be asked why states should be unwilling to ratify a treaty if it merely restates customary law. Explanations include inertia and lack of parliamentary time (if ratification requires the participation of the legislature, as it does in many countries). Moreover, only part of the treaty may codify customary law, and a state may refuse to ratify because it objects to other parts thereof.

Good examples are many (but not all) provisions of the 1969 Vienna Convention on the Law of Treaties.[39] Such a state is not bound by the treaty, but by customary law; therefore, if it can produce other evidence to show that the treaty misrepresents customary law it can disregard the rule stated in the treaty. This possibility is not open to states which are parties to the treaty, since they are bound by the treaty in their relations with other parties to the treaty, regardless of whether the treaty accurately codifies customary law or not. But treaty law and customary law can exist side by side. In the *Nicaragua* case, the International Court of Justice held that its jurisdiction was excluded with regard to the relevant treaty law (in that case the UN Charter), but nevertheless proceeded to reach a decision on the basis of customary international law, the content of which it considered to be the same as that laid down in the Charter (concerning the prohibition of the use of force).[40]

Moreover, there is the possibility that customary law may change so as to conform with an earlier treaty.[41] For instance, the Declaration of Maritime Law issued by the signatory states to the Treaty of Paris 1856[42] altered certain rules about the conduct of war at sea. It prohibited privateering, the capture of enemy goods except contraband on neutral ships, and of neutral goods except contraband on enemy ships. It also required blockades to be effective and supported by a force sufficient to actually prevent access to the coast of the enemy.[43] As a treaty, it applied only between the parties to it: Austria, France, Prussia, Russia, Sardinia, Turkey and the United Kingdom. Subsequently, however, the rules contained in the Declaration were accepted by a large number of other states as rules of customary law.

Similar problems arise with resolutions passed at meetings of international organizations, particularly resolutions of the United Nations General Assembly which will be discussed separately below.[44]

Finally, it must be noted that the debate on what constitutes proper evidence of customary law needs to be separated from procedural questions, such as the burden of proof or general rules on evidence before international courts and tribunals.[45] It is true that a state seeking to rely on a particular rule of customary law normally has the burden of proving the fact that the relevant state practice exists.[46] But an international judge or arbitrator will not rely on rules of procedure to decide whether a norm exists or not, but will rather make a value judgment.

The problem of repetition

It has sometimes been suggested that a single precedent is not enough to establish a customary rule, and that there must be a degree of repetition over a period of time; thus, in the *Asylum* case the International Court of Justice suggested that a customary rule must be based on 'a constant and uniform usage'.[47] However, this statement must be seen in the light of the facts of the *Asylum* case, where the Court said: 'The facts . . . disclose so much uncertainty and contradiction, so much fluctuation and discrepancy in the exercise of diplomatic asylum and in the official views expressed on various occasions . . . that it is not possible to discern . . . any constant and uniform usage, accepted as law.'[48] (In this case, Victor Raúl Haya de la Torre, the leader of an unsuccessful rebellion in Peru in 1948, obtained asylum in the Colombian Embassy in Lima. Peru and Colombia referred to the ICJ the question of whether Colombia had the right to grant asylum and whether he should be handed over to the Peruvian authorities or be granted safe-conduct out of the country.) In other words, what prevented the formation of a customary rule in the *Asylum* case was not the absence of repetition, but the presence of major inconsistencies in the practice.

In the *Nicaragua* case, the ICJ held:

> It is not to be expected that in the practice of States the application of the rules in question should have been perfect, in the sense that States should have refrained, with complete consistency, from the use of force or from intervention in each other's internal affairs. The Court does not consider that, for a rule to be established as customary, the corresponding practice must be in absolutely rigorous conformity with the rule. In order to deduce the existence of customary rules, the Court deems it sufficient that the conduct of States should, in general, be consistent with such rules, and that instances of State conduct inconsistent with a given rule should generally have been treated as breaches of that rule, not as indications of the recognition of a new rule.[49]

In sum, *major* inconsistencies in the practice (that is, a large amount of

43 Nussbaum, *A Concise History of the Law of Nations*, 1962, 192. See also Chapter 20 below, 350–1.

44 See text below, 52–4.

45 See M. Kazazi, *Burden of Proof and Related Issues. A Study on Evidence Before International Tribunals*, Studies and Materials on the Settlement of International Disputes (P. Malanczuk ed.), Vol. 1, 1996.

46 See Bernhardt (1992), *op. cit.*, 900–1.

47 *Asylum Case, ICJ Rep.* 1950, 266–389, at 277. The case gave rise to three decisions by the ICJ, but these decisions are not viewed as giving a precise picture of the nature of diplomatic asylum, see J.A. Barberis, Asylum, Diplomatic, *EPIL* I (1995), 281–3, at 282; A. Grahl-Madsen, Asylum, Territorial, *ibid.*, 283–7; K. Hailbronner, Haya de la Torres Cases, *ibid.*, 683–5

48 *Ibid.*

49 *Nicaragua v. US* (Merits), *ICJ Rep.* 1986, at 98, para. 186. See H.C.M. Charlesworth, Customary International Law and the Nicaragua Case, *AYIL* 11 (1984/7), 1–31; H.G. Anthony, Appraisals of the ICJ's Decision: Nicaragua v. United States (Merits), *AJIL* 81 (1987), 77–183; A. D'Amato, Trashing Customary International Law, *ibid.*, 101–5; F.L. Kirgis, Jr., Custom on A Sliding Scale, *ibid.*, 146–51; J.I. Charney, Customary International Law in the Nicaragua Case. Judgment on the Merits, *Hague YIL* 1 (1988), 16–29; W. Czaplinski, Sources of International Law in the Nicaragua Case, *ICLQ* 38 (1989), 151–66; P.P. Rijpkem, Customary International Law in the Nicaragua Case, *NYIL* 20 (1989), 91–116; J. Crawford, Military Activities Against Nicaragua Case (Nicaragua v. United States), *EPIL* III (forthcoming). On the relevance of the case for the use of force see Chapter 19 below, 311, 317, 319–22, and on the problem of the jurisdiction of the Court see Chapter 18 below, 284.

50 *UK v. Norway, ICJ Rep.* 1951, 116, at 138; see L. Gündling, Fisheries Case (U.K. *v.* Norway), *EPIL* II (1995), 381–3 and Chapter 12 below, 181.
51 See Akehurst (1974–5), Custom, *op. cit.*, 12–21.
52 The *Restatement (Third)*, Vol. 1, para. 102, 25.
53 See Chapter 12 below, 173–97.
54 See Chapter 13 below, 201–8.
55 *ILM* 35 (1996), 830, para. 96. On the case see Chapter 20 below, 347–9.
56 For a criticism see the Declaration attached to the Opinion by Judge Shi Jiuyong, *ibid.*, 832. But see also the Separate Opinion of Judge Fleischhauer, *ibid.*, 834, at 835–6.
57 Dissenting Opinion of Vice-President Schwebel, *ibid.*, 836–7.

practice which goes against the 'rule' in question) prevent the creation of a customary rule. As noted by the ICJ in the *Fisheries* case, *minor* inconsistencies (that is, a small amount of practice which goes against the rule in question) do not prevent the creation of a customary rule,[50] although in such cases the rule in question probably needs to be supported by a large amount of practice, in order to outweigh the conflicting practice in question.[51] (The *Fisheries* case concerned British claims against Norway for introducing national legislation on exclusive fishing rights in the waters surrounding Norway's entire coastline north of the Arctic Circle. The Court upheld the Norwegian method of delimitation of the territorial sea and its fixing of actual baselines.) On the other hand, where there is no practice which goes against an alleged rule of customary law, it seems that a *small* amount of practice is sufficient to create a customary rule, even though the practice involves only a small number of states and has lasted for only a short time.

There remains the question of what constitutes 'general' practice. This much depends on the circumstances of the case and on the rule at issue. 'General' practice is a relative concept and cannot be determined in the abstract. It should include the conduct of all states, which can participate in the formulation of the rule or the interests of which are specially affected. 'A practice can be general even if it is not universally accepted; there is no precise formula to indicate how widespread a practice must be, but it should reflect wide acceptance among the states particularly involved in the relevant activity.'[52] Therefore, in the law of the sea,[53] the practice of sea powers and maritime nations will have greater significance than the practice of land-locked states, while in the law governing outer space activities,[54] the practice of the United States and Russia will exert a more dominant influence than that of Burundi or Chile. This can also be seen from the Advisory Opinion of the ICJ in the *Legality of Nuclear Weapons* case in which the Court in discussing whether there is a customary rule prohibiting the use of nuclear weapons, *inter alia*, found that it could not ignore the 'practice referred to as 'policy of deterrence', to which an appreciable section of the international community has adhered for many years'.[55] Obviously, this refers to the practice of certain nuclear weapons states and not to the practice of the international community at large.[56] However, as observed by Judge Schwebel in his Dissenting Opinion:

> This nuclear practice is not a practice of a lone and secondary persistent objector. This is not a practice of a pariah Government crying out in the wilderness of otherwise international opinion. This is the practice of five of the world's major Powers, of the permanent Members of the Security Council, significantly supported for almost 50 years by their allies and other States sheltering under their nuclear umbrellas. That is to say, it is the practice of States – and a practice supported by a large and weighty number of other States – that together represent the bulk of the world's population. This practice has been recognized, accommodated and in some measure accepted by the international community. That measure of acceptance is ambiguous but not meaningless.[57]

What is certain is that general practice does not require the unanimous practice of all states or other international subjects. This means that a state can be bound by the general practice of other states even against its wishes if it does not protest against the emergence of the rule and continues persistently to do so (persistent objector).[58] Such instances are not frequent and the rule also requires that states are sufficiently aware of the emergence of the new practice and law. Thus, for example, the contention can hardly be sustained that the practice of space powers to launch their space objects into outer space after 1957 by crossing the air space under the sovereignty of other countries developed into custom by the acquiescence of those states.[59] The countries affected simply often lacked the technological capacities to find out.

What states say and what states do

It is sometimes suggested that state practice consists only of what states do, not of what they say. For instance, in his dissenting opinion in the *Fisheries* case, Judge Read argued that claims made to areas of the sea by a state could not create a customary rule unless such claims were enforced against foreign ships.[60] But in the later *Fisheries Jurisdiction* cases ten of the fourteen judges inferred the existence of customary rules from such claims, without considering whether they had been enforced.[61] (These two parallel cases dealt with the validity of the establishment by Iceland of a fifty-mile exclusive fishery zone and its effect on the fishing rights of the United Kingdom and Germany which these two states had traditionally enjoyed within this zone.) Similarly, the Nuremberg Tribunal cited resolutions passed by the League of Nations Assembly and a Pan-American Conference as authority for its finding that aggressive war was criminal according to the 'customs and practices of states'.[62] The better view therefore appears to be that state practice consists not only of what states do, but also of what they say.

This becomes even clearer if one takes the fact into account that in the modern world states have found new means of communication. As noted in a recent empirical study on state practice, Zemanek arrives at the following conclusion:

> The beloved 'real' acts become less frequent because international law, and the Charter of the UN in particular, place more and more restraints on States in this respect. And what formerly was confined to diplomatic notes is now often transmitted via new forms of communication, mainly for reasons of domestic or international policy. The present information society forces governments which seek the widest possible support for their stance to resort to publicity.[63]

Finally, state practice also includes omissions; many rules of international law forbid states to do certain acts, and, when proving such a rule, it is necessary to look not only at what states do, but also at what they do not do.[64] Even silence on the part of states is relevant because passiveness and inaction with respect to claims of other states can produce a binding effect creating legal obligations for the silent state under the doctrine of acquiescence.[65]

58 See text below, 46–8.
59 See Chapter 13 below, 206. On the doctrines of acquiescence and estoppel, see Chapter 10 below, 154–5.
60 *ICJ Rep.* 1951, 116, 191; Gündling, *op. cit.*
61 *UK v. Iceland* (Merits), *ICJ Rep.* 1974, 3, at 47, 56–8, 81–8, 119–20, 135, 161. The remaining four judges did not deal with this issue. See G. Jaenicke, Fisheries Jurisdiction Cases (U.K. v. Iceland; Federal Republic of Germany v. Iceland), *EPIL* II (1995), 386–9. See Chapter 12 below, 183.
62 *AJIL* 41 (1947), 172, 219–20. See Chapter 20 below, 354–5 and *Nicaragua v. USA, op. cit.*, 99–104, 106–8.
63 K. Zemanek, What is 'State Practice' and Who Makes It?, in *FS Bernhardt*, 289–306, at 306.
64 Similarly, the Draft Articles on State Responsibility for Internationally Wrongful Acts adopted by the ILC in its first reading in 1980 (text in *Brownlie BDIL*, 426), in defining an 'internationally wrongful act', *inter alia*, refer to 'conduct consisting of an action or omission' that is attributable to the state under international law, draft Article 3(a). See Chapter 17 below, 257–60.
65 See Müller/Cottier, *op. cit.*

66 *North Sea Continental Shelf* cases, *ICJ Rep.* 1969, 3, at 44; G. Jaenicke, North Sea Continental Shelf Cases, *EPIL* 2 (1981), 205–8. See also Chapter 12, 184–91 and text below, 46.

67 See L.D. Paul, Comity in International Law, *Harvard ILJ* 32 (1991), 1–79; P. Macalister-Smith, Comity, *EPIL* I (1992), 671–4. See also Chapter 4 below, 73.

68 J.L. Slama, Opinio juris in Customary International Law, *Okla. CULR* 15 (1990), 603–56; Elias (1995), *op. cit.*

69 See Chapter 7 below, 110–15.

70 See *Restatement (Third)*, Vol. 1, para. 101, 25.

71 See W. Karl, Protest, *EPIL* 9 (1986), 320–2.

72 *Lotus Case*, PCIJ, series A, no. 10, 28 *et seq.* See K. Herndl, Lotus, The, *EPIL* 2 (1981), 173–7. See also Chapter 12 below, 190–1.

The psychological element in the formation of customary law (*opinio iuris*)

When inferring rules of customary law from the conduct of states, it is necessary to examine not only what states do, but also why they do it. In other words, there is a psychological element in the formation of customary law. State practice alone does not suffice; it must be shown that it is accompanied by the conviction that it reflects a legal obligation. For instance, there are many international acts performed habitually, such as flag salutes greeting a foreign ship on the high seas, or in the field of ceremony and protocol, which are motivated solely by courtesy or tradition, 'but not by any sense of legal duty'.[66] Such behaviour is based merely on what is called 'comity' or '*courtoisie*' in the relations between states.[67]

The technical name given to this psychological element is *opinio iuris sive necessitatis* (*opinio iuris* for short).[68] It is usually defined as a conviction felt by states that a certain form of conduct is required by international law. This definition presupposes that all rules of international law are framed in terms of duties. But that is not so; in addition to rules laying down duties, there are also permissive rules, which permit states to act in a particular way (for example, to prosecute foreigners for crimes committed within the prosecuting state's territory) without making such actions obligatory.[69] In the case of a rule imposing a duty, the traditional definition of *opinio iuris* is correct; in the case of a permissive rule, *opinio iuris* means a conviction felt by states that a certain form of conduct is *permitted* by international law.

There is clearly something artificial about trying to analyse the psychology of collective entities such as states. Indeed, the modern tendency is not to look for direct evidence of a state's psychological convictions, but to infer *opinio iuris* indirectly from the actual behaviour of states. Thus, official statements are not required; *opinio iuris* may be gathered from acts or omissions.[70] For these purposes, it must be remembered that rules of international law govern the behaviour of states in their relations with other states; it is therefore necessary to examine not only what one state does or refrains from doing, but also how other states react. If conduct by some states provokes protests from other states that such conduct is illegal, the protests can deprive such conduct of any value as evidence of customary law.[71]

Permissive rules can be proved by showing that some states have acted in a particular way (or have claimed that they are entitled to act in that way) and that other states, whose interests were affected by such acts (or claims), have not protested that such acts (or claims) are illegal.

In the case of rules imposing duties, it is not enough to show that states have acted in the manner required by the alleged rule, and that other states have not protested that such acts are illegal. It also needs to be proved that states regard the action as obligatory. Recognition of the obligatory character of particular conduct can be proved by pointing to an express acknowledgment of the obligation by the states concerned, or by showing that failure to act in the manner required by the alleged rule has been condemned as illegal by other states whose interests were affected.

The difference between permissive rules and rules imposing duties can be clearly seen in the *Lotus* case.[72] The facts of the case were as follows: a

French merchant ship collided with a Turkish merchant ship on the high seas, and as a result (allegedly) of negligence on the part of Lieutenant Demons, an officer on the French ship, several people on the Turkish ship lost their lives. France had jurisdiction to try Lieutenant Demons for manslaughter, but the question was whether Turkey also had jurisdiction to try him. Turkey argued that there was a permissive rule empowering it to try him; France argued the exact opposite, namely, that there was a rule imposing a duty on Turkey not to try him. The Permanent Court of International Justice accepted the Turkish argument and rejected the French argument because, first, although there were only a few cases in which states in Turkey's position had instituted prosecutions, the other states concerned in those cases had not protested against the prosecutions; and secondly, although most states in Turkey's position had refrained from instituting prosecutions, there was no evidence that they had done so out of a sense of legal obligation.

Moreover, if states are clearly divided on whether a certain conduct (such as non-recourse to nuclear weapons over the past fifty years) constitutes the expression of an *opinio iuris* (in this case that the use of nuclear weapons is illegal), it is impossible to find that there is such *opinio iuris*.[73]

Opinio iuris is sometimes interpreted to mean that states must believe that something is already law before it can become law. However, that is probably not true; what matters is not what states believe, but what they say. If some states claim that something is law and other states do not challenge that claim, a new rule will come into being, even though all the states concerned may realize that it is a departure from pre-existing rules.

Customary law has a built-in mechanism of change. If states are agreed that a rule should be changed, a new rule of customary international law based on the new practice of states can emerge very quickly; thus the law on outer space developed very quickly after the first artificial satellite was launched.[74] If the number of states supporting a change, or the number of states resisting a change, is small, they will probably soon fall into line with the practice of the majority. The real difficulty comes when the states supporting the change and the states resisting the change are fairly evenly balanced. In this case change is difficult and slow, and disagreement and uncertainty about the law may persist for a long time until a new consensus emerges, as, for example, in the dispute about the width of the territorial sea.[75] Another example is the case of the *Legality of Nuclear Weapons* in which the ICJ found:

> The emergence, as *lex lata*, of a customary rule specifically prohibiting the use of nuclear weapons as such is hampered by the continuing tensions between the nascent *opinio juris* on the one hand, and the still strong adherence to the practice of deterrence on the other.[76]

'Instant' customary law

A special problem is the existence or non-existence of the category of '*diritto spontaneo*' or 'instant customary international law' which has been brought to the forefront by some authors, such as Roberto Ago[77] and Bin

73 See *Advisory Opinion on the Legality of the Threat or Use of Nuclear Weapons, op. cit.*, 826, para. 67. On this case see Chapter 20 below, 347–9.

74 See Chapter 13 below, 201–7.

75 See Chapter 12 below, 176–82.

76 *Advisory Opinion on the Legality of the Threat or Use of Nuclear Weapons, op. cit.*, 827, para. 73. However, the Court also noted in this case: 'In the long run, international law, and with it the stability of the international order which it is intended to govern, are bound to suffer from the continuing difference of views with regard to the legal status of weapons as deadly as nuclear weapons. It is consequently important to put an end to this state of affairs; the long-promised complete nuclear disarmament appears to be the most appropriate means of achieving that result.' *Ibid.*, 830, para. 98.

77 R. Ago, *Science juridique et droit international, RdC* (1956-II), 849–955, at 932 *et seq.*

78 B. Cheng, United Nations
Resolutions on Outer Space: 'Instant'
International Customary Law?, *Indian
JIL* (1965), 23 *et seq.*

79 *ICJ Rep.* 1969, at 4.

80 See Jennings (1984), *op. cit.,* 285.

81 For a discussion of the Italian
doctrine see F. Münch, *A Propos du
Droit Spontane, Studi in Onore di
Guiseppe Sperduti,* 1984, 149–62.

82 See P. Malanczuk, Space Law as a
Branch of International Law, *NYIL* 25
(1994), 143–80, 160–1.

83 *ICJ Rep.* 1969, 43.

84 *ICJ Rep.* 1986, 97 *et seq.*

85 Bernhardt (1992), *op. cit.,* 902.

Cheng.[78] The result is to deny the significance of state practice and the relevance of the time factor in the formation of customary international law and to rely solely on *opinio iuris*, as expressed in non-binding resolutions and declarations, as the constitutive element of custom.

It is true that the International Court of Justice has clarified in the *North Sea Continental Shelf* cases that customary law may emerge even within a relatively short passage of time.[79] It may also be noted that changes in the international law-making process have modified the concept of modern customary law in several respects, including the tendency that it is made with relative speed, written in textual form, and is more elaborate than traditional custom.[80] The possibility of 'instant' customary international law, or '*droit spontane*',[81] based upon *opinio iuris* only and without the requirement of any practice, however, has remained a matter of dispute.[82] In view of the nature of the decentralized international legal system and the elementary role of state practice as the objective element in the formation of customary law, enabling one to distinguish it from non-binding commitments, *opinio iuris* on its own, even if clearly established for some states as the subjective element, does not suffice to establish general custom in controversial areas. In addition, the very notion of 'custom' implies some time element and 'instant custom' is a contradiction in terms, although it appears that this is more a matter of appropriate terminology than of substance.

This view is confirmed by the jurisprudence of the ICJ. In the *North Sea Continental Shelf* cases the Court insisted that 'an indispensable requirement would be that within the period in question, short though it might be, State practice, including that of States whose interests are specially affected, should have been both extensive and uniform'.[83] In other words, the reduction of the time-element requirement is carefully balanced with a stronger emphasis on the scope and nature of state practice. An even clearer implicit rejection of the doctrine of 'instant custom' can be found in the following words of the Court in the *Nicaragua* case:

> The mere fact that States declare their recognition of certain rules is not sufficient for the Court to consider these as being part of customary international law . . . Bound as it is by Article 38 of its Statute . . . the Court must satisfy itself that the existence of the rule in the *opinio iuris* of States is confirmed by practice.[84]

Bernhardt also denies that under the traditional concepts of international law 'instant' custom is possible, but he can imagine 'exceptional cases and situations in which such instant law is useful or even necessary: If, for instance, the community of States unequivocally and without any dissent considers certain acts, which have not been known before, to be illegal, the *opinio juris* might suffice even if no practice could evolve.'[85] There may indeed be a need for this, but then it is not custom but some other (new) source of international law.

Universality and the consensual theory of international law

It has already been suggested that the practice followed by a small number of states is sufficient to create a customary rule, if there is no practice which conflicts with that rule.[86] But what if some states oppose the alleged rule? Can the opposition of a single state prevent the creation of a customary rule? If so, there would be very few rules, because state practice differs from state to state on many topics. On the other hand, to allow the majority to create a rule against the wishes of the minority would lead to insuperable difficulties. How large must the majority be? In counting the majority, must equal weight be given to the practice of Guatemala and that of the United States? If, on the other hand, some states are to be regarded as more important than others, on what criteria is importance to be based? Population? Area? Wealth? Military power? In a different context, the same questions have arisen with regard to the reform of the composition of the UN Security Council currently under discussion.[87]

In the *Lotus* case, the Permanent Court of International Justice said: 'The rules of law binding upon states . . . emanate from their own free will as expressed in conventions or by usages generally accepted as expressing principles of law.'[88] This consensual theory, as it is called, has been criticized in the West, but it has been accepted with enthusiasm by Soviet lawyers. Soviet doctrine used to teach that international law is the result of an agreement between states, and that the only difference between treaties and custom is one of form, treaties representing an express agreement and custom representing an implied agreement.[89] The merit of this approach is that it explains divergences in state practice; just as different treaties can be in force between different groups of states, so different rules of customary law can apply between different groups of states. The International Court of Justice came some way towards the Soviet approach in the *Asylum* case, where it recognized the existence of regional customs applying among groups of states in Latin America.[90]

The consensual theory explains divergences in state practice, but it is rather unconvincing when it is applied to new states. The orthodox rule is that new states are automatically bound by generally accepted international law. The problem of the relation of new states to existing international law is primarily a matter belonging to the area of state succession, and will be taken up later.[91] As far as customary law is concerned, the prevailing view is, with different reasoning, that new states cannot in principle escape existing customary obligations. One cannot select rights granted by a legal system '*à la carte*' and at the same time reject the duties one dislikes. However, the reservations of the decolonized new states towards the international legal order created by the old colonial powers have had a considerable impact in particular areas, such as international economic law[92] and the law of the sea,[93] which, at a minimum, has led to legal uncertainty. It has become more and more difficult to find the required general practice and *opinio iuris* for customary international law to retain its universal significance.[94]

The element of consent[95] can also become fictitious when one is dealing with the emergence of new rules of customary law among existing states. The International Court of Justice has emphasized that a claimant state which seeks to rely on a customary rule must prove that the rule has become binding on the defendant state.[96] The obvious way of doing this is

86 See text above, 41–3.
87 See Chapter 21 below, 376–7.
88 PCIJ, series A, no. 10, 18. See text above, 44–5.
89 On Soviet doctrine in general see Chapter 2 above, 23, 33.
90 *ICJ Rep.* 1950, 266, 277, 293–4, 316. See text above, 41.
91 See Chapter 11 below, 161–72.
92 See Chapter 15 below, 233–40 and Chapter 2 above, 28–30.
93 See Chapter 12 below, 173–97.
94 On regional customary international law see Chapters 1, 2–3 and 2, 30–2 above.
95 B. Simma, Consent: Strains in the Treaty System, in Macdonald/Johnston (eds), *op. cit.*, 485 *et seq.*; D.W. Greig, Reflections on the Role of Consent, *AYIL* 12 (1992), 125–76; A. Pellet, The Normative Dilemma: Will and Consent in International Law-Making, *ibid.*, 22–53.
96 *Asylum* case, *op. cit.*, 276–7; *Rights of Nationals of the United States in Morocco* case, *ICJ Rep.* 1952, 176, at 200.

97 *Fisheries* case, *op. cit.*, at 131.

98 See text below, 57–8.

99 See Bernhardt (1992), *op. cit.*, 904; O. Elias, Some Remarks on the Persistent Objector Rule in Customary International Law, *Denning LJ* (1991), 37–51; C. Tomuschat, Obligations Arising for States Without or Against Their Will, *RdC* 241 (1993-IV), 195–374.

100 J.I. Charney, Universal International Law, *AJIL* 87 (1993), 529–51, at 538 *et seq.*; see also ILA Committee on the Formation of Customary (General) International Law, *ILA Rep.* 1992, 366 *et seq.*

101 For the historical background see, Chapter 2 above, 12–14.

102 See B. Cheng, *General Principles of Law as Applied by International Courts and Tribunals*, 1987; G. Hanessian, 'General Principles of Law' in the Iran–US Claims Tribunal, *Colum. JIL* 27 (1989), 309; M.C. Bassiouni, A Functional Approach to 'General Principles of International Law', *Mich. JIL* 11 (1990), 768–818; J.A. Westberg/B.P. Marchais, General Principles Governing Foreign Investment as Articulated in Recent International Tribunal Awards and Writings of Publicists, *ICSID Rev.* 7 (1992), 453–96; V.-D. Degan, General Principles of Law (A Source of General International Law), *FYIL* 3 (1992), 1–102; L. Ferrari-Bravo, Considérations sur la méthode de recherche des principes généraux du droit international de l'environnement, *Hague YIL* 7 (1994), 3–10; H. Mosler, General Principles of Law, *EPIL* II (1995), 511–27.

to show that the defendant state has recognized the rule in its own state practice (although recognition for this purpose may amount to no more than failure to protest when other states have applied the rule in cases affecting the defendant's interests). But it may not be possible to find any evidence of the defendant's attitude towards the rule, and so there is a second – and more frequently used – way of proving that the rule is binding on the defendant: by showing that the rule is accepted by other states. In these circumstances the rule in question is binding on the defendant state, unless the defendant state can show that it has expressly and consistently rejected the rule since the earliest days of the rule's existence; dissent expressed after the rule has become well established is too late to prevent the rule binding the dissenting state. Thus, in the *Fisheries* case, the International Court of Justice held that a particular rule was not generally recognized, but added: 'In any event, the . . . rule would appear to be inapplicable as against Norway, inasmuch as she has always opposed any attempt to apply it to the Norwegian coast.'[97]

The problem of the 'persistent objector', however, has recently attracted more attention in the literature. Can a disagreeing state ultimately and indefinitely remain outside of new law accepted by the large majority of states? Do emerging rules of *ius cogens*[98] require criteria different to norms of lesser significance? Such questions are far from settled at this point in time.[99] The view of Charney, who dispenses with the 'persistent objector' altogether, however, is an exceptional one.[100]

General principles of law

The third source of international law listed in the Statute of the international Court of Justice is 'the general principles of law recognized by civilized nations'. (All nations are now considered as 'civilized';[101] the new term is 'peace-loving', as stated in Article 4 of the UN Charter as a requirement for admission to the organization.) This phrase was inserted in the Statute of the Permanent Court of International Justice, the forerunner of the International Court of Justice, in order to provide a solution in cases where treaties and custom provided no guidance; otherwise, it was feared, the Court might be unable to decide some cases because of gaps in treaty law and customary law. However, there is little agreement about the meaning of the phrase. Some say it means general principles of international law; others say it means general principles of national law. Actually, there is no reason why it should not mean both; the greater the number of meanings which the phrase possesses, the greater the chance of finding something to fill gaps in treaty law and customary law – which was the reason for listing general principles of law in the Statute of the Court in the first place. Indeed, international tribunals had applied general principles of law in both these senses for many years before the PCIJ was set up in 1920.[102]

According to the first definition (general principles of international law), general principles of law are not so much a source of law as a method of using existing sources – extending existing rules by analogy, inferring the existence of broad principles from more specific rules by means of inductive reasoning, and so on. According to the second definition of general principles of law (general principles of national law), gaps in international law may be filled by borrowing principles which are common to all or most national systems of law; specific rules of law usually vary from country to country, but the basic principles are often similar.[103]

In reality, the matter is more complicated. Not all general principles applied in international practice stem from domestic legal systems and have been transplanted to the international level by recognition.[104] Some are based on 'natural justice' common to all legal systems (such as the principles of good faith,[105] estoppel[106] and proportionality[107]), others simply apply logic familiar to lawyers (such as the rules *lex specialis derogat legi generali*, *lex posterior derogat legi priori*[108]), and another category is related to 'the specific nature of the international community', as expressed in principles of *ius cogens*.[109] Therefore, a real transplantation of domestic law principles to the international level is limited to a number of procedural rules, such as the right to a fair hearing, in *dubio pro reo*, denial of justice,[110] or the exhaustion of local remedies,[111] and some substantive principles, such as prescription[112] and liability for fault.[113] The mechanism by which such transformation takes place in practice goes through the mind of the international judge or arbitrator who has to decide a particular case. This is known as the 'creative role' of the judge, which is not at all peculiar to the international legal system.

On the other hand, the difficulty of proving that a principle is common to most or all legal systems is not as great as might be imagined. Legal systems are grouped in families; the law in most English-speaking countries is very similar, simply because the settlers took with them the law they knew, just as the law in most Latin American countries is very similar. Once one has proved that a principle exists in English law, one is fairly safe in assuming that it also exists in New Zealand and Australia. The problem is, of course, what do we do about the other systems in the world. In fact, what sometimes happens in practice is that an international judge or arbitrator makes use of principles drawn from the legal system in his own country, without examining whether they are also accepted by other countries. The practice is obviously undesirable, but it is too common to be regarded as illegal. In the election of the judges of the International Court of Justice, the electors are required to bear in mind that 'in the body as a whole the representation of the main forms of civilization and of the principal legal systems of the world should be assured'.[114]

General principles of law have proved most useful in 'new' areas of international law. When the modern system of international law was beginning to develop in the sixteenth and seventeenth centuries, writers like Grotius drew heavily on Roman law,[115] and a Roman ancestry can still be detected in many of the rules which have now been transformed into customary law (for example, concerning the acquisition of title to territory).[116] In the nineteenth century international arbitration, which had previously been rare, became more common, and the need for rules of judicial procedure was met by borrowing principles from national law (for example, the principle that a tribunal is competent to decide whether or not it has jurisdiction in cases of doubt, and the principle that claims

103 On comparative legal studies see Chapter 1 above, 6. On the relationship between international law and national law see Chapter 4 below, 63–74.

104 See H. Mosler, *The International Society as a Legal Community*, rev. edn 1980, 136 *et seq.*

105 A. D'Amato, Good Faith, *EPIL* II (1995), 599–601; J.F. O'Connor, *Good Faith in International Law*, 1991. In the *Nuclear Tests* case (*Australia v. France*), judgment of 20 December 1974 (*ICJ Rep.* 1974, 268, para. 46), the Court held: 'one of the basic principles governing the creation and performance of legal obligations, whatever their source, is the principle of good faith. Trust and confidence are inherent in international cooperation, in particular in an age when this cooperation in many fields is becoming increasingly essential.' See also Art. 26 of the 1969 Vienna Convention on the Law of Treaties, discussed in Chapter 9 below, 141.

106 See Chapter 10 below, 154–5.

107 See Chapter 1 above, 4 and Chapters 17, 271–2 and 19, 316–17 below.

108 See text below, 56.

109 K.-J. Partsch, International Law and Municipal Law, *EPIL* II (1995), 1188. On *ius cogens* see text below, 57–8.

110 S. Verosta, Denial of Justice, *EPIL* I (1992), 1007–10.

111 See Chapter 17 below, 267–8.

112 See Chapter 10 below, 150–1.

113 See Chapter 17 below, 258.

114 Art. 9, Statute of the ICJ, text in Brownlie *BDIL*, 438. See Chapter 18 below, 282.

115 D.J. Ibbetson, *The Roman Law Tradition*, 1994. On Grotius see Chapter 2 above, 15–16.

116 See Chapter 10 below, 147–58.

117 See Chapters 2 above, 20 and 17, 269 and 18, 293–8 below.

118 See Chapters 6, 103 and 21, 381 below.

119 See text above, 38–9.

120 See Chapter 18 below, 289.

121 v. Hecke, *op. cit.*, 818.

122 *ICJ Rep.* 1950, 148. See also M. Shahabuddeen, Municipal Law Reasoning in International Law, in Lowe/Fitzmaurice (eds), *op. cit.*, 90–103. On the *South-West Africa* case see Chapters 18, 284 and 19, 328–9 below.

123 See J. Stone, *Non Liquet* and the Function of Law in the International Community, *BYIL* 1959, 145; Fastenrath (1991), *op. cit.*; and compare the Declaration of Judge Vereshchetin in the ICJ's *Advisory Opinion on the Legality of the Threat or Use of Nuclear Weapons, op. cit.*, 833 with the Dissenting Opinions of Judge Schwebel, *ibid.*, 836, at 840, Judge Shahabuddeen, *ibid.*, 861, at 866, and Judge Koroma, *ibid.*, 925, at 930.

124 See the Separate Opinion of Judge Fleischhauer, *ibid.*, 835.

125 See Dissenting Opinion of Judge Higgins, *ibid.*, 934.

126 R. Jennings/A. Watts (eds), *Oppenheim's International Law*, Vol. I, part 1, 9th edn 1992, 13.

brought before a tribunal after an unreasonable delay must be dismissed as inadmissible).[117]

In the present century international law, or something closely resembling international law, has come to regulate certain contracts made by individuals or companies with states or international organizations – for example, contracts of employment in international organizations,[118] and oil concessions.[119] Treaties and customary law contain few rules applicable to such topics, and the gap has been filled by recourse to general principles of commercial and administrative law, borrowed from national legal systems. For instance, international administrative tribunals, which try disputes between international organizations and their staff, have consistently applied the principle, borrowed from national law, that an official must be informed of criticisms made against him and must be given an opportunity to reply to those criticisms before the international organization employing him takes a decision to his detriment on the basis of those criticisms.[120] In the case of 'internationalized contracts' between a state and foreign companies, the purpose of referring to general principles in connection with an arbitration clause is primarily (from the viewpoint of the investing company) to prefer to trust the arbitrator's (s') discretion to discover relevant rules of law creatively, rather than being at the mercy of the contracting state's national legislation.[121]

However, it must be remembered that the environment in which international law operates is very different from the one in which national law operates, and principles of national law can be used to fill gaps in international law only if they are suited to the international environment. As noted by Judge McNair in the *South-West Africa* case:

> The way in which international law borrows from this source is not by means of importing private law institutions 'lock, stock and barrel', ready-made and fully equipped with a set of rules. It would be difficult to reconcile such a process with the application of 'the general principles of law'.[122]

Finally, it should be pointed out that the issue of whether an international court is obliged to fill in gaps in substantive international law in order to provide for the 'completeness' of the legal system, to render a concrete decision and thus to avoid declaring *non liquet* ('the matter is unclear'), has remained controversial.[123] It is interesting to note that the ICJ in its rather inconclusive Advisory Opinion in the *Legality of Nuclear Weapons* case did not make any use of the general principles of law recognized in all legal systems.[124] In fact, what the Court has done in this decision is that it pronounced a *non liquet* on the central issue on the grounds of uncertainty in the current state of international law, and of the facts.[125] It is submitted that the concept of *non liquet* is an unhealthy one for the judicial function and courts misunderstand their duties if they plead *non liquet* in any given case. In international law one does not always discover a

> clear and specific rule readily applicable to every international situation, but . . . every international situation is capable of being determined as a *matter of law*.[126]

Judicial decisions

Article 38(1)(d) of the Statute of the International Court of Justice directs the Court to apply 'judicial decisions ... as subsidiary means for the determination of rules of law'. This direction is made 'subject to the provisions of Article 59', which state that 'the decision of the Court has no binding force except between the parties and in respect of that particular case'. In other words, there is no formal *stare decisis* doctrine, as known in common law systems; in international law international courts are not obliged to follow previous decisions, although they almost always take previous decisions into account.[127]

We have already seen that judicial and arbitral decisions can be evidence of customary law.[128] But it is probably true to say that judges can also create new law. The International Court of Justice is particularly important in this respect. Many of its decisions introduced innovations into international law which have subsequently won general acceptance – for instance, the *Reparation for Injuries* case,[129] the *Genocide* case[130] and the *Fisheries* case.[131] There is a very strong probability that the International Court (and other tribunals) will follow such decisions in later cases, since judicial consistency is the most obvious means of avoiding accusations of bias. Thus, it is generally questionable whether at least decisions of the International Court of Justice can in fact still be regarded as only 'subsidiary' means of determining the law.[132]

One aspect which will require more attention in the future arises from the recent proliferation of international tribunals and courts, such as various regional courts, courts on human rights,[133] international criminal courts[134] and the Tribunal for the Law of the Sea.[135] This proliferation is likely to lead to conflicting decisions on international law and there is no ultimate legal authority in the sense of a supreme court to harmonize such conflicts. The ICJ is not in such a position because it lacks any formal relations with other international courts and tribunals.[136]

Judgments of national courts are also covered by Article 38(1)(d); many of the rules of international law on topics such as diplomatic immunity[137] have been developed by judgments of national courts. But judgments of national courts need to be used with caution; the judges may look as if they are applying international law (and may actually believe that they are doing so), when in fact all that they are applying is some peculiar rule of their own national law.[138]

Learned writers

Article 38(1)(d) also directs the Court to apply 'the teachings of the most highly qualified publicists of the various nations, as subsidiary means for the determination of rules of law'. The word 'publicists' means 'learned writers'. Like judicial decisions, learned writings can be evidence of customary law, but they can also play a subsidiary role in developing new rules of law.

In the past, writers like Grotius exercised influence of a sort which no writer could hope to exercise nowadays. But writers have not entirely lost

127 See V. Röben, Le Précédent dans la jurisprudence de la Cour internationale, *GYIL* 32 (1989), 382–407; M. Shahabuddeen, *Precedent in the World Court*, 1996.

128 See text above, 39.

129 See Chapter 6 below, 93.

130 See Chapter 9 below, 136.

131 See text above, 42 and Chapter 12 below, 181.

132 See Jennings (1984), *op. cit.*, 287; H. Lauterpacht, *The Development of International Law by the International Court*, 1982.

133 See Chapter 14 below, 217–19.

134 See Chapter 20 below, 253–61.

135 See Chapter 18 below, 298–300.

136 See R.Y. Jennings, The International Court of Justice after Fifty Years, *AJIL* 89 (1995), 493–505, at 504.

137 See Chapter 8 below, 123–9.

138 See further K. Doehring, The Participation of International and National Courts in the Law-Creating Process, *SAYIL* 17 (1991/2), 1–11; R.Y. Jennings, The Judiciary, International and National, and the Development of International Law, *ICLQ* 45 (1996), 1–12.

139 See Chapter 12 below, 182–3.

140 A. Oraison, Réflexions sur 'la doctrine des publicistes les plus qualifiés des différentes nations', *RBDI* 24 (1991), 507–80.

141 See C. Gray/B. Kingsbury, Developments in Dispute Settlement: Inter-State Arbitration Since 1945, *BYIL* 63 (1992), 97, 129.

142 S. Rosenne, *The Law and Practice of the International Court of Justice*, 2nd edn 1985, 614–6.

143 See Chapter 18 below, 292, 302.

144 For a discussion see K. Skubiszewski, Resolutions of the U.N. General Assembly and Evidence of Custom, in *Études en l'honneur de R. Ago*, 1987, Vol. I, 503 et seq; B. Sloan, General Assembly Resolutions Revisited (Forty Years After), *BYIL* 58 (1987), 39 *et seq*.; C. Economidès, Les Actes institutionnels internationaux et les sources du droit international, *AFDI* (1988), 142 *et seq*.; J.A. Frowein, The Internal and External Effects of Resolutions by International Organizations, *ZaöRV* 49 (1989), 778–90; B. Sloan, *United Nations General Assembly Resolutions in Our Changing World*, 1991; J.A. Barberis, Les Résolutions des organisations internationales en tant que source du droit de gens, in *FS Bernhardt*, 21–39; H.G. Schermers, International Organizations, Resolutions, *EPIL* II (1995), 1333–36.

145 See Chapter 9 below, 136–7.

their influence. They still continue to provide the sort of conceptual framework which is necessary for any legal discussion; for instance, states had been claiming limited rights in areas adjacent to their territorial sea long before Gidel started writing about such claims, but it was Gidel who produced the concept of the contiguous zone as a framework for discussing the validity of these claims.[139] Moreover, one finds that states in diplomatic controversies still quote profusely from writers (although the quotations are not always acknowledged), because writers provide a comprehensive, succinct and (with luck) impartial summary of state practice. (A summary which is deliberately made as brief as possible, like the Harvard draft conventions, is particularly useful for purposes of quotation.) In a nutshell, writers quote states and states quote writers, at least when it suits their interests.

Generally speaking, in a multicultural world the problem of identifying those 'teachings' of writers which are the most authoritative is no longer likely to lead to easy universal acceptance of certain propositions. This has become difficult also due to the large quantity of publications that are nowadays produced by writers on international law.[140] While international arbitral tribunals frequently cite textbooks and authors,[141] the International Court of Justice refrains from doing so in its decisions,[142] as distinct from the dissenting or concurring opinions of individual judges.[143]

Other possible sources of international law

Having completed our examination of the list of sources in the Statute of the International Court of Justice, we must now examine whether there are any other sources which have been omitted from that list.

Acts of international organizations

The growth of international organizations since the First World War has been accompanied by suggestions that the acts of international organizations should be recognized as a source of international law.[144] But most of the organs of international organizations are composed of representatives of member states, and very often the acts of such organs are merely the acts of the states represented in those organs. For instance, a resolution of the United Nations General Assembly can be evidence of customary law because it reflects the views of the states voting for it; it would probably have exactly the same value if it had been passed at a conference outside the framework of the United Nations, and, if many states vote against it, its value as evidence of customary law is correspondingly reduced.

However, international organizations usually have at least one organ which is not composed of representatives of member states, and the practice of such organs is capable of constituting a source of law. For instance, the United Nations Secretariat often acts as a depositary of treaties and its practice as depositary has already affected the law of treaties on such topics as reservations.[145]

Sometimes an international organization is authorized to take decisions (often by majority vote) which are binding on member states. Apart from 'internal' questions relating to the budget, the admission and expulsion of members, and so on, the only clear example in the United Nations Charter is in Chapter VII, which empowers the Security Council to give orders to states as part of its action to deal with threats to the peace, breaches of the peace and acts of aggression.[146] In some other organizations powers to take binding decisions can be exercised more frequently; this is particularly true of the European Community.[147] But it is questionable whether such decisions should be treated as a separate source of law, because the power to take such decisions is conferred by the constituent *treaty* of the organization concerned. The same applies to the power of the International Monetary Fund to take binding decisions on the maintenance or alteration of exchange rates or depreciation of currency,[148] or the authority of the International Civil Aviation Authority to adopt binding standards for navigation or qualifications of flight personnel.[149]

Most resolutions have nothing to do with international law; an obvious example would be a resolution recommending research into the causes of cancer. Even when resolutions do touch upon international law, they may simply be recommending changes, and the text of such a resolution clearly cannot be interpreted as representing the existing law; a resolution declaring that X *ought* to be the law is obviously not evidence that X *is* the law. If a resolution declares that X is the law, it can be used as evidence of customary law. But the value of such a resolution varies in proportion to the number of states voting for it; if many states vote against it, its value as evidence of customary law is correspondingly reduced.

It has been said that, in the *Nicaragua* case,[150] the International Court of Justice extensively referred to resolutions of international organizations as a 'source of law',[151] but under the particular circumstances of the case concerning the issue of the jurisdiction of the Court, it is doubtful whether it used these resolutions as sources in the technical sense. A resolution passed at a meeting of an international organization is never conclusive evidence of customary law. It has to be examined in conjunction with all the other available evidence of customary law, and it may thus be possible to prove that the resolution is not a correct statement of customary law.[152] In the end, if there is no corresponding practice, the mere statement on what the law is supposed to be is not sufficient evidence, but nothing more than an attempt on the part of states to clarify their respective positions.[153]

Nevertheless, as stated by the International Court of Justice in its 1996 *Advisory Opinion on the Legality of the Threat or Use of Nuclear Weapons* with reference to the series of General Assembly resolutions since 1961[154] that affirm the illegality of nuclear weapons:

> General Assembly resolutions, even if they are not binding, may sometimes have normative value. They can, in certain circumstances, provide evidence important for establishing the existence of a rule or the emergence of an *opinio juris*. To establish whether this is true of a given General Assembly resolution, it is necessary to look at its content and the conditions of its adoption; it is also necessary to see whether an *opinio juris* exists as to its normative character. Or a series of resolutions may show the gradual evolution of the *opinio juris* required for the establishment of a new rule.[155]

146 See Chapter 22 below, 387–90.
147 See Chapter 6 below, 95–6.
148 See Chapter 15 below, 225–7.
149 See Chapter 13 below, 200.
150 See text above, 39, 40, 41.
151 Noted by Bernhardt (1992), *op. cit.*, 904.
152 For further discussion of resolutions of international organizations as evidence of customary law, see Akehurst (1974–5), Custom, *op. cit.*, 5–7.
153 See T. Schweisfurth, The Influence of the Third United Nations Conference on the Law of the Sea on International Customary Law, *ZaöRV* 43 (1983), 566–84, 577.
154 UNGA Res. 1653 (XVI) of 24 November 1961.
155 *Legality of Nuclear Weapons Case*, *op. cit.*, at 826, para. 70.

156 *Ibid.*, para. 71. See also the Dissenting Opinion of Judge Schwebel, which is much clearer, *ibid.*, 839.
157 R. Bierzanek, Some Remarks on 'Soft' International Law, *PYIL* 17 (1988), 21–40; C.M. Chinkin, The Challenge of Soft Law: Development and Change in International Law, *ICLQ* 38 (1989), 850–66; P.-M. Dupuy, Soft Law and the International Law of the Environment, *Mich. ILJ* 12 (1991), 420–35; H.E. Chodosh, Neither Treaty Nor Custom: The Emergence of Declarative International Law, *Texas ILJ* 26 (1991), 87–124; W. Heusel, *'Weiches' Völkerrecht: Eine vergleichende Untersuchung typischer Erscheinungsformen*, 1991; F. Francioni, International 'Soft Law': A Contemporary Assessment, in Lowe/ Fitzmaurice (eds), *op. cit.*, 167–78.
158 See Chapter 6 below, 102–3.
159 See I. Seidl-Hohenveldern, International Economic 'Soft Law', *RdC* 163 (1979), 165 *et seq.*; W.E. Burhenne (ed.), *International Environmental Soft Law. Collection of Relevant Instruments*, 1993; M.A. Fitzmaurice, International Environmental Law as a Special Field, *NYIL* 25 (1994), 181–226, at 199–201. See Chapters 15, 222–3 and 16, 241–7 below.
160 For the Rio documents see *ILM* 31 (1992), 818 *et seq.* See P. Malanczuk, Sustainable Development: Some Critical Thoughts in the Light of the Rio Conference, in K. Ginther/E. Denters/ P.J.I.M.de Waart (eds), *Sustainable Development and Good Governance*, 1995, 23–52. See also Chapter 16 below, 247–8.
161 See T. Schweisfurth, Zur Frage der Rechtsnatur, Verbindlichkeit und völkerrechtlicher Relevanz der KSZE Schlußakte, *ZaöRV* 36 (1976), 681 *et seq.*; For a recent analysis, see I. Seidl-Hohenveldern, Internationale Organisationen aufgrund von soft law, in *FS Bernhardt*, 229–39; T. Schweisfurth, Die juristische Mutation der KSZE – Eine internationale Organisation in statu nascendi, *ibid.*, 213–28; M. Sapiro, Changing the CSCE into the OSCE: Legal Aspects of a Political Transformation, *AJIL* 89 (1995), 631–7. See Chapter 6 below, 94.
162 See also M. Bothe, Legal and Non-Legal Norms – A Meaningful Distinction in International Relations?, *NYIL* 11 (1980), 65–95.
163 See Chapter 2 above, 33.
164 See text above, 35.

However, in view of the substantial numbers of negative votes and abstentions with which several of the General Assembly resolutions on the illegality of nuclear weapons have been adopted, the Court held that they still fall short of establishing the existence of an *opinio juris* on the illegality of the use of such weapons.[156]

'Soft' law

The controversy on the status of certain declarations and resolutions of international organizations is connected with the phenomenon of 'soft law'.[157] Without being able to enter into the general discussion here, it may be noted that the term 'soft law', as distinct from 'hard law', is not very helpful from a legal perspective. It is known that 'soft law', in the sense of guidelines of conduct (such as those formulated by the United Nations concerning the operations of transnational companies[158]) which are neither strictly binding norms of law, nor completely irrelevant political maxims, and operate in a grey zone between law and politics, is considered a special characteristic of international economic law and of international environmental law.[159] Such provisions can be found, for example, in treaties not yet in force or in resolutions of international conferences or organizations, which lack legally binding quality.

The emergence of 'soft law' also has to do with the fact that states in agreement frequently do not (yet) wish to bind themselves legally, but nevertheless wish to adopt and test certain rules and principles before they become law. This often facilitates consensus which is more difficult to achieve on 'hard law' instruments. A peculiar example of this practice is the Forest Declaration adopted at the 1992 Rio Conference on Environment and Development, which carries the illuminating title 'A Non-legally binding Authoritative Statement of Principles for a Global Consensus on the Management, Conservation and Sustainable Development of all Types of Forests'.[160] States may even decide to create international organizations with their own organs and structures to fulfil international tasks without accepting any legally binding obligations, as was done in the case of the Conference on Security and Cooperation in Europe on the basis of the 1975 Helsinki Final Act.[161]

Such guidelines, although explicitly drafted as non-legal ones, may nevertheless in actual practice acquire considerable strength in structuring international conduct.[162] 'Soft law' may also be relevant from a sociological perspective of international law with regard to the process of the formation of customary law or treaty law and the related issue of 'legitimacy' in the international legal system.[163] But the result of this law-making process at any given moment of legal decision is either binding law or not. In essence, under any meaningful concept of law, it remains essential to maintain the distinction between the law *de lege lata* and the law *de lege ferenda*,[164] between the codification of existing law and the progressive development of law, between legal norms and non-legal norms as regards their binding effect, and ultimately between the legal system and the political system. Otherwise, it would become rather difficult to distinguish ideologically or politically motivated claims from the accepted rules and principles of international law. However, certain principles and rules which are emerging as new norms in the process of law-making, without yet having become accepted as legally binding, may nevertheless have limited 'anticipatory' effect in judicial or arbitral decision-making as supporting arguments in interpreting the law as it stands.

Equity

'Equity', in the present context, is used not in the technical sense which the word possesses in Anglo-American legal systems in the distinction between law and equity as separate bodies of law, but as a synonym for 'justice'. Moreover, those who look to equity as a source of international law often appeal to natural law[165] in order to strengthen their arguments and to escape accusations of subjectivism. Thus the three terms – 'equity', 'justice' and 'natural law' – tend to merge into one another.

During the sixteenth and seventeenth centuries natural law was a major source of international law. In the nineteenth and twentieth centuries arbitrators have often been authorized to apply justice and equity as well as international law (such authorizations were more common before 1920 than they are today); even in the absence of such authorization, judges and arbitrators sometimes invoke equitable considerations.[166]

In the *River Meuse* case (*Netherlands v. Belgium*) (1937),[167] for example, the Netherlands claimed that Belgium had violated a treaty by building canals that changed the flow of water in the River Meuse. One of the issues was whether the Netherlands had lost the right to bring the claim because of similar earlier conduct by itself. In this connection the Individual Opinion of Judge Hudson recognized the principle of equity as part of international law. He noticed that there was no express authority in the Statute of the PCIJ to apply equity as distinguished from law. But he pointed to Article 38 of the Statute which allowed the application of general principles and argued that principles of equity are common to all national legal systems.

Thus, a judge or arbitrator can always use equity to interpret or fill gaps in the law, even when he has not been expressly authorized to do so. But he may not give a decision *ex aequo et bono* (a decision in which equity overrides all other rules) unless he has been expressly authorized to do so. Article 38(2) of the Statute of the International Court of Justice provides that the list of sources in Article 38(1) 'shall not prejudice the power of the Court to decide a case *ex aequo et bono*, if the parties agree thereto'. Article 38(2) has never been applied, but other tribunals have occasionally been authorized to decide *ex aequo et bono*; for instance, two Latin American boundary disputes were decided in this way by arbitrators in the 1930s.[168]

Whatever the position may have been in the past, it is doubtful whether equity forms a source of international law today. It cannot be assumed that a judge is using equity as a source of law every time he describes a rule as equitable or just. Counsel and judges in national courts frequently appeal to considerations of equity and justice when the authorities are divided on a point of law, but that does not lead to equity being regarded as a source of national law; nor should appeals by international lawyers to considerations of equity be interpreted as meaning that equity is a source of international law.

165 See Chapter 2 above, 15–17, 32.
166 See M. Akehurst, Equity and General Principles of Law, *ICLQ* 25 (1976), 801 *et seq.*; V. Lowe, The Role of Equity in International Law, *AYIL* 12 (1988/9), 125–76; C.M. Fombad, Equity in Current International Practice, *REDI* 45 (1989), 1–27; C.R. Rossi, *Equity as a Source of International Law?: A Legal Realist Approach to the Process of International Decision-Making*, 1993; M. Lachs, Equity in Arbitration and in Judicial Settlement of Disputes, *LJIL* 6 (1993), 323–9; T.M. Franck/D.M. Sughrue, The International Role of Equity-as-Fairness, *Geo. LJ* 81 (1993), 563–95; P. Weil, L'Équité dans la jurisprudence de la Cour Internationale de Justice, in Lowe/Fitzmaurice (eds), *op. cit.*, 121–44; Equity in International Law, *EPIL* II (1995), 109–13; T.M. Franck, *Fairness in International Law*, 1995, Chapter 3: Equity as Fairness, 47 *et seq.*
167 PCIJ, series A/B, no. 70, 76–7.
168 *RIAA* II, 1307 and III, 1817.

169 See Janis, *op. cit.*
170 See L.D.M. Nelson, The Roles of Equity in the Delimitation of Maritime Boundaries, *AJIL* 84 (1990), 837–58; M. Miyoshi, *Considerations of Equity in the Settlement of Territorial Boundary Disputes*, 1993; B. Kwiatkowska, Equitable Maritime Boundary Delimitation, in Lowe/Fitzmaurice (eds), *op. cit.*, 264–92. See Chapter 12 below, 135–7.
171 See Chapter 15 below, 233–40.
172 See Akehurst (1976), *op. cit.*, C. Tomuschat, Ethos, Ethics and Morality in International Relations, *EPIL* II (1995), 120–7.
173 M. Akehurst, The Hierarchy of the Sources of International Law, *BYIL* 47 (1974–5), 273 *et seq.*; W. Karl, Treaties, Conflicts between, *EPIL* 7 (1984), 467–73; W. Czapliński/G. Danilenko, Conflicts of Norms in International Law, *NYIL* 21 (1990), 3–42.
174 See Harris *CMIL*, 25.
175 For a good discussion see Schachter, *op. cit.*, 70–6, 335–42; Villiger, *op. cit.*
176 See text below, 57–8.
177 See Chapter 9 below, 141–2.
178 See N. Kontou, *The Termination and Revision of Treaties in the Light of New Customary International Law*, 1994.

In recent times the meaning of equity in international law has been discussed in two rather different contexts.[169] The first context is the application of equitable principles by the ICJ in the delimitation of maritime boundaries between states.[170] The other area is the controversial claim of developing countries for a new international economic order which should be based on equitable principles to achieve a fairer distribution of wealth between rich and poor states.[171] One of the problems about equity is that it can often be defined only by reference to a particular ethical system. Consequently, although references to equity are meaningful in a national society which can be presumed to hold common ethical values, the position is entirely different in the international arena, where the most mutually antagonistic philosophies meet in head-on conflict.[172]

The hierarchy of the sources

What happens if a rule derived from one source of international law conflicts with a rule derived from another source?[173] Which prevails over the other? Is there an order of application of the sources listed in Article 38 of the Statute of the ICJ? In the drafting history of this provision the proposal was made that the sources listed should be considered by the Court 'in the undermentioned order' (a–d). This proposal was not accepted and the view was expressed that the Court may, for example, draw on general principles before applying conventions and customs.[174]

The relationship between treaties and custom is particularly difficult.[175] Clearly a treaty, when it first comes into force, overrides customary law as between the parties to the treaty; one of the main reasons why states make treaties is because they regard the relevant rules of customary law as inadequate. Thus, two or more states can derogate from customary law by concluding a treaty with different obligations, the only limit to their freedom of law-making being rules of *ius cogens*, which will be discussed below.[176]

But treaties can come to an end through desuetude – a term used to describe the situation in which the treaty is consistently ignored by one or more parties, with the acquiescence of the other party or parties.[177] Desuetude often takes the form of the emergence of a new rule of customary law, conflicting with the treaty.[178]

Thus, treaties and custom are of equal authority; the later in time prevails. This conforms to the general maxim of *lex posterior derogat priori* (a later law repeals an earlier law). However, in deciding possible conflicts between treaties and custom, two other principles must be observed, namely *lex posterior generalis non derogat priori speciali* (a later law, general in nature, does not repeal an earlier law which is more special in nature) and *lex specialis derogat legi generali* (a special law prevails over a general law).

Since the main function of general principles of law is to fill gaps in treaty law and customary law, it would appear that general principles of law are subordinate to treaties and custom (that is, treaties and custom prevail over general principles of law in the event of conflict).

Judicial decisions and learned writings are described in Article 38(1)(d) as 'subsidiary means for the determination of rules of law', which suggests that they are subordinate to the other three sources listed: treaties, custom and general principles of law. Judicial decisions usually carry more weight than learned writings, but there is no hard-and-fast rule; much depends on the quality of the reasoning which the judge or writer employs.

It is doubtful whether equity is a source of international law at all; even if it is, the existence of such doubts would appear to indicate that it is, at most, a very low-ranking source. (However, when a tribunal is authorized to decide *ex aequo et bono*, the tribunal is allowed to substitute its own ideas of equity for any and every rule of international law.)

In sum, the different sources of international law are not arranged in a strict hierarchical order. Supplementing each other, in practice they are often applied side by side. However, if there is a clear conflict, treaties prevail over custom and custom prevails over general principles and the subsidiary sources.[179]

Ius cogens

Some of the early writers on international law said that a treaty would be void if it was contrary to morality or to certain (unspecified) basic principles of international law. The logical basis for this rule was that a treaty could not override natural law. With the decline of the theory of natural law,[180] the rule was largely forgotten, although some writers continued to pay lip-service to it.

Recently there has been a tendency to revive the rule, although it is no longer based on natural law; the state most in favour of the rule was the Soviet Union (which would never have supported the semi-religious theory of natural law). Moreover, the rule is now said to limit the liberty of states to create local custom, as well as their liberty to make treaties; the rule thus acts as a check on the tendency of international law to disintegrate into different regional systems.[181] The technical name now given to the basic principles of international law, which states are not allowed to contract out of, is 'peremptory norms of general international law', otherwise known as *ius cogens*.[182]

Article 53 of the Convention on the Law of Treaties, signed at Vienna in 1969,[183] provides as follows:

A treaty is void if, at the time of its conclusion, it conflicts with a peremptory norm of general international law. For the purposes of the present Convention, a peremptory norm of general international law is a norm accepted and recognized by the international community of States as a whole as a norm from which no derogation is permitted and which can be modified only by a subsequent norm of general international law having the same character.

What is said about treaties being void would also probably apply equally to local custom. The reason why local custom is not mentioned is because the purpose of the Convention was to codify the law of treaties only.

Although cautiously expressed to apply only 'for the purposes of the present Convention', the definition of a 'peremptory norm' is probably valid for all purposes. The definition is more skilful than appears at first sight. A rule cannot become a peremptory norm unless it is 'accepted and

179 Bernhardt (1992), *op. cit.*, 899.

180 See Chapter 2 above, 15–17, 32.

181 See Chapter 2 above, 30–2.

182 P. Weil, Towards Relative Normativity in International Law?, *AJIL* 77 (1983), 413–42, is critical of the concept of '*ius cogens*'. See further J.A. Frowein, Jus Cogens, *EPIL* 7 (1984), 327, at 328–9; L. Hannikainen, *Peremptory Norms (jus cogens) in International Law: Historical Development, Criteria, Present Status*, 1988; H.A. Strydom, *Ius Cogens*: Peremptory Norm or Totalitarian Instrument?, *SAYIL* 14 (1988/9), 42–58; A. D'Amato, It's a Bird, It's a Plane, It's jus cogens!, *Conn. JIL* 6 (1990), 1–6; G.M. Danilenko, International jus cogens: Issues of Law-Making, *EJIL* 2 (1991), 42–65; J. Paust, The Reality of jus cogens, *Conn. JIL* 7 (1991), 81–5; S. Kadelbach, *Zwingendes Völkerrecht*, 1992; J. Kasto, *Jus Cogens and Humanitarian Law*, 1994.

183 Text in *ILM* 8 (1969), 679; *AJIL* 63 (1969), 875; *Brownlie BDIL*, 388. See Chapter 9 below, 140–1, 145.

184 A. Cassese, *International Law in a Divided World*, 1986, 179. The recent study by Hannikainen, *op. cit.*, goes even further.

185 See R. Kühner, Torture, *EPIL* 8 (1985), 510. See Chapter 14 below, 216–17, 220.

186 *Barcelona Traction* case (*Belgium v. Spain*), *ICJ Rep.* 1970, 3, paras. 33 and 34. See Chapter 14 below, 220.

187 See Chapter 19 below, 309–11.

188 See Chapter 20 below, 342–63.

189 *ILM* 35 (1996), 828, para. 83 stating that '[t]he question whether a norm is part of the *jus cogens* relates to the legal character of the norm.'

190 Akehurst (1974–5), Hierarchy, *op. cit.*, 281–5.

191 See Chapter 17 below, 254–6.

192 See Chapter 1 above, 4 and Chapter 17 below, 271–2.

recognized [as such] by the international community of states *as a whole*' – a requirement which is too logical and reasonable to be challenged, but which is well worth stating expressly, because there have already been cases of states trying to evade rules of international law which they found to be inconvenient by arguing that those rules were contrary to some exotic examples of *ius cogens*; this danger should, with luck, be averted by requiring such states to prove that the alleged rule of *ius cogens* has been 'accepted and recognized [as such] by the international community of states *as a whole*'. It must find acceptance and recognition by the international community at large and cannot be imposed upon a significant minority of states. Thus, an overwhelming majority of states is required, cutting across cultural and ideological differences.

At present very few rules pass this test. Many rules have been suggested as candidates. Some writers suggest that there is considerable agreement on the prohibition of the use of force, of genocide, slavery, of gross violations of the right of people to self-determination, and of racial discrimination.[184] Others would include the prohibition on torture.[185] In an obscure *obiter dictum* in the *Barcelona Traction* case in 1970, the ICJ referred to 'basic rights of the human person', including the prohibition of slavery and racial discrimination and the prohibition of aggression and genocide, which it considered to be 'the concern of all states', without, however, expressly recognizing the concept of *ius cogens*.[186] But, apart from the 'basic rights of the human person' mentioned in the *Barcelona Traction* case, the only one which at present receives anything approaching general acceptance is the rule against aggression.[187] In its Advisory Opinion in the *Legality of Nuclear Weapons* case, the ICJ did not find a need to address the question whether universally recognized principles of international humanitarian law (applicable in time of armed conflict[188]) are part of *ius cogens* as defined in Article 53 of the Vienna Convention.[189] It should also be noted that in the preparatory work on Article 53 no agreement was possible on which international norms belong to *ius cogens*. France even refused to accept the Convention because of Article 53. The vagueness of *ius cogens* induced Western and Latin-American states to insist on the procedural safeguard in Article 66 lit. a of the same Convention, under which disputes on the application of Article 53 are to be settled by the International Court of Justice or an arbitral tribunal. State practice and international decisions have indeed been cautious in accepting the relevance of the concept.

Although the question is controversial, the better view appears to be that a rule of *ius cogens* can be derived from custom and possibly from treaties, but probably not from other sources.[190]

Obligations *erga omnes* and 'international crimes'

The problem of *ius cogens* is connected with the concept of *erga omnes* obligations and the acceptance of the notion of 'international crimes' by the International Law Commission in its project codifying state responsibility.[191] Under the international law of reprisals,[192] the general rule is that only the directly injured state is entitled to act against the violation of an international obligation by another state. Obligations *erga omnes* are concerned with the enforceability of norms of international law, the violation of which is deemed to be an offence not only against the state directly affected by the breach, but also against all members of the international community.[193]

As noted above, the existence of norms which are 'the concern of all states' was recognized by the ICJ in the *Barcelona Traction* case in 1970. But the decision also contains a remarkable reservation: 'However, on the universal level, the instruments which embody human rights do not confer on States the capacity to protect the victims of infringements of such rights irrespective of their nationality.'[194] Thus it offers little clarity on the issue of possible reactions by third states to the violation of such *erga omnes* obligations, the enforceability of which all states have a legal interest in. Although the Court was confronted in a number of other cases with *erga omnes* obligations, it has so far never addressed the legal consequences of the breach of such an obligation. This has been recently noted by Judge Weeramantry in his Dissenting Opinion in the *East Timor* case, in which for jurisdictional reasons the Court dismissed the claim of Portugal against Australia for concluding an agreement with Indonesia affecting the rights of East Timor, but confirmed that the principle of self-determination was an obligation *erga omnes*:

> In the Court's view, Portugal's assertion that the right of peoples to self-determination, as it evolved from the Charter and from United Nations practice, has an *erga omnes* character, is irreproachable. The principle of self-determination of peoples has been recognized by the United Nations Charter and in the jurisprudence of the Court ... ; it is one of the essential principles of contemporary international law. However, the Court considers that the *erga omnes* character of a norm and the rule of consent to jurisdiction are two different things. Whatever the nature of the obligations invoked, the Court could not rule on the lawfulness of the conduct of a State when its judgment would imply an evaluation of the lawfulness of the conduct of another State which is not a party to the case. Where this is so, the Court cannot act, even if the right in question is a right *erga omnes*.[195]

With reference to the *Barcelona Traction* case, the International Law Commission (ILC) in its draft on state responsibility has come up with a problematic distinction concerning internationally wrongful acts that can be committed by states: 'international delicts' and 'international crimes'.[196] Article 19 of the Draft Articles on State Responsibility[197] stipulates:

1 An act of a State which constitutes a breach of an international obligation is an internationally wrongful act, regardless of the subject matter of the obligation breached.

2 An internationally wrongful act which results from the breach by a State of an international obligation so essential for the protection of fundamental interests of the international community that its breach is recognized as a crime by that community as a whole constitutes an international crime.

3 Subject to paragraph 2, and on the basis of the rules of international law in force, an international crime may result, *inter alia*, from:

193 See J.A. Frowein, Die Verpflichtungen *erga omnes* im Völkerrecht und ihre Durchsetzung, in R. Bernhardt *et al.* (eds), *Festschrift für Hermann Mosler*, 1983, 241 *et seq.*; P. Malanczuk, Countermeasures and Self-Defence in the ILC's Draft Articles on State Responsibility, in M. Spinedi/B. Simma (eds), *United Nations Codification of State Responsibility*, 1987, 231 *et seq.*; A.J.J. de Hoogh, The Relationship between *jus cogens*, Obligations *erga omnes* and International Crimes: Peremptory Norms in Perspective, *AJPIL* 42 (1991), 183–214; B. Simma, Does the UN Charter Provide an Adequate Legal Basis for Individual or Collective Responses to Violations of Obligations *erga omnes?*, in J. Delbrück (ed.), *The Future of International Law Enforcement: New Scenarios – New Law?*, 1993, 125 *et seq.*; C. Annacker, The Legal Regime of *Erga Omnes* Obligations in International Law, *AJPIL* (1994), 131 *et seq.*; J.A. Frowein, Reactions by Not Directly Affected States to Breaches of Public International Law, *RdC* 248 (1994-IV), 345–437; C. Annacker, *Die Durchsetzung von erga omnes Verpflichtungen vor dem Internationalen Gerichtshof*, 1994; A.J.J. de Hoogh, *Obligations erga omnes and International Crimes: A Theoretical Inquiry into the Implementation and Enforcement of the International Responsibility of States*, 1996.

194 *Barcelona Traction* case, *op. cit.*, at 47, para. 91.

195 *East Timor* case (*Portugal v. Australia*), judgment of 30 June 1995, *ICJ Rep.* 1995, 90; *ILM* 34 (1995), 1581–91, para. 29. See Chapters 18, 286–7 and 19, 331–2 below.

196 See M. Spinedi, *Les Crimes internationaux de l'Etat dans les travaux de codification de la responsabilité des Etats entrepris par les Nations Unies*, 1984; R. Hofmann, Zur Unterscheidung Verbrechen und Delikt im Bereich der Staatenverantwortlichkeit, *ZaöRV* 45 (1985), 195 *et seq.*; M. Mohr, The ILC's Distinction Between 'International Crimes' and 'International Delicts' and Its Implications, in Spinedi/Simma (eds), 1987, *op. cit.*, 115; Malanczuk (1987), *op. cit.*, at 230 *et seq.*; J.H.H. Weiler/A. Cassese/M. Spinedi (eds), *International Crimes of States. A Critical Analysis of the ILC's Draft Article 19 on State Responsibility*, 1989; G. Gilbert, The Criminal Responsibility of States, *ICLQ* 39 (1990), 345 et seq; de Hoogh, *op. cit.* On the ILC see text below, 61.

197 Text in *Brownlie BDIL*, 426. See Chapter 17 below, 255–72.

198 See *ILCYb* 1976, Vol. 2, part 2, 120.

199 See the criticism by B. Simma, Bilateralism and Community Interest in the Law of State Responsibility, in Y. Dinstein/M. Tabory (eds), *International Law at a Time of Perplexity*, 1989, 821. In the ILC, Art. 19 and its legal consequences have remained up to now highly controversial, see ILC 48th Session, Provisional Summary Record of the 2452nd Meeting, UN Doc. A/CN.4/SR. 2452, 22 July 1996. See Chapter 17 below, 271–2.

200 See Chapter 20 below, 353–63.

201 S. Rosenne, Codification of International Law, *EPIL* I (1992), 632–40; M. Schröder, Codification and Progressive Development of International Law within the UN, in *Wolfrum UNLPP I*, 100–9; A. Pellet, La formation du droit international dans le cadre des Nations Unies, *EJIL* 6 (1995), 401–25; H. Torrone, *L'Influence des conventions de codification sur la coutume en droit international public*, 1989.

202 See Chapter 2 above, 21–2 and Chapter 20 below, 344.

203 See Chapter 17 below, 263–6.

204 See Chapter 12 below, 173–4, 176–82.

205 See Chapter 17 below, 255–72.

206 See Chapter 12 below, 173.

207 See Chapter 8 below, 123–7.

208 See Chapter 9 below, 130–1.

209 See Chapter 11 below, 161–2.

(a) a serious breach of an international obligation of essential importance for the maintenance of international peace and security, such as that prohibiting aggression;

(b) a serious breach of an international obligation of essential importance for safeguarding the right of self-determination of peoples, such as that prohibiting the establishment or maintenance by force of colonial domination;

(c) a serious breach on a widespread scale of an international obligation of essential importance for safeguarding the human being, such as those prohibiting slavery, genocide and *apartheid*;

(d) a serious breach of an international obligation of essential importance for the safeguarding and preservation of the human environment, such as those prohibiting massive pollution of the atmosphere or of the seas.

4   Any international wrongful act which is not an international crime in accordance with paragraph 2 constitutes an international delict.

According to the ILC, while an international crime always constitutes the violation of an *erga omnes* obligation, the breach of an *erga omnes* obligation does not necessarily imply an international crime. The concept of 'international crimes', therefore, is narrower than the notion of *ius cogens*.[198] The precise implications of Article 19 in terms of legal consequences remain to be seen when the work of the Commission should reach a more definite stage.[199] Only two remarks may be added here. First, the terminology is unfortunate because it tends to confuse the international criminal responsibility of individuals[200] with the criminal responsibility of states, which, as such, does not exist in international law. Second, the prohibition of the massive pollution of the environment has not been accepted by state practice even as a *ius cogens* norm.

Codification of international law

Since the end of the nineteenth century there have been public and private attempts to codify customary international law in order to clarify the existing rules and to improve them.[201] The Hague Conventions of 1899 and 1907 dealt with the laws of war and neutrality,[202] the 1930 Codification Conference in The Hague under the League of Nations addressed the law of nationality,[203] territorial waters,[204] and state responsibility.[205] But it was largely unsuccessful; agreement was possible only on the law of nationality. In recent years there has been a stronger tendency to codify customary law. Four conventions on the law of the sea were signed at Geneva in 1958;[206] a convention on diplomatic relations and immunities[207] was signed at Vienna in 1961; a convention on consular relations and immunities was signed at Vienna in 1963; conventions on the law of treaties were signed at Vienna in 1969 and 1986;[208] and conventions on state succession were signed at Vienna in 1978 and 1983.[209] A major enterprise in multilateral conference diplomacy has been the 1982 Law of the Sea Convention which took ten years of protracted negotiations to adopt and more than another ten years to enter into force.[210]

There are obvious advantages to be gained from codifying customary law in a treaty. The rules become more precise and more accessible; and new states are more willing to accept rules which they themselves have helped to draft. But, in view of the divergences between the practice of different states, codification often means that a compromise is necessary, and there is a limit to the number of compromises that states are willing to accept at any one time. Consequently, codification will succeed only if it proceeds slowly; acceleration produces the risk of failure, as happened at the codification conference organized by the League of Nations in 1930, and the failure of a codification scheme may cast doubt on customary rules which were previously well established. (This is what happened to the three-mile rule concerning the width of the territorial sea after the failure of the 1930 conference.[211])

The preparatory work for the Geneva and Vienna conventions was carried out by the International Law Commission (ILC), established in 1947 by the United Nations.[212] It is a body of thirty-four (originally fifteen) international lawyers elected by the United Nations General Assembly for a five-year term. The members of the ILC, who serve in their individual capacity, are supposed to represent the world's principal legal systems. The ILC is entrusted not only with the codification of international law, but also with its progressive development (that is, the drafting of rules on topics where customary law is non-existent or insufficiently developed); in practice the distinction between codification and progressive development is often blurred. Special rapporteurs are assigned to propose work programmes and draft articles chosen by the Commission itself or referred to it by the General Assembly.

Sometimes the Commission seeks to codify the law, not by preparing a draft convention, which may be later incorporated into a binding multilateral agreement, but simply by summarizing the law in a report to the General Assembly. Such reports are not binding in the same way as treaties, but they do constitute valuable evidence of customary law; the Commission's members base their work on extensive research and on an attempt to ascertain and reconcile the views of the member states of the United Nations (for example, by circulating questionnaires and by inviting states to comment on their draft reports – the same procedure is followed during the preliminary work on draft conventions). The effectiveness of the work of the ILC has more recently been called into question by some of its own distinguished members,[213] and with regard to the new topics under consideration its working methods may require adjustment to meet acceptance of drafts it produces by the majority of states.[214] However, it is notable that the ILC managed to respond to the request of the General Assembly and complete its draft on the Statute for an International Criminal Court within the short period of 1992 to 1994.[215]

Unofficial bodies have also tried their hand at codification. For instance, Harvard Law School has produced a number of draft conventions; these are not intended to be ratified by states, but are simply used as

210 See Chapter 12 below, 173–5.

211 See Chapter 12 below, 178–80.

212 See S. Goswami, *Politics in Law Making: A Study of the International Law Commission of the UN*, 1986; I. Sinclair, *The International Law Commission*, 1987; S. Vallat, International Law Commission, *EPIL* II (1995), 1208–16.

213 See S. Sucharitkul, The Role of the International Law Commission in the Decade of International Law, *LJIL* 3 (1990), 15–42; B. Graefrath, The International Law Commission Tomorrow: Improving Its Organization and Methods of Work, *AJIL* 85 (1991), 595–612; R. Ago, Some New Thoughts on the Codification of International Law, in E.G. Bello/B.A. Ajibola (eds), *Essays in Honour of Judge Taslim Elias*, 1992, 36–61.

214 See M. Brus, *Third Party Dispute Settlement in an Interdependent World*, 1995, 159–63.

215 See Chapter 20 below, 360–1.

216 See Chapter 2 above, 22.

a convenient means of restating the law. They derive their value from the eminence of the professors who have helped to draw them up. Finally, the private organizations of the Institute of International Law and of the International Law Association, both founded in 1873, should be mentioned.[216]

4   International law and municipal law

'Municipal law' is the technical name given by international lawyers to the national or internal law of a state. The question of the relationship between international law and municipal law can give rise to many practical problems, especially if there is a conflict between the two.[1] Which rule prevails in the case of conflict? How do rules of international law take effect in the internal law of states?

Dualist and monist theories

There are two basic theories, with a number of variations in the literature, on the relationship between international and domestic law. The first doctrine is called the dualist (or pluralist) view, and assumes that international law and municipal law are two separate legal systems which exist independently of each other. The central question then is whether one system is superior to the other. The second doctrine, called the monist view, has a unitary perception of the 'law' and understands both international and municipal law as forming part of one and the same legal order. The most radical version of the monist approach was formulated by Kelsen.[2] In his view, the ultimate source of the validity of all law derived from a basic rule ('Grundnorm') of international law. Kelsen's theory led to the conclusion that all rules of international law were supreme over municipal law, that a municipal law inconsistent with international law was automatically null and void and that rules of international law were directly applicable in the domestic sphere of states.

In reality, the opposing schools of dualism and monism did not adequately reflect actual state practice and were thus forced to modify their original positions in many respects, bringing them closer to each other, without, however, producing a conclusive answer on the true relationship between international law and municipal law. As a rule of thumb, it may be said that the ideological background to dualist doctrines is strongly coloured by an adherence to positivism and an emphasis on the theory of sovereignty, while monist schools are more inclined to follow natural law thinking and liberal ideas of a world society.[3]

It is also notable that the controversy was predominantly conducted among authors from civil law countries.[4] Authors with a common law background tended to pay lesser attention to these theoretical issues and preferred a more empirical approach seeking practical solutions in a given

1 See *Harris CMIL*, 69–101; L. Ferrari-Bravo, International Law and Municipal Law: The Complementarity of Legal Systems, in R.St.J. Macdonald/D.M. Johnston (eds), *The Structure and Process of International Law*, 1983, 715–44; G. Pau, *Le droit interne dans l'ordre international*, 1985; G.I. Tunkin/R. Wolfrum (eds), *International Law and Municipal Law*, 1988; M. Fitzmaurice/C. Flintermann (eds), *L. Erades, Interactions Between International and Municipal Law: A Comparative Case Law Study*, 1993; B. Conforti, *International Law and the Role of Domestic Legal Systems*, 1993; C. Economides, *The Relationship between International and Domestic Law*, 1993; E. Benevisti, Judicial Misgivings Regarding the Application of International Law: An Analysis of Attitudes of National Courts, *EJIL* 4 (1993), 159–83; Y. Iwasawa, The Relationship Between International Law and National Law: Japanese Experiences, *BYIL* 64 (1993), 333–9; E. Benvenisti, Judges and Foreign Affairs: A Comment on the Institut de Droit International's Resolution on 'The Activities of National Courts and the International Relations of Their State', *EJIL* 5 (1994), 423–39; P. Chandrasekhara Rao, *The Indian Constitution and International Law*, 1994; K.J. Partsch, International Law and Municipal Law, *EPIL* II (1995), 1185–202; P. Rambaud, International Law and Municipal Law: Conflicts and Their Review by Third States, *ibid.*, 1202–6; C. Schreuer, International Law and Municipal Law: Law and Decisions of International Organizations and Courts, *ibid.*, 1228–33; W. Czaplinski, International Law and Polish Municipal Law. A Case Study, *Hague YIL* 8 (1995), 31–46; J.J. Paust, *International Law as Law of the United States*, 1996; P.M. Eisemann (ed.), *The Integration of International and European Community Law into the National Legal Order*, 1996.

2 See H. Kelsen, Die Einheit von Völkerrecht und staatlichem Recht, *ZaöRV* 41 (1958), 234–48; Kelsen, *Principles of International Law*, 2nd edn 1966 (Tucker ed.), 553–88.
3 On positivism and natural law theory see Chapter 2 above, 15–17, 32.
4 On the variety of legal systems in the world see Chapter 1 above, 6.
5 G. Fitzmaurice, The General Principles of International Law Considered from the Standpoint of the Rule of Law, *RdC* 92 (1957-II), 1, at 71.
6 See Chapter 3 above, 39–50.
7 See Chapter 17 below, 263–6.
8 PCIJ, series A/B, no. 46, 167. See L. Weber, Free Zones of Upper Savoy and Gex Case, *EPIL* II (1995), 483–4.
9 Text in *ILM* 8 (1969), 679; *AJIL* 63 (1969), 875; *Brownlie BDIL*, 388, at 400. See Chapter 9 below, 131.

case. Lecturing at the Hague Academy of International Law in 1957, Fitzmaurice considered that

> the entire monist-dualist controversy is unreal, artificial and strictly beside the point, because it assumes something that has to exist for there to be any controversy at all – and which in fact does not exist – namely a *common field* in which the two legal orders under discussion both simultaneously have their spheres of activity.[5]

It is more useful to leave this dogmatic dispute aside here and to turn to the general attitude of international law to municipal law and then briefly describe the various approaches taken by national legal systems towards international law in practice.

The attitude of international law to municipal law

International law does not entirely ignore municipal law. For instance, as we have seen, municipal law may be used as evidence of international custom or of general principles of law, which are both sources of international law.[6] Moreover, international law leaves certain questions to be decided by municipal law; thus, in order to determine whether an individual is a national of state X, international law normally looks first at the law of state X, provided that the law of state X is not wholly unreasonable.[7]

However, the general rule of international law is that a state cannot plead a rule of or a gap in its own municipal law as a defence to a claim based on international law. Thus, in the *Free Zones* case, the Permanent Court of International Justice said: 'It is certain that France cannot rely on her own legislation to limit the scope of her international obligations.'[8] This is particularly true when, as often happens, a treaty or other rule of international law imposes an obligation on states to enact a particular rule as part of their own municipal law. A similar rule can be found in Article 27 of the Vienna Convention on the Law of Treaties:[9] 'A party may not invoke the provisions of its internal law as justification for its failure to perform a treaty.'

In other words, all that international law says is that states cannot invoke their internal laws and procedures as a justification for not complying with their international obligations. States are required to perform their international obligations in good faith, but they are at liberty to decide on the modalities of such performance within their domestic legal systems. Similarly, there is a general duty for states to bring domestic law into conformity with obligations under international law. But international law leaves the method of achieving this result (described in the literature by varying concepts of 'incorporation', 'adoption', 'transformation' or 'reception') to the domestic jurisdiction of states. They are free to decide how best to translate their international obligations into internal law and to determine which legal status these have domestically. On this issue, in practice there is a lack of uniformity in the different national legal systems.

The attitude of national legal systems to international law

The attitude of municipal law to international law is much less easy to summarize than the attitude of international law to municipal law. For one thing, the laws of different countries vary greatly in this respect. If one examines constitutional texts, especially those of developing countries which are usually keen on emphasizing their sovereignty, the finding is that most states do not give primacy to international law over their own municipal law.[10] However, this does not necessarily mean that most states would disregard international law altogether. Constitutional texts can form a starting point for analysis. What also matters is internal legislation, the attitude of the national courts and administrative practice, which is often ambiguous and inconsistent. The prevailing approach in practice appears to be dualist, regarding international law and internal law as different systems requiring the incorporation of international rules on the national level. Thus, the effectiveness of international law generally depends on the criteria adopted by national legal systems.

The most important questions of the attitude of national legal systems to international law concern the status of international treaties and of international customary law, including general principles of international law. The analysis of municipal law in relation to the European Community is a special area beyond the scope of the following.[11]

Treaties

The status of treaties in national legal systems varies considerably.[12] In the United Kingdom, for example, the power to make or ratify treaties belongs to the Queen on the advice of the Prime Minister, a Minister of the Crown, an Ambassador or other officials, though by the so-called Ponsonby Rule, as a matter of constitutional convention, the Executive will not normally ratify a treaty until twenty-one parliamentary days after the treaty has been laid before both Houses of Parliament. Consequently, a treaty does not automatically become part of English law; otherwise the Queen could alter English law without the consent of Parliament, which would be contrary to the basic principle of English constitutional law that Parliament has a monopoly of legislative power. There is an exception concerning treaties regulating the conduct of warfare[13] which is probably connected with the rule of English constitutional law which gives the Queen, acting on the advice of her ministers, the power to declare war without the consent of Parliament. If a treaty requires changes in English law, it is necessary to pass an Act of Parliament in order to bring English law into conformity with the treaty. If the Act is not passed, the treaty is still binding on the United Kingdom from the international point of view, and the United Kingdom will be responsible for not complying with the treaty.

An Act of Parliament giving effect to a treaty in English law can be repealed by a subsequent Act of Parliament; in these circumstances there is a conflict between international law and English law, since international law regards the United Kingdom as still bound by the treaty, but English courts cannot give effect to the treaty.[14] However, English courts usually

10 See A. Cassese, Modern Constitutions and International Law, *RdC* 192 (1985-III), 331 *et seq.*

11 See F. Caportorti, European Communities: Community Law and Municipal Law, *EPIL* II (1995), 165–70. See Chapter 6 below, 95–6.

12 See, for example, F.G. Jacobs/S. Roberts (eds), *The Effect of Treaties in Domestic Law* (UK National Committee of Comparative Law), 1987; M. Duffy, Practical Problems of Giving Effect to Treaty Obligations – The Cost of Consent, *AYIL* 12 (1988/9), 16–21; W.K. Hastings, New Zealand Treaty Practice with Particular Reference to the Treaty of Waitangi, *ICLQ* 38 (1989), 668 *et seq.*; R. Heuser, Der Abschluß völkerrechtlicher Verträge im chinesischen Recht, *ZaöRV* 51 (1991), 938–48; Zh. Li, Effect of Treaties in Domestic Law: Practice of the People's Republic of China, *Dalhouse LJ* 16 (1993), 62–97; Interim Report of the National Committee on International Law in Municipal Courts [Japan], *Jap. Ann. IL* 36 (1993), 100–62; T.H. Strom/ P. Finkle, Treaty Implementation: The Canadian Game Needs Australian Rules, *Ottawa LR* 25 (1993), 39–60; G. Buchs, *Die unmittelbare Anwendbarkeit völkerrechtlicher Vertragsbestimmungen am Beispiel der Rechtsprechung der Gerichte Deutschlands, Österreichs, der Schweiz und der Vereinigten Staaten von Amerika*, 1993; K.S. Sik, *The Indonesian Law of Treaties 1945–1990*, 1994; C. Lysaght, The Status of International Agreements in Irish Domestic Law, *ILT* 12 (1994), 171–3; M. Leigh/M.R. Blakeslee (eds), *National Treaty Law and Practice*, 1995; P. Alston/M. Chiam (eds), *Treaty-Making and Australia: Globalisation versus Sovereignty*, 1995.

13 See Lord McNair, *The Law of Treaties*, 1961, 89–91, and *Porter v. Freudenberg*, [1915] 1 KB 857, 874–80.

14 *Inland Revenue Commissioners v. Collco Dealings Ltd*, [1962] AC 1. Would English courts apply subsequent Acts of Parliament which conflicted with the European Communities Act 1972? See E.C.S. Wade/W. Bradley, *Constitutional and Administrative Law*, 10th edn 1985, 136–8.

15 *Inland Revenue Commissioners v. Collco Dealings Ltd*, [1962] AC 1 (*obiter*). This rule is not limited to treaties which have been given effect in English law by previous Acts of Parliament. See *R. v. Secretary of State for Home Affairs, ex p. Bhajan Singh*, [1975] 2 All ER 1081; *R. v. Chief Immigration Officer, Heathrow Airport, ex p. Salamat Bibi*, [1976] 3 All ER 843, 847; and *Pan-American World Airways Inc. v. Department of Trade* (1975), *ILR*, Vol. 60, 431, at 439. See also P.J. Duffy, English Law and the European Convention on Human Rights, *ICLQ* 29 (1980), 585–618; A.J. Cunningham, The European Convention on Human Rights, Customary International Law and the Constitution, *ICLQ* 43 (1994), 537–67.

16 See M.W. Janis, *An Introduction to International Law*, 2nd edn 1993, 96.

17 *Australia & New Zealand Banking Group Ltd et al. v. Australia et al.*, House of Lords, judgment of 26 October 1990, *ILM* 29 (1990), 671, at 694; see Chapter 6 below, 94. On the interpretation of treaties see R. Gardiner, Treaty Interpretation in the English Courts Since *Fothergill v. Monarch Airlines* (1980), *ICLQ* 44 (1995), 620–9.

18 For details, see *Restatement (Third)*, Vol. 1, part III, ch. 2, 40–69; Janis, *op. cit.*, 85–94; H.A. Blackmun, The Supreme Court and the Law of Nations, *Yale LJ* 104 (1994), 39–49; A.M. Weisburd, State Courts, Federal Courts and International Cases, *Yale JIL* 20 (1995), 1–64.

19 *U.S. v. Alvarez-Machain*, *ILM* 31 (1992), 902, 112 S. Ct. 2188, 119 L. edn 2d 441 (1992), at 453. See Janis, *op. cit.*, 91–2. In the end the case against the Mexican doctor was dismissed by the federal trial judge. See also B. Baker/V. Röbe, To Abduct or To Extradite: Does a Treaty Beg the Question? The Alvarez-Machain Decision in U.S. Domestic Law and International Law, *ZaöRV* 53 (1993), 657–88; D.C. Smith, Beyond Indeterminacy and Self-Contradiction in Law: Transnational Abductions and Treaty Interpretation in *U.S. v. Alvarez-Machain*, *EJIL* 6 (1995), 1–31; M.J. Glennon, State-Sponsored Abduction: A Comment on *United States v. Alvarez-Machain*, *AJIL* 86 (1992), 746–56; M. Halberstam, In Defense of the Supreme Court Decision in *Alvarez-Machain*, *ibid.*, 736–46; L. Henkin, Correspondence, *AJIL* 87 (1993), 100–2.

try to interpret Acts of Parliament so that they do not conflict with earlier treaties made by the United Kingdom.[15]

As far as the United Kingdom is concerned, there is a very clear difference between the effects of a treaty in international law and the effects of a treaty in municipal law; a treaty becomes effective in international law when it is ratified by the Queen, but it usually has no effect in municipal law until an Act of Parliament is passed to give effect to it. In other countries this distinction tends to be blurred. Most other common law countries, except the United States, as will be discussed below, follow the English tradition and strictly deny any direct internal effect of international treaties without legislative enactment. This is the case, for example, in Canada and India.[16] The House of Lords recently reaffirmed this rule in 1989 in the *International Tin* case, in which Lord Oliver of Aylmerton noted:

> as a matter of constitutional law of the United Kingdom, the Royal Prerogative, whilst it embraces the making of treaties, does not extend to altering the law or conferring rights upon individuals or depriving individuals of rights which they enjoy in domestic law without the intervention of Parliament. Treaties, as it is sometimes expressed, are not self-executing. Quite simply, a treaty is not part of English law unless and until it has been incorporated into the law by legislation.[17]

In the vast majority of democratic countries outside the Commonwealth, the legislature, or part of the legislature, participates in the process of ratification, so that ratification becomes a legislative act, and the treaty becomes effective in international law and in municipal law simultaneously. For instance, the Constitution of the United States provides that the President 'shall have power, by and with the advice and consent of the Senate, to make treaties, provided two-thirds of the Senators present concur' (Article II (2)). Treaties ratified in accordance with the Constitution automatically become part of the municipal law of the United States. However, this statement needs some qualification.[18] Under the US Constitution, treaties of the Federal Government (as distinct from the states) are the 'supreme Law of the Land', like the Constitution itself and federal law (Article VI). Cases arising under international treaties are within the judicial power of the United States and thus, subject to certain limitations, within the jurisdiction of the federal courts (Article III (2)). International agreements remain subject to the Bill of Rights and other requirements of the US Constitution and cannot be implemented internally in violation of them. If the United States fails to carry out a treaty obligation because of its unconstitutionality, it remains responsible for the violation of the treaty under international law.

A recent controversial decision of the US Supreme Court was given in the *Alvarez-Machain* case. A Mexican doctor accused of torturing an American narcotics agent was kidnapped in Mexico by US agents and brought to trial in the United States. The Court held that this action was not covered by the terms of the 1978 US–Mexico Extradition Treaty, because its language and history would 'not support the proposition that the Treaty prohibits abductions outside of its terms'.[19] This awkward interpretation of the treaty by the majority of the Supreme Court shows a remarkable disrespect for international law and understandably provoked a strong protest by the government of Mexico, which demanded that the treaty be renegotiated.

Another complicating aspect, particularly under United States law, is the distinction between 'self-executing' and 'non-self-executing agreements'.[20] In essence, the distinction concerns the issue whether an agreement, or certain provisions thereof, should be given legal effect without further implementing national legislation and is relevant when a party seeks to rely on the agreement in a case before an American court. Moreover, it is important to note that most United States treaties are not concluded under Article II of the Constitution with the consent of the Senate, but are 'statutory' or 'congressional-executive agreements' signed by the President under ordinary legislation adopted by a majority of both the House of Representatives and the Senate. There are also treaties called 'executive agreements' which the President concludes alone without the participation of Congress.[21]

In the United States and in those countries following the legal traditions of continental Europe, treaties enjoy the same status as national statutes. This means that they generally derogate pre-existing legislation (the principle of *lex posterior derogat legi priori*), but are overruled by statutes enacted later. It is difficult, however, to generalize in this area in view of considerable national modifications to this rule.

Some constitutions even make treaties superior to ordinary national legislation and subordinate law, but rarely superior to constitutional law as such. The operation of this rule in practice depends on who has the authority to give effect to it. This may be reserved to the legislature, a political body, excluding any review by the courts. In other cases, where constitutional courts exist or where courts have the power of judicial review of legislative action, the situation is often different. There are also countries in which the authoritative interpretation of the meaning of international treaties is a privilege of the executive branch, to secure the control of the government over foreign affairs. To a certain extent this is also the case in France with the result that the power of the French courts is in effect curtailed to reject the validity of a national statute because of a conflict with an international treaty. Thus, the view that numerous countries following the model of the French legal system have recognized the priority of treaties is at least open to doubt.[22]

In the Netherlands the situation is somewhat peculiar. The Dutch Constitution of 1953, as revised in 1956, clearly provided that all internal law, even constitutional law, must be disregarded if it is incompatible with provisions of treaties or decisions of international organizations that are binding on all persons.[23] Although there is no system of judicial review of legislative acts in the Netherlands,[24] which in this respect follows the tradition of the United Kingdom, Dutch courts thus obtained the authority to overrule acts of Parliament, not on grounds of unconstitutionality, but on the ground that they may conflict with certain treaties or resolutions of international organizations. However, there is a safeguard built into constitutional procedures. The Dutch Parliament has to consent to treaties

20 The case law started in 1829 with Chief Justice John Marshall's decision in *Foster & Elam v. Neilson*, 27 US (2 Pet.) 253 (1829). See T. Buergenthal, Self-Executing and Non-Self-Executing Treaties in National and International Law, *RdC* 235 (1992-IV), 303–400; C.M. Vázquez, The Four Doctrines of Self-Executing Treaties, *AJIL* 89 (1995), 695–723 and the comment by M. Dominik, *AJIL* 90 (1996), 441.
21 See Janis, *op. cit.*, 92; L. Wildhaber, Executive Agreements, *EPIL* II (1995), 312–18.
22 See Partsch, *op. cit.*, 1195.
23 Netherlands Constitution, Article 66, as amended in 1956. See H.H.M. Sondaal, Some Features of Dutch Treaty Practice, *NYIL* 19 (1988), 179–257; H. Schermers, Some Recent Cases Delaying the Direct Effect of International Treaties in Dutch Law, *Mich. JIL* 10 (1989), 266 *et seq.*
24 Article 120 of the Dutch Constitution provides: 'The constitutionality of acts of Parliament and treaties shall not be reviewed by the courts.'

25 Cassese, *op. cit.*, at 411, views the new text as 'a step backwards'. Dutch authors do not agree, see M.C.B. Burkens, The Complete Revision of the Dutch Constitution, *NILR* (1982), 323 *et seq.*; E.A. Alkema, Foreign Relations in the 1983 Dutch Constitution, *NILR* (1984), 307, at 320 *et seq.*; see also the study by E.W. Vierdag, *Het nederlandse verdragenrecht*, 1995. On recent developments see J. Klabbers, The New Dutch Law on the Approval of Treaties, *ICLQ* 44 (1995), 629–42.

26 See, e.g., Article 24 of the 1978 USSR Law of the Procedure for the Conclusion, Execution and Denunciation of International Treaties, *ILM* 17 (1978), 1115.

27 On the general lack (with the exception of the former German Democratic Republic) of constitutional provisions or general legislation on the effect of international law in the internal laws of the Comecon states, see K. Skubizewski, Völkerrecht und Landesrecht: Regelungen und Erfahrungen in Mittel- und Osteuropa, in W. Fiedler/G. Ress (eds), *Verfassungsrecht und Völkerrecht: Gedächtnisschrift für Wilhelm Karl Geck*, 1988, 777 *et seq.*

28 G.M. Danilenko, The New Russian Constitution and International Law, *AJIL* 88 (1994), 451–70. See also A. Kolodkin, Russia and International Law: New Approaches, *RBDI* 26 (1993), 552–7.

29 M.F. Brzezinski, Toward 'Constitutionalism' in Russia: The Russian Constitutional Court, *ICLQ* 42 (1993), 673 *et seq.*

30 Text in *ILM* 34 (1995), 1370 with an Introductory Note by W.E. Butler. See T. Beknazar, Das neue Recht völkerrechtlicher Verträge in Russland, *ZaöRV* 56 (1995), 406–26.

31 1978 USSR Law, *op. cit.*

32 E. Stein, International Law in Internal Law: Toward Internationalization of Central-Eastern European Constitutions?, *AJIL* 88 (1994), 427–50, at 447. See also E. Stein, International Law and Internal Law in the New Constitutions of Central-Eastern Europe, in *FS Bernhardt*, 865–84; V.S. Vereshchetin. New Constitutions and the Old Problem of the Relationship between International Law and National Law, *EJIL* 7 (1996), 29–41.

which conflict with the Constitution by a majority necessary for constitutional amendments. The new text of the 1983 Constitution retained this power of the courts in Article 94, but has given rise to some dispute as to whether it departs from the previous text as far as the relationship between international treaties and the Constitution is concerned.[25] The unusual, 'monist' Dutch openness to the internal effect of international law, not only in the case of treaties, may find some explanation in the fact that, as a small country with considerable global trading and investment interests, the Netherlands places more emphasis on the rule of law in international relations.

The strictly 'dualist' tradition of the former socialist countries has been to require a specific national legislative act before treaty obligations could be implemented and had to be respected by national authorities.[26] Thus, their courts were not required to decide on conflicts between treaty norms and municipal law, and international law could generally not be invoked before them or administrative agencies, unless there was an express reference to it in domestic law.[27]

With the constitutional reforms in Eastern Europe there have been some important changes. The new Russian Constitution of 1993, for example, contains the following revolutionary clause (Article 15(4)):

> The generally recognized principles and norms of international law and the international treaties of the Russian Federation shall constitute part of its legal system. If an international treaty of the Russian Federation establishes other rules than those stipulated by the law, the rules of the international treaty shall apply.[28]

Although this clause is comparatively broad, because it includes not only treaties but also 'generally recognized principles and norms of international law', it does not give priority to these sources over the Constitution itself. What this means in practice and what the role of the new Constitutional Court of the Russian Federation in this respect will be, remain to be seen.[29] On 16 June 1995, the State Duma of the Russian Federation adopted a Federal Law on International Treaties[30] which replaced the 1978 Law on the Procedure for the Conclusion, Execution, and Denunciation of International Treaties of the former Soviet Union.[31]

Moreover, in a recent study of fifteen constitutions or draft constitutions of Central-Eastern European States, Eric Stein concludes that

> most incorporate treaties as an integral part of the internal order, and although this is not clear in all instances, treaties have the status of ordinary legislation. In five (probably seven) instances treaties are made superior to both prior and subsequent national legislation, while in three documents this exalted rank is reserved for human rights treaties only.[32]

In the end, the actual implementation of such provisions by the courts and administration will matter more than lofty constitutional texts.

Custom and general principles

There are some significant differences in the rules for the application of customary international law and general principles in municipal law as compared with treaties. There is no problem of internal conflict between the executive branch and the legislative branch of government on the conclusion of a treaty. Rules for the recognition of customary international law in the internal sphere are either laid down in advance in the constitution or are gradually formulated by the national courts. A procedure by which a legislature would have to transform customary international law into municipal law would be impracticable, simply because it would require a regular review of all changes of norms and principles of international law, a task which no body can master for legislative purposes. Custom is also less clear than treaties and has decreased in its significance as a source of international law.

The differences between common law and civil law countries with regard to the incorporation of customary international law and general principles of international law into their domestic law are much less pronounced than in the case of treaties. Even the practice of the United States, which is markedly different from other common law jurisdictions as regards treaties, is rather similar to the prevailing principle in Great Britain and the Commonwealth, namely

> that customary rules are to be considered part of the law of the land and enforced as such, with the qualification that they are incorporated only so far as is not inconsistent with Acts of Parliament or prior judicial decisions of final authority.[33]

The traditional rule in Britain is that customary international law automatically forms part of English and Scots law; this is known as the doctrine of incorporation. Lord Chancellor Talbot said in *Barbuit*'s case in 1735 that 'the law of nations in its fullest extent is and forms part of the law of England'.[34] Strictly speaking, this statement is too wide, because it is not true of treaties; but, as far as customary international law is concerned, it was repeated and applied in a large number of cases between 1764 and 1861, and was reaffirmed by Lord Denning.[35]

However, it is possible to interpret some recent cases as discarding the doctrine of incorporation in favour of the doctrine of transformation, that is, the doctrine that rules of customary international law form part of English law only in so far as they have been accepted by English Acts of Parliament and judicial decisions.[36] In short, the theory of English law is in favour of the incorporation doctrine, but, since English courts look to English judgments as the main evidence of customary international law, practice approximates to the transformation theory. Quite apart from the problem of ascertaining the content of customary international law, there are a number of situations which constitute exceptions to the general rule, and in which English courts cannot apply customary international law. For example, if there is a conflict between customary international law and an Act of Parliament, the Act of Parliament prevails.[37] However, where possible, English courts will interpret Acts of Parliament so that they do not conflict with customary international law.[38] Moreover, if there is a conflict between customary international law and a binding judicial precedent laying down a rule of English law, the judicial precedent prevails.[39] But English courts are probably free to depart from earlier judicial precedents

33 I. Brownlie, *Principles of Public International Law*, 4th edn 1990, 43 with references.
34 25 ER 77. But see J.C. Collier, Is International Law Really Part of the Law of England?, *ICLQ* 38 (1989), 924–34.
35 *Trendtex Trading Corporation v. Central Bank of Nigeria*, [1977] QB 529, 553–4.
36 See Akehurst, 6th edn of this book, Chapter 4.
37 *Mortensen v. Peters* (1906), 8 F. (J.C.) 93. For an account of the background and sequel to this case, see H.W. Briggs, *The Law of Nations*, 2nd edn 1953, 52–7. The case is not absolutely conclusive, because the Court doubted the scope of the relevant rule of customary international law.
38 *Maxwell's Interpretation of Statutes*, 12th edn 1969, 183–6; *Halsbury's Laws of England*, 4th edn 1983, Vol. 44, para. 908.
39 *Chung Chi Cheung v. R.*, [1939] AC 160, 168; *Trendtex Trading Corporation v. Central Bank of Nigeria*, [1977] QB 529, 557.

40 *Trendtex Trading Corporation v. Central Bank of Nigeria*, [1977] QB 529, 554, 557, 576–9, rejecting the contrary view in *The Harmattan*, *WLR* 1 (1975), 1485, at 1493–5. For the relevance of the act of state doctrine and of Foreign Office certificates, see further Akehurst, 6th edn of this book, Chapter 4.
41 See Janis, *op. cit.*, 100; F.L. Kirgis, Federal Statutes, Executive Orders and 'Self-Executing Custom', *AJIL* 81 (1987), 37–75; H.G. Maier, The Authoritative Sources of Customary International Law in the United States, *Mich. JIL* 10 (1989), 450; J.J. Paust, Customary International Law: Its Nature, Sources and Status as Law of the United States, *Mich. JIL* 12 (1990), 59–91.
42 *Paquete Habana* case, 175 US 677, 686–711 (1900).
43 *Amerada Hess v. Argentine Republic*, 830 F. 2d 421 (2d Cir. 1987).
44 *Echeverria-Hernandez v. United States Immigration & Naturalization Serv.*, 923 F. 2d 688, 692–3 (9th Cir. 1991), vacated, 946 F. 2d 1481 (9th Cir. 1991).
45 See *Banco Nacional de Cuba v. Sabbatino*, 376 US 398, 425–6 (1964).
46 See Janis, *op. cit.*, 102.
47 Cassese, *op. cit.*, 383.
48 L. Wildhaber/S. Breitenmoser, The Relationship between Customary International Law and Municipal Law in Western European Countries, *ZaöRV* 48 (1988), 163–207, 204.
49 *Ibid.*, 206.

laying down a rule of international law if international law has changed in the meantime.[40]

The legal system in the United States shares the English common-law tradition in this respect and considers international law other than treaties as a part of the common law itself. But US courts do not clearly distinguish between the various sources of international law, and their reasoning has been properly described as a 'potpourri approach'.[41] It seems that they are more inclined to apply international customary rules in cases of disputes between individuals and states than in such between states themselves. Sufficient state practice to establish the existence of an international customary rule has been found, for example, to exempt coastal fishing vessels from seizure[42] and to protect neutral ships in international waters from attack in the Falklands war.[43] No such rule was found to require the United States to provide temporary asylum to all persons fleeing from foreign civil wars, because such state practice would only reflect 'understandable humanitarian concern'.[44]

Conflicts between 'international common law' and US domestic law are very much dealt with on the same level as conflicts between international treaties and national legislation. The US Supreme Court has the ultimate authority in this respect, both with regard to federal courts and state courts.[45] Whether 'international common law' in the United States has the same quality to override earlier municipal law, as in the case of treaties, is a matter of dispute.[46] At any rate, US courts, like other national courts, generally attempt to avoid an interpretation of a legislative act which would bring it into conflict with the law of nations. However, this is often a matter of national perception of what international law says.

With regard to Western European countries in the civil law tradition, there is some controversy on the evaluation of recent constitutional developments. In a survey presented in 1985, Cassese saw a tendency, not only in developing and socialist countries, but also in states such as France, Spain and the Netherlands, to downgrade customary international law.[47] This view has been questioned by a more recent investigation of Western European constitutions and state practice conducted by Wildhaber and Breitenmoser. Their examination of Germany, Italy, Austria, Greece, France, Portugal, Switzerland, Liechtenstein, the Netherlands, Belgium, and Spain concludes that

> both the written and nonwritten constitutional law of Western European countries recognize conventional and customary international law as 'part of the law of the land', and that the practice in states without an explicit provision concerning the relationship between international law and municipal law is no different from the practice in states with such a clause in their constitutions.[48]

The authors also show that most Western European countries give priority to customary international law over conflicting rules of statutory domestic law and that national courts tend to find harmonization between obligations of international law and internal law by way of interpretation under the principle of 'friendliness to international law'.[49] The main problem with this analysis, however, is that its basis appears to be restricted to the two central principles of *pacta sunt servanda* (treaties must be adhered to) and good faith (on the part of states in performing their international obligations). It is more likely that considerable diversity will emerge with regard to an analysis of what national courts consider customary international law or general principles in many other controversial areas.

The new states created in the process of decolonization generally mistrust customary international law developed by their former colonial masters and insist on the codification of new rules with their participation.[50] Therefore, it is not surprising that their constitutions rarely expressly recognize customary international law or general principles.

Similarly, the former socialist countries were not disposed to accept general rules of international law not developed by themselves in internal practice. The new Russian Constitution distinguishes between the effect of treaties and 'the generally recognized principles and norms of international law'. Treaty rules, without differentiating between 'self-executing' and 'non-self-executing' provisions, have a higher status than contrary domestic laws, disregarding whether the treaty is earlier or later; however, not above the federal Constitution itself.[51] The 'generally recognized principles and norms of international law' do not enjoy the same status, probably because they are not considered as specific enough. With regard to human rights, the Constitution recognizes that they are ensured 'according to the generally recognized principles and norms of international law'.[52] But the practical meaning of this and other similar provisions is, as yet, unclear.[53]

Conclusions

From what has been said above, it is clear that in many countries the law will sometimes fail to reflect the correct rule of international law. But this does not necessarily mean that these states will be breaking international law. Very often the divergence between national law and international law simply means that the respective state is unable to exercise rights which international law entitles (but does not require) that state to exercise. Even when a rule of municipal law is capable of resulting in a breach of international law, it is the application of the rule, and not its mere existence, which normally constitutes the breach of international law; consequently, if the enforcement of the rule is left to the executive, which enforces it in such a way that no breach of international law occurs, all is well. For instance, there is no need to pass an Act of Parliament in order to exempt foreign diplomats from customs duties;[54] the government can achieve the same result by simply instructing customs officers not to levy customs duties on the belongings of foreign diplomats.

Public international law and private international law

Laws are different in different countries. If a judge in state X is trying a case which has more connection with state Y than with state X, he is likely to feel that the case should have been tried in state Y, or (since some judges are reluctant to forgo the sense of self-importance which comes from trying cases) that he himself should try the case in accordance with the law of state Y. Feelings of this sort have produced a complicated set of rules in

50 See Chapter 2 above, 28–30.
51 Danilenko, *op. cit.*, 465.
52 Article 17, 1993 Russian Constitution.
53 See Danilenko, *op. cit.*, 467.
54 See Chapter 8 below, 126–7.

55 See U. Drobnig, Private International Law, *EPIL* 10 (1987), 330–5; L. Collins (ed.), *Dicey and Morris on the Conflict of Laws*, 12th edn 1993; E.F. Scoles/P. Hay, *Conflict of Laws*, 1992.
56 See Chapter 1 above, 1–2.
57 I. Strenger, La Notion de *lex mercatoria* en droit du commerce international, *RdC* 227 (1991-II), 207–355; T. E. Carbonneau, *Lex Mercatoria and Arbitration*, 1993.
58 But see P.D. Trooboff, The Growing Interaction between Private and Public International Law, *Hague YIL* 6 (1993), 107–14. See further A.F.M. Maniruzzaman, Conflict of Law Issues in International Arbitration, *AI* 9 (1993), 371–403; W. Meng, *Extraterritoriale Jurisdiktion im öffentlichen Wirtschaftsrecht*, 1994.
59 See K. Lipstein, Recognition and Execution of Foreign Judgments and Arbitral Awards, *EPIL* 9 (1986), 322–6, with reference to bilateral and multilateral treaties on the matter; for the situation in the United States see *Restatement (Third)*, Vol. 1, Chapter 8, 591 *et seq.*

almost every country, directing the courts when to exercise jurisdiction in cases involving a foreign element, when to apply foreign law in cases involving a foreign element, and when to recognize or enforce the judgments of foreign courts. These rules are known as private international law, or the conflict of laws.[55]

The type of international law to which this book is mainly devoted is often called public international law, in order to distinguish it from private international law; the expression 'international law', used without any qualification, almost always means public international law, not private international law. International law, as noted above,[56] primarily governs the relationships between states, whereas in the nineteenth century private international law was thought of as regulating transborder relationships between individuals, in the sense of the old 'law merchant' (or *lex mercatoria*),[57] the usages among traders. Similar names can mislead and the only true connection between public international law and private international law is the transborder element of the facts being regulated.

Although some authors have advocated the idea of 'transnational law' comprising both systems, in reality, there is no such thing. No legal order exists above the various national legal systems to deal with transborder interactions between individuals (as distinct from states). The problem is, therefore, which of the various domestic laws should apply. States have taken the attitude that cases involving a foreign element should not necessarily be governed by their own law, the *lex fori*, and have adopted special conflict rules which indicate the national law to be applied in such cases. For example, if a Spanish court has to decide on the validity of a contract concluded between a French company and an Italian merchant to be performed in Madrid, it would have to apply the rules of Spanish private international law to find the applicable law of contracts (French, Italian, Spanish, or other national law, depending on the circumstances on the case). These rules do not have an international nature and there are as many systems of private international law as there are states.

There appears to be little connection between public international law and the various municipal systems of private international law.[58] Private international law originated from a belief that in certain circumstances it would be appropriate to apply foreign law or to let a foreign court decide the case. The trouble is that each state has its own idea of what is appropriate. For instance, English courts are very ready to enforce foreign judgments; the courts in the Netherlands and several other countries seldom do so, unless there is a treaty to that effect.[59] The rules determining the jurisdiction of a state's own courts in civil cases involving a foreign element differ so much that it is impossible to discern any common pattern. Even the rules about the application of foreign law differ. For instance, before 1800 a man's 'personal law' (that is, the law governing legitimacy, capacity to marry and other questions of family law) was the law of his religion in Muslim countries, and the law of his domicile (permanent home) in Western countries; one reason for this difference was that there was greater religious tolerance in Muslim countries than in Christian countries. After 1800, in Napoleon's time, France went through an intensely nationalistic phase, and decided that French law should be the personal law of all

French nationals; after some hesitation, French courts inferred from this rule, by way of analogy, that *everyone's* personal law should be his national law, as distinct from the law of his domicile. The same thing happened in other continental countries at a slightly later date. England adhered to the old rule of domicile, but a series of nineteenth-century judicial decisions introduced a lot of artificiality and complexity into the rules about acquisition and loss of domicile. The consequence is extreme diversity between the rules of private international law in different countries, with resulting hardship; for instance, if a Spanish national domiciled in England gets an English divorce, it will be recognized in most English-speaking countries, but not in most continental countries. The significant thing, however, is that no country protested when France and other countries started abandoning the old rule of domicile; and it is submitted that the absence of protest constitutes a tacit admission that states are free to alter their rules of private international law at will.

Admittedly the differences between the rules of private international law in different countries must not be exaggerated; there *are* rules which are more or less the same in the vast majority of countries. An example is the rule concerning transfers of property; the validity of the transfer depends on the law in force at the place where the property was at the time of the alleged transfer (*lex situs* or *lex rei sitae*). But this similarity could be due to coincidence or to commercial convenience, rather than to any rules of public international law. Similarity between the laws in different countries does not necessarily reflect a rule of public international law; for instance, the law of contract is much the same in most English-speaking countries – simply because the original settlers in most English-speaking countries came from England.[60] In order to prove that public international law requires states to incorporate a particular rule in their municipal laws, it is not enough to show that rule does in fact exist in their municipal laws; it is also necessary to show an *opinio iuris*,[61] a conviction that public international law requires states to incorporate the rule in question in their municipal laws. This is what is lacking. When judges apply the *lex situs*, or any rule of private international law, they do not ask what the practice is in other countries, or attempt to bring their decisions into line with it; nor do they suggest that their actions are governed by any rule of public international law. When a state departs from a generally accepted rule of private international law, it is not denounced as a law-breaker by judges or diplomats in other countries. English judges sometimes say that their actions are dictated by 'comity'. This is an unusual word, and gives the impression of being a technical term; but it is unclear what, if anything, English judges mean when they use it. Its literal meaning is 'courtesy', and in this sense comity is regarded as something different from law of any sort; rules of comity are customs which are normally followed but which are not legally obligatory. At other times it is used as a synonym for private international law; as a synonym for public international law; or as a totally meaningless expression. It is a wonderful word to use when one wants to blur the distinction between public and private international law, or to avoid clarity of thought.[62]

It is therefore submitted that the rules of private international law do

60 J.N. Matson, The Common Law Abroad, *ICLQ* 42 (1993), 753 *et seq.*
61 See Chapter 3 above, 44–5.
62 On comity see Chapters 1, 2 and 3, 44 above.

63 See H. Kötz, Unification and Harmonization of Laws, *EPIL* 10 (1987), 513–18.

64 See A. Dyer, Hague Conventions on Private International Law, *EPIL* II (1995), 663–70; Dyer, Hague Conventions on Civil Procedure, *ibid.*, 658–63; T.M.C. Asser Instituut (ed.), *The Influence of the Hague Conference on Private International Law*, 1993; K. Lipstein, One Hundred Years of Hague Conferences on Private International Law, *ICLQ* 42 (1993), 553 *et seq.* On the status (signatures and ratifications) of Conventions adopted by the Hague Conference, see *ILM* 35 (1996), 526. Furthermore, for the work of UNCITRAL see G. Herrmann, United Nations Commission on International Trade Law, *EPIL* 5 (1983), 297–301.

not form part of public international law, or vice versa. However, it should be noted that states sometimes make treaties to unify their rules of private international law; and, when this happens, the content of private international law does come to be regulated by public international law.[63] The continuing work of the Hague Conference on Private International Law, founded in 1893, has been important in this connection.[64]

5   States and governments

States

Since international law is primarily concerned with the rights and duties of states, it is necessary to have a clear idea of what a state is, for the purposes of international law.[1] The answer to this question is less simple than one might suppose. However, it should be noted that in practice, disputes tend to focus on factual issues rather than on the relevant legal criteria.[2]

The 1933 Montevideo Convention on Rights and Duties of States provides in Article 1:

> The State as a person of international law should possess the following qualifications:
>
> (a) a permanent population;
> (b) a defined territory;
> (c) government; and
> (d) capacity to enter into relations with other States.[3]

The first three criteria (a)–(c) correspond to established international practice and to the so-called doctrine of the three elements ('Drei-Elementen-Lehre') formulated by the German writer Georg Jellinek at the end of the nineteenth century.[4] They will be considered first before discussing suggestions for additional criteria.

Defined territory

The control of territory is the essence of a state.[5] This is the basis of the central notion of 'territorial sovereignty', establishing the exclusive competence to take legal and factual measures within that territory and prohibiting foreign governments from exercising authority in the same area without consent. A leading case in this connection is the *Island of Palmas* case. The case concerned a dispute between the Netherlands and the United States on sovereignty over an island about halfway between the Philippines and the now Indonesian Nanusa Islands. The parties referred the issue to the Permanent Court of Arbitration in The Hague. Max Huber, the President of the Permanent Court of International Justice, was appointed as the sole arbitrator. In his award of 4 April 1928 Judge Huber noted on the concept of territorial sovereignty:

> Territorial sovereignty . . . involves the exclusive right to display the activities of a State. This right has as a corollary a duty: the obligation to protect within the territory the rights of other States, in particular their right to integrity and

1 *Harris CMIL*, 102–26; J. Crawford, The Criteria for Statehood in International Law, *BYIL* 48 (1976–7), 93–182; J.A. Andrews, The Concept of Statehood and the Acquisition of Territory in the Nineteenth Century, *LQR* 94 (1978), 408–27; Crawford, *The Creation of States in International Law*, 1979; 30–86; H. Mosler, Subjects of International Law, *EPIL* 7 (1984), 442–59; J.A. Barberis, *Los sujetos del derecho internacional actual*, 1984; K. Doehring, State, *EPIL* 10 (1987), 423–8; P.K. Menon, The Subjects of Modern International Law, *Hague YIL* 3 (1990), 30–86; N.L. Wallace-Bruce, *Claims to Statehood in International Law*, 1994; S. Magiera, Government, *EPIL* II (1995), 603–7. On state sovereignty see the literature in Chapter 2 above, 17–18.
2 I. Brownlie, *Principles of Public International law*, 4th edn 1990, 72. On the need for a simplified definition in international law to be able to conform to the principle of equality of states, see Doehring, *op. cit.*, 423–4.
3 165 LNTS 19.
4 G. Jellinek, *Allgemeine Staatslehre*, 3rd edn 1914, 396 *et seq.*
5 M.N. Shaw, Territory in International Law, *NYIL* 13 (1982), 61–91; S. Torres Bernardez, Territorial Sovereignty, *EPIL* 10 (1987), 487–94; C.K. Rozakis, Territorial Integrity and Political Independence, *ibid.*, 481–7. On the acquisition of territory see Chapter 10 below, 147–8.

6 *Island of Palmas* case, *RIAA* II 829, at 839 (1928). See See also P.C. Jessup, The Palmas Island Arbitration, *AJIL* 22 (1928), 735–52; R. Lagoni, Palmas Island Arbitration, *EPIL* 2 (1981), 223–4; *Harris CMIL*, 173–83. See also Chapters 7, 109–10 and 10, 148, 150, 156 below.

7 See Chapter 13 below, 206.

8 See Chapter 12 below, 178–80.

9 M. Bothe, Boundaries, *EPIL* I (1992), 443–9.

10 See the articles by E.J. de Aréchaga, T. Schweisfurth, I. Brownlie, W. Hummer, R. Khan, and H.D. Treviranus/R. Hilger in *EPIL* I (1992), 449 *et seq.*

11 Judgment of 20 February 1969, *ICJ Rep.* 1969, 3, at 33, para. 46. On the cases see Chapters 3, 44, 46 above and 12 below, 193, 196.

12 See P. Malanczuk, Israel: Status, Territory and Occupied Territories, *EPIL* II (1995), 1468–508; Malanczuk, Jerusalem, *EPIL* 12 (1990), 184–95. On the Arab–Israeli conflict see also Chapters 10, 153 and 22, 417, 422–3 and text below, 77.

13 Brownlie (1990), *op. cit.*, 73.

14 See *Restatement (Third)*, Vol. 1, para. 201, at 73.

15 See D. Orlow, Of Nations Small: The Small State in International Law, *Temple ICLJ* 9 (1995), 115–40; J. Crawford, Islands as Sovereign Nations, *ICLQ* 38 (1989), 277 *et seq.* On the membership of mini-states in the United Nations, see Chapter 21 below, 370.

16 See H.F. Köck, Holy See, *EPIL* II (1995), 866–9; K. Oellers-Frahm, Grenzen hoheitlichen Handelns zwischen der Republik Italien und dem Vatikan, *ZaöRV* 47 (1987), 489 *et seq.* For a recent international treaty concluded by the Holy See establishing diplomatic relations with a state see Holy See-Israel: Fundamental Agreement of 30 December 1993, *ILM* 33 (1994), 153–9.

inviolability in peace and war, together with the rights which each State may claim for its nationals in foreign territory. Without manifesting its territorial sovereignty in a manner corresponding to circumstances, the State cannot fulfill this duty. Territorial sovereignty cannot limit itself to its negative side, i.e. to excluding the activities of other States; for it serves to divide between the nations the space upon which human activities are employed, in order to assure them at all points the minimum of protection of which international law is the guardian .[6]

It is important to note that the concept of territory is defined by geographical areas separated by borderlines from other areas and united under a common legal system (e.g. Denmark and Greenland; France and Martinique, East and West Pakistan before the secession of Bangladesh in 1971). It includes the air space above the land (although there is no agreement on the precise upper limit)[7] and the earth beneath it, in theory, reaching to the centre of the globe. It also includes up to twelve miles of the territorial sea adjacent to the coast.[8]

Thus, the delimitation of state boundaries is of crucial importance.[9] But absolute certainty about a state's frontiers is not required; many states have long-standing frontier disputes with their neighbours.[10] In the *North Sea Continental Shelf* cases, the International Court of Justice held:

> The appurtenance of a given area, considered as an entity, in no way governs the precise determination of its boundaries, any more than uncertainty as to boundaries can affect territorial rights. There is for instance no rule that the land frontiers of a State must be fully delimited and defined, and often in various places and for long periods they are not .[11]

What matters is that a state consistently controls a sufficiently identifiable core of territory. Thus, Israel was soon clearly recognized as a state, in spite of the unsettled status of its borders in the Arab-Israeli conflict.[12]

Population

The criterion of a 'permanent population' is connected with that of territory and constitutes the physical basis for the existence of a state.[13] For this reason alone, Antarctica, for example, cannot be regarded as a state. On the other hand, the fact that large numbers of nomads are moving in and out of the country, as in the case of Somalia, is in itself no bar to statehood, as long as there is a significant number of permanent inhabitants.[14]

The size of the population, as well as the size of territory, may be very small. This raises the problem of so-called mini-states which have been admitted as equal members to the United Nations.[15] The Vatican City, the government of which is the Holy See, the administrative centre of the Catholic Church, is a special case. In spite of its small population, the Vatican (or the Holy See) entertains diplomatic relations with many other states, has concluded international agreements and joined international organizations (but it is not a UN member). Many state functions, however, are actually performed by Italy.[16]

Who belongs to the 'permanent population' of a state is determined by the internal law on nationality, which international law leaves to the discretion of states, except for a number of limited circumstances.[17] Many states have a multinational composition as regards population. Thus, it would be absurd to legally require any ethnic, linguistic, historical, cultural or religious homogeneity in the sense of the antiquated political concept of the nation-state.[18] Issues connected with such factors again arise under the topic of self-determination and the rights of minorities and indigenous peoples,[19] but are not relevant as criteria to determine the existence of a state. A state exercises territorial jurisdiction over its inhabitants and personal jurisdiction over its nationals when abroad.[20] The essential aspect, therefore, is the common national legal system which governs individuals and diverse groups in a state.

Effective control by a government

Effective control by a government over territory and population is the third core element which combines the other two into a state for the purposes of international law.[21] There are two aspects following from this control by a government, one internal, the other external. Internally, the existence of a government implies the capacity to establish and maintain a legal order in the sense of constitutional autonomy. Externally, it means the ability to act autonomously on the international level without being legally dependent on other states within the international legal order.

The mere existence of a government, however, in itself does not suffice, if it does not have effective control. In 1920, the International Committee of Jurists submitted its Report on the status of Finland and found that it had not become a sovereign state in the legal sense

> until a stable political organisation had been created, and until the public authorities had become strong enough to assert themselves throughout the territories of the State without the assistance of foreign troops. It would appear that it was in May 1918, that the civil war ended and that the foreign troops began to leave the country, so that from that time onwards it was possible to re-establish order and normal political and social life, little by little.[22]

Thus, the 'State of Palestine' declared in 1988 by Palestinian organizations was not a state, due to lack of effective control over the claimed territory.[23] However, the historic Israeli–Palestinian accord concluded on 14 September 1993 and the subsequent agreements may ultimately, if the peace process is sustained, result in some form of Palestinian statehood, although this issue is controversial between the parties and subject to further negotiations.[24]

The requirement of effective control over territory is not always strictly applied; a state does not cease to exist when it is temporarily deprived of an effective government as a result of civil war or similar upheavals. The long period of *de facto* partition of the Lebanon did not hinder its continued legal appearance as a state. Nor did the lack of a government in Somalia, which was described as a 'unique case' in the resolution of the Security Council authorizing the United Nations humanitarian intervention,[25] abolish the international legal personality of the country as such. Even when all of its territory is occupied by the enemy in wartime, the state continues

17 See Chapter 17 below, 263–6.

18 See Th. M. Franck, Clan and Superclan: Loyalty, Identity and Community in Law and Practice, *AJIL* 90 (1996), 359–83.

19 See Chapters 6, 105–8 and 19, 338–41 below.

20 See Chapter 7 below, 110–11.

21 See Magiera, *op. cit.*

22 LNOJ, Special Supp. No. 3 (1920), 3.

23 See J. Salmon, Declaration of the State of Palestine, *Palestine YIL* 5 (1989), 48–82; F. Boyle, The Creation of the State of Palestine, *EJIL* 1 (1990), 301–6; J. Crawford, The Creation of the State of Palestine: Too Much Too Soon?, *ibid.*, 307–13; Malanczuk (1995), *op. cit.*, at 1491–2.

24 For the documents see *ILM* 32 (1993), 1525 *et seq.*; *ILM* 34 (1995), 455 *et seq.*; see also E. Benevisti, The Israeli-Palestinian Declaration of Principles: A Framework for Future Settlement, *EJIL* 4 (1993), 542–54; R. Shihadeh, Can the Declaration of Principles Bring About a 'Just and Lasting Peace'?, *ibid.*, 555–63; A. Cassese, The Israel-PLO Agreement and Self-Determination, *ibid.*, 555–63; Y.Z. Blum, From Camp David to Oslo, *Israel LR* 28 (1994), 211 *et seq.*; F.A.M. Alting v. Geusau, Breaking Away Towards Peace in the Middle East, *LJIL* 8 (1995), 81–101; E. Cotran/C. Mallat (eds), *The Arab-Israeli Accords: Legal Perspectives*, 1996; P. Malanczuk, Some Basic Aspects of the Agreements Between Israel and the PLO from the Perspective of International Law, *EJIL* 7 1996, 485–500.

25 See Chapter 22 below, 402–5.

26 See Chapter 10 below, 151. See also M. Rotter, Government-in-Exile, *EPIL* II (1995), 607–11.

27 See Chapter 10, 151–2 and text below, 83–4.

28 C. Haverland, Secession, *EPIL* 10 (1987), 384.

29 See Crawford (1979), *op. cit.*, 103–6, 247–68 and Chapter 19 below, 326–41.

30 See Chapter 19 below, 319–22, 336–8.

31 P. Malanczuk, American Civil War, *EPIL* I (1992), 129–31.

32 See M. Weller, The International Response to the Dissolution of the Socialist Republic of Yugoslavia, *AJIL* 86 (1992), 569–607; P. Radan, Secessionist Self-Determination: The Cases of Slovenia and Croatia, *AJIA* 48 (1994), 183–95. See also Chapters 11, 167 and 22, 409–15 and text, 89–90 below.

33 On the theory of sovereignty, see Chapter 2 above, 17–18.

34 See Brownlie (1990), *op. cit.*, 73–4.

to exist, provided that its allies continue the struggle against the enemy, as in the case of the occupation of European states by Germany in the Second World War.[26] The allied occupation of Germany and Japan thereafter also did not terminate their statehood.[27]

The circumstance that the temporary ineffectiveness of a government does not immediately affect the legal existence of the state not only makes it clear that it is necessary to distinguish between states and governments, but also reflects the interest of the international system in stability and to avoid a premature change of the status quo, since the government may be able to restore its effectiveness. The other side of the same coin is that the requirement of government is strictly applied when part of the population of a state tries to break away to form a new state. There is no rule of international law which forbids secession from an existing state; nor is there any rule which forbids the mother state from crushing the secessionary movement, if it can. Whatever the outcome of the struggle, it will be accepted as legal in the eyes of international law.[28] These propositions (and some others in the present chapter) may need modification when one side is acting contrary to the principle of self-determination, but the principle of self-determination has a limited scope, and the propositions remain true in most cases.[29] But, so long as the mother state is still struggling to crush the secessionary movement, it cannot be said that the secessionary authorities are strong enough to maintain control over their territory with any certainty of permanence. Intervention by third states in support of the insurgents is prohibited.[30] Traditionally, therefore, states have refrained from recognizing secessionary movements as independent states until their victory has been assured; for instance, no country recognized the independence of the southern states during the American civil war (1861–5).[31] In recent years, however, states have used (or abused) recognition as a means of showing support for one side or the other in civil wars of a secessionary character; thus in 1968 a few states recognized Biafra as an independent state after the tide of war had begun to turn against Biafra; recognition was intended as a sign of sympathy. Particularly controversial in the context of the Yugoslavian conflict has been the drive for early recognition of Slovenia and Croatia, which Germany and Austria justified as being an attempt to contain the civil war, but which was seen by other states as premature action which actually stimulated it.[32]

The notion of effective government is interlinked with the idea of independence, often termed 'state sovereignty',[33] in the sense that such government only exists if it is free from direct orders from and control by other governments. Indeed, some authors require independence as an additional criterion for statehood.[34] In international law, however, the distinction between independent and dependent states is based on external appearances and not on the underlying political realities of the situation; as long as a state appears to perform the functions which independent states normally perform (sending and receiving ambassadors, signing treaties, making and replying to international claims and so on), international law treats the state as independent and does not investigate the possibility that the state may be acting under the direction of another state. An independent state becomes a dependent state only if it enters into a treaty or some other legal commitment whereby it agrees to act under the direction of another state or to assign the management of most of its international relations to another state. It may seem artificial to have described Afghanistan, for instance, as an independent state, at the time when everybody knew that Afghanistan was forced to follow Soviet policy on all important questions;[35] however, if international law tried to take all the political realities into account, it would be impossible to make a clear distinction between dependent and independent states, because all states, even the strongest, are subject to varying degrees of pressure and influence from other states. Therefore, although sometimes amounting to little more than a mere legal fiction, the vast majority of states are considered to be 'independent' in this sense.

Moreover, it is important to note that, in principle, international law is indifferent towards the nature of the internal political structure of states, be it based on Western conceptions of democracy and the rule of law, the supremacy of a Communist Party, Islamic perceptions of state and society, monarchies or republics, or other forms of authoritarian or non-authoritarian rule.[36] The rule is crude and only demands that a government must have established itself in fact. The legality or legitimacy of such an establishment are not decisive for the criteria of a state. Although the Holy Alliance in Europe after the Napoleonic Wars had sought a different solution,[37] revolutions and the overthrow of governments have become accepted in international law; the only relevant question is whether they are successful. The choice of a type of government belongs to the domestic affairs of states and this freedom is an essential pre-condition for the peaceful coexistence in a heterogeneous international society. Thus, international law also does not generally inquire into the question whether the population recognizes the legitimacy of the government in power. Nor is it concerned with the actual form of government, democratic in one sense or another or not so. Certain qualifications in this respect may arise from the recognition of the principle of self-determination of peoples,[38] but this is not pertinent to the question of whether or not a state exists.[39]

Capacity to enter into relations with other states

The last criterion (d) in the Montevideo Convention suggested by the Latin American doctrine finds support in the literature[40] but is not generally accepted as necessary. Guinea-Bissau, for example, was recognized in the 1970s by the United States and by Germany on the basis of only the first three elements. The *Restatement (Third)* of the American Law Institute, however, basically retains this criterion, although with certain qualifications:

> An entity is not a state unless it has competence, within its own constitutional system, to conduct international relations with other states, as well as the political, technical, and financial capabilities to do so.[41]

In fact, even the Montevideo Convention suggests a different perspective in Article 3:

> The political existence of the State is independent of recognition by the other

35 See I. Jahn-Koch, Conflicts, Afghanistan, in *Wolfrum UNLPP I*, 176–88. See Chapter 19 below, 322–3.
36 But on new theories on the requirements of democracy, see Chapter 2 above, 31.
37 See Chapter 2 above, 11–12.
38 See Chapter 19 below, 326–40.
39 On the UN sponsored intervention to restore an elected government in Haiti, see Chapter 22 below, 407–9.
40 See also Akehurst, 6th edn of this book, 53.
41 See *Restatement (Third)*, Vol. 1, para. 201, Comment e, at 73.

42 Article 3, Montevideo Convention.
43 See text below, 83–6.
44 See Chapter 2 above, 28.
45 G. Hoffmann, Protectorates, *EPIL* 10 (1987), 336–9.
46 See Chapter 19 below, 327–32.
47 See also M.N. Shaw, *International Law*, 3rd edn 1991, 138.
48 See text below, 82–90.
49 See Chapter 22 below, 393–5.

States. Even before recognition the State has the right to defend its integrity and independence, to provide for its conservation and prosperity, and consequently to organise itself as it sees fit, to legislate upon its interests, administer its services, and to define the jurisdiction and competence of its courts. The exercise of these rights has no other limitation than the exercise of the rights of other States according to international law.[42]

Although this statement is more directly relevant to the dispute on various theories of the legal effect of recognition,[43] it also implies that the existence of a state does not primarily rest on its relations to other states and its own foreign policy capacity.

There are several examples of dependent states, which have only a limited capacity to enter into international relations and are usually mentioned as a special category. For example, colonies in the process of becoming independent[44] often had a limited capacity to enter into international relations. In practice, the formal grant of independence was usually preceded by a period of training, during which the colonial power delegated certain international functions to the colony, in order to give the local leaders experience of international relations. Protectorates were another example.[45] The basic feature of a protectorate is that it retains control over most of its internal affairs, but agrees to let the protecting state exercise most of its international functions as its agent. However, the exact relationship depends on the terms of the instrument creating the relationship, and no general rules can be laid down. Protectorates were generally a by-product of the colonial period, and most of them have now become independent. Trusteeships and 'associated territories' that were placed under the control of the United Nations after the Second World War were also limited in their capacity to conduct foreign relations.[46]

Self-determination and recognition as additional criteria

Some authors refer to other additional factors that may be relevant as criteria for states, such as self-determination and recognition. These, however, are not generally regarded as constitutive elements for a state and it is agreed that what matters in essence is territorial effectiveness.[47]

For reasons which will be explained later,[48] the better view appears to be that recognition is usually no more than evidence that the three requirements listed above are satisfied. In most cases the facts will be so clear that recognition will not make any difference, but in borderline cases recognition can have an important effect. For instance, recognition of very small states such as Monaco and the Vatican City is important, because otherwise it might be doubted whether the territory and population of such states were large enough to make them states in the eyes of international law. Similar considerations apply in the case of secessionary struggles; outright victory for one side or the other will create a situation which international law cannot ignore, and no amount of recognition or non-recognition will alter the legal position; but in borderline cases such as Rhodesia (now Zimbabwe) between 1965 and 1979, where the mother state's efforts to reassert control are rather feeble, recognition or non-recognition by other states may have a decisive effect on the legal position.[49]

Federal states

Unions of states can take several forms, but one of the most important forms nowadays is the federal state (or federation), as exemplified, for example, by the constitutional systems of the United States, Canada, Australia, Switzerland and Germany.[50] There is no uniform model of federal states, many of which are 'federal' in name only, due to effective centralization, but the basic feature of a federal state is that authority over internal affairs is divided by the constitution between the federal authorities and the member states of the federation, while foreign affairs are normally handled solely by the federal authorities.[51]

International law is concerned only with states capable of carrying on international relations; consequently the federal state is regarded as a state for the purposes of international law, but the member states of the federation are not. If a member state of the federation acts in a manner which is incompatible with the international obligations of the federal state, it is the federal state which is regarded as responsible in international law. For instance, when a mob lynched some Italian nationals in New Orleans in 1891, the United States admitted liability and paid compensation to Italy, even though the prevention and punishment of the crime fell exclusively within the powers of the State of Louisiana, and not within the powers of the federal authorities.[52]

Although the normal practice is for foreign affairs to be handled solely by the federal authorities, there are a few federal constitutions which give member states of the federation a limited capacity to enter into international relations. For instance, in 1944 the constitution of the former USSR was amended so as to allow the Ukraine and Byelorussia (two member states of the USSR) to become members of the United Nations alongside the USSR; the purpose and effect of this device was to give the USSR three votes instead of one.[53] There has been no other comparable example of a member state of a federation exchanging diplomats on this level. The representation of the German Bundesländer on the European level in Brussels is of a different nature.[54] The constitution of the United States permits a constituent state to make compacts or agreements with foreign powers – with certain minor exceptions – only with the consent of Congress, but these are limited in scope and content. It does not allow the exchange of ambassadors (only commercial representatives) or to generally engage in relations with a foreign government.[55] In recent years the province of Quebec has signed treaties on cultural questions with France and other French-speaking countries, under powers reluctantly delegated by the federal authorities of Canada.[56] In Europe, however, there have been interesting developments of direct transfrontier cooperation between entities on the local and regional level.[57]

Governments

A state cannot exist for long, or at least cannot come into existence, unless it has a government. But the state must not be identified with its government; the state's international rights and obligations are not affected by a

50 For the international law aspects see W. Rudolf, Federal States, *EPIL* II (1995), 362–75; R. Dehousse, *Fédéralisme et Relations Internationales*, 1991.

51 For the situation in the United States see *Restatement (Third)*, Vol. 1, para. 202, Reporters' Notes, 76.

52 J.B. Moore, *A Digest of International Law*, 1906, Vol. 6, 837–41. On state responsibility see Chapter 17 below, 255–72.

53 See J.N. Hazard, Soviet Republics in International Law, *EPIL* 10 (1987), 418–23.

54 See P. Malanczuk, European Affairs and the 'Länder' (States) of the Federal Republic of Germany, *CMLR* 22 (1985), 237–72; D. Rauschning, The Authorities of the German Länder in Foreign Relations, *Hague YIL* 2 (1989), 131–9; A. Kleffner-Riedel, Die Mitwirkung der Länder und Regionen im EU-Ministerrat, *BayVBl.* 126 (1995), 104–8.

55 *Restatement (Third)*, Vol. 1, para. 201, Reporters' Notes, 76.

56 R. Lane/P. Malanczuk, Verfassungskrise und Probleme des Föderalismus in Kanada, *Der Staat* 20 (1981), 539–70; on recent secessionist tendencies see S. Dion, The Dynamic of Secessions: Scenarios After a Pro-Separatist Vote in a Quebec Referendum, *CJPS* 28 (1995), 533–51; Ch. F. Doran, Will Canada Unravel?, *FA* 75 (1996), 97–109.

57 U. Beyerlin, *Rechtsprobleme der lokalen grenzüberschreitenden Zusammenarbeit*, 1988; N. Levrat, *Le Droit applicable aux accords de coopération transfrontière entre collectivités publiques infra - étatiques*, 1994.

58 *RIAA* I 369, 375. See H. Bülck, Tinoco Concessions Arbitration, *EPIL* 2 (1981), 275–6. For further discussion of the *Tinoco* case, see text below, 84, 88.

59 On arbitration see Chapter 18 below, 293–8.

60 See *Harris CMIL*, 139–51; H. Lauterpacht, *Recognition in International Law*, 1947; I. Brownlie, Recognition in Theory and Practice, in R.St.J. Macdonald/D.M. Johnston (eds), *The Structure and Process of International Law*, 1983, 627–42; J.A. Frowein, Recognition, *EPIL* 10 (1987), 340–8; Frowein, Non-Recognition, ibid, 314–6; C. Warbrick, Recognition of States, *ICLQ* 41 (1992), 473–82; Part 2, *ICLQ* 42 (1993), 433–42; J. Verhoeven, La Reconnaisssance internationale: déclin ou renouveau?, *AFDI* 39 (1993), 7–40; P.K. Menon, *The Law of Recognition in International Law: Basic Principles*, 1994.

61 In other countries the legal effects of recognition are not the same as in Great Britain: D.P. O'Connell, *International Law*, 2nd edn 1970, 172–83. For the legal effects of recognition under English law, see Akehurst, 6th edn of this book, 67–9. See also F.A. Mann, The Judicial Recognition of an Unrecognised State, *ICLQ* 39 (1990), 348 *et seq.* and text below, 86–8.

62 On the relation between international law and national law see Chapter 4 above, 63–74.

63 See Chapter 10 below, 154–5.

64 E.H. Riedel, Recognition of Belligerency, *EPIL* 4 (1982), 167–71; Riedel, Recognition of Insurgency, *ibid.*, 171–3. See also Chapters 6, 104–5 and 19, 319–22, below.

65 See F.L.M. van de Craen, Palestine Liberation Organization, *EPIL* 12 (1990), 278–82 and Chapters 6, 104–5 and 19, 336–8 below.

66 See W. Meng, Recognition of Foreign and Legislative Acts, *EPIL* 10 (1987), 348–52; K. Lipstein, Recognition and Execution of Foreign Judgments and Arbitral Awards, *EPIL* 9 (1986), 322–6.

67 See *Restatement (Third)*, Vol. 1, para. 202, 84–5.

change of government. Thus the post-war governments of West Germany and Italy have paid compensation for the wrongs inflicted by the Nazi and Fascist regimes. The same principle is also illustrated by the *Tinoco* case.[58] Tinoco, the dictator of Costa Rica, acting in the name of Costa Rica, granted concessions to British companies and printed banknotes, some of which were held by British companies. After his retirement, Costa Rica declared that the concessions and banknotes were invalid. The United Kingdom protested on behalf of the British companies, and the two states referred the case to arbitration.[59] The arbitrator held that Tinoco had been the effective ruler of Costa Rica, and that his acts were therefore binding on subsequent governments; the fact that his regime was unconstitutional under Costa Rican law, and that it had not been recognized by several states, including the United Kingdom, was dismissed as irrelevant.

Recognition of states and governments in international law

Recognition is one of the most difficult topics in international law.[60] It is a confusing mixture of politics, international law and municipal law. The legal and political elements cannot be disentangled; when granting or withholding recognition, states are influenced more by political than by legal considerations, but their acts do have legal consequences. What is not always realized, however, is that the legal effects of recognition in international law are very different from the legal effects of recognition in municipal law.[61] Once this distinction is grasped, the whole topic of recognition should become easier to understand; apparent conflicts between two sets of cases will be easily resolved when it is realized that one set is concerned with international law and the other with national law.[62]

Another reason why recognition is a difficult subject is because it deals with a wide variety of factual situations; in addition to recognition of states and governments, there can also be recognition of territorial claims,[63] the recognition of belligerency or of insurgents,[64] the recognition of national liberation movements, such as the Palestine Liberation Organization,[65] or the recognition of foreign legislative and administrative acts.[66] In the present section of the book it is proposed, for purposes of simplicity, to concentrate on recognition of states and governments.

Today a clear distinction must be made between the recognition of a *state* and the recognition of a *government*. The recognition of a state acknowledges that the entity fulfils the criteria of statehood. The recognition of a government implies that the regime in question is in effective control of a state. The basic difference is that the recognition of a government necessarily has the consequence of accepting the statehood of the entity which the regime is governing, while the recognition of a state can be accorded without also accepting that a particular regime is the government of that state.[67]

Recognition of states

When a new state comes into existence, other states are confronted with the problem of deciding whether or not to recognize the new state.

Recognition means a willingness to deal with the new state as a member of the international community. The first example in history was the recognition in 1648 by Spain of the United Netherlands, which had declared their independence in 1581. Another well-known example is the dispute between France and Britain on the status of the United States when it declared its independence. At that time Britain took the view that title to territory could never be established by revolution or war without recognition by the former sovereign. It was the view of France, however, which was based on the doctrine of effectiveness, that became the accepted principle in the nineteenth century.[68]

Legal effects of recognition in international law

The question of the legal effects of recognition has given rise to a bitter theoretical quarrel. According to the constitutive theory, advanced in particular by Anzilottii and Kelsen, a state or government does not exist for the purposes of international law until it is recognized; recognition thus has a constitutive effect in the sense that it is a necessary condition for the 'constitution' (that is, establishment or creation) of the state or government concerned. Thus, an entity is not a state in international law until it has secured its general recognition as such by other states. The constitutive theory is opposed by the declaratory theory, according to which recognition has no legal effects; the existence of a state or government is a question of pure fact, and recognition is merely an acknowledgment of the facts. If an entity satisfies the requirements of a state objectively, it is a state with all international rights and duties and other states are obliged to treat it as such. An intermediate position was formulated by Lauterpacht who, on the basis of the constitutive theory, argued that other states had an obligation to recognize an entity meeting the criteria of a state.[69]

Historically, the constitutive theory has more to be said for it than one might suppose. During the nineteenth century, international law was often regarded as applying mainly between states with a European civilization; other countries were admitted to the 'club' only if they were 'elected' by the other 'members' – and the 'election' took the form of recognition. There were also occasions (for example, during the period of the Holy Alliance, immediately after 1815) when some states tended to treat revolutionary governments as outlaws, which were likewise excluded from the 'club' until they were recognized.[70]

Even today, recognition can sometimes have a constitutive effect, although state practice is not always consistent. If the establishment of a state or government is a breach of international law, the state or government is often regarded as having no legal existence until it is recognized. For instance, for many years the Western powers refused to recognize the existence of the German Democratic Republic (East Germany), mainly because they considered that its establishment by the Soviet Union was a breach of the Soviet Union's obligations under treaties made between the allies concerning the administration of Germany after the Second World War. The recognition of the German Democratic Republic by the Western powers in 1973 had a constitutive effect as far as the Western powers were

68 Frowein (1987), *op. cit.*, 341.
69 Lauterpacht, *op. cit.*, 47.
70 See Chapter 2 above, 11–12.

71 See G. Ress, Germany, Legal Status After the Second World War, *EPIL* II (1995), 567–81; T. Schweisfurth, Germany, Occupation After the Second World War, *ibid.*, 582–90; T. Eitel, Germany, Federal Republic of, Treaties with Socialist States (1970–4), *ibid.*, 561–7; G.v. Well, Germany and the United Nations, in *Wolfrum UNLPP I*, 558–65. On the reunification of Germany and the problems of state succession see Chapter 11 below, 167–8.
72 See text above, 78 and Chapter 19 below, 326–40.
73 *Tinoco* case, *op. cit.*
74 *Ibid.*, at 381.
75 See Frowein (1987), *op. cit.*, 342; *Restatement (Third)*, Vol. 1, para. 202, Comment b, at 77–8, noting, however, 'As a practical matter, however, an entity will fully enjoy the status and benefits of statehood only if a significant number of other states consider it to be a state and treat it as such, in bilateral relations or by admitting it to major international organizations.'
76 Article 3, see text above, 79–80.
77 On the OAS see Chapter 6 below, 95.
78 Frowein (1987), *op. cit.*, 343.

concerned; recognition cured the illegality of the German Democratic Republic's origins, and converted it from a legal nullity into a state.[71]

However, in most cases the establishment (even the violent establishment) of a new state or government is not a breach of international law; there is no general rule of international law which forbids a group of people from overthrowing the government of their state, or to break away and form a new state, if they have the strength to do so.[72] In such cases the existence of a state or government is simply a question of fact, and recognition and non-recognition usually have no legal effects. For instance, in the *Tinoco* case, Chief Justice Taft, the arbitrator, held that Tinoco's regime was the government of Costa Rica because it was clearly in effective control of Costa Rica, and the fact that it had not been recognized by several states, including the United Kingdom, made no difference. Nevertheless, Chief Justice Taft indicated that recognition or non-recognition would have assumed greater importance if the effectiveness of Tinoco's control over Costa Rica had been less clear, because 'recognition by other powers is an important evidential factor in establishing proof of the existence of a government'.[73] Similarly, recognition can play an evidentiary role when it is uncertain whether a body claiming to be a state fulfils the factual requirements of statehood. Where the facts are clear, as in the *Tinoco* case, the evidential value of recognition or non-recognition is not strong enough to affect the outcome; in such circumstances recognition is declaratory. But in borderline cases, where the facts are unclear, the evidential value of recognition can have a decisive effect; in such circumstances recognition is semi-constitutive.

On the other hand, recognition has little evidential value if the granting or withholding of recognition by other nations is not based on an assessment of the government's control over the country:

> when recognition *vel non* of a government is by such nations determined by inquiry, not into its . . . governmental control, but into its illegitimacy or irregularity of origin [as in the *Tinoco* case], their non-recognition loses something of evidential weight on the issue with which those applying the rules of international law are alone concerned.[74]

The prevailing view today is that recognition is declaratory and does not create a state.[75] This was already laid down in the Montevideo Convention of 1933 on the Rights and Duties of States[76] and has also been taken up in Article 12 of the Charter of the Organization of American States:

> The political existence of the State is independent of recognition by other States. Even before being recognized, the State has the right to defend its integrity and independence.[77]

It has been observed that the two theories are of little assistance in explaining recognition or determining the position of non-recognized entities in practice, and that the practical differences between them are not very significant.[78] Under the declaratory theory, it is still in fact left to other states to decide whether an entity satisfies the criteria of statehood. The declaratory theory leaves unresolved the difficulty of who ultimately determines whether an entity meets the objective test of statehood or not. Granting formal recognition to another state is a unilateral act which is in fact left to the political discretion of states, mostly to the executive branches which national courts generally tend to follow.[79]

The relevance of the constitutive theory, on the other hand, has been diminished by the acceptance of the obligation of other states to treat an entity with the elements of statehood as a state.[80] The main reasons in state practice for delays in recognition have been, in particular, the question whether the new state was viable, really independent from another state which had helped to create it, or established in violation of Article 2(4) of the UN Charter prohibiting the use of force.[81]

The viability of a new state is especially at issue in cases of secession leading to a longer period of civil war. Premature recognition in such cases may even constitute a violation of international law and of the rights of the mother country. Most states refused to recognize the secession of Biafra form Nigeria in 1967–70. On the other hand, in the decolonization process there were many examples of the recognition of a territory as a new state while the colonial power was still in military control of it (e.g. Algeria, Guinea-Bissau).[82] In the case of Rhodesia, where a white minority government declared independence without the consent of the colonial power and backing of the whole population, the United Nations Security Council called upon 'all states not to recognize this illegal act'.[83] This was a mandatory decision taken under Chapter VII of the Charter and binding upon all members of the UN under Article 25 of the Charter. The Smith regime remained unrecognized for a long period until the state of Zimbabwe was established and accepted under a majority government in 1979–80.

Examples of the perceived lack of independence of a new entity are the non-recognition by other states of the pre-war puppet-state of Manchukuo created by Japan, of Croatia established by Nazi Germany, the long delay of Western states in recognizing East Germany due to the influence of the USSR, and the refusal of the international community to recognize the South African homelands declared to be sovereign states by South Africa.[84] In the cases of the independence of Transkei, declared by South Africa,[85] and of the independent state in northern Cyprus in 1983 by Turkish Cypriot authorities,[86] the UN Security Council called for non-recognition, which was generally followed by the international community.

In most of the relatively few cases in which entities claiming statehood have allegedly come into existence by an illegal threat or use of force by another state, the dispute often cannot be resolved authoritatively. The secession of Bangladesh from Pakistan, supported by India's armed intervention, gave rise to different views on the legality of the intervention, but states nevertheless generally recognized or treated Bangladesh as a state, which was also admitted to the United Nations and the British Commonwealth.[87]

It should be emphasized that non-recognition as a state by other states does not imply that a *de facto* regime is entirely outside the realm of international law. Many rules are applicable in spite of non-recognition, such as the prohibition of the use of force.[88] Although the United States, which was in control of the unified command of the UN forces, refused to

79 *Restatement (Third)*, Vol. 1, para. 202, Reporters' Notes, 80.

80 But see, in view of recent developments, C. Simmler, Kehrt die Staatengemeinschaft zur Lehre von der konstitutiven Anerkennung zurück?, *Schr.-Reihe Dt. Gruppe AAA* 9 (1994), 75–102.

81 See Chapters 10, 154–5 and 19, 309–11 below.

82 *Restatement (Third)*, Vol. 1, 81.

83 SC Res. 216 and 217 of 12 and 20 November 1965. Frowein (1987), *op. cit.*, at 342, notes that the lack of self-determination by the whole population was seen as justifying non-recognition. See also Chapter 22 below, 393–5.

84 See Chapter 22 below, 394.

85 SC Res. 402 (1976). See E. Klein, South African Bantustan Policy, *EPIL* 10 (1987), 393–7.

86 SC Res. 541 (1983). See Chapter 22 below, 420–2.

87 See *Restatement (Third)*, Vol. 1, 81–2 with further references; and Chapter 19 below, 319–22.

88 Frowein (1987), *op. cit.*, 342 and 347.

89 See Chapter 22 below, 351–2.

90 *Restatement (Third)*, Vol. 1, 81. See J. Kokott, Pueblo Incident, *EPIL* 11 (1989), 268–71.

91 Frowein (1987), *op. cit.*, 343. See also Chapter 8 below, 123–4.

92 See *Harris CMIL*, 151–72.

93 See Akehurst, 6th edn of this book, Chapter 5. See also the Statement of Interest, dated 29 November 1995, of the US Department of State in *Meridien International Bank Ltd v. Government of Liberia* which declared that allowing the (second) Liberian National Transitional Government (LNTG II) access to American courts was consistent with US foreign policy, M. Nash (Leich), *AJIL* 90 (1996), 263–5.

94 See text above, 82, 84.

recognize North Korea as a state – as well as the governments of China and North Korea – this was no bar to signing an armistice agreement ending the Korean War in 1953.[89] The non-recognition of North Korea was also no obstacle in the later Pueblo incident to the contention raised by the United States that North Korea had violated international law by attacking a US ship.[90]

Recognition of another state does not lead to any obligation to establish full diplomatic relations or any other specific links with that state.[91] This remains a matter of political discretion. Nor does the termination of diplomatic relations automatically lead to de-recognition.

Legal effects in domestic law

If state A recognizes state B, this usually entails that the courts of state A will apply the law of state B and give effect to its sovereign acts.[92] In the case of non-recognition, national courts will not accept the right of the foreign state or government to sue or claim other rights of a governmental nature, but as regards private parties (for example, whether non-recognition extends to the registration of births, deaths and marriages in the foreign state), the situation varies to some extent, depending on the national framework.

Courts in Switzerland and Germany have always applied the effective law governing a foreign territory even if it was not recognized as a state. English and American courts originally had a tendency to completely disregard the law and sovereign acts of a foreign state, unless it was recognized by their governments. However, changes in the United States and Britain then went in the direction that courts could apply the law of a non-recognized entity if the executive confirmed that this was not harmful to the foreign policies behind the non-recognition.[93]

Recognition of governments

International law allows states to exercise great discretion when granting or withholding recognition, especially when a new government comes into power in an existing state by violent means. Recognition is accorded to the head of state, and so no problem of recognition arises when a revolution does not affect the head of state (for example, the military coup in Greece in April 1967, which overthrew the Prime Minister but not the King). Nor does any problem of recognition arise when there is a constitutional change in the head of state, for example, when a British monarch dies and is succeeded by the eldest son, or when a new President of the United States is elected. States have often used recognition as an instrument of policy; for instance, the United States has often regarded recognition as a mark of approval, and in President Wilson's time it withheld recognition from Latin American regimes which had come to power by unconstitutional means, such as Tinoco's regime in Costa Rica.[94]

A refusal to recognize is sometimes based on a belief that the new state or government is not in effective control of the territory which it claims, but a refusal to recognize can also be based on other factors; for instance, the United States at one time refused to recognize foreign governments simply because it disapproved of them; in the eyes of the United States, recognition was a mark of approval. The United Kingdom, on the other hand, usually recognized all governments which were in actual control of their territory, without necessarily implying any approval of such governments.

Because non-recognition of foreign governments has often been used as a mark of disapproval, recognition of a foreign government has sometimes been misinterpreted as implying approval, even in cases where no approval was intended. In order to avoid such misinterpretations, some states have adopted the policy of never recognizing governments (although they continue to grant or withhold recognition to foreign states). This policy originated in Mexico, where it is known as the Estrada Doctrine. In 1930, the Secretary of Foreign Relations of Mexico declared that: 'the Mexican Government is issuing no declarations in the sense of grants of recognition, since that nation considers that such course is an insulting practice.'[95]

This statement reflects the fact that the change of government in a state is legally an internal matter, whether in conformity with the national constitution or not, and does not concern international law or other states. The same policy has been applied in recent years by several other states, including France, Spain and the United States; in 1977 the Department of State Bulletin noted that

> in recent years US practice has been to deemphasize and avoid the use of recognition in cases of changes of governments and to concern ourselves [instead] with the question of whether we wish to have diplomatic relations with the new governments.[96]

In 1980 the British Foreign Secretary announced that the United Kingdom also would adopt this policy:

> we have decided that we shall no longer accord recognition to governments.
>
> The British government recognise states . . .
>
> Where an unconstitutional change of régime takes place in a recognised state, governments of other states must necessarily consider what dealings, if any, they should have with the new régime, and whether and to what extent it qualifies to be treated as the government of the state concerned. Many of our partners and allies take the position that they do not recognise governments and that therefore no question of recognition arises in such cases. By contrast, the policy of successive British governments has been that we should make and announce a decision formally 'recognising' the new government.
>
> This practice has sometimes been misunderstood, and, despite explanations to the contrary, our 'recognition' interpreted as implying approval. For example, in circumstances where there may be legitimate public concern about the violation of human rights by the new régime . . . it has not sufficed to say that an announcement of 'recognition' is simply a neutral formality.
>
> We have therefore concluded that there are practical advantages in following the policy of many other countries in not according recognition to governments. Like them, we shall continue to decide the nature of our dealings with régimes which come to power unconstitutionally in the light of our assessment of whether they are able . . . to exercise effective control of the territory of the state concerned, and seem likely to continue to do so.[97]

95 M. Whiteman, *Digest of International Law*, Vol. 2, 1963, at 85.
96 J.A. Boyd, *Digest of United States Practice of International Law*, 1977, 19.
97 *House of Lords Debates*, Vol. 408, cols 1121–2, announcement made on 28 April 1980.

98 The Foreign Secretary seems to have adopted this interpretation in his subsequent statement on 23 May 1980. For a discussion of British practice see Akehurst, 6th edn of this book, Chapter 5 and M. Aristodemou, Choice and Evasion in Judicial Recognition of Governments: Lessons from Somalia, *EJIL* 5 (1994), 532–55; S. Talmon, Recognition of Governments: An Analysis of the New British Policy and Practice, *BYIL* 63 (1992), 231–97, and the literature cited above. On the practice in New Zealand, for example, see S. Davidson, Recognition of Foreign Governments in New Zealand, *ICLQ* 40 (1991), 162 *et seq.*
99 Frowein (1987), *op. cit.*, 342. See also J.A. Frowein, De facto Régime, *EPIL* I (1992), 966–8.
100 Ch. Rousseau, *Droit international public*, 1977, Vol. 3, 555–7.
101 See also Chapters 10, 152 and 11, 165–6 below.
102 See Chapter 10 below, 155.
103 See text above, 82, 84, 86.

At first sight the Estrada Doctrine appears to abolish the entire system of recognition of governments. In practice, however, it probably merely substitutes implied recognition for express recognition; recognition is not announced expressly, but can be implied from the existence of diplomatic relations or other dealings with a foreign government.[98] In fact, implied recognition is a long accepted practice. However, recognition should only be deduced from acts which clearly show an intention to that effect. The establishment of full diplomatic relations is probably the only one unequivocal act from which full recognition can be inferred. All other forms of contact do not necessarily imply recognition.[99]

Most states which have adopted the Estrada Doctrine in the past have not applied it consistently; sooner or later they succumb to the temptation of announcing recognition of a foreign government, in order to demonstrate their support for it, or in the hope of obtaining its goodwill.[100]

De jure and *de facto* recognition

One of the most confused aspects of recognition is the distinction between *de jure* and *de facto* recognition. For a start, the expressions '*de jure* recognition' and '*de facto* recognition', although commonly used, are technically incorrect; '*de jure* recognition' really means recognition of a *de jure* government; the words *de jure* or *de facto* describe the government, not the act of recognition. The terminology implies that a *de facto* government does not have the same legal basis as a *de jure* government. But it is difficult to find any body of legal rules by which this legal basis can be determined.

The distinction between *de jure* and *de facto* recognition usually arises in the case of governments. It is sometimes said that a state can be recognized only *de jure*, but there are a few examples of states being recognized *de facto*; for instance, Indonesia was recognized *de facto* by several states while it was fighting for its independence against the Dutch in 1945–9. Similarly there are a few examples of territorial claims being given only *de facto* recognition; the United Kingdom, for example, granted only *de facto* recognition to the Soviet annexation of Estonia, Latvia and Lithuania in 1940.[101] *De facto* recognition of states and territorial claims is governed by roughly the same rules, and gives rise to roughly the same problems, as *de facto* recognition of governments. When recognition is granted by an express statement, it should probably always be treated as *de jure* recognition, unless the recognizing state announces that it is granting only *de facto* recognition. When recognition is not express, but implied, there will often be uncertainty as to the intentions of the recognizing state: did it intend to grant *de jure* recognition, or did it intend to grant *de facto* recognition?

Whatever the basis for the distinction between *de jure* and *de facto* recognition, the effects of the two types of recognition are much the same. However, if a state or government has been established (or a territorial change brought about) in violation of international law, it seems that only *de jure* recognition can cure the illegality; *de facto* recognition is insufficient to cure it.[102] If, like Chief Justice Taft in the *Tinoco* case,[103] one thinks of recognition as having an evidential value, then presumably *de jure* recognition would have greater evidential force than *de facto* recognition; but the difference is probably not very great.

In reality, the distinction between *de jure* and *de facto* recognition has always been a source of difficulty, and in practice in most cases of the recognition of states it will not be qualified in either of these terms.[104] In the case of the recognition of governments the distinction has also become obsolete.[105] The *Restatement (Third)* thus avoids these uncertain terms.[106]

A separate matter altogether that has become more important since 1945 is the impact of the United Nations and other international organizations on the recognition of states and governments.[107] The developments in Eastern Europe, the Soviet Union and in former Yugoslavia induced the European Community and its member states to adopt a common position on guidelines for the formal recognition of new states in these areas on 16 December 1991.[108] These guidelines start from reaffirming the principles of the Helsinki Act of 1975[109] and of the Charter of Paris of 1990,[110] 'in particular the principle of self-determination'.[111] The Community and its member states

> affirm their readiness to recognize, subject to the normal standards of international practice and the political realities in each case, those new states which, following the historic changes in the region, have constituted themselves on a democratic basis, have accepted the appropriate international obligations and have committed themselves in good faith to a peaceful process and to negotiations.

Specific requirements laid down in the European Community guidelines for recognition and the establishment of diplomatic relations are:

- respect for the provisions of the Charter of the United Nations and the commitments subscribed to in the Final Act of Helsinki and in the Charter of Paris, especially with regard to the rule of law, democracy and human rights;
- guarantees for the rights of ethnic and national groups and minorities in accordance with the commitments subscribed to in the framework of the CSCE;
- respect for the inviolability of all frontiers which can only be changed by peaceful means and by common agreement;
- acceptance of all relevant commitments with regard to disarmament and nuclear non-proliferation as well as to security and regional stability;
- commitment to settle by agreement, including where appropriate by recourse to arbitration, all questions concerning state succession and regional disputes.[112]

Recognition of 'entities which are the result of aggression' is expressly excluded and the 'effects of recognition on neighbouring states' are also to be taken into account. While non-recognition of 'entities which are the result of aggression' reflects the principle of not accepting the acquisition of territory by the use of force,[113] the meaning of the phrase that the European Union also intended to take into account the 'effects of recognition on neighbouring states' remains rather cryptic. At any rate, these guidelines, as applied by the Badinter Arbitration Commission, served to

104 Frowein (1987), *op. cit.*, 342.

105 *Ibid.*, 345.

106 *Restatement (Third)*, Vol. 1, 80.

107 See Frowein (1987), *op. cit.*, 343–4; 345–6; J. Dugard, *Recognition and the United Nations*, 1987; V. Gowlland-Debbas, Collective Responses to the Unilateral Declarations of Independence of Southern Rhodesia and Palestine: An Application of the Legitimizing Function of the United Nations, *BYIL* 61 (1990), 135 *et seq.* On membership in the UN, see Chapter 21 below, 363–73.

108 See European Community: Declaration on Yugoslavia and on the Guidelines on the Recognition of New States, *ILM* 31(1992), 1485–7; A. Pellet, The Opinions of the Badinter Arbitration Committee. A Second Breath for the Self-Determination of Peoples, *EJIL* 3 (1992), 178–85; L.S. Eastwood, Secession: State Practice and International Law after the Dissolution of the Soviet Union and Yugoslavia, *Duke JCIL* 3 (1993), 299–349, M.M. Kelly, The Rights of Newly Emerging Democratic States Prior to International Recognition and the Serbo-Croatian Conflict, *Temple ICLJ* 23 (1993), 63–88; R. Rich, Recognition of States: The Collapse of Yugoslavia and the Soviet Union, *EJIL* 4 (1993), 36–65; D. Türk, Recognition of States: A Comment, *ibid.*, 66–71; P. Hilpold, Die Anerkennung der Neustaaten auf dem Balkan, *AVR* 31 (1993), 387–408; Weller, *op. cit.*; Radan, *op. cit.*; S. Hille, Mutual Recognition of Croatia and Serbia (& Montenegro), *EJIL* 6 (1995), 598–610. See also text above, 78 and Chapters 11, 165–7 and 22, 409–15 below.

109 Text in *ILM* 14 (1975), 1292–1325. See M. Coccia/K. Oellers-Frahm, Helsinki Conference and Final Act on Security and Cooperation in Europe, *EPIL* II (1995), 693–705. See also Chapter 3 above, 54 and Chapter 6 below, 94.

110 Charter of Paris for a New Europe, *ILM* 30 (1991), 190–228.

111 Guidelines on the Recognition of New States, *op. cit.*, at 1487. On the principle of self-determination, see Chapter 19 below, 326–40.

112 *Ibid.*, at 1487.

113 See Chapter 10 below, 151–5.

114 The Advisory Opinion No. 6 of 11 January 1992 of the Arbitration (Badinter) Commission of the European Community (Carrington) Conference on Peace in Yugoslavia concerning the status of Macedonia is in *ILM* 31 (1992), 1507.
115 See D.M. Poulakides, Macedonia: Far More Than a Name to Greece, *Hastings ICLR* 18 (1995), 397–443.
116 UN Doc. GA 47/225.
117 *ILM* 34 (1995), 1461 (Introductory Note by P.C. Szasz).
118 ECJ Case No. C-120/94 R, Order of 29 June 1994.
119 *FAZ* of 18 April 1996, 1, 7. The text of the Agreement between Macedonia and the Federal Republic of Yugoslavia is in *ILM* 35 (1996), 1246. On the normalization of relations between Croatia and the Federal Republic of Yugoslavia see *ibid.*, 1219.
120 See Chapters 11, 167, 21, 372–3 and 22, 409–15 below.

determine the policy of European Union member states with regard to the recognition of the new states emerging from the break-up of former Yugoslavia. Without entering into the complicated details of the recognition process on this basis, it should only be noted that, as far as the Serbian-controlled Federal Republic of Yugoslavia was concerned, in 1995 the European Union made it one of the conditions for its recognition that all successor states to former Yugoslavia had recognized each other.

The case of the former Yugoslav Republic of Macedonia is instructive. Macedonia had held a referendum on independence on 8 September 1991 and confirmed this on 17 November 1991.[114] Greece was concerned about the name of the new state and the use of the Star of Vergina on the new republic's flag, because it feared possible claims to its own province of Macedonia.[115] The former Yugoslav Republic of Macedonia was admitted to the UN on 8 April 1993, however, leaving the dispute over the proper name of the country undecided.[116] Greece and the former Yugoslav Republic of Macedonia finally settled their dispute by an Interim Accord of 13 September 1995 and a Memorandum of 13 October 1995.[117] Greece subsequently lifted the embargo it had imposed upon Macedonia and the European Commission withdrew the case it had filed with the European Court of Justice on 22 April 1994 challenging the legality of the embargo under Community law.[118] On 8 April 1996, the Federal Republic of Yugoslavia and Macedonia accorded each other mutual recognition. The Federal Republic of Yugoslavia was subsequently recognized first by France, then by Britain and other EU member states, including by Germany on 17 April 1996.[119] The difficult problems of 'state succession' in the case of former Yugoslavia will be dealt with in a broader perspective in chapters below.[120]

6 International organizations, individuals, companies and groups

When lawyers say that an entity is a legal person, or that it is a subject of the law (these two terms are interchangeable),[1] they mean that it has a capacity to enter into legal relations and to have legal rights and duties. In modern systems of municipal law all individuals have legal personality, but in former times slaves had no legal personality; they were simply items of property.[2] Companies also have legal personality, but animals do not; although rules are made for the *benefit* of animals (for example, rules against cruelty to animals), these rules do not confer any *rights* on the animals.

In the nineteenth century states were the only legal persons in international law; international law regarded individuals in much the same way as municipal law regards animals. Writing in 1912, in his famous treatise on international law, L. Oppenheim still found: 'Since the law of nations is based on the common consent of individual States, and not of individual human beings, States solely and exclusively are subjects of international law.'[3] While states have remained the predominant actors in international law, the position has changed in the last century, and international organizations, individuals and companies have also acquired some degree of international legal personality; but when one tries to define the precise extent of the legal personality which they have acquired, one enters a very controversial area of the law.

The problem of including new actors in the international legal system is reflected in the very concept of legal personality, the central issues of which have been primarily related to the capacity to bring claims arising from the violation of international law, to conclude valid international agreements, and to enjoy privileges and immunities from national jurisdictions.[4] Thus, the International Court of Justice has noted that '[t]he subjects of law in any legal system are not necessarily identical in their nature or in the extent of their rights, and their nature depends upon the needs of the community'.[5] It is the international legal system which determines which are the subjects of international law and which kind of legal personality they enjoy on the international level.

Legal personality can be unlimited, in the sense that, in principle, *all* international rights and obligations can be accorded to a subject. This is so only in the case of states, the original, primary and universal subjects of international law. States have exclusive jurisdiction with respect to their

1 The *Restatement (Third)*, Vol. 1, part II, 70, dealing with 'persons in international law', however, rejects the term 'subjects' because it may have more limited implications meaning that such entities have only rights and duties, and not also, to varying extents, legal status and personality under international law. See further *Harris CMIL*, 126–38; H. Mosler, Subjects of International Law, *EPIL* 7 (1984), 442–59; J.A. Barberis, *Los sujetos del derecho internacional actual*, 1984; P.K. Menon, The Subjects of Modern International Law, *Hague YIL* 3 (1990), 30–86; I. Brownlie, *Principles of Public International Law*, 4th edn 1990, 58 *et seq.*; Conference on Changing Notions of Sovereignty and the Role of Private Actors in International Law, *AUJILP* 9 (1993-4), 1–213. See further the literature below.
2 See Chapter 2 above, 21 on the slave trade and its prohibition in the nineteenth century.
3 L. Oppenheim, *International Law. A Treatise*, 2nd edn 1912, Vol. I (Peace), 19.
4 Brownlie (1990), *op. cit.*, 58.
5 Reparations for Injuries Case, *ICJ Rep.* 1949, 178. See text below, 93–4.

6 See F. Morgenstern, Legality in International Organizations, *BYIL* 48 (1976–7), 241–58; E. Osieke, Ultra Vires Acts in International Organizations – The Experience of the International Labour Organization, *ibid.*, 259–80; and Chapters 18, 289, 292–3 and 22, 426 below.

7 H. G. Schermers, *International Institutional Law*, 3rd edn 1995; D.W. Bowett, *The Law of International Institutions*, 4th edn 1982; R.-J. Dupuy (ed.), *A Handbook on International Organizations*, 1988; C. Archer, *International Organizations*, 2nd edn 1992; I. Seidl-Hohenveldern/G. Loibl, *Das Recht der Internationalen Organisationen einschließlich der Supranationalen Gemeinschaften*, 5th edn 1992; W.J. Feld, *International Organizations: A Comparative Approach*, 3rd edn 1994; V. Rittberger, International Organizations, Theory of, in *Wolfrum UNLPP II*, 760–70; R.L. Bindschedler, International Organizations, General Aspects, *EPIL* II (1995), 1289–309; R. Wolfrum, International Administrative Unions, *ibid.*, 1041–7; H.G. Schermers, International Organizations, Membership, *ibid.*, 1320–4; L. Louis-Jacques/J.S. Korman, *Introduction to International Organizations*, 1996.

8 D. Bindschedler-Robert, Red Cross, *EPIL* 5 (1983), 248–54; A. Schlögel, Geneva Red Cross Conventions and Protocols, *EPIL* II (1995), 531–41; A. Schlögel, IRC, in *Wolfrum UNLPP II*, 814–9. See also Chapter 20 below, 344–5.

9 See text below, 96–100.

10 See Chapter 2 above, 22.

11 On the debate on the nature of these treaties see E. Suy, The Constitutional Character of Constituent Treaties of International Organizations and the Hierarchy of Norms, in *FS Bernhardt*, 267–77; T. Sato, *Evolving Constitutions of International Organizations*, 1996. On the UN Charter see Chapter 21 below, 364–7.

12 Article 104, UN Charter, text in *Brownlie BDIL*, 1. See I. Seidl-Hohenveldern, Article 104, in *Simma CUNAC*, 1125–36; R. Wolfrum, International Organizations, Headquarters, *EPIL* II (1995), 1309–12.; P.H.F. Bekker, *The Legal Position of Intergovernmental Organizations*, 1994; A.S. Muller, *International Organizations and their Host States – Aspects of their Legal Relationship*, 1995; H.-J. Schultz, Host State Agreements, in *Wolfrum UNLPP I*, 581–91. On the legal situation in the UK see G. Marston, The Origin of the Personality of International

territory and personal jurisdiction over their nationals. Other subjects of international law, such as international organizations created by states, have legal personality only with respect to *certain* international rights and obligations. The legal personality of international organizations is limited as to substance by the treaty which states have concluded to constitute them and to accord them rights and duties to achieve their specific tasks. It is also relative in the sense that it exists only with regard to the member states of the organization and with respect to non-member states acknowledging the organization. Such secondary subjects act *ultra vires*, meaning that their acts are legally void, if they operate beyond the authority given to them by the constitutive treaty.[6]

Individuals have acquired a certain status under international law with the development of human rights, but they cannot make treaties or create rules of customary international law. Other questions concern the status of multinational companies, insurgents and national liberation movements, ethnic minorities and indigenous peoples under international law, and these questions will also be addressed below.

International organizations

The term 'international organization' is usually used to describe an organization set up by agreement between two or more states.[7] It is different from the term 'non-governmental organization' (NGO), which is set up by individuals or groups of individuals (such as Amnesty International or Greenpeace), although some non-governmental organizations are entrusted with certain functions by states; the outstanding example is the International Committee of the Red Cross, which plays an important role in supervising the application of the Geneva Conventions to the laws of war.[8] The following deals with inter-governmental organizations created by states. NGOs will be discussed separately below.[9]

International organizations, in the sense of inter-state organizations, have existed since 1815, if not earlier,[10] but it is only since the First World War that they have acquired much political importance. The idea that they have international legal personality is even more recent.

Treaties setting up international organizations[11] often provide, as does Article 104 of the United Nations Charter, that 'the organization shall enjoy in the territory of each of its members such legal capacity as may be necessary for the exercise of its functions and the fulfilment of its purposes'.[12] All that this means is that the organization enjoys legal personality under the municipal laws of its member states; it can own property, enter into contracts, and so on. There is no corresponding article in the Charter expressly giving the United Nations personality under *international* law. Nevertheless, it is generally agreed that the United Nations does have at least some degree of international personality; for instance, Article 43 of the Charter empowers the United Nations to make certain types of treaties with member states[13] – a power which could not exist if the United Nations had no international personality.

When states create an international organization, they set it up for specific purposes and give it limited powers. For this reason, legal personality must be treated as a relative concept, not as an absolute concept. It is futile to ask whether an international organization has legal personality in the abstract; instead, one should ask, 'What specific rights, duties and powers is it capable of exercising?' An organization may have a power to make treaties concerning one topic, for instance, but not about others.[14] Similarly, powers may vary from organization to organization. The United Nations can take military action (in certain circumstances),[15] but the World Health Organization (WHO) cannot.

The leading judicial authority on the personality of international organizations is the advisory opinion given by the International Court of Justice in the *Reparation for Injuries* case. The case arose out of the murder of Count Bernadotte, the United Nations mediator[16] in Palestine, in 1948. The United Nations considered that Israel had been negligent in failing to prevent or punish the murderers, and wished to make a claim for compensation under international law. There was uncertainty over the preliminary problem of whether the United Nations had the legal capacity to make such a claim, and so the following question was put to the Court:

In the event of an agent of the United Nations in the performance of his duties suffering injury in circumstances involving the responsibility of a State, has the United Nations, as an organization, the capacity to bring an international claim against the responsible *de jure* or *de facto* government with a view to obtaining the reparation due in respect of the damage caused (a) to the United Nations, (b) to the victim?

The Court answered both parts of the question in the affirmative.[17] The Court began by saying that the United Nations organization had international personality in principle; its functions were so important that the organization could not carry them out unless it had some degree of international personality. The Court then went on to advise that the organization's personality included the capacity to bring the type of claim mentioned in the request to the Court. It decided without much argument that the organization could claim for the loss suffered by the organization itself as a result of the breach of an international obligation owed to it. The capacity to claim for the loss suffered by the organization's agents raised a more difficult problem, but the Court nevertheless advised that the organization had an *implied* power to make such a claim, because the organization could not work effectively without the help of loyal and efficient agents, who would not serve it loyally and efficiently unless they were sure of its protection. (The Court dealt with the abstract question of the capacity to claim, not with the facts of the *Bernadotte* case. Although the UN has capacity to make a claim, it cannot enforce that claim through the ICJ, since Article 34 of the Statute of the ICJ provides that only states may be parties in contentious cases before the Court[18]. In the end the *Bernadotte* case was settled by negotiation; Israel agreed to pay compensation, while denying that it was under an obligation to do so.)

The Court's reasoning is of the utmost importance for the law of international organizations generally, because it shows that the powers of international organizations need not necessarily be conferred expressly

Organisations in United Kingdom Law, *ICLQ* 40 (1991), 366; I. Cheyne, Status of International Organisations in English Law, *ibid.*, 981.
13 See Chapter 22 below, 389.
14 K. Zemanek, International Organizations, Treaty-Making Power, *EPIL* II (1995), 1343–6.
15 See Chapter 22 below, 387–90.
16 On mediation as a method of dispute settlement see Chapter 18 below, 275–7.
17 *ICJ Rep.* 1949, 174. See E. Klein, Reparations for Injuries Suffered in Service of UN (Advisory Opinion), *EPIL* 2 (1981), 242–4.
18 On the difference between contentious and advisory proceedings see Chapter 18 below, 281–90.

19 M. Zuleeg, International Organizations, Implied Powers, *EPIL* II (1995), 1312–14. See also Chapter 21 below, 367–8.

20 See Chapter 8 below.

21 K. Ginther, International Organizations, Responsibility, *EPIL* II (1995), 1336–40. On state responsibility see Chapter 17 below, 254–72.

22 See M. Herdegen, The Insolvency of International Organizations and the Legal Position of Creditors: Some Observations in the Light of the International Tin Council Crisis, *NILR* 35 (1988), 135–44; H.G. Schermers, Liability of International Organizations, *LJIL* 1 (1988), 3–14; I. Seidl-Hohenveldern, Piercing the Corporate Veil of International Organizations: The International Tin Council Case in the English Court of Appeals, *GYIL* 32 (1989), 43–54; I.A. Mallory, Conduct Unbecoming: The Collapse of the International Tin Agreement, *AUJILP* 5 (1990), 835–92; C.F. Amerasinghe, Liability to Third Parties of Member States of International Organizations: Practice, Principle and Judicial Precedent, *AJIL* 85 (1991), 259–80; M. Hirsch, *The Responsibility of International Organizations Toward Third Parties. Some Basic Principles*, 1995.

23 H.J. Hahn, International Organizations, Succession, *EPIL* II (1995), 1340–3; O.M. Ribbelink, *Opvolging van internationale organisaties van Volkenbond – Vereinigde Naties tot ALALC – ALADI*, 1988; P. Myers, *Succession Between International Organizations*, 1993. On state succession see Chapter 11 below, 161–72.

24 See Chapter 21 below, 364–84.

25 See Chapter 21 below, 382–4.

26 On the various organizations see *EPIL* and Wolfrum *UNLPP* and the literature cited above, 92.

27 See Chapter 15 below, 224–33.

28 See Chapter 13 below, 202–3.

29 See Chapter 22 below, 388.

30 P.v. Dijk, Regional Cooperation and Organization: Western Europe, *EPIL* 6 (1983), 330–6; F.V. García-Amador, American States, *ibid.*, 308–14; E.G. Bello, African States, *ibid.*, 301–8; R. Khan, Asian States, *ibid.*, 314–9; I.A. Shearer, Pacific Region, *ibid.*, 319–24.

31 See text below, 96.

32 A.H. Robertson, Council of Europe, *EPIL* I (1992), 843–50. See also J.-F. Flauss, Les Conditions d'admission des pays d'Europe centrale et orientale au sein du Conseil de l'Europe, *EJIL* 5 (1994), 401–22; R. Bernhardt *et al.*,

in the organization's constituent treaty; an organization also has such implied powers as are necessary for the most efficient performance of its functions.[19] Other aspects related to the legal personality of international organizations are that they can also enjoy privileges and immunities,[20] may engage international responsibility and liability[21] (which can be rather complicated, as was seen in the collapse of the commodity agreement governed by the International Tin Council in 1985 and the controversy on the liability of the member states[22]), pose problems of succession (when an international organization is replaced by a new one),[23] and that their relations to states require legal definition in many other aspects.

There are now some 500 international organizations of very different types. This proliferation reflects the need for increasing cooperation between states to solve problems of a transnational nature. They can be classified under various criteria – for example, according to whether their membership is global or regional or according to their functions and tasks.

The United Nations is the most important global organization, with almost universal membership of states, and will be treated separately in Chapter 21 below.[24] The UN hosts a large number of so-called Specialized Agencies[25] within the UN family, such as the International Labour Organization (ILO), the International Civil Aviation Organization (ICAO), the United Nations Educational, Scientific and Cultural Organization (UNESCO), the World Health Organization (WHO), the Universal Postal Union (UPU), the International Telecommunication Union (ITU), the International Maritime Organization (IMO), the World Intellectual Property Organization (WIPO), the International Atomic Energy Agency (IAEA), or the World Meteorological Organization (WMO) and other organizations,[26] as provided for in Article 57 of the UN Charter. In addition, there are a number of international economic and financial organizations, which will be dealt with in Chapter 15 below.[27] To take a rather different field, another group of international organizations, for example, is concerned with the exploration and use of outer space.[28]

Moreover, there are political regional organizations, some of which are supposed to interact with the United Nations in one way or another, as envisaged in Article 52 of the Charter.[29] There are now many forms of institutionalized regional cooperation and organization in Europe, the Americas, Asia, Africa, and the Pacific.[30] The various forms of regional organization in Europe include the European Union[31] and the Council of Europe, which had thirty-nine member states in 1996, following the admission of countries from Eastern Europe, and under the auspices of which, *inter alia*, the regional system of the protection of human rights under the European Human Rights Convention has developed.[32] Furthermore the Organization for Cooperation and Security in Europe (OCSE), including the United States and Canada, emerged recently as a new organization from the Helsinki Process that had been established in 1975.[33] Under the hegemony of the Soviet Union, the former bloc of socialist states had its own forms of regional organization and cooperation.[34] Following the demise of the USSR, in 1991 the Commonwealth of Independent States (CIS) was formed by Russia, Belarus and Ukraine on the basis of the Minsk Agreement, the preamble of which stated that the

Soviet Union 'as a subject of international law and geopolitical reality no longer exists'.[35] The CIS then expanded to eleven members (excluding Georgia and the Baltic states).[36] In 1993 seven CIS states signed the CIS Charter which was later ratified by five other states (now in force for all former USSR republics, excluding the Baltic states).[37] In April 1996, Russia, Belarus, Kazakhstan and Kyrgyzstan signed a document proclaiming their intention to create a 'Commonwealth of Integrated States' and Russia and Belarus signed a treaty establishing a 'Commonwealth of Sovereign Republics'.[38]

The main forms of political regional organization in other parts of the world include the Organization of American States (OAS), the Organization of Central American States (ODECA), the Organization of African Unity (OAU), the Association of South East Asian Nations (ASEAN) and the Arab League. Islamic countries have also established their own organization with the Islamic Conference in 1973 and in the Persian (or Arabian) Gulf, Arab oil-producing states have sought to create a counterweight to the Islamic Republic of Iran in the Gulf Cooperation Council, after the war between Iraq and Iran. The Commonwealth, which is the present name of what was formerly the British Empire, is a unique case with many forms of functional cooperation, such as the Commonwealth Fund for Technical Cooperation, without an organizational or constitutional framework, apart from the existence of the Commonwealth Secretariat, which has no executive functions.[39]

These political regional organizations are (or have been) often interacting to various degrees with defence alliances, such as NATO, the dissolved Warsaw Pact, the still largely defunct Western European Union (WEU), and the now obsolete CENTO Pact. They have been to a large extent children of the Cold War and have now lost much of their previous military significance to organizations aimed at dealing with the economic aspects of the relations between states. NATO is currently in a process of restructuring itself with the prospect of including certain Eastern European states (against opposition from Russia) which is interconnected with the question of their admission as new member states of the European Union.[40]

Most international organizations are of the traditional type, meaning that they are in essence based on inter-governmental cooperation of states which retain control of the decision-making and finance of the organization.[41] To distinguish a new type of independent international organization created on a higher level of integration of member states, the term 'supranational organization'[42] has been coined. While there are different views on the criteria for distinguishing supranational organizations from traditional forms of international institutions, it may be said that the transfer of sovereignty from the member states to the international level is more extensive as to the scope and nature of delegated powers and is characterized by the cumulative presence of the following elements:

1   the organs of the organization are composed of persons who are not government representatives;
2   the organs can take decisions by majority vote;[43]
3   they have the authority to adopt binding acts;

Report on the Conformity of the Legal Order of the Russian Federation with Council of Europe Standards, *HBLJ* 15 (1994), 249–300; Russia Joins the Council of Europe, *ILM* 35 (1996), 808. On the European Human Rights Convention see Chapter 14 below, 217–19.

33 See A. Bloed (ed.), *The Conference on Security and Cooperation in Europe: Analysis and Basic Documents, 1972–1993*, 2nd edn 1993; D. McGoldrick, The Development of the CSCE after the 1992 Conference, *ICLQ* 42 (1993), 411 et seq.; A. Bloed (ed.), *The Challenges of Change: The Helsinki Summit of the CSCE and its Aftermath*, 1994; J. Borawski, The Budapest Summit Meeting, *HM* 6/1 (1995), 5–17; W. Höynck, From the CSCE to the OSCE. The Challenges of Building New Stability, *HM* 6/3, (1995), 11–22; M. Oswald, Potentialities for the CSCE in the Changing International System, *AJPIL* 49 (1995), 361–78. See also Chapter 3 above, 54.

34 B. Meissner, Regional Cooperation and Organization: Socialist States, *EPIL* 6 (1983), 324–30.

35 *ILM* 31 (1992), 138.

36 Alma-Ata Declaration and Protocol, *ILM* 31 (1992), 147. See M.R. Lucas, Russia and the Commonwealth of Independent States: The Role of the CSCE, *HM* 5/4 (1994), 5–3; .S.A. Voitovich, The Commonwealth of Independent States: An Emerging Institutional Model, *EJIL* 3 (1993), 403–17.

37 Commonwealth of Independent States Charter, *ILM* 34 (1995), 1279. See also the Council of Heads of States Decisions on Settlement of Conflicts, Peacekeeping Forces and Military Training of 19 January 1996, *ILM* 35 (1996), 783.

38 *FAZ* of 3 April 1996, 1, 3. The Treaty on the Formation of the Community of Belarus and Russia is reprinted in *ILM* 35 (1996), 1190.

39 For more information and references on these organizations see *EPIL* and the literature above, 92. On the British Commonwealth see also Chapter 2 above, 23.

40 See L.S. Kaplan, *NATO and the United States: The Enduring Alliance*, 1994; W. Goldstein (ed.), *Security in Europe: Role of NATO after the Cold War*, 1994; P. Williams, *North Atlantic Treaty Organization*, 1994. M. Rühle/N. Williams, NATO Enlargement and the European Union, *The World Today* 51 (1995), 84–8. See also A. Bloed (ed.), *The Changing Functions of the Western European Union (WEU)*, 1994.

41 R. Wolfrum, International Organizations, Financing and Budgeting, *EPIL* II (1995), 1284–9.

42 F. Capotorti, Supranational Organizations, *EPIL* 5 (1983), 262–9.

43 See H.G. Schermers, Voting Rules in International Conferences and Organizations, *EPIL* 5 (1983), 395–8; K. Zemanek, Majority Rule and Consensus Technique in Law-Making Diplomacy, in R.St.J. Macdonald/D.M. Johnston (eds), *The Structure and Process of International Law*, 1983, 875–88.

44 H.G. Schermers, International Organizations, Legal Remedies against Acts of Organs, *EPIL* II (1995), 1318–20.

45 Text of the Treaty on European Union and Final Act in *ILM* 31 (1992), 247; it entered into force on 1 November 1993, *ILM* 32 (1993), 1693. See R.B. Lake (ed.), *European Union Law After Maastricht*, 1996; J.A. Winter et al. (eds), *Reforming the Treaty on European Union*, 1996. For further literature see Chapter 1 above, 8.

46 See L. Hancher, Constitutionalism, the Community Court and International Law, *NYIL* 25 (1994), 259–98; B. de Witte, Rules of Change in International Law: How Special is the European Community?, *ibid.*, 299–336.

47 G. Guillaume, *The Future of International Organizations*, 1995.

48 See Chapter 3 above, 52–5.

49 See J.S. Ignarski, Amnesty International, *EPIL* I (1992), 151–3; P.R. Baehr, Amnesty International and Its Self-Imposed Limited Mandate, *NQHR* 12 (1994), 5 *et seq.*

50 H. H.-K. Rechenberg, Non-Governmental Organizations, *EPIL* 9 (1986), 276–82; Y. Beigbeder, *Le Rôle international des organisations non gouvernementales*, 1992; C. Ritchie, The Relation Between the State and NGOs, *TA* 46 (1994), 210; K. Hüfner, Non-Governmental Organizations, in *Wolfrum UNLPP* II, 927–35; L. Gordenker/T. Weiss (eds), *NGOs, the UN, and Global Governance*, 1996; P. Willetts (ed.), '*The Conscience of the World'. The Influence of Non-Governmental Organizations in the UN System*, 1996.

4   some of which have direct legal effect on individuals and companies;

5   the constituent treaty of the organization and the measures adopted by its organs form a new legal order; and

6   compliance of member states with their obligations and the validity of acts adopted by the organs of the organization are subject to judicial review by an independent court of justice.[44]

The only existing international organization which currently meets all of these criteria in a sufficient degree is the European Community, or in other words, since the Treaty of Maastricht, the European Union (the terminology has become rather confusing since Maastricht; the term 'European Community' is now limited to the previous European Economic Community and its treaty).[45] Community organs, especially those of the European Community, have extensive (and ever-increasing) powers of regulation *vis-à-vis* the member states and individuals and companies. The agreements establishing the European Communities and the 'secondary' law created by Community organs on the basis of these treaties form an independent legal order which can no longer be adequately grouped with categories of general international law. European Community law claims absolute priority over any conflicting national law of the member states. All other international organizations are more or less based upon inter-governmental cooperation where states have retained their control over the organization and have not submitted to the decisions of independent organs. In fact the criteria for a 'supranational organization' have been taken from the example of the European Community, which is often described as an entity *sui generis* in the contemporary pattern of the international organization of states.[46]

The broad spectrum of international organizations has led to duplication in many areas, especially in the social and economic fields, raising problems of coordination, costs and efficiency. However, there is no doubt that the future development of the international legal system will not only rest on the activities of states, but also increasingly on the international organizations they have created themselves to overcome the limits of the capacity of national governments to deal effectively with transnational problems.[47] One element of this process is that administrations and bureaucracies, also international ones, once established, tend to develop interests as well as a life and dynamic of their own. The important role of international organizations in international law-making has been discussed above in Chapter 3.[48]

Non-governmental organizations (NGOs)

Private international organizations, such as Amnesty International,[49] Greenpeace or Médecins Sans Frontières (MSF), are very much in the news these days because of their active role in international affairs. They belong to the category of so-called non-governmental organizations (NGOs) because they are not established by a government or by an agreement between states and their members are private citizens or bodies corporate.[50] International NGOs have proliferated considerably in the past decades and are engaged in a broad variety of different areas, ranging from politics, the legal and judicial field, the social and economic domain, human rights and humanitarian relief, education, women, to the environment and sports. In the field of international business, important NGOs, incorporated under the law of a particular state, include the International Chamber of Commerce in Paris (ICC), the International Air Transport Association (IATA), and the international federations of trade unions and employers. Multinational companies can also be classified as non-governmental international organizations under certain aspects, but because they are primarily profit-orientated and due to their considerable impact on the international economy, they form a different species altogether and will therefore be dealt with separately below.[51]

The role of NGOs in the international legal system is primarily an informal one. They have some effect on international law-making in certain areas by adding additional expertise and making procedures more transparent, and a stronger effect with regard to supervision and fact-finding as to the implementation of international norms, most visibly in the area of human rights.[52] For instance, at the United Nations Conference on Environment and Development (UNCED), held in Rio de Janeiro in 1992, which was attended by 170 countries and 103 heads of government, some 2,000 NGOs were engaged in lobbying on the side-lines and at a so-called Global Forum, a shadow conference, they negotiated among themselves more than thirty 'treaties' to impress governments. Their 'partnership role' was recognized in Agenda 21[53] and NGOs were later given enhanced standing in the work of the new UN Commission on Sustainable Development. However, the criteria for making the inevitable choice of which of the numerous NGOs should be selected to participate in the activities of the Commission are far from clear.

From a formal point of view, on the global level there are no international legal standards governing the establishment and status of NGOs. The relevant law is that of the state where an NGO is based and this may cause problems in the case of international activities because national laws are different. Inter-governmental organizations may agree to grant NGOs a certain consultative or observer status[54] (such as the exceptional case of the observer status granted by the UN General Assembly to the International Committee of the Red Cross in 1991) and thereby a limited international status, but this does not make them a subject of international law. In accordance with Article 71 of the UN Charter, the UN Economic and Social Council (ECOSOC) has adopted a number of resolutions concerning arrangements for consulting with NGOs. The enhanced recognition of their role in international affairs can be detected from the fact that in 1994 about 1,000 NGOs had consultative status with the Council, as compared with only forty-one in 1948.[55]

Since the beginning of this century, efforts have been made by bodies such as the Institute of International Law (itself being an NGO)[56] to improve the international legal standing of NGOs, but such efforts have remained fruitless in view of the doctrine of sovereignty. On the regional level, however, within the framework of the Council of Europe a common status for NGOs has been recently laid down in the European Convention

51 See text below, 100–4.

52 H. Thoolen/B. Verstappen, *Human Rights Missions: A Study of the Fact-Finding Practice of Non-Governmental Organizations*, 1986; T.v. Boven, The Role of Non-Governmental Organizations in International Human Rights Standard-Setting: A Prerequisite of Democracy, *CWILJ* 20 (1989), 207–25; P.H. Kooijmans, The Non-Governmental Organizations and the Monitoring Activities of the United Nations in the Field of Human Rights, in *The Role of Non-Governmental Organizations in the Protection of Human Rights, Symposium International Commission of Jurists*, 1990, 15–22; H.J. Steiner, *Diverse Partners: Non-Governmental Organizations in the Human Rights Movement*, 1991; C.E. Welch, *Protecting Human Rights in Africa – Strategies and Roles of Non-Governmental Organizations*, 1995. On human rights see Chapter 14 below, 209–21.

53 Agenda 21, Chapter 27.5: Strengthening the Role of Non-Governmental Organizations: Partners for Sustainable Development. On Agenda 21 and the results of the Rio Conference see Chapter 16 below, 247–53.

54 H.G. Schermers, International Organizations, Observer Status, *EPIL* II (1995), 1324–5; B. Bartram/D.P. López, Observer Status, in *Wolfrum UNLPP II*, 936–46.

55 P. Macalister-Smith, Non-Governmental Organizations, Humanitarian Action and Human Rights, in *FS Bernhardt*, 477–501, at 485; see also The United Nations Partnership with the Non-Governmental Sector (ECOSOC, UNESCO, UNICEF, GATT), *TA* 46 (1994), 214; L.A. Kimball, General Developments, *YIEL* 5 (1994), 135–6, also with regard to the involvement of NGOs in the Global Environmental Facility (GEF) of the World Bank. On ECOSOC see Chapter 21 below, 382–3.

56 See Chapter 3 above, 62.

57 *ETS*, no. 124.

58 See also Chapter 20 below, 349–50, on the *Nuclear Test* cases brought before the ICJ.

59 See M. Pugh, Legal Aspects of the Rainbow Warrior Affair, *ICLQ* 36 (1987), 655.

60 See also Chapter 7 below, 110, 117.

61 *Rainbow Warrior* (*New Zealand v. France*) Case, *ILR* 74 (1987), 241; United Nations Secretary-General: Ruling Pertaining to the Differences between France and New Zealand arising from the *Rainbow Warrior* Affair, *ibid.*, 256; *ILM* 26 (1987), 1346.

on the Recognition of the Legal Personality of International Non-Governmental Organizations.[57] The Convention, signed in 1986 and in force since 1991, recognizes, among the states which have ratified it, the legal personality and attached rights and duties as acquired by an NGO by its establishment in any one of the states parties.

The international activities of NGOs are not always without problems, as the 1995 campaign by Greenpeace against Shell to prevent the sinking of the Brent-Spar oil platform in the North Atlantic, although Shell was licensed to do so by the British government, has shown. Using the media and spectacular stunts, Greenpeace persuaded consumers (for example, in Germany) to boycott Shell's products and Shell (to the embarrassment of the British government) gave in, although it remained convinced by the evidence of technical expertise that its decision was not only reasonable from the economic point of view, but also environmentally tolerable. (Later Greenpeace apologized to Shell for using wrong information in its campaign.) Shortly afterwards, Greenpeace engaged in another spectacular campaign against the resumption of nuclear tests by the French in the Pacific, a matter which has a delicate precedent in the *Rainbow Warrior* affair ten years previously, which involved the first international case in history of an agreement between a sovereign state and an NGO to submit a dispute to arbitration.

The facts of the *Rainbow Warrior* affair are briefly as follows. For many years France had been conducting underground nuclear tests on the Mururoa Atoll in French Polynesia, alleging that these tests had no real consequences for the environment.[58] Greenpeace had led protests against the French tests for more than fifteen years, including attempts, opposed by the French navy, to send vessels into the waters prohibited for navigation by France which surround the Mururoa Atoll, particularly in 1973 and 1982. In 1985 Greenpeace again planned to send several ships, including the *Rainbow Warrior*, registered in Britain, into the neighbourhood of the nuclear testing area. On 10 July 1985, an undercover operation ordered by the French military security service sank the *Rainbow Warrior* in New Zealand's Auckland Harbour with two explosive devices and thereby also killed a crewman.[59] Two French agents caught in New Zealand were sentenced to ten years' imprisonment for manslaughter and seven years for wilful damage (the terms to run concurrently). The French government refused to extradite to New Zealand other French officials involved, and sought negotiations for the release and return to France of the two agents who, it argued, had acted under military orders.[60]

New Zealand suspended the negotiations in May 1986 after France had imposed economic sanctions by impeding New Zealand imports. In June 1986 the two states agreed to refer all issues to the Secretary-General of the United Nations for a ruling. Perez de Cuéllar achieved a quick settlement in July 1986.[61] It required France to convey to New Zealand 'a formal and unqualified apology for the attack, contrary to international law', to pay compensation to New Zealand in the amount of US$7 million (New Zealand had demanded US$9 million and France had offered US$4 million), and to discontinue opposing New Zealand imports into the European Community. New Zealand was required to transfer the two agents to the French military authorities, who were to keep them isolated under military discipline for a period of three years on the island of Hao in French Polynesia. They were to be prohibited from leaving the island, 'for any reason, except with the mutual consent of the two Governments'. Finally, the ruling of the Secretary-General provided for an agreement of the two parties on a mechanism of binding arbitration on further disputes concerning the implementation of the matter.[62]

These terms to settle a most remarkable affair between two friendly states were originally carried out by the governments, but at the end of 1987 and some months later in 1988 France unilaterally allowed the two agents to return to France from the island of Hao, partly for alleged medical reasons. This led to a decision of an arbitral tribunal on 30 April 1990,[63] distinguishing between the two cases of repatriation of the agents. In the first case, France was not found to be in violation of its obligations towards New Zealand by repatriating the agent on 13 December 1987, but by failing to order his return to Hao by 12 February 1988. In the second case, France was held responsible for a breach by failing to make an effort in good faith on 5 May 1988 to obtain the consent of New Zealand and by failing to return the agent on 5 and 6 May 1988. In a way following the spirit of the ancient Jewish King Solomon, the Tribunal also made the recommendation that the two governments should establish a fund for the purpose of promoting friendly relations between the citizens of both countries, into which the French government was asked to pay US$2 million.

With regard to the private claims, in November 1985 France had already reached a settlement with the family of the dead crewman, including a formal apology, compensation to the total amount of 2.3 million francs, and reimbursement of the insurers. In December 1985, France had also admitted legal liability to Greenpeace and both sides agreed to negotiate on damages. Failing to reach agreement, they referred the matter to a panel of three arbitrators on 10 July 1986. On 2 October 1987, the tribunal awarded Greenpeace US$8,159,000 against France in damages (US$5 million for the loss of the ship and US$1.2 million for aggravated damages, the rest for expenses, interest and legal fees).[64]

One problem as regards NGOs is that most of them are based in the industrialized part of the world, concentrating in a few home countries (predominantly in the UK, France, Belgium, Switzerland and the United States) which implies that there is a certain geographical imbalance. Although these home countries are democracies, guaranteeing freedom of association, NGOs are sometimes used (and misused) by governments in their international dealings, *inter alia*, through their necessary collaboration with inter-governmental organizations which are controlled by states.

The question has been raised whether it is really advisable that these non-territorial entities should seek to obtain a formal international status on the universal level, which in effect might undermine their strength in the future, or whether it is not better that they rather continue to rely on their independence to act as a social bridge between the state-dominated international legal system and individual human beings.[65] The constructive role of NGOs, especially in the field of human rights, in providing

62 On arbitration see Chapter 18 below, 293–8.

63 *Rainbow Warrior* Arbitration, *ILR* 82 (1990), 499–90. The Arbitration Tribunal was composed of J. de Aréchaga, Sir K. Keith and Prof. J.-D. Bredin. See J.S. Davidson, The *Rainbow Warrior* Arbitration Concerning the Treatment of the French Agents Mafart and Prieur, *ICLQ* 40 (1991), 446 *et seq.*

64 *Greenpeace Press Release*, Lewes, UK, 2 October 1987.

65 For thoughts in this direction see Macalister-Smith (1995), *op. cit.*, at 500–1.

66 M. Brus, *Third Party Dispute Settlement in an Interdependent World*, 1995.; 202. But see D. Shelton, The Participation of Nongovernmental Organizations in International Judicial Proceedings, *AJIL* 88 (1994), 611.
67 See Chapter 2 above, 15–16.
68 See Chapter 4 above, 63–74.
69 C.A. Norgaard, *The Position of the Individual in International Law*, 1962; R.A. Mullerson, Human Rights and the Individual as a Subject of International Law, *EJIL* 1 (1990), 33–43; K.J. Partsch, Individuals in International Law, *EPIL* II (1995), 957–62; P.K. Menon, The Legal Personality of Individuals, *Sri Lanka JIL* 6 (1994), 127–56; see also the literature above, 91.
70 D. Kokkini-Iatridou/P.J.I.M. de Waart, Foreign Investments in Developing Countries – Legal Personality of Multinationals in International Law, *NYIL* 14 (1983), 87–131; P. Fisher, Transnational Enterprises, *EPIL* 8 (1985), 515–19; A.A. Fatouros, National Legal Persons in International Law, *EPIL* 10 (1987), 299–306; I. Seidl-Hohenveldern, *Corporations in and under International Law*, 1987; United Nations Centre on Transnational Corporations, *Transnational Corporations in World Development: Trends and Prospects*, 1988; P. Mercial, *Les Entreprises multinationales en droit international*, 1993; R. Higgins, International Law and Foreign Corporations, in *New Diplomacy in the Post Cold War World: Essays for Susan Strange*, 1993; D.W. Bachmann, Transnational Corporations, in *Wolfrum UNLPP II*, 1239–47; P.T. Muchlinski, *Multinational Enterprises and the Law*, 1995.
71 See Chapter 20 below, 353–61.
72 See Chapter 14 below, 208–21.

information, analysis and public support, and active engagement in humanitarian relief operations and alleviating poverty in developing countries, for instance, is now generally acknowledged. At least with regard to international law-making in general, however, it is unlikely that NGOs will be included in the formal process in the near future and, as noted by one recent author, this may also be undesirable, 'as they are not democratically authorized to realize the common good, and often neglect the common good in the pursuance of their specific interests'.[66]

Individuals and companies

In the seventeenth century, when all law was regarded as derived from natural law,[67] no sharp distinction was made between international law and municipal law,[68] and it was easy to assume that individuals had legal personality under international law.[69] But in the nineteenth century, when positivism had become the dominant philosophy, states were usually regarded as the only subjects of international law.

The present century has seen a growing tendency to admit that individuals – and companies[70] – have some degree of international personality, but the whole subject is extremely controversial. Soviet international lawyers admitted that individuals can be guilty of crimes (for example, war crimes) against international law,[71] but usually denied that individuals and companies have any *rights* under international law; they probably feared that such rights would undermine the powers of states over their own nationals. In Western countries writers and governments are usually prepared to admit that individuals and companies have some degree of international legal personality; but the personality is usually seen as something limited – much more limited than the legal personality of international organizations. Individuals and companies may have various rights under special treaties, for instance, but it has never been suggested that they can imitate states by acquiring territory, appointing ambassadors, or declaring war. As in the case of international organizations, it is useless to treat legal personality as an absolute concept; one must break it down into specific rights and duties.

Very many rules of international law exist for the benefit of individuals and companies, but that does not necessarily mean that the rules create *rights* for the individual and companies, any more than municipal rules prohibiting cruelty to animals confer rights on animals. Even when a treaty expressly says that individuals and companies shall enjoy certain rights, one has to read the treaty very carefully to ascertain whether the rights exist directly under international law, or whether the states party to the treaty are merely under an obligation to grant municipal law rights to the individuals or companies concerned.

The international rules concerning the protection of human rights (which will be dealt with separately in Chapter 14 below[72]) are a good example of the difficulty of deciding whether individuals derive rights from international law, or whether they merely derive benefits. Indeed, there is an even greater problem of classification in this context, since many of the commitments undertaken by states are expressed in such vague and idealistic language that it is uncertain whether they enunciate legal obligations at all, as distinct from merely moral aspirations.

One way of proving that the rights of the individuals or companies exist under international law is to show that the treaty conferring the rights gives the individuals or companies access to an international tribunal in order to enforce their rights. Most international tribunals are not open to individuals or companies; for instance, Article 34 of the Statute of the International Court of Justice provides that only states may be parties to contentious cases before the Court.[73] But there are exceptions; thus, the International Bank for Reconstruction and Development (the World Bank) has set up an international arbitral tribunal to hear disputes arising out of investments between states and the nationals of other states (ICSID).[74] At the Iran–United States Claims Tribunal, individuals and companies which are nationals of one of the two parties have legal standing under certain conditions.[75] The procedure of the United Nations Compensation Commission (UNCC), set up by the UN Security Council in Geneva in 1991 after the defeat of Iraq in the Second Gulf War, even attempts to give priority to the masses of claims of individual victims rather than to the claims of big companies against Iraq (it is not, however, really operating as an arbitral or judicial body).[76] The Permanent Court of Arbitration (PCA) in The Hague in 1993 modified its procedure to encourage access of 'Parties of which only one is a State'.[77] Under the 1988 Canada-United States Free Trade Agreement (FTA)[78] private parties have access to binational panels which can reach binding decisions in certain cases.[79] The procedure has also been made part of the North American Free Trade Agreement (NAFTA).[80] On the other hand, proposals to grant private parties which are directly affected by alleged breaches of GATT rules access to the GATT dispute settlement system,[81] in order to relieve them from the discretion of their home governments to take up the complaint, have not been included in the reform of the dispute settlement mechanism under the WTO arrangements.[82] Similarly, in the European Communities individuals and companies can bring claims before the Court of Justice of the European Communities; but this is not a very good example, because, as noted above, the powers exercised by the Communities over the governments and nationals of the member states are so extensive that 'Community law' is almost a hybrid between international law and federal law.[83] One could also mention certain limited examples in the law of the sea and in environmental law.[84]

In the field of human rights individuals have under certain conditions access to international dispute settlement procedures,[85] but these depend on treaties consented to by their governments and such consent can be qualified or withdrawn. Moreover, in most cases human rights disputes involve the complaints of individuals against their own government, whereas in investment disputes under international law a foreign government is involved. In this connection it is important to note that under the customary law of diplomatic protection and state responsibility for the treatment of aliens,[86] the claim of a national of state X, for example, against state Y for denial of justice or wrongful expropriation of property is not a claim belonging to the individual citizen (or company) of state X which has

73 Criticism of this limitation: E. Lauterpacht, *Aspects of the Administration of International Justice,* 1991. See also Chapter 18 below, 282–7.
74 See Chapter 18 below, 295–6.
75 See Chapter 18 below, 296–8.
76 See Chapter 22 below, 398–9.
77 See Chapter 18 below, 294.
78 Text in *ILM* 27 (1988), 281. See Chapters 15, 225 and 18, 300 below.
79 For example, in disputes concerning investment, anti-dumping and countervailing measures (Article 1904 FTA). See J.-G. Castel, The Settlement of Disputes under the 1988 Canada–United States Free Trade Agreement, *AJIL* 83 (1989), 118–28.
80 See Chapters 15, 225 and 18, 300 below.
81 See Chapters 15, 233 and 18, 300 below and Brus, *op. cit.,* 207–8 with references.
82 For a brief survey see Brus, *ibid.* 28–37. See also Chapter 15 below, 233.
83 See text above, 96 and Chapter 1 above, 8.
84 On the law of the sea see Chapter 12, 172–97 and Chapter 18, 298–300, below, on international environmental law see Chapter 16 below, 241–53.
85 See Chapter 14 below, 207–21.
86 See Chapter 17 below, 256–72.

87 See Chapter 17 below, 267–8.
88 For a critical discussion see L. Henkin, 'Nationality' at the Turn of the Century, in *FS Bernhardt*, 89–102, at 92 *et seq.*
89 See Chapter 3 above, 38–9.
90 For a different view see M. Herdegen, *Internationales Wirtschaftsrecht*, 2nd edn 1995, 58, referring to an advancing view that such contracts may grant the company limited international personality; see also 205 *et seq.*
91 See P. Kennedy, *Preparing for the Twenty-First Century*, 1993, Chapter 3, noting that the large multinational corporations have 'more global reach than global responsibility' (at 47), have 'international rather than national interests' (at 49) and that 'the real 'logic' of the borderless world is that nobody is in control – except, perhaps, the managers of multinational corporations, whose responsibility is to their shareholders, who, one might argue, have become the new sovereigns, investing in whatever company gives the highest returns' (at 55).
92 A. Cassese, *International Law in a Divided World*, 1986, 103.

actually suffered the harm itself, but to its home state X. This means that under international law, unless there are special agreements to the contrary, it is up to the government of state X to decide whether it wants to pursue the claim diplomatically or in an international forum against state Y. Compensation is paid to state X and international law does not demand that state X pays any of it to the injured individual (or company). State X is free to waive the claim or to arrive at a settlement which leaves the individual without international remedy. Awkwardly, this construction, which seeks to preserve the control of states over their international affairs, nevertheless depends on the individual concerned under certain aspects: the individual can also waive the right to the claim; the individual has to exhaust available local remedies[87] under the national law of state Y before state X can raise the claim on the international level; and the compensation that state Y has to pay is measured by the injury caused to the individual.[88]

It has sometimes been suggested that individuals (or companies) can acquire rights under international law by making agreements with states (or international organizations) containing a provision that the agreements should be governed by international law. This suggestion has given rise to considerable controversy, especially in connection with oil concessions before the oil crisis in 1973, as has already been discussed above with regard to the nature of 'internationalized contracts' between a state and a foreign investor.[89] But even such contracts are at the discretion of the host state and they do not confer international legal personality on the foreign country.[90] A unilateral elevation by the host state of the foreign company to the international level is not possible because it would also interfere with the rights of the home state of the company.

Even the influential group of the few outstanding global multinational companies (such as IBM, ITT or Unilever), which already hold more economic and political power than many states and, in connection with the globalization of the economy under the communications and financial revolution, are likely to become stronger still in the next century,[91] have not been upgraded by states to international subjects proper.[92] States prefer to maintain control over these corporations, rather than accepting them on a legally equal footing, although it is often difficult in practice to effectively regulate on the national level the activities of such global companies, due to their extensive network of decision-making and operational structures formed by their headquarters, branches, subsidiaries and other forms of investment in independent company units throughout the world and their flexibility in transferring seats of production as well as profits within the framework of the organization as a whole.

The emergence of transnational companies reflects the globalization of economic activities and new forms of specialization and the international division of labour requiring direct investment in foreign markets. Some states, however, for obvious economic reasons, are more favourable to the operations of multinational companies based in their own territory than other states where these companies are operating. Developing countries especially have expressed concern about the dominance of TNCs in national economies, in contract negotiations and in other respects concerning company interests, including interference in the domestic politics of the host state. Industrialized countries, on the other hand, tend to be more worried about the protection of the investments of their multinationals in foreign countries and about legal certainty for their transactions.

Various international bodies have been engaged in finding a compromise by formulating so-called codes of conduct of a recommendatory nature, for example the International Chamber of Commerce, the International Labour Organization and the OECD.[93] Of particular importance have been the protracted negotiations in the United Nations since 1977 on a UN Draft Code of Conduct on Transnational Corporations and the work of the UN Centre on TNCs.[94] The issue has meanwhile lost much of its former political significance, since a number of developing countries now have transnational companies of their own and almost all of them have become more interested in the flow of private foreign investment into their economies, and because of the changes in the former socialist countries after the end of the Cold War. Significantly, following the shift in 1993 of the UN programme on TNCs from New York to UNCTAD in Geneva,[95] in 1994 ECOSOC installed the renamed Commission on International Investment and TNCs as an advisory body to the Trade and Development Board.[96]

Some other treaties provide for a different means of enforcement; individuals take their complaints, not to an international tribunal, but to a political organ of an international organization, which investigates the complaint and takes such action as it considers necessary and feasible against the offending state. (For instance, the 1919 Peace Treaties allowed members of certain national minorities in Central and Eastern Europe to complain to the Council of the League of Nations, if they considered that they were victims of discrimination.)[97] The individual initiates the proceedings, but thereafter has no control over them and plays no active part in the proceedings. If the political organ refuses to take up his case, he has no remedy; but if it does take up his case, it may be able to protect his interests more effectively than he could ever hope to do by appealing to an international tribunal – apart from anything else, this indirect system of enforcement spares the individual the costs of litigation. Moreover, the system is popular with states, because it provides a speedier means of rejecting frivolous claims. However, it is doubtful whether the individual's interests which are protected by such a system can be regarded as rights conferred on him by international law; there is room for argument about what is meant by a legal right, but most lawyers would probably agree that in such cases the rights are vested in the political organ and not in the individual.

Similar problems arise in connection with employment in international organizations, which is generally not governed by municipal law, but by an elaborate set of rules enacted by the organization and interpreted in the light of general principles of administrative law. International administrative tribunals, which decide disputes between organizations and their officials, have sometimes described this body of law as the 'internal law of the organization', without saying whether the 'internal law' represents part of international law or a separate system of law.[98]

In conclusion, it should be noted that the international legal personality

93 See E.-U. Petersmann, Codes of Conduct, *EPIL* I (1992), 627–32.
94 On the drafts see *ILM* 23 (1984), 626; *ICSID Rev.* 4 (1989), 135. See W. Spröte, Negotiations on a United Nations Code of Conduct on Transnational Corporations, *GYIL* 33 (1990), 331.
95 *YIEL* 4 (1993), 103.
96 *YIEL* 5 (1994), 136.
97 See Chapter 2 above, 24.
98 See M. Akehurst, *The Law Governing Employment in International Organizations*, 1967, especially 3–10, 249–63; S. Bastid, United Nations Administrative Tribunal, *EPIL* 5 (1983), 281–7; C.F. Amerasinghe, *The Law of the International Civil Service as Applied by International Administrative Tribunals*, 2 vols, 2nd edn 1988; C.F. Amerasinghe (ed.), *Documents on International Administrative Tribunals*, 1989; G. Vandersanden, Administrative Tribunals, Boards and Commissions in International Organizations, *EPIL* I (1992), 27–31; R. Bernhardt, International Organizations, Internal Law and Rules, *EPIL* II (1995), 1314–18. See also Chapter 18 below, 289.

99 See Chapter 1 above, 1 and Chapter 19 below, 318–22.

100 Text in *Brownlie BDIL*, 426.

101 See Chapter 17 below, 254–60.

102 See Chapter 2 above, 28.

103 See Cassese, *op. cit.*, 90 *et seq.*

104 K. Ginther, Liberation Movements, *EPIL* 3 (1982), 245–9; S.v. Schorlemer, Liberation Movements, in *Wolfrum UNLPP II*, 854–64. See also Chapter 19 below, 28.

105 See Chapter 20 below, 344–5.

of individuals and companies (and, indeed, of international organizations) is still comparatively rare and limited. Moreover, it is derivative, in the sense that it can be conferred only by states; it is states which set up international organizations; it is states which make treaties or adopt customary rules giving international rights to individuals and companies; it is only states (or international organizations, created by states) which can make contracts with individuals or companies governed by international law. Consequently, when some states say that individuals are subjects of international law, and when other states disagree, both sides may be right; if states in the first group confer international rights on individuals, then individuals are subjects of international law as far as those states are concerned; states in the second group can, for practical purposes, prevent individuals from acquiring international personality, by refraining from giving them any rights which are valid under international law.

Insurgents and national liberation movements

Insurgents in a civil war have long been recognized in international law as subjects having certain rights and duties because they control some territory and might become the effective new government of the state.[99] This is also reflected in Articles 14 and 15 of the UN International Law Commission's Draft Articles on State Responsibility,[100] according to which, as long as the old government is still in power, a wrongful act of an insurrectional movement established in the territory of the state shall not be considered as an act of that state under international law (involving responsibility to other states for it). However, it will be considered as an act of that state (in a retroactive sense) if the insurrectional movement becomes the new government.[101]

New problems emerged in the process of decolonization[102] concerning the international legal status of liberation movements of 'peoples under colonial, alien or racist domination', having a representative organization (such as SWAPO, the ANC or the PLO).[103] With regard to such national liberation movements,[104] the situation is different from that of the traditional category of insurgents, although in practice there has been some overlap. There have been conflicting positions of states on this issue in the past, which has now lost most of its former relevance. The controversy reveals that the international status of the three aforementioned distinct types of national liberation movement does not rest primarily on the control of territory, but rather on the international recognition of their political goals of freedom from colonial domination, racist oppression or alien occupation. Nevertheless, at least the future prospect of gaining effective control over population in a given territory appears to be a central element of their recognition as subjects of the international community, or at least as a lawful belligerent, although there was much dissent on this detail in connection with the negotiations on the 1977 Additional Protocols to the Geneva Red Cross Conventions.[105]

The problems of recognition of such liberation movements by states and international organizations are similar to those discussed above with regard to the effect of the recognition of states among themselves in international law.[106] Some movements were even granted observer status[107] at the United Nations. In the case of the PLO[108] this led to difficulties with the host state of the United Nations[109] in 1988 when the United States, invoking its Anti-Terrorism Act, intended to close the PLO office in New York. A US court declared the act of its government to be a violation of the Headquarters Agreement of the United States with the UN.[110]

Ethnic minorities and indigenous peoples

With the rise of ethno-nationalism in many parts of the world, not only in the Balkans and in the former Soviet Union, the status of ethnic minorities and other groups in international law has again become a central issue.[111] This is witnessed in various recent efforts on the global and regional level to improve their legal protection. The issue of self-determination of ethnic, cultural and linguistic minorities and of indigenous peoples will be treated in more detail below in Chapter 19.[112] The only relevant aspect in the present chapter is the question to what extent such groups have acquired international legal personality.

Minorities

As we have seen, the problem of protecting national minorities in Europe confronted the League of Nations after the First World War.[113] After the Second World War certain rights were granted to the individual members of ethnic, linguistic or cultural minorities to have their language and identity respected by the state as part of the process of the development of human rights in general.[114] But as far as nation states were at all willing to accept that such minorities were in fact existing on their territory, they remained reluctant to take any steps which might increase the danger of claims to independence and secession. Recent developments have again raised the question of what legal status should be accorded to minorities on various levels. On the global level we have the 1992 UN Declaration on the Rights of Persons Belonging to National or Ethnic, Religious and Linguistic Minorities.[115] On the regional level in Europe one should mention the creation of a High Commissioner for National Minorities in the CSCE process[116] and other initiatives, such as the European Charter for Regional or Minority Languages adopted by the Council of Europe in 1992,[117] and the 1995 Council of Europe Framework Convention for the Protection of National Minorities.[118] As of 5 March 1996, the Framework Convention (which needs twelve ratifications to enter into force) was ratified by four states and signed by twenty-eight other states.[119]

However, the question of what constitutes a 'minority' in terms of international law has remained a vexed one to which, as yet, no completely satisfactory answer has been found. The main reason is that no abstract definition is fully capable of covering the broad variety of relevant situations in the world involving some 3,000 to 5,000 different groups qualified as minorities in existing states. The most frequently cited proposition is the one offered by Capotorti, as the United Nations Special Rapporteur, in his *Study on the Rights of Persons Belonging to Ethnic, Religious and Linguistic Minorities* of 1977:

106 See Chapter 5 above, 82–90.

107 See text above, 97.

108 F.v. de Craen, Palestine Liberation Organization, *EPIL* 12 (1990), 278–82.

109 See the literature cited above, 92.

110 Documents on the Controversy Surrounding the Closing of the Palestine Liberation Organization Observer Mission to the United Nations, *ILM* 27 (1988), 712–834; US District Court for the Southern District of New York Decision in *United States v. Palestine Liberation Organization*, *ILM* 27 (1988), 1055–91. See also *United Nations Headquarters Agreement Case*, *ICJ Rep.* 1988, 12–35; T. Fitschen, Closing the PLO Observer Mission to the United Nations in New York, *GYIL* 31 (1988), 595–620; R. Pinto, La Fermeture du bureau de l'OLP auprès de l'Organisation des Nations Unies à New York, *JDI* 116 (1989), 329–48; W.M. Reisman, The Arafat Visa Affair: Exceeding the Bounds of Host State Discretion, *AJIL* 83 (1989), 519–27; S. Sadiq Reza, International Agreements: United Nations Headquarters Agreement – Dispute Over the United States Denial of a Visa to Yassir Arafat, *Harvard ILJ* 30 (1989), 536–48.

111 See P. Thornberry, *International Law and the Rights of Minorities*, 1991; Y. Dinstein/M. Tabory (eds), *The Protection of Minorities and Human Rights*, 1991; I.M. Cuthbertson/J. Leibowitz (eds), *Minorities: The New Europe's Old Issue*, 1993; T.R. Gurr, *Minorities at Risk: A Global View of Ethnopolitical Conflicts*, 1993; C. Hillgruber/M. Jestaedt, *The European Convention on Human Rights and the Protection of National Minorities*, 1994; P. Malanczuk, Minorities and Self-Determination, in N. Sybesma-Knol/J.v. Bellingen (eds), *Naar een nieuwe interpretatie van het Recht op Zelfbeschikking*, 1995, 169–93; F. Capotorti, Minorities, in *Wolfrum UNLPP* II, 892–903; L.-A. Sicilianos (ed.), *New Forms of Discrimination*, 1995; A. Phillips/A. Rosas (eds), *Universal Minority Rights*, 1995; H. Hannum, *Autonomy, Sovereignty and Self-Determination. The Accommodation of Conflicting Rights*, rev. edn 1996.

112 See Chapter 19 below, 338–40.

113 See Chapter 2 above, 24.

114 See Chapters 14, 209–21 and 19, 338–40 below.

115 *ILM* 32 (1993), 911; A. Phillips/A. Rosas (eds), *The UN Minority Rights Declaration*, 1993; P. Thornberry, The UN Declaration on the Rights of Persons Belonging to National or Ethnic, Religious and Linguistic Minorities:

Background, Analysis, Observations, and an Update, in Phillips/Rosas (eds), 1995, op. cit.; I.O. Bokatola, L'Organisation des Nations Unies et la protection des minorités, 1992.
116 E. Klein (ed.), The Institution of a Commissioner for Human Rights and Minorities and the Prevention of Human Rights Violations, 1994.
117 G. Gilbert, The Legal Protection Accorded to Minority Groups in Europe, NYIL 23 (1992), 67–104.
118 ILM 34 (1995), 351–9. See P. Thornberry/M.A.M. Estebanez, The Work of the Council of Europe in the Protection of Minorities, RIA 46 (1995), 28–32; A. Rönquist, The Council of Europe Framework Convention for the Protection of National Minorities, HM 6 (1995), 38–44; M.A. Martín Estébanez, International Organizations and Minority Protection in Europe, 1996.
119 ILM 35 (1996), 807.
120 F. Capotorti, Study on the Rights of Persons belonging to Ethnic, Religious and Linguistic Minorities, 1991, 96.
121 See Chapter 19 below, 326–40.
122 See N.S. Rodley, Conceptual Problems in the Protection of Minorities: International Legal Developments, HRQ 17 (1995), 48–71.
123 H.-J. Heintze, Völkerrecht und Indigenous Peoples, ZaöRV 50 (1990), 39–70; I. Brownlie, Treaties and Indigenous Peoples, 1992. G. Alfredsson, Indigenous Populations, Protection, EPIL II (1995), 946; Indigenous Populations, Treaties With, ibid., 951; E. Spiry, From 'Self-Determination' to a Right to 'Self-Development' for Indigenous Groups, GYIL 38 (1995), 129–52; W.M. Reismann, Protecting Indigenous Rights in International Adjudication, AJIL 89 (1995), 350–62; S.J. Anaya, Indigenous Peoples in International Law, 1996.
124 See M.C. v. Walt v. Praag, The Position of UNPO in the International Legal Order, in C. Brölmann/R. Lefeber/ M. Zieck (eds), Peoples and Minorities in International Law, 1993, 313 et seq.
125 Sub-Commission on Prevention of Discrimination and Protection of Minorities, ILM 34 (1995), 541; see E. Gayim, The UN Draft Declaration on Indigenous Peoples: Assessment of the Draft Prepared by the Working Group on Indigenous Populations, 1994; C.M. Brölmann/M.Y.A. Zieck, Some Remarks on the Draft Declaration on the Rights of Indigenous Peoples, LJIL 8 (1995), 103 et seq.; R.T. Coutler, The Draft UN Declaration on the Rights of Indigenous

> A group numerically inferior to the rest of the population of a State, in a non-dominant position, whose members – being nationals of the State – possess ethnic, religious or linguistic characteristics differing from those of the rest of the population and show, if only implicitly, a sense of solidarity, directed towards preserving their culture, traditions, religion or language.[120]

The question of the international legal personality of minorities is more complicated than the issue of the international legal personality of individuals or companies. The problem of minorities has quite a different political and legal dimension for two main reasons. First, it is related to the meaning and legal consequences of the principle of self-determination[121] and implies, in the view of states, the danger of secession of a minority and thus may lead to the loss of territory and control over part of the population. Second, it is connected with the problem of possible intervention of a mother country into a neighbouring state to protect 'its' minorities, as, for example, was the pretext in the case of the Sudeten Germans, when Hitler invaded Czechoslovakia. It is no accident that in the development of international law since the Second World War, the rights of minorities have been conceived as a category of human rights which are to be exercised by the individual belonging to a minority, rather than as group rights attributed to a collective entity as such.[122]

Indigenous peoples

Special issues have arisen in recent years with regard to the category of so-called 'indigenous peoples'.[123] Examples are the Aborigines in Australia, the Indians (Native Americans) in America, the Inuit (also known as Eskimos), the Maori in New Zealand and the Sami (Lapps) in Scandinavia and Russia. A total of 100 to 200 million people in more than forty states are estimated to fall within this category. An independent NGO to further the claims of indigenous peoples has been established in The Hague under the name Unrepresented Nations and Peoples Organization (UNPO).[124] Recent results of the quest of such groups have been the Draft UN Declaration on the Rights of Indigenous Peoples adopted by the UN Commission on Human Rights on 26 August 1994[125] and the establishment of a Working Group on the Draft Declaration by the Commission on 3 March 1995.[126]

The definitional obstacles are in principle of the same nature as in the case of minorities. An elaborate definition was formulated by J.R. Martinez Cobo, appointed by the UN as Special Rapporteur to undertake a *Study of the Problem of Discrimination against Indigenous Populations*, in 1983:

> Indigenous communities, peoples and nations are those which, having a historical continuity with pre-invasion and pre-colonial societies that developed on their territories, consider themselves distinct from other sectors of the societies now prevailing in those territories, or parts of them. They form at present non-dominant sectors of society and are determined to preserve, develop and transmit to future generations their ancestral territories, and their ethnic identity, as the basis of their continued existence as peoples, in accordance with their own cultural patterns, social institutions and legal systems.

... On an individual basis, an indigenous person is one who belongs to these indigenous populations through self-identification as indigenous (group consciousness) and is recognized and accepted by these populations as one of its members (acceptance by the group).[127]

From a legal perspective, it is difficult to see, even on the basis of this more elaborate definition, what exactly should distinguish 'indigenous peoples' from the definition of 'minorities', as proposed by Capotorti, or, from the equally unclear and disputed general term of 'peoples'. A. Cristescu once attempted to clarify it as follows: 'The term "people" denotes a social entity possessing a clear identity and its own characteristics. It implies a relationship with a territory, even if the people in question has been wrongfully expelled from it and artificially replaced by another population.'[128] While at least the criterion of numerical inferiority in the case of minorities offers a clear distinguishing feature from the category of 'people', whatever its precise meaning, the definition of 'indigenous peoples' seems to combine the elements of both.[129] Of course, the definitional problems should not be exaggerated because often the legal meaning of such terms becomes clear from the relevant legal context and instrument. But whether 'indigenous peoples', special attention to which has been given primarily within the framework of the International Labour Organization and the United Nations,[130] really form a separate legal category is doubtful. To solve the problem, suggestions have been made to include the alleged characteristic dependence on the land in the definition of 'indigenous peoples'.[131] However, it seems difficult not to apply the same considerations, in one form or another, to other groups, such as, for example the Kurds, the Armenians, the Scots or the Welsh. The only valid distinguishing criterion so far appears to be a purely subjective and political one, namely the refusal of 'indigenous peoples' to be identified as simple 'minorities' in order to be able to claim more far-reaching rights.

Such a claim seems to be gaining some recognition. Principle 22 of the non-binding 1992 Rio Declaration on Environment and Development states:

> Indigenous people and their communities, and other local communities, have a vital role in environmental management and development because of their knowledge and traditional practices. States should recognize and duly support their identity, culture and interests and enable their effective participation in the achievement of sustainable development.[132]

The aforementioned UN Draft Declaration on Indigenous Peoples seems to go a step further than documents on protecting members of minorities by recognizing group rights for indigenous peoples who are considered to be 'equal in dignity and rights to all other peoples' (preamble) and who should have the right of self-determination. But, first, it is still a draft and, second, even if it becomes a declaration accepted by states in the General Assembly, it would be a resolution of an international organization and thus not necessarily an expression of the law as it stands.[133] In sum, like in the case of individuals and companies, the question of the international legal personality of minorities and indigenous

Peoples: What Is It? What Does It Mean?, *NQHR* 13 (1995), 123–38.;38.

126 *ILM* 34 (1995), 535.

127 M. Cobo, *Study of the Problem of Discrimination Against Indigenous Populations*, UN Doc. E/CN.4/Sub.2/1983/21/Add. 8, paras. 379 and 381.

128 A. Cristescu, *The Right to Self-Determination, Historical and Current Development on the Basis of United Nations Instruments*, UNP Sales No. 80.XIV.3, para. 279. See also J. Crawford (ed.), *The Rights of Peoples*, 1992.

129 See C.M. Brölmann/M.Y.A. Zieck, Indigenous Peoples, in Brölmann/Lefeber/Zieck (eds), *op. cit.*, 187 et seq., at 196.

130 *Ibid.*, 197 et seq., discussing ILO Conventions 107 and 169 and the 1992 UN Draft Declaration on the Rights of Indigenous Peoples, *op. cit.*

131 *Ibid.*, at 196.

132 *ILM* 31 (1992), 876–80, at 880. On the Rio Declaration see Chapter 16 below, 247, 250.

133 See Chapter 3 above, 52–5.

peoples is in reality a question of the specific rights attributed to them by states, but the point is that these entities pose a different set of problems under international law *de lege ferenda* because of claims to self-determination. They are not subjects of international law in any meaningful sense of the term and have not (yet) achieved an international legal status any higher than that of individuals.

7 Jurisdiction

Forms of jurisdiction

'Jurisdiction' is a word which must be used with extreme caution. It sounds impressively technical, and yet many people think that they have a vague idea of what it means; there is therefore a temptation to use the word without stopping to ask what it means. In fact, it can have a large number of different meanings.[1] Sometimes it simply means territory; for instance, in cases concerning the custody of children, British courts may order a party not to take the child 'out of the jurisdiction of the court', which means 'out of Britain'. The phrase 'domestic jurisdiction', as used in the United Nations Charter, has a specialized meaning.[2] But most often 'jurisdiction' refers to powers exercised by a state over persons, property, or events. But, here again, the term is ambiguous, for the powers under consideration may be powers to legislate in respect of the persons, property, or events in question (legislative or prescriptive jurisdiction), the powers of a state's courts to hear cases concerning the persons, property or events in question (judicial or adjudicative jurisdiction), or the powers of physical interference exercised by the executive, such as the arrest of persons, seizure of property, and so on (enforcement jurisdiction).

It is essential to differentiate between these three groups of powers, particularly between the second and third groups, although the distinctions are not always rigid in practice. For instance, if a man commits a murder in England and escapes to France, the English courts have jurisdiction to try him, but the English police cannot enter French territory and arrest him there; they must request the French authorities to arrest him and to surrender him for trial in England. (This distinction between the right to arrest and the right to try is fairly obvious in the case of crimes committed on land, but can easily be overlooked in the case of crimes committed on ships.[3]) What has been said follows from the principle of territorial sovereignty, according to which a state may not perform any governmental act in the territory of another state without the latter's consent. As noted by Max Huber in the *Palmas Island* case:

> Sovereignty in the relations between States signifies independence. Independence in regard to a portion of the globe is the right to exercise therein, to the exclusion of any other State, the functions of a State. The development of the national organization of States during the last few centuries and, as a corollary, the development of international law, have established this principle of the exclusive competence of the State in regard to its own territory in such a way as

1 See *Harris CMIL*, 250–86; F.A. Mann, The Doctrine of Jurisdiction in International Law, *RdC* 111 (1964-I), 9–162; M. Akehurst, Jurisdiction in International Law, *BYIL* 46 (1972–3), 145–257; D.W. Bowett, Jurisdiction: Changing Patterns of Authority over Activities and Resources, *BYIL* 53 (1982), 1; F.A. Mann, The Doctrine of Jurisdiction Revisited After Twenty Years, *RdC* 186 (1984-III), 9–116; *Restatement (Third)*, Vol. 1, 230 *et seq.*; B.H. Oxman, Jurisdiction of States, *EPIL* 10 (1987), 277–83; G. Marston, Maritime Jurisdiction, *EPIL* 11 (1989), 221–4; L. Henkin, *RdC* 216 (1989-IV), 277–330; R.S.J. Martha, *The Jurisdiction to Tax in International Law: Theory and Practice of Legislative Fiscal Jurisdiction*, 1989; T. Mundiya, Extraterritorial Injunctions against Sovereign Litigants in US Courts: The Need for a *Per Se* Rule, *ICLQ* 44 (1995), 893–904; F. Münch, Consular Jurisdiction, *EPIL* I (1992), 763–5. On the relevant jurisprudence of the ICJ see H. Fox, Jurisdiction and Immunities, in V. Lowe/M. Fitzmaurice (eds), *Fifty Years of the International Court of Justice*, 1996, 210–36.
2 A. D'Amato, Domestic Jurisdiction, *EPIL* I (1992), 1090–6. See also Chapter 21 below, 368–9.
3 See Chapter 12 below, 186–91.

4 *Island of Palmas* Case, *RIAA* II 829, at 838. On the case see also Chapter 5 above, 75–6 and Chapter 10 below, 148.

5 For a discussion see, for example, A.F. Lowenfeld, U.S. Law Enforcement Abroad: The Constitution and International Law, *AJIL* 83 (1980), 880; Continued, *AJIL* 84 (1990), 444–93; E.A. Nadelmann, *Cops Across Borders: The Internationalization of U.S. Criminal Enforcement*, 1993.

6 *RGDIP* (1960), 772.

7 See Chapter 4 above, 66–7. See also the interesting discussion in the ILA Committee on Extraterritorial Jurisdiction, *ILA Rep.* 1994, 679 *et seq.*

8 See Chapter 6 above, 98–9.

9 It is sometimes suggested that such acts are permissible in exceptional circumstances if their purpose is to prosecute crimes against humanity, B. Stern, L'Extraterritorialité revisitée: où il est question des affaires Alvarez-Machain, Pâté de bois et de quelques autres, *AFDI* 38 (1992), 239–313, at 288.

10 See generally T. Oppermann, Intervention, *EPIL* II (1995), 1436–9.

11 See also V.P. Nanda, The Validity of United States Intervention in Panama under International Law, *AJIL* 84 (1990), 494–503, at 502; S.B.v. Ellington, *United States v. Noriega* as a Reason for an International Criminal Court, *Dick. JIL* 11 (1993), 451–75; R. Rayfuse, International Abduction and the United States Supreme Court: The Law of the Jungle Reigns, *ICLQ* 42 (1993), 882 *et seq.*

12 See Chapter 8 below, 118–25.

13 See Akehurst, *op. cit.*, 170–7. But see I. Brownlie, *Principles of Public International Law*, 4th edn 1990, 299, who argues that there is no great difference between the problems arising from the assertion of civil and criminal jurisdiction over aliens because the enforcement of civil jurisdiction in the end involves criminal sanctions.

14 On territory see Chapter 5 above, 73–6.

to make it the point of departure in settling most questions that concern international relations.[4]

There are many cases in which states have claimed the right to their own law enforcement abroad.[5] But the (open or secret) performance of state acts on the territory of another state without its consent, such as the kidnapping of the Nazi criminal Eichmann in Argentina by Israel in 1960[6] and the kidnapping in the *Alvarez-Machain* case by US agents,[7] or the sinking of *Rainbow Warrior* by French agents in a New Zealand harbour,[8] although some are disputed,[9] generally constitute violations of the principles of territorial integrity and non-intervention.[10] No state has the authority to infringe the territorial integrity of another state in order to apprehend an alleged criminal, even if the suspect is charged with an international crime, such as drug trafficking as in the case of General Manuel Noriega who was brought to the United States for the purpose of criminal prosecution after President Bush had ordered the military invasion of Panama (on rather dubious grounds of legal justification) on 20 December 1989.[11]

Criminal jurisdiction of national courts

The remainder of this chapter is restricted to the limitations imposed by international law on the jurisdiction of municipal *courts*. It is comparatively rare for international law to *require* a municipal court to hear a case; most of the relevant rules of international law consist of *prohibitions*. If a municipal court exercises jurisdiction in violation of one of these prohibitions, the national state of the injured individual adversely affected by the decision may make an international claim, and it is no excuse for the defendant state to plead that the exercise of jurisdiction was lawful under municipal law, or that the trial was fair and just. But in most cases international law neither forbids nor requires municipal courts to hear cases; it makes an *offer* of jurisdiction, so to speak, which municipal courts need not accept if they do not want to. The jurisdiction of municipal courts is determined mainly by municipal law, and international law confines itself to placing a few limitations on the discretion of states.

Apart from cases of sovereign and diplomatic immunity, and so on, which will be dealt with in the next chapter,[12] international law does not seem to impose any restrictions on the jurisdiction of courts in civil cases;[13] it restricts jurisdiction only in criminal cases. As far as criminal trials are concerned, the bases of jurisdiction most frequently invoked by states are as follows (some of them being more widely accepted than others).

Territorial principle

Every state claims jurisdiction over crimes committed in its own territory,[14] even by foreigners. Sometimes a criminal act may begin in one state and be completed in another: for instance, a man may shoot across a frontier and kill someone on the other side. In such circumstances both states have jurisdiction; the state where the act commenced has jurisdiction under the subjective territorial principle, and the state where the act is completed has jurisdiction under the objective territorial principle (also sometimes called the 'effects doctrine', based on the fact that the injurious effect, although not the act or omission itself, occurred on the territory of the state).[15]

Nationality principle

Whether a person has the nationality of a particular state is determined by the municipal law of that state. International law only lays down certain limits for states to prescribe which criteria are relevant for nationality.[16] A state may prosecute its nationals for crimes committed anywhere in the world (active nationality principle). This rule is universally accepted, and continental countries make extensive use of it. English law gives jurisdiction on this ground to English courts as regards only a few crimes, such as treason, murder and bigamy, but the United Kingdom does not challenge the extensive use of this principle by other countries. The courts of the United States also accept nationality as a basis for jurisdiction.[17] The *Restatement (Third)* provides that a state may exercise jurisdiction through its courts to adjudicate if the person is a national of the state,[18] but US courts 'may try a person only for violation of United States law, not for violation of the penal law of a foreign state'.[19] Similarly, English courts will generally not enforce the criminal laws of foreign states.[20] Some countries claim jurisdiction on the basis of some personal link other than nationality (for example, long residence by the accused in the state exercising jurisdiction), and other states have not protested against such jurisdiction.

Some states, such as Mexico, Brazil and Italy, claim criminal jurisdiction also on the basis of the passive nationality principle to try an alien for crimes committed abroad affecting one of their nationals. *Inter alia* on this principle, in the *Cutting* case (1886), a court in Mexico assumed criminal jurisdiction over an American citizen for the publication of a defamatory statement against a Mexican citizen in a Texas newspaper.[21] At the time the United States protested against this, but in the end the case was dropped because the affected Mexican citizen withdrew the charges. The United States and the United Kingdom have consistently opposed this principle in the past and it may indeed be argued that the mere fact that the national of a state has been the victim of a crime committed in another country does not necessarily concern the general interests of the home state. On the other hand, if the state where the crime has occurred is unwilling or unable to prosecute the offender, one could also argue that the home state is entitled to protect its own citizens once the foreign suspect comes under its control. Recent developments in the United States have come to accept the passive nationality principle with regard to terrorist activities and similar serious crimes.[22] The *Restatement (Third)* notes:

> The principle has not been generally accepted for ordinary torts or crimes, but it is increasingly accepted as applied to terrorist and other organized attacks on a state's nationals by reason of their nationality, or to assassination of a state's diplomatic representatives or other officials.[23]

Protective principle

This allows a state to punish acts prejudicial to its security, even when they are committed by foreigners abroad – for example, plots to overthrow its

15 For example, see the *Lotus* case, PCIJ, series A, no. 10 (see Chapter 3 above, 44–5 and Chapter 12 below, 490–1); Akehurst, *op. cit.*, 152–6. On the controversial application of the 'effects doctrine' by some states to exercise extensive extraterritorial jurisdiction in economic regulation, see O. Schachter, *International Law in Theory and Practice*, 1991, 261–4 and text below, 116–17.
16 See Chapter 17 below, 263–7.
17 See, for example, *Blackmer v. United States*, 284 US 421 (1932) in which an American citizen who had taken refuge in France was ordered to return to the United States to testify in criminal proceedings.
18 *Restatement (Third)*, para. 421(1), (2)(d), at 305.
19 *Ibid.*, para. 422(1), at 313.
20 See *Huntington v. Attrill*, [1893] AC 150.
21 Moore, *Digest of International Law*, Vol. 2, 1906, 228–42.
22 See, for example, the 1986 Diplomatic Security and Anti-Terrorism Act, adopted after the *Achille Lauro* incident, and *US v. Yunis (No. 2)*, 681 F. Supp. 896 (1988); 82 *ILR* 344, where the Court held that the international community would recognize the legitimacy of the passive personality principle, although it was the most controversial basis of assuming criminal jurisdiction. On the international measures adopted to combat terrorism on the high seas after the *Achille Lauro* affair, see Chapter 12 below, 188.
23 *Restatement (Third)*, para. 402, Comment g and Reporter's Note 3, at 240.

24 *Ibid.*, Comment f, at 240, notes that '[t]he protective principle does not support application to foreign nationals of laws against political expression, such as libel of the state or of the chief of state.' See generally I. Cameron, *The Protective Principle of International Criminal Jurisdiction*, 1994.

25 See Chapter 17 below, 256–7, 263.

26 *Lotus* case, *op. cit.*

27 See Chapter 20 below, 353–61.

28 See Chapter 12 below, 189.

29 Akehurst, *op. cit.*, 161–2. See also Chapter 13 below, 201.

30 See M.C. Bassiouni, Hostages, *EPIL* 8 (1985), 264–8; M. Feinrider, Kidnapping, *ibid.*, 355–8; R.A. Friedlander, Terrorism, *EPIL* 9 (1986), 371–6; A. Cassese, The International Community's 'Legal' Response to Terrorism, *ICLQ* 38 (1989), 589–608; G. Guillaume, Terrorisme et droit international, *RdC* 215 (1989-III), 287–416; J.J. Lambert, *Terrorism and Hostages in International Law – A Commentary on the Hostages Convention 1979*, 1990; P. Hortatos, *International Law and Crimes of Terrorism Against the Peace and Security of Mankind*, 1993; H.H. Han, *Terrorism & Political Violence: Limits & Possibilities of Legal Control*, 1993; G. Gilbert, The Law and International Terrorism, *NYIL* 26 (1995), 3–32.

31 *Restatement (Third)*, para. 404, at 254.

32 *Ibid.*, Comment a.

33 Adopted by UNGA Res. 3068 (XXVIII) of 30 November 1973, text in *ILM* 13 (1974), 50. See J. Delbrück, Apartheid, *EPIL* I (1992), 192–6.

government, espionage, forging its currency and plots to break its immigration regulations. Most countries use this principle to some extent, and it therefore seems to be valid, although there is a danger that some states might try to interpret their 'security' too broadly. For instance, if a newspaper published in state A criticizes state B, it would be unreasonable to suggest that state B has jurisdiction to try the editor for sedition.[24] Also not covered by any sense of the protective principle is the death sentence (backed by the reward offered) that was imposed by the *fatwa* issued by the Iranian leader Ayatollah Khomeini on 14 February 1989 against the writer Salman Rushdie (who had to go into hiding under police protection in his domicile in England) for 'blasphemy' in his book *The Satanic Verses*, which had aroused great anger in parts of the Muslim world.

The protective principle of jurisdiction must not be confused with 'diplomatic protection', which refers to the right of a state to intervene diplomatically or to raise an international claim on behalf of its nationals against another state.[25]

Universality principle

Some states claim jurisdiction over all crimes, including all crimes (or at least serious crimes) committed by foreigners abroad. English-speaking countries consider that such universal jurisdiction is normally forbidden by international law. The Permanent Court of International Justice refrained from discussing the validity of such jurisdiction in the *Lotus* case,[26] but individual judges declared that it was normally contrary to international law. The universality principle can obviously lead to unjust results when an individual is punished elsewhere for an act which was lawful under the law of the place where it was committed. The universality principle is less objectionable when it is applied to acts which are regarded as crimes in all countries; indeed, even English-speaking countries, which consider that the universality principle is normally contrary to international law, accept that international law allows states to exercise universal jurisdiction over certain acts which threaten the international community as a whole and which are criminal in all countries, such as war crimes,[27] piracy,[28] hijacking[29] and various forms of international terrorism.[30]

The United States (according to the *Restatement (Third)*) also accepts that

[a] state has jurisdiction to define and prescribe punishment for certain offenses recognized by the community of nations as of universal concern, such as piracy, slave trade, attacks on or hijacking of aircraft, genocide, war crimes, and perhaps certain acts of terrorism.[31]

The *Restatement (Third)* views these offences as being subject to universal jurisdiction as a matter of customary law.[32] Additional offences may be subject to universal jurisdiction on the basis of international agreements, such as, for example, the 1973 International Convention on the Suppression and Punishment of the Crime of 'Apartheid'[33] or the 1984 Convention against Torture and other Cruel, Inhuman and Degrading Treatment or Punishment.[34] But such agreements only apply between the states that are parties to them, unless it can be shown that customary law has also come to accept these offences as subject to universal jurisdiction.

The concept of universal jurisdiction in its broad sense of the power of a state to punish certain crimes, wherever and by whomsoever they have been committed, without any required connection to territory, nationality or special state interest, however, raises a number of problems. First, it is frequently said that universal jurisdiction has been (at least implicitly) recognized after the Second World War in multilateral treaties with regard to crimes considered to be of international concern, in particular, war crimes, which the courts of one state have prosecuted even if they were committed by foreign nationals on the territory of another state. Reference is especially made to the 1949 Geneva Conventions and the obligations of state parties to punish persons guilty of war crimes and crimes against humanity.[35] Thus, in the *Eichmann* case, apart from the issue of the legality of the kidnapping, the jurisdiction assumed by Israeli courts for war crimes and crimes against humanity was generally recognized, although the crimes were committed in Europe during the Second World War before Israel came into existence, and concerned people who were not citizens of the State of Israel.[36] Such crimes are a violation of international law, directly punishable under international law itself (and thus universal crimes), and they may be dealt with by national courts or by international tribunals, such as the Tribunals that were recently established by the UN Security Council for crimes committed in former Yugoslavia or Rwanda, or the envisaged creation of a permanent International Criminal Court.[37] But, in a strict sense, they are not a reflection of the universality principle of jurisdiction, granting states the liberty to prosecute persons under their national law for certain acts which, as such, are not criminal under international law.[38]

Second, apart from piracy, the slave trade, war crimes and crimes against humanity, other crimes of international concern established by more recent conventions, extending to the hijacking of aircraft, sabotage, apartheid, crimes against internationally protected persons, terrorism, hostage-taking, drug trafficking, counterfeiting of currency and others, raise perplexing issues concerning the legal basis of the alleged universal jurisdiction.[39] Such conventions create an obligation to prosecute or to extradite the accused (*aut dedere aut judicare*) and thereby confer jurisdiction under the provisions of the relevant treaty.[40] But how can such treaties, which are binding only among the parties to them, by themselves create true universal jurisdiction in relation to non-parties?

Universal jurisdiction of national courts over crimes against human rights

Moreover, there is a recent tendency in some states to claim universal jurisdiction over crimes against human rights. But here one has to be clear whether one is speaking of criminal law jurisdiction or of non-criminal law jurisdiction (torts or other civil proceedings for compensation for damages). In principle, under international law, universal jurisdiction is not limited to criminal law; states can provide other remedies for victims of crimes against universally accepted interests.[41]

34 *ILM* 23 (1984), 1027, amended text in *ILM* 24 (1985), 535. See Chapter 14 below, 216.

35 See Chapter 20 below, 353–61.

36 *Eichmann v. Att.-Gen. of Israel* (1962), 36 *ILR* 277.

37 See Chapter 20 below, 353–61.

38 See Brownlie (1990), *op. cit.*, 305.

39 See Schachter, *op. cit.*, 268. See also G. Gilbert, Crimes *Sans Frontières*: Jurisdictional Problems in English Law, *BYIL* 63 (1992), 415–42.

40 See M. Chapter Bassiouni/E.M. Wise, *Aut Dedere aut Judicare: The Duty to Extradite or Prosecute in International Law*, 1995.

41 See *Restatement (Third)*, para. 404, Comment b, 255.

42 630 F. 2d 876, 890 (2d Cir. 1980).
43 On the case see the Symposium – Federal Jurisdiction, Human Rights, and the Law of Nations: Essays on Filartiga v. Peña-Irala, *Ga. JICL* 11 (1981), 305–41; F. Hassan, A Conflict of Philosophies: The Filartiga Jurisprudence, *ICLQ* 32 (1983), 250–8.
44 See A.-M. Burley, The Alien Tort Statute and the Judiciary Act of 1789: A Badge of Honor, *AJIL* 83 (1989), 461–93.
45 See also *Restatement (Third)*, para. 702, Reporters' Note 5, at 171.
46 *Siderman de Blake v. Republic of Argentina*, 965 F. 2d 699 (9th Cir. 1992).
47 See Chapter 8 below, 118–23.
48 See R.B. Lillich, Damages for Gross Violations of International Human Rights Awarded by US Courts, *HRQ* 15 (1993), 207, at 220–1.
49 See Chapter 8 below, 118.
50 *Siderman* case, *op. cit.*, at 713.
51 *Argentine Republic v. Amerada Hess Shipping Corp.*, 488 US 428; 109 S. Ct. 683; see Chapter 8 below, 120.

It appears that the first case of this type that was decided by a national court was *Filartiga v. Peña-Irala* (1980) in which a citizen of Paraguay filed a suit in the United States against a former Paraguayan police officer (who was living illegally in New York when the suit was filed) for the torture and death of the plaintiff's brother by acts committed in Paraguay three years earlier. The US Court of Appeals for the Second Circuit found that 'for purposes of civil liability, the torturer has become – like the pirate and slave trader before him – *hostis humani generis*, an enemy of mankind.'[42] The decision held that torture under the guise of official authority, even if it could not be clearly attributed to the government, is a violation of international law and that foreign torturers discovered in the United States might be sued before an American court, regardless of where the act occurred.[43] It is important to note that the suit was based on the US Alien Tort Statute which grants district courts jurisdiction over 'any civil action by an alien for a tort only, committed in violation of the law of nations or a treaty of the United States'. The decision was hailed as a landmark in human rights litigation in support of President Carter's human rights foreign policy, but subsequent attempts to extend jurisdiction to violations of human rights other than torture have proved less successful.[44] At any rate, whether torture has in fact become a crime subject to universal jurisdiction under customary international law, has remained uncertain.[45]

A recent decision of 22 May 1992 by the US Court of Appeals for the Ninth Circuit in the *Siderman* case[46] should also be mentioned because it demonstrates well the close interaction between the concept of 'jurisdiction' and the concept of 'state immunity' exempting a foreign state from the judicial power of the courts of another state (which will be dealt with in more detail in the next chapter[47]). In 1982 the Siderman family sued Argentina for the torture of José Siderman and the expropriation of the family's property, which had taken place immediately after the military seized power in 1976. As far as the torture claim was concerned, in 1984 the lower District Court for the Central District of California awarded the family some US$2.7 million damages in a default judgment (Argentina not taking part in the proceedings).[48] In 1985, however, the District Court vacated the default judgment and dismissed the action after Argentina had claimed immunity under the US Foreign Sovereign Immunity Act (FSIA).[49] While a foreign state can invoke its immunity under the FSIA, it cannot do so in all circumstances, because the Act lays down certain exceptions. In 1992, the US Court of Appeals reversed the decision of the District Court and sent the case back for further proceedings on the grounds that jurisdiction existed prima facie (meaning that the burden of proof lay on Argentina to show 'by a preponderance of evidence'[50] that none of the exceptions to immunity laid down in the FSIA apply).

In its reasoning, the Court of Appeals extensively tried to demonstrate that the prohibition of torture has the nature of *ius cogens*, but in view of a pertinent ruling of the higher US Supreme Court,[51] which it had to follow, the Court of Appeals had no choice but to find that jurisdiction overcoming the immunity defence raised by Argentina could neither be based upon a general exception of the 'violation of *ius cogens*', nor upon the existing treaty exception of section 1604 FSIA. Nevertheless, the Court was able to find jurisdiction under the 'implied waiver' provision of section 1605(a)(1) FSIA, in short, because Argentina was seeking the assistance of US courts in pressing criminal charges against José Siderman. This was seen as sufficient evidence for an implied waiver of immunity by Argentina in the case brought by the Siderman family. The further details of the argument may here be overlooked. The case illuminates the general legal difficulties in human rights litigation in the United States in connection with foreign sovereign immunity.

Because of the problems individual victims face under US foreign sovereign immunity law to bring suits against foreign states for gross violations of human rights, in recent years a number of cases have been filed directly against individuals for such acts, often committed in the exercise of some form of governmental authority. They include the *Marcos* case[52] and suits filed against the Argentinian General Carlos Gúillermo Suárez-Mason, the ex-President of Haiti (Lt.-Gen. Prosper Avril), the former Defence Minister of Guatemala (General Hector Alejandro Gramajo Morales), the Indonesian General Panjaitan, a former official of the Government of Ethiopia (Negowo), and the Serbian leader Dr Karadžić.[53] In response to these difficulties, on 12 March 1992, the US Congress adopted the Torture Victim Protection Act of 1991. The Act allows victims to file claims for damages in a civil action against individuals who 'under actual or apparent authority, or color of law, of any foreign nation' subjects an individual to torture or extrajudicial killing.[54] It remains to be seen what this means in actual judicial practice with regard to foreign sovereign immunity and the related 'act of state doctrine' (which will be discussed in the next chapter[55]) if such acts are also clearly attributable to a foreign government.

'Ivan the Terrible' – The trial of John Demjanuk

Instructive lessons on the difficulties of effectively prosecuting war criminals arising from the application of strict rules on due process and evidence in national legal systems based upon the respect for the rule of law can be learnt from the recent case of John Demjanuk.[56] Demjanuk was accused of being 'Ivan the Terrible', a name given by victims to a sadistic operator of gas chambers who assisted in murdering thousands of Jews at the Treblinka death camp set up by Nazi Germany in Poland during the Second World War.

In 1977 proceedings were commenced against Demjanuk in the United States to deprive him of the US citizenship he had allegedly gained on the basis of lies concerning his wartime activities on his visa application. After Israel had requested his extradition under a treaty with the United States,[57] while deportation proceedings were still pending, in 1983 Demjanuk was finally extradited to stand trial in Israel in 1986. In 1988 he was sentenced to death by hanging by the District Court of Jerusalem.[58] Damjanuk appealed against the decision on the grounds that, as he had stated from the beginning, he was a victim of mistaken identity. He remained in solitary confinement in a cell near Tel Aviv for five years until his appeal was decided. Following the break-up of the Soviet Union, in 1991 new evidence emerged from Soviet archives identifying another man

52 See R.G. Steinhardt, Fulfilling the Promise of Filartiga: Litigating Human Rights Claims Against the Estate of Ferdinand Marcos, *Yale JIL* 20 (1995), 65–103.

53 See G. Ress, Final Report, International Committee on State Immunity, *ILA Rep.* 1994, 466–7, nn. 62 and 63 with references.

54 Section 2(a), P.L. 102–256, 102d Congress, 106 Stat. 73.

55 See Chapter 8 below, 121–3.

56 L.J. Del Pizzo, Not Guilty – But Not Innocent: An Analysis of the Acquittal of John Demjanuk and Its Impact on the Future of Nazi War Crimes Trials, *BCICLR* 18 (1995), 137–78.

57 On extradition, see text below, 117.

58 Del Pizzo, *op. cit.*, 138.

59 *Ibid.*, 139.
60 *Ibid.*, 140.
61 See Chapter 14 below, 209–21.
62 A.T.S. Leenen, Extraterritorial
Application of the EEC Competition Law,
NYIL 15 (1984), 139–66; P.M. Barlow,
*Aviation Antitrust. The Extraterritorial
Application of the United States
Antitrust Laws and International Air
Transportation,* 1988; J.-G. Castel,
*Extraterritoriality in International Trade.
Canada and United States of America
Practices Compared,* 1988; I. Seidl-
Hohenveldern, Extraterritorial Respect
for State Acts, *Hague YIL* 1 (1988),
152–63; F.A. Mann, The Extremism of
American Extraterritorial Jurisdiction,
ICLQ 39 (1990), 410 *et seq.*; A. Bianchi,
Extraterritoriality and Export Controls:
Some Remarks on the Alleged Antinomy
Between European and U.S.
Approaches, *GYIL* 35 (1992), 366; P.M.
Roth, Reasonable Extraterritoriality:
Correcting the 'Balance of Interests',
ICLQ 41 (1992), 245 *et seq.*; W. Meng,
*Extraterritoriale Jurisdiktion im
öffentlichen Wirtschaftsrecht,* 1994; A.
Robertson/M. Demetriou, 'But that was
another country . . . ': The Extra-
Territorial Application of the US Antitrust
Laws in the US Supreme Court, *ICLQ* 43
(1994), 417–24; W. Meng,
Extraterritorial Effects of Administrative,
Judicial and Legislative Acts, *EPIL* II
(1995), 337–43.
63 Text in *ILM* 35 (1996), 357. See
also the Iran and Libya Sanctions Act
adopted by the United States in 1996,
ILM 35 (1996), 1273.
64 See also Chapter 13 below, 200.

named Ivan Marchenko as 'Ivan the Terrible'. In 1993 the Israeli Supreme Court[59] acquitted Demjanuk of all charges, although it found that Demjanuk had served as an SS guardsman in the Trawniki unit, participating in the killings of thousands of Jews, and that he had also been active at the Sobibor death camp in Poland.

A group of survivors of the Holocaust petitioned the Court to institute new criminal proceedings against Demjanuk on the basis of the evidence concerning Trawniki and Sobibor. However, the decision not to bring new charges against Demjanuk was in the end upheld. The United States Court of Appeals for the Sixth Circuit then reopened Demjanuk's extradition case and permitted him to return to the United States. In 1993 the Court found that there had been procedural misconduct during the extradition hearings and that exculpatory evidence had been withheld by the Justice Department's Office of Special Investigations. It revoked the extradition order. In 1994 the US Supreme Court[60] denied review of this decision and Demjanuk returned to free life in Ohio. Thus, an expensive and time-consuming process occupying more than seventeen years, involving two friendly countries both known to be seriously disposed to prosecute Nazi war criminals, in the end led to no conviction.

Conflicts of jurisdiction

The existence of different grounds of jurisdiction invoked by national courts means that several states may have concurrent jurisdiction – that is, the criminal may be tried and punished by several different countries. A conviction or acquittal in a foreign country is treated as a bar to a subsequent prosecution in some countries, but not in all. International law is silent on this point, and the result may be great hardship, unless the protection of international human rights can be invoked.[61]

The inherent conflict between the nationality principle and the effects doctrine (or objective territoriality principle) with the concurrent jurisdiction of the state in whose territory the act or omission has occurred (subjective territoriality principle) often leads to more general difficulties in quite a variety of areas when the laws of the states involved reach different results in permitting, prohibiting or even requiring a certain act. Delicate issues in this respect have arisen particularly in international economic relations, in view of the negative response by a number of states (by enacting so-called blocking statutes) to the attempt by the United States to apply its antitrust and securities laws to foreign subsidiaries of American companies with 'extraterritorial effect'.[62] Similar problems have emerged with the more recent application of regulations of the European Community to nationals outside of the Community. The controversial issue of economic sanctions through exercise of extraterritorial jurisdiction by the United States has re-emerged most recently with the adoption of the Cuban Liberty and Democratic Solidarity (Libertad) Act of 1996 (the Helms-Burton Act).[63] The Act was signed by President Clinton in response to the shooting down by the Cuban Air Force of two light planes flown by a Cuban-American organization based in Florida in February 1996.[64] Under the Act, nationals of third states dealing with American property expropriated by Cuba, using such property or making benefit of it, may be sued for damages before American courts and even barred from entering the United States. This far-reaching extension of US jurisdiction to acts undertaken on foreign territory caused international protests[65] because it is seen to violate obligations of the United States under multilateral trade agreements and under general international law. A discussion of this complicated but in practice increasingly relevant legal area is beyond the scope of an introductory textbook.[66]

Extradition

Finally, it should be pointed out that a certain cooperation exists between different countries in civil, criminal and administrative matters, based upon multilateral and bilateral treaties.[67] This includes cooperation with regard to extradition: a criminal may take refuge in a state which has no jurisdiction to try him, or in a state which is unable or unwilling to try him because all the evidence and witnesses are abroad. To meet this problem, international law has evolved the practice of extradition; individuals are extradited (that is, handed over) by one state to another state, in order that they may be tried in the latter state for offences against its laws. Extradition also includes the surrender of convicted criminals who have escaped before completing their punishment.

Despite occasional statements to the contrary, there is no duty to extradite in the absence of a treaty. It is sometimes said that asylum ends where extradition begins; in other words, a state has a right to grant asylum (refuge) to fugitive criminals unless it has bound itself by treaty to extradite them. The right of asylum means the right of a state to grant asylum; an individual has no right to demand asylum.[68] On the other hand, there is no rule of international law which prevents states from extraditing in the absence of a treaty.[69] The problem of the duty to extradite in the absence of an extradition treaty has recently arisen in view of the United Nations Security Council action taken under Chapter VII of the UN Charter against Libya for the alleged responsibility for the terrorist bombing of the aircraft which crashed over Lockerbie in Scotland. The case brought by Libya in this connection against the United States and the United Kingdom before the International Court of Justice[70] is still pending at the time of writing and raises some fundamental issues with respect to the limits of the legal authority of the Security Council and the role of the Court. They will be taken up later in a broader perspective.[71]

Commonwealth Initiative, *ICLQ* 37 (1988), 177; D. McClean, *International Judicial Assistance*, 1992; W.C. Gilmore, *Mutual Assistance in Criminal and Business Regulatory Matters*, 1995.

68 See Weis, The Draft UN Convention on Territorial Asylum, *BYIL* 50 (1979), 151. For the special problems of asylum in embassies and warships, see D.P. O'Connell, *International Law*, 2nd edn 1970, Vol. 2, 734–40. See further J.A. Barberis, Asylum, Diplomatic, *EPIL* I (1992), 281–3; A. Grahl-Madsen, Asylum, Territorial, *ibid.*, 283–7;.

69 For further study see A.V. Lowe/C. Warbrick, Extraterritorial Jurisdiction and Extradition, *ICLQ* 36 (1986), 398–423; I. A. Shearer, *Extradition in International Law*, 1971; I. Stanbrook/C. Stanbrook, *The Law and Practice of Extradition*, 1980. See also the 6th edn of this book, 107–10; *Restatement (Third)*, Vol. 1, 556 *et seq.*; L.C. Green, Terrorism, the Extradition of Terrorists and the 'Political Offence' Defence, *GYIL* 31 (1988), 337–71; G. Gilbert, *Aspects of Extradition Law*, 1991; B. Swart, Refusal of Extradition and the United Nations Model Treaty on Extradition, *NYIL* 23 (1992), 175–222; Y. Dinstein, Some Reflections on Extradition, *GYIL* 36 (1993), 36–59; G. Gilbert, Extradition, *ICLQ* 42 (1993), 442 *et seq.*; T. Stein, Extradition, *EPIL* II (1995), 327–34; Extradition Treaties, *ibid.*, 334–7.

70 *Lockerbie* case, Order of 14 April 1992, *ICJ Rep.* 1992, 114; *ILM* 31 (1992), 662. See C.C. Joyner/W.P. Rothbaum, Libya and the Aerial Incident at Lockerbie: What Lessons for International Extradition Law, *Mich. JIL* 14 (1993), 222.

71 See Chapter 18 below, 292–3. On the issue of the obligation of states to surrender fugitives to the War Crimes Tribunals for Yugoslavia and Rwanda, see Chapter 20 below, 355–60.

65 See, for example, the European Union Démarches in *ILM* 35 (1996), 397. See also the opinion of the OAS Inter-American Juridical Committee, *ILM* 35 (1996), 1322.

66 See A.F. Lowenfeld, Congress and Cuba: The Helms-Burton Act, *AJIL* 90 (1996), 419–34; for a counter-argument see B.M. Clagett, Title III of the Helms-Burton Act is Consistent with International Law, *ibid.*, 434–40. On the issue of extraterritorial legislative jurisdiction see also A.F. Lowenfeld, Conflict, Balancing of Interest and the Exercise of Jurisdiction to Prescribe: Reflections on

the Insurance Antitrust Case, *AJIL* 89 (1995), 42–53; P.R. Trimble, The Supreme Court and International Law: The Demise of Restatement Section 403, *ibid.*, 53–7, L. Kramer, Extraterritorial Application of American Law after the Insurance Antitrust Case: A Reply to Professors Lowenfeld and Trimble, *ibid.*, 750–8.

67 On legal assistance between states in criminal, civil and administrative matters, see the articles by R. Geiger, *EPIL* 9 (1986), 248–55; 241–8; 235–41; *Restatement (Third)*, Vol. 1, 525 *et seq.*, 591 *et seq.*; D. McClean, Mutual Assistance in Criminal Matters: The

8 Immunity from jurisdiction

1 See *Harris CMIL*, 286–319; *Restatement (Third)*, Vol. 1, 390 *et seq.*; S. Sucharitkul, Immunities of Foreign States Before National Authorities, *RdC* 149 (1976), 87; I. Sinclair, The Law of Sovereign Immunity: Recent Developments, *RdC* 167 (1980), 113; UN Materials on the Jurisdictional Immunities of States and Their Property, UN Doc. ST/LEG/SER.B/20 (1982), 297–321; J. Crawford, International Law and Foreign Sovereigns: Distinguishing Immune Transactions, *BYIL* 54 (1983), 75; G.M. Badr, *State Immunity: An Analytical and Prognostic View*, 1984; H. Steinberger, State Immunity, *EPIL* 10 (1987), 428–46; P.D. Trooboff, Foreign State Immunity: Emerging Consensus on Principles, *RdC* 200 (1986-V), 235–431; R. Jennings, *The Place of the Jurisdictional Immunity of States in International and Municipal Law*, 1987; C. Schreuer, *State Immunity: Some Recent Developments*, 1988; W. Tsutsui, Subjects of International Law in the Japanese Courts, *ICLQ* 37 (1988), 325–36; M.W. Gordon, *Foreign State Immunity in Commercial Transactions*, 1991; R. Donner, Some Recent Caselaw concerning State Immunity Before National Courts, *FYIL* 5 (1994), 388–428. A. Zimmermann, Sovereign Immunity and Violations of International *Jus Cogens* – Some Critical Remarks, *Mich. JIL* 16 (1995), 433–40; H. Fox, Jurisdiction and Immunities, in V. Lowe/ M. Fitzmaurice (eds), *Fifty Years of the International Court of Justice*, 1996, 210–36.

2 L. Bouchez, The Nature and Scope of State Immunity from Jurisdiction and Execution, *NYIL* 10 (1979), at 4.

3 For a German case see German Bundesverfassungsgericht, Decision of 3 December 1977, BverfGE 46, 342; H. Steinberger, Immunity Case (German Federal Constitutional Court, 1977), *EPIL* II (1995), 943–5; see also Ch. J. Oehrle, German Sovereign Immunity Defense, *Fla. JIL* 6 (1991), 445–74.

There are certain categories of persons and bodies which, under international law, are immune from the jurisdiction of municipal courts. The two principal categories are foreign states (sovereign or state immunity) and their diplomatic agents (diplomatic immunity); but other categories are of growing importance and need to be noted, such as the immunity of international organizations. Although the latter two areas are relevant to state immunity, they are of a different kind and must be kept distinct in order not to mix apples with pears.

Sovereign (or state) immunity

In international law state immunity refers to the legal rules and principles determining the conditions under which a foreign state may claim freedom from the jurisdiction (the legislative, judicial and administrative powers) of another state (often called the 'forum state').[1] In practice, problems of state immunity, which seem to occupy national courts more than any other question of international law,[2] primarily arise on two different levels. The first level concerns the immunity of a foreign state from the jurisdiction of municipal courts of another state to adjudicate a claim against it, arising, for example, from a contract or a tort. The second level concerns the exemption of a foreign state from enforcement measures against its state property, especially to execute a municipal court decision, for example, by attaching the bank account of the embassy of that state.[3] Rules on state immunity form part of customary law and are sometimes incorporated in international treaties like the 1972 European Convention on State Immunity.[4] On the national level, a number of states with a common law background have enacted special statutes, such as the 1976 Foreign Sovereign Immunities Act (FSIA) of the United States,[5] the 1978 State Immunity Act of the United Kingdom (SIA)[6] or the 1985 Foreign States Immunities Act of Australia.[7] In civil law countries the courts have also been advancing their doctrines on various aspects of the issue during the past twenty years. Although there are similarities between the principles adopted on the national level and those to be found on the international plane,[8] both levels must be distinguished for systematic reasons (unless, of course, one follows the 'monist' approach to the relation between international and municipal law[9]).

Since states are independent and legally equal,[10] no state may exercise jurisdiction over another state without its consent; in particular, the courts of one state, as a principle, may not assume jurisdiction over another state.

Historically, the ruler was equated with the state, and to this day the head of a foreign state possesses complete immunity, even for acts done by him in a private capacity.[11] Originally, under customary international law the doctrine of absolute state immunity applied, covering all areas of state activity and recognizing only very narrow exceptions. The prevailing trend nowadays, at least in the practice of many states, is to adopt a doctrine of qualified immunity – that is, they grant immunity to foreign states only in respect of their governmental acts (acts *iure imperii*), not in respect of their commercial acts (acts *iure gestionis*). This distinction reflects the fact of the increasing activity of states in economic affairs, both internally and externally, particularly since the nineteenth century.

For a long time English-speaking countries upheld a rule of absolute immunity, which enabled foreign states to enjoy immunity in respect of all their activities, including commercial activities. It is remarkable that the common law world persisted much longer than most civil law countries in sustaining the old theory of absolute sovereignty. However, in 1952 the United States abandoned the absolute immunity rule and adopted the qualified immunity rule.[12] English courts continued to follow the absolute immunity rule even after 1952, out of deference to earlier English cases applying that rule; in the mid-1970s they began moving towards the qualified immunity rule, but the resulting conflict between the old cases and the new cases made English law very uncertain. In 1978 the British Parliament intervened and passed the State Immunity Act, section 3 of which provides that foreign states do not enjoy immunity in respect of their commercial transactions.[13] A number of other states, such as Canada, Pakistan and South Africa, followed and enacted legislation on the basis of the restrictive theory. In other countries the courts moved in the same general direction. Nowadays most states apply the qualified immunity rule, although the absolute immunity rule is still followed by some countries, especially in South America.[14] With the demise of the Soviet Empire and the change from state planning to market economy, the number of former communist countries adhering to the absolute theory has also diminished considerably. China, again, is still a special case.[15]

International instruments, such as the rather complicated European Convention on State Immunity 1972, which states have been reluctant to ratify,[16] or the Montreal Draft Convention on State Immunity approved by the International Law Association in 1982,[17] equally start from the principle of qualified immunity. By 1992, the consensus in the International Law Commission of the United Nations on its Draft Articles on the Jurisdictional Immunities of States and Their Property was also developing in favour of the restrictive theory of immunity.[18] However, this does not mean that the significant divergence in details of applying the restrictive theory in the varying practice of states has been overcome. This explains the need for agreement and codification in an international treaty on the matter, with which various bodies are still concerned.[19] Nor does it necessarily mean that any particular restrictive theory of immunity has become the standard of international customary law. Some scholars take the view that under contemporary general international law states are still only obliged to grant other states immunity from jurisdiction of

4 *ILM* 11 (1972), 470. See H. Damian, European Convention on State Immunity, *EPIL* II (1995), 197–201.
5 P.L. 94–583 (1976), 90 Stat. 2891, *ILM* 15 (1976), 1388; amended text in P.L. 100–699 (1988). See also M.B. Feldman, The United States Foreign Sovereign Immunities Act of 1976: A Founder's View, *ICLQ* 35 (1986), 302; G.R. Delaume, The Foreign Sovereign Immunities Act and Public Debt Litigation: Some Fifteen Years Later, *AJIL* 88 (1994), 257.
6 *ILM* 17 (1978), 1123. See F.A. Mann, The State Immunity Act 1978, *BYIL* 50 (1979), 43; H. Fox, A 'Commercial Transaction' under the State Immunity Act 1978, *ICLQ* 43 (1994), 193; D. Hockl, The State Immunity Act 1978 and its Interpretation by the English Courts, *AJPIL* 48 (1995), 121–59.
7 *ILM* 25 (1986), 715.
8 See the instructive analysis by Jennings, *op. cit.*
9 See Chapter 4 above, 63–4.
10 See Chapter 1 above, 3.
11 *Mighell v. Sultan of Johore*, [1894] 1 QB 149 (breach of promise of marriage). If the sultan had abdicated or had been deposed, he could probably have been sued for private (that is, non-official) acts done by him during his reign; see the analogous case of former diplomats, below, 125–6. English law on the legal position of foreign heads of state is now contained in the State Immunity Act 1978, sections 14(1)(a) and 20. See also J.A. Barberis, Representatives of States in International Relations, *EPIL* 10 (1987), 353–8; C.A. Whomersley, Some Reflections on the Immunity of Individuals for Official Acts, *ICLQ* 41 (1992), 848 *et seq.*; A. Watts, The Legal Position in International Law of Heads of States, Heads of Governments and Foreign Ministers, *RdC* 247 (1994-III).
12 See Letter of Acting Legal Adviser, J.B. Tate to Department of Justice, May 19, 1952, *Dept. State Bull.* 26 984 (1952), 1985.
13 1978 State Immunity Act, *op. cit.* The Act also provides for various other exceptions to sovereign immunity; see sections 3–11.
14 See the Inter-American Draft Convention on Jurisdictional Immunity of States, approved by the Inter-American Juridical Committee on 21 January 1983, *ILM* 22 (1983), 292.
15 See J.V. Feinerman, Sovereign Immunity in the Chinese Case and Its Implications for the Future of International Law, in R.St.J. Macdonald (ed.), *Essays in Honour of Wang Tieya*, 1994, 251–84.

16 Text in *ILM* 11 (1972), 470, *AJIL* 66 (1972), 923. See Damian, *op. cit.*

17 See *ILA Rep*, 1994, 454 (by G. Ress). Revised text of the 1982 Montreal Draft Convention at 488.

18 Text in *ILM* 30 (1991), 1565. On the work of the ILC, see D.W. Greig, Forum State Jurisdiction and Sovereign Immunity under the International Law Commission's Draft Articles, *ICLQ* 38 (1989), 243–76; Specific Exceptions to Immunity under the International Law Commission's Draft Articles, *ibid.*, 560–88; C. Kessedjian/C. Schreuer, Le Project de la Commission du Droit International des Nations-Unies sur les immunités des États, *RGDIP* (1992), 299–341; M. Byers, State Immunity: Article 18 of the International Law Commission's Draft, *ICLQ* 44 (1995), 882–93.

19 In addition to the other aforementioned codification attempts one could refer to the Institut de Droit International, 14th Commission, Contemporary Problems Concerning the Immunity of States in Relation to Questions of Jurisdiction and Enforcement, Basel Resolution of 31 August 1991, *Ann. IDI* 64 (1991-I), 430, or the Afro-Asian Consultative Commission.

20 Steinberger (1987), *op. cit.*, at 432.

21 For an example, see *Buttes Gas and Oil Co. v. Hammer (No. 3)*, [1982] AC 888, and see below, 121–3 on the act of state doctrine.

22 Steinberger (1987), *op. cit.*, 443.

23 *Argentine Republic v. Amerada Hess Shipping Corp.*, 109 S. Ct. 683 (1989).

24 This is the approach adopted in the United States (1976 Foreign Sovereign Immunities Act, section 1603(d)) and in the UK (*Trendtex Trading Corporation v. Central Bank of Nigeria*, [1977] QB 529, 558, 579; *I Congreso del Partido*, [1981] 3 *WLR* 328, 335, 337, 345, 349, 350, 351; section 3(3) SIA.

25 See the instructive cases discussed by M. Herdegen, *Internationales Wirtschaftsrecht*, 2nd. edn 1995, 69 *et seq.*

26 See, for example, H. Ogunniran, The Successive Demise of the Doctrine of State Immunity from Tort Liability: A Comparative Appraisal with Emphasis on the Nigerian Experience, *AJICL* 4 (1992), 369–94; M.H.J. Krent, Reconceptualizing Sovereign Immunity, *Vand. LR* 45 (1992), 1529–80.

27 See Chapter 7 above, 114–15. See also W.F. Pepper, Iraq's Crimes of State Against Individuals and Sovereign Immunity, *Brooklyn JIL* 18 (1992), 313–84.

national courts if the claim against the foreign state is based on its conduct *de jure imperii* and immunity from execution if it is sought against property of the foreign state which serves public (not commercial) purposes.[20] With regard to conduct or property *de jure gestionis* of a foreign state, this view implies that states are free to, but not obliged to, grant immunity.

It is sometimes suggested that the rule of qualified immunity somehow implies that it is improper for states to engage in commercial activities. This is not so. From the policy point of view, the distinction between governmental and commercial activities is not based on the propriety of state acts, but on the appropriateness of municipal courts to decide disputes arising out of those acts. Acts which, by their nature, can only be performed by states, such as expropriating property or testing nuclear weapons, are likely to involve delicate issues of international politics, which make them unsuitable for adjudication by municipal courts. This consideration may lead a municipal court to decline jurisdiction even in cases where the foreign state in question is not a party to the court proceedings.[21] On the other hand, acts which can be performed equally well by states or by private individuals, such as entering into contracts for the purchase of wheat, are clearly suitable for adjudication by municipal courts, and it would cause unjustified hardship for the other contracting party if municipal courts refused to hear such cases.

A more serious objection to the qualified immunity rule is that the distinction between governmental and commercial acts is not always precise and has made the law on state immunity much more complicated than under the theory of absolute sovereignty.[22] If the area in question concerns the exercise of 'classical' state functions, such as the use of the army in an armed conflict, the matter is rather simple. In 1989, in *Argentine Republic v. Amerada Hess Shipping Corp.*, for example, the US Supreme Court found no difficulty in granting immunity to Argentina against a claim filed by the owner of a tanker which had been attacked and damaged on the high seas by the Argentinian air force in the Falklands war.[23] The Court also rejected the contention raised by the claimant against sovereign immunity that the Argentinian act had been a violation of international law.

The matter becomes more complicated in cases in which foreign states have selected forms of private commercial activities to pursue public purposes. Some states base the distinction between acts *de jure imperii* and acts *de jure gestionis* on the 'nature' of the act (objective test),[24] others base it on the purpose of the act (subjective test); for instance, the purchase of boots for the army would be regarded as a commercial act under the first test and as a governmental act under the second test. It may seem that such borderline cases are exceptional and that they are more easy to settle under the current trend to look at the 'nature' of the activity (objective test). But in actual practice, considerable difficulties and controversial (or unclarified) issues remain,[25] including the commercial exception in the field of public debt/foreign central bank litigation, the relationship between the immunity exception for commercial transactions on the one hand and for torts on the other,[26] the availability of the defence of immunity against claims for the gross violation of human rights by a foreign government (torture),[27] and with regard to the question whether individuals can also invoke immunity (as distinct from foreign states or their instrumentalities).[28]

In any case, under the absolute immunity rule, the old vexed question, now less virulent, whether nationalized industries form part of the state (and thus enjoy immunity like the state itself) gives rise to just as many borderline cases, most of which would be avoided if the qualified immunity rule were applied, because the vast majority of the acts of nationalized industries would then be regarded as commercial and not covered by immunity, thus making it unnecessary to decide whether the nationalized industries form part of the state.

So far we have only been considering cases in which legal proceedings are brought against the foreign state. But immunity also applies to proceedings involving property in which the foreign state has an interest, even though the foreign state may not necessarily be a party to the proceedings. (Under the qualified immunity rule, no immunity applies if the foreign state is using the property for commercial purposes.)[29] For instance, if A sues B, disputing B's title to property which a foreign state has hired from B, the foreign state may intervene to have the proceedings stopped, because judgment in A's favour would deprive the foreign state of its interest in the property. This rule applies if the foreign state claims to own the property,[30] or if it claims some right less than ownership, such as possession[31] or the right to immediate possession.[32]

Clearly a court cannot allow a foreign state to halt proceedings between two private individuals by simply asserting an interest in property, unsupported by evidence. On the other hand, to require the foreign state to prove its title would make nonsense of the idea of immunity, because it would mean forcing the state to submit to the court's jurisdiction on the merits of the case. English courts, for example, take the middle course of requiring the foreign state to prove that its alleged interest in the property has a prima facie validity; the foreign state must 'produce evidence to satisfy the court that its claim is not merely illusory nor founded on a title manifestly defective'.[33]

Finally, the question of what constitutes a 'state' for the purposes of immunity is a difficult one. If the British government certifies that it recognizes a particular entity as a sovereign state, then English courts will grant immunity to that entity.[34] But the difficulties do not stop there. For instance, the fact that Ruritania may be recognized as a sovereign state does not help us to decide whether the political subdivisions of Ruritania, such as provinces and town councils, form part of the state for the purposes of entitlement to sovereign immunity; the cases on this point conflict.[35] Again, should nationalized industries and similar bodies in Ruritania be treated as part of the state for the purposes of entitlement to sovereign immunity? Here, too, the cases conflict, and they conflict even within the line of jurisprudence of one particular national jurisdiction.

The act of state doctrine

Closely connected in the practice of some states with the principle of sovereign immunity, particularly in the United States, is the so-called 'act

28 See the cases reviewed by Ress, *op. cit.*, 452 *et seq.*

29 For other exceptions to the general principle stated in the main text, see I. Brownlie, *Principles of Public International Law*, 4th edn 1990, Chapter XV; sections 6 and 7 SIA.

30 *The Parlement Belge* (1880), 5 PD 197.

31 *The Cristina*, [1938] AC 485; *The Arantzazu Mendi*, [1939] AC 256.

32 *USA and France v. Dollfus Mieg et Compagnie*, [1952] AC 582.

33 *Juan Ysmael & Co. v. Republic of Indonesia*, [1955] AC 72.

34 Section 21 SIA.

35 Brownlie (1990), *op. cit.*; section 14 SIA.

36 J.-P. Fonteyne, Acts of State, *EPIL* I (1992), 17–20; *Restatement (Third)*, Vol. 1, 366 *et seq.*

37 See Chapter 4 above, 71–4.

38 See Lipstein, Recognition of Governments and the Application of Foreign Law, *Trans. Grot. Soc.* 35 (1949), 157.

39 M. Akehurst, Jurisdiction in International Law, *BYIL* 46 (1972–3), 145, 240–4.

40 See Chapter 20 below, 353–61.

41 See Chapter 6 above, 98–9.

42 See M. Pugh, Legal Aspects of the *Rainbow Warrior* Affair, *ICLQ* 36 (1987), 655–69, at 660–3.

of state' doctrine.[36] Under this doctrine, the acts of a state, carried out within its own territory, cannot be challenged in the courts of other states (not even if the acts are contrary to international law, according to the most extreme version of the doctrine). The doctrine overlaps with private international law,[37] and there have been cases in England in which courts have applied the doctrine and private international law as alternative grounds for their decision, with the result that private international law and the act of state doctrine are sometimes confused with one another. (If Ruritania expropriates property situated in Ruritania, do English courts accept the expropriation as legal because it is legal under the laws of the place where the property is situated (private international law), or because the expropriation has been carried out by a foreign state (act of state doctrine)?[38]) But there is a difference; the act of state doctrine is in one sense wider than private international law, because it covers acts performed by a foreign state within its own territory *which are contrary to its own law*; but the doctrine is in another sense also much narrower than private international law, because it covers only acts of a *state* and not, for instance, a sale of goods between two private individuals.

Opinions differ as to whether the act of state doctrine is a rule of public international law. The disagreement is probably caused by a failure to perceive that the doctrine really covers two very different types of situation:

1   The first situation is where an individual is sued or prosecuted in the courts of one state for acts which he or she performed as a servant or agent of another state. In this situation the act of state doctrine is a sort of corollary to the principle of sovereign immunity, and is an established rule of international law. All servants or agents (or former servants or agents) of a foreign state are immune from legal proceedings in respect of acts done by them on behalf of the foreign state. The reason is that such proceedings indirectly implead the state, because the state would probably feel honour-bound to stand behind the individual concerned and to indemnify him for any damages which he had to pay. Also, such proceedings would be likely to involve delicate issues of international politics, which would make them unsuitable for adjudication by municipal courts. However, there are various exceptions to the immunity conferred by the act of state doctrine;[39] for instance, it cannot be pleaded as a defence to charges of war crimes, crimes against peace, or crimes against humanity.[40] In the *Rainbow Warrior* case,[41] for example, there was no commission of crimes of this nature by the two French agents. The incident rather falls within the category of cases in which immunity from local jurisdiction (in this case that of New Zealand) over official agents entering another country illegally with the official purpose of committing unlawful acts cannot be established. Thus, the French government made no formal immunity claim for the two French agents in the New Zealand proceedings, even after French state responsibility for the attack was admitted.[42]

2   The second situation is where a state expropriates property situated within its territory and sells it to a private individual, who is then

sued by the original owner in the courts of another state. Different considerations apply here; the purchaser is not forced to buy the property in the same way that a servant or agent is forced to carry out the orders of the state. Many of the cases applying the act of state doctrine in this situation are American, and the leading US case regards the doctrine, not as a rule of public international law, but as a rule of US constitutional law, derived from the principle of the separation of powers;[43] the courts should not embarrass the executive in its conduct of foreign relations by questioning the acts of foreign states. It is notable that in the United States the doctrine has been primarily developed with respect to an act of a government expropriating foreign property allegedly violating international law, although the case law is inconsistent as regards the aspect of what the limits are for judicial interference with policy options available to the American government in international affairs.[44] The application of the doctrine by English courts is different.[45]

Civil law countries, such as France and Germany and those countries following their legal tradition, normally do not work with the act of state concept, but rather have used their conflict of laws principles to determine, in particular, the effect to be accorded to foreign nationalization decrees.

Diplomatic immunity

The rules of diplomatic immunity[46] sometimes arouse indignation in ordinary people, but are almost always observed by states, because states have a common interest in preserving the rules. A state may be under pressure from its internal public opinion to limit the immunity of foreign diplomats, but it usually resists the pressure, because otherwise it would create a precedent which would be used against its own diplomats in foreign countries. All states are both 'sending states' (that is, states which send diplomatic missions to foreign countries) and 'receiving states', and consequently the rules on diplomatic immunity work much more smoothly than the rules on expropriation, for instance, which are sometimes regarded as favouring the rich states at the expense of the poor states. The rules of diplomatic immunity are 'essential for the maintenance of relations between states and are accepted throughout the world by nations of all creeds, cultures and political complexions'.[47] Major breaches of these rules, such as Iran's behaviour towards the United States diplomats who were held as hostages in 1979–81, while extremely rare, receive disproportionate publicity because of that rarity.[48]

Most of the modern law on diplomatic immunity is contained in the 1961 Vienna Convention on Diplomatic Relations.[49] Accession to the Convention by states is almost universal, which shows the importance attached to its subject matter. Most of the provisions of the Convention seek to codify customary law, and can therefore be used as evidence of customary law even against states which are not parties to the Convention.

Diplomatic relations are established by mutual consent between the two states concerned.[50] However, they may be broken off unilaterally (often as

43 *Banco Nacional de Cuba v. Sabbatino* (1964), 376 US 398, which held that US courts could not challenge the Cuban nationalization of US-owned sugar plantations. The effect of this decision was subsequently reversed by an Act of Congress. See the case note by K.R. Simmonds, *ICLQ* 14 (1965), 452 and by J.P. Fonteyne, *EPIL* 10 (1987), 381–3.

44 For a good summary of the present state of affairs see M.W. Janis, *An Introduction to International Law*, 2nd edn 1993, 359–66.

45 See Akehurst, *op. cit.*, 240–57 and the 6th edn of this book, at 47.

46 See *Harris CMIL*, 319–46; *Restatement (Third)*, Vol. 1, 455 *et seq.*

47 *Tehran Hostages* case (*USA v. Iran*), *ICJ Rep.* 1980, 3, at 24. See Chapter 17, 259–60 and text below, 126–7.

48 See text below, 126–7.

49 Text in 500 UNTS 95, *AJIL* 55 (1961), 1064, *Brownlie BDIL*, 217. See also M. Hardy, *Modern Diplomatic Law*, 1968; E. Denza, *Diplomatic Law: Commentary on the Vienna Convention on Diplomatic Relations*, 1976; G.E. do Nascimento e Silva, Vienna Convention on Diplomatic Relations (1961), *EPIL* 9 (1986), 393–8; J. Brown, Diplomatic Immunity: State Practice under the Vienna Convention on Diplomatic Relations, *ICLQ* 37 (1988), 53–88; G.V. McClanahan, *Diplomatic Immunity – Principles, Practices, Problems*, 1989; S.E. Nahlik, Development of Diplomatic Law. Selected Problems, *RdC* 222 (1990-III), 187–363; C.J. Lewis, *State and Diplomatic Immunity*, 3rd edn 1990; F. Orrego Vicuna, Diplomatic and Consular Immunities and Human Rights, *ICLQ* 40 (1991), 34–4; M. Richtsteig, *Wiener Übereinkommen über diplomatische und konsularische Beziehungen: Entstehungsgeschichte, Kommentierung, Praxis*, 1994.

50 Article 2, 1961 Vienna Convention. See L. Gore-Booth (ed.), *E. Satow's Guide to Diplomatic Practice*, 6th edn 1988; B. Sen, *A Diplomat's Handbook of International Law and Practice*, 3rd edn 1988; L. Dembinski, *The Modern Law of Diplomacy: External Missions of States and International Organizations*, 1988; B.S. Murty, *The International Law of Diplomacy*, 1989; D.D. Newson, *Diplomacy Under a Foreign Flag: When Nations Break Relations*, 1990; A. James, Diplomatic Relations and Contacts, *BYIL* 62 (1991), 347 *et seq.*; H. Blomeyer-Bartenstein, Diplomatic Relations, Establishment and Severance, *EPIL* I (1992), 1070–2; Y.Z. Blum, Diplomatic Agents and Missions, ibid., 1034–40; E. Denza, Diplomatic Agents and Missions, Privileges and Immunities, ibid., 1040–5; J. Salmon, Manuel de droit diplomatique, 1994.

a mark of disapproval of an illegal or unfriendly act by the other state); when state A breaks off diplomatic relations with state B, it not only withdraws its own diplomatic mission from state B, but also requires state B to withdraw its mission from state A. The receiving state's consent is necessary for the selection of the head of mission (who nowadays usually has the title of ambassador) but not for the selection of his subordinates (although there are exceptions). The receiving state may at any time declare a diplomat *persona non grata* or not acceptable, which forces the sending state to withdraw him; this is a step which can be employed as a sanction if immunities are abused, although the receiving state has a complete discretion and can take this step in other circumstances also. Article 11 of the Vienna Convention provides that 'the receiving state may require that the size of a mission be kept within limits considered by it to be reasonable and normal' – a desirable innovation.

Article 3(1) of the Convention states:

The functions of a diplomatic mission consist *inter alia* in:

(a) representing the sending State in the receiving State;

(b) protecting in the receiving State the interests of the sending State and of its nationals, within the limits permitted by international law;

(c) negotiating with the Government of the receiving State;

(d) ascertaining by all lawful means conditions and developments in the receiving State, and reporting thereon to the Government of the sending State;

(e) promoting friendly relations between the sending State and the receiving State, and developing their economic, cultural and scientific relations.

In modern times, promotion of exports has become a major function of diplomatic missions. So, too, have public relations (less euphemistically known as propaganda) – a practice which occasionally degenerates into interference in the internal affairs of the receiving state (such interference is forbidden by Article 41(1) of the Convention).

Throughout history diplomats and other envoys have needed privileges and immunities for the effective performance of their functions in the receiving state. The preamble to the Vienna Convention recites that 'the purpose of such privileges and immunities is not to benefit individuals but to ensure the efficient performance of the functions of diplomatic missions *as representing states*' (emphasis added). There is thus a double basis for diplomatic immunities; they are needed for the efficient performance of diplomatic functions, and they are also given because diplomats are representatives of states. The 'representative basis', although accepted as the basis of diplomatic immunities in previous centuries, is nowadays rather doubtful; it would suggest that diplomats, like states, are not immune from suit in respect of the commercial activities of states, whereas in fact diplomats *are* immune from suit in respect of such activities. The modern view is to treat immunities as having a 'functional basis' – that is, as being necessary 'to ensure the efficient performance of the functions of diplomatic missions'.

51 *BPIL* 1964, 74.
52 See text above, 124.

Immunity from the jurisdiction of courts

Article 31(1) of the Vienna Convention provides:

> A diplomatic agent shall enjoy immunity from the criminal jurisdiction of the receiving State. He shall also enjoy immunity from its civil and administrative jurisdiction, except in the case of:
>
> (a) a real action relating to private immovable property situated in the territory of the receiving State, unless he holds it on behalf of the sending State for the purposes of the mission;
>
> (b) an action relating to succession in which the diplomatic agent is involved . . . as a private person . . . ;
>
> (c) an action relating to any professional or commercial activity exercised by the diplomatic agent in the receiving State outside his official functions.

The same immunity is enjoyed by a diplomat's family, if they are not nationals of the receiving state. The existence of immunity does not mean that people injured by diplomats are wholly without remedy. A diplomat's hopes of promotion are usually dependent on scrupulous good behaviour, and this will induce him not to abuse his immunity; he will probably be willing to settle private claims against him before they come to the attention of his superiors. Alternatively, the injured individual or the government of the receiving state can ask the ambassador to waive his subordinate's immunity, which often happens. The injured party can also commence legal proceedings against the diplomat in the sending state. Most claims arise out of road accidents, and often diplomats are expected to insure their vehicles and the insurance companies do not try to hide behind their clients' immunity.[51] In extreme cases of abuse a diplomat can be declared *persona non grata*.[52]

One of the most striking features of the Vienna Convention is that it does not grant full immunity to *all* the staff of a diplomatic mission. In addition to diplomatic agents, the Convention speaks of administrative and technical staff (for example, clerical assistants, archivists and radio technicians) and of service staff (for example, drivers and receptionists). These two categories of subordinate staff have complete immunity from criminal jurisdiction, but their immunity from civil and administrative jurisdiction is limited to their official acts. The same is true of diplomatic agents who are nationals or permanent residents of the receiving state (and see Article 38(2) of the Vienna Convention concerning other members of the staff who are nationals or permanent residents of the receiving state). The limitation was an innovation as far as English law was concerned, although it was not unknown in some other countries. It demonstrates the functional character of immunities; since the functions of subordinate staff are less important than those of diplomats, there is less need for the interests of private litigants in the receiving state to be sacrificed in order to enable the subordinate staff of the diplomatic mission to carry out their duties efficiently.

When an individual ceases to be a member of the staff of a diplomatic mission, his immunity continues for a reasonable time thereafter, in order

53 Article 39(2), 1961 Vienna
Convention.
54 See Chapter 17 below, 257–60.
55 See Chapter 7 above, 110–11.
56 See R. Higgins, The Abuse of
Diplomatic Privileges and Immunities:
Recent United Kingdom Experience,
AJIL 79 (1985), 641; M. Herdegen, The
Abuse of Diplomatic Privileges and
Countermeasures not Covered by the
Vienna Convention on Diplomatic
Relations. Some Observations in the
Light of Recent British Experience,
ZaöRV 46 (1986), 734. For an
interesting discussion of possible ways
of preventing various abuses of
diplomatic privileges and immunities,
see Higgins, UK Foreign Affairs
Committee Report on the Abuse of
Diplomatic Immunities and Privileges:
Government Response and Report, AJIL
80 (1986), 135–40. See also I.
Cameron, First Report of the Foreign
Affairs Committee of the House of
Commons, ICLQ 34 (1985), 610–20; A.
Akinsanya, The Dikko Affair and Anglo-
Nigerian Relations, ibid., 602–9.
57 L.A.N.M. Barnhoorn, Diplomatic
Law and Unilateral Remedies, NYIL 25
(1994), 39–81.
58 Article 23, 1961 Vienna
Convention.
59 Article 34.
60 Article 36.
61 Tehran Hostages case, op. cit.,
at 42.

to give him time to leave the country. After that, he may be sued for private acts done during his period of office, but not for official acts.[53]

Other privileges and immunities

In addition to immunity from the jurisdiction of the courts, diplomats possess other privileges and immunities (the meanings of the words 'privilege' and 'immunity' overlap so much that it is impracticable to distinguish between them). In the interests of simplicity, discussion will be confined to diplomatic agents *stricto sensu* who are not nationals or permanent residents of the receiving state. (For the more limited immunities of other persons attached to a diplomatic mission, see Articles 37 and 38 of the Vienna Convention.)

Thus, the premises of a diplomatic mission and the private residence of a diplomat are inviolable; agents of the receiving state are not allowed to enter such places without the permission of the sending state, and must take appropriate steps to protect them from harm.[54] On the other hand, diplomatic premises are not extraterritorial; acts occurring there are regarded as taking place on the territory of the receiving state, not on that of the sending state, and criminals who take refuge there are usually handed over to the police of the receiving state.[55] The sending state is not allowed to imprison people on diplomatic premises.

Archives, documents and other property belonging to a diplomatic mission or diplomat are inviolable. The mission must have unimpeded communication with the sending state by all appropriate means, including diplomatic couriers and messages in code or cipher (but it may not use a radio transmitter without the receiving state's consent). The mission's official correspondence is inviolable, and the diplomatic bag must not be opened or detained. The diplomatic bag ought to contain only diplomatic documents or articles intended for official use; the problem is what to do if such privileges are abused for smuggling weapons, drugs or even live bodies.[56] Invoking an exceptional right to inspect (apart perhaps from infra-red scrutiny) and to open suspicious diplomatic bags is likely to provoke corresponding reprisals.[57] 'Bugging' of diplomatic premises, which is not mentioned in the Vienna Convention, is contrary to the spirit of the Convention, but is probably too widespread to be regarded as illegal.

The premises of the mission are exempt from all taxes, except those which represent payment for specific services rendered (for example, water rates).[58] Diplomats are also exempt from all taxes, with certain exceptions.[59] The receiving state must allow the importation, free of customs duties, of articles for the official use of the mission and of articles for the personal use of a diplomat or his family;[60] before 1961 this rule was generally observed, but was regarded as a rule of comity, not of law.

Article 29 of the Vienna Convention provides that diplomats shall not be liable to any form of arrest or detention, and that appropriate steps must be taken to protect them from attack. Terrorists often attack diplomats, but receiving states almost always do their best to protect diplomats in such circumstances. The approval given by Iran to the 'militants' who seized United States diplomats in Iran in November 1979 was correctly described by the International Court of Justice as 'unique',[61] and was condemned

unanimously by the Court and the Security Council.[62] Iran tried to excuse
its behaviour by claiming that the United States and its diplomats had
acted unlawfully towards Iran (for example, by intervening in Iran's
internal affairs, starting from the CIA-supported overthrow of the government of Mossadegh in 1951 to protect American and British oil interests), but the Court held that these charges, even if they had been proved,
would not have justified Iran's violation of diplomatic immunity; the obligation to respect the rules of diplomatic immunity is an absolute obligation
which must be obeyed in all circumstances.[63]

Consular immunity

Consuls, like diplomats, represent their state in another state, but, unlike
diplomats, they are not concerned with political relations between the two
states. They perform a wide variety of non-political functions: issuing
passports and visas, looking after the shipping and commercial interests of
their states, and so on. Consulates often are based in provincial towns as
well as in capital cities.

In 1963 the United Nations convened a conference at Vienna, which
drew up the Vienna Convention on Consular Relations[64] and many states
subsequently became parties to the Convention. According to the International Court of Justice, the 1963 Convention codified the law on consular
relations;[65] but some writers have argued that the immunities conferred on
consuls by the Convention are wider than the immunities enjoyed by consuls under customary law. Be that as it may, even if the Convention does
not reflect the customary law relating to consuls, it often does reflect post-
war bilateral consular conventions. This is particularly true of Article 36,
which gives consuls a right to communicate with nationals of the sending
state in the territory of the receiving state, especially when those nationals
are in prison before trial or after conviction in a criminal case.

To a large extent the Convention assimilates the status of consuls to
that of diplomats, but this is not surprising, because it is becoming increasingly common nowadays for a state to amalgamate its diplomatic and consular services. People who act simultaneously as diplomats and as consuls
have diplomatic immunity. Consuls who do not act as diplomats have many
of the same privileges and immunities as diplomats, according to the Convention, but they are immune from the civil or criminal jurisdiction of the
receiving state's courts only in respect of official acts. In addition, they may
import articles for their personal use, free of duty, only at the time of their
first appointment.

Immunities of international organizations

It is uncertain to what extent international organizations enjoy immunities
under customary law; in practice the matter is usually regulated by treaties,
such as the 1946 General Convention on the Privileges and Immunities of
the United Nations, or by the headquarters agreements concluded with
the host state where the organization is seated.[66] The purpose of immunity
in the case of international organizations is a purely functional one, related

62 *Ibid.*, 29–45; SC Res. 460, 21
December 1979, *UN Chronicle*, 1980,
no. 1, 13, at 14. See B.V.A. Röling,
Aspects of the Case concerning United
States Diplomatic and Consular Staff in
Tehran, *NYIL* 11 (1980), 125 *et seq.*;
G.T. McLaughlin/L.A. Teclaff, The
Iranian Hostages Agreements, *Fordham
ILJ* 4 (1980), 223–64; K. Oellers-
Frahm, United States Diplomatic and
Consular Staff in Tehran Case, *EPIL* 2
(1981), 282–6; W. Christopher *et al.*,
*American Hostages in Iran: The Conduct
of A Crisis*, 1985; S.A. Riesenfeld,
United States-Iran Agreement of
January 19, 1981 (Hostages and
Financial Arrangements), *EPIL* 8 (1985),
522–6. See also Chapter 17 below,
259–60.

63 *Tehran Hostages* case, *op. cit.*, at
38–41.

64 596 UNTS 261.

65 *Ibid.*, at 24. See also E. Kussbach,
Vienna Convention on Consular
Relations (1963), *EPIL* 9 (1986), 388–
93; F. Matscher, Marriages Performed
by Diplomatic and Consular Agents,
ibid., 258–62; L.T. Lee, *Consular Law
and Practice*, 2nd edn 1991; C.
Economidès, Consular Treaties, *EPIL* I
(1992), 768–70; F. Münch, Consular
Jurisdiction, *ibid.*, 763–5.

66 Text in 1 UNTS 15. See P.C. Szaz,
International Organizations, Privileges
and Immunities, *EPIL* II (1995), 1325–
33; P.H.F. Bakker, *The Legal Position of
Intergovernmental Organizations: A
Functional Necessity Analysis of Their
Legal Status and Immunities*, 1994;
Restatement (Third), Vol. 1, 492 *et seq.*;
M. Wenckstern, *Eine Analyse der
Immunitätsbestimmungen
internationaler Organisationen und der
völkerrechtlichen Praxis*, 1994.

67 Sections 11–16. For a special case see *Applicability of Article VI, Section 22, of the Convention on the Privileges and Immunities of the United Nations* (Advisory Opinion), *ICJ Rep.* 1989, 177–221 and the article on the case by S. Richter, *EPIL* I (1992), 823–5.
68 Discussion will be confined to sovereign and diplomatic immunity, since the rules are more clearly established with regard to these types of immunity than with regard to other types. However, the rules governing sovereign and diplomatic immunity are probably applicable by analogy to other types of immunity from the jurisdiction of courts.
69 *R. v. Kent*, [1941] 1 KB 454.
70 *R. v. Madan*, [1961] 2 QB 1; see also section 2(7) SIA.

to the specific tasks of the organization, as set out in the constituent treaty, and serves to secure its ability to perform them. It is not a reflection of sovereignty, except only in the very indirect sense of also serving to protect the interests of the member states of the respective organization. For the purposes of this introduction, it may be instructive to summarize the provisions of the General Convention, as an example of the immunities enjoyed by international organizations.

The UN has complete immunity from all legal process (section 2 of the 1946 Convention); otherwise a combination of eccentric litigants and biased courts could interfere with the performance of its functions. Its premises, assets, archives and documents are inviolable (sections 3 and 4). It is exempt from direct taxes and customs duties (section 7), and its staff are exempt from income tax on their salaries (section 18); otherwise income tax would be levied on staff members' salaries by the states where those staff members worked, and states contributing to the UN's budget would in effect be making indirect payments to the states in which the UN had its principal offices (the United States and Switzerland). The Secretary-General and the Assistant Secretaries-General have diplomatic immunity (section 19); the member states were not prepared to go as far as this in the case of other staff members, who only have limited immunities, such as immunity from legal process in respect of their official acts, and exemption from military service (section 18). The Secretary-General must waive a staff member's immunity if in his opinion immunity would impede the course of justice and can be waived without prejudice to the interests of the UN (section 20). The UN must 'make provisions for appropriate modes of settlement of' claims against it (section 29); it has done so by insuring itself against tortious liability, entering into arbitration agreements, and so on.

Representatives of member states attending UN meetings are granted almost the same privileges and immunities as diplomats, except that their immunity from legal process applies only to their official acts, and they are immune from customs duties only in respect of their personal baggage.[67]

Waiver of immunity

Immunity from the jurisdiction of courts does not mean that the holder of the immunity is above municipal law. The obligations of municipal law remain binding on him, but are unenforceable. (This is true as regards immunity from the jurisdiction of courts. However, some of the other immunities discussed in the present chapter, for example, immunities from tax, are immunities from obligations, not merely immunities from enforcement.) Consequently, both sovereign and diplomatic immunity can be waived;[68] the effect is to change an unenforceable obligation into an enforceable one. The immunity is conferred in the interests of the state, and can be waived only by the state. A state may waive the immunity of one of its diplomats against the diplomat's wishes.[69] Conversely, waiver by a diplomat is ineffective unless authorized by his superiors.[70] Immunity can be waived either 'in the face of the court' (that is, after proceedings have been commenced), or by an agreement made before proceedings are commenced.[71]

Waiver 'in the face of the court' can take two forms: express (that is, expressly stating to the court that immunity is waived) or implied (that is, defending the action without challenging the jurisdiction of the court). Article 32(2) of the Vienna Convention 1961 says that waiver must always be express, but it is doubtful whether this provision reflects customary law, so it cannot necessarily be applied by analogy to sovereign immunity.

If states or diplomats appear as plaintiffs, they are deemed to waive their immunity in respect of counter-claims arising out of the same subject matter. For instance, in the days when English law conferred sovereign immunity on foreign states in respect of their commercial activities, a state which sold goods to an individual and sued him for not paying the price was deemed to have waived its immunity from a counter-claim by the individual that the goods were defective. But a claim by a state for repayment of money lent did not constitute an implied waiver of immunity from a counter-claim for slander, because the counter-claim was entirely unrelated to the original claim.[72]

Waiver of immunity in a court of first instance also covers appeals from the judgment of that court; if a state wins on the merits in a court of first instance, it cannot revive its immunity in order to prevent the other party appealing to a higher court.[73] But waiver of immunity from the jurisdiction of courts does not entail waiver of immunity from enforcement of judgments; a separate act of waiver of immunity from enforcement is necessary before execution can be levied against the property of a foreign state or diplomat in order to satisfy an unpaid judgment debt.[74] In most cases a state which waives its immunity from jurisdiction will be prepared to carry out an adverse judgment; otherwise it would not have waived its immunity from jurisdiction in the first place. In most countries where foreign states do not enjoy sovereign immunity in respect of their commercial activities, property which foreign states use for commercial purposes does not usually enjoy immunity from execution, and in such cases the question of waiving immunity from execution does not arise.[75]

[71] Sections 2(2) and 17(2) SIA.
[72] *High Commissioner for India v. Ghosh*, [1960] 1 QB 134; see also Article 32(3) Vienna Convention and section 2(6) SIA.
[73] Section 2(6) SIA
[74] Article 32(4) Vienna Convention; section 13(3) SIA.
[75] See Sinclair, *op. cit.*, 218–42 (especially at 242), 255–7, 263–5, H. Fox, Enforcement Jurisdiction, Foreign State Property and Diplomatic Immunity, *ICLQ* (1985), 114.

9 Treaties

1 *Harris CMIL*, 729–812; *Restatement (Third)*, Vol. 1, part III, 144 *et seq.*; Lord McNair, *The Law of Treaties*, 2nd edn 1961; T.O. Elias, *The Modern Law of Treaties*, 1974; S. Rosenne, Vienna Convention on the Law of Treaties, *EPIL* 7 (1984), 525–33; R. Bernhardt, Treaties, *ibid.*, 459–64; L. Wildhaber, Treaties, Multilateral, *ibid.*, 480–4; S.K. Chatterjee, International Law of Treaties: Substance or Shadow?, *Indian JIL* 27 (1987), 13; T.M. Franck, Taking Treaties Seriously, *AJIL* 82 (1988), 67–8; S. Rosenne, *Developments in the Law of Treaties 1945–1986*, 1989; A.Z. Hertz, Medieval Treaty Obligation, *Conn. JIL* 6 (1991), 425–43; J. Klabbers, Informal Agreements in International Law: Towards a Theoretical Framework, *FYIL* 5 (1994), 267–387; P. Reuter, *Introduction to the Law of Treaties*, 3rd edn 1995; E.W. Vierdag, The International Court of Justice and the Law of Treaties, in V. Lowe/M. Fitzmaurice (eds), *Fifty Years of the International Court of Justice*, 1996, 145–66; Klabbers, *The Concept of Treaties*, 1996. See also Chapter 3 above, 36–9.
2 *Nuclear Tests Case (Australia v. France)*, *ICJ Rep.* 1974, 253, 267–8 (although it is submitted that the Court was wrong in holding that France's statement that it would conduct no more nuclear tests in the atmosphere was intended to be a legally binding promise). See also Chapter 20 below, 349.
3 Text in *ILM* 8 (1969), 679, *AJIL* 63 (1969), 875. See I. Sinclair, *The Vienna Convention on the Law of Treaties*, 2nd edn 1984.
4 See Chapter 3 above, 61.
5 Text in *AJIL* 61 (1967), 285.

States make treaties about every conceivable topic.[1] By and large, all treaties, regardless of their subject matter, are governed by the same rules, and the law of treaties therefore tends to have a rather abstract and technical character; it is a means to an end, not an end in itself. For the same reasons, the greater part of the law of treaties is not affected by conflicts of interests between states; every state is a party to hundreds of treaties and has an interest in ensuring that treaties work effectively, just as all states have a common interest in preserving the rules of diplomatic immunity in order to facilitate diplomatic relations.

It should be noted, however, that a treaty is not the only means by which a state can enter into a legal obligation. A unilateral promise is binding in international law on the state making the promise, if that state intended its promise to be legally binding.[2] Similarly a state can lose a legal right by unilaterally waiving it, provided its intention to do so is sufficiently clear.

A convenient starting-point for discussing treaties is the 1969 Vienna Convention on the Law of Treaties which came into force on 27 January 1980.[3] The preliminary research and drafting were carried out by the International Law Commission,[4] whose commentary is a useful guide to the interpretation of the Convention, and indicates the extent to which different articles of the Convention reflect the pre-existing customary law and the agreed views of states.[5] Since 1969 many provisions of the Convention have been frequently cited in judgments and in state practice as accurate statements of the customary rules relating to treaties.

However, the Convention applies only to treaties made after its entry into force (Article 4). *As a convention*, therefore, its value initially has been rather limited. Its importance lies in the fact that most of its provisions attempt to codify the customary law relating to treaties, although there are other provisions which represent a 'progressive development' rather than a codification of the law. Unless otherwise stated, the provisions mentioned in this chapter codify the pre-existing law.

Article 2(1)(a) of the 1969 Vienna Convention defines a treaty, for the purposes of the Convention, as 'an international agreement concluded between States in written form and governed by international law, whether embodied in a single instrument or in two or more related instruments, and whatever its particular designation'. This definition excludes agreements between states which are governed by municipal law and agreements between states which are not intended to create legal relations at all. The exclusion of these two types of agreement from the definition of treaties is fairly orthodox, but the definition given in the Vienna Convention is more controversial in so far as it excludes oral agreements between states, and agreements of any sort between international organizations or between states and international organizations. Such agreements are usually called treaties, and the only reason why they are not regarded as treaties – for the purposes of the Convention – is that the rules of international law governing them differ in a few respects from the rules governing written treaties between states; they were therefore not covered by the Convention, in order to prevent the Convention becoming too complicated. A special convention, the Convention on the Law of Treaties Between States and International Organizations or Between International Organizations, was signed in 1986 but has not yet entered into force.[6] In any case, treaties made by international organizations are more usefully studied as part of the law of international organizations,[7] and oral treaties are extremely rare nowadays.

Conclusion and entry into force of treaties

When lawyers talk about the conclusion of a treaty, they are not talking about its termination, but about its coming into effect or formation.[8]

Adoption of the text of a treaty

Article 9 of the 1969 Vienna Convention provides:

1   The adoption of the text of a treaty takes place by the consent of all the States participating in its drawing up except as provided in paragraph 2.
2   The adoption of the text of a treaty at an international conference takes place by the vote of two-thirds of the States present and voting, unless by the same majority they shall decide to apply a different rule.

Article 9(2) describes what actually happens at most modern conferences (in earlier times unanimity was the normal practice), but each conference adopts its own rules concerning voting procedures, and there is no general rule of customary law governing voting procedures; Article 9(2) therefore represents progressive development rather than codification.

The adoption of the text does not, by itself, create any obligations. A treaty does not come into being until two or more states consent to be bound by it, and the expression of such consent usually comes after the adoption of the text and is an entirely separate process.

Consent to be bound by a treaty

Article 11 of the Vienna Convention provides:

The consent of a State to be bound by a treaty may be expressed by signature, exchange of instruments constituting a treaty, ratification, acceptance, approval or accession, or by any other means if so agreed.

The multiplicity of methods of expressing consent has unfortunately introduced much confusion into the law. Traditionally, *signature and*

6 Text in *ILM* 25 (1986), 543. See also E. Klein/M. Pechstein, *Das Vertragsrecht internationaler Organisationen*, 1985; G. Gaja, A 'New' Vienna Convention on Treaties Between States and International Organizations or Between International Organizations: A Critical Commentary, *BYIL* 58 (1987), 253 *et seq.*; P.K. Menon, *The Law of Treaties between States and International Organizations*, 1992; K. Zemanek, International Organizations, Treaty-Making Power, *EPIL* II (1995), 1343–6.

7 See the literature in Chapter 6 above, 32–6.

8 S. Rosenne, Treaties, Conclusion and Entry into Force, *EPIL* 7 (1984), 464–7; E.W. Vierdag, The Time of the 'Conclusion' of A Multilateral Treaty: Article 30 of the Vienna Convention on the Law of Treaties and Related Provisions, *BYIL* 59 (1988), 75 *et seq.*

9 See Chapter 4 above, 66–7.
10 See Articles 2(1)(b) and 16, 1969 Vienna Convention.

ratification are the most frequent means of expressing consent. In some cases the diplomats negotiating a treaty are authorized to bind their states by signing the treaty; in other cases their authority is more limited, and the treaty does not become binding until it is ratified (that is, approved) by the head of state. In some countries (including the United States but not the United Kingdom), the constitution requires the head of state to obtain the approval of the legislature, or of part of the legislature (for example, the Senate in the United States), before ratifying a treaty.[9]

Strictly speaking, ratification occurs only when instruments of ratification are exchanged between the contracting states, or are deposited with the depositary.[10] In the case of a multilateral treaty, it is obviously impractical to exchange instruments of ratification between a large number of states, and so, instead, the treaty usually provides that instruments of ratification shall be deposited with a state or international organization which is appointed by the treaty to act as the depositary. Ratifications, accessions, reservations, denunciations and similar communications from states concerning the treaty must be sent to the depositary, which notifies the other states concerned whenever such a communication is received.

The relationship between signature and ratification can be understood only in the light of history. In days when slow communications made it difficult for a diplomat to keep in touch with his sovereign, ratification was necessary to prevent diplomats exceeding their instructions; after receiving the text of the treaty and checking that his representatives had not exceeded their instructions, the sovereign was obliged to ratify their signatures. By 1800, however, the idea of a duty to ratify was obsolete, and ratification came to be used for a different purpose – to give the head of state time for second thoughts. With the rise of democracy, the delay between signature and ratification also gave a chance for public opinion to make itself felt; this was particularly true if important negotiations had been conducted secretly, or if the treaty necessitated changes in municipal law, or if the constitution of the state concerned required the consent of the legislature for ratification.

During the nineteenth century a further change occurred. By this time many states had adopted constitutions requiring the consent of the legislature for ratification, but states also began to conclude an increasing number of routine treaties which legislatures had no time to discuss. The modern practice therefore grew up of treating many treaties as binding upon signature alone. There is much to be said for this practice. Even in the United Kingdom, where the consent of the legislature is not needed for ratification, many treaties which are subject to ratification are never ratified, simply as a result of the inertia inherent in any large administrative machine; treaties are negotiated in a spirit of popular enthusiasm which soon wanes afterwards, so that there is no pressure for ratification.

The subject matter of a treaty has little bearing on the question whether it requires ratification. One might have imagined that politically important treaties would always require ratification, but practice is not consistent; for instance, in urgent cases ratification is sometimes dispensed with, because there is no time for it. Treaties usually state expressly whether or not ratification is necessary, and this makes it difficult to know what rule to apply if the treaty is silent. Some writers are of the opinion that the general rule is that treaties need ratification; other writers say the general rule is that treaties do *not* need ratification. But each group of writers recognizes that there are many exceptions to the general rule, and so in practice the effects of the difference between the two theories are comparatively slight. The Vienna Convention adopts a 'neutral' attitude; everything depends on the intentions of the parties, and Articles 12(1) and 14(1) of the Convention provide guidelines for ascertaining the intentions of the parties. Article 12(1) provides:

The consent of a State to be bound by a treaty is expressed by the signature of its representative when:

(a) the treaty provides that signature shall have that effect;

(b) it is otherwise established that the negotiating States were agreed that signature should have that effect;[11] or

(c) the intention of the State to give that effect to the signature appears from the full powers[12] of its representative or was expressed during the negotiations.

Article 14(1) provides:

The consent of a State to be bound by a treaty is expressed by ratification when:

(a) the treaty provides for such consent to be expressed by ratification;

(b) it is otherwise established that the negotiating States were agreed that ratification should be required;

(c) the representative of the State has signed the treaty subject to ratification; or

(d) the intention of the State to sign the treaty subject to ratification appears from the full powers of its representative or was expressed during the negotiations.

It should also be added that performance of a treaty can constitute tacit ratification. In particular, if a state successfully claims rights under an unratified treaty, it will be estopped from alleging that it is not bound by the treaty.

In addition to signature and ratification, a state can also become a party to a treaty by *accession* (otherwise known as adhesion or adherence). The difference between accession, on the one hand, and signature or ratification, on the other, is that the acceding state did not take part in the negotiations which produced the treaty, but was invited by the negotiating states to accede to it. Accession is possible only if it is provided for in the treaty, or if all the parties to the treaty agree that the acceding state should be allowed to accede. Accession has the same effects as signature and ratification combined.

These, then, were the traditional methods of expressing consent to a treaty: signature, ratification and accession. However, modern developments have complicated the situation in several different ways.

11 This can be readily inferred if the treaty provides that it shall come into force at once, or on a fixed date in the very near future.

12 Full powers are defined in Article 2 (1)(c) of the 1969 Vienna Convention as 'a document emanating from the competent authority of a State designating a person or persons to represent the State for negotiating, adopting or authenticating the text of a treaty, for expressing the consent of the State to be bound by a treaty, or for accomplishing any other act with respect to a treaty'.

13 Article 24. For a special case see R. Platzöder, Substantive Changes in a Multilateral Treaty Before its Entry into Force: The Case of the 1982 United Nations Convention on the Law of the Sea, *EJIL* 4 (1993), 390–402. See also Chapter 12 below, 174–5.

In the first place, treaties are nowadays often concluded by an exchange of correspondence (usually called an exchange of notes) between the two states. Each note is signed by a representative of the state sending it, and the two signatures are usually enough to establish the consent of the states to be bound; however, exchanges of notes require ratification in the few cases where it can be proved that that was the intention of the states concerned.

Second, the modern practice of leaving certain treaties open for long periods for signature by states which may or may not have participated in the drafting of the treaty has blurred the distinction between accession, on the one hand, and signature and ratification, on the other. For instance, Article 81 of the Vienna Convention provides that the Convention shall be open for nearly a year for signature by certain categories of states, not all of which attended the Vienna Conference; Article 83 provides that the Convention 'shall [thereafter] remain open for accession by any State belonging to any of the categories mentioned in article 81'.

Third, *acceptance* or *approval* is sometimes used nowadays in place of ratification (or, alternatively, in place of accession). This innovation is more a matter of terminology than of substance. Acceptance and approval perform the same function on the international plane as ratification and accession; in particular, they give a state time to consider a treaty at length before deciding whether to be bound. The main reason for the popularity of these terms is that they enable a state to evade provisions in its own constitution requiring the consent of the legislature for ratification. Article 14(2) of the Vienna Convention recognizes the similarity between ratification and acceptance and approval by providing that 'the consent of a State to be bound by a treaty is expressed by acceptance or approval under conditions similar to those which apply to ratification'.

Finally, it sometimes happens that the text of a treaty is drawn up by an organ of an international organization (for example, the UN General Assembly) and that the treaty is then declared open for 'accession', 'ratification', 'acceptance', or 'approval' by member states. The terminological confusion here becomes complete, because 'accession', 'ratification', 'acceptance' and 'approval' are used interchangeably; different terms are used in different treaties to describe a process which is absolutely identical.

Entry into force

A treaty normally enters into force as soon as all the negotiating states have expressed their consent to be bound by it.[13] But the negotiating states are always free to depart from this general rule, by inserting an appropriate provision in the treaty itself.

Thus, the entry into force of a treaty may be delayed by a provision in the treaty, in order to give the parties time to adapt themselves to the requirements of the treaty (for example, in order to enable them to make the necessary changes in their municipal laws). The treaty may provide for its entry into force on a fixed date, or a specified number of days or months after the last ratification.

When very many states participate in drafting a treaty, it is unlikely that they will all ratify it, and it is therefore unreasonable to apply the normal rule that the treaty does not enter into force until all the negotiating states have ratified it. Accordingly, such a treaty often provides that it shall enter into force when it has been ratified by a specified number of states (the number is frequently as high as a third of the number of the negotiating states, because the treaty might not be any use if it were only ratified by a very small number of states). Even when the minimum number of ratifications is reached, the treaty is, of course, in force only between those states which have ratified it; it does not enter into force for other states until they in turn have also ratified it.

A treaty can apply retroactively, but only if the contracting states clearly intend it to do so. In the same way, the contracting states may agree to apply a treaty provisionally between its signature and entry into force; this is a useful device when a treaty deals with an urgent problem but requires ratification. Under the Vienna Convention, however, 'unless . . . the negotiating States have otherwise agreed, the provisional application of a treaty . . . with respect to a State shall be terminated if that State notifies the other States between which the treaty is being applied provisionally of its intention not to become a party to the treaty'.[14]

Article 18 of the Vienna Convention provides:

A State is obliged to refrain from acts which would defeat the object and purpose of a treaty when:

(a) it has signed the treaty or has exchanged instruments constituting the treaty subject to ratification, acceptance or approval, until it shall have made its intention clear not to become a party to the treaty; or

(b) it has expressed its consent to be bound by the treaty, pending the entry into force of the treaty and provided that such entry into force is not unduly delayed.

There is some authority for this rule in customary law, but the matter is controversial.

Reservations

A state may be willing to accept most of the provisions of a treaty, but it may, for various reasons, object to other provisions of the treaty. In such cases states often make reservations when they become parties to a treaty.[15] For example, the United States made a reservation concerning the death penalty when it signed the International Covenant on Civil and Political Rights.[16] Article 2(1)(d) of the Vienna Convention defines a reservation as

a unilateral statement . . . made by a State, when signing, ratifying, accepting, approving or acceding to a treaty, whereby it purports to exclude or to modify the legal effect of certain provisions of the treaty in their application to that State.

The effect of a reservation depends on whether it is accepted or rejected by the other states concerned. A reservation to a bilateral treaty presents no problems, because it is, in effect, a new proposal reopening the negotiations between the two states concerning the terms of the treaty; and, unless agreement can be reached about the terms of the treaty, no

14 Article 25(2), 1969 Vienna Convention.
15 D.W. Bowett, Reservations to Non-Restricted Multilateral Treaties, *BYIL* 48 (1976–7), 67–92; R.L. Bindschedler, Treaties, Reservations, *EPIL* 7 (1984), 496–9; R. Kühner, *Vorbehalte zu multilateralen völkerrechtlichen Verträgen*, 1986; F. Horn, *Reservations and Interpretative Declarations to Multilateral Treaties*, 1988; R.W. Edwards, Jr., Reservations to Treaties, *Mich. JIL* 10 (1989), 362; C. Redgwell, Universality or Integrity? Some Reflections on Reservations to General Multilateral Treaties, *BYIL* 64 (1993), 245–82. The ILC decided in 1993 to take up the topic of the law and practice relating to reservations to treaties and a preliminary report was submitted by Alain Pellet (A/CN.4/470) in 1995.
16 See E.F. Sherman, The U.S. Death Penalty Reservation to the International Covenant on Civil and Political Right: Exposing the Limitations of the Flexible System Governing Treaty Formation, *Texas ILJ* 29 (1994), 69–93. On reservations to human rights treaties see Chapter 14 below, 215.

17 *ICJ Rep.* 1951, 15, at 29. See E. Klein, Genocide Convention (Advisory Opinion), *EPIL* II (1995), 544–6.
18 Article 102(1) UN Charter (text in *Brownlie BDIL*, 1). See M. Brandon, Analysis of the Terms 'Treaty' and 'International Agreement' for Purposes of Registration under Article 102 of the United Nations Charter, *AJIL* 47 (1953), 46–69; U. Knapp, Article 102, in *Simma CUNAC*, 1103–16.
19 K. Zemanek, Treaties, Secret, *EPIL* 7 (1984), 505–6.
20 For other collections see Chapter 3 above, 36–7.

treaty will be concluded. In the case of a multilateral treaty the problem is more complicated, because the reservation may be accepted by some states and rejected by others.

The traditional rule was that a state could not make a reservation to a treaty unless the reservation was accepted by all the states which had signed (but not necessarily ratified) or adhered to the treaty. However, this rule was undermined by the advisory opinion of the International Court of Justice in the *Genocide* case.[17] The Court said that the traditional theory was of 'undisputed value', but was not applicable to certain types of treaty. More specifically, it was not applicable to the Genocide Convention, which sought to protect individuals, instead of conferring reciprocal rights on the contracting states. The Court therefore advised that

> a State which has made . . . a reservation which has been objected to by one or more of the parties to the [Genocide] Convention but not by others, can be regarded as a party to the Convention if the reservation is compatible with the object and purpose of the Convention.

Since different states may reach different conclusions about the compatibility of a reservation, the practical effect of the Court's opinion is that a state making a reservation is likely to be regarded as a party to the treaty by some states, but not by others.

Articles 19–21 of the Vienna Convention follow the principles laid down by the Court in the *Genocide* case, but make a concession to the supporters of the traditional rule by recognizing that *every* reservation is incompatible with *certain types* of treaty unless accepted unanimously. The International Law Commission's proposals to this effect met a favourable response from member states of the United Nations, and it is probable that the rules contained in Articles 19–21 will be followed in the future, even by states which are not parties to the Vienna Convention on the Law of Treaties.

Registration

Article 102(1) of the United Nations Charter provides that

> [e]very treaty . . . entered into by any Member of the United Nations after the present Charter comes into force shall as soon as possible be registered with the Secretariat and published by it.[18]

Treaties between non-member states are not covered by Article 102, but are often transmitted voluntarily to the Secretariat for 'filing and recording'; Article 80 of the Vienna Convention seeks, for the first time, to make such transmission obligatory. Article 102 was intended to prevent states entering into secret agreements without the knowledge of their nationals, and without the knowledge of other states, whose interests might be affected by such agreements.[19] An additional advantage of Article 102 is that treaties are published in the United Nations Treaty Series (UNTS), which is a useful work of reference.[20] If states fail to register a treaty, as sometimes happens, the treaty is not void; but '[n]o party to any such treaty . . . may invoke that treaty . . . before any organ of the United Nations'. [21]

Application of treaties

Territorial scope of treaties

Article 29 of the Vienna Convention states: 'Unless a different intention appears from the treaty or is otherwise established, a treaty is binding upon each party in respect of its entire territory.'[22] This general rule is often altered by a specific provision in a treaty. For instance, older treaties often contained a 'colonial clause', which provided that the treaty shall apply automatically only to each party's metropolitan (that is, non-colonial) territory, but that each party shall have the option of extending it to one or more of its colonies. One advantage of a colonial clause was that it enabled the wishes of the inhabitants of a colony to be considered before the treaty was extended to the colony.

The interpretation of treaties is dealt with briefly in Articles 31–3 of the Vienna Convention and will be taken up later when dealing with the interpretation of the UN Charter.[23]

Treaties and third states

The general rule is that a treaty creates neither rights nor obligations for third states (that is, states which are not parties to the treaty).[24] But there are exceptions to this general rule, which are laid down in detail in Articles 35–7 of the Convention. It is sometimes suggested that Article 2(6) of the United Nations Charter (which is a treaty) imposes obligations on states without their consent.[25] What Article 2(6) actually says is that:

> The Organization shall ensure that States which are not Members of the United Nations act in accordance with these Principles [that is, the principles of the United Nations, set out in Article 2 of the Charter] so far as may be necessary for the maintenance of international peace and security.[26]

In reality, Article 2(6) does not even purport to impose obligations on non-members; it merely announces the policy which the United Nations will follow in its relations with non-members.

Application of successive treaties relating to the same subject matter

It sometimes happens that a party to a treaty subsequently enters into another treaty relating to the same subject matter, and that the provisions of the two treaties are mutually inconsistent; the position is complicated by the fact that the other party or parties to the second treaty may or may not also be parties to the first treaty. Article 30 of the Vienna Convention lays down detailed rules to deal with the resulting problems.[27]

Invalid treaties

Article 42(1) of the Vienna Convention provides:

21 Article 102(2) UN Charter. See D.N. Hutchinson, The Significance of the Registration or Non-Registration of an International Agreement in Determining Whether or Not It Is a Treaty, *CLP* 46 (1993), 257–90.

22 M.B. Akehurst, Treaties, Territorial Application, *EPIL* 7 (1984), 510–11.

23 See Chapter 21 below, 364–8.

24 H. Ballreich, Treaties, Effect on Third States, *EPIL* 7 (1984), 476–80; C. Tomuschat/H.-P. Neuhold/J. Kropholler, *Völkerrechtlicher Vertrag und Drittstaaten*, 1988.

25 On the nature and interpretation of the UN Charter, see Chapter 21 below, 364–8.

26 Article 2(6), UN Charter. See W. Graf Vitzthum, Article 2(6), in *Simma CUNAC*, 131–9.

27 W.G. Grewe, Treaties, Revision, *EPIL* 7 (1984), 499–505; W. Karl, Treaties, Conflicts between, *ibid.*, 467–73; B.M. Carnahan, Treaty Review Conferences, *AJIL* 81 (1987), 226–30. See also Articles 39–41 of the Vienna Convention on the amendment and modification of treaties, and Articles 58(1) and 59 on the termination or suspension of treaties.

28 M. Schröder, Treaties, Validity, *EPIL* 7 (1984), 511–4; B. Conforti/A. Labella, Invalidity and Termination of Treaties: The Role of National Courts, *EJIL* 1 (1990), 44–66.
29 See L. Wildhaber, *Treaty-Making Power and Constitution: An Interpretational and Comparative Study*, 1971.

The validity of a treaty or of the consent of a State to be bound by a treaty may be impeached only through the application of the present Convention.[28]

This is to prevent states attempting to evade inconvenient treaty obligations by making far-fetched allegations that the treaty is invalid.

Provisions of municipal law regarding competence to conclude treaties

The constitutions of many countries provide that the head of state may not conclude (or, at least, may not ratify) a treaty without the consent of a legislative organ.[29] What happens if the head of state disregards such a rule when entering into a treaty? Is the treaty valid or not? Opinion is divided. One school of thought says that the treaty is void, although this conclusion is sometimes limited to cases where the constitutional rule in question is well known – an imprecise qualification which would be difficult to apply in practice. Another school of thought considers that the treaty is valid, but some supporters of this school are prepared to make exceptions when one party to the treaty *knew* that the other party was acting in breach of a constitutional requirement. Most states favour the latter point of view, which is reflected in Article 46 of the Vienna Convention:

1 A State may not invoke the fact that its consent to be bound by a treaty has been expressed in violation of a provision of its internal law regarding competence to conclude treaties as invalidating its consent unless that violation was manifest and concerned a rule of its internal law of fundamental importance.

2 A violation is manifest if it would be objectively evident to any State conducting itself in the matter in accordance with normal practice and in good faith.

Treaties entered into by persons not authorized to represent a state

Article 46 is essentially concerned with the relationship between the executive and the legislature within a state. But it is one thing to say, as Article 46 in effect does, that the executive's act in making a treaty is binding on the state; it is another thing to decide which particular members of the executive are authorized to act in the name of the state. It would be absurd to suppose that a state could be bound by the acts of a junior clerk in the same way that it is bound by the acts of the Minister for Foreign Affairs.

Accordingly, Article 7(1) of the Vienna Convention provides:

A person is considered as representing a State for the purpose of . . . expressing the consent of the State to be bound by a treaty if:

(a) he produces appropriate full powers; or

(b) it appears from the practice of the States concerned or from other circumstances that their intention was to consider that person as representing the State for such purposes and to dispense with full powers.

Article 7(2) provides that heads of state, heads of government and ministers for foreign affairs are, by virtue of their functions and without having to produce full powers, considered as representing their state for the purpose of performing all acts relating to the conclusion of a treaty.

Article 8 provides:

> An act relating to the conclusion of a treaty performed by a person who cannot be considered under article 7 as authorized to represent a State for that purpose is without legal effect unless afterwards confirmed by that State.

Specific restrictions on authority to express the consent of a state

Although a person may be authorized to enter into a treaty on behalf of a state, in accordance with Article 7, it sometimes happens that a specific restriction is imposed on his authority; for example, he may be instructed not to enter into a treaty unless it contains a particular provision to which his state attaches importance. What happens if he disregards such a restriction? Article 47 provides:

> If the authority of a representative to express the consent of a State to be bound by a particular treaty has been made subject to a specific restriction, his omission to observe that restriction may not be invoked as invalidating the consent expressed by him unless the restriction was notified to the other negotiating States prior to his expressing such consent.

Coercion of a representative of a state

Article 51 of the Vienna Convention provides:

> The expression of a State's consent to be bound by a treaty which has been procured by the coercion of its representative through acts or threats directed against him shall be without any legal effect.[30]

Coercion of a state by the threat or use of force

Before the First World War, customary international law imposed no limitations on the right of states to go to war,[31] and consequently a treaty procured by the threat or use of force against a state was as valid as any other treaty. Since the First World War there has been a growing tendency to regard aggression as illegal, and the corollary would seem to be that treaties imposed by an aggressor are void. Accordingly, Article 52 of the Vienna Convention provides:

> A treaty is void if its conclusion has been procured by the threat or use of force in violation of the principles of international law embodied in the Charter of the United Nations.

Article 52 is an accurate statement of the modern law.[32] When Article 52 of the Vienna Convention speaks of 'the threat or use of force in violation of the principles . . . embodied in the Charter of the United Nations', it is obviously referring to Article 2(4) of the Charter, which prohibits 'the threat or use of force . . . in any . . . manner inconsistent with the Purposes of the United Nations'. The communist states and the more militant Third World countries used to argue that 'force' in Article 2(4) covers economic and political pressure as well as military force, and that treaties imposed by economic or political pressure were therefore void. The Western countries disagreed. The International Law Commission adopted

30 H.G. de Jong, Coercion in the Conclusion of Treaties, *NYIL* 15 (1984), 209–47.
31 See Chapter 2 above, 13–20 and Chapter 19 below, 306–7.
32 *Fisheries Jurisdiction Case* (*UK v. Ireland*) (Jurisdiction), *ICJ Rep.* 1973, 3, at 14, *obiter*. On this case see Chapter 3 above, 93 and Chapter 12 below, 183.

33 W. Morvay, Unequal Treaties, *EPIL* 7 (1984), 514–7; C.v. Katte, Denunciation of Treaty of 1865 between China and Belgium (Orders), *EPIL* I (1992), 1010; C. Ku, Change and Stability in the International System: China Secures Revision of the Unequal Treaties, in R.St.J. Macdonald (ed.), *Essays in Honour of Wang Tieya*, 1994, 447–62. See also B.W. Morse/K.A. Hamid, American Annexation of Hawaii: An Example of the Unequal Treaty Doctrine, *Conn. JIL* 5 (1990), 407–56; L. Caflisch, Unequal Treaties, *GYIL* 35 (1992), 52.
34 See also Chapter 10 below, 155–7.
35 See Chapter 3 above, 57–8.

a neutral attitude in its commentary on the law of treaties, saying that the meaning of 'force' 'should be left to be determined in practice by interpretation of the relevant provisions of the Charter'. However, it is submitted that the interpretation placed on the word 'force' by the communist states and the more militant Third World countries is an extremely strained interpretation. Article 2(4) of the Charter gives effect to the principle, stated in the preamble to the Charter, that '*armed* force shall not be used, save in the common interest', and a Brazilian amendment to extend Article 2(4) to include economic and political coercion was rejected at the San Francisco conference, which drew up the United Nations Charter in 1945.

Such treaties are often called 'unequal treaties', although the term is also used to describe treaties whose terms are unfair, regardless of the circumstances of their conclusion.[33] States which argue that unequal treaties are void seldom define their terms. Despite occasional suggestions to the contrary by communist and militant Third World countries, the modern rules against force do not operate retroactively. In other words, if a treaty was procured by force at a time when force was not illegal, the validity of the treaty is not affected by subsequent changes in the law which declare that force is illegal and that treaties procured by force are void.[34]

Other causes of invalidity

According to the Vienna Convention, a state's consent to be bound by a treaty can be invalidated by mistake (in certain circumstances, specified in Article 48), by the fraud of another negotiating state (Article 49), or by the corruption of its representative by another negotiating state (Article 50). It is uncertain whether these causes of invalidity existed in customary international law. A treaty is void if it conflicts with *ius cogens* (Article 53).[35]

The consequences of invalidity

The consequences of invalidity vary according to the precise nature of the cause of invalidity. In cases covered by Articles 8 and 51–3 of the Vienna Convention, the treaty is void, or the expression of consent to be bound by the treaty is 'without legal effect', which comes to the same thing. In cases covered by Articles 46–50, however, the Vienna Convention says that a state may merely *invoke* the vitiating factor as invalidating the treaty; the effect of this formula is that the treaty is probably voidable rather than void; the treaty is valid until a state claims that it is invalid, and the right to make such a claim may be lost in certain circumstances (Article 45). The vitiating factors mentioned in Articles 8 and 51–3 are more serious than those mentioned in Articles 46–50, so this distinction is logical; but it is doubtful whether it is as clearly established in customary law as the Vienna Convention suggests.

In both cases, however, Articles 65–8 of the Vienna Convention provide that a party challenging the validity of a treaty must notify the other parties to the treaty and give them time to make objections before it takes any action (although there are exceptions to this rule). If objections are made, and if the resulting dispute is not settled within twelve months,

Article 66 confers jurisdiction on the International Court of Justice over disputes arising from Article 53 (*ius cogens*) and confers jurisdiction over other disputes on a special conciliation commission set up under an annex to the Convention. These provisions are obviously desirable in order to prevent abuse of the rules concerning causes of invalidity, but they represent an almost complete innovation when one compares them with the pre-existing customary law; in particular, under customary law, international courts and conciliation commissions do not have jurisdiction over all cases concerning claims that a treaty is invalid, but only over those cases which the parties *agree* to refer to the court or conciliation commission.

Termination of treaties

Article 26 of the Vienna Convention provides: 'Every treaty in force is binding upon the parties to it and must be performed by them in good faith.' In other words, a state cannot release itself from its treaty obligations whenever it feels like it; if it could, legal relations would become hopelessly insecure. But the words 'in force' must not be overlooked; few treaties last for ever, and, unless some provision is made for the termination of treaties, the law will become hopelessly rigid. The rules of law concerning the termination of treaties try to steer a middle course between the two extremes of rigidity and insecurity.[36] They work fairly well, because every state is a party to hundreds of treaties on a wide range of topics, and therefore has an interest in ensuring that the right balance between security and flexibility is maintained in practice. Article 42(2) of the Vienna Convention seeks to protect the security of legal relations by providing: 'The termination of a treaty, its denunciation or the withdrawal of a party, may take place only as a result of the application of the provisions of the treaty or of the present Convention. The same rule applies to suspension of the operation of a treaty.'

Termination in accordance with the provisions of a treaty
Article 54 of the Vienna Convention provides: 'The termination of a treaty or the withdrawal of a party may take place; (a) in conformity with the provisions of the treaty.'[37] Indeed, the majority of modern treaties contain provisions for termination or withdrawal. Sometimes it is provided that the treaty shall come to an end automatically after a certain time, or when a particular event occurs; other treaties merely give each party an option to withdraw, usually after giving a certain period of notice.

Termination by consent of the parties
Article 54 of the Vienna Convention provides: 'The termination of a treaty or the withdrawal of a party may take place: (a) . . . (b) at any time by consent of all the parties.' At one time it used to be thought that the treaty could be terminated only in exactly the same way as it was made; thus, a ratified treaty could be terminated only by another ratified treaty, and not by a treaty which came into force on signature alone. But this formalistic view is no longer accepted. Indeed, the International Law Commission thought that an agreement to terminate could even be *implied* if it was

36 M.B. Akehurst, Treaties, Termination, *EPIL* 7 (1984), 507–10; A. Vamvoukos, *Termination of Treaties in International Law. The Doctrines of Rebus Sic Stantibus and Desuetude*, 1985; R. Plender, The Role of Consent in the Termination of Treaties, *BYIL* 57 (1986), 133–68; L.-A. Sicilianos, The Relationship Between Reprisals and Denunciation or Suspension of a Treaty, *EJIL* 4 (1993), 341–59; N. Kontou, *The Termination and Revision of Treaties in the Light of New Customary Law*, 1994. But termination must be distinguished from the amendment of treaties, see M.J. Bowmann, The Multilateral Treaty Amendment Process – A Case Study, *ICLQ* 44 (1995), 540–59.
37 A similar rule applies to suspension of the operation of a treaty (Articles 57 and 58(1) Vienna Convention).

38 *AJIL* 61 (1967), 388.
39 See also Article 59 of the Vienna Convention and Vamvoukos, *op. cit.*
40 See K. Widdows, The Unilateral Denunciation of Treaties Containing No Denunciation Clause, *BYIL* 53 (1982), 83–114.
41 *Nicaragua Case* (Jurisdiction), *ICJ Rep.* 1984, 392, at 420. On this case see Chapter 3 above, 40–1 Chapters 18, 284 and 19, 319 below.
42 *Ibid.*
43 S. Rosenne, *Breach of Treaty*, 1985; D.N. Hutchinson, Solidarity and Breaches of Multilateral Treaties, *BYIL* 59 (1988), 151 *et seq.*; R. Morrison, Efficient Breach of International Agreements, *Denver JILP* 23 (1994), 183–222; M.M. Gomaa, *Suspension or Termination of Treaties on Grounds of Breach*, 1996.

clear from the conduct of the parties that they no longer regarded the treaty as being in force.[38] The technical name for this method of termination is 'desuetude'.[39]

Implied right of denunciation or withdrawal

Article 56 of the Vienna Convention provides:

1 A treaty which contains no provision regarding its termination and which does not provide for denunciation or withdrawal is not subject to denunciation or withdrawal unless:

   (a) it is established that the parties intended to admit the possibility of denunciation or withdrawal; or

   (b) a right of denunciation or withdrawal may be implied by the nature of the treaty.

2 A party shall give not less than twelve months' notice of its intention to denounce or withdraw from a treaty under paragraph 1.

It follows from the wording of Article 56 that a right of denunciation or withdrawal can never be *implied* if the treaty contains an *express* provision concerning denunciation, withdrawal, or termination.

It is uncertain to what extent Article 56 reflects customary law;[40] this is particularly true of paragraph l(b), which was added to the text of Article 56 at the Vienna conference by twenty-six votes to twenty-five with thirty-seven abstentions. The provisions of Article 56 (especially paragraph 1(b)) reflect the views of most British writers, but many continental writers thought that there could never be an implied right of denunciation or withdrawal under customary international law. However, in *Nicaragua v. USA*, the International Court of Justice seems to have accepted that Article 56 was an accurate statement of customary law.[41]

Treaties of alliance and certain types of commercial treaties are often cited as the main examples of the kind of treaty in which a right of denunciation or withdrawal can be inferred from the nature of the treaty, within the meaning of Article 56(1)(b). A similar inference can also probably be made in the case of treaties conferring jurisdiction on international courts.[42]

Customary international law requires reasonable notice to be given whenever an implied right of denunciation or withdrawal is exercised. Article 56(2) adds greater precision by requiring notice of at least twelve months.

Termination or suspension of a treaty as a consequence of its breach (discharge through breach)

Article 60(1) of the Vienna Convention provides: 'A material breach of a bilateral treaty by one of the parties entitles the other to invoke the breach as a ground for terminating the treaty or suspending its operation in whole or in part.'[43] The injured state's power to terminate or suspend a treaty is one of the main sanctions for breach of a treaty, but it is not the only one; there is nothing to prevent the injured state claiming compensation instead of, or in addition to, exercising its rights under Article 60(1).

The problem is more complicated if the treaty is multilateral. Obviously, breach by state A cannot entitle state B to denounce the treaty, because that would not be fair to states C, D, E, and so on. Accordingly, Article 60(2) provides:

44 See Chapter 20 below, 342.

A material breach of a multilateral treaty by one of the parties entitles:

(a) the other parties by unanimous agreement to suspend the operation of the treaty in whole or in part or to terminate it either:

  (i) in the relations between themselves and the defaulting State, or

  (ii) as between all parties;

(b) a party specially affected by the breach to invoke it as a ground for suspending the operation of the treaty in whole or in part in the relations between itself and the defaulting State;

(c) any party other than the defaulting State to invoke the breach as a ground for suspending the operation of the treaty in whole or in part with respect to itself if the treaty is of such a character that a material breach of its provisions by one party radically changes the position of every party with respect to the further performance of its obligations under the treaty.

An example of the type of treaty contemplated by paragraph 2(c) is a disarmament treaty.[44] Clearly, breach of a disarmament treaty by one party constitutes a very serious threat to each of the other parties. But should this entitle one of the injured parties to create a similar threat to the other injured parties? Would it not be more appropriate to deal with the problem under paragraph 2(a)? It is in any case doubtful whether paragraph 2(c) really reflects customary law.

It is generally agreed that a right to terminate does not arise unless the breach is a material (that is, serious) one. Article 60(3) defines a material breach as: '(a) a repudiation of the treaty not sanctioned by the present Convention; or (b) the violation of a provision essential to the accomplishment of the object or purpose of the treaty'. This definition is defective, because it does not make clear that violation of an essential provision does not constitute a material breach unless it is a serious violation. If a state makes a treaty to deliver 5,000 tons of tin and delivers only 4,999 tons, a literal interpretation of Article 60(3) would imply that the other party could denounce the treaty because of this minor violation of an essential provision – which is repugnant to common sense.

Breach does not automatically terminate a treaty; it merely gives the injured party or parties an option to terminate or suspend the treaty, and, according to Article 45, an injured party loses the right to exercise this option

if, after becoming aware of the facts:

(a) it shall have expressly agreed that the treaty . . . remains in force or continues in operation, as the case may be; or

(b) it must by reason of its conduct be considered as having acquiesced . . . in its [that is, the treaty's] maintenance in force or in operation, as the case may be.

The power of the injured party or parties to terminate or suspend a treaty may also be modified or excluded by the treaty itself.[45]

Supervening impossibility of performance

Article 61 of the Vienna Convention provides:

1 A party may invoke the impossibility of performing a treaty as a ground for terminating or withdrawing from it if the impossibility results from the permanent disappearance or destruction of an object indispensable for the execution of the treaty. If the impossibility is temporary, it may be invoked only as a ground for suspending the operation of the treaty.

2 Impossibility of performance may not be invoked by a party as a ground for terminating, withdrawing from or suspending the operation of a treaty if the impossibility is the result of a breach by that party either of an obligation under the treaty or of any other international obligation owed to any other party to the treaty.

It is not hard to think of examples; for instance, a treaty providing that the waters of a particular river be used for irrigation would become impossible of performance if the river dried up. The Vienna Convention regards the impossibility not as automatically terminating the treaty, but as merely giving a party an option to terminate; this point was controversial in customary law.

Fundamental change of circumstances (*rebus sic stantibus*)

A party is not bound to perform a treaty if there has been a fundamental change of circumstances since the treaty was concluded. In previous centuries writers tried to explain this rule by saying that every treaty contained an implied term that it should remain in force only as long as circumstances remained the same (*rebus sic stantibus*) as at the time of conclusion. Such an explanation must be rejected, because it is based on a fiction, and because it exaggerates the scope of the rule. In modern times it is agreed that the rule applies only in the most exceptional circumstances; otherwise it could be used as an excuse to evade all sorts of inconvenient treaty obligations.

Article 62 of the Vienna Convention confines the rule within very narrow limits:

1 A fundamental change of circumstances which has occurred with regard to those existing at the time of the conclusion of a treaty, and which was not foreseen by the parties, may not be invoked as a ground for terminating or withdrawing from the treaty unless:

(a) the existence of those circumstances constituted an essential basis of the consent of the parties to be bound by the treaty; and

(b) the effect of the change is radically to transform the extent of obligations still to be performed under the treaty.

2 A fundamental change of circumstances may not be invoked as a ground for terminating or withdrawing from the treaty:

(a) if the treaty established a boundary; or

(b) if the fundamental change is the result of a breach by the party invoking it either of an obligation under the treaty or of any other international obligation owed to any other party to the treaty.

3   If, under the foregoing paragraphs, a party may invoke a fundamental change of circumstances as a ground for terminating or withdrawing from a treaty it may also invoke the change as a ground for suspending the operation of the treaty.

In the *Fisheries Jurisdiction* case the International Court of Justice said that Article 62 'may in many respects be considered as a codification of existing customary law on the subject'.[46]

Some writers consider that the change of circumstances automatically terminates the treaty; others hold that it merely gives a state an option to terminate. The Vienna Convention adopts the latter approach; moreover, the option to terminate may be lost in certain circumstances under Article 45.[47]

No doubt treaties often need to be altered, to bring them into line with changing conditions. But the *rebus sic stantibus* rule is an unsuitable method for achieving this end; it applies only in extreme cases, and, when it does apply, its effect is not to alter a treaty, but to terminate it. Alterations, as opposed to termination, can be brought about only by agreement, and not all states are prepared to agree to amendments which go against their interests; sometimes they fear that making concessions to one state will induce other states to demand similar changes in other treaties. But the desire of states to obtain the goodwill of other states often induces them to make the necessary concessions. Moreover, the United Nations General Assembly has a power to recommend alterations of treaties, under Article 14 of the United Nations Charter, which provides: 'the General Assembly may recommend measures for the peaceful adjustment of any situation, regardless of origin, which it deems likely to impair the general welfare or friendly relations among nations.'[48]

Emergence of a new peremptory norm (*ius cogens*)

Article 64 of the Vienna Convention provides: 'If a new peremptory norm of general international law emerges, any existing treaty which is in conflict with that norm becomes void and terminates.' The treaty does not, however, become void retroactively.[49]

Outbreak of war

The Vienna Convention does not deal with the effects of war[50] on treaties, apart from stating that 'the provisions of the present Convention shall not prejudice any question that may arise in regard to a treaty . . . from the outbreak of hostilities between States' (Article 73). The problem is extremely complicated.[51] Originally, war was regarded as ending all treaties between belligerent states, but this rule has now been partly abandoned. Maybe it is not so much the rule which has changed, as the nature of the treaties to which the rule applies. It was sensible to say that war ended all treaties between belligerent states when most treaties were bilateral

46 *UK v. Iceland* (Jurisdiction), *ICJ Rep.* 1973, 3, 18, para. 36; on this case see Chapter 3, 43 above and Chapter 12, 183 below. See also the *Free Zones* case (1932), PCIJ, series A/B, no. 46, 156–8.

47 See text above, 143.

48 See Chapter 22 below, 387.

49 See Article 71(2), Vienna Convention. On *ius cogens* generally, see Chapter 3 above, 57–8.

50 See Chapter 19 below, 309.

51 J. Delbrück, War, Effect on Treaties, *EPIL* 4 (1982), 310–15.

52 See Chapter 3 above, 37–8.
53 See text above, 140–1.

'contract treaties'; the rule has to be altered when many treaties are multilateral 'law-making treaties',[52] to which neutrals as well as belligerents are parties.

In any case, this tangled branch of the law is less important now than it used to be, for two reasons. First, when states are engaged in hostilities nowadays, they seldom admit that they are in a state of war in the technical sense; and, unlike war, hostilities falling short of war do not generally terminate treaties between the hostile states. Second, the peace treaty or other instrument which terminates a modern war usually provides what is to happen to pre-war treaties (or at least bilateral treaties) between the belligerent states, so that it is unnecessary to apply the rules of customary law on this point.

Consequences of termination or suspension

Rules concerning the consequences of termination or suspension of a treaty are laid down in Articles 70, 71(2) and 72 of the Vienna Convention, which are too detailed to be discussed here. Many of the rules in the Vienna Convention laying down the procedure to be followed when a treaty is alleged to be invalid also apply, *mutatis mutandis*, to termination or suspension; this is particularly true of Articles 65–8.[53]

10   Acquisition of territory

'Acquisition of territory' is an abbreviated way of describing acquisition of sovereignty over territory.[1] Sovereignty, that much abused word,[2] is here used in a specialized sense; sovereignty over territory means 'the right to exercise therein, to the exclusion of any other state, the functions of a state'.[3] But it is not necessarily unlimited. Other states may, by treaty or local custom, acquire minor rights over the territory, such as a right of way across it. Even the right of a state to transfer its territory to another state, which is often regarded as the acid test of sovereignty over territory, may be limited by treaty. For instance, by the 1955 State Treaty for the Re-Establishment of an Independent and Democratic Austria, Austria agreed not to enter into political or economic union with Germany.[4] Again, under the 1713 Treaty of Utrecht, Great Britain agreed to offer Gibraltar to Spain before attempting to transfer sovereignty over Gibraltar to any other state.[5]

Modes of acquisition of territory

The traditional view is that there are several distinct modes by which sovereignty can be acquired over territory. The classification of these modes was originally borrowed from the Roman law rules on the acquisition of property, which is not surprising, since sovereignty over territory bears some resemblance to ownership of property; and in the sixteenth and seventeenth centuries, when modern international law began to develop, the then current theories of absolute monarchy tended to regard a state's territory as the private estate of the monarch. But there are several ways in which this use of private law concepts produces a distorted view of modern international law. In particular, it presupposes that transfers of territory take place between already existing states, just as transfers of property take place between already existing individuals. In recent years, however, the most frequent form of transfer of territory (more precisely: the transfer of sovereignty over territory) has occurred when a colony has become independent;[6] since territory is an essential ingredient of statehood,[7] the birth of the state and the transfer of territory are inseparable – a state *is* its territory. In the pages which follow, an attempt will be made to fit the emergence of new states into the traditional list of modes of acquisition of territory; but it must be confessed that the emergence of new states does not fit very well into that list.

Another preliminary point to notice about modes of acquisition is that

1 G. Schwarzenberger, Title to Territory: Response to a Challenge, *AJIL* 51 (1967), 308–24; J.A. Andrews, The Concept of Statehood and the Acquisition of Territory in the Nineteenth Century, *LQR* 94 (1978), 408–27; R.Y. Jennings, *The Acquisition of Territory in International Law*, 1962; Y. Z. Blum, *Historic Titles in International Law*, 1965; M.N. Shaw, Territory in International Law, *NYIL* 13 (1982), 61–91; S.T. Bernardez, Territorial Sovereignty, *EPIL* 10 (1987), 487–94; Bernardez, Territory, Acquisition, *ibid.*, 496–504; *Harris CMIL*, 173 *et seq.*; R. Jennings/A. Watts (eds), *Oppenheim's International Law*, 9th edn 1992, 679 *et seq.*; G. Distefano, La Notion de titre juridique et les différends territoriaux dans l'ordre international, *RGDIP* 99 (1995), 335–66.

2 See Chapter 2 above, 17–18.

3 *Island of Palmas Case* (1928), *RIAA* II 829, 838. On this case see also Chapters 5, 75–6 and 7, 109–10 above and text below, 148, 150, 156, 157–8.

4 Text in 217 UNTS 223 (1955). See G. Stourzh, Austrian State Treaty (1955), *EPIL* I (1992), 301–5.

5 Text of the Treaty in 28 CTS 295 (1713–4). On the status of Gibraltar see *Harris CMIL*, 209–10; H.S. Levie, Gibraltar, *EPIL* II (1995), 596–9; P. Gold, *Stone in Spain's Shoe? Search for a Solution to the Problem of Gibraltar*, 1994; S.J. Lincoln, The Legal Status of Gibraltar: Whose Rock is it Anyway?, *Fordham ILJ* 18 (1994), 285–31.

6 J. G. Starke, The Acquisition of Title to Territory by Newly Emerged States, *BYIL* 41 (1965–66), 411–16; see Chapter 2 above, 28.

7 See Chapter 5 above, 75–6.

8 *Island of Palmas Case, op. cit.*

9 See text below, 150, 156, 157–8.

10 J. Simsarian, The Acquisition of Legal Title to Terra Nullis, *Political Science Quarterly* 53 (1938), 111–28.

11 *Clipperton Island Case* (1932) (*France v. Mexico*), *RIAA* XI 1105, 1110–11. See also *Harris CMIL*, 183–6; I.v. Münch, Clipperton Island Arbitration, *EPIL* I (1992), 622–3; S.T. Bernardez, *Territory, Abandonment, EPIL* 10 (1987), 494–6.

12 See *Harris CMIL*, 196–201; P. Beck, *The Falkland Islands as an International Problem*, 1988; M. Evans, The Restoration of Diplomatic Relations Between Argentina and the United Kingdom, *ICLQ* 40 (1991), 473 *et seq.*; A. Donchev (ed.), *International Perspectives on the Falkland Conflict: A Matter of Life and Death*, 1992; R. Dolzer, *The Territorial Status of the Falkland Islands (Malvinas): Past and Present*, 1992; A. Norman, *The Falkland Islands. Their Kinship Isles, the Antarctic Hemisphere and the Freedom of the Two Great Oceans*, Vols 1–4, 1986–1993. For the 1989 Joint Statement between Argentina and the UK on Relations and a Formula on Sovereignty with Regard to the Falkland Islands, South Georgia and South Sandwich Islands, see *ILM* 29 (1990), 1291. See also the 1995 Joint Declaration of both sides on cooperation over offshore activities in the South West Atlantic, *ILM* 35 (1996), 301. See also Chapter 19 below, 315.

13 See Chapter 2 above, 12–14. But such attitudes were rarer than is sometimes supposed; see the *Western Sahara Case, ICJ Rep.* 1975, 12, 390; *Harris CMIL*, 190–2; K. Oellers-Frahm, Western Sahara (Advisory Opinion), *EPIL* 2 (1981), 291–3; D.P. O'Connell, *International Law*, 2nd edn 1970, Vol. 1, 408–9.

they are fully relevant only when title to territory is uncertain. For instance, the Shetland Isles have been part of the United Kingdom for so long that all states recognize them as part of the United Kingdom, and no one bothers to ask how the United Kingdom first acquired it.

Cession

Cession is the transfer of territory, usually by treaty, from one state to another. If there were defects in the ceding state's title, the title of the state to which the territory is ceded will be vitiated by the same defects; this is expressed by the Latin maxim, *nemo dat quod non habet* (nobody gives what he does not have). For instance, in the *Island of Palmas* case,[8] Spain had ceded the Philippine islands to the United States by the Treaty of Paris 1898; the treaty described the island of Palmas as forming part of the Philippines. But when the United States went to take possession of the island, it found it under Dutch control. In the ensuing arbitration between the United States and the Netherlands, the United States claimed that the island had belonged to Spain before 1898, and that the United States had acquired the island from Spain by cession. The arbitrator, Max Huber, held that, even if Spain had originally had sovereignty over the island (a point which he left open), the Netherlands had administered it since the early eighteenth century, thereby supplanting Spain as the sovereign over the island.[9] Since Spain had no title to the island in 1898, the United States could not acquire title from Spain.

Except for territorial changes following the conclusion of peace treaties, cession of territory (such as France's cession of Louisiana to the United States for 60 million francs in 1803, or Britain's cession of the island of Heligoland to Germany, in exchange for Zanzibar, in 1890) has now become rare and concerns marginal areas, such as, for example, the transfer of the Swan Islands in 1971 by the United States to Honduras.

Occupation

Occupation is the acquisition of *terra nullius* – that is, territory which, immediately before acquisition, belonged to no state.[10] The territory may never have belonged to any state, or it may have been abandoned by the previous sovereign. Abandonment of territory requires not only failure to exercise authority over the territory, but also an intention to abandon the territory.[11] This corresponds roughly to the distinction in municipal law between losing property and throwing it away. Nowadays there are hardly any parts of the world that could be considered as *terra nullius*, because most of the land areas of the globe are at present placed under the territorial sovereignty of an existing state. But many modern disputes over territory have their roots in previous centuries, when territory was frequently acquired by occupation, for example, the sovereignty dispute between Argentina and the UK over the Falkland Islands.[12] In previous centuries European international lawyers were sometimes reluctant to admit that non-European societies could constitute states for the purposes of international law, and territory inhabited by non-European peoples was sometimes regarded as *terra nullius*.[13]

Territory is occupied when it is placed under effective control. The requirements of effective control have become increasingly strict in international law, as unoccupied territory has become increasingly scarce. In the sixteenth century, when large areas of unoccupied territory were being discovered,[14] effective control was interpreted very liberally; indeed, mere discovery gave a state an 'inchoate title', that is, an option to occupy the territory within a reasonable time, during which time other states were not allowed to occupy the territory. As time went on, international law demanded more and more in order to constitute effective control.[15] However, even in modern times, effective control is a relative concept; it varies according to the nature of the territory concerned. It is, for instance, much easier to establish effective control over barren and uninhabited territory than over territory which is inhabited by fierce tribes; troops would probably have to be stationed in the territory in the latter case, but not in the former. Effective control is also relative in another sense, which was stressed by the Permanent Court of International Justice in the *Eastern Greenland* case:

> Another circumstance which must be taken into account . . . is the extent to which the sovereignty is also claimed by some other Power. In most of the cases involving claims to territorial sovereignty which have come before an international tribunal, there have been two competing claims to sovereignty, and the tribunal has had to decide which of the two is the stronger . . . in many cases the tribunal has been satisfied with very little in the way of actual exercise of sovereign rights, provided that the other State could not make out a superior claim. This is particularly true in the case of claims to sovereignty over areas in thinly populated or unsettled countries.[16]

(In this case the Court held that Denmark had sovereignty over all of Greenland and dismissed the claim of Norway that a certain area known as Eirik Raudes Land was *terra nullius* when Norway issued a declaration of occupation in 1931.)

Some cases say that a state, in order to acquire territory by occupation, must not only exercise effective control, but must also have 'the intention and will to act as sovereign'.[17] Consequently,

> the independent activity of private individuals is of little value unless it can be shown that they have acted in pursuance of . . . some . . . authority received from their Governments or that in some other way their Governments have asserted jurisdiction through them.[18]

Sometimes states may agree not to make claims to particular territory, so that the territory in effect remains *terra nullius*. Examples can be found in Article 2 of the 1967 Treaty on Principles Governing the Activities of States in the Exploration and Use of Outer Space including the Moon and Other Celestial Bodies (Outer Space Treaty)[19] and in the 1959 Antarctica Treaty.[20] Before 1959 several states had laid claims to various areas of Antarctica, but the area claimed by one state sometimes overlapped with an area claimed by another state, and none of the areas was subject to effective control by the states concerned. The 1959 treaty has been ratified by all the states actively interested in Antarctica, and no

14 F.A. Frhr. v.d. Heydte, Discovery, Symbolic Annexation and Virtual Effectiveness in International Law, *AJIL* 29 (1935), 448–71; A.-M. de Zayas, Territory, Discovery, *EPIL* 10 (1987), 504–7. See also *Harris CMIL*, 181, n. 3.
15 See A.S. Keller/O.J. Lissitzyn/F.J. Mann, *Creation of Rights of Sovereignty through Symbolic Acts 1400–1800* (1938).
16 *Eastern Greenland Case* (1933), PCIJ, series A/B, no. 53, at 46. See I.v. Münch, Eastern Greenland Case, *EPIL* II (1995), 7–9; *Harris CMIL*, 186, n. 2. See text below, 150–1, 155.
17 *Ibid.*, 45; but see I. Brownlie, *Principles of Public International Law*, 4th edn, 1990, 142–4, 145–6, 150.
18 *Fisheries Case, ICJ Rep.* 1951, 116, 184, per Judge McNair. On this case see Chapter 3, 42, 43, 47, 51, 181 above and Chapter 12 below; *Harris CMIL*, 182–3.
19 610 UNTS 205; *Harris CMIL*, 222–32. See Chapter 13 below, 202, 204, 205
20 Text in 402 UNTS 71; *AJIL* 54 (1960), 477; *ILM* 19 (1980), 860. See *Harris CMIL*, 211–7; F. Francioni/T. Scovazzi, *International Law for Antarctica*, 1987; C. Joyner/S.K. Chopra (eds), *The Antarctic Legal Regime*, 1988; R. Lefeber, The Exercise of Jurisdiction in the Antarctic Region and the Changing Structure of International Law: The International Community and Common Interests, *NYIL* 21 (1990), 81–138; E.J. Sahurie, *The International Law of Antarctica*, 1992; R. Wolfrum/U.-D. Klemm, Antarctica, *EPIL* I (1992), 173–82; A. Berg, Antarctica Cases (U.K. v. Argentina; U.K. v. Chile), *ibid.*, 182–3; A. Watts, *International Law and the Antarctic Treaty System*, 1992; K.R. Simmonds, *The Antarctic Conventions*, 1993; M.C.W. Pinto, Governance of Antarctica, in R.St.J. Macdonald (ed.), *Essays in Honour of Wang Tieya*, 1994, 587–609. With regard to the Arctic, the eight Arctic states (Canada, Denmark, Finland, Iceland, Norway, Russia, Sweden, United States) established the Arctic Council as an intergovernment forum on 19 September 1996. See *ILM* 35 (1996), 1382.

21 G.D. Triggs (ed.), *The Antarctic Treaty Regime: Law, Environment and Resources*, 1987; M. Howard, The Convention on the Conservation of Antarctic Marine Living Resources: A Five Year Review, *ICLQ* 38 (1989), 104–50; A.D. Watts, The Convention on the Regulation of Antarctic Mineral Resource Activities 1988, *ICLQ* 39 (1990), 169 *et seq.*; I.D. Hendry, The Antarctic Minerals Act 1989, *ibid.*, 183 *et seq.*; R. Wolfrum, *The Convention on the Regulation of Antarctic Mineral Resource Activities*, 1991; J. Verhoeven/ P. Sands/M. Bruce (eds), *The Antarctic Environment and International Law*, 1992; C.C. Joyner, *Antarctica and the Law of the Sea*, 1992; M.T. Infante, Maritime Conventions in Antarctica, *GYIL* 35 (1992), 249; C. Redgwell, Environmental Protection in Antarctica: The 1991 Protocol, *ICLQ* 43 (1994), 599–756; see also the documents reproduced in *ILM* 35 (1996), 1165–89.
22 For discussion of this principle see Chapter 13 below, 207–8.
23 See D. Johnson, Acquisitive Prescription in International Law, *BYIL* 27 (1950), 332–54; R. Pinto, La Prescription en droit international, *RdC* 87, 1995–I), 390-452; C.A. Fleischhauer, Prescription, *EPIL* 10 (1987), 327–30.
24 W. Karl, Protest, *EPIL* 9 (1986), 320–2.
25 Brownlie (1990), *op. cit.*, 153 *et seq.* See also *Harris CMIL*, 195–6, nn. 3 and 4.
26 *Island of Palmas Case, op. cit.*, at 868.
27 *Eastern Greenland Case, op. cit.*

state party to the treaty might withdraw from it during the first thirty years. The treaty provides for freedom of movement and scientific exploration throughout Antarctica; the parties agree to cooperate with one another and not to use Antarctica for military purposes. Existing claims to sovereignty in Antarctica are not affected by the treaty, but Article IV provides:

> No acts or activities taking place while the present Treaty is in force shall constitute a basis for asserting, supporting or denying a claim to territorial sovereignty in Antarctica or create any rights of sovereignty in Antarctica. No new claim, or enlargement of an existing claim, to territorial sovereignty in Antarctica shall be asserted while the present Treaty is in force.

Meanwhile, Antarctica has been placed under an international treaty regime aiming at the protection of its resources and environment.[21] With other areas beyond national jurisdiction, such as the high seas, the deep sea-bed and outer space, Antarctica is now viewed as belonging to the 'international commons' governed by the ambiguous principle of the 'common heritage of mankind'.[22]

Prescription

Like occupation, prescription[23] is based on effective control over territory. As in the case of occupation, effective control probably needs to be accompanied by 'the intention and will to act as sovereign'. The difference between prescription and occupation is that prescription is the acquisition of territory which belonged to another state, whereas occupation is acquisition of *terra nullius*. Consequently the effective control necessary to establish title by prescription must last for a longer period of time than the effective control which is necessary in cases of occupation; loss of title by the former sovereign is not readily presumed.

Effective control by the acquiring state probably needs to be accompanied by acquiescence on the part of the losing state; protests,[24] or other acts or statements which demonstrate a lack of acquiescence, can probably prevent acquisition of title by prescription.[25] This explains why, in the *Island of Palmas* case, the arbitrator emphasized the absence of Spanish protests against Dutch acts on the island.[26]

Although occupation and prescription can be distinguished from one another in theory, the difference is usually blurred in real life, because often one of the very points in dispute is whether the territory was *terra nullius* or was subject to the sovereignty of the 'first' state before the 'second' state arrived on the scene. For instance, the judgment in the *Island of Palmas* case does not make clear whether the island was under Spanish sovereignty before the Dutch began to exercise control. Many of the cases which textbooks classify as cases on occupation could equally well be regarded as cases on prescription, and vice versa. When faced with competing claims, international tribunals often decide in favour of the state which can prove the greater degree of effective control over the disputed territory, without basing their judgment on any specific mode of acquisition. For instance, in the *Eastern Greenland* case,[27] the Permanent Court of

International Justice gave judgment to Denmark because Denmark had exercised greater control than Norway over Eastern Greenland, but the court did not specify the mode whereby Denmark had acquired sovereignty.

Operations of nature

A state can acquire territory through operations of nature – for example, when rivers silt up, or when volcanic islands emerge in a state's internal waters or territorial sea. Such events are rare and unimportant, and there is little point in discussing the detailed rules.[28]

Adjudication

Adjudication is sometimes listed as a mode of acquisition, but its status is doubtful.[29] In theory, a tribunal's normal task is to declare the rights which the parties already have, not to create new rights; in theory, therefore, adjudication does not give a state any territory which it did not already own. A number of such cases have also recently beeen brought to the International Court of Justice.[30] Another important recent case was decided by an arbitral tribunal in the *Taba* dispute between Israel and Egypt, involving a small piece of land on the western shore of the Gulf of Aqaba, where Israelis had constructed a hotel during the period of military occupation.[31]

On the other hand, it sometimes happens that states set up a boundary commission to mark out an agreed boundary, but empower it to depart to some extent from the agreed boundary (for example, to prevent a farm being cut in two); however, this power of the boundary commission is derived from the treaty setting it up, and the transfer of territory may therefore be regarded as a sort of indirect cession.[32] A different matter is the determination of a boundary by the United Nations Security Council in exercise of its powers under Chapter VII of the United Nations Charter, as in the case of the demarcation of the border between Iraq and Kuwait by a Commission after the Gulf War.[33]

Conquest

Normally a state defeated in a war used to cede territory to the victor by treaty, but conquest alone, without a treaty, could also confer title on the victor under the traditional law.[34] However, acquisition of territory by conquest was not lawful unless the war had come to an end. If the defeated state entered into a peace treaty which ceded territory to the victor, or which recognized the victor's title, it was clear that the war had come to an end. In the absence of a peace treaty, it was necessary to prove that the war had come to an end in a different way, by producing clear evidence that all resistance by the enemy state and by its allies had ceased; thus the German annexation of Poland during the Second World War was invalid, because Poland's allies continued the struggle against Germany.[35] In law, Germany was merely the belligerent occupant of Poland, and its rights were very much more limited than they would have been if the annexation had been valid. In addition, the conqueror acquired territory only if he intended to do so; in 1945 the Allies expressly disclaimed the intention of annexing

28 See *The Anna Case* (1805), 165 ER 809; *Chamizal Arbitration (USA v. Mexico)* (1911), RIAA XI 316; on this case see *Harris CMIL*, 193–6; M. Dingley, Eruptions in International Law: Emerging Volcanic Islands and the Law of Territorial Acquisition, *Cornell ILJ* 9 (1975), 121–35; L.J. Bouchez, River Deltas, *EPIL* 10 (1987), 380–1.

29 See A. L.W. H. Munkman, Adjudication and Adjustment – International Judicial Decision and the Settlement of Territorial and Boundary Disputes, *BYIL* 46 (1972–73), 1–116.

30 See H. Post, Adjudication as Mode of Acquisition of Territory? Some Observations on the Iraq-Kuwait Boundary Demarcation in Light of the Jurisprudence of the international Court of Justice, in V. Lowe/M. Fitzmaurice (eds), *Fifty Years of the International Court of Justice*, 1996, 237–63. See Chapter 18 below, 291.

31 *Taba Arbitration*, Award of the Egypt-Israel Tribunal, *ILM* 27 (1988), 1427. See E. Lauterpacht, The Taba Case: Some Recollections and Reflections, *Israel LR* 23 (1989), 443–68; R. Lapidoth, Taba Arbitration, *EPIL* 12 (1990), 365–7; Lapidoth, Some Reflections on the Taba Award, *GYIL* 35 (1992), 224. For another arbitration case see D.W. Bowett, The Dubai/ Sharjah Boundary Arbitration of 1981, *BYIL* 65 (1994), 103–34.

32 On boundary disputes in general see the entries by M. Bothe, E.J. de Aréchaga, T. Schweisfurth, I. Brownlie, W. Hummer, R. Khan and H.-D. Treviranus, *EPIL* I (1992), 443–79.

33 Final Report on the Demarcation of the International Boundary Between the Republic of Iraq and the State of Kuwait Boundary Demarcation Commission, *ILM* 32 (1993), 1425; D.H. Finnie, *Shifting Lines in the Sand: Kuwait's Elusive Frontier with Iraq*, 1992; M.H. Mendelson/S.C. Hulton, The Iraq-Kuwait Boundary, *BYIL* 64 (1993), 135–95; J. Bulloch, *United Nations Demarcation of the Iraq-Kuwait Border*, 1993; J. Klabbers, No More Shifting Lines? The Report of the Iraq-Kuwait Boundary Demarcation Commission, *ICLQ* 43 (1994), 904–13; Post, *op. cit.* See Chapter 22 below, 398, 425.

34 E. Kussbach, Conquest, *EPIL* I (1992), 756–9. On the controversial meaning of the concept of *debellatio* as one of the ways of ending war and acquiring territory when one of the belligerent states has been defeated totally see K.-U. Meyn, Debellatio, *EPIL* I (1992), 969–71.

35 See L. Oppenheim, *International Law*, Vol. 2, 7th edn (H. Lauterpacht ed.), 1952, 432–56; R.L. Bindschedler, Annexation, *EPIL* I (1992),168–72.
36 For literature see Chapter 5 above, 84, n. 71.
37 See Andrews, *op. cit.* and Chapter 2 above, 19–20.
38 See Chapter 19 below, 309–18.
39 See Chapter 9 above, 139–40.
40 On the general problems of recognition in international law see Chapter 5 above, 82–90.
41 See Q. Wright, The Stimson Note of January 7, 1932, *AJIL* 26 (1932), 342–8; A.D. McNair, The Stimson Doctrine of Non-Recognition, *BYIL* 14 (1993), 65–74; W. Meng, Stimson Doctrine, *EPIL* 4 (1982), 230–5.
42 See Chapter 2 above, 25–6.
43 See Chapter 2 above, 32.
44 See W.J. Hough, The Annexation of the Baltic States and Its Effect on the Development of Law Prohibiting Forcible Seizure of Territory, *NYL. Sch. JICL* 6 (1985), 301-533; B. Meissner, Baltic States, *EPIL* I (1992), 328–37. See also Chapter 11 below, 165–6.
45 See *Harris CMIL*, Appendix IV, 1010–17; J.A. Frowein, Gulf Conflict (1990/1991), *EPIL* II (1995), 643–7; R. Schofield, *Kuwait and Iraq: Historical Claims and Territorial Disputes*, 2nd edn 1993; Schofield (ed.), *The Iraq-Kuwait Dispute*, Vols 1–7, 1994. See Chapter 22, 396 below.

Germany, although they had occupied all of Germany's territory and defeated all of Germany's allies.[36]

In the nineteenth century, it was inevitable that international law should allow states to acquire territory by conquest, because at that time customary international law imposed no limit on the right of states to go to war.[37] During the twentieth century there has been a growing movement, culminating in the United Nations Charter, to restrict the right of states to go to war; as a general rule, the use of force is now illegal, with certain exceptions such as self-defence.[38] What effect has this revolutionary change in the law had upon the possibility of acquiring territory by conquest?

We have already seen that the better view is that a treaty imposed by an aggressor is now void.[39] Since an aggressor state cannot acquire territory by conquering another state and forcing it to sign a treaty of cession, it must follow *a fortiori* that an aggressor cannot acquire territory by conquest alone. Some authors indeed argue that such annexation cannot even be recognized as legal by other states.[40] This view was prepared by the Stimson Doctrine. In 1931 Japanese troops set up the puppet state of Manchukuo in Manchuria, which had until then formed part of China. Almost all states considered that Japan was guilty of aggression, and the American Secretary of State, Stimson, announced that his government would not recognize situations brought about by aggression.[41] The following year the Assembly of the League of Nations passed a resolution stating that 'it is incumbent upon the members of the League of Nations not to recognize any situation, treaty or agreement which may be brought about by means contrary to the Covenant of the League of Nations or to the Pact of Paris'.[42] In 1970 the United Nations General Assembly declared that it was a basic principle of international law that 'no territorial acquisition resulting from the threat or use of force shall be recognized as legal'.[43] These resolutions suggest that there is a duty to withhold recognition, but states have not always acted in accordance with them. For instance, three years after the Italian conquest of Ethiopia in 1936, the conquest was recognized *de jure* by the United Kingdom; and the United Kingdom also recognized (although only *de facto*) the Soviet conquest of the Baltic republics in 1940.[44] The only effect of the Stimson Doctrine seems to have been to delay the grant of recognition, not to prevent it. An example for the practice of non-recognition of territorial change through annexation has been the case of the Baltic states. The view that any annexation based upon the unauthorized use of force is illegal and is not to be recognized seems to find support in recent developments in connection with the annexation of Kuwait by Iraq. In Resolution 662/1990 of 9 August 1990 the UN Security Council unanimously declared the annexation null and void and called upon states and institutions not to recognize it and to refrain from any action that might be interpreted as indirect recognition.[45]

But, until such time as the international community is determined to consistently prevent aggressors from enjoying the fruits of their crimes, the idea that an aggressor cannot acquire a good title to territory is liable to produce a serious discrepancy between the law and the facts. Ideally, the facts should be brought into line with the law, but, if states are not prepared to take action to alter the facts, the only alternative is to bring the law into line with the facts. One view is that this can be done by means of recognition: an aggressor's title is invalid, simply because it is based on aggression, but its defects are cured when it is recognized *de jure* by other states. In this exceptional situation recognition would have a constitutive effect.[46]

It is true that *de jure* recognition excludes claims for reparations and the invocation of invalidity of the title to territory by the state granting such recognition. But the concept of recognition by third states in itself is not a sufficient explanation for the possibility of the acquistion of territory in spite of unlawful forceful annexation. The real reason is the principle of effectiveness,[47] based upon the passage of time and the requirements of legal stability, which comes into play if it is impossible within a certain period to achieve a reversal of the illegal situation. The mere passage of time and undisturbed possession, whereby the reaction or non-reaction by third states naturally is a significant factor, leads to a 'historical consolidation', as referred to by the International Court of Justice in the *Fisheries* case.[48]

What about the 'innocent' parties to a war? Can they still acquire territory by conquest? The Declaration on Principles of International Law concerning Friendly Relations and Cooperation among States in Accordance with the Charter of the United Nations, passed by the General Assembly in 1970, suggests that they cannot:[49]

> The territory of a State shall not be the object of military occupation resulting from the use of force in contravention of the provisions of the Charter. The territory of a State shall not be the object of acquisition by another State resulting from the threat or use of force.

In these words, the Declaration makes a significant distinction between military occupation and acquisition of territory. Military occupation (this is the same as belligerent occupation)[50] is unlawful only if it results from the use of force in contravention of the Charter; *any* threat or use of force, whether it is in contravention of the Charter or not, invalidates acquisition of territory.[51]

After the Arab–Israeli hostilities of June 1967, the Security Council and General Assembly of the United Nations did not condemn either side for committing aggression: draft resolutions condemning Israel were defeated. But the General Assembly and the Security Council have repeatedly declared by overwhelming majorities that Israel is not entitled to annex any of the territory which it overran in 1967[52] – which provides further support for the view that the modern prohibition of the acquisition of territory by force applies to all states, and not merely to aggressor states. However, just as titles based on conquests by aggressors can be validated by the principle of effectiveness, so can titles based on conquests by non-aggressor states.

The modern rules prohibiting acquisition of territory by conquest are concerned only with international wars, not with civil wars.[53] No breach of international law is therefore committed when part of a state's inhabitants

46 See the sixth edition of this book, at 149.

47 See R.Y. Jennings, Nullity and Effectiveness in International Law, *Cambridge Essays in International Law* (1965), 64-87; C. de Visscher, *Les Effectivités en droit international public*, 1967, 101-11; K. Doehring, Effectiveness, *EPIL* II (1995), 43–8.

48 *Fisheries Case, op. cit.*

49 Friendly Relations Declaration 1970, *Brownlie BDIL*, 36-45, 40. See Chapters 2 above, 32 and 19 below, 314–15.

50 See text above, and Chapter 20 below, 151–2.

51 See also *Harris CMIL*, 20.

52 See P. Malanczuk, Das Golan-Gesetz im Lichte des Annexionsverbots und der occupatia bellica, *ZaöRV* 42 (1982), 261–94; Malanczuk, Jerusalem, *EPIL* 12 (1990), 184–95; *idem*, Israel, Status, Territory and Occupied Territories, *EPIL* II (1995), 1468–508. See also *Harris CMIL*, 205–8.

53 See Chapter 19 below, 318–19.

54 C. Haverland, Secession, *EPIL* 10 (1987), 384–9.

55 See Chapter 11 below, 163. On the controversial issue of the status of Tibet under the rule of China see M.C.v.W.v. Praag, *The Status of Tibet: History, Rights and Prospects in International Law*, 1987; A.D. Hughes, Tibet, *EPIL* 12 (1990), 375–7. On East Timor, occupied by Indonesia, see Chapter 3 above, 59 and Chapters 18, 286–7 and 19, 331–2 below.

56 See I.C. MacGibbon, The Scope of Acquiescence in International Law, *BYIL* (1954), 143–86; D.W. Bowett, Estoppel Before International Tribunals and Its Relation to Acquiescence, *BYIL* 33 (1957), 176–202; J.P. Müller/T. Cottier, Acquiescence, *EPIL* I (1992), 14–16. The doctrine of 'acquiescence' is difficult to distinguish from the related concepts of 'estoppel', 'prescription' and 'waiver', see A.M. Trebilcock, Waiver, *EPIL* 7 (1984), 533–6; T. Nöcker/G. French, Estoppel: What's the Government's Word Worth? An Analysis of German Law, Common Law Jurisdictions, and of the Practice of International Arbitral Tribunals, *IL* 24 (1990), 409–37; J.P. Müller/T. Cottier, Estoppel, *EPIL* II (1995), 116–19; I. Sinclair, Estoppel and Acquiescence, in Lowe/Fitzmaurice (eds), *op. cit.*, 104–20. See also Chapter 3 above, 49. On prescription see text above, 150–1. On recognition see Chapter 5 above, 82–90.

57 *Island of Palmas Case, op. cit.*, 843. See also the *Frontier Land Case (Belgium v. The Netherlands)*, *ICJ Rep.* 1959, 209; *Harris CMIL*, 194, n. 2.

58 See Judge Fitzmaurice (Separate Opinion) in the *Preah Vihear Temple Case, ICJ Rep.* 1962, 6, 63–4; A. Rustemeyer, Temple of Preah Vihear Case, *EPIL* 2 (1981), 273–4.

59 *Eastern Greenland Case, op. cit.*, at 68; Lord McNair, *The Law of Treaties*, 1961, 485.

60 *ICJ Rep.* 1984, 246, 309. On the case see Chapter 18 below, 288 and K. Oellers-Frahm, Gulf of Maine Case, *EPIL* 11 (1989), 131–5.

61 *Ibid.*, 305. On equity and on the principle of good faith see Chapter 3 above, 55–6.

62 *Preah Vihear Temple Case, op. cit.*; *Eastern Greenland Case, op. cit.*

succeed in setting up a new state by winning a civil war of secession,[54] as happened in Algeria in 1956–62, or, of course, if secession occurs with the consent of the government in power, as in the case of the independence of Eritrea from Ethiopia in 1993.[55]

Acquiescence, recognition and estoppel

Acquiescence, recognition and estoppel[56] play a very important role in the acquisition of territory, although they are not, strictly speaking, modes of acquisition. Where each of the rival claimants can show that it has exercised a certain degree of control over the disputed territory, an international tribunal is likely to decide the case in favour of the state which can prove that its title has been recognized by the other claimant or claimants. Such recognition may take the form of an express statement, or it may be inferred from acquiescence (that is, failure to protest against the exercise of control by one's opponent). Recognition of a state does not necessarily entail recognition of all the territorial claims made by that state. But in every case recognition or acquiescence by one state has little or no effect unless it is accompanied by some measure of control over the territory by the other state; failure to protest against a purely verbal assertion of title unsupported by any degree of control does not constitute acquiescence.[57]

It is sometimes said that recognition or acquiescence gives rise to an estoppel. Estoppel is a technical rule of the English law of evidence; when one party makes a statement of fact and another party takes some action in reliance on that statement, the courts will not allow the first party to deny the truth of his statement if the party who acted in reliance on the statement would suffer some detriment in the event of the statement being proved to be false. Transposed into the context of international disputes over territory, the rule would mean that a state which had recognized another state's title to particular territory would be estopped from denying the other state's title if the other state had taken some action in reliance on the recognition, for example by constructing roads in the territory concerned, because the state constructing the roads would have been wasting its money if its title turned out to be unfounded. The attitude of international law towards estoppel is not always consistent. Sometimes international law insists on the English requirements of reliance and detriment;[58] at other times it does not.[59] In the *Gulf of Maine* case, the International Court of Justice said that 'the element of detriment . . . distinguishes estoppel *stricto sensu* from acquiescence';[60] in other words, detriment is necessary for estoppel but not for acquiescence. But estoppel and acquiescence probably have the same effects as one another, because the Court also said that acquiescence and estoppel were 'different aspects of one and the same institution', since both concepts 'follow from the fundamental principles of good faith and equity'.[61]

Again, estoppel in international law sometimes has the effect of making it *impossible* for a party to contradict its previous acts, behaviour or statements, as in English law;[62] in other cases it is merely evidential (that is, its effect is simply to make it *difficult* for a party to contradict its previous conduct).[63] In the dispute between Thailand and Cambodia over the ancient Temple of Preah Vihear, which is located on the Danrek mountains forming part of the boundary between the two countries, the International Court of Justice held that the Siamese authorities had acquiesced for many years by failing to object to a map that had been drawn up by a mixed commission in 1908, showing the temple as being on the Cambodian side.[64]

We have already seen that acquiescence and recognition play a crucial role in cases of prescription.[65] But they are equally relevant to other modes of acquisition. For instance, in the *Eastern Greenland* case, Norway claimed to have acquired Eastern Greenland by occupation – a claim which presupposed that Eastern Greenland had been *terra nullius* before the Norwegian claim was made. Norway lost because Denmark had exercised more control over Eastern Greenland than Norway had done, and because Norway, by its actions, had recognized Denmark's title to the whole of Greenland.[66] Acquiescence and recognition can also be important in interpreting treaties of cession.

States are no longer allowed to acquire territory by conquest, but the invalidity of such acquisitions of territory can be cured by recognition by the victim of the conquest. In an attempt to prevent such acquisitions being validated by recognition, in the Friendly Relations Declaration of 1970 the General Assembly has declared that 'no territorial acquisition resulting from the threat or use of force shall be recognized as legal'.[67] But it remains to be seen whether states will withhold recognition indefinitely from such territorial acquisitions. However, recognition is subject to special rules in this context. First, it must take the form of an express statement, and cannot be implied.[68] Second, it cannot validate acquisition of territory by conquest unless it is *de jure*; if the recognizing state says that it recognizes the conquest only *de facto*, it is saying in effect that it regards the conqueror's title as defective, and such a statement obviously cannot give the conqueror a good title to the territory. Third, recognition by the victim of the conquest needs to be supplemented by recognition by third states, partly because the acquisition of territory by force is a matter of concern to the whole international community,[69] and partly because recognition by third states is needed to provide evidence that the victim granted recognition freely and without duress. In the case of other modes of acquisition of territory, recognition by rival claimants is what counts, although recognition by third states does have a slight evidential value.[70]

Intertemporal law

The rules governing acquisition of territory have changed over the centuries. This produces a problem of 'intertemporal law': which century's law is to be applied to determine the validity of title to territory? The generally accepted view is that the validity of an acquisition of territory depends on the law in force at the moment of the alleged acquisition; this solution is really nothing more than an example of the general principle that laws should not be applied retroactively.[71]

63 *Minquiers and Ecrehos Case* (*France v. UK*), *ICJ Rep.* 1953, 47, 71; *Harris CMIL*, 187–90; K. Herndl, Minquiers and Ecrehos Case, *EPIL* 2 (1981), 192–4.
64 *Preah Vihear Temple Case, op. cit.*
65 See text above, 150–1.
66 *Eastern Greenland Case, op. cit.*, at 68.
67 Friendly Relations Declaration, *op. cit.*, 40. See Chapter 2 above, 32.
68 H. Lauterpacht, *Recognition in International Law*, 1947, 395.
69 Lauterpacht, *ibid.*, 428–30.
70 Jennings (1962), *op. cit.*, 34–9, 42.
71 See the *Western Sahara Case, ICJ Rep.* 1975, 12, 37–40. See also *Harris CMIL*, 182, n. 5.

72 *Island of Palmas Case, op. cit.,* 845–6.
73 Friendly Relations Declaration, *op. cit.*; The UN Charter entered into force on 24 October 1945. See Chapter 2 above, 27–8. On the prohibition of the use of force see Chapter 19 below, 309–11. On unequal treaties imposed by the threat of the use of force see text below, 158 and Chapter 9 above, 139–40.
74 For extracts from the Security Council debate see *Harris CMIL,* 202–5.

But the generally accepted view has to some extent been undermined by the *Island of Palmas* case, where the arbitrator, Max Huber, said:

> a distinction must be made between the creation of rights and the existence of rights. The same principle which subjects the act creative of a right to the law in force at the time the right arises, demands that the existence of right, in other words its continued manifestation, shall follow the conditions required by the evolution of law.[72]

Therefore, as the requirements of the law for the maintenance of territory become stricter, a state has to do more and more in order to retain its title – it must continue to run all the time in order to stay in the same place. Max Huber's decision was clearly correct on the facts; increased Spanish action on the island of Palmas was necessary to prevent the Dutch gaining a title by prescription. But the wide terms in which Max Huber expressed himself seem to virtually deny the effect of the rule that the validity of an acquisition of territory depends on the law in force at the time of the alleged acquisition.

This problem is particularly acute in the case of titles based on conquest. Nowadays conquest cannot confer title; in the past it could. Do old titles based on conquest now become void? If so, the results could be very startling; carried to its logical conclusion, this suggestion would mean that North America would have to be handed back to the Indian nations, and that the English would have to hand Wales back to the Welsh. It is therefore not surprising that the General Assembly declared in 1970 that the modern prohibition against the acquisition of territory by conquest should not be construed as affecting titles to territory created 'prior to the Charter regime and valid under international law'.[73] On the other hand, if state A conquered part of state B's territory in the nineteenth century, state B may suffer from a sense of injustice and be tempted to break the law if it is told that it is not allowed to reconquer that territory now.

The Indian invasion of Goa in 1961 demonstrates the difficulties of doing justice in such a situation. Portugal acquired Goa by conquest in the sixteenth century, and India recognized the Portuguese title after becoming independent in 1947. However, in the Security Council debates which followed the invasion, India argued that Portugal's title was void because it was based on colonial conquest. Such a view is correct under twentieth-century notions of international law, but hardly under sixteenth-century notions. The sympathies of most of the members of the United Nations lay with India, and neither the Security Council nor the General Assembly condemned India's action.[74] But this does not necessarily mean that they thought that India's action was legally justified. Where a rule of law works well in most cases but causes injustice in isolated cases, the best solution may be to turn a blind eye to violations of the rule in those isolated cases. In some municipal legal systems the authorities often exercise a good deal of discretion in deciding whether or not to prosecute. The United Nations seems to have reacted in the same way to India's invasion of Goa.

India's invasion of Goa had an ironic sequel. A year later China invaded some areas in the Himalayas held by India, arguing that these areas had originally been seized from China by a colonial power (Britain), that Britain's title was invalid because it was based on colonial conquest, that the title which India had inherited from Britain was similarly invalid, and that China was entitled to use force to recover the territory in question, just as India had done in Goa.[75] The argument that conquests in previous centuries are invalid is an argument which cuts both ways, and most states therefore do not accept it. Even communist China has shown itself less interested in regaining lost territory than in securing admissions from its neighbours that the boundaries between them and China were established by imperialist aggression; once such an admission has been made (for example, by Pakistan and Burma), China has been prepared to negotiate a new boundary which is almost indistinguishable from the old. If India and the Soviet Union had been prepared to make such an admission, they could probably have avoided their boundary disputes with China.[76]

Legal and political arguments

In territorial disputes, legal and political arguments are often used side by side – so much so that it is sometimes difficult to distinguish one from the other. There are good reasons for this; a state which has relied solely on legal arguments might be suspected of having a weak case politically, and a state which has relied solely on political arguments might be suspected of having a weak case legally. Besides, territorial disputes arouse extraordinary passions – people are prepared to fight and die rather than surrender an inch of their territory, however useless the territory in dispute may be – and in these circumstances it is hardly to be expected that people will be able to distinguish between what the law is and what it ought to be. Sometimes the confusion is deliberate. As noted by Jennings: 'If a political argument can be made to possess legal overtones, and the legal distinction between *meum* and *tum* blurred, the claimant may be enabled to convey the impression to others and, perhaps more importantly, to himself that he already possesses a claim in the sense of a legal title.'[77]

The main political arguments which are used in territorial disputes are the principles of geographical contiguity, of historical continuity and of self-determination.[78] The meaning and function of these principles can be understood by considering briefly the position of Northern Ireland.[79] It is generally agreed that Northern Ireland forms part of the United Kingdom from the point of view of international law; but the Republic of Ireland argues that Northern Ireland should be reunited with the Republic, because the two halves of Ireland form a natural geographical unit (geographical contiguity) and were administered as a political unit for centuries until 1922 (historical continuity); the United Kingdom replies that the majority of the population of Northern Ireland wishes to remain part of the United Kingdom (self-determination).

Such principles cannot, by themselves, create a legal title to territory. In the *Island of Palmas* case, the arbitrator said of the principle of contiguity:

It is impossible to show the existence of a rule of positive international law to the

75 A. Siehr, Conflicts, Indian Subcontinent, in *Wolfrum UNLPP I*, 243–54, at 245–6; S. Vohra, *The Northern Frontier of India: The Border Dispute with China*, 1993; X. Liu, *Sino-Indian Border Dispute and Sino-Indian Relations*, 1994. See also Chapter 19 below, 314–15.

76 T. Schweisfurth, Boundary Disputes between China and USSR, *EPIL* I (1992), 453–60; R. Khan, Boundary Disputes in the Indian Subcontinent, *ibid.*, 473–5.

77 Jennings (1962), *op. cit.*, 73.

78 See H. Kelsen, Contiguity as a Title to Territorial Sovereignty, in W. Schätzel/ H.-J. Schlochauer (eds), *Festschrift für H. W. Wehberg*, 1956, 200–10. On self-determination see Chapter 19 below, 324–40.

79 P. Macallister-Smith, Northern Ireland, *EPIL* 12 (1990), 249–64; I.S. Lustick, *Unsettled States, Disputed Lands: Britain and Ireland, France and Algeria, Israel and the West Bank-Gaza*, 1993; P. Arthur, The Anglo-Irish Joint Declaration: Towards a Lasting Peace?, *Gov. & Oppos.* 29 (1994), 218–30; K. Boyle/T. Hadden, The Peace Process in Northern Ireland, *IA* 71 (1995), 269–83.

80 *Island of Palmas Case, op. cit.,* at 854.
81 Jennings (1962), *op. cit.,* 73. See also the *Eastern Greenland Case, op. cit.,* 45–52.
82 P. Schneider, Condominium, *EPIL* I (1992), 732–5.
83 S. Less, New Hebrides, *EPIL* 12 (1990), 241–7.
84 J.A. Frowein, Lake Constance, *EPIL* 12 (1990), 216–9.
85 C. Rumpf, Territory, Lease, *EPIL* 10 (1987), 507–9.
86 A.D. Hughes, Hong Kong, *EPIL* II (1995), 870–3; *Harris CMIL,* 235, n. 4; on the (draft) agreement see *ILM* 23 (1984), 1366–87; see further G. Ress, The Legal Status of Hong Kong after 1997. The Consequences of the Transfer of Sovereignty According to the Joint Declaration of December 19, 1984, *ZaöRV* 46 (1986), 647; D.R. Fung, The Basic Law of the Hong Kong Special Administrative Region of the People's Republic of China, *ICLQ* 37 (1988), 701; J.-P. Béjà, *Hong Kong 1997: fin de siècle, fin d'un monde,* 1993; J.Y.S. Cheng, Sino-British Negotiations on Hong Kong During Chris Patten's Governorship, *AJIA* 48 (1994), 229–45; A. Goodlad, Hong Kong: Britain's Legacy, China's Inheritance, *The World Today* 50 (1994), 112–15.
87 See W. Rudolf, Macau, *EPIL* 12 (1990), 223–5; P. Fifoot, One Country, Two Systems – Mark II: From Hong Kong to Macao, *IR* 12 (1994), 25–58.
88 T. Oppermann, Cyprus, *EPIL* I (1992), 923–6. On the right granted by the 1960 Treaty concerning the Establishment of the Republic of Cyprus between Greece, Turkey and the UK to the UK to maintain military bases in Cyprus, see *Harris CMIL,* 234, n. 3. See also Chapter 22 below, 420–2.
89 U. Fastenrath, Servitudes, *EPIL* 10 (1987), 389–92.

effect that islands situated outside territorial waters should belong to a State from the mere fact that its territory forms the *terra firma* (nearest continent or island of considerable size).[80]

That does not mean, however, that such principles have no legal relevance:

Contiguity is no more than evidence raising some sort of presumption of effective occupation – a presumption that may be rebutted by better evidence of sovereign possession by a rival claimant.[81]

In other words, the principle of contiguity can be taken into account by international tribunals in borderline cases. So, presumably, can the principles of self-determination and historical continuity; where there is genuine doubt about the effectiveness of a state's control over territory, the loyalties of the inhabitants, or the fact that the territory has traditionally formed part of a larger administrative unit, may constitute evidence of effective control by a claimant state.

Minor rights over territory

So far we have been considering the situation where a state exercises full and exclusive sovereignty over territory. But there are also lesser rights over territory, which, although rare, deserve brief mention. Two states may agree to exercise sovereignty jointly over a certain territory. This is known as a condominium,[82] and resembles co-ownership in municipal law. The New Hebrides Islands (now Vanuatu) in the Pacific were a Franco-British condominium before they became independent in 1980.[83] Today, the relevance of the concept is still an issue in the dispute on the division of sovereignty over Lake Constance (Bodensee, Lac de Constance) which is surrounded by Germany, Switzerland and Austria.[84]

Occasionally a state leases part of its territory to another state; this is, in effect, a temporary transfer of sovereignty, because the state to which the territory is leased can exercise full sovereignty over the territory as long as the lease remains in force.[85] Part of the British colony of Hong Kong is held by the United Kingdom under a lease from China which is due to expire in 1997 when Hong Kong is to be returned under an agreement reached by the two countries in 1984.[86] Similarly, Portugal agreed in 1987 to return Macau to China in 1999.[87]

A state may also, by treaty, be given the right to administer part of the territory of another state. For instance, the Treaty of Berlin 1878 gave the United Kingdom the right to administer the Turkish island of Cyprus (the subsequent British annexation of Cyprus in 1915 was recognized by Turkey in the Treaty of Lausanne 1923).[88]

Servitudes

A servitude is said to arise when territory belonging to one state is, in some particular way, made to serve the interests of territory belonging to another state.[89] The state enjoying the benefit of the servitude may be entitled to do something on the territory concerned (for example, exercise a right of way, or remove water for irrigation); alternatively, the state on whom the burden of the servitude is imposed may be under an obligation to abstain from certain action (for example, not to fortify or station forces on the territory in question). Servitudes are usually created by treaty, although they may also be derived from local custom.[90]

The term 'servitude' is borrowed from the Roman law of property, and many writers criticize its use in international law, on the grounds that so-called international servitudes are not subject to the same rules as servitudes in Roman law. The essential feature of servitudes in Roman law (and of equivalent institutions in modern systems of municipal law) was that they 'ran with the land' – that is, all successors in title to the owner of the 'servient' land were subject to the burden of the servitude, and all successors in title to the owner of the 'dominant' land could claim the benefit of the servitude. Do the same rules apply to so-called international servitudes?

There are many cases of successor states being bound by territorial obligations entered into by predecessor states. For instance, in the *Free Zones of Upper Savoy and District of Gex* case, the Permanent Court of International Justice held that France was obliged to perform a promise made by Sardinia to maintain a customs-free zone in territory which France had subsequently acquired from Sardinia.[91]

Recorded examples of the benefit of an international servitude 'running with the land' in the same way are harder to find. But if obligations can 'run with the land', as in the *Free Zones* case, logic suggests that rights can also 'run with the land'. Moreover, it would be highly inconvenient if such rights did not survive changes in sovereignty; where the population of a particular area is economically dependent on obtaining water, for instance, from a neighbouring area, their livelihood ought not to be endangered by changes in sovereignty over either of the areas concerned.

International servitudes can sometimes exist, not for the benefit of a single state, but for the benefit of many states, or even for the benefit of all the states in the world. For instance, in 1856 Russia entered into a treaty obligation not to fortify the Aaland Islands in the Baltic; the islands lie near Stockholm, but Sweden was not a party to the treaty.[92] In 1918 the islands became part of Finland, which started fortifying them. Sweden, feeling threatened by the fortifications, complained to the Council of the League of Nations. The Council appointed a Committee of Jurists to report on the legal issues involved. The Committee of Jurists advised the Council that Finland had succeeded to Russia's obligations, and that Sweden could claim the benefit of the 1856 treaty, although it was not a party to it, because the treaty was designed to preserve the balance of power in Europe, and could therefore be invoked by all the states which were 'directly interested', including Sweden.[93]

Servitudes are particularly important in connection with rivers and canals.[94] In the eighteenth century states used to exclude foreign ships from using waterways within their territory. This caused great hardship, especially to landlocked states lying upstream, and since 1815 various treaties have been concluded, opening most of the major rivers of the world to

90 *Right of Passage Case (Portugal v. India)*, ICJ Rep. 1960, 6; *Harris CMIL*, 235–8; L. Weber, Right of Passage over Indian Territory Case, *EPIL* 2 (1981), 244–6. See also the *North Atlantic Fisheries Arbitration Case* (1910) (*U.S. v. Great Britain*), RIAA XI 167; extract in *Harris CMIL*, 232–3.

91 PCIJ, series A/B, no. 46; L. Weber, Free Zones of Upper Savoy and Gex Case, *EPIL* II (1995), 483–4.

92 T. Modeen, Aaland Islands, *EPIL* I (1992), 1–3.

93 LNOJ, Special Supplement No. 3, 1920, 18–9. See *Harris CMIL*, 234, n. 2 and Chapter 3 above, 59.

94 R. Lagoni, Canals, *EPIL* I (1992), 523–7; J.A. Barberis, International Rivers, *EPIL* II (1995), 1364–8.

95 *Harris CMIL*, 240–2; B. Broms, Suez Canal, *EPIL* 12 (1990), 360–5. See also Chapter 2 above, 27–8.

96 M. Hartwig, Panama Canal, *EPIL* 12 (1990), 282–9; J. Major, *Prize Possession: The United States and the Panama Canal, 1903–1979*, 1993. On the Kiel Canal, see *The Wimbledon Case* (1923) (France, Italy, Japan and the UK *v.* Germany), PCIJ, series A, n. 1; *Harris CMIL*, 239–40. See Chapter 2 above, 18.

97 Text in *AJIL* 53 (1957), 673; *Harris CMIL*, 241.

navigation, either by the ships of all states, or by the ships of all riparian states, or by the ships of all states parties to the treaty (the treaties vary in their terms). The Convention of Constantinople, signed in 1888 by Turkey and nine other states, declared the Suez Canal open to the ships of all nations.[95] The same rule was applied to the Panama Canal by treaties concluded by the United States with the United Kingdom and Panama in 1901 and 1903.[96] Egypt accepts that it has succeeded to Turkey's obligations under the 1888 Convention, and, after the nationalization of the canal, it filed a declaration with the United Nations Secretariat in 1957, reaffirming its intention 'to respect the terms and the spirit of the Constantinople Convention', and agreeing to accept the jurisdiction of the International Court of Justice in all disputes between Egypt and the other parties to the Convention which might arise out of the Convention.[97]

11 Legal consequences of changes of sovereignty over territory (state succession)

The term 'state succession' is used to describe that branch of international law which deals with the legal consequences of a change of sovereignty over territory.[1] When one state acquires territory from another, which of the rights and obligations of the 'predecessor state' pass to the 'successor state'? What happens to existing bilateral and multilateral treaties, to membership of international organizations, to international claims, to the nationality of the affected persons, to public and private property, to contractual rights, to national archives and to the national debt? This problem is complicated because it can arise in several different forms. A state may lose part of its territory, or it may lose all of it. Similarly, the loss of territory may result in the enlargement of one or more existing states, or it may result in the creation of one or more new states. These distinctions are vital, because different rules of law apply to different types of situation; for instance, the legal effects of the creation of a new state are different from the legal effects of the enlargement of an existing state.

The importance of classifying the situation is exceeded only by the difficulty of doing so. For instance, with regard to the creation of Yugoslavia after the First World War, one was faced with the question of whether it was a new state, or merely an enlargement of Serbia? Judicial decisions on the status of Yugoslavia indeed varied. Again, whether, after the recent dissolution of former Yugoslavia, the Federal Republic of Yugoslavia (Serbia/Montenegro) is now to be seen as a new state or a continuation of the Socialist Federal Republic of Yugoslavia is not easy to answer (see below). The only safe way of dealing with such problems is to ask, first, does the state concerned claim to be a new state, or does it claim to be a continuation of a previously existing state? And, second, how far have its claims been accepted by other states?

The status of the law on state succession has been aptly described as 'chaotic'.[2] In the 1970s, stimulated by the process of decolonization,[3] the International Law Commission made an attempt to codify major areas of the law of state succession which materialized in two draft Conventions: the 1978 Vienna Convention on State Succession in Respect of Treaties,[4] and the 1983 Vienna Convention on State Succession in Respect of State Property, Archives and Debts.[5] The codification attempt is generally viewed as a failure (although valuable research was produced in the course of preparing the draft articles), the main reason being that it focused far too much on the special problems and interests of the 'newly independent states' and disregarded other relevant situations. Also, the

1 D.P. O'Connell, *State Succession in Municipal and International Law*, 2 vols, 1967; *Restatement (Third)*, Vol. 1, paras. 208–210; W. Fiedler, State Succession, *EPIL* 10 (1987), 446–56; *Harris CMIL*, 813–6; P.K. Menon, *The Succession of States in Respect to Treaties, State Property, Archives and Debts*, 1991; M. Bothe/C. Schmidt, Sur quelques questions de succession posées par la dissolution de l'URSS et celle de la Yugoslavia, *RGDIP* 96 (1992), 811–42; D.F. Vagts, State Succession: The Codifiers' View, *Virginia JIL* 33 (1993), 275–97; O. Schachter, State Succession, The Once and Future Law, *ibid.*, 253–60; E.D. Williamson/J.E. Osborn, A U.S. Perspective on Treaty Succession and Related Issues in the Wake of the Breakup of the USSR and Yugoslavia, *ibid.*, 261 *et seq.*; W. Czapliński, La Continuité, l'identité et la succession d'Etats – Evaluation de cas récents, *RBDI* 26 (1993), 374–92; R. Mullerson, The Continuity and Succession of States by Reference to the Former USSR and Yugoslavia, *ICLQ* 42 (1993), 473–93; M.N. Shaw, State Succession Revisited, *FYIL* 5 (1994), 34–98; S. Bolderson/A. Verdonk, Treaty Status in the Commonwealth of Independent States, the Baltic States and the Former Czechoslovakia, *ET* 34 (1994), 50–60; P.R. Williams, The Treaty Obligations of the Successor States of the Former Soviet Union, Yugoslavia and Czechoslovakia: Do They Continue in Force?, *Denver JILP* 23 (1994), 1–42; G. Burdeau (ed.), *Dissolution, continuation et succession en Europe de l'Est*, 1994; *Annual Meeting of the Dutch Society of International Law*, 1995, Preadviezen by A. Bos and O.M. Ribbelink; L.H.W. Sandick, *Statenopvolging, Mededelingen NVIR* 1995; O.M. Ribbelink, On the Uniting of States in Respect to Treaties, *NYIL* 26 (1995), 139–69.
2 S. Oeter, German Unification and State Succession, *ZaöRV* 51 (1991), 349–83, at 352 *et seq.*

3 See Chapter 2 above, 28.
4 Text in *ILM* 17 (1978), 1488; *AJIL* 72 (1978), 971. See H.D. Treviranus, Vienna Convention on Succession of States in Respect of Treaties, *EPIL* 10 (1987), 523–6. For the useful Commentary of the ILC see *ILCYb* 1974, Vol. 2, part 1, 174–269.
5 Text in *ILM* 23 (1983), 306; Commentary in *ILCYb* 1981, Vol. 2, part 2, 20–113. See J. Oesterhelt, Vienna Convention on Succession of States in Respect of State Property, Archives and Debts, *EPIL* 10 (1987), 521–3.
6 Articles 11 and 12, 1978 Vienna Convention.
7 See Chapter 10 above, 158–60. For a discussion in the context of state succession, see Bos, *op. cit.*, 15–16.
8 See Kaikobad, Some Observations on the Doctrine of Continuity and Finality of Boundaries, *BYIL* 54 (1983), 119, 126–36.
9 See Touval, The OAU and African Borders, *IO* 21 (1967), 102, and *Case Concerning the Continental Shelf* (Tunisia/Libya), *ICJ Rep.* 1982, 18, 65–6 (para. 84), 131. See also Chapter 19 below, 335.
10 I. Brownlie, *African Boundaries: A Legal and Diplomatic Encyclopaedia*, 1979, 9–12; Y. Makonnen, State Succession in Africa: Selected Problems, *RdC* 200 (1986-V), 92–234; F. Wooldridge, *Uti possidetis* Doctrine, *EPIL* 10 (1987), 519–21; R. McCorquodale, Self-Determination Beyond the Colonial Context and its Potential Impact on Africa, *AJICL* 4 (1992), 592–608; J. Klabbers/R. Lefeber, Africa: Lost Between Self-Determination and Uti Possidetis, in C. Brölmann/R. Lefeber/M. Zieck (eds), *Peoples and Minorities in International Law*, 1993, 37–76; P. Malanczuk, Minorities and Self-Determination, Reflections on International Law in General Including Some Recent Developments in Ethiopia, in N. Sybesma-Knol/J. Van Bellingen (eds), *Naar een nieuwe interpretatie van het recht op Zelfbeschikking*, 1995, 169–93, 188 *et seq.*

rules in the draft treaties have not always been followed by actual state practice. Significantly, neither of the two conventions has so far received the necessary fifteen ratifications by states to enter into force. The 1978 Convention has been signed by twenty states and ratified by three (Ethiopia, Iraq and Yugoslavia); seven states acceded (Dominican Republic, Egypt, Estonia, Morocco, Seychelles, Tunisia and Ukraine). Bosnia-Herzegovina, Croatia, Slovenia and Slovakia are registered as successor states. The 1983 Convention has been signed by only six states. However, the topic of state succession has unexpectedly moved into the forefront again recently in view of the unifications of Yemen and of Germany, the dissolution of the Soviet Union, Yugoslavia and Czechoslovakia, and the secession of Eritrea from Ethiopia.

Treaties

Treaties dealing with rights over territory

In the case of 'dispositive' treaties (that is, treaties which deal with rights over territory), succession to rights and obligations always occurs. Such treaties 'run with the land' and are unaffected by changes of sovereignty over the territory.[6] Servitudes[7] are one important example. Boundary treaties are another. If a treaty delimits a boundary between two states, and if the territory on one side of the boundary is acquired by a third state, the third state is bound by the boundary treaty. The rule of automatic succession to boundary treaties is part of a wider principle that a state acquiring territory automatically succeeds to the boundaries of that territory, whether the boundaries are fixed by a treaty or whether they are fixed by the application of rules of customary law concerning title to territory and acquisition of territory.[8]

One consequence of this rule is that newly independent states inherited boundaries drawn by the former colonial powers; this consequence was accepted by almost all newly independent states, who had no wish to see their boundaries called into question. Colonial boundaries, particularly in Africa, were often unnatural, disregarding ethnic divisions and cutting through areas which form a natural economic unit, but, since the newly independent states could not agree on a radical redrawing of boundaries, they were wise to avoid uncertainty and conflict by preserving their existing boundaries.[9]

In 1964 the Organization of African Unity adopted a resolution which declared that 'all member states pledge themselves to respect the borders existing on their achievement of national independence'. This resolution reflects the so-called *uti possidetis* principle, which originally developed in South America in connection with the independence of states from Spanish and Portuguese rule to protect territorial integrity under the existing former administrative boundaries.[10] In the territorial dispute between Burkina Faso and Mali, the International Court of Justice recognized the obligation to respect existing borders in cases of state succession with the following words:

There is no doubt that the obligation to respect pre-existing international frontiers in the event of a State succession derives from a general rule of international law, whether or not the rule is expressed in the formula of *uti possidetis*.[11]

Similarly, the Conference on Yugoslavia Arbitration Commission that was established in 1991 upon the initiative of the European Community, supported by the United States and the former USSR, to render opinions on questions arising from the dissolution of Yugoslavia held:

> Except where otherwise agreed, the former boundaries become frontiers protected by international law. This conclusion follows from the principle of respect for the territorial status quo and, in particular, from the principle of *uti possidetis*. *Uti possidetis*, though initially applied in settling decolonization issues in America and Africa, is today recognized as a general principle, as stated by the International Court of Justice.[12]

The Commission also emphasized that '[a]ll external frontiers must be respected' with reference to the UN Charter and other international documents, including Article 11 of the 1978 Vienna Convention, that boundaries between the parties to the conflict cannot be altered except by free agreement, and that 'the alteration of existing frontiers or boundaries by force is not capable of producing any legal effects'.[13]

In Africa, the secession of Eritrea after thirty years of war and a referendum supervised by the United Nations and with the consent of the new Ethiopian government which had overthrown the Soviet-backed regime of Colonel Mengistu, has raised concern with regard to the 'sanctity of African borders' and the *uti possidetis* principle.[14] Eritrea was admitted as the fifty-first state of Africa to the United Nations on 28 May 1993.

Other types of treaties

With respect to other types of treaties, the rules vary according to the nature of the territorial change which has occurred.

The principle of 'moving treaty boundaries'

When a state loses territory, it loses its rights and obligations under treaties, in so far as those treaties used to apply to the lost territory. Thus, when the United Kingdom granted independence to Nigeria, the United Kingdom was no longer bound by an Anglo-American extradition treaty to extradite criminals from Nigeria, nor did it have a right to require the extradition of criminals from the United States for crimes committed in Nigeria. (But treaties made by the United Kingdom will normally continue to apply to territory retained by the United Kingdom after it granted independence to Nigeria.)

When an existing state acquires territory, it does not succeed to the predecessor state's treaties; but its own treaties normally become applicable to that territory. For instance, there are many decisions by French and Belgian courts holding that French treaties applied to Alsace and Lorraine after they were ceded to France in 1919. This rule is codified by Article 15 of the 1978 Vienna Convention.

The above rules are reflected in the so-called principle of 'moving treaty boundaries' which is thought to apply in the case when an existing state

11 *ICJ Rep.* 1986, 566.

12 Opinion No. 3 of 11 January 1992, *ILM* 31 (1992), 1499, at 1500. See also Chapter 19 below, 335.

13 *Ibid.*

14 See Malanczuk (1995), *op. cit.*; R. Goy, L'Indépendence de l'Erythrée, *AFDI* 39 (1993), 337–56. See generally E. Gayim, *The Eritrean Question: The Conflict between the Right of Self-Determination and the Interest of States*, 1993.

15 See Articles 29, 61 and 62, 1969 Vienna Convention on the Law of Treaties (text in *ILM* 8 (1969), 679; *AJIL* 63 (1969), 875); Article 15, 1978 Vienna Convention, *op. cit.*
16 See Bos, *op. cit.*, 12. See also below, 167–8.
17 See Chapter 2 above, 28–30.
18 Article 17, 1978 Vienna Convention.
19 Article 24.
20 For the meaning of estoppel, see Chapters 3, 49 and 10, 154–5 above.
21 See Chapter 5 above, 80.

transfers sovereignty over a part of its territory to another state (as distinct from the cases of the confederation of independent states or the unification into one state of two previously independent states). It means that the treaties concluded by the predecessor state are no longer applicable to that territory, while the treaties of the successor state automatically apply to it. This rule of the law of state succession reflects the law of treaties and knows only an exception if the application of a particular treaty to a certain territory is incompatible with the object and purpose of the treaty.[15] The rule, however, is controversial because it may be too restrictive to deal with cases in which one state is completely extinguished by fusion with another state, a view particularly advanced by Germany in the discussions on the 1978 Convention with the possible eventual reunification of the two German states in mind.[16]

Decolonization and new states

As regards new states which have come into being through decolonization,[17] the Vienna Convention lays down the following rules:

1   A new state can succeed to a multilateral treaty, to which the predecessor state was a party, by notifying the depositary that it regards itself as succeeding to the treaty. There are some exceptions to this rule; for instance, a new state cannot succeed to a multilateral treaty if that would be incompatible with the intentions of the parties to the treaty. A new state is under no obligation to succeed to a multilateral treaty if it does not want to do so.[18]
2   A new state succeeds to a bilateral treaty, which the predecessor state made with another state, only if that other state and the new state both agree.[19] However, agreement can be inferred from conduct; for instance, if both sides claim rights, or grant rights to one another, on the basis of the treaty, they will be estopped from denying that succession has occurred.[20] Such implied agreements often occur, because both sides often find that it is in their mutual interests to continue to apply treaties made by the predecessor state.

As we have seen, colonies were frequently given a limited treaty-making power before becoming independent.[21] Treaties which they themselves had made under such a power were not affected by independence. For instance, India joined the UN in 1945 but did not become independent until 1947; independence did not affect India's membership of the UN. (Pakistan, however, was regarded as a new state and had to apply to be admitted as a new member.) Whether India succeeded to treaties made by the United Kingdom, however, is a much more difficult problem.

It may also seem paradoxical and inconsistent that succession to a bilateral treaty requires the consent of the other party, but that succession to a multilateral treaty does not require the consent of the other parties. However, the paradox and inconsistency are more apparent than real. The parties to most multilateral treaties welcome the participation of as many states as possible, and so their consent to succession by a new state can be taken for granted; that is why Article 17 makes no express mention of their consent. However, Article 17 does require the consent of the other parties if it is clear that succession without their consent would be incompatible with the intentions of the parties to the treaty.

These rules apply only if the new state was formerly a dependent territory (for example, a colony) of the predecessor state. A new state formed by secession from the metropolitan (that is, non-'colonial') territory of the predecessor state, or by the disintegration of the predecessor state's metropolitan territory into two or more new states, succeeds automatically to most of the predecessor state's treaties.[22] When a new state is formed by the merger of two or more existing states, treaties made by the predecessor states continue to apply to the territory to which they applied before the merger, subject to certain exceptions.[23]

Under Articles 17 and 24, a new state is under no obligation to succeed to a treaty if it does not want to do so; it can start life with a 'clean slate'. The 'clean slate' doctrine was well established in customary international law before 1945. Developments after 1945 cast some doubt on the 'clean slate' doctrine, because some of the states which became independent after 1945 seemed to accept that they succeeded automatically to treaties made by their predecessor states. However, it is submitted that this practice of automatic succession was insufficient to destroy the 'clean slate' doctrine, because:

1   only some of the states which became independent after 1945 followed this practice, while others followed the 'clean slate' doctrine;
2   some of the states which followed the practice of automatic succession applied it to only some of the treaties made by their predecessors, and not to others;
3   the states which followed the practice of automatic succession appear to have done so because they found it convenient, not because they considered themselves obliged to do so.[24]

By reaffirming the 'clean slate' doctrine, Articles 17 and 24 of the Vienna Convention 1978 are therefore probably in accordance with customary law.

The provisions of Articles 34 and 31 concerning disintegration and merger, respectively, are also probably in accordance with customary law, although examples of disintegration and merger have been too few to justify a firm conclusion. On the other hand, the provisions of Article 34 concerning secession probably conflict with customary law, which seems to have permitted a secessionary state to start life with a 'clean slate'.[25]

Recent practice

Secession

Baltic states

The Baltic states (Estonia, Latvia and Lithuania)[26] that had been annexed by the Soviet Union in 1940 declared their independence in 1990 and 1991.[27] A number of states recognized their independence, including the

22 Article 34, 1978 Vienna Convention.

23 Article 31.

24 On the requirements of consistency and *opinio iuris* for the creation of rules of customary law, see Chapter 3 above, 41–5.

25 See Z. Meriboute, *La Codification de la succession d'état aux traites*, 1984, 141–64 (secession), 182–6 (merger), 206–17 (disintegration).

26 B. Meissner, Baltic States, *EPIL* I (1992), 328–37. See also Chapter 10 above, 152.

27 Lithuania on 11 March 1990, Estonia on 20 August 1991, and Latvia one day later. See R. Yakemtchouk, Les Républiques baltes en droit international – Echec d'une annexation operée en violation de droit international, *AFDI* 37 (1991), 259; A. Spruds (ed.), *The Baltic Path to Independence: An International Reader of Selected Articles*, 1994.

28 See Bos, *op. cit.*, 27–9.

29 On the concept see B. Schloh, Dismemberment, *EPIL* I (1992), 1083–5.

30 See generally C. Haverland, Secession, *EPIL* 10 (1987), 384–9.

31 But see Mullerson, *op. cit.*, 483 concerning the agreement between Finland and Estonia on the provisional application of certain treaties or parts thereof.

32 On the cases of the Federation of Mali 1950, the United Arab Republic 1961, and Bangladesh 1971, see Ribbelink, Preadviezen, *op. cit.*, 81 *et seq.*

33 See Mullerson, *op. cit.*; Bos, *op. cit.*, 30 *et seq.*; Ribbelink, Preadviezen, *op. cit.*, 85 *et seq.*; Bothe/Schmidt, *op. cit.*; T. Schweisfurth, Vom Einheitsstaat (UdSSR) zum Staatenbund (GUS), *ZaöRV* 52 (1992), 541–702. See generally W. Fiedler, Continuity, *EPIL* I (1992), 806–9.

34 *ILM* 31 (1992), 138. See also Chapter 6 above, 94–5.

35 See Lukašuk, Rußland als Rechtsnachfolger in völkerrechtliche Verträge der USSR, *Osteur.-Recht* 39 (1993), 235.

36 *ILM* 31 (1992), 151. See Y. Blum, Russia Takes Over the Soviet Union's Seat at the United Nations, *EJIL* 3 (1992), 354–51; M.P. Scharf, Musical Chairs: The Dissolution of States and Membership in the United Nations, *Cornell ILJ* 28 (1995), 29–69. See also Chapter 21 below, 373.

37 UN Doc. 1991/Russia.

38 *AJIL* 90 (1996), 448.

39 See Chapter 5 above, 89–90.

40 See T. Schweisfurth, Ausgewählte Fragen der Staatensukzession im Kontext der Auflösung der UdSSR, *AVR* 32 (1994), 99–129, 105; Bos, *op. cit.*, 33.

41 G. Bunn/J.B. Rhinelander, The Arms Control Obligations of the Former Soviet Union, *Virginia JIL* 33 (1993), 323–50; L.S. Wolosky/J.M. Malis/D.A. Schwimmer, START, START II, and Ownership of Nuclear Weapons: The Case for a 'Primary' Successor State, *Harvard ILJ* 34 (1993), 581–95.

Soviet Union on 6 September 1991, and they were admitted to the United Nations. Whether the Baltic states may be regarded as new independent states in the sense of the 1978 Convention is unclear because the Convention fails to provide a definition of 'dependent territories'.[28] States take different positions on whether the Baltic States should be recognized as new states following their independence from the Soviet Union, as well as on the issue of whether this is a case of the 'dismemberment' of a state[29] or a case of 'secession'.[30] The Baltic states themselves do not regard themselves as successor states to the USSR and have refused to be bound by any doctrine of treaty succession to bilateral or multilateral treaties concluded by the former Soviet Union.[31]

Dismemberment[32]

Soviet Union

When Mikhail Gorbachov came to power in the Soviet Union in 1985, a process was initiated which, following the abortive coup d'état in August 1991, ultimately led to the disintegration of the USSR. It is disputed whether the claim of the Russian Federation to continuity with the former Soviet Union is justified.[33] However, there is no doubt that the former USSR ended with the establishment of the Commonwealth of Independent States (CIS) based upon the Alma Ata Declaration, signed on 21 December 1991 by eleven Soviet republics.[34] The CIS states declared themselves willing to guarantee, in accordance with their constitutional procedures, 'the discharge of the international obligations deriving from treaties and agreements concluded by the former Union of Soviet Republics' (concerning some 16,000 instruments)[35] and to support 'Russia's continuance' of the membership of the USSR in the United Nations, including permanent membership of the Security Council, and other international organizations.[36] A corresponding declaration on the latter point was transmitted by Russia to the UN Secretary-General on 24 December 1991.[37] There was no objection by anyone to Russia taking the seat of the USSR at the United Nations. On 17 January 1992, the Russian Ministry of Foreign Affairs informed diplomatic missions in Moscow that the Russian Federation would continue to carry out obligations under international treaties concluded by the USSR, and that the Russian Government would perform the functions of depository for corresponding multilateral agreements in place of the Government of the USSR.[38]

Whether the position adopted by the European Union on the basis of its 'Guidelines on the Recognition of New States in Eastern Europe and in the Soviet Union'[39] amounts to an implicit recognition of the Russian Federation's claim to continuity with the former USSR is controversial.[40] At any rate, a major consideration of the West in dealing with the issue of the disintegration of the USSR was to secure the continued applicability of a number of multilateral treaties which are of prime importance to international security. One aspect was the control of the arsenal of nuclear weapons on the territories of Russia, Ukraine, Belarus and Kazakstan. While Russia appeared as the successor state to the Soviet Union as a nuclear power[41] and entered into the rights and obligations of the

Non-Proliferation Treaty,[42] the other three states declared that they would aim for a non-nuclear status.[43] With respect to the 1991 Treaty on Conventional Armed Forces in Europe, the Russian Federation declared that all its relevant armaments and equipment, on or after 19 November 1990, still provisionally on the territories of Estonia, Latvia and Lithuania, were subject to the provisions of the treaty. At the same time, the Baltic states were taken out of the Treaty's territorial scope of application.[44]

Yugoslavia

The case of Yugoslavia is also a complex one.[45] The independence declared by Slovenia and Croatia on 25 June 1991 (the implementation of these declarations was later postponed until 8 October 1991) as the first units of former Yugoslavia, was recognized by the European Union and a number of other states in January 1992, followed by the recognition of Bosnia-Herzegovina on 7 April 1992. On 27 April 1992, Serbia and Montenegro set up the Federal Republic of Yugoslavia with the explicit claim of continuing the former Socialist Federal Republic of Yugoslavia.[46] On 1 May 1992, the European Union expressed its willingness to recognize Macedonia as an independent state under a name acceptable to all parties (thereby taking into consideration the objections raised by Greece).[47]

Soon thereafter, on 22 May 1992, the new republics of Slovenia, Bosnia-Herzegovina and Croatia were admitted as members of the United Nations.[48] The Security Council, however, denied the claim of the Federal Republic of Yugoslavia (Serbia and Montenegro) to automatically succeed to the membership of former Yugoslavia and required it to make a new application for admission because former Yugoslavia had ceased to exist.[49] Much of the following dispute in New York had to do with the right of whom to raise which flag in front of the United Nations building. The same negative attitude towards Serbia's and Montenegro's claim to continuity was adopted by the Arbitration Commission set up within the framework of the Conference on Yugoslavia.[50] The only major states willing to recognize the claim of the Federal Republic of Yugoslavia were Russia and China. In the General Assembly Kenya, Swaziland, Tanzania, Zimabwe, Zambia and Yugoslavia voted against the recommendation of the Security Council.[51] Moreover, the practice of the successor states to former Yugoslavia with regard to international treaties has been rather inconsistent.[52]

Czechoslovakia

The separation of Czechoslovakia created two new states on 1 January 1993, and occurred much in line with the provisions of the 1978 Convention. The Czech Republic and Slovakia declared themselves as successor states and to be willing to take over the respective international obligations of the predecessor state.[53]

Unification[54]

Germany

The unification of Germany on 3 October 1990 is an almost unique case.[55] The procedure adopted under Article 23 of the Constitution of the Federal

42 See Chapter 20 below, 349.

43 For details see Bos, *op. cit.*, 34.

44 For further information on other treaties and on the position of the other CIS states see Bos, *op. cit.*, 35 *et seq.*

45 See, for example, M. Weller, The International Response to the Dissolution of the Socialist Federal Republic of Yugoslavia, *AJIL* 86 (1992), 569–607; Y.Z. Blum, UN Membership of the 'New' Yugoslavia: Continuity or Break?, *ibid.*, 830–33; Agora: UN Membership of the Former Yugoslavia, *AJIL* 87 (1993), 240–51; W. Hummer, Probleme der Staatennachfolge am Beispiel Jugoslawiens, *RSDI* 4 (1993), 425–59. See also the literature above, 161 and Chapter 5, 89–90 above and Chapters 21, 372–3 and 22, 409–15 below.

46 See UN Doc. S/23877 of 5 May 1992.

47 See also Chapter 5 above, 90 and Chapters 21, 372 and 22, 409–15 below.

48 UN Doc. GA Res. 46/238; 46/236 and 46/237.

49 UN Doc. S/Res 757, 30 May 1992; UN Doc. S/Res 777 (1992). See Ribbelink, Preadviezen, *op. cit.*, 95 *et seq.*

50 See Chapter 5 above, 89–90.

51 See *UNYb* 1992, 139; Czapliński, *op. cit.*

52 See Bos, *op. cit.*, 42 *et seq.*; H. Tichy, Two Recent Cases of State Succession – An Austrian Perspective, *AJPIL* 44 (1992), 125. See also Art. 5 of the 1996 Agreement on the Normalization of Relations between Croatia and the Federal Republic of Yugoslavia, *ILM* 35 (1996), 1219, and Art. 4 of the 1996 Agreement between Macedonia and Yugoslavia, *ibid.*, 1246.

53 See M. Hoškova, Die Selbstauflösung der CSFR – Ausgewählte rechtliche Aspekte, *ZaöRV* 53 (1993), 697. The separation of Czechoslovakia is a pertinent case in which the predecessor state was extinguished; see generally U. Fastenrath, State Extinction, *EPIL* 10 (1987), 465–7.

54 For the older cases of the United Arab Republic (Egypt and Syria) 1958, Tanzania 1964 (Tanganyika and Zanzibar), and Vietnam 1976, see Ribbelink, Preadviezen, *op. cit.*, 71 *et seq.*; see also Ribbelink (1995), *op. cit.*, 139–69.

55 Text of the Treaty on the Final Settlement with respect to Germany of 12 September 1990 in *ILM* 29 (1990), 1186. Documents Relating to Germany's Unification are reprinted in

ZaöRV 51 (1991), 494. See also Taking Reichs Seriously: German Unification and the Law of State Succession, Harvard LR 104 (1990), 588–606; J.A. Frowein, Germany Reunited, ZaöRV 51 (1991), 333–48; Oeter (1991), op. cit.; G.E. Wilms, The Legal Status of Berlin after the Fall of the Wall and German Reunification, ZaöRV 51 (1991), 470–93; K. Hailbronner, Legal Aspects of the Unification of the Two German States, EJIL 2 (1991), 18–41; F.G. v.d. Dunk/P.H. Kooijmans, The Unification of Germany and International Law, Mich. JIL 12 (1991), 510–37; J.A. Frowein, The Reunification of Germany, AJIL 86 (1992), 152–63; R. Wittkowski, Die Staatensukzession in völkerrechtliche Verträge unter besonderer Berücksichtigung der Herstellung der staatlichen Einheit Deutschlands, 1992; U. Fastenrath, Der deutsche Einigungsvertrag im Lichte des Rechts der Staatennachfolge, AJPIL 44 (1992), 1–54; F. Elbe, Resolving the External Aspects of German Unification, The 'Two-Plus-Four' Process, GYIL 36 (1993), 371–84; Bos, op. cit., 48 et seq.; Ribbelink, Preadviezen, op. cit., 76 et seq.; R. Bernhardt, Germany, Unification of, EPIL II (1995), 590–5. On the occupied status of Germany after the Second World War see Chapters 5, 83–4 and 10 above, 151–2.

56 See T. Giegerich, The European Dimension of German Reunification: East Germany's Integration into the European Communities, ZaöRV 51 (1991), 384–450; J.-P. Jacqué, German Unification and the European Community, EJIL 2 (1991), 1–17; P.J. Kuyper, The Community and State Succession in Respect of Treaties, in D. Curtin/T. Heukels (eds), International Dynamics of European Integration, Vol. II, 1994, 619–40; J.F. Weiss, Succession of States in Respect of Treaties Concluded by the European Communities, SEW 10 (1994), 661–79.

57 See text above, 163–4.

58 Bos, op. cit., 48 et seq.

59 See Ribbelink, Preadviezen, op. cit., 77 et seq. On UN peacekeeping see Chapter 22 below, 416–25.

60 See the letter of 3 October 1990 from the German Foreign Minister to the UN Secretary-General, ILM 30 (1991), 457.

61 See R. Goy, La Réunification du Yemen, AFDI 36 (1990), 249–65. Text of the Agreement on the Establishment of the Republic of Yemen in ILM 30 (1991), 820.

Republic of Germany (West Germany) provided for the accession of the German Democratic Republic (East Germany, which ceased to exist) while retaining the identity and continuity of the Federal Republic. The alternative option under Article 146 of the *Grundgesetz* to adopt a new constitution was considered unfeasible – a view shared by the Commission of the European Community – because of the problems that might have arisen concerning the question of whether the united Germany would then have to be seen as a new international legal personality.[56]

From the German point of view, succession took place on the basis of the 'moving treaty boundaries' rule,[57] although East Germany was an independent subject of international law (having a *sui generis* character as a state, as emphasized by the Federal Republic) and the unification involved the complete incorporation of one state into another state, instead of the transfer of a part of state territory.[58] But the principle of 'moving treaty boundaries' was not really fully applied in the process. In practice, negotiations with all treaty partners of the former German Democratic Republic were held concerning the fate of treaties that had been concluded by East Germany.

The continuation of membership in international organizations did not raise any special problems in the case of the United Nations, except for the refusal of the united Germany to pay for the outstanding contributions of East Germany to two peacekeeping operations in the Middle East (UNDOF and UNIFIL).[59] The UN argued that Germany was liable to pay for the debts of the predecessor state to the extent that it had inherited property rights and interests. From the date of unification, in the United Nations the Federal Republic of Germany, to which the German Democratic Republic had acceded, simply acted under the designation 'Germany'.[60] More complications became apparent in other international organizations, particularly with regard to the European Community. While the Community in principle accepted the 'moving treaty boundary' rule, meaning that the territory of the Community was enlarged and the territorial scope of the application of Community law thus extended to former East Germany, it did not accept that all treaties concluded by East Germany had automatically been terminated. Moreover, the Community was in a position to argue that it had to be involved in negotiations on East German treaties, at least where exclusive competences had been transferred to Community organs. The alternative would have been a very complicated and time-consuming admission and amendment procedure concerning the European Community treaties.

Yemen

The unification of Yemen in 1990 took a different form with two states merging into a single state.[61] They declared that united Yemen is to be considered as a party to all treaties which had been concluded by one of the predecessor states with effect from the date upon which the first of the two had become party to the treaty.

International claims

International claims for compensation for illegal acts are regarded as being intensely 'personal', and no succession occurs to the rights of the claimant state or to the obligations of the defendant state. The claims are unaffected by expansion or contraction of the claimant state or of the defendant state; new states commence with a 'clean slate';[62] and extinction of either the claimant state or the defendant state results in extinction of the claim. This last proposition is exemplified by *Brown's* claim. Brown, a United States citizen, suffered a denial of justice in the South African Republic in 1895, but, before the claim was settled, the Boer War broke out and the Republic was annexed by the United Kingdom. The United States presented a claim against the United Kingdom, but the arbitrator held that the United Kingdom had not succeeded to the South African Republic's liabilities for international claims.[63]

Nationality

It is sometimes said that a change of sovereignty over territory means that the subjects of the predecessor state, who inhabit the territory, automatically lose their old nationality and acquire the nationality of the successor state.[64] But what is meant by the 'inhabitants' of a territory? Does birth on the territory suffice, or is residence to be taken as the criterion? Or are both birth and residence necessary? Or are they alternatives? If residence is taken into account, what are the critical dates or periods of time for determining whether someone is a resident? In practice, such problems can be regulated only by treaties or by municipal legislation. Treaties sometimes allow the individuals concerned to choose whether they want to retain their old nationality or acquire the nationality of the successor state.

It must be admitted, however, that much of the area is unclear.[65] In 1993 therefore, the International Law Commission decided to include on its agenda the topic of state succession and its impact on the nationality of natural and legal persons. The preliminary conclusions of a working group submitted in 1995 start from the premise that, in situations resulting from state succession, every person whose nationality might be affected by the change in the international status of the territory has a right to nationality and that states have the obligation to prevent statelessness, as the most serious potential consequence of state succession. Other potential detrimental effects considered are dual nationality, the separation of families as a result of the attribution of different nationalities to their members, military service obligations, pensions and the right of residence.[66]

Public property

When a state acquires all the territory of another state, it succeeds to all the public property of that state (that is, all property belonging to the state, as distinct from property belonging to its nationals or inhabitants), wherever that property may be situated.[67]

On the other hand, if a state merely loses some of its territory, the

62 See text above, 165.
63 *RIAA* VI 120. See E.H. Riedel, Lighthouses Cases, *EPIL* 2 (1981), 171–2. But the orthodox principle applied in this and other cases was not followed by the Permanent Court of Arbitration in the *Lighthouses Arbitration, ILR* 23 (1956), 81, 90–3.
64 On nationality under international law see Chapter 17 below, 263–7.
65 See L. Barrington, The Domestic and International Consequences of Citizenship in the Soviet Successor States, *Eur.-Asia Stud.* 47 (1995), 731–63; G. Ginsburg, The Issue of Dual Citizenship Among the Successor States, *Osteur.-Recht* 41 (1995), 1–29.
66 A/CN.4/L.507..V. Mikulka was appointed as Special Rapporteur.
67 *Haile Selassie v. Cable & Wireless Ltd,* [1939] ChD 182.

68 *ILCYb* 1981, Vol. 2, part 2, 25–71; *Peter Pazmany University* case (1933), PCIJ, series A/B, no. 61, 237. See V.-D. Degan, State Succession. Especially in Respect of State Property and Debts, *FYIL* 4 (1993), 3–21; S. Oeter, State Succession and the Struggle over Equity. Some Observations on the Laws of State Succession with Respect to State Property and Debts in Cases of Separation and Dissolution of States, *GYIL* 38 (1995), 73–102.

69 *United States v. Percheman* (1833), 32 US 51, 86–8; *German Settlers* case (1923), PCIJ, series B, no. 6; *Certain German Interests in Polish Upper Silesia* (1926), PCIJ, series A, no. 7, 21–2; *Chorzow Factory* case (1928), PCIJ, series A, no. 17, 46–8. In the two latter cases the question was regulated by a treaty, but the Court said that the rules of customary law were the same as those contained in the treaty. On the minimum standard for the treatment of aliens, with special reference to expropriation, see Chapter 15 above, 235–9 and Chapter 17 below, 260–9.

70 C. Schreuer, Unjust Enrichment, *EPIL* 9 (1986), 381–3.

71 For example, Friedmann, *AJIL* (1963), 279, 295.

72 See Chapter 15 below, 237.

73 [1905] 2 KB 291.

successor state succeeds to much less of the predecessor's public property. Most of the public property situated in territory retained by the predecessor state, or in third states, continues to belong to the predecessor state, while most of the public property situated in the transferred territory passes to the successor state.[68]

Private property

Private property rights do not lapse automatically when territory is transferred. If the successor state subsequently wishes to expropriate privately owned property in the territory which it has acquired, the extent of its power to do so depends on the nationality of the owner. If the owner has (or has acquired) the nationality of the successor state, the successor state's right to expropriate his property is unlimited under customary international law (although it may be limited by treaties on human rights). On the other hand, if the owner is a national of the predecessor state or of a third state, the successor state must comply with the minimum international standard for the treatment of aliens; expropriation must be for a public purpose and must be accompanied by compensation.[69]

Such, at any rate, are the traditional rules accepted by Western countries. Most Third World countries, however, have rejected these rules. Even when they were prepared to accept that the 'Western' rules are applicable to investments made in newly independent countries *after* independence, they maintained that different considerations apply to investments made *before* independence, at a time when those countries were unable to protect their own interests. Such investments, they argued, were often made on unequal terms and amounted to a form of colonialist exploitation. Some Western writers have tried to counter this point by suggesting that the rule requiring compensation in the event of expropriation is designed to prevent unjust enrichment,[70] and that it is therefore logical, in certain cases, to reduce the amount of compensation payable for the act of expropriation, in order to take account of the extent to which the expropriated foreigner has unjustly enriched himself in the past.[71] Unfortunately words like 'unjust enrichment' and 'exploitation' are so subjective that there are bound to be constant disputes about the application of a rule drafted in such terms; enrichment which seems just to one party will seem unjust to the other. And Western investors are hardly likely to make new investments in newly independent countries if they feel that those countries have enriched themselves unjustly at the expense of old investments. It is therefore questionable whether a relaxation of the traditional rules would really be in the long-term interests of the newly independent countries, and recent developments in foreign investment have shown that this is indeed true.[72]

Contractual rights

Even before the modern era of decolonization, some authorities doubted whether a successor state succeeded to the contractual obligations of the predecessor state. For instance, in *West Rand Central Gold Mining Co. v. The King*,[73] the English High Court held that the Crown did not succeed to the contractual liabilities of the South African Republic after it had been annexed by the United Kingdom. This case has been criticized, and it was not followed by the Permanent Court of International Justice in the *German Settlers* case.[74]

It is sometimes said that the successor state cannot logically be bound by a contract to which it is not a party.[75] But, if the alien has benefited the territory by spending money and effort in performing his contract, it is only fair that a state acquiring sovereignty over that territory should allow him to reap the rewards of his investment. On this analysis, the successor state's liability is probably not contractual but quasi-contractual – a term used to describe a situation where there is no contract, but where the law requires the parties to behave *as if* there were a contract, in order to prevent unjust enrichment. It does not matter much whether the successor state's liability is regarded as contractual or as quasi-contractual, because the results are the same in both cases; either the successor state must allow the alien to obtain the benefits due to him under the original contract, or, if it wishes to deprive him of some or all of those benefits, it must compensate him for expropriating his rights.[76]

The problem of contractual rights has arisen chiefly in connection with concessions and the national debt. A concession is a right granted by a state to a company or individual to operate an undertaking on special terms defined in an agreement between the state and the concessionaire; the undertaking usually consists of extracting oil or other minerals, or of providing a public utility (supplying gas, water, or electricity, running a canal or railway, and so on).[77] The concessionaire's rights are semi-proprietorial, semi-contractual. Practice is not entirely consistent, but the better view is that a successor state must pay compensation if it revokes a concession granted by the predecessor state.[78]

The problems which arise in connection with the national debt are more complex, and can be discussed only in outline here.[79] If state A annexes the whole of state B's territory, it succeeds to the obligations which state B owed to foreign creditors in respect of state B's national debt. If state B loses only part of its territory, it is right that the successor state or states should take over part of B's debt, otherwise B, with reduced territory and economic resources, might be unable to meet its debts. For example, when British colonies became independent, they were made liable for the debts raised by the local colonial administration, but not for any part of the British national debt (even while they were colonies they did not contribute towards the cost of the British national debt).[80] However, when the Irish Free State became independent in 1922, it took over part of the British national debt;[81] otherwise independence would have relieved taxpayers in the Irish Free State of their previous responsibility for paying interest on the national debt, and would have increased the burdens falling on taxpayers in the remaining parts of the United Kingdom.

Similarly, if state B loses all its territory as a result of being dismembered by several other states, it is only fair that responsibility for state B's debt should be split up among the successor states. The difficulty in these last two cases is deciding what proportion of the debt should be

74 PCIJ, series B, no. 6.

75 On state contracts in general see Chapters 3, 38–9 and 6, 102 above.

76 On the consequences of German reunification, for example, see F. Drinhausen, *Die Auswirkungen der Staatensukzession auf Verträge mit privaten Partnern*, 1995.

77 See P. Fisher, Concessions, *EPIL* I (1992), 715–21.

78 *Mavrommatis* case (1924), PCIJ, series A, no. 2, 28. See K. Doehring, Mavrommatis Concessions Cases, *EPIL* 2 (1981), 182–5. This is the rule accepted by Western countries, but it is rejected by most Third World countries.

79 See H.-E. Folz, State Debts, *EPIL* 8 (1985), 484–8; P.R. Williams, State Succession and the International Financial Institutions, Political Criteria v. Protection of Outstanding Financial Obligations, *ICLQ* 43 (1994), 776–808; Degan, *op. cit.* As to valuation difficulties even on a treaty basis, see H.J. Hahn, Value Maintenance in the Young Loan Arbitration. History and Analysis, *NYIL* 14 (1983), 3–39.

80 See also *ILCYb* 1981, Vol. 2, part 2, 91–105, on the legal position of former colonies in connection with national debts.

81 O'Connell, *op. cit.*, Vol. 1, 40.

82 See *ILCYb* 1981, Vol. 2, part 2, 72–113.

83 See P. Juillard, La Dette extérieure de l'ancienne Union Soviétique: succession ou continuation?, in Burdeau (ed.), *op. cit.*, 201, 210 *et seq.*, discussing the Memorandum of 28 October 1991, the Treaty of 4 January 1992 and the Joint Declarations of 2 April 1993.

84 1983 Vienna Convention, *op. cit.*

borne by each of the states concerned; in practice this problem can only be settled by treaty.[82] The successor states to the former Soviet Union, for example, agreed that most of the property and the major part of the debt of the USSR were to be taken over by the Russian Federation. The other states were accorded small percentages and a remaining part was transferred to the Baltic States and Georgia.[83]

Finally, it should be noted that Western states refused to sign or ratify the 1983 Vienna Convention on Succession of States in Respect of State Property, Archives and Debts[84] mainly because it deals with succession to debts owed only to other states and international organizations, and says nothing about succession to debts owed to individuals and companies.

12 The law of the sea

For legal purposes the sea (which covers more than 70 per cent of the surface of the globe) has traditionally been divided into three different zones, each of which is subject to different rules.[1] Moving outwards from land, these zones are (1) internal waters, (2) territorial sea, and (3) high seas. In recent years the position has been complicated by the tendency of coastal states to claim limited rights over areas of the high seas adjacent to their territorial sea (contiguous zones, exclusive fishery zones, exclusive economic zones and the continental shelf).

The law of the sea was to a large extent codified by the first United Nations Conference on the Law of the Sea (UNCLOS I) at Geneva in 1958, which drew up four conventions: the Convention on the Territorial Sea and the Contiguous Zone, the Convention on the High Seas, the Convention on Fishing and Conservation of the Living Resources of the High Seas, and the Convention on the Continental Shelf.[2] These conventions were ratified or acceded to by forty-six, fifty-seven, thirty-six and fifty-four states respectively, while thirty-eight states became parties to the Optional Protocol on the compulsory settlement of disputes.[3] Most of the provisions of the first two conventions, and some of the provisions of the Convention on the Continental Shelf, codified customary law. Consequently, although the conventions as such are binding only on states which are parties to them, many of their provisions can be used as evidence of customary law even against states which are not parties to them. (However, provisions which were declaratory of customary law in 1958 are not necessarily declaratory of customary law today, because, as we shall see, some rules of customary law have changed since 1958.)

The 1958 conference failed to reach agreement on a number of questions (especially the question of the width of the territorial sea; a second conference in 1960, UNCLOS II, also failed to reach agreement on this question). Moreover, some states became dissatisfied with various rules which were laid down in the 1958 Conventions; and technological advances created a need for new rules. Consequently a third United Nations Conference on the Law of the Sea (UNCLOS III) was convened in 1973, to draw up a new comprehensive convention on the law of the sea. After meeting intermittently for nine years (with 144 states and eight Specialized Agencies participating), the Conference finally adopted the text of the United Nations Convention on the Law of the Sea in 1982.[4] One reason for the slow progress made at the Conference was that so many of the issues were interrelated; states were often willing to support a proposal on one issue only if other states were willing to support another proposal on

1 Harris CMIL, 347–459; Restatement (Third), Vol. 2, part V, 3–98; R.P. Anand, Origin and Development of the Law of the Sea. History of International Law Revisited, 1983; D.P. O'Connell, The International Law of the Sea (I.A. Shearer ed.), Vol. 1, 1982; Vol. 2, 1984; M.N. Nordquist/S. Rosenne/L.B. Sohn (eds), United Nations Convention on the Law of the Sea 1982. A Commentary, 5 vols, 1985–90; E.D. Brown/R.R. Churchill (eds), The UN Convention on the Law of the Sea: Impact and Implementation, 1987; R.R. Churchill/A.V. Lowe, The Law of the Sea, 2nd edn 1988; G. Jaenicke, Law of the Sea, EPIL 11 (1989), 174–91; E.D. Brown, Law of the Sea, History, ibid., 191–6; R. Platzöder, Conferences on the Law of the Sea, EPIL I (1992), 748–55; T. Treves, Codification du droit international et pratique des États dans le droit de la mer, RdC 223 (1990-IV), 13–302; R.-J. Dupuy/D. Vignes (eds), A Handbook on the New Law of the Sea, 2 vols, 1991–2; T. Kuribayashi/E.L. Miles (eds), The Law of the Sea in the 1990s: A Framework for Further International Cooperation, 1992; E.D. Brown, The International Law of the Sea. Introductory Manual, 1994; R. Wolfrum, Law of the Sea, in Wolfrum UNLPP II, 834–47; for a useful collection of documents issued each year by international organizations see A.H.A. Soons/B. Kwiatkowska et al. (eds), International Organizations and the Law of the Sea. Documentary Yearbook.
2 Texts in AJIL 52 (1958), 834, 842, 851 and 858; Brownlie BDIL, 87–123.
3 Text in UNTS 450, 169.
4 Text in ILM 21 (1982), 1261.

5 See E. Suy, Consensus, *EPIL* I (1992), 759–61.
6 See text below, 193–5.
7 They only signed the Final Act (*ILM* 21 (1982), 1245), not the Convention.
8 M.H. Nordquist/J.N. Moore (eds), *Entry into Force of the Law of the Sea Convention*, 1995; see also R. Platzöder, Substantive Changes in a Multilateral Treaty Before its Entry into Force: The Case of the 1982 United Nations Convention on the Law of the Sea, *EJIL* 4 (1993), 390–402.
9 See the report of the UN Secretary-General, UN Doc. A/50/713, *UN Chronicle* 1996, no. 1, 76. On 5 December 1995, the UN General Assembly adopted Resolution 50/23 by a vote of 132 to 1 (Turkey), with three abstentions, calling upon all states to become parties to the Convention.
10 For an account of the consultations see D.H. Anderson, Efforts to Ensure Universal Participation in the United Nations Convention on the Law of the Sea, *ICLQ* 42 (1993), 654–64; Anderson, Further Efforts to Ensure Universal Participation in the United Nations Convention on the Law of the Sea, *ICLQ* 43 (1994), 886–93.
11 See J.R. Stevenson/B.H. Oxman, The Future of the United Nations Convention on the Law of the Sea, *AJIL* 88 (1994), 488–99; B.H. Oxman, The 1994 Agreement and the Convention, *ibid.*, 687–96; L.B. Sohn, The 1994 Agreement on Implementation of the Seabed Provisions of the Convention on the Law of the Sea. International Law Implications of the 1994 Agreement, *ibid.*, 696–705; D.H. Anderson, Legal Implications of the Entry into Force of the UN Convention on the Law of the Sea, *ICLQ* 44 (1995), 313–26; G. Jaenicke, The United Nations Convention on the Law of the Sea and the Agreement Relating to the Implementation of Part XI of the Convention, in *FS Bernhardt*, 121–34. See also the contributions by D.H. Anderson, K. Davidson and K. Rattrey, *ZaöRV* 55 (1995), 275 *et seq.*; A. de Marffy-Mantuano, The Procedural Framework of the Agreement Implementing the 1982 United Nations Convention on the Law of the Sea, *AJIL* 89 (1995), 814–24.
12 GA Res. 48/263.
13 See President's Transmittal of the UN Convention on the Law of the Sea and the Agreement Relating to the Implementation of Part XI to the U.S. Senate with Commentary [October 7, 1994], *ILM* 34 (1995), 1393. On the US position see M.G. Schmidt, *Common*

another issue ('package-deal' principle), and the result was that deadlock on one issue also tended to produce a deadlock on many other issues. Moreover, whenever possible, UNCLOS III (unlike the two previous conferences) tried to take decisions by consensus,[5] and not by majority vote; and this caused further delays.

The 1982 Convention was closed for signature on 9 December 1984, having received 159 signatures. According to its Article 308(1), the Convention was to 'enter into force twelve months after the date of deposit of the sixtieth instrument of ratification or accession'. However, many Western states refused to sign or ratify the Convention because they were dissatisfied with some of its provisions in Part XI about exploitation of the deep seabed.[6] Among the states which did not sign were the United States, the United Kingdom and Germany.[7] Belgium, France, Italy, Luxembourg and the European Community made declarations to the effect that the deep seabed mining regime was deficient and needed revision. For a long time a universally or generally acceptable convention on the law of the sea seemed to be beyond reach because of the continuing dispute between developing and industrialized countries. The 1982 Convention finally entered into force on 16 November 1994, one year after it had obtained the necessary sixty ratifications.[8] But the only Western state to ratify it was Iceland. As of 1995, thirteen more states had deposited their instruments of ratification, accession or succession, bringing the total number of parties to eighty-one.[9] However, in order to achieve a universally acceptable solution and meet the objections of industrialized states, the UN Secretary-General initiated consultations among interested states, which were held from 1990 to 1994.[10] These finally resulted in an Agreement Relating to the Implementation of Part XI of the Convention, providing for a modification of the deep seabed mining regime which found general acceptance.[11] It was adopted by the UN General Assembly on 29 July 1994 by a vote of 121 in favour, none against with seven abstentions.[12] As of 23 January 1995, the Agreement had been signed by seventy-one states, including the United States,[13] and by the European Community. In addition, twelve states had consented to be bound by it, including Germany and Italy.

Thus, there is now a good prospect that much of the uncertainty which surrounded many parts of the law of the sea before 1982 is likely to diminish. Some of the provisions of the 1982 Convention codify the customary international law of the sea; this is particularly true of those provisions of the 1982 Convention which are identical to those provisions of the 1958 Conventions which codified customary law. But many of the provisions of the 1982 Convention represent a departure from the pre-existing customary law. It is possible that future state practice, even by states which are not (yet) parties to the 1982 Convention, will imitate provisions of the 1982 Convention, thus creating new rules of customary law,[14] but there is no certainty that all of the provisions of the 1982 Convention will pass into customary law in this way. At the moment, many of the provisions of the 1982 Convention probably do not represent existing law for states not parties to it;[15] rather, they indicate the directions in which the law may evolve in the future. However, now that universal acceptance of the

Convention under the modified terms has been secured, it is reasonable to give prominence to its provisions.

According to Article 311(1) of the 1982 Convention, among the states parties to it, the Convention will prevail over the four 1958 Conventions. Almost all of the provisions of these older Conventions are either repeated, modified or replaced by the 1982 Convention. The latter now establishes a comprehensive framework concerning the use of the oceans and covers all marine areas, including the airspace above and the seabed and subsoil below. It deals, *inter alia*, with the rights and duties of states in the territorial sea and the exclusive economic zone, the right of transit passage in international straits, the use of fishing resources, the exploration and exploitation of natural resources in the seabed and subsoil of the continental shelf, navigation and overflight rights, deep seabed mining under the regime of an International Seabed Authority and marine scientific research. As will be discussed separately in later chapters, it also provides for the most comprehensive regime of environmental protection so far agreed upon by states[16] and an elaborate system of dispute settlement, which in most cases ultimately leads to a binding decision by an independent body.[17]

Internal waters

Internal waters consist of ports, harbours, rivers, lakes and canals (and also water on the landward side of the baselines[18] used for measuring the width of the territorial sea). Internal waters are scarcely mentioned in the 1958 Convention Territorial Sea and the Contiguous Zone or the 1982 Convention on the Law of the Sea; the relevant rules are to be found mainly in customary international law.[19] Article 8(1) of the 1982 Convention defines internal waters as the waters on the landward side of the baseline from which the width of the territorial sea is measured and corresponds to Article 5 of the 1958 Convention.

It is clear that the sovereignty of coastal states extends to internal waters.[20] A coastal state is therefore entitled to prohibit entry into its ports by foreign ships, except for ships in distress (for example, ships seeking refuge from a storm, or ships which are severely damaged)[21] and in certain cases in which previously a right of innocent passage had existed.[22] Although a coastal state has the right to forbid foreign merchant ships to enter its ports, most states are keen to support trade, and therefore welcome foreign ships to their ports. The important question is not whether a ship has a right of entry to a port, but its legal status once it has got there. Here, as in virtually every branch of the law of the sea, a distinction must be made between merchant ships[23] on the one hand, and warships[24] and other foreign state ships in non-commercial service, on the other.[25]

Broadly speaking, the coastal state may apply and enforce its laws in full against foreign merchant ships in its internal waters. (In addition, under Articles 218 and 220 of the 1982 Convention, port states are authorized to take enforcement action within internal waters for pollution offences that have occurred elsewhere.) This principle is subject to a number of exceptions, most of which are more apparent than real:

Heritage or Common Burden? The United States Position on the Development of a Regime for Deep Sea-Bed Mining in the Law of the Sea Convention, 1989; Panel on the Law of Ocean Uses, United States Interests in the Law of the Sea Convention, *AJIL* 88 (1994), 167; J.I. Charney, The 1994 Agreement on Implementation of the Seabed Provisions of the Convention on the Law of the Sea. U.S. Provisional Application of the 1994 Deep Seabed Agreement, *ibid.*, 705–14; G. Galdorisi, The United Nations Convention on the Law of Sea: A National Security Perspective, *AJIL* 89 (1995), 208–13.

14 For an example of a case where this has already happened, see the text on the continental shelf below, 191–3.

15 R. Bernhardt, Custom and Treaty in the Law of the Sea, *RdC* 205 (1987-V), 251–394; R. Wolfrum, The Emerging Customary Law of Marine Zones: State Practice and the Convention on the Law of the Sea, *NYIL* 18 (1987), 121 *et seq.*; T.A. Clingan, The Law of the Sea in Prospective: Problems of States not Parties to the Law of the Sea Treaty, *GYIL* 30 (1987), 101; T. Schweisfurth, The Influence of the Third United Nations Conference on the Law of the Sea on International Customary Law, *ZaöRV* 43 (1983), 566–84. On the dispute about which provisions reflect and which do not reflect customary law, see also the literature above, 174.

16 See Chapter 16 below, 242–3.

17 Part XII of the 1982 Convention, Articles 192–237. See Chapter 18 below, 298–30.

18 See text below, 180–1.

19 See V.D. Degan, Internal Waters, *NYIL* 17 (1986), 3–44; P. Badura, Ports, *EPIL* 11 (1989), 262–6; D.H.N. Johnson, Navigation, Freedom of, *ibid.*, 233–5; B. Vitanyi, Navigation on Rivers and Canals, *ibid.*, 235–40; R. Lagoni, Internal Waters, *EPIL* II (1995), 1034–6; Lagoni, Internal Waters, Seagoing Vessels in, *ibid.*, 1036–41; Lagoni, Canals, *EPIL* I (1992), 523–7.

20 See Article 2, 1982 Convention.

21 See A.F. de Zayas, Ships in Distress, *EPIL* 11 (1989), 287–9.

22 See Article 8(2) 1982 Convention and text below, 176–7.

23 See R. Lagoni, Merchant Ships, *EPIL* 11 (1989), 228–33.

24 See W.K. Geck, Warships, *EPIL* 4 (1982), 346–52.

25 See G.C. Rodriguez Iglesias, State Ships, *EPIL* 11 (1989), 320–3.

26 See Chapter 7 above, 109–17.
27 See text below, 185–6.
28 See Chapter 8 above, 118–23.
29 See Article 30, 1982 Convention.
30 See Chapter 8 above, 128–9.
31 See S.P. Sharma, Territorial Sea, *EPIL* 11 (1989), 328–33; G. Marston, The Evolution of the Concept of Sovereignty Over the Bed and Subsoil of the Territorial Sea, *BYIL* 48 (1976–7), 321–32.
32 See also Article 1 of the 1958 Convention.
33 See F. Ngantcha, *The Right of Innocent Passage and the Evolution of the Law of the Sea*, 1990; D.H.N. Johnson, Innocent Passage, Transit Passage, *EPIL* II (1995), 994–7.

1   The jurisdiction[26] of the coastal state's courts is not exclusive. The courts of the flag state[27] may also try people for crimes committed on board the ship.
2   The coastal state will not interfere with the exercise of disciplinary powers by the captain over his crew.
3   If a crime committed by a member of the crew does not affect the good order of the coastal state or any of its inhabitants, the coastal state will usually allow the matter to be dealt with by the authorities of the flag state, instead of trying the criminal in its own courts. This abstention from exercising jurisdiction is probably a matter of grace and convenience, rather than obligation.
4   Ships in distress possess some degree of immunity;[28] for instance, the coastal state cannot profit from their distress by imposing harbour duties and similar taxes which exceed the cost of services rendered.

While a coastal state may use its full enforcement procedures against a foreign commercial vessel found without permission in its internal waters, the powers of the coastal state over foreign warships are much less than its powers over foreign merchant ships. Warships are immune from enforcement, but they can be required by the coastal state to leave its internal waters immediately.[29] In general, a foreign warship is expected to observe the coastal state's laws on navigation and health regulations, but the authorities of the coastal state cannot even set foot on the ship, or carry out any act on board, without the permission of the captain or of some other authority of the flag state. Members of the crew are immune from prosecution by the coastal state for crimes committed on board the ship and for crimes committed on shore, if they were in uniform and on official business at the time of the crime. However, the flag state may waive its immunity.[30]

Territorial sea

The territorial sea (otherwise known as territorial waters, or the maritime belt) extends for an uncertain number of miles beyond internal waters.[31] The width of the territorial sea has been one of the most controversial questions in international law and, before studying it, it will be helpful to examine what rights the coastal state and other states have over the territorial sea. In this way it will be possible to understand the conflict of interests which has arisen between states concerning the width of the territorial sea; for it is this conflict of interests which is at the root of the legal controversies.

The right of innocent passage

Article 2(1) of the 1982 Convention[32] says that the coastal state exercises sovereignty over its territorial sea. But the coastal state's sovereignty is subject to a very important limitation; foreign ships have a right of innocent passage through the territorial sea.[33]

Passage is innocent so long as it is not prejudicial to the peace, good order, or security of the coastal state; fishing vessels[34] must comply with laws enacted by the coastal state to prevent them from fishing, and submarines[35] must navigate on the surface and show their flag.[36] The coastal state must not hamper innocent passage, and must give warning of known dangers to navigation in the territorial sea.[37] It may prevent non-innocent passage; and it may also, for security reasons, temporarily suspend innocent passage in specified areas of its territorial sea, provided that the areas do not constitute 'straits which are used for international navigation between one part of the high seas and another part of the high seas or the territorial sea of a foreign state'.[38] No charges may be levied upon foreign ships except for specific services rendered.[39]

Western states maintain that the right of innocent passage extends to warships, but this is denied by some other countries. In the *Corfu Channel* case[40] the International Court of Justice held that warships have a right of passage through international straits, but did not decide the wider question of passage through the territorial sea in general. In the Geneva Convention, the rules mentioned in the previous paragraph (with the exception of the prohibition against levying charges) appear under the heading 'rules applicable to all ships', which includes warships by implication; but the USSR and six other communist countries, together with Colombia, made reservations to the Convention, denying the right of innocent passage for warships. However, in 1984 the USSR recognized that foreign warships have a right of innocent passage.[41]

Following a 1989 USSR/USA Joint Statement[42] on the uniform interpretation of norms of international law governing innocent passage, the USSR amended its regulations to exclude arbitrary discriminatory restriction of the right of warships to innocent passage.[43] However, the new law on the territorial sea and the contiguous zone adopted by China in 1992 requires permission for warships to enter the twelve-mile territorial sea.[44]

Rights of the coastal state over the territorial sea

The coastal state's sovereignty over the territorial sea includes the following rights:

1 An exclusive right to fish, and to exploit the resources of the seabed and subsoil of the territorial sea.[45]
2 Exclusive enjoyment of the air space above the territorial sea; unlike ships, foreign aircraft have no right of innocent passage.[46]
3 The coastal state's ships have the exclusive right to transport goods and passengers from one part of the coastal state to another (cabotage).[47]
4 If the coastal state is neutral in a time of war,[48] belligerent states may not engage in combat, or capture merchant ships, in the coastal state's territorial sea.
5 The coastal state may enact regulations concerning navigation, health, customs duties and immigration, which foreign ships must obey.
6 The coastal state has certain powers of arrest over merchant ships

34 G. Hafner, Fishing Boats, *EPIL* II (1995), 400–1.
35 I.A. Shearer, Submarines, *EPIL* 11 (1989), 326–8.
36 Article 14, 1958 Convention; Article 19, 1982 Convention.
37 Article 15, 1958 Convention; Article 24, 1982 Convention.
38 Article 16, 1958 Convention; Articles 25, 44 and 45, 1982 Convention.
39 Article 18, 1958 Convention; Article 26, 1982 Convention.
40 *ICJ Rep.* 1949, 4, 29–30. See R. Bernhardt, Corfu Channel Case, *EPIL* I (1992), 831–4.
41 *ILM* 24 (1985), 1715.
42 See *LOS Bull.*, No. 14, at 12.
43 Apparently confirmed after the break-up of the USSR by the Russian Federation in 1991; see UN Secretary-General Report on the Law of the Sea, UN Doc. A/47/623 of 24 November 1992, at 10, para. 16.
44 Article 6 of the 1992 Law of the People's Republic of China on the Territorial Sea and the Contiguous Zone. See H.-S. Kim, The 1992 Chinese Territorial Sea Law in the Light of the UN Convention, *ICLQ* 43 (1994), 894–904. On the uncertainties remaining under the 1982 Convention see *Wolfrum UNLPP* II, 839.
45 R. Wolfrum, Coastal Fisheries, *EPIL* 11 (1989), 61–3.
46 See also Chapter 13 below, 198–200.
47 See R.C. Lane, Cabotage, *EPIL* I (1992), 519–21.
48 See Chapter 20 below, 350–1.

49 Articles 19 and 20, 1958 Convention; Articles 27 and 28, 1982 Convention.
50 In *R. v. Keyn* (1876), 2 ExD 63, the English Court of Crown Cases Reserved held that there was no English court with jurisdiction to try people for crimes committed on board foreign merchant ships in the English territorial sea; but this decision, which was based on a gap in English law rather than on any prohibition by international law, was reversed two years later by the Territorial Waters Jurisdiction Act 1878. Unless the Act is to be regarded as going beyond what is permitted by customary international law, it would seem that coastal states have a general power to try crimes committed on foreign merchant ships in the territorial sea. (The flag state has concurrent jurisdiction, however.)
51 *Chung Chi Cheung v. R.*, [1939] AC 160. See text above, 176.
52 On the new regulations on fisheries in the law of the sea see text below, 183–5.
53 See text below, 183–4.

exercising a right of innocent passage, and over persons on board such ships.[49] No similar powers of arrest exist in relation to warships, which are regarded, for certain purposes, as if they were floating islands of the flag state; but, according to Article 30 of the 1982 Convention, 'if any warship does not comply with the regulations of the coastal state concerning passage through the territorial sea and disregards any request for compliance which is made to it, the coastal state may require the warship to leave the territorial sea'. The same rule is laid down in Article 23 of the 1958 Convention on the Territorial Sea and the Contiguous Zone. In other words, the floating island may be told to go and float somewhere else![50]

Members of the crew of foreign warships may be tried by the courts of the flag state for crimes committed on the warship while the warship was in the territorial sea, but they are immune from the jurisdiction of the coastal state's courts, unless the flag state waives immunity.[51]

The width of the territorial sea

In the sixteenth and seventeenth centuries, some states made extravagant claims to large areas of the sea. But these claims were gradually discredited, and in the eighteenth century it came to be generally accepted that the width of the territorial sea should be the same as the range of a cannon (the cannon-shot rule). During the Napoleonic Wars the practice grew up of regarding the territorial sea as being three nautical miles wide (The nautical mile is equivalent to 1,000 fathoms, 6,080 feet, or 1,853 metres.) The three-mile rule is popularly thought of as a rationalization of the cannon-shot rule, but it was more probably a new rule substituted for the cannon-shot rule.

In the nineteenth century the three-mile rule was accepted by most states, although the Scandinavian states claimed four miles of territorial sea and Spain and Portugal claimed six. During the twentieth century there has been a progressive abandonment of the rule. The states supporting the rule were in the majority at the unsuccessful codification conference organized by the League of Nations in 1930, but the rule was accepted by only twenty-one of the eighty-six states attending the Geneva conference in 1958.

Why have so many states abandoned the three-mile rule? And why has agreement on a new rule been so difficult to reach? The answer to both questions is that a wide territorial sea is in the interests of some states, but against the interests of other states.

The most obvious conflict of interests concerns fishing.[52] Areas of the sea close to shore are particularly rich in fish, and modern improvements in trawling techniques, coupled with the development of refrigeration, have made it possible for fishing vessels from one state to catch huge quantities of fish near the coasts of distant countries. Nowadays states are entitled to claim exclusive fishery zones beyond their territorial seas,[53] but this rule is of recent origin; until about 1960, the only way a state could extend its fishing limits was by extending its territorial sea. Consequently, poor states which were dependent on local fisheries (because they could not afford the large trawlers and refrigerating equipment which are needed for fishing in *distant* waters) sought to extend their territorial seas in order to exclude foreign fishing vessels, particularly when there was a danger of over-exploitation by foreign fishing vessels causing exhaustion of local fishing stocks. On the other hand, rich states with large and technologically advanced fishing fleets, such as the United Kingdom, the United States and Japan, favoured a narrow territorial sea; the losses which they suffered by allowing other states to fish near their coasts were outweighed by the gains which they made by fishing off the coasts of other states.

The economic interests which affect the attitudes of states are not confined to fisheries; for instance, since aircraft have no right of innocent passage through the air space above the territorial sea, an extension of the territorial sea, particularly for straits, was opposed by some states on the grounds that it would force aircraft to make expensive detours.

But, apart from fishing, the main clash of interests relates to questions of security. Some Third World states wanted a wide territorial sea because they were afraid that the three-mile rule would enable a great power to exert psychological pressure in times of crisis by an ostentatious display of naval force just beyond the three-mile limit. On the other hand, Western states, which are traditionally dependent on sea-power and on sea-borne trade, feared that an extension of the territorial sea, especially if coupled with a denial of innocent passage for warships, would restrict the freedom of movement of their fleets, and thus place them at a strategic disadvantage. They also feared that extensive neutral territorial seas could be used as a sanctuary by enemy (that is, Russian) submarines in wartime. (Such use would be a violation of the legal rights of the neutral state, but the neutral state might be too weak to stop it.)

At the Geneva Conference of 1958 the United Kingdom suggested, as a compromise, that the width of the territorial sea should be fixed at six miles. This suggestion was later withdrawn in favour of a United States proposal for a six-mile territorial sea, with a further six-mile zone in which the coastal state would have exclusive fishing rights, subject to the right of other states to continue to fish in the outer zone without limit of time if they had fished there regularly during the previous five years. Other states suggested that the width of the territorial sea should be fixed at twelve miles. No agreement was reached; the United States proposal received more support than any other proposal (with forty-five votes in favour, thirty-three against and seven abstentions), but fell short of the two-thirds majority required by the rules of the conference. UNCLOS II in 1960 attempted to solve the deadlock, and the United States proposal of 1958 was amended in the hope of obtaining more support; the 'traditional' fishing rights of other states in the outer six-mile zone were now not to last indefinitely, but only for ten years. The amended proposal received fifty-four votes in favour, with twenty-eight against and five abstentions – narrowly missing the required two-thirds majority.

Given the diversity of state practice, and the failure of the conferences of 1958 and 1960 to reach agreement on this point, it became difficult to say what the customary law was concerning the width of the territorial sea. Almost all states agreed that international law imposes a limit on the width

54 *ILM* 34 (1995), 1401. For an overview of state claims to maritime zones (territorial sea, contiguous zone, exclusive economic zone, continental shelf), see the Report of the UN Secretary-General, *op. cit.*, 7–8; J.A. Roach/R.W. Smith, *Excessive Maritime Claims*, 1994.
55 See *AJIL* 74 (1980), 48–121; O'Connell (1982), *op. cit.*, 299–337, argues that Articles 34–45 are more or less declaratory of pre-existing customary law, but in 1978 the British government said: 'At present there is no right of overflight over territorial waters, including those which constitute the waters of straits used for international navigation' (*BYIL* 49 (1978), 418). On the right of overflight see P. de Vries Lentsch, The Right of Overflight over Strait States and Archipelagic States: Developments and Prospects, *NYIL* 14 (1983), 165–225; H. Caminos, The Legal Régime of Straits in the 1982 UN Convention on the LOS, *RdC* 205 (1987-V), 12–245; D.H.N. Johnson, Straits, *EPIL* 11 (1989), 323–6; S.N. Nandan/D.H. Anderson, Straits Used for International Navigation: A Commentary on Part III of the United Nations Convention on the Law of the Sea 1982, *BYIL* 60 (1989), 159 *et seq.*
56 See W.M. Reismann/G.S. Westerman, *Straight Baselines in International Maritime Boundary Delimitation*, 1992; P.B. Beazley, Baselines, *EPIL* I (1992), 354–7; D.D. Caron, When Law Makes Climate Change Worse: Rethinking the Law of Baselines in Light of a Rising Sea Level, *ELQ* 17 (1990), 621–53.

of the territorial sea (a Peruvian proposal at the 1958 conference that each state should be allowed to claim whatever it considered reasonable, that is, in effect, to claim as much territorial sea as it liked, received so little support that it was never put to the vote); but states continued to disagree as to what that limit was.

The adoption of the 1982 Convention significantly influenced state practice. Article 3 provides that '[e]very State has the right to establish the breadth of its territorial sea up to a limit not exceeding twelve nautical miles'. Before 1982, twenty-five states had claimed a territorial sea wider than twelve miles, while thirty states claimed less than twelve miles. Since the adoption of the 1982 Convention, states have largely respected the twelve-mile limit. The United States extended its territorial sea to twelve miles in 1988 and had been recognizing the claims of other states up to a maximum of twelve miles since President Reagan's Ocean Policy Statement of 10 March 1983. Thus, as of 1 January 1994, 128 states claimed a territorial sea of twelve miles or less and only seventeen states claimed a wider area.[54]

However, major maritime powers such as the United States and the UK made it clear, at UNCLOS III, that they would not accept Article 3 of the 1982 Convention unless a special regime was adopted for international straits. Extension of the territorial sea to twelve miles would mean that many international straits (for example, the Straits of Dover), through which there was a high seas passage, would fall within the territorial seas of the coastal states. The normal rule is that foreign aircraft have no right to fly over the territorial sea, but the major maritime powers wanted an exception to be made to this rule in the case of international straits. They also wanted the rules governing passage of foreign ships through international straits to be more favourable to foreign ships than the normal rules concerning innocent passage through the territorial sea. For instance, they wanted submarines to be allowed to pass through an international strait under water – something which is normally forbidden in the territorial sea. Articles 34–45 of the 1982 Convention go a long way towards meeting the wishes of the major maritime powers on these points, apart from an ambiguous silence on the question of submarines.[55]

The line from which the territorial sea is measured

The rules for measuring the territorial sea rest on the concept of 'baselines'[56] and are now laid down in Articles 5–11, 13 and 14 of the 1982 Convention. The normal baseline from which the width of the territorial sea is measured is the low-water line (that is, the line on the shore reached by the sea at low tide), and this rule is codified in Article 3 of the 1958 Convention on the Territorial Sea and the Contiguous Zone and Article 5 of the 1982 Convention.

But in certain geographical circumstances it is permissible to draw straight lines across the sea, from headland to headland, or from island to island, and to measure the territorial sea from those straight lines. Article 4 of the Geneva Convention provides:

1   In localities where the coastline is deeply indented and cut into, or if there is a

fringe of islands along the coast in its immediate vicinity, the method of straight baselines joining appropriate points may be employed in drawing the baseline from which the breadth of the territorial sea is measured.

2   The drawing of such baselines must not depart to any appreciable extent from the general direction of the coast.

3   . . .

4   Where the method of straight baselines is applicable under the provisions of paragraph 1, account may be taken, in determining particular baselines, of economic interests peculiar to the region concerned, the reality and the importance of which are clearly evidenced by a long usage.

57 *ICJ Rep.* 1951, 116. On this case see Chapter 3 above, 43.
58 See C.J. Bouchez, Bays and Gulfs, *EPIL* I (1992), 357–9.

Article 4 restates the principle laid down by the International Court of Justice in the *Fisheries* case,[57] but attributes less importance than the Court did to the coastal region's economic interests. At the time, the Court's decision was regarded as an innovation, but the principle laid down in Article 4 has come to be generally accepted, and since 1964 the United Kingdom (which was the losing party in the *Fisheries* case) has used straight baselines off the west coast of Scotland.

Article 5 of the Convention provides:

1   Waters on the landward side of the baseline . . . form part of the internal waters of the State.

2   Where the establishment of a straight baseline in accordance with Article 4 has the effect of enclosing as internal waters areas which previously had been considered as part of the territorial sea or of the high seas, a right of innocent passage . . . shall exist in those waters.

Articles 7 and 8 of the 1982 Convention are substantially the same as Articles 4 and 5 of the 1958 Convention.

Bays are restrictively defined and regulated in great detail by Article 7 of the 1958 Convention (Article 10 of the 1982 Convention).[58] Long before the *Fisheries* case, it had been customary to draw straight baselines across the mouth of a bay and to measure the width of the territorial sea from such lines. But there was controversy about the maximum permissible length of such lines. After considerable argument, the Geneva Conference laid down twenty-four miles as the maximum length; and this limit is repeated in Article 10 of the 1982 Convention.

The provisions of Article 7 of the 1958 Convention (and of Article 10 of the 1982 Convention) are stated not to apply to historic bays. Historic bays are bays which the coastal state claims to be entitled to treat as internal waters, not by virtue of the general law, but by virtue of a special historic right. For instance, Canada claims historic rights over Hudson Bay, which has an area of 580,000 square miles and is fifty miles wide at the entrance. According to a study published by the UN Secretariat in 1962, it would seem that under customary international law a state may validly claim title to a bay on historic grounds if it can show that it has 'for a considerable period of time' claimed the bay as internal waters and effectively exercised its authority therein, and that during this time the claim has received the acquiescence of other states.

59 Y.Z. Blum, Sidra, Gulf of, *EPIL* 12 (1990), 343–5.

60 See Y.Z. Blum, The Gulf of Sidra Incident, *AJIL* 80 (1986), 668.

61 *Land, Island and Maritime Frontier Dispute Case*, ICJ Rep. 1992, 351. See A. Gioia, The Law of Multinational Bays and the Case of the Gulf of Fonseca, *NYIL* 24 (1993), 81–138.

62 See generally H.W. Jayewardene, *The Regime of Islands in International Law*, 1990; D.W. Bowett, Islands, *EPIL* II (1995), 1455–7; see also R. Symmons, The Maritime Zones Around the Falkland Islands, *ICLQ* 37 (1988), 283; B. Kwiatkowska/A.H.A. Soons, Entitlement to Maritime Areas of Rocks Which Cannot Sustain Human Habitation or Economic Life of Their Own, *NYIL* 21 (1990), 139–84; C.R. O'Keefe, Palm-Fringed Benefits: Island Dependencies in the New Law of the Sea, *ICLQ* 45 (1996), 408–20. On the Falkland Islands, see Chapter 10 above, 148 and Chapter 19 below, 315.

63 L.F.E. Goldie, Archipelagos, *EPIL* II (1995), 239–44; M. Munawar, *Ocean States, Archipelagic Regimes in the Law of the Sea*, 1995.

64 F. Wooldridge, Contiguous Zone, *EPIL* I (1992), 779–83.

Since 1973 Libya has claimed the Gulf of Sirte (or Sidra), which is 290 miles wide, as a historic bay.[59] The period since 1973 does not constitute 'a considerable period of time', and Libya's claim has not been recognized by other states. The United States was therefore entitled to treat the Gulf of Sirte as high seas and to hold naval manoeuvres there in 1981 and 1986, even though the manoeuvres led to armed clashes with Libya on both occasions. However, it is submitted that the United States did not need to hold naval manoeuvres in the Gulf of Sirte in order to preserve the legal status of the Gulf as part of the high seas; the United States could have preserved the status of the Gulf equally well by simply protesting against Libya's claim.[60]

In the case of the *Gulf of Fonseca* a Chamber of the International Court of Justice decided that it is an historic bay held in sovereignty jointly by El Salvador, Honduras and Nicaragua, but excluding the existing three-mile belt held under the exclusive sovereignty of each state. The Bay, including the three-mile belt, was found to continue to be subject to the right of innocent passage.[61]

Article 10(2) of the 1958 Convention on the Territorial Sea and the Contiguous Zone states that 'the territorial sea of an island is measured in accordance with the provisions of these articles'.[62] The British government regarded this as an implied condemnation of the practice (followed by the Philippines and Indonesia) of measuring the territorial sea from straight baselines drawn round the outer edge of an archipelago.[63] In fact, however, the 1958 conference evaded the question of archipelagos because discussion tended to turn too much on the facts of specific cases, rather than on general principles. Articles 46–54 of the 1982 Convention accept the claims made by states such as the Philippines and Indonesia, subject to certain conditions (for example, concerning transit by ships and aircraft of other states), but the position under customary international law is still uncertain.

The contiguous zone

At various periods of history different states have claimed limited rights in areas of the high seas adjacent to their territorial seas, or have claimed different widths of territorial sea for different purposes. Between the two World Wars the French writer Gidel propounded the theory of the contiguous zone as a means of rationalizing the conflicting practice of states.[64] At that time the British government attacked the contiguous zone as a surreptitious means of extending the territorial sea, and failure to agree about the contiguous zone was one of the main reasons for the failure of the League of Nations Codification Conference in 1930. However, opposition has faded away since then, and Article 24 of the 1958 Convention on the Territorial Sea and the Contiguous Zone provides:

1   In a zone of the high seas contiguous to its territorial sea, the coastal State may exercise the control necessary to:
     (a)   Prevent infringement of its customs, fiscal, immigration or sanitary regulations within its territory or territorial sea;

(b)   Punish infringement of the above regulations committed within its territory or territorial sea.

2   The contiguous zone may not extend beyond twelve miles from the baseline from which the breadth of the territorial sea is measured.

Article 33(1) of the 1982 Convention is basically the same as Article 24(1) of the 1958 Convention. Article 33(2) of the 1982 Convention provides that '[t]he contiguous zone may not extend beyond 24 nautical miles from the baselines from which the breadth of the territorial sea is measured'; in other words, if a state has a territorial sea of twelve miles, it will be entitled to a contiguous zone of a further twelve miles.

The rules of customary law concerning the width of the contiguous zone, and the rights which a state may exercise therein, are somewhat uncertain; but the matter is not of great practical importance, because in 1986 only twenty-seven states claimed a contiguous zone (the widths claimed varied considerably – one state claimed six miles, one claimed ten miles, three claimed twelve miles, four claimed eighteen miles, seventeen claimed twenty-four miles and one claimed forty-one miles). In the case of the United States the territorial sea and the contiguous zone became coterminous in 1988 when the territorial sea was extended from three to twelve miles.

Exclusive fishery zones and exclusive economic zones

Since about 1960 there has been a tendency for states to claim exclusive fishery zones beyond their territorial seas.[65] In the *Fisheries Jurisdiction* case between the United Kingdom and Iceland, the International Court of Justice held in 1974 that a rule of customary law had developed since 1960 which permitted states to claim exclusive fishery zones of twelve miles (this width of twelve miles included the territorial sea; thus, if a state claimed a territorial sea of three miles, it was entitled to an exclusive fishery zone of a further nine miles). The Court also held that a coastal state had a *preferential* right over fish in adjacent areas of sea beyond the twelve-mile limit, at least if the coastal state was (like Iceland) economically dependent on local fisheries, but that the coastal state could not wholly exclude other states from fishing in such areas, especially if they had traditionally fished there and if part of their population was economically dependent on fishing there.[66]

However, it soon became apparent that UNCLOS III would approve a territorial sea of twelve miles, with an exclusive economic zone extending for a further 188 miles, making a total of 200 miles.[67] Article 56(1)(a) of the 1982 Convention gives the coastal state sovereign rights over all the economic resources of the sea, seabed and subsoil in its exclusive economic zone; this includes not only fish, but also minerals beneath the seabed.[68] In fact, most of the existing fish resources are thus brought under the control of coastal states (about 90 per cent of living marine resources are caught within 200 miles of the coast). To some extent the word 'exclusive' is misleading, because Articles 62 and 69–71 of the 1982 Convention provide that a coastal state which cannot exploit the fish or

65 J.-P. Quéneuduc, Les Rapports entre zone de pêche et zone économique exclusive, *GYIL* 32 (1989), 138–55; F.O. Vicuña, The 'Presential Sea': Defining Coastal States' Special Interests in High Seas Fisheries and Other Activities, *GYIL* 35 (1992), 264; J. Carroz, Fishery Zones and Limits, *EPIL* II (1995), 397–400.

66 *Fisheries Jurisdiction Case (UK v. Iceland)* (Merits), *ICJ Rep.* 1974, 3, at 23–9. On this case see Chapter 3 above, 43.

67 P. Peters/A.H.A. Soons/L.A. Zima, Removal of Installations in the Exclusive Economic Zone, *NYIL* 15 (1984), 167–207; R.W. Smith, *Exclusive Economic Zone Claims: An Analysis and Primary Documents*, 1986; D. Attard, *The Exclusive Economic Zone in International Law*, 1987; M. Dahmani, *The Fisheries Regime of the Exclusive Economic Zone*, 1987; F. Orrego Vicuna, The Contribution of the Exclusive Economic Zone to the Law of Maritime Delimitation, *GYIL* 31 (1988), 120–37; F. Vicuna, *The Exclusive Economic Zone: Regime and Legal Nature under International Law*, 1989; B. Kwiatkowska, *The 200 Mile Exclusive Economic Zone in the New Law of the Sea*, 1989; S. Oda, Exclusive Economic Zone, *EPIL* II (1995), 305–12.

68 See also text below, 193–5.

69 Article 62(4)(a), 1982 Convention.
70 Articles 211(5) and (6), 220, 246–55.
71 Article 58. See R. Lagoni, Cables, Submarine, *EPIL* I (1992), 516–9.
72 Under EEC Regulation 170/83, member states of the EEC have agreed to share their exclusive fishery zones with one another, apart from a small area (usually twelve miles in width) around the coast, which is reserved for local fishermen. In the interests of conservation of fish stocks, the Council of the European Communities may fix quotas limiting the amount of fish which each member state may catch. See R.R. Churchill, *EEC Fisheries Law*, 1987. On the Common Fisheries Policy and its external effect see also M. Fitzmaurice, Common Market Participation in the Legal Regime of the Baltic Seas Fisheries, *GYIL* 33 (1990), 214–35.
73 See *AFDI* 1978, 851, 858–65, or R.P. Barston/P. Birnie, *The Maritime Dimension*, 1980, 45–6.
74 See text above, 183.
75 *Continental Shelf Case (Tunisia v. Libya)*, ICJ Rep. 1982, 18, at 74.
76 *Continental Shelf Case (Libya v. Malta)*, ICJ Rep. 1985, 13, at 33, 35.
77 *ILM* 34 (1995), 1402. On the practice of ASEAN states see R.S.K. Lim, EEZ Legislation of ASEAN States, *ICLQ* 40 (1991), 170 *et seq.*
78 See text above, 183.
79 See text above, 182–3.
80 Article 1, 1958 Convention on the High Seas; but see also Article 86, 1982 Convention. See T. Treves, High Seas, *EPIL* II (1995), 705–10.

other living resources of its exclusive economic zone to the full must make arrangements to share the surplus with other states; however, it can require payment for allowing foreign vessels to fish in its exclusive economic zone.[69] The coastal state also has limited powers to prevent pollution and to control scientific research in its exclusive economic zone.[70] But foreign states enjoy freedom of navigation and overflight, and the right to lay submarine cables and pipelines, in the coastal state's exclusive economic zone.[71]

Since 1976 most states have anticipated the outcome of the conference by claiming exclusive fishery zones or exclusive economic zones of 200 miles. In 1986, out of 138 coastal states, 101 claimed exclusive fishing rights for 200 miles (thirteen claimed a territorial sea of 200 miles, sixty-seven claimed an exclusive economic zone of 200 miles and twenty-one claimed an exclusive fishery zone of 200 miles); twelve other states claimed a territorial sea, exclusive fishery zone, or exclusive economic zone exceeding twelve miles but less than 200 miles. The states claiming exclusive fishing rights for 200 miles include the United States, the USSR, Japan and the EEC countries (including the UK),[72] which had previously opposed wide fishery zones. Most states which claim exclusive fishing rights for 200 miles have made treaties permitting other states to fish there, but only if those other states are prepared to offer something in return.[73]

The practice of claiming exclusive fishing rights for 200 miles, although recent, is now so widespread that it can probably no longer be regarded as illegal. In other words, the rules laid down by the International Court of Justice in 1974[74] have now been replaced by a new rule of customary international law permitting states to claim exclusive fishing rights for 200 miles. Indeed, in 1982 the International Court said that 'the concept of the exclusive economic zone . . . may be regarded as part of modern international law',[75] and in 1985 it accepted that the exclusive economic zone could extend for 200 miles.[76]

As of 1 March 1994, ninety-three states claimed an exclusive economic zone, none of which claimed more than 200 miles, although some claim the right to restrict activities within their zones beyond what the 1982 Convention allows.[77] The largest exclusive economic zone in the world is enjoyed by the United States in the Atlantic, Pacific and Arctic Oceans, including those areas surrounding US island territories.

Foreign ships which violate the rights of a coastal state in its exclusive fishery zone or exclusive economic zone[78] may be arrested by the coastal state. The coastal state also has certain powers of arrest in its contiguous zone.[79]

The high seas

'The term "high seas" means all parts of the sea that are not included in the territorial sea or in the internal waters of a state.'[80] The high seas may be used freely by the ships of all nations; Article 2 of the 1958 Geneva Convention on the High Seas states that freedom of the high seas comprises, *inter alia*, freedom of navigation, freedom of fishing, freedom to lay submarine cables and pipelines, and freedom to fly over the high seas. (Some of these freedoms are limited where a coastal state claims an exclusive fishery zone, an exclusive economic zone, or a contiguous zone.[81]) These freedoms may also be enjoyed by land-locked states, which are given the right to sail ships under their own flags on the high seas;[82] states lying between land-locked states and the sea should negotiate agreements with land-locked states in order to give the latter the right to use their ports and rights of transit through their territory.[83] UN GA Res. 46/212 of 20 December 1991 reaffirmed the right of access of land-locked states to and from the sea and freedom of transit through the territory of transit states by all means of transport.

As far as the freedom of fishing is concerned, certain limitations have been introduced by the 1993 FAO Agreement to Promote Compliance with International Conservation and Management Measures by Fishing Vessels on the High Seas[84] and the 1995 UN Agreement for the Implementation of the Provisions of the United Nations Convention on the Law of the Sea of 10 December 1982 Relating to the Conservation and Management of Straddling Fish Stocks and Highly Migratory Fish Stocks.[85] As of 31 January 1996, the Agreement had been signed by thirty-one states.[86]

As a general rule, a ship on the high seas is subject only to international law and to the laws of the flag state.[87] This makes it important to know which state is the flag state. The 'flag state' really means the state whose nationality the ship possesses; it is nationality which creates the right to fly a country's flag, and not vice versa. The nationality of warships does not give rise to any problems, but the same is not true of merchant ships. Apart from very small ships, the nationality of merchant ships is determined in virtually all countries by registration; a ship has French nationality, for instance, if it is registered in France. Article 6 of the 1958 Convention on the High Seas provides:

1   Ships shall sail under the flag of one State only . . . A ship may not change its flag . . . save in the case of a real transfer of ownership or change of registry.

2   A ship which sails under the flags of two or more States, using them according to convenience, may not claim any of the nationalities in question with respect to any other State, and may be assimilated to a ship without nationality.

These rules are repeated in Article 92 of the 1982 Convention. The conditions which states lay down before placing a ship on their register vary from state to state. The traditional shipowning countries like the United Kingdom lay down stringent requirements about the nationality of the shipowners, the nationality of the crew, and the place of construction. Other states – the so-called 'flags of convenience' countries – are prepared to register virtually any ship in return for the payment of a fee.[88]

Flags of convenience are mainly used as a means of avoiding payment of taxes and statutory wage-rates. But they can also be used for more sinister purposes. A vast amount of the law of the sea is contained in treaties –

81 See text above, 183–4.

82 Article 4, 1958 Convention. See L. Calfisch, Land-Locked and Geographically Disadvantaged States, *EPIL* 11 (1989); S. Vasciannie, *Land-Locked and Geographically Disadvantaged States in the International Law of the Sea*, 1990.

83 Article 3, 1958 Convention. Articles 87, 90 and 125 of the 1982 Convention contain provisions similar to Articles 2, 3 and 4 of the 1958 Convention.

84 Text in *ILM* 33 (1994), 1461.

85 See UN Doc. A/CONF.164/33 (1995), and the note in *AJIL* 90 (1996), 270–2.

86 *UN Chronicle* 1996, no. 1, 77. See also United States: Fisheries Act of 1995, *ILM* 35 (1996), 379. See further W.T. Burke, *The New International Law of the Fisheries*, 1994; C. Dominguez Diaz, Towards a New Regime for High Sea Fisheries?, *Hague YIL* 7 (1994), 25–34; R. Wolfrum, Fisheries, International Regulation, *EPIL* II (1995), 383-6; D.H. Anderson, The Straddling Stocks Agreement of 1995 – An Initial Assessment, *ICLQ* 45 (1996), 463 *et seq.*

87 See D.D. Caron, Ships, Nationality and Status, *EPIL* 11 (1989), 289–97; Flags of Vessels, *EPIL* II (1995), 405–7.

88 J.S. Ignarski, Flags of Convenience, *EPIL* II (1995), 404–5.

89 See, for example, G. Breuer, Maritime Safety Regulations, *EPIL* 11 (1989), 224–8.
90 The provisions of Article 5 of the 1958 Convention are repeated, with slight differences, in Articles 91 and 94(1) of the 1982 Convention. See further H.W. Wefers Bettink, Open Registry, the Genuine Link and the 1986 Convention on Registration Conditions for Ships, *NYIL* 18 (1987), 69–119.
91 Articles 6, 8, 9, 1958 Convention; Articles 92, 95, 96, 1982 Convention. See G. Marston, Maritime Jurisdiction, *EPIL* 11 (1989), 221–4.
92 [1948] AC 351.

dealing with such matters as ships' lights, safety regulations, the slave trade, compulsory insurance, 'pirate' radio stations, pollution and the conservation of fisheries – which, of course, are binding only on states parties to them.[89] It is dangerously easy for shipowners to avoid compliance with such treaties by registering their ships in states which are not parties to them.

The popularity of flags of convenience is shown by the fact that Liberia has been the largest shipowning nation (in terms of registered tonnage) since 1967. (But Liberia has ratified all the relevant major treaties.) Most countries with flags of convenience are developing countries, but in recent years the majority of developing countries have demanded the abolition of flags of convenience. Opinion among developed countries is equally divided; France is strongly opposed to flags of convenience, but the United States is not; as long as US shipowners are prepared to allow the United States government to requisition their ships in time of war, the government does not care where the ships are registered, and many of the ships concerned would operate at a loss if their owners were forced to pay US wage-rates.

Flags of convenience were an explosive issue at the Geneva Conference of 1958. Article 5 of the High Seas Convention emerged as an ambiguous compromise: 'There must exist a genuine link between the [flag] State and the ship; in particular, the State must effectively exercise its jurisdiction and control in administrative, technical and social matters over ships flying its flag.' Obviously, the fact that a ship is owned by foreigners does not necessarily prevent a flag state from exercising control in administrative, technical and social matters over the ship; but the Convention uses the words 'in particular', and it may therefore be that exercise of such control is not enough by itself to constitute a genuine link.

What happens if there is no genuine link between the ship and the flag state? Does this affect the nationality of the ship? Here again, Article 5 is badly drafted, because it provides no answer to this question.[90]

Interference with ships on the high seas

As a general rule, no one but the flag state may exercise jurisdiction (in the sense of powers of arrest or other acts of physical interference) over a ship on the high seas.[91] As regards interference with warships, there is only one exception, which was too obvious to be mentioned in the Conventions; in a time of war, a warship of a belligerent state is liable to be attacked by enemy warships. In the case of merchant ships, the same general rule applies; but there are a large number of exceptional cases where a warship of one state may interfere with a merchant ship of another state:

1   *Stateless ships.* Since the high seas are open to the ships of all *nations*, the Judicial Committee of the Privy Council held in the *Asya* case[92] that it was lawful to seize a *stateless* ship on the high seas. Although the decision was probably correct on the facts of the case, the Privy Council's reasoning should not be carried to its logical conclusion; it is possible that arbitrary confiscation or destruction of a stateless

ship would entitle the national state of the shipowners to make an international claim.

2   *Hot pursuit.*[93] As we have seen, the coastal state has certain powers of arrest over foreign merchant ships in its internal waters, territorial sea and contiguous zone. The right of hot pursuit is designed to prevent the ship avoiding arrest by escaping to the high seas. It is regulated in some detail by Article 23 of the 1958 Convention on the High Seas, the most important provisions of which read as follows:

1   The hot pursuit of a foreign ship may be undertaken when the competent authorities of the coastal State have good reason to believe that the ship has violated the laws and regulations of that State. Such pursuit must be commenced when the foreign ship or one of its boats is within the internal waters or the territorial sea or the contiguous zone of the pursuing State, and may only be continued outside the territorial sea or the contiguous zone if the pursuit has not been interrupted . . . If the foreign ship is within a contiguous zone, as defined in Article 24 of the Convention on the Territorial Sea and the Contiguous Zone, the pursuit may only be undertaken if there has been a violation of the rights for the protection of which the zone was established.

2   The right of hot pursuit ceases as soon as the ship pursued enters the territorial sea of its own country or of a third State.

3   . . . . The pursuit may only be commenced after a visual or auditory signal to stop has been given at a distance which enables it to be seen or heard by the foreign ship.

4   The right of hot pursuit may be exercised only by warships or military aircraft, or other ships or aircraft on government service specially authorized to that effect.

These rules are repeated, in almost the same words, in Article 111 (paragraphs 1, 3, 4 and 5) of the 1982 Convention. Hot pursuit may also begin in the coastal state's exclusive fishery zone if the foreign ship was illegally fishing there.[94] Article 111(2) of the 1982 Convention lays down a similar rule for the exclusive economic zone. According to the *I'm Alone* case,[95] the right of hot pursuit does not include the right to sink the pursued vessel deliberately; but accidental sinking in the course of arrest may be lawful.

3   *The right of approach.* The general rule is that merchant ships on the high seas are subject to control only by warships of the flag state. If a merchant ship is doing something which it ought not to be doing, it may try to escape the control of warships from its own state, by flying a foreign flag or no flag at all. Consequently, if a warship encounters a merchant ship on the high seas and has reasonable grounds for suspecting that the merchant ship is of the same nationality as the warship, it may carry out investigations on board the merchant ship in order to ascertain its nationality. This power is reaffirmed in Article 22 of the 1958 Convention on the High Seas and Article 110 of the 1982 Convention.

4   *Treaties* often give the contracting parties a reciprocal power of arrest over one another's merchant ships. Examples may be found in treaties for the conservation of fisheries, or for the protection of

93 F. Wooldridge, Hot Pursuit, *EPIL* II (1995), 881–4; Gilmore, Hot Pursuit: The Case of *R. v. Mills and Others, ICLQ* 44 (1995), 949–58.

94 *AJIL* 70 (1976), 95.

95 *RIAA* III 1609, 1615. See P. Seidl, I'm Alone, *EPIL* 2 (1981), 133–4.

96 See Chapter 2 above, 21.

97 A. Cassese, Achille Lauro Affair, *EPIL* I (1992), 10–4. See also Chapter 7 above, 111 n. 22.

98 See Chapter 6 above, 94.

99 *ILM* 27 (1988), 668 (1988 Convention) and 685 (1988 Protocol). See N. Ronzitti (ed.), *Maritime Terrorism and International Law*, 1990. See further C.C. Joyner, The 1988 IMO Convention on the Safety of Maritime Navigation, *GYIL* 31 (1988), 230–62; F. Francioni, Maritime Terrorism and International Law, *GYIL* 31 (1988), 289–306; G. Plant, The Convention for the Suppression of Unlawful Acts Against the Safety of Maritime Navigation, *ICLQ* 39 (1990), 27 *et seq.*

100 Text in *ILM* 28 (1989), 493. On the need to strengthen international cooperation to deal with the growing incidence of crimes at sea, including drug trafficking, smuggling of aliens, piracy and armed robbery, see the report of the UN Secretary-General, UN Doc. A/50/713 of 1 November 1995.

101 See J. Fawcett, Broadcasting, International Regulation, *EPIL* I (1992), 506–9.

102 *Financial Times*, 27 March 1995, 6; P.G.G. Davies, The EC/Canadian Fisheries Dispute in the Northwest Atlantic, *ICLQ* 44 (1995), 927–38.

103 Agreed Minute on the Conservation and Management of Fish Stocks, *ILM* 34 (1995), 1260.

104 *ICJ Communiqué* no. 95/8 of 29 March 1995; Order of 2 May 1995, *ICJ Communiqué* no. 95/12 of 2 May 1995.

submarine cables. Such provisions used to be particularly common in treaties for the suppression of the slave trade;[96] but Article 22 of the 1958 Convention on the High Seas and Article 110 of the 1982 Convention suggest that the power to search foreign ships suspected of engaging in the slave trade has now become a rule of customary law. Following the hijacking of the Italian cruise ship *Achille Lauro* in October 1985 by terrorists,[97] Italy took an initiative in the International Maritime Organisation (IMO)[98] which culminated in the adoption of the 1988 Rome Convention for the Suppression of Unlawful Acts Against the Safety of Maritime Navigation and the 1988 Rome Protocol for the Suppression of Unlawful Acts Against the Safety of Fixed Platforms Located on the Continental Shelf.[99] Furthermore, under Article 17(3) of the 1988 UN Convention Against Illicit Traffic in Narcotic Drugs and Psychotropic Substances a state party which has reason to suspect that a vessel of another party is engaged in illicit traffic has to request authorization from the flag state to take appropriate measures in regard to that vessel.[100] Article 17(9) encourages the parties to the Convention to enter into bilateral or regional agreements to carry out, or to enhance the effectiveness of the provisions of Article 17.

It is important to note that states, in most of such cases, have only a reciprocal power of arrest; after arrest, the offenders must be handed back to their flag state for trial. (Theoretically a treaty could provide for reciprocal powers of trial, as well as reciprocal powers of arrest; examples are rare, but see Articles 109 and 110(1)(c) of the 1982 Convention, which deal with unauthorized broadcasting.[101])

A case which illuminates this is the 'fish war' between Canada and the European Union in 1995 because of measures taken by Canada against Spanish trawlers acting outside Canada's 200-mile economic zone in an area governed by the treaty on the North Atlantic Fisheries Organization (NAFO). The conflict started with the seizure by Canada of the Spanish trawler *Estai* fishing for turbot (also known as Greenland halibut) in defiance of a sixty-day moratorium imposed by Canadian conservation regulations. The vessel was only released a week later after its owners had posted a C$500,000 bond.[102] The relevant provisions of the Canadian Coastal Fisheries Protection Act, as amended on 12 May 1994, and the unilateral Canadian enforcement measures on the high seas, including arrest and the use of 'warp-cutters' to sever the cables holding foreign trawler's nets, were clearly illegal, although meant to protect a common interest. The NAFO agreement gives states parties certain control and inspection rights over each others' fishing vessels, but only the flag state has the right (and is obliged) to take enforcement measures. The conflict was settled by an agreement between Canada and the European Community which was reached on 20 April 1995.[103] However, in March 1995 Spain had brought a case against Canada before the ICJ which was still pending at the time of writing.[104]

5   *Piracy*[105] is dealt with at length in Articles 14–21 and 22 of the 1958 Geneva Convention on the High Seas and Articles 100–10 of the 1982 Convention. According to Article 15 of the 1958 Geneva Convention on the High Seas, piracy consists of any of the following acts:

1   Any illegal acts of violence, detention or any act of depredation, committed for private ends by the crew or the passengers of a private ship or a private aircraft, and directed:

   (a)   On the high seas, against another ship or aircraft, or against persons or property on board such a ship or aircraft;

   (b)   Against a ship, aircraft, persons or property in a place outside the jurisdiction of any State.

2   Any act of voluntary participation in the operation of a ship or of an aircraft with knowledge of facts making it a pirate ship or aircraft.

3   Any act of inciting or of intentionally facilitating an act described in subparagraph 1 or sub-paragraph 2 of this Article.

The definition in Article 101 of the 1982 Convention is almost identical. If a warship has reasonable grounds for suspecting that a merchant ship is engaged in piracy, it may board it on the high seas for purposes of investigation, regardless of the merchant ship's nationality.[106] If the suspicions are justified, the merchant ship may be seized and the persons on board may be arrested and tried.[107] Every state is entitled to arrest and to try a pirate, without being limited by any of the rules which are often regarded as restricting the jurisdiction of municipal courts in criminal cases.[108]

Laymen often use the word 'piracy' loosely to include all sorts of acts which international law does not regard as piracy. For instance, mutiny (seizure of a ship by its crew or passengers) is not piracy within the meaning of international law: under Article 15(1)(a) of the Geneva Convention on the High Seas (Article 101(a)(i) of the 1982 Convention) piracy on the high seas must be directed 'against *another* ship'. Indeed, in the laws of some countries, mutiny is described as piracy. But since mutiny is not piracy within the meaning of international law, a ship under the control of mutineers may be arrested on the high seas only by the flag state and not by other states (unless there is a treaty authorizing arrest by other states).

6   *Belligerent rights*. In a time of war a warship belonging to a belligerent state may seize enemy merchant ships and also, in certain circumstances, neutral merchant ships trading with the enemy.[109]

7   *Self-defence*. Even when there is no war, states sometimes claim a right to interfere with foreign merchant ships on the grounds of self-defence, but the law on this point is uncertain. For instance, France cited self-defence as a justification for seizing foreign merchant ships carrying arms to the rebel movement in Algeria in the 1950s, but such seizures were condemned as illegal by most of the flag states concerned.[110] On the other hand, when a foreign

105 A.P. Rubin, *The Law of Piracy*, 1988; Rubin, Piracy, *EPIL* 11 (1989), 259–62; C. Touret, *La Piraterie au vingtième siecle*, 1992
106 Article 22, 1958 Convention; Article 110, 1982 Convention.
107 Article 19, 1958 Convention; Article 105, 1982 Convention.
108 See Chapter 7 above, 109–15.
109 See Chapter 20 below, 350–1.
110 For details of this and earlier incidents, see *ICLQ* 10 (1961), 785, 791–8, and O'Connell (1984), *op. cit.*, 803–6. On the issue of civilian protest ships, such as the vessels sent by Greenpeace to disturb French nuclear tests in the Pacific (see the *Rainbow Warrior* case in Chapter 6 above, 98–9), see G. Plant, Civilian Protest Vessels and the Law of the Sea, *NYIL* 14 (1983), 133–63.

111 *Hague Academy of International Law, Colloquium*, 1973, 39–50. See also Article 221 of the 1982 Convention and O'Connell (1984), *op. cit.*, 1006–8. The International Law Commission found that Britain's reaction against the *Torrey Canyon* was an expression of the doctrine of 'necessity', see Article 33 of the Draft Articles on State Responsibility, in *Brownlie BDIL*, 436. See Chapter 17 below, 256.

112 R.H. Stansfield, Torrey Canyon, The, *EPIL* 11 (1989), 333–5.

113 Text in UNTS 970, 212.

114 Text in UNTS 973, 3. See Chapter 16 below, 242.

115 See Chapter 22 below, 387–415.

116 See Chapter 7 above, 107–15.

117 *Lotus Case* (1927), PCIJ, series A, no. 10. See Chapter 3 above, 44–5.

merchant ship has been involved in an accident which creates an imminent threat of massive oil pollution on neighbouring coasts, it is possible that the coastal state is entitled to seize or destroy the ship in order to prevent pollution;[111] thus the Liberian government did not protest in 1967 when the United Kingdom bombed the *Torrey Canyon*, a Liberian oil tanker which had run aground on a reef in the English Channel.[112] Perhaps the distinction lies in the differing degrees of urgency in the two situations; France could have waited until the ships carrying arms entered the French territorial sea before arresting them, whereas immediate destruction of a wrecked oil tanker is often the only way to prevent the pollution of coasts. The *Torrey Canyon* incident led to the adoption in 1969 of the Convention Relating to Intervention on the High Seas in Cases of Oil Pollution Casualties[113] and of the Convention on Civil Liability for Oil Pollution Damage.[114]

8   *Action authorized by the United Nations.*[115]

Jurisdiction of municipal courts over crimes committed on the high seas

Apart from the special case of piracy, the ordinary rules of international law concerning criminal jurisdiction[116] apply to crimes committed on the high seas. For this purpose, a ship is treated as if it were the territory of the flag state. For instance, if an Englishman on a French ship fires a fatal shot at someone on a German ship, he can be tried in England (nationality principle), France (subjective territorial principle) and Germany (objective territorial principle).

However, controversies have arisen in connection with criminal liability for collisions at sea. In the *Lotus* case, a French ship, the *Lotus*, collided with a Turkish ship on the high seas, and, as a result, people on the Turkish ship were drowned; when the *Lotus* reached a Turkish port, Lieutenant Demons, who had been at the helm of the *Lotus* at the time of the collision, was arrested and prosecuted for manslaughter. France complained that this exercise of jurisdiction by Turkey was contrary to international law, but the Permanent Court of International Justice held that Lieutenant Demons could be tried, not only by his own flag state, France, but also by Turkey, because the effects of his actions had been felt on the Turkish ship.[117] This decision, based on the objective territorial principle, produced alarm among seafarers, and a long campaign against the rule in the *Lotus* case culminated in Article 11(1) of the 1958 Geneva Convention on the High Seas which provides:

> In the event of collision or of any other incident of navigation concerning a ship on the high seas, involving the penal [that is, criminal] or disciplinary responsibility of the master or of any other person in the service of the ship, no penal or disciplinary proceedings may be instituted against such persons except before the judicial or administrative authorities either of the flag State or of the State of which such person is a national.

This provision, which is repeated in Article 97(1) of the 1982 Convention, reverses the effect of the *Lotus* decision, in so far as that decision dealt with collisions and other 'incidents of navigation'. But the wider principles laid down in the *Lotus* case, concerning the objective territorial principle, jurisdiction in general, and the nature of customary law, remain valid.

The continental shelf

Before 1945 the freedom of the high seas meant, among other things, that every state had the right to exploit the seabed and subsoil of the high seas. This right was enjoyed by all states; no state could claim an exclusive right to any part of the seabed or subsoil of the high seas.

However, the law began to change when it became technologically and economically feasible to exploit oil deposits beneath the sea by means of offshore oil wells. In 1945 President Truman of the United States issued a proclamation that the United States had the exclusive right to exploit the seabed and subsoil of the continental shelf off the coasts of the United States. The term, 'the continental shelf', requires some explanation.[118] In most parts of the world the seabed slopes gently away from the coast for quite a long distance before it plunges steeply down to the great ocean depths. This gently sloping seabed, covered by shallow water, is called the continental shelf by geologists, and in prehistoric times was dry land. For the purposes of President Truman's proclamation, the continental shelf was defined as being those offshore areas of the seabed which were not more than 100 fathoms deep.

President Truman's proclamation was copied by certain other states, and offshore drilling for oil and natural gas became common in the Caribbean and the Persian Gulf. No protests were made by other states, except when Chile and Peru made claims which went far beyond the scope of President Truman's proclamation. Chile and Peru have no continental shelf in the geological sense; the seabed off their coasts drops sharply down to the great ocean depths. Therefore, instead of claiming a continental shelf, they claimed sovereignty over the seabed and subsoil for a distance of 200 miles from their coasts; and they also claimed sovereignty over the superjacent waters and air space, which had been expressly excluded from the proclamations issued by the United States and other countries.

The history of the continental shelf in the years after 1945 is a classic example of the formation of a new rule of customary law. The action of the United States created a precedent which other states followed – and in some cases tried to extend. Claims to exclusive rights to exploit the seabed and subsoil were copied, or at least not challenged, by other states and thus gave rise to a new rule of customary law; claims to sovereignty over superjacent waters did not give rise to a new rule of customary law, because they met with protests from other states. (Even the 200-mile exclusive economic zone, a concept of much more recent origin,[119] gives the coastal state fewer rights than the sovereignty over superjacent waters claimed by Chile and Peru.)

Before 1958 customary law on the continental shelf was still rather vague and controversial; the 1958 Geneva Convention on the Continental Shelf added more precision and detail to the rules. Article 1 defines the continental shelf as: 'the seabed and subsoil of the submarine areas adjacent to the coast but outside the area of the territorial sea, to a depth of

118 See H. Kelsen, *On the Issue of the Continental Shelf*, 1986; G.J. Tanja, *The Legal Determination of International Maritime Boundaries*, 1990; S.V. Scott, The Inclusion of Sedentary Fisheries Within the Continental Shelf Doctrine, *ICLQ* 41 (1992), 788–807; C. L. Rozakis, Continental Shelf, *EPIL* I (1992), 783–92; U.-D. Klemm, Continental Shelf, Outer Limits, *ibid.*, 804–6; *International Boundary Cases: The Continental Shelf*, 2 vols, 1992; S.A. Alexandrov, Delimitation of the Continental Shelf in an Enclosed Sea, *Hague YIL* 5 (1992), 3–32; C.R. Symmons, The 1992 Protocol to the 1988 Anglo-Irish Agreement on the Continental Shelf, *ICLQ* 42 (1993), 970–5; B. Kwiatkowska, A Regional Approach Towards the Management of Marine Activities, *ZaöRV* 55 (1995), 479–519, at 488 *et seq.*; G. Marston, The Incorporation of Continental Shelf Rights into United Kingdom Law, *ICLQ* 45 (1996), 13–51. See also the 1995 Russian Federation Law on the Continental Shelf, *ILM* 35 (1996), 1498.
119 See text above, 183–4.

200 metres, or, beyond that limit, to where the depth of the superjacent
waters admits of the exploitation of the natural resources of the said areas'.
Article 2 provides:

1   The coastal State exercises over the continental shelf sovereign rights for the
    purpose of exploring it and exploiting its natural resources.
2   The rights referred to in paragraph 1 of this Article are exclusive in the sense
    that if the coastal State does not explore the continental shelf or exploit its
    natural resources, no one may undertake these activities, or make a claim to
    the continental shelf, without the express consent of the coastal State.
3   The rights of the coastal State over the continental shelf do not depend on
    occupation, effective or notional, or on any express proclamation.
4   The natural resources referred to in these Articles consist of the mineral and
    other non-living resources of the seabed and subsoil together with living
    organisms belonging to sedentary species, that is to say, organisms which, at
    the harvestable stage, either are immobile on or under the seabed or are
    unable to move except in constant physical contact with the seabed or the
    subsoil.

Article 3 provides that 'the rights of the coastal State over the continental shelf do not affect the legal status of the superjacent waters at high
seas, or that of the air space above those waters'.

Article 5 states that the exploration and exploitation of the continental
shelf must not cause unreasonable interference with navigation, fishing,
conservation of fisheries, or scientific research (paragraph 1). Subject to
paragraph 1, the coastal state may construct installations for the purpose
of exploiting the natural resources of the continental shelf. The installations may protrude above the surface of the sea, but they do not have the
legal status of islands (for example, they have no territorial sea), although
the coastal state may establish safety zones with a radius of 500 metres
around each installation. There are further provisions to prevent the installations being dangerous (for example, there must be an adequate system of
warning of their presence, and they must be dismantled when disused).

Articles 2 and 3 of the Geneva Convention on the Continental Shelf are
repeated, with slight alterations, in Articles 77 and 78 of the 1982 Convention. Many of the provisions of Article 5 of the Geneva Convention
reappear, in a rather different form, in Articles 60 and 80 of the 1982
Convention. Article 76 of the 1982 Convention differs considerably from
Article 1 of the Geneva Convention on the Continental Shelf.

What are the outer limits of the continental shelf for legal purposes?
Does it have any outer limits at all, or do the coastal state's exclusive rights
over the seabed and subsoil extend to mid-ocean, regardless of the depth of
the ocean? This is a vital question, because in the future the deep seabed
(or ocean floor) is likely to be of great economic importance. The ocean
floor in many areas is covered with manganese nodules, averaging about 4
cm in diameter and containing up to 50 per cent manganese, with significant traces of copper, nickel, cobalt and other metals. It is estimated that
there are 1,500,000 million tons of these nodules on the floor of the Pacific
alone, sometimes in concentrations of up to 100,000 tons per square mile.

Article 1 of the 1958 Geneva Convention on the Continental Shelf speaks of exploitability as a criterion for fixing the outer limit of the continental shelf. This might suggest that the continental shelf could, for legal purposes, extend to mid-ocean; but such an interpretation is unsound, for several reasons. The Geneva Convention defines the continental shelf as 'submarine areas *adjacent* to the coast', and areas in mid-ocean cannot be regarded as adjacent to any of the coastal states. Again, the International Court of Justice emphasized in the *North Sea Continental Shelf* cases[120] that the continental shelf was a prolongation of land territory – the deep seabed is too deep, and too far from shore, to be regarded as a prolongation of land territory. Finally, the continental shelf is a geological concept as well as a legal concept, and, from the geological point of view, to say that the deep seabed forms part of the continental shelf is as absurd as saying that Africa forms part of Australia. Article 76(1) of the 1982 Convention provides:

> The continental shelf of a coastal State comprises the sea-bed and subsoil of the submarine areas that extend beyond its territorial sea throughout the natural prolongation of its land territory to the outer edge of the continental margin, or to a distance of 200 nautical miles from the baselines from which the breadth of the territorial sea is measured where the outer edge of the continental margin does not extend up to that distance.

Article 76 also contains complicated and controversial provisions for delineating the outer edge of the continental margin. The continental margin consists not only of the continental shelf, but also of the continental slope, a steeply sloping area beyond the continental shelf, and the continental rise, a gently sloping area between the continental shelf and the deep seabed. The minimum limit of 200 miles, which was copied from the provisions on the exclusive economic zone[121] is probably already part of customary international law.[122]

The deep seabed

Resolution 2749 (XXV), passed by the General Assembly on 17 December 1970 by 108 votes to nil with fourteen abstentions, declared that the deep seabed was the common heritage of mankind,[123] and laid down various principles to govern the future exploitation of its resources.[124] These principles are elaborated in detail in Articles 133–91 and Annexes III and IV of the 1982 Convention. According to the 1982 Convention, control of the deep seabed (that is, the seabed beyond the continental shelf, as defined in Article 76) would be vested in an International Seabed Authority, which will exploit the deep seabed and its subsoil or grant licences for such exploitation to states or commercial companies.[125] (The powers of the Authority will apply only to the seabed and subsoil; Article 135 of the 1982 Convention declares that the provisions of the 1982 Convention concerning the deep seabed and the Authority shall not affect the legal status of the superjacent waters (high seas) or the air space above those waters.) The International Seabed Authority will also receive part of the revenue from the exploitation of the continental shelf beyond the 200-mile limit; the coastal state will receive the remainder of such

120 *North Sea Continental Shelf Cases, ICJ Rep.* 1969, 3–257, at 31, 47, 53. See Chapter 3 above, 44, 46 and text below, 196. See also *Arbitration between the United Kingdom of Great Britain and Northern Ireland and the French Republic on the Delimitation of the Continental Shelf,* Cmnd. 7438 (1979), *ILM* 18 (1979), 397–494; *Continental Shelf (Libya v. Malta) Case, ICJ Rep.* 1985, 13–187; *Continental Shelf (Tunisia v. Libya) Case, ICJ Rep.* 1982, 18–323. See the relevant articles by G. Jaenicke, *EPIL* 2 (1981), 205–8, and U.-D. Klemm, R. Oellers-Frahm, *EPIL* I (1992), 792–5; 795–8; 798–804.

121 See text above, 183–4.

122 *ICJ Rep.* 1985, at 33, 35. See D.N. Hutchinson, The Seaward Limit to Continental Shelf Jurisdiction in Customary International Law, *BYIL* 56 (1985), 11118.

123 See B.H. Oxman, The High Seas and the International Seabed Area, *Mich. JIL* 10 (1989), 526–42; F. Zegers Santa Cruz, Deep Sea-Bed Mining Beyond National Jurisdiction in the 1982 UN Convention on the Law of the Sea: Description and Prospects, *GYIL* 31 (1988), 107–19; W.G. Vitzthum, International Sea-Bed Area, *EPIL* II (1995), 1372–76. On the 'common heritage of mankind' concept see also Chapter 13 below, 207–8.

124 Text in *Brownlie BDIL,* 124–8.

125 See R. Wolfrum, International Sea-Bed Authority, in *Wolfrum UNLPP II,* 789–96.

126 Article 82, 1982 Convention.
127 See Chapter 15 below, 233–5.
128 See the 1980 draft of the 1982 Convention in *ILM* 19 (1980), 1129.
129 See text above, 174.
130 Text in *ILM* 19 (1980), 1003.
131 *ILM* 23 (1984), 1354.
132 See *AJIL* 73 (1979), 30–8.
133 See text above, 174–5.

revenue.[126] Revenue, royalties and profits received by the Authority will be used for the benefit of mankind as a whole, taking into particular consideration the needs of developing countries, whether coastal or landlocked.

The developing countries hoped to benefit financially from the International Seabed Authority and hailed Part XI of the 1982 Convention as a significant victory in their quest for a 'New International Economic Order'.[127] But the developed countries, which are the only countries with the advanced technology and huge amounts of capital needed to exploit the resources of the seabed, insisted on getting a fair return on the money and effort which they will put into exploiting those resources. This clash of interests affected many provisions of the 1982 Convention concerning the functions, powers, structure and voting procedure of the International Seabed Authority and the relations between mining companies and the Authority. Until 1981 it seemed likely that the UN Conference on the Law of the Sea would reach agreement on a compromise between the interests of the developed states and the interests of the developing states.[128] But in 1981 President Reagan of the United States demanded that some amendments should be made to the provisions of the 1980 draft concerning the deep seabed and the Authority, in order to make them more favourable to the developed states. The Conference made a few changes to the text of the 1980 draft in order to make it more acceptable to the developed states, but most Western states (including the United States and the UK) remained unsatisfied and refused to sign or ratify the 1982 Convention.[129]

Even before President Reagan took office in 1981, the United States had become so impatient with the disagreements and delays at the conference that it passed a law authorizing United States companies to start exploiting the deep seabed.[130] Similar laws have also been passed by several other developed states, such as France, West Germany, Italy, Japan, the UK and the USSR. There is an agreement between most of the states which have passed such laws (but not the USSR) that companies from one 'reciprocating state' (to use the terminology of the law passed by the United States) will not be authorized to operate in an area covered by a licence issued by another 'reciprocating state'.[131] The laws in question do not purport to create rights over any part of the deep seabed which will be exclusive as against states which have not passed such laws; moreover, the laws are intended to apply only during the period before the entry into force of a convention on the law of the sea to which the legislating state is a party, and they provide that all or part of the revenue received by the government concerned from the exploitation of the seabed will be shared with developing countries or transferred to the International Seabed Authority. In spite of that, these laws were condemned by developing countries as a violation of General Assembly resolution 2749 (XXV).[132]

As noted above, the 1994 Agreement Relating to the Implementation of Part XI of the 1982 Convention changed the deep seabed mining regime to the satisfaction of almost all parties.[133] The reasons for the amendment were basically twofold. First, it had become apparent that relatively low metal prices over the last decade had led to a decline in commercial interest in deep seabed mining. The huge bureaucratic structure based on detailed provisions laid down in Part XI appeared unnecessary. Second, the end of the Cold War and the global move towards market principles gave further impetus to reform willingness. The details of the amended regime, as well as the technical problems of the provisional application of the Agreement (before it enters into force, as provided for by Article 25 of the Vienna Convention on the Law of Treaties),[134] are beyond the scope of this book.

Maritime boundaries

Many disputes have arisen in recent years over the location of boundaries between areas of sea claimed by one state and areas of sea claimed by another state.[135] They have also occupied international tribunals and the ICJ.[136] Article 12(1) of the 1958 Geneva Convention on the Territorial Sea provides as follows:

> Where the coasts of two States are opposite or adjacent to each other, neither of the two States is entitled, failing agreement between them to the contrary, to extend its territorial sea beyond the median line every point of which is equidistant from the nearest points on the baselines from which the breadth of the territorial seas of each of the two States is measured. The provisions of this paragraph shall not apply, however, where it is necessary by reason of historic title or other special circumstances to delimit the territorial seas of the two States in a way which is at variance with this provision.

The same rules are laid down in Article 15 of the 1982 Convention. In the case of the contiguous zone, Article 24(3) of the Geneva Convention on the Territorial Sea lays down the same rule as Article 12(1), except that it omits the final sentence of Article 12(1). The 1982 Convention contains no provision for delimiting contiguous zones claimed by opposite or adjacent states.

Article 6(1) of the 1958 Geneva Convention on the Continental Shelf provides as follows:

> Where the same continental shelf is adjacent to the territories of two or more States whose coasts are opposite each other, the boundary of the continental shelf appertaining to such States shall be determined by agreement between them. In the absence of agreement, and unless another boundary line is justified by special circumstances, the boundary is the median line, every point of which is equidistant from the nearest point of the baselines from which the breadth of the territorial sea of each State is measured.

Article 6(2) applies the same rules '[w]here the same continental shelf is adjacent to the territories of two adjacent States'.

Articles 12(1) and 24(3) of the Geneva Convention on the Territorial Sea place primary emphasis on the equidistance principle. By contrast, Article 6 of the Geneva Convention on the Continental Shelf places primary emphasis on delimitation by agreement. Both Article 12(1) of the Geneva Convention on the Territorial Sea and Article 6 of the Geneva Convention on the Continental Shelf provide for a 'special circumstances'

134 See Marffy-Mantuano, *op. cit.*, 821–4.

135 See S.P. Jagota, *Maritime Boundary*, 1985; P. Weil, *The Law of Maritime Delimitation – Reflections*, 1989; L. Caflisch, Maritime Boundaries, Delimitation, *EPIL* 11 (1989), 212–9; D.M. Johnston/M.J. Valencia, *Pacific Ocean Boundary Problems: Status and Solutions*, 1991; M. Habibur Raiman, *Delimitation of Maritime Boundaries*, 1991; E.M.D. Evans, Maritime Delimitation and Expanding Categories of Relevant Circumstances, *ICLQ* 40 (1991), 1 *et seq.*; D.H. Anderson, Recent Boundary Agreements in the Southern North Sea, *ICLQ* 41 (1992), 414–23; M.D. Evans, Delimitation and the Common Maritime Boundary, *BYIL* 64 (1993), 283–332; E. Franckx, *Maritime Claims in the Arctic: Canadian and Russian Perspectives*, 1993; P.J.I. Charney/L.M. Alexander, *International Maritime Boundaries*, 2 vols, 1993; F.A. Ahnish, *The International Law of Maritime Boundaries and the Practice of States in the Mediterranean*, 1993; G.H. Blake (ed.), *World Boundaries*. Vol. 5: Maritime Boundaries, 1994; J.I. Charney, Progress in International Maritime Boundary Delimitation Law, *AJIL* 88 (1994), 227.

136 On the *Arbitration between Canada and France on the Delimitation of Maritime Areas (St. Pierre et Miquelon)*, see the Decision of 10 June 1992, *ILM* 31 (1992), 1145, and M.D. Evans, Less Than an Ocean Apart: The St Pierre and Miquelon and Jan Mayen Islands and the Delimitation of Maritime Zones, *ICLQ* 43 (1994), 678. For the most recent case decided by the ICJ concerning *Maritime Delimitation and Territorial Questions between Qatar and Bahrain*, see *ICJ Rep.* 1995, 6, *ILM* 34 (1995), 1204; for the judgment on jurisdiction and admissibility see *ICJ Rep.* 1994, 112, *ILM* 33 (1994), 1461 The *East Timor* case between Portugal and Australia (see Chapter 3 above, 59 and Chapter 18 below, 286–7) was dismissed on grounds of jurisdiction. For the contribution of the ICJ to the law of the sea, see Kwiatkowska (1995), *op. cit.*, 488 *et seq.*; Kwiatkowska, Equitable Maritime Boundary Delimitation, in V. Lowe/M. Fitzmaurice (eds), *Fifty Years of the International Court of Justice*, 1996, 264–92.

137 *North Sea Continental Cases, op. cit.,* 16–8. See text above, 193.
138 *Ibid.,* especially 46–54.
139 *ILR,* Vol. 54, 6, 8–10, 54–9, 101–3, 123–4. For further discussion of these two cases, and a comparison between them and later cases, see P. Birnie, Delimitation of Maritime Boundaries: Emergent Legal Principles and Problems, in G.H. Blake (ed.), *Maritime Boundaries and Ocean Resources,* 1987.
140 For the text of Article 38(1) of the Statute of the ICJ, see Chapter 3 above, 36.

exception to the equidistance principle, but in practice the 'special circumstances' exception is likely to be invoked more often in delimiting the continental shelf than in delimiting the territorial sea, because continental shelves stretch further than territorial seas; maritime boundaries based on the equidistance principle are often distorted by the presence of islands or by curvatures of the coast, and the effect of such distortions increases as one moves further out to sea.[137] Such distortions may be tolerable if they enable one state to extend its territorial sea at the expense of another state by a few miles, but not if they enable one state to extend its continental shelf at the expense of another state by hundreds of miles.

In the *North Sea Continental Shelf* cases the International Court of Justice held that the rules contained in Article 6(2) of the Geneva Convention on the Continental Shelf were not rules of customary law, and were therefore not binding on West Germany, which was not a party to the Convention. Instead, the Court said that the relevant rule of customary law required the parties (West Germany, Denmark and the Netherlands) to negotiate in good faith in order to reach an agreement on an equitable delimitation.[138] However, the arbitral award in a later case between the United Kingdom and France, concerning the delimitation of the continental shelf in the English Channel, suggests that the difference between customary law and Article 6 of the Geneva Convention on the Continental Shelf is slight; the United Kingdom and France were both parties to the Convention, but the arbitrators held that the position of the Channel Islands and of the Isles of Scilly constituted 'special circumstances' within the meaning of Article 6 of the Convention and that the boundary should be based on equitable considerations (which involved departing from the median (equidistance) line) wherever such special circumstances existed.[139]

The downgrading of the equidistance principle has been carried a stage further by Article 83(1) of the 1982 Convention which provides: 'The delimitation of the continental shelf between States with opposite or adjacent coasts shall be effected by agreement on the basis of international law, as referred to in Article 38 of the Statute of the International Court of Justice, in order to achieve an equitable solution.' Article 74(1) of the 1982 Convention applies the same rule to the delimitation of exclusive economic zones.[140] Articles 83(1) and 74(1) are vague, but that is inevitable; the whole question of delimitation was a source of acute controversy at UNCLOS III. Judicial and arbitral decisions in the future will probably clarify the concept of 'an equitable solution', but that is bound to be a slow process; what is equitable in one geographical situation will not be equitable in other geographical situations, and there is therefore a danger that each decided case will be unique and incapable of serving as a precedent for other cases.

Article 121(3) of the 1982 Convention provides that 'rocks which cannot sustain human habitation or economic life of their own shall have no exclusive economic zone or continental shelf'. This innovation is regarded as desirable by most states (but presumably not by the United Kingdom, which claims an exclusive fishery zone of 200 miles around Rockall, an uninhabitable rock 180 miles west of the Hebrides). However, Article 121 implies that such rocks will continue to possess a territorial sea and a contiguous zone.

Among the regional disputes still unsettled, some of the most serious ones with a very real potential for conflict are in the South-East Asian region, especially with regard to the competing claims to the Spratly Islands in the South China Sea.[141]

141 See G. Marston, Abandonment of Territorial Claims: The Cases of Bouvet and Spratly Islands, *BYIL* 57 (1986), 337–56; H. Chiu, Spratly Archipelagos, *FPIL* 12 (1990), 357-60; J. Greenfield, *China's Practice in the Law of the Sea*, 1992; 1992 UN Secretary-General Report, *op. cit.*, paras. 31–7; J.I. Charney, *China and the South China Sea Disputes: Conflicting Claims and Potential Solutions in the South China Sea*, 1995; Charney, Central East Asian Maritime Boundaries and the Law of the Sea, *AJIL* 89 (1995), 724–49.

13 Air space and outer space

1 *Harris CMIL*, 217–22; P.S. Dempsey, *Law and Foreign Policy in International Aviation*, 1987; K.-G. Park, *La Protection de la souveraineté aérienne*, 1991; B. Cheng, Air Law, *EPIL* I (1992), 66–72; I.H. P. Diederiks-Verschoor, *An Introduction to Air Law*, 5th edn 1993; S. Shubber, The Contribution of the International Court of Justice to Air Law, in V. Lowe/M. Fitzmaurice (eds), *Fifty Years of the International Court of Justice*, 1996, 316–26.
2 See K. Hailbronner, Airspace over Maritime Areas, *EPIL* I (1992), 90–4 and Chapter 12 above, 176–8.
3 Text in 15 UNTS 295. See L. Weber, Chicago Convention, *EPIL* I (1992), 571–3.
4 *U.S. v. Hungary*, *ICJ Rep.* 1954, 99–105; Aerial Incident of 7 October 1952, *ICJ Rep.* 1956, 9–11; Aerial Incident of 10 March 1953, *ibid.*, 6–8; Aerial Incident of 4 September 1954, *ICJ Rep.* 1958, 158–61; Aerial Incident of 7 November 1954, *ICJ Rep.* 1959, 276–8. See K. Hailbronner, Aerial Incident Cases (U.S. v. Hungary; U.S. v. U.S.S.R.; U.S. v. Czechoslovakia), *EPIL* I (1992), 50–2.
5 See Chapter 18 below, 282–7.
6 Aerial Incident of 27 July 1955 (*Israel v. Bulgaria*), *ICJ Rep.* 1959, 127–204. See K. Hailbronner, Aerial Incident of 27 July 1955 Cases (Israel v. Bulgaria; U.S. v. Bulgaria; U.K. v. Bulgaria), *EPIL* I (1992), 52–4.
7 See *AJIL* 54 (1960), 836, and *AJIL* 56 (1962), 135; *Colum. LR* (1961), 1074. On the unregulated area of espionage see J. Kish, *International Law and Espionage*, 1995.
8 *AJIL* 47 (1953), 559, 586. See J.N. Hyde, Oliver J. Lissitzyn (1912–1994), *AJIL* 89 (1995), 88–90.

Air space

Between 1900 and 1914 academic lawyers proposed various theories about the legal status of air space.[1] But from 1914 onwards it was clear that states would be content with nothing less than complete sovereignty over their air space, unlimited by any right of innocent passage; and a new rule of customary law to that effect arose very quickly. The military potential of aircraft for bombing and reconnaissance, demonstrated during the First World War, meant that any other rule would have been unacceptable to states, on security grounds. (In fact, it was the neutral states which were most insistent on their right to exclude foreign aircraft during the First World War, in order to prevent aerial battles taking place over their territory.) Since then, the customary rule has been that aircraft from one state have a right to fly over the high seas, but not over the territory or territorial sea of another state.[2] This rule is reaffirmed in Article 1 of the 1944 Chicago Convention on International Civil Aviation which states that 'every State has complete and exclusive sovereignty over the airspace above its territory'.[3]

It is a serious breach of international law for a state to order its aircraft to violate the air space of another state. In the period between 1950 and 1960 a number of aerial incidents occurred in which American military aircraft were attacked, forced to land or shot down and their crews interned by Hungary, the USSR and Czechoslovakia.[4] The United States took the view that the use of force was unjustified because the aircraft were either flying over international waters or had strayed inadvertently into foreign airspace. The cases filed by the United States against the states in question, which refused to admit liability, were dismissed by the International Court of Justice because the respondent states had not accepted its jurisdiction.[5] The Court also denied its jurisdiction in cases brought by Israel, the United States and the United Kingdom against Bulgaria for shooting down in 1955 an Israeli aircraft on a regular commercial flight between Austria and Israel which was carrying passengers of various nationalities.[6]

In May 1960, when a United States U2 reconnaissance aircraft was shot down over the Soviet Union, the Soviet Union cancelled a summit conference with the United States in protest against the violation of its air space.[7] Apparently the United States did not protest against the shooting down of the U2. But that does not mean that states have an unlimited right to attack intruding aircraft in all circumstances. In 1953 Lissitzyn[8] suggested that the following rule of customary law could be inferred from state practice: 'In its efforts to control the movements of intruding aircraft the territorial sovereign must not expose the aircraft and its occupants to unnecessary or unreasonably great danger – unreasonably great, that is, in relation to the reasonably apprehended harmfulness of the intrusion.' This is a very flexible principle. It implies that a state must not attack an intruding aircraft unless it has reason to suspect that the aircraft constitutes a real threat to its security (military aircraft are obviously more likely to present such a threat than civil aircraft); it also implies that a warning to land or change course should be given before the aircraft is attacked, unless there is reason to suspect that the aircraft constitutes an immediate and very serious threat to the security of the state, or unless it is impracticable to give such a warning.

Lissitzyn's flexible approach is probably still an accurate statement of the law in the case of military aircraft which enter the air space of another state without that state's consent. However, as we have just seen, there is some disagreement about the action which can be taken against civil aircraft which enter the air space of another state without that state's consent; some states still seem to support the application of Lissitzyn's flexible approach to civil aircraft (as well as to military aircraft), but other states (and the International Civil Aviation Organization (ICAO), a specialized agency of the United Nations)[9] believe that civil aircraft must never be attacked in such circumstances. On the other hand, civil aircraft which enter the air space of another state without that state's consent can be ordered to leave or to land, and the state whose air space has been violated can protest to the state in which the aircraft are registered if such orders are ignored; the rule (if it is indeed a rule) that trespassing civil aircraft must never be attacked does not mean that they have a legal right to trespass.

In 1981 ICAO recommended to its member states that 'intercepting aircraft should refrain from the use of weapons in all cases of interception of civil aircraft'.[10] In 1983 the Soviet Union shot down a South Korean civil airliner which had entered Soviet air space; in the United Nations Security Council a draft resolution condemning the Soviet action[11] received nine votes in favour, but was vetoed by the Soviet Union (Poland also voted against, and China, Guyana, Nicaragua and Zimbabwe abstained). The preamble to the draft resolution contained a paragraph 'reaffirming the rules of international law that prohibit acts of violence which pose a threat to the safety of international civil aviation', which implies that attacks on civil aircraft are never permitted (the position is obviously different if military aircraft enter the air space of another state). This 'absolute' rule was supported by statements made by the United States, South Korea, Australia, Togo, Ecuador and Portugal,[12] while Canada, Zaire, West Germany and Fiji echoed Lissitzyn's more flexible approach by saying that the Soviet reaction was 'disproportionate' in the circumstances.[13] Even the Soviet Union did not claim that it had an unlimited right to shoot down intruding aircraft; instead, it claimed that it had mistaken the South Korean airliner for a United States military reconnaissance aircraft, and that the South Korean airliner had acted suspiciously and had ignored Soviet orders to land.[14]

9 See text below, 200–1 and Chapter 6 above, 94 and Chapter 21 below, 382–4.
10 *ILM* 22 (1983), 1185, 1187.
11 *Ibid.*, 1148.
12 *Ibid.*, 1110, 1114, 1118, 1129, 1133–4, 1139.
13 *Ibid.*, 1117, 1120, 1133.
14 *Ibid.*, 1126–8, cf. 1074; J.H.H. Weiler, Korean Airlines Incident, *EPIL* 11 (1989), 167–9. See also the 1993 ICAO Report on the Completion of the Fact-Finding Investigation with Regard to the 31 August 1983 Destruction of Korean Airlines Aircraft, *ILM* 33 (1994), 310.

15 Text in 15 UNTS 295, amended text in 1175 UNTS 297.

16 Text in *ILM* 23 (1984), 705.

17 See I.F. Dekker/H.H.G. Post (eds), *The Gulf War of 1980–1988*, 1992.

18 *AJIL* 83 (1989), 912–3. See also ICAO Resolution and Report Concerning the Destruction of Iran Air Bus, 3 July 1988, *ILM* 28 (1989), 896–943.

19 *ILM* 28 (1989), 842; Aerial Incident of 3 July 1988 (*Iran v. USA*) Case, Order of 13 December 1989, *ICJ Rep.* 1989, 132, *ILM* 29 (1990), 123.

20 See Chapter 18 below, 284 n. 78.

21 See *ILM* 35 (1996), 553; *AJIL* 90 (1996), 278.

22 See *ILM* 35 (1996), 493; *AJIL* 90 (1996), 448–54.

23 See Chapter 7 above, 116–17.

24 See K. Hailbronner, International Civil Aviation Organization, *EPIL* II (1995), 1070–4. For other institutions concerned with international civil aviation see S.J. Fawcett, Inmarsat, *ibid.*, 991–4; K. Hailbronner, International Air Transport Association, *ibid.*, 1047–50; L. Weber, European Civil Aviation Conference, *ibid.*, 137–9; European Organization for the Safety of Air Navigation (Eurocontrol), *ibid.*, 270–73.

25 J. Ducrest, Legislative and Quasi-Legislative Functions of ICAO: Towards Improved Efficiency, *AASL* 20 (1995), 343–66.

In 1984 the Assembly of ICAO adopted an amendment (Article 3*bis*) to the 1944 Chicago Convention on the International Civil Aviation[15] (the constitution of ICAO) which confirms 'that every State, in the exercise of its sovereignty, is entitled to require the landing at some designated airport of a civil aircraft flying above its territory without authority'. But it also states that 'the Contracting States recognize that every State must refrain from resorting to the use of weapons against civil aircraft in flight and that, in case of interception, the lives of persons on board and the safety of aircraft must not be endangered'.[16]

During the war between Iraq and Iran (1980–8),[17] on 3 July 1988, the US warship *Vincennes* in an engagement with Iranian gunboats in the Persian Gulf, believing it was being attacked from the air, shot down the civilian Iran Air Flight 655, killing 290 passengers from six countries and crew members. Although the United States did not admit its liability under international law, it later offered to pay *ex gratia* compensation (which means without recognizing any legal obligation to do so) to the families of the victims (US$250,000 per full-time wage-earning victim, and US$100,000 for each of all the other victims).[18] Iran, however, declined to accept the offer and in 1989 filed an application for compensation in the International Court of Justice.[19] On 22 February 1996, Iran and the United States settled Iran's claims concerning the downing of Iran Air Flight 655 in connection with the settlement of other Iranian claims against the United States concerning certain banking matters, filed before the Iran–United States Claims Tribunal.[20] Under the terms of the settlement agreement, the survivors of each Iranian victim will be paid US$300,000 (for wage-earning victims) or US$150,000 (for non-wage-earning victims).[21]

In another recent incident, on 24 February 1996, Cuban military aircraft shot down two civilian aircraft registered in the United States which led to a Statement by the President of the UN Security Council condemning the act with reference to Article 3*bis* of the Chicago Convention and calling for an investigation of the incident by ICAO.[22] In addition, on 12 March 1996, President Clinton approved sanctions against Cuba under the controversial Cuban Liberty and Democratic Solidarity (Libertad) Act of 1996 (Helms-Burton Act).[23]

The general legal and institutional framework for international civil aviation is nowadays laid down in the 1944 Chicago Convention and the rules adopted by ICAO which now has practically universal membership.[24] ICAO is the main forum for the development of international air law and thereby also of domestic air law. It has quasi-legislative powers with regard to laying down 'international standards' (as distinct from mere 'recommended practices'), especially in the field of air navigation.[25] But the attempt since 1944 to establish on a multilateral basis rights of aircraft of contracting states to fly into each others' territories, whether engaged in scheduled air services or in non-scheduled flights, has largely failed. The current system of the exchange of lucrative traffic rights is essentially based upon a complex web of bilateral treaties, by which one state gives aircraft from another state the right to fly through its air space (usually in return for a similar concession from the other state in favour of the first state's aircraft, which constitutes a barter of rights of equivalent commercial value).[26] Air transport disputes between states are frequently decided by arbitration.[27]

Many of the rules governing aircraft have been copied from the rules governing ships.[28] For instance, the nationality of aircraft[29] is based on registration, and an aircraft cannot be registered in two or more states at the same time; the problem of flags of convenience, which has caused so much controversy in connection with merchant ships, has scarcely arisen in the context of aircraft – maybe because most airlines are owned or subsidized by governments. Similarly, the rules concerning the power to try crimes committed on aircraft resemble the rules concerning the power to try crimes committed on ships.[30] For the purposes of the territorial principle of jurisdiction, a civil aircraft in flight may be treated as if it were a part of the state of registration (a sort of 'flying island', so to speak), but it may also be regarded as present within the subjacent state, so that both the state of registration and the subjacent state may try the offender. This resembles the concurrent jurisdiction exercised by the flag state and the coastal state over crimes committed on foreign merchant ships in internal waters or the territorial sea.[31]

The most common offences committed against civil aviation safety are hijacking, sabotage and forced flights to seek asylum in another state.[32] These are not acts of piracy in the technical sense, involving universal jurisdiction,[33] because they are rarely committed from one aircraft against another or in an area beyond the jurisdiction of any state. Since the 1960s, international legal instruments have been adopted to deal with unlawful interference with civil aviation, including the 1963 Toyko Convention,[34] the 1970 Hague Convention,[35] and the 1971 Montreal Convention.[36] These have been ratified by a large number of states and require that the parties provide for severe penalties and far-reaching jurisdiction in most cases. But no effective international machinery was created providing for enforcement measures against states refusing to cooperate in suppression of acts of hijacking and in international terrorism.[37]

Outer space

'Need I apologize for my choice of subject? Some may say it belongs to the realm of exotics of law. Some may ask: Why deal with issues so remote when there are so many much closer to us still awaiting a solution? Why reach so far?' With these words the late Judge Manfred Lachs introduced his 1964 lecture at the Hague Academy of International Law on the topic 'The International Law of Outer Space'.[38] Exotic the subject is no longer.[39] Within the four decades following the launch of Sputnik 1 in 1957 (the first artificial satellite, launched by the USSR), the use of space technology has become widespread, not only for military but also for civilian purposes, including satellites for communications, meteorology, television and radio broadcasting and other applications.[40] Remote sensing of data is employed in agriculture and resource management as well as in environmental monitoring. Some states, such as the United States, the United Kingdom and

26 J. Naveau, *International Air Transport in a Changing World*, 1989; P. Mendes de Leon (ed.), *Air Transport Law and Policy in the 1990s*, 1991; L. Weber, Air Transport Agreements, *EPIL* I (1992), 75–8. See also M. Milde, Air Transport, Regulation of Liability, *ibid.* 78–82; P.M. de Leon, *Cabotage in International Air Transport*, 1992; M. Zylicz, *International Air Transport Law*, 1992. See also the United States Model Bilateral Air Transport Agreement, *ILM* 35 (1996), 1479.

27 K.-H. Böckstiegel, Italy-United States Air Transport Arbitration (1965), *EPIL* II (1995), 1508–10; Böckstiegel, France-United States Air Transport Arbitration (1963), *ibid.*, 459–61; K. Oellers-Frahm, France-United States Air Transport Arbitration (1978), *ibid.*, 461–3. On the US/UK Arbitration Concerning Heathrow Airport User Charges, see J. Skilbeck, *ICLQ* 44 (1995), 171–9; J.J. van Haersolte-van Hof, *LJIL* 8 (1995), 203 and S.M. Witten, *AJIL* 89 (1995), 174–92. On arbitration see Chapter 18 below, 293–8.

28 See Chapter 12 above, 185–6.

29 See M. Milde, Aircraft, *EPIL* I (1992), 86–7; K. Hailbronner, State Aircraft, *EPIL* 11 (1989), 317–20.

30 See Chapter 12 above, 185–9.

31 See also M. Akehurst, Hijacking, *Indian JIL* (1974), 81–9.

32 See E. McWhinney, *Aerial Piracy and International Terrorism: the Illegal Diversion of Aircraft and International Law*, 2nd edn 1987; K. Hailbronner, Civil Aviation, Unlawful Interference with, *EPIL* I (1992), 583–6; M.N. Leich, Aircraft Crimes, Multilateral Conventions – Montreal Protocol, *AJIL* 82 (1988), 569–71.

33 See Chapters 7, 112–13 and 12, 105 above.

34 Convention on Offences and Certain Other Acts Committed on Board Aircraft, *ILM* 2 (1963), 1042.

35 Convention for the Suppression of Unlawful Seizure of Aircraft, *ILM* 10 (1971), 133.

36 Convention for the Suppression of Unlawful Acts against the Safety of Civil Aviation, *ILM* 10 (1971), 1151.

37 See the 1978 Declaration of Bonn by Western heads of government, *ILM* 17 (1978), 1285; R.A. Friedländer, Terrorism, *EPIL* 9 (1986), 371–6. On the *Lockerbie* case see Chapter 18 below, 292–3.

38 M. Lachs, The International Law of Outer Space, *RdC* 113 (1964-III), 7. On the life of Judge Lachs who, *inter alia*, chaired the Legal Sub-Committee on Outer Space in the United Nations and fostered the development of the consensus on the major aspects of space law, see the contributions by O. Schachter, S.M. Schwebel, T.M. Franck and S.K. Chopra, In Memoriam: Judge Manfred Lachs (1914–1993), *AJIL* 87 (1993), 414–23.

39 K.-H. Böckstiegel, Prologue, in T.L. Zwaan (ed.), *Space Law: Views of the Future*, 1988, 1. See also *Harris CMIL*, 222–32; S.M. Williams, *Derecho internacional contemporáneo: La utilización del espacio ultraterrestre*, 1990; K.-H. Böckstiegel (ed.), *Handbuch des Weltraumrechts*, 1991; H.A. Wassenbergh, *Principles of Outer Space Law in Hindsight*, 1991; P.-M. Martin, *Le Droit de l'espace*, 1991; C.Q. Christol, *Space Law: Past, Present and Future*, 1991; S. Gorove, *Developments in Space Law: Issues and Policies*, 1991; N. Jasentuliyana, *Space Law: Development and Scope*, 1992; M. Andem, *International Legal Problems in the Peaceful Exploration and Use of Outer Space*, 1993; M. Couston, *Droit spatial économique, Régimes applicables à l'exploration de l'espace*, 1993; I.H. Ph. Diederiks-Verschoor, *An Introduction to Space Law*, 1993; L. Peyrefitte, *Droit de l'espace*, 1993; P. Malanczuk, Space Law as a Branch of International Law, *NYIL* 25 (1994), 143–80; S. Gorove, *United States Space Law – National and International Regulation, 1982–1996*; Gorove, *Cases on Space Law: Texts, Comments and References*, 1996.

40 For a good survey on the current applications of space technology, see R. Gibson, *Space*, 1992.

41 G.M. Danilenko, Outer Space and the Multilateral Treaty-Making Process, *High Tech. LJ* 4 (1990), 217; M. Benkö/ K.U. Schrogl, *International Space Law in the Making*, 1994.

42 B. Cheng, *The Military Use of Outer Space and International Law*, Vol. 1, 1992, 63–75; W.v. Kries, Anti-Missile Defense for Europe and the Law of Outer Space, *ZLW* 42 (1993), 271.

43 See P. Malanczuk, Telecommunications Satellites and International Law, Comments, *RBDI* 21(1988), 262–72; F. Lyall, *Law and Space Telecommunications*, 1989; M.L. Smith, *International Regulation of Satellite Communication*, 1990; I.H.P. Diederiks-Verschoor, Legal Aspects Affecting Telecommunications Activities in Space, *TSJ* 1 (1994), 81–91; S. White, International Regulation of the Radio Frequency Spectrum and Orbital Positions, *TSJ* 2 (1995), 329–50. See also text below, 202, 208.

Sweden, have even adopted specific national legislation relating to outer space activities.

The law-making process in the field of space law[41] has some special characteristics. Since 1958, in practice it has primarily relied upon the work of a special international body, the United Nations Committee on the Peaceful Uses of Outer Space (UNCOPUOS) with its two sub-committees, the Scientific and Technical Subcommittee and the Legal Subcommittee. The administrative arm of the Committee is the United Nations Office for Outer Space Affairs, now based in Vienna. Due to the function of UNCOPUOS, the institutional framework of space law-making enables more consistency in law-making than in many other fields of international law. UNCOPUOS, however, is a limited club with only a quarter of the members of the United Nations participating.

It should be noted that UNCOPUOS is not the only body concerned with the law of outer space. Thus, the important issue of the military use of outer space is considered by the major space powers to be outside the mandate of UNCOPUOS and to properly belong to the fora dealing with disarmament and arms control issues.[42] Furthermore, albeit controversial at the beginning, the competence to deal with the regulation of the use of radio frequencies and satellite positions in the geostationary orbit (a highly advantageous orbit 36,000 km above the Earth's equator) for space communications[43] rests with the International Telecommunication Union (ITU), with its global membership – a rather successful international organization, due to the technical necessities of cooperation in the field of telecommunications.[44]

The United Nations General Assembly started studying the legal problems posed by outer space activities in 1959[45] and adopted Resolution 1721 in December 1961 to give guidance to the subsequent evolution of space law.[46] This culminated in the 1963 Declaration of Legal Principles Governing the Activities of States in the Exploration and Use of Outer Space[47] and led to the adoption of four major multilateral treaties[48] governing outer space activities from 1967 to 1975: the 1967 Treaty on Principles Governing the Activities of States, Including the Moon and Other Celestial Bodies (Outer Space Treaty),[49] the 1968 Agreement on the Rescue of Astronauts, the Return of Astronauts and the Return of Objects Launched into Outer Space (Rescue Agreement),[50] the 1972 Convention on Liability for Damage Caused by Objects Launched into Outer Space (Liability Convention),[51] and the 1974 Convention on Registration of Objects Launched into Outer Space (Registration Convention).[52] In addition, in 1979 the Agreement Governing the Activities of States on the Moon and Other Celestial Bodies (Moon Treaty) was adopted.[53] But there are also special conventions dealing with certain aspects of space-based activities, such as the 1963 Treaty Banning Nuclear Weapon Tests in the Atmosphere, in Outer Space and Under Water,[54] the 1977 Convention on the Prohibition of Military or Any Other Hostile Use of Environmental Modification Techniques[55] and the Convention and Regulations of the International Telecommunication Union.

The technical necessities of jointly using resources,[56] as well as the immense financial and technological requirements of conducting activities in outer space, necessitate international cooperation[57] more than in many other fields of international law and tend to induce a stronger pressure towards integrationist solutions in international organization in this area. Regulatory needs became most obvious in the fields of satellite communications[58] and remote sensing.[59] The development of the substantive and procedural aspects of space law was accompanied by innovations in international organization concerned with the exploration and use of outer space (ESA),[60] especially with regard to satellite communications systems providing global and regional networks (INTELSAT, INMARSAT, EUTELSAT, ARABSAT).[61] Recently, there has also been some discussion even on creating a global space agency.[62]

In its initial formative phase, space law has developed in anticipation of outer space activities at a time when such activities were still rather limited in practice. This process was successful because only the two major powers, the United States and the Soviet Union, were at the time actively engaged in outer space activities, while most other states failed to perceive that any of their substantial interests would be affected in this connection in the near future. While the major space powers seek to retain their monopoly positions and technological edge as much as possible, this has now clearly changed. Meanwhile, more and more states have become directly or indirectly involved in outer space or consider that their political and economic interests require the taking of a position. Conflicts of interest, especially between industrialized and developing countries, have made achieving a consensus in the law-making process increasingly difficult.

One peculiar highlight of this process has been the 1976 Bogota Declaration by eight equatorial countries claiming sovereign rights to segments of the geostationary orbit 36,000 km above their territory, which was met by rejection by the international community.[63] Equatorial countries subsequently began abandoning this untenable position; however, the controversial issue of whether there should be a special legal regime for the geostationary orbit, in addition to the existing regulations of the ITU, which should provide for certain preferential rights for developing countries, is still on the agenda of UNCOPUOS.[64]

All of the major treaty instruments were prepared on the basis of the consensus method (instead of majority decision-making) to ensure the participation of the space powers.[65] The same applies to all other resolutions of the General Assembly prepared by UNCOPUOS with the single exception of the controversial principles on direct satellite television broadcasting adopted by majority against the votes of Western states in 1982, mainly because they refused to accept the requirement of 'prior consent' of the receiving state to foreign satellite broadcasting.[66] UNCOPUOS thereafter returned to the consensus method, as in the case of the 1986 principles on remote sensing[67] or the most recently adopted principles on the use of nuclear power sources in outer space.[68]

Conflicts of interest also became evident with the adoption of the still largely defunct Moon Treaty of 1979,[69] attempting to establish an international regime for the exploitation of mineral resources,[70] which was opposed by the major space powers. It has been accepted only by a small number of states without any significant independent space capabilities,

44 A. Noll, International Telecommunication Union, *EPIL* II (1995), 1379–85; P. Malanczuk, Telecommunications, International Regulation of, *EPIL* 9 (1986), 367–71; Malanczuk, Information and Communication, Freedom of, *EPIL* II (1995), 976-91; A. Tegge, *Die Internationale Telekommunikations-Union*, 1994; M.W. Zacher/B.A. Sutton, *Governing Global Networks. International Regimes for Transportation and Communications*, 1995. See also text below, 208.

45 International Co-operation in the Peaceful Uses of Outer Space, UN GA Res. 1472 (XIV), 12 December 1959. See also the earlier Resolution on the Question of the Peaceful Use of Outer Space, UN GA Res. 1348 (XIII), 13 December 1958.

46 UN GA Res. 1721 (XVI), 20 December 1961. See Kopal, The Role of United Nations Declarations of Principles in the Progressive Development of Space Law, *JSpaceL* 16 (1988), 5 *et seq.*

47 UN GA Res. 1962 (XVIII), 13 December 1963.

48 B.C.M. Reijnen, *The United Nations Space Treaties Analyzed*, 1992.

49 610 UNTS 205 (1967); *ILM* 6 (1967), 386. See also N.M. Matte, Outer Space Treaty, *EPIL* 11 (1989), 251–3; M. Lachs, The Treaty on Principles of the Law of Outer Space, 1967–92, *NILR* 39 (1992), 291–302.

50 Text in *AJIL* 63 (1969), 382.

51 Text in *ILM* 10 (1971), 965.

52 1023 UNTS 15 (1976).

53 *ILM* 18 (1979), 1434–41. See N. Mateesco-Matte, The Moon Agreement: What Future?, *AFDMAS* 12 (1993), 345.

54 480 UNTS 43.

55 1108 UNTS 151.

56 S.M. Williams, The Law of Outer Space and Natural Resources, *ICLQ* 36 (1987), 142–51; B.E. Helm, Exploring the Last Frontiers for Mineral Resources: A Comparison of International Law Regarding the Deep Seabed, Outer Space, and Antarctica, *Vand. JTL* 23 (1990), 819–49; D.A. Barritt, A 'Reasonable' Approach to Resource Development in Outer Space, *Loyola LAICLJ* 12 (1990), 615–42.

57 See R. Müller/M. Müller, Co-operation as a Basic Principle of Legal Regimes for Areas Beyond National Sovereignty – With Special Regard to Outer Space Law, *GYIL* 31 (1988), 553 *et seq.*

58 See text above, 202–3.

59 See P. Malanczuk, Satelliten-

Fernerkundung der Erde: politische und rechtliche Aspekte, in K. Kaiser/Frhr. v. Welck (eds), *Weltraum und internationale Politik*, 1987, 57–71; Malanczuk, Erdfernerkundung, in Böckstiegel (ed.), 1991, *op. cit.*, 425–55; H. Heintze (ed.), *Remote Sensing Under Changing Conditions*, 1992; S. Courteix, *Droit télédétection et environnement*, 1994.

60 K.J. Madders, European Space Agency, *EPIL* II (1995), 295–300.

61 S.J. Fawcett, Intelsat, *EPIL* II (1995), 1000–4; S. J. Fawcett, Inmarsat, *ibid.*, 991–4; R. Wolfrum, Eutelsat, *ibid.*, 300–2; M. Snow, *The International Telecommunication Satellite Organization. Economic Challenges Facing an International Organization*, 1987; International Maritime Satellite Organization: Amendments to the Agreement of INMARSAT, *ILM* 27 (1988), 691.

62 K.S. Pederson, Is It Time to Create A World Space Agency?, *SP* 9 (1993); M. Bourély et al. *Faut-il créer une organisation mondiale de l'espace?*, 1992.

63 K.-H. Böckstiegel/M. Benkö (eds), *Space Law. Basic Legal Documents*, 1990, Vol. 1, B.IV.

64 See UN Doc. A/AC. 105/573 of 14 April 1994, 15 *et seq.* and Annex IV, working paper A/AC. 105/C.2/L. 192 of 30 March 1993, submitted by Columbia.

65 See E. Galloway, Consensus Decision-Making by the United Nations Committee on the Peaceful Uses of Outer Space, *JSpaceL* 7 (1979), 3 *et seq.* On the general function of consensus in international law-making see E. Suy, Consensus, *EPIL* I (1992), 759–61; K. Zemanek, Making Rule and Consensus Technique in Law-Making Diplomacy, in R.St.J. Macdonald/D.M. Johnston (eds), *The Structure and Process of International Law*, 1983, 857–87.

66 P. Malanczuk, Das Satellitenfernsehen und die Vereinten Nationen, *ZaöRV* 44 (1984), 257–89 with the text of the principles; J.A. Frowein, Satellite Broadcasting, *EPIL* 11 (1989), 273–6; D. Fisher, *Prior Consent to International Direct Satellite Broadcasting*, 1990; M.L. Stewart, *To See the World: The Global Dimension in International Direct Television Broadcasting by Satellite*, 1991.

67 See text above, 203.

68 M. Benkö/G. Gruber/K. Schrogl, The UN Committee on the Peaceful Uses of Outer Space: Adoption of Principles Relevant to the Use of Nuclear Power

with the exception of France.[71] In essence, the politics of the New World Economic Order[72] advocated by the former so-called Third World also entered the domain of space law. The demands of developing countries to share in the benefits of the use of outer space technology are reflected in the continuing dispute in UNCOPUOS on the item 'Consideration of the legal aspects related to the application of the principle that the exploration and utilization of outer space should be carried out for the benefit and in the interests of all states, taking into particular account the needs of developing countries'.[73]

The basic substantive framework of the present law on outer space is contained in the Outer Space Treaty of 1967.[74] The treaty provides that outer space is free for exploration and use by all states (Article 1) and cannot be annexed by any state (Article 2). The exploration and use of outer space must be carried out for the benefit of all countries (Article 1) and in accordance with international law (Article 3). Activities in outer space must not contaminate the environment of the Earth or of celestial bodies, and must not interfere with the activities of other states in outer space (Article 9). States must disclose information about their activities in outer space (Articles 10–12). Activities of non-governmental entities in outer space require governmental authorization, and the state concerned is responsible for all activities which it authorizes (Article 6). A state which launches (or authorizes the launching of) an object into outer space is liable for any damage caused by that object (Article 7). States must assist astronauts in distress; an astronaut from one state who makes a forced landing in another state must be returned to the former state (Article 5). Ownership of objects launched into outer space is not altered by their presence in outer space or by their return to Earth; if found, such objects must be returned to the state of origin (Article 8). The rules in Articles 7, 5 and 8 were subsequently laid down in greater detail by the Rescue Agreement 1968, the Liability Convention 1972, and by the Registration Convention 1974 (see above).

Article 4 of the Outer Space Treaty provides that the moon and other celestial bodies 'shall be used . . . exclusively for peaceful purposes'. However, as regards spacecraft orbiting around the Earth, Article 4 merely provides that nuclear weapons and other weapons of mass destruction must not be placed in orbit around the Earth. This difference between the rules applicable to spacecraft in Earth orbit and the rules applicable to celestial bodies justifies the inference that spacecraft in Earth orbit may be used for military purposes which do not involve nuclear weapons or other weapons of mass destruction; in particular, they may be used for purposes of reconnaissance. During the negotiations leading up to the conclusion of the Outer Space Treaty, the Soviet Union (which, as a 'closed society', had most to lose from being observed by satellites) argued that the use of satellites for reconnaissance purposes was illegal and should be prohibited by the treaty; but the United States disagreed. One advantage of the use of reconnaissance satellites is that they provide an efficient means of verifying compliance with disarmament treaties; in the past, avoidance of inspection has always been a major obstacle to disarmament.[75]

While general international law, in principle, does not hold states responsible for the activities of private individuals,[76] in space law, Article VI of the Outer Space Treaty establishes the rule that state parties bear international responsibility for national activities in outer space, including activities carried out by non-governmental entities. However, in view of the tendency towards commercialization and privatization of outer space activities, a number of problems require further clarification. They include the exact definition of the 'responsible' state and the scope of discretion accorded to states in fulfilling their obligations of supervision.[77]

The aspect of responsibility/liability of states for actual damage in space law[78] is particularly interesting because Article 2 of the 1972 Liability Convention provides for 'absolute' liability of states for damage caused by a space object on the surface of the Earth or to aircraft in flight, which means they are obliged to pay compensation regardless of fault. Although some have argued that there is already a precedent for such type of liability in Article 22(3) of the 1958 Geneva Convention on the High Seas,[79] this is truly an innovation in international law, which, apart from the instances of treaty-based indirect civil liability of operators engaged in hazardous activities, has previously not known direct strict state liability in these terms.

According to Article XXII of the Liability Convention, an intergovernmental organization active in space is liable as a state, if a corresponding declaration is made and the majority of member states are parties both to the Liability Convention and the Outer Space Treaty. So far, the European Space Agency (ESA) and Eutelsat have made such declarations. International organizations are primarily, their member states secondarily, under a regime of joint liability to protect claimants. 'Piercing the veil' to gain recovery from member states directly is admissible only if the organization fails to pay the agreed or determined amount of compensation within six months.

With the increasing use of outer space for practical applications of space technology and the proliferation of states, agencies, international organizations and private actors involved, the settlement of international disputes with regard to outer space activities is no longer a mere academic topic, as it was in the past.[80] As to disputes between states, the existing international instruments governing outer space activities all suffer from the deficiency that none of them provide for a mechanism which arrives at binding decisions for the parties. In effect, they do not progress beyond the non-binding methods of dispute settlement available as options to the parties according to Article 33 of the United Nations Charter, if they do not agree on international arbitration or adjudication.[81] A proposal by the United States to adopt compulsory dispute settlement by the International Court of Justice in the 1967 Outer Space Treaty was not acceptable to the USSR.

The 1972 Liability Convention is no exception, although some progress has been made by at least including some provisions on dispute settlement. The Convention provides for the establishment of a Claims Commission at the request of either party, if diplomatic negotiations fail. Although the details laid down in the Convention for the Claims Commission resemble in a number of aspects what is known from international arbitration, the decisive difference is that the decision of the Commission is final and binding only if the parties have so agreed. Thus, the procedure in fact

Sources in Outer Space and Other Recent Developments, ZLW (1993), 35.

69 See text above, 202.

70 Article 11, 1979 Moon Treaty.

71 The Treaty entered into force on 12 July 1984, see C.Q. Christol, The Moon Treaty Enters into Force, AJIL 79 (1985), 163–8.

72 See Chapter 15 below, 233–5.

73 See UN Doc. A/AC.105/573 of 14 April 1994, 8 et seq.

74 Op. cit.

75 See Chapter 20 below, 342.

76 See Chapter 17 below, 259–60.

77 See H. Bittlinger, Private Space Activities: Questions of International Responsibility, Proc. IISL 30 (1987), 191 et seq.; P. Malanczuk, The Actors: States, International Organizations, Private Entities, in G. Lafferrenderie (ed.), An Outlook for Outer Space Law in the Coming 30 Years (forthcoming).

78 See P. Malanczuk, Die völkerrechtliche Haftung für Raumfahrtschäden, in Böckstiegel (ed.), 1991, op. cit., 755–803; B.A. Hurwitz, State Liability for Outer Space Activities in Accordance with the 1972 Convention on International Liability for Damage Caused by Space Objects, 1992.

79 See Chapter 12 above, 173.

80 On the discussion of reforming the system of dispute settlement in international space law see ILA Rep. 1984, 325, 334 et seq.; K.-H. Böckstiegel, Proposed Draft Convention on the Settlement of Space Law Disputes, JSpaceL 12 (1984), 136–62; H.v. Traa-Engelman, Settlement of Space Law Disputes, LJIL 3 (1990), 139–55; K.-H. Böckstiegel, Developing a System of Dispute Settlement Regarding Space Activities, Proc. IISL 35 (1993), 27 et seq.; idem, Settlement of Disputes Regarding Space Activities, JSpaceL 21 (1993), 1–10; K.M. Gorove, Settlement of Space Law Disputes, ibid., 64–5; Malanczuk (1994), op. cit., at 166 et seq.; M. Williams, Report on Dispute Settlement Regarding Space Activities, ILA Space Law Committee, Helsinki Conference 1996 (K.-H. Böckstiegel, Chairman).

81 See Chapter 18 below, 281–98.

82 For details see Böckstiegel (1993), Settlement of Disputes, *op. cit.*, 3 *et seq.*

83 See Böckstiegel/Benkö (eds), 1990, *op. cit.*, Vol. 1, A.VI.2.

84 Böckstiegel (1993), Settlement of Disputes, *op. cit.*, 9 *et seq.*; K.-H. Böckstiegel/W. Stoffel, Private Outer Space Activities and Dispute Settlement, *TSJ* 1 (1994), 327–37. See Chapter 18 below, 293.

85 But see V.S. Vereshchetin/G.M. Danilenko, Custom as a Source of International Law of Outer Space, *JSpaceL* 13 (1985), 22–35. See also Chapter 3 above, 39–46.

86 See Chapter 12 above, 173–97.

87 Vereschchetin/Danilenko, *op. cit.*, 25.

88 P.-M. Martin, Les Définitions absentes du droit de l'espace, *RFDAS* 46 (1992), 105–17; R.F.A. Goedhart, *The Never Ending Dispute: Delimitation of Air Space and Outer Space*, 1996.

89 See Diederiks-Verschoor (1993), Space Law, *op. cit.*, 12. For a differentiated analysis see Vereshchetin/Danilenko, *op. cit.*, 27 *et seq.*

90 Malanczuk (1994), Space Law, *op. cit.*

amounts to no more than conciliation. The same effect results, for example from the general cross-waiver of liability between the parties to the 1988 Permanently Manned Civil Space Station Agreement.[82] In actual practice the settlement procedures of the Liability Convention have not yet been used. The *Cosmos 954* case, in which a Soviet nuclear-powered satellite disintegrated in 1978 over the north-west of Canada contaminating a territory of the size of Austria, was settled through diplomatic negotiations.[83]

Disputes between states and private enterprises are likely to occur with the increasing trend towards commercialization and privatization of outer space activities, in particular in satellite communications, remote sensing and microgravity, but the trend seems to move into the direction of using available procedures of international commercial arbitration. The existing national and international procedures of commercial arbitration are certainly preferable for disputes between private enterprises among themselves.[84]

Customary law is of far lesser importance than treaties and other instruments and its significance for outer space activities is not secured in many respects.[85] For such a new area, in comparison with, for example, the 'classical' area of the law of the sea,[86] this is not surprising. Nevertheless, it may not be excluded that some customary law has developed in the relatively short historical period since 1957. This appears to be true for the essential principles of the Outer Space Treaty which have been accepted by all states active in outer space by practice and with *opinio iuris* after ratification, and where no evidence of dissenting practice of non-ratifying states is available. It seems agreed that such principles include the freedom of exploration and use of outer space by all states and the prohibition of national appropriation of outer space, but whether they also include the principles on responsibility and liability, as laid down in the Outer Space Treaty, or rather the principle that states retain jurisdiction and control over space objects launched into outer space,[87] is unclear.

Since Sputnik 1, artificial satellites have passed over the territory of other states on innumerable occasions; for many years no state has ever protested that this constituted a violation of its air space. The conduct of the states launching satellites, coupled with the acquiescence of other states, may have given rise to a new permissive rule of customary international law; states are entitled to put satellites in orbit over the territory of other states, but not necessarily to pass through their air space to get into orbit in outer space. The rule concerning outer space is thus different from the rule concerning air space (see above).

The precise location of the point where air space ends and outer space begins, however, is uncertain but unimportant, because the minimum height at which satellites can remain in orbit is at least twice the maximum height at which aircraft can fly.[88] However, the alleged general customary nature of the rule allowing free passage of space objects through the national air space of other states, contrary to some views in the literature, is difficult to establish.[89] Such a rule would at least require the knowledge of states that their airspace has been used by a foreign space object, which is not likely to be often the case.

Space law is a rapidly evolving new branch of international law.[90]

Unresolved problems include the delimitation of outer space and air space (the issue is still on the agenda of UNCOPUOS), the definition of space objects and the related issues of jurisdiction, control and ownership,[91] and legal problems pertaining to space transportation.[92] Manned space flight and space station projects have also raised issues of international criminal law.[93] In addition, new issues have emerged by the commercialization of certain activities and the emergence of private operators, such as in the fields of satellite communications, remote sensing, and microgravity.[94] The development has led into areas of the law which were previously remote and now requires consideration of private international law, of insurance problems, and of details of intellectual property law and its further development.[95] It is also venturing into areas of European Community Law and international trade law.[96]

A further new topic concerns environmental problems arising from outer space activities, especially the problem of man-made pollution of outer space by space debris.[97] Even the evolving concept of 'sustainable development' is having an impact on space law in connection with the follow-up process of the 1992 Rio Conference on Environment and Development (UNCED) and the contribution of space activities to the implementation of Agenda 21, in particular, to environmental monitoring and sustainable development in the areas of land-use planning and management, deforestation, desertification, water resource assessment and the scientific study of environmental dynamics.[98]

After the ending of the Cold War, there are some indications that cooperation may acquire a new stimulus among the major space powers. There are also trends in the direction of enhancing cooperation among developing countries in the use of outer space.[99] The changing context of international space activities has further led to the consideration of convening a Third UN Conference on the Exploration and Peaceful Uses of Outer Space as a follow-up to the 1968 and 1982 UNISPACE events.[100]

The 'common heritage of mankind' principle

Within the general framework of international law, there is the close link of space law to the law governing other areas beyond national jurisdiction, such as the high seas, the deep sea floor, and Antarctica.[101] Indeed, the legal regime of outer space has been described as 'analogous' to the basic status of the high seas, discarding special rules which only apply to the latter.[102]

Related to this is the interesting general discussion on the controversial common heritage of mankind principle.[103] The term has emerged in connection with the progressive development of international law and has found reflection in the reform of the law of the sea, in space law, and in the legal framework for Antarctica. In space law (much earlier than in the context of the law of the sea negotiations), the principle was first mentioned in UN General Assembly Resolution 1962 (XVIII) of 13 December 1963[104] and was then incorporated in the 1967 Outer Space Treaty in Article 1, which, however, uses its own terminology, stating that the exploration and use of outer space shall be the common province of all

91 B. Cheng, Spacecraft, Satellites and Space Objects, *EPIL* 11 (1989), 309–17; C.Q. Christol, The Aerospace Plane: Its Legal and Political Future, *SP* 9 (1993), 35.

92 P.D. Nesgos, Commercial Space Transportation: A New Industry Emerges, 16 *AASL* 16 (1991), 393–422; B. Stockfish, Space Transportation and the Need for a New International Legal and Institutional Regime, *AASL* 17 (1992), 323–68.

93 K.-H. Böckstiegel (ed.), *Space Stations – Legal Aspects of Scientific and Commercial Use in a Framework of Transnational Cooperation*, 1985; A.J. Young, *Law and Policy in the Space Stations' Era*, 1989; K.-H. Böckstiegel/ V. Vereshchetin/S. Gorove, Draft for a Convention on Manned Space Flight, *ZLW* 40 (1991), 3–8; Böckstiegel (ed.), *Manned Space Flight*, 1993.

94 Qizhi He, Certain Legal Aspects of Commercialization of Space Activities, *AASL* 15 (1990), 33–42; H.L.v. Traa-Engelman, *Commercial Utilization of Outer Space, Law and Practice*, 2nd edn 1993; P. Malanczuk, Independent Private Enterprise and Satellite Communications: The Evolving European Legal Framework, *Space Comm.* 13 (1995), 269–74; S. Hobe, *Die rechtlichen Rahmenbedingungen der wirtschaftlichen Nutzung des Weltraums*, 1995.

95 See, for example, J. Klucka, The Role of Private International Law in the Regulation of Outer Space, *ICLQ* 39 (1990), 918–22 and Chapter 4 above, 71–4; I.I. Kuskuvelis, The Space Risk and Commercial Space Insurance, *SP* 9 (1993), 109; P. Malanczuk, Introduction and Conclusions by the Chairman, Recent Developments in the Field of Protection and Distribution of Remote Sensing Data, *Proceedings of the 3rd Dutch NPOC/ECSL Workshop*, ESTEC, Noordwijk, The Netherlands, 15 April 1994; Malanczuk, Ten Years of European Telecommunications Law and Policy – A Review of the Past and of Recent Developments, *TSJ* 1 (1994), 27–51.

96 See P. Malanczuk, Satellite Communications and the GATT, *Space Comm.* 9 (1992), 231–9; P. Malanczuk/ H. de Vlaam, International Trade in Telecommunications Services and the Results of the Uruguay Round of GATT, *TSJ* 3 (1996), 269–90.

97 Report of the Legal Subcommittee on the Work of its Thirty-Third Session (21 March–5 April 1994), UN Doc A/AC.105/ 573 of 14 April 1994, 17. See I.H.P. Diederiks-Verschoor, , Environmental

Protection in Outer Space, *GYIL* 30 (1987), 144; H.A. Baker, *Space Debris: Legal and Policy Implications*, 1989; P. Malanczuk, Outer Space, *YIEL* 1 (1990), 173–5; 2 (1991), 184–9; 3 (1992), 299–300; 4 (1993), 224–8; 5 (1994), 227–9; 6 (1995), 291–3; Malanczuk, International Law Association (ILA) Continues Work on Draft Instrument to Protect the Environment from Damage Caused by Space Activities, *JSpaceL* 20 (1992), 164–8; *idem*, Review of the Regulatory Regime Governing the Space Environment: The Problem of Space Debris, *ZLW* 45 (1996), 37–62.
98 See the report prepared by the Office for Outer Space Affairs in 1993, UN Doc. A/AC.105/547 and Add. 1. See also Chapter 16 below, 247–53.
99 See P. Malanczuk, Report on the UN/IAF Workshop on 'Organising Space Activities in Developing Countries' (Graz, October 1993), *JSpaceL* 21 (1993), 175–8.
100 See UN Doc. A/AC.105/575 of 9 May 1994.
101 See Chapters 10, 149–50 and 12, 184–91, 193–5 above.
102 B. Cheng, Astronauts, *EPIL* I (1992), 278–81.
103 S. Errin, Law in a Vacuum: The Common Heritage Doctrine in Outer Space Law, *BICLR* 7 (1984), 403–31; D. Wotter, The Peaceful Purpose Standard of the Common Heritage of Mankind Principle in Outer Space Law, *ASILS ILJ* 9 (1985), 117–46; A. Casesse, *International Law in a Divided World*, 1986, Chapter 14; R. Wolfrum, Common Heritage of Mankind, *EPIL* I (1992), 692–5; M.Y.A. Zieck, The Concept of 'Generations' of Human Rights and the Right to Benefit from the Common Heritage of Mankind with Reference to Extraterrestrial Realms, *VRÜ* 25 (1992), 161–98; T. Fitschen, Common Heritage of Mankind, in *Wolfrum UNLPP* I, 149–59.
104 Article 1, *op. cit.*
105 On the negotiations, see Casesse, *op. cit.*, 387–91.
106 Malanczuk (1994), Space Law, *op. cit.*, 171–5; R.St.J. Macdonald, The Common Heritage of Mankind, in *FS Bernhardt*, 153–71.
107 See Chapter 12 above, 174–5.
108 See Chapter 3 above, 42–3.
109 See Chapters 19, 328 and 22, 373 below.
110 See V. Morris/M.-C. Bourloyannis-Vrailas, The Work of the Sixth Committee at the Fiftieth Session of the UN General Assembly, *AJIL* 90 (1996), 491–500, at 500.
111 Article 33.

mankind. Article 11 of the Moon Treaty refers to the common heritage principle more explicitly. Article 4 of the same treaty combines both notions in laying down that the exploration and use of the moon 'shall be the province of all mankind and shall be carried out for the benefit and in the interests of all countries, irrespective of their degree of economic or scientific development'.[105]

The legal content of the common heritage of mankind principle has remained obscure.[106] First of all, it is clear that the alleged legal consequences flowing from the principle are not specific at all, as they are in fact left to the discretion of states. The second objection, however, to the purported customary law nature of the principle is more fundamental. If one looks at its basis in the 1982 Law of the Sea Convention, the opposition of important affected states to the deep seabed mining regime in Part XI of the Convention and their reluctance to sign or ratify the Convention stands in the way of assuming that the principle reflects general customary international law.[107] Many of the provisions in Part XI were clearly an attempt to codify new law in a hitherto unknown area. They are not customary law and, at best, may be of some legal relevance to the states supporting the principle.

Furthermore, the Moon Treaty, which is far weaker in its attempt to implement the principle than the 1982 Law of the Sea Convention, has been accepted by only a few states, none of which is a significant space power. Therefore, it is difficult to see what the basis is for regarding the principle as a part of general customary law. Treaties as such, under treaty law, bind only states which are parties to them by an agreed form of acceptance or ratification. They do not generally create obligations for states not parties to them, certainly not for those absenting states particularly affected by the subject matter. Whether they may in certain provisions reflect existing customary law or later develop into custom, is a different matter. At any rate, even if new customary law emerges, it does not bind states persistently objecting to it.[108]

In sum, the common heritage of mankind principle, as applied to the utilization of resources in areas beyond national jurisdiction, has certainly brought a new and useful dimension into the general development of international law, but in essence it is still a controversial and vague political principle. (In 1996 Malta proposed that the UN General Assembly should consider designating the UN Trusteeship Council[109] as 'trustee of the common heritage of humankind to ensure the necessary coordinated approach to this matter of common concern'.[110]) It has found some form of legal recognition only in a restricted number of treaties and other instruments for a restricted number of states parties to them or supporting them. This is also true for space law, even if one considers the qualification of radio frequencies and satellite positions in the geostationary orbit as 'limited natural resources' which should be distributed equitably, as laid down in the Convention of the International Telecommunication Union,[111] in one way or another, as an expression of that principle.

14   Human rights

International concern for what we nowadays call human rights,[1] in the sense of fundamental and inalienable rights essential to the human being, is nothing new. The early Spanish school of international law (i.e. Vitoria and Suarez) was heavily engaged in the discussion on which rights are to be accorded to every human being under any circumstances, with particular reference to the treatment of the native inhabitants of America by the Spanish colonizers.[2] In state practice, as early as 1815 the United Kingdom tried to persuade states to make treaties for the suppression of the slave trade.[3] During the following century treaties were made to protect individuals against various forms of injustice. A big step forward came with the peace treaties of 1919, which provided guarantees of fair treatment for the inhabitants of mandated territories[4] and for certain national minorities in Eastern and Central Europe, and which set up the International Labour Organization to promote improvements in working conditions throughout the world.[5]

However, until 1945 international action tended to concentrate on remedying particular abuses or on protecting particular minority groups or aliens.[6] In general, the relationship between states and their own nationals was considered to be an internal matter for each state. The Second World War brought about a change, heralded by the 'four freedoms' (freedom of speech and expression, freedom of religion, freedom from economic want, freedom from fear of aggression) listed as the foreign policy goals of the United States in a message to Congress by President Roosevelt in 1941 and which were included in the Atlantic Charter.[7] Following the horrific and systematic abuse of human rights under the rule of National Socialism, it was only after the United Nations Charter was signed in 1945 that an attempt was made to provide more comprehensive protection for all individuals.

The concept of human rights

The concept of human (or fundamental) rights is certainly a dynamic one and has been subject to change and expansion, as can be seen from the constitutional history of Western states. But it is important to retain the essence of the concept, which is that every individual has certain inalienable and legally enforceable rights protecting him or her against state interference and the abuse of power by governments. These so-called civil rights and fundamental freedoms are, for example, the right to a fair trial, freedom of religion or freedom of speech.

Unfortunately, the discussion on human rights has become confusing

1 Harris CMIL, 600–728; Restatement (Third), Vol. 2, 152–83; I. Brownlie (ed.), Basic Documents on Human Rights, 3rd edn, 1992. See further T. Meron (ed.), Human Rights in International Law: Legal and Policy Issues, 2 vols 1984; B.G. Ramcharan, The Concept and Present Status of the International Protection of Human Rights Forty Years After the Universal Declaration, 1989; A. Cassese, Human Rights in a Changing World, 1990; L. Henkin, The Age of Rights, 1990; R.B. Lillich, International Human Rights: Problems of Law, Policy and Practice, 2nd edn 1991; R. Blackburn/J. Taylor (eds), Human Rights for the 1990s, 1991; M.T. Kamminga, Inter-State Accountability for Violations of Human Rights, 1992; H. Hannum, Guide to International Human Rights Practice, 2nd edn 1992; R.P. Claude/B.H. Weston (eds), Human Rights in the World Community, 1992; P. Alston (ed.), The United Nations and Human Rights. A Critical Appraisal, 1992; F. Ermarcora/ M. Nowak/H. Tretter, International Human Rights, 1993; D.P. Forsythe, Human Rights and Peace – International and National Dimensions, 1993; C. Muzaffar, Human Rights and the New World Order, 1993; S. Davidson, Human Rights, 1993; R. Provost, Reciprocity in Human Rights and Humanitarian Law, BYIL 65 (1994), 383 et seq.; J. Henkin/J.L. Hargrove (eds), Human Rights: An Agenda for the Next Century, 1994; L. Henkin, Human Rights, EPIL II (1995), 886–93; S.P. Marks, Human Rights, Activities of Universal Organizations, ibid., 893– 902; B. Simma, Human Rights, in C. Tomuschat (ed.), The United Nations at Age Fifty, 1995, 263–80; The United Nations and Human Rights, 1948–1994 (UN Blue Book Series), 1995; M.C. Bassiouni, The Protection of Human Rights in the Administration of Justice, 1995; H. Hannum/R.B. Lillich, International Human Rights: Problems of Law, Policy and Process, 3rd edn

1995; M. O'Flaherty, *Human Rights and the UN: Practice Before the Treaty Bodies*, 1996. H. Steiner/P. Alston, *International Human Rights in Context. Law, Politics, Morals*, 1996. On international humanitarian law see, Chapter 20 below, 342–63.

2 See Chapter 2 above, 15–16.

3 See Chapter 2 above, 21.

4 See Chapter 19 below, 327–8.

5 See Chapter 2 above, 24.

6 See Chapter 2 above, 24 and Chapter 17 below, 260–9.

7 See Chapter 2 above, 26–7.

8 See Chapter 19 below, 326–41.

9 See Chapter 13 above, 207–8.

10 See Chapter 15 below, 239–40.

11 See Chapter 6 above, 105–8 and Chapter 19 below, 338–40.

12 See Chapter 16 below, 241–53.

13 See R. Bernhardt, The International Enforcement of Human Rights, General Report, in R. Bernhardt/J.A. Jolowicz (eds), *International Enforcement of Human Rights*, 1987, 143–58, at 145 with reference to K.-J. Partsch.

14 See Chapter 1 above, 3–5 and Chapter 18 below, 273–305.

15 See L. Kühnhardt *Die Universalität der Menschenrechte*, 1987; P.H. Koojmans, *Human Rights, Universal Values*, 1993; C. Muzaffar, *Human Rights and the New World Order*, 1993; G.J.H.v. Hoof, Human Rights in a Multi-Cultural World: The Need for Continued Dialogue, in R.St.J. Macdonald (ed.), *Essays in Honour of Wang Tieya*, 1994, 877–91; A.E. Mayer, Universal Versus Islamic Human Rights: A Clash of Cultures or a Clash with a Construct, *Mich. JIL* 15 (1994), 307–404; A.A. An-Na'im, *Human Rights in Cross-Cultural Perspectives. A Quest for Consensus*, 1995. On cultural diversity see also Chapter 2 above, 31–2.

by the new habit of speaking of different 'generations' of human rights. The distinction between civil rights in the sense of individual freedoms from state interference ('first generation'), on the one hand, and social rights in the sense of rights to claim welfare benefits from the state, such as the right to work or the right to education ('second generation'), on the other hand, is now a traditional one. But, as we shall see, these are two rather different kinds of rights. In recent years, a 'third generation' of human rights has been proposed which, according to the advocates of the notion, should comprise, for example, the right to peace, the right to self-determination,[8] the common heritage of mankind principle,[9] the right to development,[10] minority rights[11] and the right to a clean environment.[12]

It is submitted that the concept of successive 'generations' of human rights replacing each other is unsound because it, in effect, abolishes the concept of human rights as basic rights of the individual human being. Moreover, with regard to the so-called third generation of human rights it is entirely unclear who is supposed to be the subject and who is the addressee of a right to peace, a right to a clean environment, etc. It makes no sense to combine these issues, important as they undoubtedly are, with a discussion on human rights. The real question is only whether individual rights are, or should be, complemented by other rights or values, and be seen in connection with the obligations of the individual towards society (e.g. military service or the duty to pay taxes).[13]

This becomes clear when one considers the problems of implementation. National courts and international decision-making bodies can only effectively protect civil rights as freedoms from state interference. An investigation can take place whether or not state organs have abused a certain right in a given case and the individual concerned is entitled to a remedy or to compensation. In the case of social and economic rights, binding decisions in individual cases are hardly available because the enforcement of this kind of right, as a rule, requires the allocation of finances and resources and policy decisions by legislative and executive bodies. It is no accident, therefore, that both on the universal as well as on the regional level there are different treaties with different enforcement mechanisms for civil rights, on the one hand, and for social rights, on the other. In the case of the alleged 'third generation' rights, there are no special enforcement procedures available at all, apart from the usual mechanisms in inter-state relations.[14]

The aforementioned confusion is part of the problem of finding a consensus on defining human rights on the universal level.[15] The Western tradition, following Western countries' own constitutional models, as they have developed since the Age of Enlightenment, emphasizes civil and political rights as liberal fundamental rights and freedoms in the sense of negative rights directed against the state and the abuse of power. The socialist concept of human rights, on the other hand, is based upon the proposition that rights have to be guaranteed by the state and emphasis is placed not upon individual freedom, but on collective aspects and social and economic rights. Developing countries tend to focus upon their problems of poverty and economic development and argue that it is more important for a human being to have enough to eat than to enjoy the freedom of speech. Islamic countries have their own views on the meaning of the freedom of religion and the rights of women. The universality of Western human rights values, allegedly associated with excessive individualism and decadence, has been most vigorously challenged recently in certain parts of Asia.[16]

It is obvious that the cultural, economic and political diversity of the international community leads to difficulties in finding a true global consensus on the meaning of human rights in many areas. Is there any common philosophy behind the common texts adopted at the universal level by Christians, Muslims, Marxists, etc.? Some think that such questions lead to a dangerous cultural relativism in the field of human rights. But it appears that the common denominator on the universal level at the present stage of the (comparatively still recent) development of international human rights law is only a very general one, namely that the individual deserves to be protected and that the international community should contribute to this protection. In addition, in spite of commendable and abstract verbal commitments, in practice, many states still regard the treatment of their own nationals as an internal matter and reject foreign reaction to alleged human rights violations, at least if it reaches a certain level of intensity, as an unjustified form of intervention.[17] The principle of state sovereignty[18] is in a continuing state of tension with the goal of the effective international protection of human rights. This is different on the regional level where human rights conventions are based on a more homogeneous democratic tradition and understanding of basic values (such as the rule of law) in the member states, such as is the case in Europe.

The development of human rights on the international level is one of the most startling innovations in modern international law, because it has the potential to unleash explosive forces challenging the basic tenet of the system, the principle of state sovereignty. However, a closer look at the now considerable body of international rules and documents concerning the protection of human rights reveals that there is still the difficulty of deciding whether individuals derive rights from international law, or whether they merely derive benefits.[19] Indeed, there is an even greater problem of classification in this context, since many of the commitments undertaken by states are expressed in such vague and idealistic language that it is uncertain whether they enunciate legal obligations at all, as distinct from merely moral aspirations.

The protection of the civil rights of the individual against state interference still remains an important task today and it is in this area where international law and the development of an enforcement machinery has made most progress. It is upon these rights which the following will concentrate. This is not to deny that in many parts of the world social and economic rights have the same or even greater importance for the individual than the rights of liberty.[20]

Human rights on the universal level

The United Nations Charter

The goals of the United Nations listed in Article 1 of the UN Charter include the promotion and encouragement of respect for human rights and

16 D.A. Bell, The East Asian Challenge to Human Rights: Reflections on an East West Dialogue, *HRQ* 18 (1996), 641–67.
17 T. Oppermann, Intervention, *EPIL* II (1995), 1436–9.
18 See Chapter 2 above, 17–18.
19 See Chapter 6 above, 91–2, 100–4.
20 See for example, I. Brownlie, *The Human Right to Food*, 1987; J. Delbrück, The Right to Education as an International Human Right, *GYIL* 35 (1992), 92.

21 Article 1, UN Charter, text in *Brownlie BDIL*, 1. See also Chapter 21 below, 368.
22 Article 55. See K.J. Partsch, Article 55(c), in *Simma CUNAC*, 776–93.
23 Article 56. See R. Wolfrum, Article 56, *ibid.*, 793–5.
24 *Namibia Case* (1971), *ICJ Rep.* 1971, 16–345, at 57, para. 131. See J. Delbrück, Apartheid, *EPIL* I (1992), 192–6. See also text below, 214, 220 and Chapters 18, 284 and 19, 328–9 below.
25 See Articles 13(1), 73 and 76.
26 See Chapter 21 below, 368–9.
27 UN GA Res. 217 A(III), UN Doc. A/810, at 71; text reprinted in *Brownlie BDIL*, 255. See N. Robinson, *The Universal Declaration of Human Rights*, 1958; A. Verdoodt, *Naissance et signification de la Déclaration Universelle des Droits de l'Homme*, 1964; A. Eide (ed.), *The Universal Declaration of Human Rights: A Commentary*, 1992; A. Eide *et al.* (eds), *The Universal Declaration of Human Rights*, 1992; J.C. Salcedo, Human Rights, Universal Declaration (1948), *EPIL* II (1995), 922–6; K.-J. Partsch, Human Rights in General, in *Wolfrum UNLPP I*, 603–11.

fundamental freedoms for all without distinction as to race, sex, language or religion.[21] Article 55 of the United Nations Charter states that 'the United Nations shall promote . . . universal respect for, and observance of, human rights and fundamental freedoms for all without distinction as to race, sex, language, or religion'.[22] In Article 56, '[a]ll Members pledge themselves to take joint and separate action in cooperation with the Organization for the achievement of the purposes set forth in Article 55.'[23] The use of the word 'pledge' ('s'engagent' in the French text) implies a legal obligation, but the obligation is probably not to observe human rights *now* (the rights are not defined or listed in any case), but to work towards their fulfilment in the *future*; the vagueness of the language probably leaves a wide discretion to states about the speed and means of carrying out their obligations, and it is notorious that in many countries no perceptible progress, and in others little visible progress, has been made towards the realization of human rights.

On the other hand, a state which deliberately moved backwards as far as human rights are concerned would probably be regarded as having broken Article 56; certainly this was the attitude of most members of the United Nations towards the South African policy of apartheid. In its Advisory Opinion in the *Namibia* case, the ICJ held:

> To establish . . . and to enforce, distinctions, exclusions, restrictions and limitations exclusively based on grounds of race, colour, descent or national or ethnic origin which constitute a denial of fundamental human rights is a flagrant violation of the purposes and principles of the Charter.[24]

Whatever legal obligations may or may not be imposed by Articles 55 and 56 of the Charter, it is clear that these provisions confer no international rights on individuals, but only benefits. In countries, such as the United States, where the ratification of the Charter has the effect of transforming it into municipal law, courts have generally held that Articles 55 and 56 are too imprecise to confer any rights on individuals.

There are other provisions in the Charter which mention human rights;[25] but all of them are weak and there is no enforcement mechanism laid down. There is also Article 2(7) stating that nothing in the Charter shall authorize the UN to intervene in matters which are essentially within the domestic jurisdiction of any state.[26] But, as we shall see, this provision was later interpreted as not preventing UN bodies from addressing human rights violations in member states.

The Universal Declaration of Human Rights

The Universal Declaration of Human Rights is a resolution which was passed by the UN General Assembly on 10 December 1948, by forty-eight votes to nil, with eight abstentions (the communist countries, plus Saudi Arabia and South Africa).[27] Its provisions fall into two main categories.

First, there are provisions enunciating what have subsequently come to be known as civil and political rights. They prohibit slavery, inhuman treatment, arbitrary arrest and arbitrary interference with privacy, together with discrimination on grounds of race, colour, sex, language, religion, political or other opinion, national or social origin, property, birth, or other status. They also proclaim the right to a fair trial, freedom of movement and residence, the right to seek political asylum, the right to possess and change nationality, the right to marry, the right to own property, freedom of belief and worship, freedom of opinion and expression, freedom of peaceful assembly and association, free elections and equal opportunities for access to public positions.

The second group of provisions is concerned with what have subsequently come to be known as economic, social and cultural rights: the right to social security, to full employment and fair conditions of work, to an adequate standard of living, to education and to participation in the cultural life of the community.

After the preamble, the opening words of the resolution are as follows:

The General Assembly Proclaims this Universal Declaration of Human Rights as a common standard of achievement [*l'ideal commun a atteindre*] for all peoples and all nations, to the end that every individual and every organ of society, keeping this Declaration constantly in mind, shall strive by teaching and education to promote respect for these rights and freedoms and by progressive measures, national and international, to secure their universal and effective recognition and observance.

Many laymen imagine that states are under a legal obligation to respect the rights listed in the Declaration. But most of the states which voted in favour of the Universal Declaration regarded it as a statement of a relatively distant ideal, which involved little or nothing in the way of legal obligations. The Declaration merely recommends states to keep it in mind and to 'strive . . . by progressive [not immediate] measures . . . to secure . . . universal and effective recognition and observance' of its provisions. At most, the Declaration is simply a list of the human rights which member states 'pledge' themselves to 'promote' under Articles 55 and 56 of the Charter; but, as we have seen, the Charter leaves a wide discretion to states concerning the speed and means of fulfilling their pledge.

It is possible, however, that the Universal Declaration of Human Rights, at least in some parts (like the prohibition of torture),[28] may subsequently have become binding as a new rule of customary international law. For instance, the United Nations Conference on Human Rights at Teheran in 1968 passed a resolution proclaiming, *inter alia*, that 'the Universal Declaration of Human Rights . . . constitutes an obligation for the members of the international community'.[29]

United Nations bodies active in the field of human rights

Under Article 13 of the Charter the UN General Assembly can initiate studies and make recommendations on human rights issues.[30] An important body in this connection is the Economic and Social Council (ECOSOC), which consists of fifty-four members elected by the General Assembly.[31] Under Article 62 of the Charter ECOSOC can make recommendations on human rights, draft conventions, and convene international human rights conferences. It hears reports from a wide range of bodies.

In 1946 the United Nations set up a Commission on Human Rights

28 See Chapter 3 above, 58 and text below, 216.

29 Text in *AJIL* 63 (1969), 674. See also Filartiga *v.* Peña-Irala, *ILM* 19 (1980), 966, 971 and 973, discussed in Chapter 7 above, 114.

30 See C.-A. Fleischhauer, Article 13, in *Simma CUNAC*, 265–79.

31 See A. Eide/T. Opsahl (eds), *The Human Right Organs of the United Nations*, 1985; R. Lagoni, Article 62, in *Simma CUNAC*, 843; K.J. Partsch, Article 55(c), *ibid.*, 776–93; Partsch, Article 68, *ibid.*, 888–92. On ECOSOC see Chapter 21 below, 382–3.

32 1967 ECOSOC Res. 1235 (XLII).

33 1971 ECOSOC Res. 1503 (XXVIII).

34 M. Nowak, Country-Oriented Human Rights Protection by the UN Commission on Human Rights and its Sub-Commission, *NYIL* 22 (1991), 91–162; On the recent activity of the Commission, see J.R. Crook, The Fiftieth Session of the UN Commission on Human Rights, *AJIL* 88 (1994), 806–21; on the 1995 Session, see *AJIL* 90 (1996), 126–38.

35 See Chapter 21 below, 378.

36 See Vienna Declaration and Programme of Action of 25 June 1993, UN Doc. A/CONF. 157/23; *ILM* 32 (1993), 1661.

37 UN GA Res. 48/141 of 20 December 1993, *ILM* 33 (1994), 303. See A. Clapham, Creating the High Commissioner for Human Rights: The Outside Story, *EJIL* 5 (1994), 556–68.

(as a subsidiary body of ECOSOC, composed now of forty-three representatives of member states on the basis of equitable geographical distribution), to carry out research and to draft treaties implementing Articles 55 and 56 of the Charter. In the first twenty years of its existence the Commission had no authority to deal with complaints that were sent to the UN Secretary-General. Against the background of the situation in Southern Africa, in 1967 it was empowered by an ECOSOC resolution 'to examine information relevant to gross violations of human rights' and to study 'situations which reveal a consistent pattern of violations of human rights'.[32] This became the basis for public investigations against particular states, either on an *ad hoc* basis (in the case of Iran in 1990) or through a standing working group (in the case of Chile under the military regime).

Furthermore, another ECOSOC Resolution adopted in 1971[33] authorized the Sub-Commission on the Prevention of Discrimination and Protection of Minorities to appoint a working group to deal with individual petitions which appear to reveal a 'consistent pattern of gross violations of human rights'. Since then the Commission has been able to debate such complaints and to make recommendations; but so far the Commission has made little use of these powers, limited though they are. It is also important to note that the procedure is not concerned with individual abuses as such, but with 'situations', although the procedure is applicable to all states and to all rights listed in the 1948 Declaration. The procedure is to a large extent ineffective; the examination takes place in private and ends with a report to the Sub-Commission. The Commission has no enforcement power; it can only make recommendations and has no right to enter territory or to hear witnesses.[34]

The UN further maintains a Human Rights Centre in Geneva; but it only has fifty experts and works to a budget of US$11 million, which is about 0.7 per cent of the UN budget.[35] Following the World Conference on Human Rights held in 1993 in Vienna,[36] the UN General Assembly (by consensus) also created the post of a High Commissioner for Human Rights, an issue which had been controversial for many years.[37] The difficulties of the negotiating process are reflected in the complicated language addressing the responsibilities of the High Commissioner in paragraph 3 of the relevant resolution. The General Assembly decided that the High Commissioner shall combine the following tasks, the objective reconciliation of all of which at the same time is difficult to imagine:

(a)   Function within the framework of the Charter of the United Nations, the Universal Declaration of Human Rights, other international instruments of human rights and international law, including the obligations, within this framework, to respect the sovereignty, territorial integrity and jurisdiction of States to promote the universal respect for and observance of all human rights, in the recognition that, in the framework of the purposes and principles of the Charter, the promotion and protection of all human rights is a legitimate concern of the international community;

(b)   Be guided by the recognition that all human rights – civil, cultural, economic, political and social – are universal, indivisible, interdependent and interrelated and that, while the significance of national and regional particularities and various historical, cultural and religious backgrounds must be borne in mind, it is the duty of States, regardless of their political, economic and cultural systems, to promote and protect all human rights and fundamental freedoms;

(c) Recognize the importance of promoting a balanced and sustainable development for all people and of ensuring realization of the right to development, as established in the Declaration on the Right to Development.[38]

Ambassador Ayala Lasso from Ecuador was appointed as the first High Commissioner in 1994 with the rank of an Under-Secretary-General of the UN. It remains to be seen to what extent the effectiveness of the international protection of human rights can really be improved by the creation of this office, but it is certainly a step in the right direction.[39]

The 1966 Covenants

On 16 December 1966, after twelve years of discussion, the United Nations completed the drafting of two treaties designed to transform the principles of the Universal Declaration of Human Rights into binding, detailed rules of law: the International Covenant on Civil and Political Rights, and the International Covenant on Economic, Social and Cultural Rights.[40] Both Covenants came into force in 1976. As of 31 July 1996, 134 states were parties to the International Covenant on Economic, Social and Cultural Rights and to the International Covenant on Civil and Political Rights.[41]

In many of their articles, the two Covenants closely follow the 1948 Universal Declaration and they also provide for monitoring systems which, however, are rather weak. The Covenant on Civil and Political Rights establishes a Human Rights Committee which is composed of eighteen members elected by the states parties.[42] They are elected as individuals, not as government representatives, which distinguishes this Committee from the UN Human Rights Commission. The only compulsory mechanism under the Covenant is a reporting system (Article 40), requiring states to submit reports on the national human rights situation every five years.[43] These reports are studied and commented upon by the Committee, which may ask for additional information. As an optional procedure (Article 41) states may grant other states the right to bring a complaint against them before the Committee alleging the violation of human rights (accepted by only forty-five states as of July 1996).[44] But both states concerned must have accepted the procedure, and local remedies[45] must first be exhausted. The procedure lacks teeth because it can ultimately only lead to a conciliation attempt and there is no reference to a judicial body which could take a binding decision. Another problem arises from the large number of various kinds of reservations (150 between the 127 states parties as of 1 November 1994) entered by contracting states to their acceptance of the obligations of the Covenant, which tend to undermine its effective implementation.[46]

38 *Ibid.*, at 305. On the right to development, see Chapter 15 below, 239–40.

39 See Z. Kędzia, The United Nations High Commissioner for Human Rights, in *FS Bernhardt*, 435–52.

40 Texts in *Brownlie BDIL*, 262, 270. See E.W. Vierdag, Some Remarks about Special Features of Human Rights Treaties, *NYIL* 25 (1994), 119–42; G.C. Jonathan, Human Rights Covenants, *EPIL* II (1995), 915–22.

41 State of Ratifications of Major Human Rights Conventions as of 31 July 1996, *NQHR* 14 (1996), 360 *et seq.* See also H. Hannum/D.D. Fisher (eds), *United States Ratification of the International Covenants on Human Rights*, 1993; L. Henkin, U.S. Ratification of Human Rights Conventions: The Ghost of Senator Bricker, *AJIL* 89 (1995), 341–9.

42 M.J. Bossuyt, *Guide to the 'Travaux Préparatoires' of the International Covenant on Civil and Political Rights*, 1987; P.R. Ghandi, The Human Rights Committee and Derogation in Public Emergencies, *GYIL* 32 (1989), 321–61; W.A. Schaba, The Omission of the Right to Property in the International Covenants, *Hague YIL* 4 (1991), 135–70; M. Nowak, *UN Covenant on Civil and Political Rights: CCPR Commentary*, 1993; D. McGoldrick, *The Human Rights Committee. Its Role in the Development of the International Covenant on Civil and Political Rights*, 2nd edn 1994. C. Tomuschat, International Covenant on Civil and Political Rights, Human Rights Committee, *EPIL* II (1995), 1115–19.

43 C. Tomuschat, Human Rights, States Reports, in *Wolfrum UNLPP I*, 628–37.

44 K.J. Partsch, Human Rights, Interstate Disputes, *ibid.*, 612–18.

45 See Chapter 17 below, 267–8.

46 See the General Comment No. 24 (52) adopted by the Human Rights Committee under Article 40(4) in 1994, *ILM* 34 (1995), 839. See further L. Lijnzaad, *Reservations to UN Human Rights Treaties: Ratify and Ruin?*, 1994; T. Giegerich, Vorbehalte zu Menschenrechtsabkommen: Zulässigkeit, Gültigkeit und Prüfungskompetenz von Vertragsgremien, *ZaöRV* 55 (1995), 713; J.P. Gardner (ed.), *Human Rights as General Norms and a State's Right to Opt out: Reservations and Objections to Human Rights Conventions*, 1996. See also I. Cameron/F. Horn, Reservations to the European Convention on Human Rights: The Belilos Case, *GYIL* 33 (1990),

69–129; On reservations to treaties in general see Chapter 9 above, 135–6.
47 See C. Tomuschat, Making Individual Communications an Effective Tool for the Protection of Human Rights, in *FS Bernhardt*, 615–34; *idem*, Human Rights and Individual Complaints, in *Wolfrum UNLPP I*, 619–27.
48 G.J. Naldi, United Nations Seeks to Abolish the Death Penalty, *ICLQ* 40 (1991), 948 *et seq.*; W.A. Schabas, *The Abolition of the Death Penalty in International Law*, 1993; C. Schreuer, Capital Punishment and Human Rights, in *FS Bernhardt*, 563–77.
49 See P. Alston, The Committee on Economic, Social and Cultural Rights, in Alston (ed.), 1992, *op. cit.*, 473; A. Eide/ C. Krause/A. Rosas (eds), *Economic, Social and Cultural Rights – A Textbook*, 1994; B. Simma, Die internationale Kontrolle des VN-Paktes über wirtschaftliche, soziale und kulturelle Rechte: neue Entwicklungen, in *FS Bernhardt*, 599–614; M.C.R. Craven, *The International Covenant on Economic, Social, and Cultural Rights – A Perspective on Its Development*, 1995.
50 78 UNTS 277; *ILM* 28 (1989), 754; See L.J. LeBlanc, *The United States and the Genocide Convention*, 1990; G. Andreapoulos, *Genocide. Conceptual and Historical Dimensions*, 1994. On the case brought by Bosnia and Herzegovina before the ICJ against Yugoslavia (Serbia and Montenegro) under the Genocide Convention, see Chapter 18 below, 292.
51 660 UNTS 13; *Brownlie BDIL*, 310.
52 1249 UNTS 13; *ILM* 19 (1980), 33. For the UN General Assembly Resolutions 50/202 and 50/203 approving an amendment to Article 20 of the Convention see *ILM* 35 (1996), 485. For the Declaration and Platform for Action (15 September 1995) of the UN Fourth World Conference on Women (Beijing), see *ILM* 35 (1996), 401. See further Cook (ed.), *Human Rights of Women: National and International Perspectives*, 1994; D.J. Sullivan, Women's Human Rights and the 1993 World Conference on Human Rights, *AJIL* 88 (1994), 152.
53 *ILM* 23 (1984), 1027; amended text in *ILM* 24 (1985), 535. See J. H. Burgers/H. Danelius, *The UN Convention Against Torture: A Handbook on the Convention against Torture and other Cruel, Inhuman or Degrading Treatment or Punishment*, 1988; A. Cassese (ed.), *The International Fight Against Torture*, 1991. On the European regional counterpart of the 1984 Torture Convention see K. Ginther, The

There is also an optional protocol to the Covenant on Civil and Political Rights, which provides for individual petitions; but all that the Human Rights Committee can do is to call upon the state concerned for explanations, and make recommendations.[47] In 1996 only eighty-one states were parties to the optional protocol. About 1,000 complaints a year are received under the optional protocol, only forty to fifty of which are officially registered. Of the about 600 complaints that were filed in the past twenty years, roughly 50 per cent were rejected as inadmissible. A Second Optional Protocol of 1989 aims at the abolition of the death penalty, but in 1996 it was in force for only twenty-nine states.[48]

The Covenant on Economic, Social and Cultural Rights only knows a reporting system. No provision is made for inter-state complaints or individual petitions. The reports from member states were originally examined by a Working Group established by ECOSOC, composed of fifteen members selected from government representatives. Since 1987 there has been a Committee on Economic, Social and Cultural Rights of eighteen independent experts who are responsible to ECOSOC.[49] The Committee prepares 'General Comments' and exchanges general views on particular rights in the Convention. It should be noted that the rights of this Covenant (different from the Covenant on Civil and Political Rights) are formulated not as directly binding obligations, but described in terms of a programme depending on the goodwill and resources of states. Article 2 states that each state party undertakes steps to the maximum of its available resources 'with a view to achieving progressively the full realization of the rights recognized in the present Covenant', which makes the legal obligation rather weak.

Other human rights instruments on the universal level

There are numerous other international human rights treaties that have been adopted under the auspices of the UN since 1948. They include the 1948 Convention on the Prevention and Punishment of Genocide[50] (121 ratifications by 1996), the 1965 International Convention on the Elimination of All Forms of Racial Discrimination[51] (147 ratifications with only twenty-two states recognizing the competence of the Committee under Article 14), the 1979 Convention on the Elimination of All Forms of Discrimination Against Women[52] (153 ratifications), the 1984 Convention Against Torture and Other Cruel, Inhuman or Degrading Treatment or Punishment[53] (ninety-six ratifications). All of these Conventions have entered into force, although the level of participation by states varies. An outstanding example is the 1989 Convention on the Rights of the Child.[54] On 31 July 1996, it had received almost universal ratification by 187 state parties. No other international treaty in history has been ratified so quickly (in only six years) by so many countries.

In addition, there are many other human rights treaties concluded under the umbrella of the International Labour Organization, UNESCO and other specialized agencies of the UN, too numerous to mention here. Furthermore, there are international instruments aiming at the protection of special groups, such as refugees,[55] minorities, indigenous and tribal peoples,[56] and the disabled. A separate category is formed by the Geneva Red Cross Conventions and the Additional Protocols thereto laying down international humanitarian law for armed conflicts. The implementation mechanisms are often different from treaty to treaty, but generally speaking they are not very effective.[57]

To what extent the proliferation of international human rights documents on the global level has led to the emergence of an international customary law of human rights binding upon all states is a matter of debate. A positive view on the issue is taken especially by American authors.[58] But this is not generally accepted[59] and, considering the problems of cultural diversity, universality and the impact of state sovereignty discussed at the beginning, a broad assertion of the customary law nature of many human rights is at least open to serious doubt. There is a widespread consensus, however, on the necessity to cultivate the whole array of international human rights instruments, to improve the coordination of the activities of the manifold institutions and bodies active in the field of international human rights, and to streamline the law-making process to avoid the apparent inconsistencies between the different treaties.[60]

Human rights on the regional level

The European Convention for the Protection of Human Rights and Fundamental Freedoms

Conflicting ideologies and interests, and mutual distrust, make it difficult to reach agreement at the United Nations about human rights. Agreement is easier to reach at the regional level, where states are more likely to trust one another and to have common values and interests. In 1950 the Council of Europe,[61] an international organization in the following years comprising almost all the non-communist states in Europe, drafted the European Convention for the Protection of Human Rights and Fundamental Freedoms, which entered into force on 3 September 1953 (thirty-three ratifications as of 31 July 1996).[62] A number of protocols (that is, supplementary agreements) were added later.[63] After the changes in Eastern Europe a number of former socialist states also joined the Council of Europe and the Convention. On 28 February 1996, Russia was admitted as the thirty-ninth member state of the Council of Europe and also signed the European Human Rights Convention (but not, however, the protocol abolishing the death penalty).[64]

The European Convention, plus the protocols, covers much the same ground as the Universal Declaration of Human Rights; one revealing difference is that Article 1 of the first protocol goes much further than Article 17 of the Universal Declaration in underlining the sanctity of property, which is not mentioned at all in the 1966 Covenant on Civil and Political Rights. Since the Convention and protocols are legally binding on the states parties to them, they are drafted in much more detail than the Universal Declaration – as one would expect in the case of a legal document. Some of the details have the effect of restricting the force of the Convention. In particular, Article 15 provides: 'In time of war or other public emergency threatening the life of the nation any . . . Party may take measures derogating from its obligations under this Convention.'[65]

There is nothing in the European Convention which corresponds to Articles 22–5 of the Universal Declaration, which deal with social security,

European Convention for the Prevention of Torture and Inhuman or Degrading Treatment or Punishment, *EJIL* 2 (1991), 123–31; M. Evans/R. Morgan, The European Convention for the Prevention of Torture: Operational Practice, *ICLQ* 41 (1992), 590 *et seq.*; J. Murdoch, The Work of the Council of Europe's Torture Committee, *EJIL* 5 (1994), 220–48; M. Evans/R. Morgan, The European Torture Committee: Membership Issues, *ibid.*, 249–58.

54 *ILM* 28 (1989), 1448. See S. Detrick (ed.) , *The United Nations Convention on the Rights of the Child – A Guide to the 'Travaux Préparatoires'*, 1992; P. Alston, *The Best Interests of the Child: Reconciling Culture and Human Rights*, 1994; G.v. Bueren, *The International Law on the Rights of the Child*, 1995; L.J. LeBlanc, *The Convention on the Rights of the Child: United Nations Lawmaking on Human Rights*, 1995.

55 See G. Goodwin-Gill, *The Refugee in International Law*, 1983; D.A. Martin (ed.), *The New Asylum Seekers: Refugee Law in the 1980s*, 1988; R. Hofmann, Refugee Law in the African Context, *ZaöRV* 52 (1992), 318–33; G. Loescher, *Beyond Charity: International Cooperation and the Global Refugee Crisis*, 1993; K. Musalo, Irreconcilable Differences? Divorcing Refugee Protections from Human Rights Norms, *Mich. JIL* 15 (1994), 1179–241; United Nations High Commissioner For Refugees, *The State of the World's Refugees – In Search of Solutions*, 1995; P. Weis (ed.), *The Refugee Convention 1951*, 1995; V. Gowlland-Debbas, *The Problem of Refugees in the Light of Contemporary Law Issues*, 1995.

56 See Chapter 6 above, 105–8 and Chapter 19 below, 338–40.

57 See Y. Dinstein, The Implementation of International Human Rights, in *FS Bernhardt*, 331–53.

58 For a purported list of such rights see *Restatement (Third)*, Vol. 2, para. 702. See also Lillich (1991), *op. cit.*, Chapter II; T. Meron, *Human Rights and Humanitarian Law as Customary Law*, 1989; O. Schachter, *International Law in Theory and Practice*, 1991, 335–42.

59 See B. Simma/P. Alston, The Sources of Human Rights Law; Custom, Ius Cogens, and General Principles, *AYIL* 12 (1992), 82, at 98.

60 See T. Meron, *Human Rights Law-Making in the United Nations*, 1986; A.A. Trindade, Co-Existence and Co-ordination of Mechanisms of International Protection of Human

Rights (At Global and Regional Levels), *RdC* 202 (1987-II), 13–435; J.S. Gibson, International Human Rights Law: Progression of Sources, Agencies and Law, *Suffolk TLJ* 4 (1990), 41–60; M.G. Schmidt, Individual Human Rights Complaints Procedures Based on United Nations Treaties and the Need for Reform, *ICLQ* 41 (1992), 645 *et seq.*; R.B. Lillich, Towards the Harmonization of International Human Rights Law, in *FS Bernhardt*, 453–76.

61 A.H. Robertson, Council of Europe, *EPIL* I (1992), 843–50. See also Chapter 6 above, 94.

62 Text in *Brownlie BDIL*, 328. See P. van Dijk/G.J.H. van Hoof, *Theory and Practice of the European Convention on Human Rights*, 2nd edn 1990; V. Berger, *Case Law of the European Court of Human Rights*, Vol. II: 1988–1990, 1992; M. Delman-Marty/C. Chodkiewicz (eds), *The European Convention for the Protection of Human Rights*, 1992; R.St.J. Macdonald/F. Matscher/H. Petzold (eds), *The European System for the Protection of Human Rights*, 1993; R. Beddard, *Human Rights and Europe*, 3rd edn 1993; J.G. Merrills, *The Development of International Law by the European Court of Human Rights*, 2nd edn 1993; A.H. Robertson/J.G. Merrills, *Human Rights in Europe*, 3rd edn 1993; L. Clements, *European Human Rights: Taking a Case under the Convention*, 1994; L. Heffernan (ed.), *Human Rights – A European Perspective*, 1994; J.A. Frowein, European Convention on Human Rights (1950), *EPIL* II (1995), 188–96; D.J. Harris/C. O'Boyle/C. Warbrick, *Law of the European Convention on Human Rights*, 1995; M. Janis/R. Kay/A. Bradley, *European Human Rights Law. Text and Materials*, 1995; I. Cameron/M.K. Eriksson, *An Introduction to the European Convention on Human Rights*, 2nd edn 1995; P. Kempees (ed.), *A Systematic Guide to the Case Law of the European Court of Human Rights 1960–1994*, 1996.

63 Texts in *Brownlie BDIL*, 347.

64 Protocol No. 6, ratified by all other parties. See D.P. Forsythe (ed.), *Human Rights in the New Europe: Problems and Progress*, 1994; A.M. Gross, Reinforcing the New Democracies: The European Convention on Human Rights and the Former Communist Countries – A Study of the Case Law, *EJIL* 7 (1996), 103–11.

65 Subject to certain conditions and expectations, see R. Higgins, Derogations under Human Rights Treaties, *BYIL* 48 (1976–7), 281–320, at 301–7, 319–20; J.M. Fitzpatrick,

full employment, fair conditions of work and adequate standards of living. These are covered in detail by a separate treaty, the European Social Charter, which was opened for signature in 1961 and entered into force in 1965 (twenty ratifications by 1996).[66] The semi-judicial enforcement machinery of the European Convention would be inappropriate for the European Social Charter, which uses a less 'legal' and more 'political' system of enforcement.[67] An attempt to improve the reporting system was made by an Additional Protocol to the European Social Charter adopted in 1988[68] (five ratifications by 1996) and by a Protocol amending the Charter signed in 1991[69] (ten ratifications by 1996). On 9 November 1995, the Council of Europe adopted a further Protocol amending the European Social Charter which provides for a system of 'collective complaints'.[70] This system is similar to that of existing arrangements of the International Labour Organization.[71] International and national organizations of employers and trade unions and other international and national NGOs can submit complaints to an independent committee of experts.

The European Human Rights Convention set up a Commission of Human Rights,[72] composed of individuals elected by the Committee of Ministers of the Council of Europe (the Committee of Ministers is a political body roughly corresponding to the General Assembly in the UN). The Commission hears complaints against state parties to the Convention who are accused of breaking it. Complaints may be made by any other state party to the Convention, although experience has shown that states have little inclination to protect other states' nationals except when their own interests are involved.[73] In addition, under Article 25, states have the option of empowering the Commission to hear complaints brought against them by individuals, groups of individuals or NGOs; all states parties to the Convention have now accepted this right of individual petition,[74] as it is called, although the United Kingdom, for example, did not accept it until 1966, even though it ratified the Convention in 1953.[75] A commitment to accept it has become *de facto* a condition for admission to the Council of Europe. There are, however, a number of obstacles to be overcome before the Commission can hear a complaint, and the obstacles are particularly severe in the case of individual petitions. For instance, if local remedies exist, they must be exhausted before the individual concerned or a state party to the Convention can refer the case to the Commission;[76] individual petitions may also be rejected for other reasons, for example, if they are anonymous or an abuse of the right of petition.

If it is admissible, the Commission investigates the complaint and tries to solve the dispute by conciliation.[77] If conciliation fails, the Commission draws up a report on the merits of the claim, which it sends to the Committee of Ministers. Unless the case is referred to the Court (see below), the Committee of Ministers may, by a two-thirds majority, decide that there has been a breach of the Convention and order the defaulting state to rectify the situation. In extreme cases, the ultimate sanction is expulsion from the organization – a threat which forced Greece to withdraw from the Council of Europe in 1969 (Greece was readmitted to the Council of Europe in 1974, after the restoration of democratic government).

After the case has been heard by the Commission, the Commission or (in certain circumstances) a state party to the Convention may refer the case to the European Court of Human Rights, if the defendant state has accepted the jurisdiction of the Court under Article 46 (which all parties have done).[78] The Court's decision is binding and may be enforced by the Committee of Ministers (Article 54).

The growing number of complaints and an increasing backlog of cases has made a reform of the supervisory machinery of the Convention an urgent matter. The urgency is enhanced by the accession of new states from Eastern Europe and the prospect that by the year 2000 there may well be some forty to forty-five states parties to the Convention. While the number of applications filed with the Commission had risen from 404 in 1981 to 2,037 in 1993, the number of pending cases before the Commission in January 1994 stood at 2,672, almost 1,500 of which had not yet even been looked at. On average it takes more than five years for a case to be finally decided by the Court or by the Committee of Ministers.

On 11 May 1994, the Council of Europe therefore decided to adopt an amending (meaning not optional) Protocol No. 11 to the Convention to restructure the control machinery by creating a new single Court which will replace the former Court and the Commission.[79] The jurisdiction of the Court will cover inter-state complaints as well as individual applications which it may receive from any person, non-governmental organization or group of individuals claiming to be the victim of a violation of the Convention by one of the states parties. Under the new system, applicants will be able to bring their cases directly before the Court without restrictions. It requires ratification by all the parties and will be established one year after the last ratification (as of 31 July 1996 there were 21 ratifications), but the Court has been asked to take preparatory measures concerning its organization, which envisage a restructuring of it on the basis of functions allocated to the plenary Court, a Grand Chamber, Chambers and committees, as early as possible.

Other regional instruments

It is fair to say that the European Convention on Human Rights is the most sophisticated and practically advanced international system of the protection of human rights. There are other regional human rights treaties, which are much less effective than the European Convention, although they partly follow its model. The American Convention on Human Rights adopted by the Organization of American States (OAS) entered into force in 1978 and had twenty-five states parties as of 31 July 1996.[80] The Convention organs have been established and have been making some progress in the promotion of human rights in the Western hemisphere.[81] The 1981 African Charter on Human and Peoples' Rights has been ratified by almost all member states of the Organization of African Unity (OAU).[82] The document signals an important development, but it is not only concerned with the rights of the individual, as its title emphasizes, and the enforcement machinery is rather weak. There are also some developments on the discussion of regional human rights instruments in other parts of the world, for example, in the Arab states and in Asia,[83] but, as yet, they have not attained any major significance.

Human Rights in Crisis: The International System for Protecting Rights During States of Emergency, 1994.

66 On the list of ratifications see ILM 34 (1995), 1714.

67 Text in 529 UNTS 89, ETS No. 35. See D.J. Harris, The European Social Charter, 1984; K. Drzewicki et al. (eds), Social Rights as Human Rights: A European Challenge, 1994; W. Strasser, European Social Charter, EPIL II (1995), 291–4.

68 ILM 27 (1988), 575.

69 ILM 31 (1992), 155. See M. Mohr, The Turin Protocol of 22 October 1991: A Major Contribution to Revitalizing the European Social Charter, EJIL 3 (1992), 363–70.

70 ILM 34 (1995), 1453.

71 See Chapters 2, 24 and 6, 94 above.

72 H.G. Schermers (ed.), The Influence of the European Commission of Human Rights, 1992; C.A. Nørgaard, European Commission of Human Rights, EPIL II (1995), 154–9.

73 G. Nolte/S. Oeter, European Commission and Court of Human Rights, Inter-State Applications, EPIL II (1995), 144–54.

74 See T. Zwart, The Admissibility of Human Rights Petitions: The Case Law of the European Commission of Human Rights and the Human Rights Committee, 1994; I. Cameron, Turkey and Article 25 of the European Convention on Human Rights, ICLQ 37 (1988), 887.

75 On the status of the Convention in the UK see A.J. Cunningham, The European Convention on Human Rights, Customary International Law and the Constitution, ICLQ 43 (1994), 537–67; R.R. Churchill/J.R. Young, Compliance with Judgments of the European Court of Human Rights and Decisions of the Committee of Ministers: The Experience of the United Kingdom, 1975–1987, BYIL 62 (1991), 283–346.

76 See B. Robertson, Exhaustion of Local Remedies in International Human Rights Litigation – The Burden of Proof Reconsidered, ICLQ 39 (1990), 191 et seq. The local remedies rule is discussed in more detail in Chapter 17 below, 267–8.

77 On conciliation, see Chapter 18 below, 278–81.

78 W.J.G. van der Meersch, European Court of Human Rights, EPIL II (1995), 201–7.

79 ILM 33 (1994), 943; text in Brownlie BDIL, 372. See R. Bernhardt, Reform of the Control Machinery under the European Convention on Human

Rights: Protocol No. 11, *AJIL* 89 (1995), 145–54.

80 C.M. Quiroga, *The Battle of Human Rights, Systematic Violations and the Inter-American System*, 1988; C. Grossman, Proposals to Strengthen the Inter-American System of Protection of Human Rights, *GYIL* 32 (1989), 264–79; S. Davidson, *The Inter-American Court of Human Rights*, 1992; C.M. Cerna, The Structure and Functioning of the Inter-American Court of Human Rights, *BYIL* 63 (1992), 135–230; T. Buergenthal, American Convention on Human Rights, *EPIL* I (1992), 131–6; T.J. Farer, Inter-American Commission on Human Rights, *EPIL* II (1995), 1004–7; T. Buergenthal, Inter-American Court of Human Rights, *ibid.*, 1008–11; B. Santoscoy, *La Commission interaméricaine des droits de l'homme et le développement de sa compétence par le système des pétitions individuelles*, 1995.

81 For the advisory opinion of 9 December 1994 by the Inter-American Court of Human Rights on international responsibility for the promulgation and enforcement of laws in violation of the Convention, see *ILM* 34 (1995), 1188.

82 There were fifty ratifications as of 31 July 1996. See M. Hamalengwa/C. Flinterman/E.V.O. Dankwa (eds), *The International Law of Human Rights in Africa – Basic Documents and Annotated Bibliography*, 1988; K. Mbaye, *Les Droits de l'homme en Afrique*, 1992; R. Coheb/G. Hyden/W.P. Nagan (eds), *Human Rights and Governance in Africa*, 1993; F. Ouguergouz, *La Charte africaine des droits de l'homme et des peuplesé*, 1993; F. Ouguergouz, *La Chartre Africaine des droits de l'homme et des peuples*, 1993; W. Benedek, *Durchsetzung von Rechten des Menschen und der Völker in Afrika auf regionaler und nationaler Ebene*, *ZaöRV* 54 (1994), 150; U.O. Umozurike, Six Years of the African Commission on Human and Peoples' Rights, in *FS Bernhardt*, 635–45; E.G. Bello, Human Rights, African Developments, *EPIL* II (1995), 902–10.

83 R. Daoudi, Human Rights Commission of the Arab States, *EPIL* II (1995), 913–15.

84 See Chapter 6 above, 34.

85 E. Klein (ed.), *The Institution of a Commissioner for Human Rights and Minorities and the Prevention of Human Rights Violations*, 1994.

86 Text of the Charter of Paris in *ILM* 30 (1991), 190; the 1992 Helsinki Summit Documents are in *ILM* 31 (1992),

Finally, one should mention the developments on the promotion of human rights within the framework of the Conference on Security and Co-operation in Europe (CSCE, now the OSCE),[84] which, starting from the 1975 Helsinki Final Act and the 1989 Vienna Follow-up Meeting, culminated in the 1990 Charter of Paris for a New Europe and the 1992 Helsinki Documents which established a High Commissioner on National Minorities[85] and laid down provisions for strengthening the Office for Democratic Institutions and Human Rights that has been set up in Warsaw with regard to the process of transition in Eastern Europe.[86]

Human rights as a matter of international concern

It is true that, on the universal level, the international protection of human rights still leaves much to be desired and that global consensus on the content and implementation of those rights often seems difficult to achieve.[87] It is also true that the Charter, as shown by the *travaux prépara-toires*, originally did not attach as much significance to the promotion and protection of human rights as to the maintenance of international peace and security.[88] But today there is no doubt, in view of the evolution of the practice of the United Nations, that at least serious human rights abuses may be taken up by various organs of the United Nations as a matter of international concern. Severe human rights violations no longer belong to the 'domain reservé' of states, irrespective of Article 2(7) of the UN Charter, and may be taken up not only within the United Nations, but also in various other multilateral or bilateral relations between states.

Thus, the investigation, discussion and condemnation ('droit de regard') of human rights violations in a state, has become compatible with the sovereignty of that state, although this has been disputed, in the past particularly by the former socialist states, while Western critics have diagnosed 'double standards' employed at times by UN bodies when dealing with allegations of human rights violations.[89] This development has succeeded, independent of whether international peace and security are affected, because of the moral, political, and legal significance attributed to the idea of human rights, the Universal Declaration of Human Rights of 1948 and the subsequent international and regional human rights treaties. It led to the recognition of, in the words of the International Court of Justice in the *Barcelona Traction* case in 1970, certain 'basic rights of the human person',[90] such as protection from slavery, racial discrimination, or genocide as obligations *erga omnes*. Furthermore, the International Law Commission of the United Nations classified in Article 19 of the draft Articles on State Responsibility, 'a serious breach on a widespread scale of an international obligation of essential importance for safeguarding the human being, such as those prohibiting slavery, genocide and apartheid' as an 'international crime'.[91] Such fundamental human rights, which perhaps also include protection from torture,[92] may even be *ius cogens*.[93] The jurisprudence of the International Court of Justice shows that the Court has clearly accepted that the obligation to respect fundamental human rights is an obligation of general international law. This, however, does not necessarily mean customary international law, but could also be interpreted as a reference to general principles of international law.[94] Moreover, questions remain open as to the content of those 'basic' or 'fundamental' human rights and their distinction from other human rights.

The right of UN bodies and states to 'take up' human rights violations, if this is meant in the sense of a 'droit de regard' and a right to criticize, however, must be distinguished from the question of which other remedies may be resorted to under customary international law by third states in response to human rights violations. The problem is that international human rights treaties have their own specific implementation mechanisms, and there are also often different treaty obligations on the part of the parties due to either reservations entered to the treaty or the signing of an additional protocol. This leads directly to the question whether they are 'self-contained regimes'[95] which may exclude the right of states parties to rely on remedies of general international law, for example, to adopt peaceful countermeasures (trade measures or other sanctions) to protect and implement fundamental human rights in another state as obligations *erga omnes* outside the specific procedures the treaty provides for.[96] This question is unclear and has not yet been decided by the International Court of Justice. Nor has it been answered in a definite sense by the International Law Commission.[97] In the end the answer depends on the interpretation of the relevant human rights treaties and their procedures.

Be that as it may, it is another matter to discuss the legality of the use of armed force or other compelling coercion by third states as a response to severe human rights violations in another state. This so-called right of humanitarian intervention (which must be distinguished from the protection of a state's own nationals who are in danger abroad)[98] has been abused in the past by strong states to pursue other political, economic or military objectives. The issue is controversial, but the better view is that a unilateral right to use force to intervene for humanitarian reasons in another state is illegal in view of the prohibition on the use of force in the UN Charter.[99] In *Nicaragua v. USA*, the International Court of Justice said that 'the use of force could not be the appropriate method to . . . ensure . . . respect' for human rights.[100] Such intervention requires the authorization by the UN Security Council as, for example, in the case of Somalia in 1992.[101]

99 See P. Malanczuk, *Humanitarian Intervention and the Legitimacy of the Use of Force*, 1993 and Chapter 19 below, 309–11. But see also F.R.Teson, *Humanitarian Intervention: An Inquiry into Law and Morality*, 1988; N.S. Rodley, Human Rights and Humanitarian Intervention: The Case Law of the World Court, *ICLQ* 38 (1989), 321–33; N.S. Rodley (ed.), *To Loose the Bands of Wickedness: International Intervention in Defence of Human Rights*, 1992; R.B. Lillich, Humanitarian Intervention Through the United Nations: Towards the Development of Criteria, *ZaöRV* 53 (1993), 557–75; N. Chandrahasan, Use of Force to Ensure Humanitarian Relief – A South Asian Precedent Examined, *ICLQ* 42 (1993), 664 *et seq.*; D. Schweigmann, Humanitarian Intervention under International Law: The Strife for Humanity, *LJIL* 6 (1993), 91–110; M. Heiberg (ed.), *Subduing Sovereignty: Sovereignty and the Right to Intervene*, 1994; Y.K. Tyagi, The Concept of Humanitarian Intervention Revisited, *Mich. JIL* 16 (1995), 883–910; U. Beyerlin, Humanitarian Intervention, *EPIL* II (1995), 926–33; G.J. Tanja, Humanitarian Intervention and Humanitarian Assistance, in *Law in Humanitarian Crises*, Vol. II: Office for Official Publications of the European Communities, 1995, 67–96. See further Chapter 2 above, 19–20 and Chapter 22 below, 309–407.
100 *ICJ Rep.* 1986, 14, 135.
101 See Chapter 22 below, 402–5.

1385; on the 1994 Budapest Summit Declaration of the OSCE see *ILM* 34 (1994), 764. See A. Bloed/P.v. Dijk, *The Human Dimension of the Helsinki Process*, 1991. W. Korey, *The Promises We Keep: Human Rights, the Helsinki Process and American Foreign Policy*, 1993. See also Chapter 6 above, 94.
87 See C. Tomuschat, Human Rights in a World-Wide Framework – Some Current Issues, *ZaöRV* 45 (1985), 547.
88 See J. Delbrück, A Fresh Look at Humanitarian Intervention Under the Authority of the United Nations, *Indiana LJ* 67 (1992), 887, 892.
89 See T.M. Franck, Of Gnats and Camels: Is There a Double Standard at the United Nations?, *AJIL* 78 (1984), 811, at 819 *et seq.*; Schachter, *op. cit.*, 345–8.
90 *Belgium v. Spain* (Second Phase), *ICJ Rep.* 1970, 3, paras. 33–4. On this case see Chapter 3 above, 59. See also S.M. Schwebel, The Treatment of Human Rights

and of Aliens in the International Court of Justice, in V. Lowe/M. Fitzmaurice (eds), *Fifty Years of the International Court of Justice*, 1996, 327–50.
91 See Chapter 3 above, 59–60.
92 R. Kühner, Torture, *EPIL* 8 (1985), 510–13.
93 See Chapter 3 above, 57–8.
94 See Simma/Alston, *op. cit.*, at 105–6.
95 See B. Simma, Self-Contained Regimes, *NYIL* 16 (1985), 12, discussing the view of W. Riphagen (the former Special Rapporteur of the ILC on State Responsibility).
96 See Chapter 3 above, 58–60 and Chapter 17 below, 271–2.
97 For strong reservations on the concept of 'self-contained regimes', see G. Arangio-Ruiz, Fourth Report on State Responsibility, UN Doc. A/CN.4/444/Add.2, 1 June 1992.
98 See Chapter 19 below, 315–16.

15 Economy

1 *Restatement (Third)*, Vol. 2, part VIII: Selected Law of International Economic Relations, 261–337; J.H. Jackson/W.J. Davey, *International Economic Relations*, 2nd edn 1989; E.-U. Petersmann, *Constitutional Functions and Constitutional Problems of International Economic Law*, 1991; I. Seidl-Hohenveldern, *International Economic Law*, 2nd edn 1992; H. Fox, *International Economic Law and Developing Countries. An Introduction*, 1992; M. Hilf/E.-U. Petersmann (eds), *National Constitutions and International Economic Law*, 1993; J.H. Jackson/ W.J. Davey/A.O. Sykes, Jr., *Legal Problems of International Economic Relations: Cases, Materials and Text*, 3rd edn 1995; J.H. Jackson, Economic Law, International, *EPIL* II (1995), 20–32; E.-U. Petersmann, International Economic Order, *ibid.*, 1129–37; For a collection of documents see S. Zamora/ R. Brand (eds), *Basic Documents of International Economic Law*, 2 vols, 1990; P. Kunig/N. Lau/W. Meng, *International Economic Law*, 2nd edn 1993.

2 See, for example, G. Schwarzenberger, The Province and Standards of International Economic Law, I, *ILQ* 2 (1948), 402–20.

3 See also M.W. Janis, *An Introduction to International Law*, 2nd edn 1993, 273.

4 For an integrated approach, see M. Herdegen, *Internationales Wirtschaftsrecht*, 2nd edn 1995, 3.

5 D. Carreau/P. Juillard/T. Flory, *Droit international économique*, 2nd edn 1980, 11.

6 *Restatement (Third)*, Vol. 2, 261.

7 See R.W. Bentham, The Law of Development: International Contracts, *GYIL* 32 (1989), 418; F.V. Garcia-Amador, *The Emerging International Law of Development: A New Dimension of International Economic Law*, 1990; A. Carty (ed.), *Law and Development*. Vol. 2: *Legal Cultures*, 1992; P. Ebow Bondzi-Simpson (ed.), *The Law and*

The law governing international economic relations is one of the most important areas in which international legal rules and principles and international institutions operate in practice. This reflects the remarkable growth of the economic interdependence of the world since the end of the Second World War and it is challenging traditional perceptions of international law.[1] The concept of 'international economic law' which has come into use over several decades[2] covers a vast terrain which is far beyond the scope of this book. But to leave it aside completely would indeed convey a rather misleading impression of the nature of modern international law as it stands today.[3]

It is still a matter of discussion among scholars what the term 'international economic law' exactly covers, the main problem being that the close interconnection with norms of the municipal law of states complicates the study of the area immensely.[4] A restrained approach suggests concentrating on the international regulation of the establishment by foreign business of various factors of production (persons and capital) on the territory of other states, on the one hand, and of international transactions concerning goods, services and capital on the other.[5] The *Restatement (Third)* takes the following view:

> The law of international economic relations in its broadest sense includes all the international law and international agreements governing economic transactions that cross state boundaries or that otherwise have implications for more than one state, such as those involving the movement of goods, funds, persons, intangibles, technology, vessels or aircraft.[6]

The subject thus includes as sub-topics the law of establishment, the law of foreign investment, the law of economic relations, the law of economic institutions, and the law of regional economic integration. But one could also include many other questions, such as the international law of economic development[7]or economic sanctions.[8] As this book is concerned with an introduction to public international law,[9] this chapter selects only some very basic features of international economic law. Other legal aspects of international economic relations, such as the problem of the extraterritorial application of national economic regulations,[10] state immunity,[11] the role of transnational enterprises,[12] air transport,[13] telecommunications,[14] the protection of the environment[15] and diplomatic protection[16] are addressed in a different context in other chapters. The following also leaves aside international commercial law which deals with the relationship between merchants and other private parties in their international business transactions and with international commercial arbitration.[17]

International economic law is to a large extent based upon reciprocal international (bilateral and multilateral) treaties reflecting the commercial principle *quid pro quo*. Customary international law in this area is insignificant. Under customary law states have always been regarded as free to regulate their economic and monetary affairs internally and externally as they see fit.[18] Some customary law limits of this freedom in the economic intercourse of states follow from the general principles of state sovereignty and state responsibility (e.g. concerning the treatment of aliens and their property).[19] Yet the principles of the freedom of commerce, the most-favoured nation treatment[20] or the principle of the convertibility of currencies are not guaranteed by customary law.

The Bretton Woods system and international economic organizations

Towards the end of the nineteenth century the international trade system had become based primarily upon liberal national legislation (e.g. on the gold standard and on the convertibility of national currencies) and on bilateral trade agreements and so-called 'FCN Treaties' on friendship, commerce and navigation.[21] The system collapsed with the First World War, which was followed by protectionism and currency instability in the inter-war period. The Atlantic Charter of 1941 envisaged the establishment of a liberal international economic order, an idea mainly supported by the United States and the United Kingdom, to increase international economic transactions on the basis of equal market access conditions.

The modern global system of international economic regulation between states rests upon the multilateral system established by the Bretton Woods Conference in 1944.[22] The two main objectives of the Conference were, first, to advance the reduction of tariffs and other barriers to international trade, and, second, to create a global economic framework to minimize the economic conflicts among nations which, at least in part, were held to have been responsible for the outbreak of the Second World War. The Conference led to the creation of the three basic international economic institutions regulating money and trade: the International Monetary Fund (IMF), the International Bank for Reconstruction and Development (IBRD), also known as the 'World Bank', and later the General Agreement on Tariffs and Trade (GATT), which will be dealt with in more detail below.

The underlying philosophy of the system is the theory of comparative advantage, which had been developed by the British economists David Ricardo and John Stuart Mill by applying the market theory of Adam Smith to international transactions. It assumes that liberalized foreign trade and the corresponding international division of labour creates benefits for all participating national economies. In a nutshell, the international economic order envisaged in the Bretton Woods system views market access and the reduction of barriers to international trade and monetary transactions as the main instruments to promote a high level of

Economic Development in the Third World, 1992; S.K. Chatterjee, International Law of Development, *EPIL* II (1995), 1247–51; R. Pritchard (ed.), *Economic Development, Foreign Investment and the Law*, 1996. For the multilateral agreement establishing the International Development Law Institute see *ILM* 28 (1989), 870. See also text below, 00–00.

8 See J. Combacau, Sanctions, *EPIL* 9 (1986), 337–41; M.P. Malloy, *Economic Sanctions and US Trade*, 1990; N. Schrijver, The Meaning and Operation of Sanctions and Other Measures Short of the Use of Force, *Ga. JICL* 22 (1992), 41–53; J.A. Frowein, Article 41, in *Simma CUNAC*, 621–8.

9 See Chapter 1 above, 7–8.

10 See Chapter 7 above, 116–17.

11 See Chapter 8 above, 118–23.

12 See Chapter 6 above, 102–3.

13 See Chapter 13 above, 200–1.

14 See Chapter 13 above, 202–3.

15 See Chapter 16 below, 241–53.

16 See Chapter 17 below, 256–63.

17 See B.M. Cremades, Commercial Arbitration, *EPIL* I (1992), 674–7.

18 E.-U. Petersmann, Rights and Duties of States and Rights and Duties of Their Citizens, in *FS Bernhardt*, 1087 at 1094. See also S. Zamora, Is There Customary International Economic Law?, *GYIL* 32 (1989), 9.

19 See text below, 235–9.

20 See text below, 229.

21 See G. Herrmann, Commercial Treaties, *EPIL* I (1992), 677–83; D. Blumenwitz, Treaties of Friendship, Commerce and Navigation, *EPIL* 7 (1984), 484–90.

22 H. Coing, Bretton Woods Conference (1944), *EPIL* I (1992), 494–5; S.A. Silard, Financial Institutions, Intergovernmental, *EPIL* II (1995), 378–81; E.-U. Petersmann, Economic Organizations and Groups, International, *ibid.*, 32–8; R.F. Mikesell, *The Bretton Woods Debates*, 1994; P.B. Kenen (ed.), *Managing the World Economy: Fifty Years after Bretton Woods*, 1994; The Bretton Woods Commission (ed.), *Bretton Woods: Looking to the Future*, 1994; J. Cavanagh/D. Wysham/M. Arruda (eds), *Beyond Bretton Woods: Alternatives to the Global Economic Order*, 1994.

23 Articles 1(3), 55(a) and (b), 56 of the Charter. See Chapter 21 below, 382–4.
24 H.G. Schermers, Weighted Voting, *EPIL* 5 (1983), 398–9.
25 H.J. Hahn, Organisation for Economic Co-operation and Development, *EPIL* 5 (1983), 214–22.
26 A.-M.d. Zayas, European Recovery Program, *EPIL* II (1995), 282–5.
27 P.-T. Stoll, Economic Commissions, Regional, in *Wolfrum UNLPP I*, 434–50; W. Meng, Economic Co-operation under the UN-System, *ibid.*, 451–60; R. Lagoni, ECOSOC, *ibid.*, 461–9. On ECOSOC see also Chapter 21 below, 382–3.
28 G. Corea, United Nations Conference on Trade and Development, *EPIL* 5 (1983), 301–7; R. Marxen, UNCTAD, in *Wolfrum UNLPP II*, 1274–83; On the latest conference, UNCTAD IX, held in South Africa from 27 April to 11 May 1996 see *UN Chronicle* 1996, no. 2, 58–60.
29 S. Marchisio/A. di Blase, *The Food and Agricultural Organization (FAO)*, 1991; J.P. Dobbert, Food and Agriculture Organization of the United Nations, *EPIL* II (1995), 413–9; H.-J. Schütz, FAO, in *Wolfrum UNLPP I*, 499–522.
30 See H. Sahlmann/B. Blank, UNDP, in *Wolfrum UNLPP II*, 1284–90.
31 P.C. Szasz, United Nations Industrial Development Organization, *EPIL* 5 (1983), 329–36; B.L. Rau-Mentzen/G.v. Koppenfels, UNIDO, in *Wolfrum UNLPP II*, 1329–34.
32 W. Benedek, International Fund for Agricultural Development, *EPIL* II (1995), 1146–9; P.M. Frankenfeld, IFAD, in *Wolfrum UNLPP I*, 694–701.
33 See B.S. Chimni, *International Commodity Agreements: A Legal Study*, 1987; C. Tomuschat, Commodities, Common Fund, *EPIL* I (1992), 683–6; Commodities, International Regulation of Production and Trade, *ibid.*, 686–92; R. Wolfrum, Commodity Agreements/ Common Fund, in *Wolfrum UNLPP I*, 138–47.

employment, to increase real income and to optimize the use of production factors. This is supplemented by the goal of monetary stability as a pre-condition for sound economic growth. In addition, the principle of non-discrimination aims at achieving the optimal allocation of resources and at preventing the distortion of competition resulting from a privileged position of particular states. However, these liberal principles often conflict with the sovereign equality of states, as laid down in Article 2(1) of the UN Charter, and their freedom to determine their economic policies and priorities, in spite of the commitments to international cooperation also in the social and economic fields mentioned in the UN Charter.[23]

Communist countries refused to join a number of the Bretton Woods institutions on the grounds that they were based on a capitalist (market economy) philosophy. Developing countries, initially critical of the alleged insensitivity of these Western institutions to poverty and problems of economic development in the Third World, gradually participated and began to play an important role in those organizations which operate on the basis of the one-state one-vote principle. The influence of industrialized countries remained overwhelming, however, in central institutions, such as the IMF or the World Bank, which make decisions according to a weighted voting system reflecting the amount of capital input into the organization and which thus dispenses with the principle of the sovereign equality of states.[24]

The Bretton Woods system was complemented by the Organization for Economic Cooperation and Development (OECD).[25] In 1960 the OECD became the successor to the Organization for European Economic Cooperation that had been set up in connection with the Marshall Plan aid given by the United States to reconstruct Europe after the Second World War.[26] The OECD comprises twenty-six of the largest industrial states in the Western world which together combine more than half of world production and more than 70 per cent of world trade. It is primarily a forum for cooperation, especially with regard to the coordination of economic and monetary policies of the members. In addition, the United Nations (which has created five regional economic commissions under ECOSOC for Europe, Asia and the Far East, Latin America, Africa, and Western Asia[27]) has set up quite a number of more specialized organizations in the economic field, the most important of which for formulating the interests of developing countries is the United Nations Conference on Trade and Development (UNCTAD), which was established in 1964.[28] Under the umbrella of the UN there are also organizations dedicated to the improvement of living standards and to industrial development in the poorer countries, such as the Food and Agriculture Organization (FAO),[29] the United Nations Development Programme (UNDP),[30] the United Nations Industrial Development Organization (UNIDO),[31] and the International Fund for Agricultural Development (IFAD).[32] Furthermore, there are a number of not very successful commodity arrangements which aim to achieve a stable price level primarily in the interest of developing countries heavily dependent on the export of raw materials (e.g. rubber, coffee, tea, metals).[33]

Apart from the OECD, other economic organizations which are

regional in nature include the Organization of Petroleum Exporting Countries (OPEC),[34] the European Communities (ECSC, EEC and Euratom), now under the umbrella of the European Union,[35] the Benelux Economic Union,[36] the European Free Trade Association (EFTA),[37] and the European Economic Area (EEA), created in 1992.[38] (The EEA agreement, governed by the principles of European Community law, was signed by the EC and ECSC and the member states and seven EFTA states. Switzerland withdrew following a referendum. With the accession of Finland, Austria and Sweden to the European Union, EFTA has been largely absorbed by European integration.) Furthermore, there is the 1988 Canada–United States Free Trade Agreement (FTA),[39] which formed the basis for the North American Free Trade Area (NAFTA),[40] concluded in 1992 between Canada, Mexico and the United States as a free trade area open to further extension to Latin America as a counterweight to the European Union and Japan. There are also a number of other free trade areas and sub-regional economic organizations in Latin America,[41] including the Andean Pact,[42] CACM, ALADI, SELA, CARICOM,[43] and MERCOSUR.[44] The Additional Protocol on the Institutional Structure of MERCOSUR, (founded by Argentina, Brazil, Paraguay and Uruguay), adopted on 17 December 1994[45] may lead to the first significant integration process undertaken by developing countries. Chile joined MERCOSUR in June 1996. In Africa, for example, we find the Economic Community of West African States (ECOWAS), founded in 1975,[46] the African Economic Community, established in 1991,[47] and the Common Market for Eastern and Southern Africa, created in 1993.[48] In the Pacific area, in 1989 the Asian-Pacific-Economic-Cooperation (APEC),[49] with its seat in Singapore, was formed by a large number of states, including Australia, Hong Kong, China, Indonesia, Japan, Canada, Brunei, Malaysia, the Philippines, New Zealand, Singapore, South Korea, Taiwan, Thailand, Mexico, Papua New Guinea and the United States. In 1992 the Czech Republic, Hungary, Poland and the Slovak Republic created the Central European Free Trade Area (CEFTA).[50] Furthermore, in 1993 the Commonwealth of Independent States (CIS),[51] which had emerged from the remains of the former Soviet Union, signed a 'Treaty on Creation of an Economic Union.'[52] Among the CIS members signing the Treaty on 24 September 1993 were Russia, Belarus, Armenia, Moldova, Kazakstan, Kyrgyzstan, Uzbekistan, Tajikistan and Azerbaijan. Ukraine and Turkmenistan joined as associated members. Georgia became full member in October 1993. Not all of such forms of cooperation in free trade areas and customs unions have led to the creation of a legally separate organization. However, there is a danger that the trend to create large trading blocs may result in a regionalization of the world economy. This trend is also reinforced by the 1994 Energy Charter Treaty;[53] which, subsequent to the non-binding European Energy Charter signed in 1991, is a novel multilateral investment and trade arrangement accepted by forty-nine states and the European Community.

The International Monetary Fund (IMF)

The main ideas that led to the creation of the IMF rest upon proposals made by the renowned economists John Maynard Keynes (UK) and

34 I.F.I. Shihata/A.R. Parra, Organization of Petroleum Exporting Countries, *EPIL* 5 (1983), 224–8. See also O. Elwan, Organization of Arab Petroleum Exporting Countries, *EPIL* 6 (1983), 281–7.

35 See Chapters 1, 8 and 6, 96 above.

36 E.D.J. Kruijtbosch, Benelux Economic Union, *EPIL* I (1992), 373–7; P. Pescatore, Belgium-Luxembourg Economic Union, *ibid.*, 367–71.

37 W. Karl, European Free Trade Association, *EPIL* II (1995), 237–40.

38 See, for example, A. Evans, *The Law of the European Community Including the EEA Agreement*, 1994; T. Blanchet/R. Piipponen/M. Westman-Clément, *The Agreement on the European Economic Area (EEA)*, 1994.

39 Text in *ILM* 27 (1988), 281. See S.A. Baker/S.B. Battram, The Canada-United States Free Trade Agreement, *IL* 23 (1989), 37–80; Canada-United States Free Trade Agreement Binational Secretariat: Background Note on the FTA Binational Secretariat and A Status Report of All Cases Filed with the Secretariat under Chapters 18 and 19, *ILM* 30 (1991), 181; M.J. Hahn, Free Trade Agreement between the United States and Canada (1988), *EPIL* II (1995), 469–73.

40 Text in *ILM* 32 (1993), 289 and 605. See F.L. Ansley, North American Free Trade Agreement: The Public Debate, *Ga JICL* 22 (1992), 469; M.D. Baer/S. Weintraub (eds), *The NAFTA Debate: Grappling with Unconventional Trade Issues*, 1994; D.C. Alexander/S.J. Rubin (eds), *NAFTA and Investment*, 1995; F. M. Abbott, *Law and Policy of Regional Integration: The NAFTA and Western Hemispheric Integration in the World Trade Organisation*, 1995.

41 M. Minker, Central American Integration: Evolution, Experience and Perspectives, *GYIL* 32 (1989), 195–240; O. Ribbelink, Institutional Aspects of Regional Economic Integration: Latin America, *Hague YIL* 4 (1991), 86–105; K.R. Simmonds, Caribbean Cooperation, *EPIL* I (1992), 533–6; K.R. Simmonds, Central American Common Market, *ibid.*, 548–50.

42 Text in *ILM* 28 (1989), 1165. See P. Nikken, Andean Common Market, *EPIL* I (1992), 155–9.

43 The Caribbean Community (CARICOM) established by a treaty in 1973, replaced the Caribbean Free Trade Association (CARIFTA) founded in 1962. Text of the CARCOM Treaty in *ILM* 12 (1973), 1033.

44 Mercado Comun del Sur, *ILM* 30 (1991), 1041.

45 *ILM* 34 (1995), 1244.

46 Text in *ILM* 14 (1975), 1200, revised text in *ILM* 35 (1996), 660. See J.E. Okolo, ECOWAS Regional Cooperation Regime, *GYIL* 32 (1989), 111; S. Ajulo, Economic Community of West African States, *EPIL* II (1995), 16–20.

47 *ILM* 30 (1991), 1241. See K.v. Walraven, Some Aspects of Regional Economic Integration in Africa, *Hague YIL* 4 (1991), 106–26; M. Ndulo, Harmonization of Trade Laws in the African Economic Community, *ICLQ* 42 (1993), 101 *et seq.*

48 Text of the Treaty in *ILM* 33 (1994), 1067; see also *ILM* 34 (1995), 864.

49 See D.K. Linnen, APEC Quo Vadis?, *AJIL* 89 (1995), 824–34. For recent steps taken by APEC towards a Voluntary Consultative Dispute Mediation Service and towards trade liberalization see the documents in *ILM* 35 (1996), 1102 and 1111.

50 *ILM* 34 (1995), 3.

51 See Chapter 6 above, 94–5.

52 Text of the Treaty in *ILM* 34 (1995), 1298. See S. Peers, From Cold War to Lukewarm Embrace: The European Union's Agreements with the CIS States, *ICLQ* 44 (1995), 829–47.

53 Text in *ILM* 34 (1995), 360; corrections in *ILM* 34 (1995), 1158; for the status of the agreements reached see *ILM* 34 (1995), 593. On the US Statement on the Energy Charter Treaty see *ILM* 34 (1995), 556.

54 J. Gold, International Monetary Fund, *EPIL* II (1995), 1271–8; *Restatement (Third)*, Vol. 2, 313–37; P. Rawert, IMF, in *Wolfrum UNLPP I*, 724–33. See also R.W. Edwards, Jr., *International Monetary Collaboration*, 1985; R.C. Tennekoon, *The Law and Regulation of International Finance*, 1991; B. Steil (ed.), *International Financial Market Regulation*, 1994.

55 2 UNTS 39, TIAS No. 1501 (1947) [original articles], amended text in 726 UNTS 266, TIAS No. 6748 (1976) [first amendment]; TIAS No. 8937 (1978) [second amendment].

56 J. Gold, *Exchange Rates in International Law and Organization*, 1989; Gold, *Legal Effects of Fluctuating Exchange Rates*, 1990.

57 M. Garritsen de Vries, *Balance of Payments Adjustment, 1945–1986: The IMF Experience*, 1987

Harry Dexter White (USA).[54] According to Article IV of the IMF Agreement, the essential purpose of the international monetary system is 'to provide a framework that facilitates the exchange of goods, services and capital among countries, and that sustains sound economic growth.'[55] Furthermore, Article I mentioned, *inter alia*, the following purposes of the IMF:

(ii)   To facilitate the expansion and balanced growth of international trade, and to contribute thereby to the promotion and maintenance of high levels of employment and real income and to the development of the productive resources of all members as primary objectives of economic policy.

(iii)   . . .

(iv)   To assist in the establishment of a multilateral system of payments in respect of current transactions between members and in the elimination of foreign exchange restrictions which hamper the growth of world trade.

As of 1995, the membership of the IMF had increased to 179 states, including states arising from the break-up of the Soviet Union. The rights and duties of members are based upon 'quotas', which are supposed to reflect the economic and financial position of the members and which also determine the level of financial contribution to be made to the Fund. The main organ of the IMF is the Board of Governors composed of one Governor and one alternate nominated by each member (usually the Minister of Finance or the Central Bank Governor are nominated). The Executive Board has at least twenty Executive Directors, five of whom are appointed and fifteen are elected. The members with the largest five quotas have the right to appoint directors (the United States, United Kingdom, Germany, France and Japan). A maximum of up to two additional directors may be appointed by other members under certain conditions. The voting system is weighted and puts the actual decision-making power into the hands of the group of Western states with the largest quotas.

The IMF has manifold functions, but the main ones concern regulatory and supervisory functions with regard to exchange rates,[56] the regulation and coordination of the multilateral system of payments and transfers for current international transactions and include a number of financial activities. With regard to the convertibility of currencies, the original Bretton Woods system was based upon a fixed gold parity of the US dollar to which the other currencies were tied. It had to be abandoned for economic reasons in 1971 which led to an amendment of the IMF Agreement in 1976 allowing members legally to introduce flexible ('floating') exchange rates under the supervision of the IMF.

One important task of the IMF is to assist member states in balance-of-payment deficit situations.[57] So-called 'special drawing rights' (SDRs) play a particular role in providing the required liquidity. The SDR is an asset allocated to members by the Fund as a reserve asset or for use in support of their currencies. It is valued by reference to a 'basket' of specified amounts of the five most important currencies (US dollar, Deutschmark, Japanese yen, French franc and pound sterling) and by reference to their exchange rates. In effect, the use of SDRs enables members to acquire 'hard' currencies against their own national currencies, but the mechanism is too complicated to be described here in any detail.

As a result of excessive lending by international institutions, Western states and private banks to developing countries which became unable to repay their huge foreign debts, a serious international debt crisis emerged at the end of the 1970s and it is still continuing.[58] A rather controversial issue in this connection is the 'conditionality' of loans offered by the IMF and the World Bank to developing countries with such huge debts. Under so-called 'stand-by arrangements' between the IMF and the debtor country (Article XXX lit. d), the debtor country must formally declare to undertake certain economic reform measures to counter its balance-of-payment deficit. This is a condition of the IMF for offering the loan, but it does not amount to a treaty obligation. Therefore, if the debtor state does not comply with the condition, legally it does not commit an internationally wrongful act.[59] However, there might be difficulties in obtaining further loans from the international institutions which in fact makes it difficult not to comply. Such required structural adjustment policies often have painful social consequences for the populations of developing countries. Whether they are really effective is a matter of debate. Many countries in the South feel that they are being put under tutelage, and regard this as an infringement of their sovereignty.[60]

The World Bank

The International Bank for Reconstruction and Development (World Bank) was set up together with the IMF at the 1994 Bretton Woods Conference.[61] As set forth in Article 1 of its Articles of Agreement, the purposes of the World Bank are to assist in the reconstruction and development of territories of members, to promote private foreign investment by means of guarantees or participation in loans and other investments made by private investors, to provide (under certain circumstances) finance for productive purposes, to promote the long-term balanced growth of international trade and the maintenance of equilibrium in balances of payment, to arrange its lending policies to give priority to the more useful and urgent projects and to conduct its operations with due regard to the effect of international investment on business conditions in the member states.[62] The Bank was originally concerned with reconstruction after the Second World War and is nowadays primarily occupied with granting loans to developing countries to finance particular projects to improve the infrastructure and economic development in the South in general.[63]

Membership of the World Bank requires membership of the IMF; therefore the two organizations have the same circle of member states. The voting system and the structure of the main organs is similar to the model of the IMF; thus the largest shareholders enjoy a privileged position according to their financial input. In essence, the Bank acts as a financial intermediary which relends funds it raises in the market or guarantees loans made to members through the commercial investment channel. It also makes loans out of its own capital funds, but this constitutes a smaller

58 See F.P. Feliciano/R. Dolzer, The International Law of External Debt Management – Some Current Aspects, *ILA Rep.* 1988, 419; P.M. Keller/N.E. Weerasinghe, *Multilateral Official Debt Rescheduling: Recent Experiences*, 1988; F. Gianviti, The IMF and External Debt, *RdC* 215 (1989-III), 205–86; P. Adams, *Odious Debts: Loose Lending, Corruption, and the Third World's Environmental Legacy*, 1991; D.H. Cole, Debt-Equity Conversions, Debt-for-Nature Swaps, and the Continuing World Debt Crisis, *Colum. JTL* 30 (1992), 57; V.P. Nanda/G.W. Shepherd, Jr./E. McCarthy-Arnolds (eds), *World Debt and the Human Condition. Structural Adjustment and the Right to Development*, 1993; H.J. Hahn, Foreign Debts, *EPIL* II (1995), 428–35; M. Bothe, Debt Crisis, in *Wolfrum UNLPP I*, 366–79; A. Reinisch, *State Responsibility for Debts*, 1995.

59 Herdegen, *op. cit.*, 229.

60 W. Meng, Conditionality of IMF and World Bank Loans: Tutelage over Sovereign States?, *VRÜ* 21 (1988), 263; H.M.G. Denters, *IMF Conditionaliteit – Juridische aspecten van betalingsbalanssteun door het IMF*, 1993; J.-M. Sorel, Sur quelques aspects juridiques de la conditonalité du F.M.I. et leurs conséquences, *EJIL* 7 (1996), 67–88.

61 I.F. Shihata, *The World Bank in a Changing World. Selected Essays*, 1991; D.D. Bradlow/S. Schlemmer-Schulte, The World Bank's New Inspection Panel: A Constructive Step in the Transformation of the International Legal Order, *ZaöRV* 54 (1994), 392–415; H. Golsong, International Bank for Reconstruction and Development, *EPIL* II (1995), 1057–64; C.v. Monbart, IBRD, in *Wolfrum UNLPP I*, 656–64; A. Broches, *Selected Essays – World Bank, ICSID, and Other Subjects of Public and Private International Law*, 1995. On regional development banks see P. Kunig, in *Wolfrum UNLPP II*, 1052–8.

62 Text in 2 UNTS 134 (1947), amended text in 606 UNTS 294 (1967).

63 See J.W. Head, Evaluation of the Governing Law for Loan Agreements of the World Bank and Other Multilateral Banks, *AJIL* 90 (1996), 214–34.

64 B.S. Brown, *The United States and the Politicization of the World Bank. Issues of International Law and Policy*, 1992; D. Bandow/I. Vásquez (eds), *Perpetuating Poverty. The World Bank, the IMF, and the Developing World*, 1994.

65 H. Golsong, International Finance Corporation, *EPIL* II (1995), 1142–4; A. Graf Keyserlingk, IFC, in *Wolfrum UNLPP I*, 702–4.

66 H. Golsong, International Development Association, *EPIL* II (1995), 1127–9; D.H. Frankenfeld, IDA, in *Wolfrum UNLPP I*, 686–93.

67 See Chapter 18 below, 295–6.

68 Convention Establishing the Multilateral Investment Guarantee Agency (MIGA), *ILM* 24 (1985), 1598. See S.K. Chatterjee, The Convention Establishing the Multilateral Investment Guarantee Agency, *ICLQ* 36 (1986), 76–91; H.G. Petersmann, Die Multilaterale Investitions-Garantie-Agentur (MIGA)., *ZaöRV* 46 (1986), 758; I.F.I. Shihata, The Multilateral Investment Guarantee Agency (MIGA) and the Legal Treatment of Foreign Investment, *RdC* 203 (1987-III), 99–320; Shihata, *MIGA and Foreign Investment: Origins, Operations, Policies and Basic Documents of the Multilateral Investment Guarantee Agency*, 1988; S.A. Riesenfeld, Foreign Investments, *EPIL* II (1995), 435–9; D.W. Bachmann, MIGA, in *Wolfrum UNLPP II*, 884–91.

69 Text of the Charter in Cmd. 7375. See G. Jaenicke, Havana Charter, *EPIL* II (1995), 679–83.

70 Text of the GATT Treaty in 55 UNTS 187. See J.H. Jackson, *World Trade and the Law of GATT*, 1969; T.J. Schoenbaum, Antidumping and Countervailing Duties and the GATT: An Evaluation and a Proposal for a Unified Remedy for Unfair International Trade, *GYIL* 30 (1987), 177; *Restatement (Third)*, Vol. 2, 263–312; K.R. Simmonds/B.H.W. Hill, *Law and Practice under the GATT*, 1988; E.-U. Petersmann, Mid-Term Review Agreements of the Uruguay Round and the 1989 Improvements to the GATT Dispute Settlement Procedures, *GYIL* 32 (1989), 280; R.E. Hudec, *The GATT Legal System and World Trade Diplomacy*, 2nd edn 1990; W. Benedek, *Die Rechtsordnung des GATT aus völkerrechtlicher Sicht*, 1990; G.R. Winham, *The Evolution of International Trade Agreements*, 1992; R.E. Hudec, *Enforcing International Trade Law: The Evolution of the Modern GATT Legal System*, 1993; GATT Secretariat, *Analytical Index: Guide to GATT law and Practice*, 6th edn 1994; P. Hallström,

part of its actual activities. In view of strong criticism directed against the pure economic criteria applied in the Bank's policy in the past,[64] it has recently become more sensitive to the social and environmental consequences of the projects it finances throughout the world.

The World Bank is complemented by the International Finance Corporation (IFC)[65] and the International Development Association (IDA);[66] these three organizations form the so-called World Bank Group. While the World Bank lends only for specific projects to member states or to an enterprise with a government guarantee at appropriate rates of interest, the IFC provides venture capital for productive private enterprises independent of a repayment guarantee by the home state of the borrower. The IDA gives concessionary loans (in fact often amounting to grants, because of the highly favourable terms) to the poorest countries which are no longer able to obtain finance under normal market conditions, and to private enterprises with suitable government guarantees. Affiliated with the World Bank Group is the International Centre for the Settlement of Investment Disputes (ICSID)[67] and the Multilateral Investment Guarantee Agency (MIGA).[68]

The GATT

Following the Bretton Woods Conference and the creation of the United Nations, a charter for a complementary International Trade Organization (ITO) to deal with trade in goods was drafted and finally completed at Havana in 1948,[69] but the US Congress, fearing that American interests and options would be limited in international trade affairs, refused to accept it and it never entered into force. Instead the GATT, a multilateral treaty which was designed to operate under the auspices of the ITO, became the central institution to liberalize trade in goods by implementing tariff reductions. But it also never entered into force and operated on the basis of a Protocol of Provisional Application, signed by twenty-three states in 1947, pending the establishment of the ITO. In the following forty years of GATT's existence, more than 130 states either became formally a 'Contracting Party' or at least applied the GATT rules *de facto*. In practice, GATT developed into something akin to an international organization, although it lacked a proper constitutional basis and the GATT Secretariat never referred to it as an international organization.

The purpose of GATT was to establish general principles and rules for the liberalization of international trade on the basis of a multilateral treaty by reducing customs barriers and other barriers to trade and by eliminating discriminatory treatment between states in international commerce.[70] The provisions of GATT, supplemented by about a dozen side agreements, form a complex web filling hundreds of pages of text, which even specialists in the area find difficult to understand. The treaty has been amended several times by successive protocols. The most important amendment added a new Part IV (Trade and Development) requiring Contracting Parties to give special regard to the economic needs of the less-developed countries and grant them preferential treatment. Most developing countries are now participating in the GATT in one way or the other, although, as distinct from UNCTAD, GATT is still perceived as a 'rich man's club', designed to operate according to the interests of the industrialized member states.[71]

GATT members have agreed upon supplementary agreements for the purpose of interpreting, implementing and even (in the case of textiles and agriculture), modifying certain provisions of GATT which have been put into operation separately. Examples are the Cotton Textiles Agreement of 1962, replaced by the Multi-Fibre Textiles Arrangement of 1973, and the Anti-Dumping Code Agreement of 1967 which was revised in 1979. One should also mention the 1979 Agreements on the interpretation of the GATT provisions dealing with export subsidies and countervailing duties, and other agreements on technical barriers to trade, on import licensing procedures, and on government procurement.

The most-favoured nation (MFN) clause is the central principle of GATT.[72] It provides for non-discrimination among trading partners by requiring all GATT members to grant all other members of the Agreement treatment (concerning any tariff or other concession) as favourable, in relation to a particular 'product', as they accord to any other country.[73] The MFN clause does not apply, however, to commercial transactions not involving 'products' (which is interpreted to mean physical items), such as transport, transfer of patents, licences and other 'invisibles', or movements of capital. Once products have passed customs, under the principle of national treatment, GATT members are obliged to treat them on the basis of complete equality with 'like' (which is not always easy to define) products of national origin.[74] This is to prevent the use of internal regulations to discriminate against imported products which would in effect undermine the reduction of tariffs and other trade liberalization measures through the back door.

In addition, there are exceptions to the MFN rule also with regard to goods under the GATT, in special circumstances. If a country wishes to protect its own producers against foreign competition, it may do so under the GATT, but only by using the customs tariffs and not in any other manner. This ensures that the actual trading conditions are transparent and predictable for all suppliers. These tariffs can further be progressively reduced on the basis of negotiations, which may result in the mutual commitment not to increase them above the agreed level ('binding'). The MFN rule does not apply if GATT members form a customs union[75] or a free trade area[76] or if they offer developing countries preferential treatment.

In order to prevent practices which undermine the aforementioned core principles, secured by obligations to use consultation and dispute settlement procedures, the GATT also prohibits the use of quantitative restrictions (for example, import or export quotas, restrictive use of import or export licences, or controls of payments concerning product transactions) as a form of protectionism.[77] There are exceptions, however; for example, in case of serious balance-of-payment difficulties under Article XIV. Developing countries are given large privileges with regard to the rules on quantitative restrictions in view of their notorious balance-of-payment problems. Other rules deal with export subsidies, internal taxation and state-owned enterprises for basically the same reason. However, the

The GATT Panels and the Formation of International Trade Law, 1994; P.J. Kuyper, The Law of GATT as a Special Field of International Law, NYIL 25 (1994), 227–57; H.v. Houtte, The Law of International Trade, 1995; G. Jänicke, General Agreement on Tariffs and Trade (1947), EPIL II (1995), 502–610.

71 See further G.M. Engblom, International Trade Centre UNCTAD/ GATT, EPIL II (1995), 1385–8; J.E. Harders, Discriminatory Measures in Economic and Trade Relations, in Wolfrum UNLPP I, 424–33.

72 E. Ustor, Most-Favoured-Nation Clause, EPIL 8 (1985), 411–6.

73 Article I GATT.

74 Article III.

75 H. Ballreich, Customs Union, EPIL I (1992), 920–3.

76 P. Fischer, Free Trade Areas, EPIL II (1995), 473–8.

77 Article IX GATT.

78 See M.J. Hahn, *Die einseitige Aussetzung von GATT-Verpflichtungen als Repressalie*, 1996.

79 E.-J. Mestmäcker, Free Trade In Services: Regional and Global Perspectives, in D. Friedmann/E.-J. Mestmäcker (eds), *Rules for Free International Trade in Services*, 1990, 9, at 17.

80 T. Oppermann/J. Molsberger (eds), *A New GATT for the Nineties and Europe '92*, 1991.

81 Ministerial Declaration of 20 September 1986, in GATT, *Basic Instruments and Selected Documents*, 33rd Suppl., 1987, 19 *et seq.*; E.-U. Petersmann/M. Hilf (eds), *The New GATT Round of Multilateral Trade Negotiations. Legal and Economic Problems*, 2nd edn 1991; J.H. Jackson, *Restructuring the GATT Legal System*, 1990; T.P. Stewart (ed), *The GATT Uruguay Round: A Negotiating History (1986–1992)*, 3 vols, 1993.

GATT also provides for a number of general exceptions, on grounds of national security, for example. Most problematic is perhaps the rule in 'safeguards' permitting GATT members, under certain circumstances, to impose restrictions on imports or to raise a 'bound' tariff in order to avoid or limit 'serious injury' to domestic producers under the so-called 'escape clause' of Article XIX.

In spite of built-in structural tension, normative contradictions and frequent resort of member states to aggressive unilateral counter-measures in their trade disputes,[78] the GATT system has worked remarkably well as an instrument against tariff protectionism for quite a long period. This is partly due to its flexible semi-legal/semi-political nature of application. Negotiations within GATT have reduced tariff levels in the principal trading nations from about 40 per cent in 1947 to about 5–10 per cent in 1986. As a result of the seven successive GATT negotiating rounds, from the Geneva Round in 1947 to the 1973–9 Tokyo Round, there has been a considerable increase in the volume of world trade (world exports in nominal US dollars were $56,000 million in 1948, $128,000 million in 1960, $312,000 million in 1970 and $1,985,000 million in 1980), almost 90 per cent of which is now covered by the GATT. But it should also be noted that this continuous expansion occurred largely among industrialized countries. The GATT managed to keep developing countries (which suffer most from global economic recession) within the system by granting them non-reciprocal preferential treatment, although this did not meet their demands for more favourable terms of trade.

However, GATT increasingly met with other problems. The progress of the multilateral approach in reducing tariffs in the 1950s and 1960s was to a large extent due to the fact that at that time the United States was committed to free trade and that tariff negotiations can be conducted with sufficient transparency and cause little transaction costs.[79] In the following decade multilateral instruments were unable to deal effectively with more complex issues of, for example, non-tariff barriers, government procurement and subsidies. In addition, the economic problems since the 1970s favoured the widespread emergence of new forms of non-tariff protectionism, such as so-called 'voluntary self-restraint' and other 'grey area measures' to restrict foreign exports. This development, together with tendencies towards a more regional economic orientation, such as in North America and in Europe as a whole, presented a formidable challenge to the basic principles of the GATT and the liberal world trading system it sought to establish on the broadest possible multilateral basis.[80]

These problems led to the eighth GATT negotiating round which was launched in 1986 by the 'Uruguay Declaration'.[81] The ambitious agenda aimed at a fundamental restructuring of the GATT including the reduction of non-tariff trade barriers, and improving the efficiency of the institutional-legal framework to reduce non-compliance with, or evasion of, GATT rules. Furthermore, the intention was to cover additional new areas, hitherto unregulated, such as trade in services, trade-related intellectual property rights (TRIPS) and trade-related investment measures (TRIMS). Further principles and guidelines clarifying the objectives of the Uruguay Round negotiations were laid down in the 1988/9 Montreal Mid-Term Review Agreements. Originally, there were as many as fifteen different negotiating groups in the Uruguay Round, which were later consolidated into six large groups. In essence, the topics can be classified into the three following areas:

1   measures to improve market access in traditional GATT areas (agriculture, textiles, government procurement, and exceptions, including safeguards, anti-dumping and subsidies);
2   new issues (services, TRIPS and TRIMS); and
3   institutional aspects (dispute settlement, surveillance, and organization).

The new World Trade Organization

After seven and a half years of protracted negotiations, the Uruguay Round of GATT was finally completed on 15 April 1994 with 111 of the 125 participating states signing the final document. The final agreement on the new World Trade Organization (WTO),[82] accepted by 104 states, entered into force on 1 January 1995 for eighty-one members, representing more than 90 per cent of international trade, including the 'Triad' of the United States, the European Union and Japan. Among the twenty-seven multilateral agreements appended to the text of the WTO accord, there is the new General Agreement on Trade in Services (GATS).

The WTO encompasses the GATT, the various supplementary agreements of 'codes' and a reform of the dispute settlement system under a common institutional umbrella. It aims at integrating the GATT (as it stood in 1947), the results of the successive multilateral negotiation rounds (where the scope of membership varies) and the new Uruguay Round agreements ('GATT 1994') into one single legal system. This means that there will be two systems in operation in the future, at least for a transitory period, because those states which do not wish to join the WTO, or in spite of their WTO membership prefer to remain contracting parties to the old system, are bound only by the previous GATT arrangements they have accepted ('GATT 1947').[83]

Membership in the WTO is restricted to states and customs territories (e.g. the European Community and Hong Kong) which accept both a GATT Schedule of trade concessions as well as a GATS Schedule of services concessions. The purpose of this requirement is to avoid the 'free-rider problem' in past GATT practice, under which many members claimed rights under the GATT but did not make any concessions themselves and often demanded far-reaching exemptions for developing countries from GATT obligations, such as the MFN clause.

The trade agreements on goods

The Uruguay Round Agreements on international trade in goods basically maintain the old GATT agreements, with a number of amendments. There are also seven 'Understandings' on the interpretation of important GATT Articles.[84] In addition, thirteen multilateral agreements contain

82 The Final Act Embodying the Results of the Uruguay Round is reprinted in *ILM* 33 (1994), 1; on the text of the WTO Agreement see *ibid.*, 13. For the Final Act, as adopted on 15 April 1994, see *ibid.*, 1125. See further P.-T. Stoll, Die WTO, *ZaöRV* 54 (1994), 241–337; E. McGovern, *International Trade Regulation*, 1995; W. Benedek, GATT – The Uruguay Round – WTO, in *Wolfrum UNLPP I*, 532–47; W. Benedek, Die neue Welthandelsorganisation (WTO) und ihre internationale Stellung, *VN* 43 (1995), 13 *et seq.*; T.J. Dillon, The World Trade Organization: A New Legal Order for World Trade? *Mich. JIL* 16 (1995), 349–402; P. Hilpold, Die Neuregelung der Schutzmaßnahmen im GATT/WTO-Recht und ihr Einfluß auf 'Grauzonenmaßnahmen', *ZaöRV* 55 (1995), 89–127; E.-U. Petersmann, The Transformation of the World Trading System through the 1994 Agreement Establishing the World Trade Organization, *EJIL* 6 (1995), 161–221; P.J. Kuijper, The Conclusion and Implementation of the Uruguay Round Results by the European Community, *ibid.*, 222–44; M. Hilf, The ECJ's Opinion 1/94 on the WTO – No Surprise, but Wise?, *ibid.*, 245–59; v. Houtte, *op. cit.*; M.J. Hahn, Eine kulturelle Bereichsausnahme im Recht der WTO?, *ZaöRV* 56 (1996), 315.
83 See P.M. Moore, The Decisions Bridging the GATT 1947 and the WTO Agreement, *AJIL* 90 (1996), 317–38.
84 Article II, XII, XVII, XVIII, XXIV, XXV, XXVIII and XXXV of GATT.

85 G. Sacerdoti, The International Regulation of Services: Basic Concepts and Standards of Treatment, in G. Sacerdoti (ed.), *Liberalization of Services and Intellectual Property in the Uruguay Round of GATT*, 1990, 6; K.P. Sauvant/J. Weber, *The International Legal Framework for Services*, 1992; M.E. Footer, Global and Regional Approaches to the Regulation of Trade in Services, *ICLQ* 43 (1994), 661–77.
86 N. Hopkinson, *Completing the GATT Uruguay Round: Renewed Multilateralism or a World of Regional Trading Blocs?*, 1992.
87 Petersmann (1995), Rights and Duties, *op. cit.*, 1111.
88 See the Second Protocol to the GATS and Related Decisions, *ILM* 35 (1996), 199.
89 P. Malanczuk/H. de. Vlaam, International Trade in Telecommunications Services and the Results of the Uruguay Round of GATT, *TSJ* 3 (1996), 269–90.
90 Annex 1C of the WTO Agreement.

concessions concerning agriculture, sanitary and phytosanitary measures, textiles and clothing, technical barriers to trade, trade-related investment measures (TRIMS), customs valuation, anti-dumping measures, pre-shipment inspection, rules of origin, import licensing procedures, subsidies and countervailing measures, and safeguards. Such detailed agreements were considered necessary to make the system more effective and to limit the trade policy discretion of governments in the interest of more predictable trade and investment conditions (in combination with a more stronger international dispute settlement mechanism and clearer guidelines for national courts) for private enterprise.

The Agreement on Services (GATS)

Before the acceptance of GATS, the regulation of trade in services had been limited to bilateral treaties dealing with the treatment of nationals of the respective parties or to regional or bilateral agreements constituting free trade areas or customs unions.[85] An important example is the Treaty of the European Economic Community, Articles 59–66 of which deal with services. Services were included in the GATT negotiations because of the growing economic importance of the sector. In terms of value of trade, services already represent a far greater proportion than, for instance, agriculture (world exports in 1990 amounted to US$4,300 billion, of which 60 per cent were in manufactures, 19 per cent in services, 11 per cent in mining and only 10 per cent in agriculture).[86] Today, over 20 per cent of world trade and 60 per cent of world production are in the area covered by the GATS.[87]

The GATS is built upon several layers. First, there is a framework agreement which applies to any service in any sector, except a service provided in the exercise of governmental authority either on a commercial basis or in competition with other suppliers. Some of the basic provisions follow the corresponding provisions in GATT law on the trade in goods. Second, there are various types of 'commitments' in 'national schedules' to take care of the fact that most barriers to international trade in services do not arise from border measures (as in the case of goods) but from domestic regulations, affecting (and discriminating), for example tourism, foreign consultants or construction workers, or the operation of subsidiaries of foreign banks on the territory of the receiving state. The GATS envisages successive rounds of negotiations on the progressive liberalization of trade in services. Third, individual (more sensitive) service sectors have found special treatment, including financial services,[88] telecommunications,[89] air transport services, maritime transport services and movement of natural persons providing services.

The Agreement on Intellectual Property Rights (TRIPS)

The Agreement on Trade-Related Aspects of Intellectual Property Rights (TRIPS)[90] is concerned with a variety of private rights, such as the protection and enforcement of copyrights and related rights, trademarks, geographical indications, industrial designs, patents, lay-out designs and undisclosed information. It is in part based on traditional legal principles of GATT (e.g. most-favoured nation clause and national treatment principle), but it also introduces many new legal elements into the multi-lateral trading system by interconnecting it with existing international agreements on intellectual property.

Institutional aspects

The highest organ of the WTO is the Ministerial Conference, which consists of all member states and meets at least every two years. The General Council is the main organ between the meetings of the Minis-terial Conference and also consists of representatives of all members. There are also special councils below the level of the General Council, a Council for Trade in Goods, a Council for Trade in Services, a Council for TRIPS and further subsidiary bodies, such as the Committee on Trade and Development, the Committee on Balance-of-Payments Restrictions and the Committee on Budget and Finance. In addition, there is a WTO-Secretariat headed by a Director-General. In contrast to GATT, it is explicitly recognized that the WTO has international legal personality.[91]

Apart from creating a single institutional framework for the numerous multilateral trade agreements, the new system also provides for a new integrated dispute settlement order[92] and a trade policy review mechan-ism[93] applicable to all multilateral trade agreements. The new dispute settlement system, including a Dispute Settlement Body and a Standing Appellate Body to review panel decisions, is much more 'judicialized' than the previous one and has considerably strengthened the legal and binding elements of the resolution of international trade conflicts. It has more teeth and is designed to limit the scope of power politics and unilateral countermeasures.[94]

Developing countries and the legal quest for a New International Economic Order

The call for a 'New International Economic Order'(NIEO) reflects the wide gap in living standards between North and South and the desire of developing countries[95] to redress the imbalance in the international eco-nomic system, in which their very position is notoriously weak.[96] The programme of a NIEO includes a complex variety of claims which have also manifested themselves in the controversy on the deep seabed mining regime in the 1982 Law of the Sea Convention[97] or on the 'common heritage of mankind principle'[98] in general, as well as in the discussion on the control of multinational enterprises,[99] and in the call for the transfer of technology[100] as well as for a 'New World Information and Communication Order' (NWICO).[101] It is generally recognized that there is a need to increase the flow of finance to developing countries, especially to those which are burdened with heavy debt, and to low-income countries depending on aid, to counter the acceleration of global poverty and an unacceptable decline in living standards. But the legal content of the idea of solidarity among states is in many respects still very ambiguous.[102]

Development assistance in the form of the transfer of money from North to South, claimed by developing countries as a 'right', has not met

91 See Chapter 6 above, 91–4.
92 Understanding on Rules and Procedures Governing the Settlement of Disputes, Annex 2 of the WTO Agreement, *ILM* 33 (1994), 112. See Chapter 18 below, 300.
93 Annex 3 of the WTO Agreement.
94 A.F. Lowenfeld, Remedies Along with Rights: Institutional Reform in the New GATT, *AJIL* 88 (1994), 477–88. On countermeasures see Chapter 17 below, 271–2.
95 On the problems of definition see J. Betz, Developing Countries, in *Wolfrum UNLPP I*, 398–406.
96 R. Caldera, The Juridical Basis of a New International Order, *RdC* 196 (1986-I), 387; D.C. Dicke (ed.), *Foreign Debts in the Present and a New International Economic Order*, 1986; Dicke (ed.), *Foreign Investment in the Present and a New International Economic Order*, 1987; T. Oppermann/ E.-U. Petersmann (eds), *Reforming the International Economic Order*, 1987; J. Makarczyk, *Principles of a New International Economic Order*, 1988; D. C. Dicke/E.-U. Petersmann (eds), *Foreign Trade in the Present and a New International Order*, 1988; H. Fox (ed.), *International Economic Law and Developing States: Some Aspects*, 1988; M. Bulijić, *Principles of International Development Law: Progressive Development of the Principles of International Law Relating to the New Economic Order*, 2nd edn 1993; U.E. Heinz, International Economic Order, in *Wolfrum UNLPP II*, 749–59; J. Betz, International Relations, North-South, ibid., 778–88; C. Tomuschat, New International Economic Order, *EPIL* III (forthcoming). On the views of developing countries on international law in general, see Chapter 2 above, 28–30.
97 See Chapter 12 above, 171–5, 193–5.
98 See Chapter 13 above, 207–8.
99 See Chapter 6 above, 102–3.
100 P.-T. Stoll, Transfer of Technology, in *Wolfrum UNLPP II*, 1229–38.
101 I. Osterdahl, *Freedom of Information in Question: Freedom of Information in International Law and the Calls for a New World Information and Communication Order* (NWICO), 1992; P. Malanczuk, Information and Communication, Freedom of , *EPIL* II (1995), 976–91; J. Delbrück, World Information and Communication Order, in *Wolfrum UNLPP II*, 1466–84.
102 R.St.J. Macdonald, The Principle of Solidarity in Public International Law, *Etudes de droit en l'honneur de Pierre Lalive*, 1993, 275–307.

103 UN Doc. A/CONF.151/PC/51 of 5 July 1991, 3, noting that the 0.7 per cent target which was reiterated in the May 1990 Bergen Joint Agenda for action, excludes funding for most Central and Eastern European countries.

104 There are also other forms of development assistance, such as the preferential treatment granted under the GATT or the Lomé agreements concluded by the European Community with developing countries. See L. Gündling, Economic and Technical Aid, *EPIL* II (1995), 9–13. See also H. Eggerstedt/H.-H. Taake, Capital Assistance, in *Wolfrum UNLPP I*, 87–93; P.-T. Stoll, Technical Assistance, *ibid.*, 1209–19; E. Opoku Awuku, A Trans-Regional Model of North-South Trade: The Lomé Convention, *Hague YIL* 8 (1995), 17–30.

105 K. Melchers, *VN* 44 (1996), 147–53, at 149.

106 See the World Bank Report, *Adjustment in Africa. Reforms, Results and the Road Ahead*, 1994; H.S. Wilson, *African Decolonization*, 1994; F. Ansprenger, Afrika – der verlorene Kontinent?, *Internationale Politik* 51 (1996), 1–10.

107 See *UN Chronicle*, 1996, no. 2, 4–9, at 5, which also notes: 'By 1994, the external debt of Africa had risen to $313 billion, equivalent to 234 per cent of export income and 83 per cent of gross domestic product (GDP) – comparatively higher than in any other region. Exports have stagnated and by 1992 real commodity prices had fallen to half their 1979–1981 average levels.' See also Y. Daudet, *Les Nations Unies et le developpement: Le cas de l'Afrique*, 1994.

108 UNGA Res. 3201 (S-VI).

109 UNGA Res. 3202 (S-VI).

110 *ILM* 13 (1974), 744.

111 UNGA Res. 3281 (XXIX). See E.-U. Petersmann, Charter of Economic Rights and Duties, *EPIL* I (1992), 561–6; see also R.L. Lawrence, A Special Session of the UN General Assembly Rethinks the Economic Rights and Duties of States, *AJIL* 85 (1991), 192–200; S.K. Chatterjee, the Charter of Economic Rights and Duties of States: An Evaluation of 15 Years, *ICLQ* 40 (1991), 669 *et seq.*

the target of 0.7 per cent of GNP set by international institutions and accepted by most OECD members,[103] albeit not as a legally binding obligation. Some countries, such as the United States and Switzerland, even reject the 0.7 per cent norm as a moral principle with the argument that such 'targetry' is based on arbitrary norms and gives too much consideration to the quantity rather than to the quality of assistance. In fact, only very few donor countries meet the 0.7 per cent norm. What actually has occurred was a reverse net outflow from the developing to the developed countries due to capital flight and high interest rate payments, as well as the fall of commodity prices.[104] The following may give some idea of the imbalance and inequality which affect the developing countries. In 1994, of the approximately 5.6 billion people living on the earth, 15 per cent were living in rich countries (with an economic power of US$24,170 per head), 28 per cent in countries with middle-size income (US$2,550 per head) and 57 per cent in poor countries (US$390 per head). This means that more than half of the humanity is surviving (or dying) under conditions of utmost poverty. According to figures presented by the World Bank for 1994, on average, a person living in a poor country received little more than US$1 per day. One-sixth of the countries in the world commands four-fifths of the global wealth.[105] The problems are most acute in Africa which has come to be called the 'lost continent'.[106] Of the forty-eight least developed countries in the world, thirty-three are in Africa. About 50 per cent of the 365 million Africans live in absolute poverty, and this number is expected to increase during this decade.[107]

The recognition of the huge development tasks that still lie ahead in most countries of the South has induced industrialized countries with market economies to give some sympathy to at least certain aspects of the legal quest of developing countries for a NIEO since the 1960s. Thus, the general idea of a NIEO found some support in the 'Declaration on the Establishment of a New International Economic Order'[108] and the 'Programme of Action on the Establishment of a New International Economic Order'[109] adopted by the UN General Assembly by consensus on 1 May 1974, although industrialized countries already showed their discontent by registering reservations.[110]

However, the subsequent 'Charter of Economic Rights and Duties' of 12 December 1974, originally intended to become legally binding, revealed the fundamental differences between North and South.[111] The General Assembly adopted the Charter as a resolution with a majority of 120 states against six votes (Belgium, Denmark, Germany, Luxembourg, the UK and the United States), with ten abstentions (Austria, Canada, France, Ireland, Israel, Italy, Japan, the Netherlands, Norway and Spain). Thus, sixteen states representing fifteen major OECD countries accounting for over two-thirds of global trade and development assistance did not vote in favour of the Charter because they felt that many of its provisions went too far. The relevance of the Charter, which like many similar documents calling for change in international economic relations is not legally binding, is thereby considerably diminished. A more balanced attempt to redress the differences of opinion between developing countries and industrialized countries was made in the 'Declaration on the Progressive

Development of Principles of Public International Law Relating to a New International Economic Order' adopted by the International Law Association in Seoul in 1986, but this is only a resolution of a non-governmental organization.[112]

The Charter emphasizes the permanent sovereignty of states over their natural resources and their jurisdiction to regulate economic activity on their territory, especially with respect to foreign investment by multinational companies. The document contains provisions which are aimed at making it an instrument of change in favour of developing countries, concerning, *inter alia*, international trade, the transfer of technology, preferential treatment, protection of commodity prices, and foreign aid. Dissent particularly arose concerning the principles laid down for compensation to be paid in the case of the expropriation of foreign investment.

Expropriation and standard of compensation

The rules on expropriation of foreign property are comprised in the so-called minimum international standard which belongs to the core of the traditional rules of state responsibility for the treatment of aliens.[113] The question is very controversial, and has been of enormous political importance in the past.[114] In many developing countries the economy is dominated by foreign companies, but this problem is not limited to developing countries.

According to Western countries, the minimum international standard contains two rules of customary law concerning expropriation. First, expropriation must be for a public purpose (for instance, it must not be an act of spite, or a means of adding to the ruler's private fortune).[115] Second, even when expropriation is for a public purpose, it must be accompanied by payment of compensation for the full value of the property – or, as it is often expressed, 'prompt, adequate and effective compensation'.[116] (Of course, no compensation need be paid when property is seized as a penalty for breaking an obligation imposed by the local law, provided that the local law does not fall below the minimum international standard by virtue of its excessive harshness.)

On the other hand, communist governments used to argue that states may expropriate the means of production, distribution and exchange without paying compensation. But their practice was not entirely consistent. Among themselves they concluded treaties providing for a mutual waiver of claims and obligations arising out of one another's expropriation programmes, which implies that claims and obligations existed until waived; even the payment of compensation between communist countries was not entirely unknown.[117]

Developing countries with left-wing regimes tended to support the communist attitude towards the legality of expropriation. Other developing countries, however, entered into treaties for the protection of investments,[118] in order to attract further foreign investment; but they showed an increasing reluctance to accept the Western view of customary international law about expropriation. Thus, the developing countries used to vacillate between the Western countries and the communist countries.

112 *ILA Rep.* 1986, 2.

113 See Chapter 17 below, 256–69.

114 N.J. Schrijver/W.D. Verwey, The Taking of Property under International Law: A New Legal Perspective?, *NYIL* 15 (1984), 3–96; R. Dolzer, *Eigentum, Enteignung und Entschädigung im geltenden Völkerrecht*, 1985; M. Sornarajah, *The Pursuit of Nationalized Property*, 1986; R.B. Lillich (ed.), *The Valuation of Nationalized Property in International Law*, Vol. IV, 1987; S.K.B. Asante, International Law and Foreign Investment: A Reappraisal, *ICLQ* 37 (1988), 588; Dolzer, Expropriation and Nationalization, *EPIL* II (1995), 319–27.

115 See the authorities cited by O'Keefe in *JWTL* 8 (1974), 257–62. Some writers add a further requirement that the expropriation must not be discriminatory, but this is probably best regarded as part of the public purpose requirement (O'Keefe, *ibid.*). Expropriation is also illegal if it is forbidden by a treaty. The United Kingdom argued that the Egyptian nationalization of the Suez Canal in 1956 was illegal because it was contrary to the Constantinople Convention of 1888, but the United Kingdom probably misinterpreted the Convention. See G. Schwarzenberger, *Foreign Investments and International Law*, 1969, 84–9; R. Delson, Nationalization of the Suez Canal Company, *Colum. LR* 57 (1957), 755.

116 *Norwegian Ships* case (1921), *RIAA* I 307, 338; *Spanish Zone of Morocco* case (1925), *RIAA* II 615, 647; *Shufeldt's* claim (1930), *RIAA* II 1079, 1095; *Mariposa's* claim (1933), *RIAA* VI 338; *de Sabla's* claim (1933), *RIAA* VI 358, 366; *Arabian-American Oil Co. v. Saudi Arabia*, *ILR* 27 (1958), 117, 144, 168, 205; *American International Group, Inc. v. Islamic Republic of Iran* (1983), *AJIL* 77 (1984), 454; *Sedco, Inc. v. National Iranian Oil Company and Iran* (1986), *ILM* 25 (1986), 629, 632–5, 641–7.

117 A. Drucker, On Compensation Treaties Between Communist States, *Law Times* 229 (1960), 279–80, 293–4. See the change as witnessed, for example, by the 1992 U.S.–Russia investment treaty, *ILM* 31 (1992), 794, and the 1995 Russian Federation Law on Production Sharing Agreements, *ILM* 35 (1996), 1251.

118 See text below, 237.

119 Text in *Brownlie BDIL*, 235. See N. Schrijver, *Sovereignty over Natural Resources. Balancing Rights and Duties*, 1997.
120 Text in *Brownlie BDIL*, 240; *ILM* 14 (1975), 251, 255.
121 Article 2(2)(c) was adopted by 104 votes to 16, with 6 abstentions; on the legal position of states which dissent from a new rule of customary law, see Chapter 3 above, 42–3.
122 For the significance of this distinction, see Chapter 3 above, 35. See also *Texaco v. Libya*, *ILM* 17 (1978), 1, 27–31, *ILR*, Vol. 53, 389, at 483–95; I. Brownlie, Legal Status of Natural Resources in International Law, *RdC* 162 (1979), 245, 255–71.

Most of them could gain a large short-term benefit by expropriating foreign-owned property without compensation, but in the long term they would lose by doing so, because they would attract no private investments in the future (or, alternatively, they would have to pay a much higher price for private investments, in order to compensate for political risks).

Some of these conflicts and contradictions were reflected in resolution 1803 (XVII) on 'permanent sovereignty over natural resources', passed by the United Nations General Assembly on 14 December 1962.[119] The very title of the resolution is peculiar, and is designed to emphasize that foreign ownership of the means of production should not deprive a state of its sovereignty or, more specifically, of its power of economic planning. The resolution also provides, *inter alia*, that states are free to restrict or prohibit the import of foreign capital. These are principles which Western lawyers might forget, but would never deny. Western lawyers are mainly interested in paragraph 4 of the resolution, which provides:

> Nationalization, expropriation or requisitioning shall be based on grounds or reasons of public utility, security or the national interest which are recognized as overriding purely individual or private interests, both domestic and foreign. In such cases the owner shall be paid appropriate compensation, in accordance with the rules in force in the State taking such measures . . . and in accordance with international law.

This corresponds to the Western position, apart from the deliberate ambiguity of the phrase 'appropriate compensation' (it is true that compensation is to be paid 'in accordance with international law', but that begs the question as to the content of the relevant rules of international law). As evidence of customary law, the value of the resolution is diminished by the fact that a Soviet amendment, stating that 'the question of compensation . . . shall . . . be decided in accordance with the national law of the [expropriating] State' (without mentioning international law), was defeated by only thirty-nine votes to twenty-eight, with twenty-one abstentions.

Resolutions passed by the General Assembly in the 1970s moved further away from the Western position. In particular, Article 2(2)(c) of the 1974 Charter of Economic Rights and Duties of States states that 'appropriate compensation should be paid by the [expropriating] State . . . taking into account its relevant laws and regulations and all circumstances that the State considers pertinent'.[120] This resolution, unlike the Soviet amendment of 1962, acknowledges that appropriate compensation should be paid; but what is appropriate is to be determined by the law of the expropriating state (the resolution makes no express mention of international law in this context), and therefore compensation is likely to be very low. However, it is doubtful whether Article 2(2)(c) can be invoked as evidence of customary law against Western states, which voted against it.[121] Indeed, it could be argued that resolution 3281 (XXIX) is not evidence of customary law at all, since it does not claim to declare what the law *is* (the General Assembly deleted a passage in the original draft of the resolution which said that the resolution was intended to codify international law); it merely says what many states think the law *ought* to be.[122]

The dispute has led to considerable legal uncertainty in this area of international economic relations. However, the question has now lost much of its practical significance, due to four main reasons. First, developing countries have come to recognize that the nationalization and expropriation of foreign property as an instrument of economic reform is detrimental to attracting the foreign capital they urgently require and to producing a favourable investment climate. Second, the collapse of the system of communist states has also reduced the leverage of developing countries. Third, many developing countries have accepted the Western standards in bilateral investment protection treaties they concluded with industrialized countries, which means that much of the dispute on the content of customary law has become academic.[123] Fourth, a number of recent arbitral decisions have confirmed that customary law requires full compensation in case of expropriation of foreign property.[124] Of particular importance in this connection is the jurisprudence of the Iran–United States Claims Tribunal concerning the nationalization of American investment in Iran after the Islamic Revolution in 1979, although the three different Chambers of the Tribunal have not always taken the same view.[125]

When disputes arise between states which believe that full compensation must be paid for expropriation and states which think otherwise, they are usually settled by a compromise; the expropriating state pays part of the value of the expropriated property. The compromise usually takes the form of a global settlement or 'lump sum agreement', so called because it covers all the claims made by one state arising out of a particular nationalization programme of the other state, instead of dealing with each individual's claim separately.[126] A disadvantage of global settlements, in the eyes of Western countries, is that only a fraction of the property's value is recovered; on the other hand, if claims were settled in the old way, by arbitration, many of them would be lost through lack of proof, and the expense of proving hundreds of separate claims would be enormous.

In any case, even an arbitral tribunal would often find it difficult to define the true value of expropriated property; the value of a productive enterprise, for instance, is based on its profit-earning capacity, which depends on local factors, and varies from year to year. Share prices could theoretically be used in assessing compensation, but everyone knows how share prices fluctuate. The principle is, however, that the amount of (full) compensation must be based upon the market value of the property. In the case of income-generating property, like a factory, modern arbitral practice tends not to accept mere 'net book value' (value of the investment minus depreciation) but to look for the actual market value, including 'goodwill' (value of the business contacts, name of the company, etc.). According to the decision in the *Starrett Housing Corporation* case, the Iran–United States Claims Tribunal used the following formula as a starting-point to determine the appropriate market value:

> The price that a willing buyer would pay to a willing seller in circumstances in which each had good information, each desired to maximize his financial gain, and neither was under duress or threat.[127]

123 On the status of more than 1000 bilateral and 8 multilateral investment treaties see *ILM* 35 (1996), 1130. See further M. Banz, *Völkerrechtlicher Eigentumsschutz durch Investitionsschutzabkommen* (practice of Germany since 1959), 1988; E. Denza/S. Brooks, Investment Protection Treaties: United Kingdom Experience, *ICLQ* 39 (1990), 908 *et seq.*; P. Peters, Dispute Settlement Arrangements in Investment Treaties, *NYIL* 22 (1991), 91–162; M.I. Khalil, Treatment of Foreign Investment in Bilateral Investment Treaties, *ICSID Rev.* 7 (1992), 272; K.J. Vandevelde, *United States Investment Treaties: Policy and Practice*, 1992; B. Kishaiyian, The Utility of Bilateral Investment Treaties in the Formulation of Customary International Law, *NJILB* 14 (1994), 327–75; R. Dolzer/M. Stevens, *Bilateral Investment Treaties*, 1995. On legal problems of foreign investment in general see B. Sen, Investment Protection and New World Order, *ZaöRV* 48 (1988), 419; R.B. Lillich, Joint Ventures and the Law of International Claims, *Mich. JIL* 10 (1989), 430; M. Sornarajah, *Law of International Joint Ventures*, 1992; I.F.I. Shihata, *The Legal Framework for Foreign Investment: The World Bank Guidelines*, 1993; M. Sornarajah, *The International Law on Foreign Investment*, 1994; M.A. Geist, Toward a General Agreement on the Regulation of Foreign Direct Investment, *Law and Policy in International Business*, 26 (1995), 677–717; T.L. Brewer, International Investment Dispute Settlement Procedures: The Evolving Regime for Foreign Direct Investment, *ibid.*, 633; P.E. Comeaux/N.S. Kinsella, *Protecting Foreign Investment Under International Law: Legal Aspects of Political Risk*, 1996.
124 See P.M. Norton, A Law of the Future or a Law of the Past? Modern Tribunals and the International Law of Expropriation, *AJIL* 85 (1991), 474; J. Westberg/B. Marchais, General Principles Governing Foreign Investment as Articulated in Recent International Tribunal Awards and Writings of Publicists, *ICSID Rev.* 7 (1992), 453–96; C.F. Amerasinghe, Issues of Compensation for the Taking of Alien Property in the Light of Recent Cases and Practice, *ICLQ* 41 (1992), 22 *et seq.*
125 M. Fitzmaurice/M. Pellonpää, Taking of Property in the Practice of the Iran-United States Claims Tribunal, *NYIL* 19 (1988), 53–178; J.A. Westberg, Applicable Law, Expropriatory Takings

and Compensation in Cases of Expropriation: ICSID and Iran-United States Claims Tribunal Case Law Compared, *ICSID Rev.* 8 (1993), 1–28; A. Mouri, *The International Law of Expropriation as Reflected in the Work of the Iran-United States Claims Tribunal*, 1994; G.H. Aldrich, What Constitutes a Compensable Taking: The Decisions of the Iran-United States Claims Tribunal, *AJIL* 88 (1994), 585–610; G.H. Aldrich, *The Jurisprudence of the Iran–United States Claims Tribunal*, 1996, 171–276. See Chapter 18 below, 296–8.

126 See R.B. Lillich/B.H. Weston, *International Claims: Their Settlement by Lump Sum Agreements*, 1995; C. Warbrick, Addendum: Protection of Nationals Abroad: Lump-Sum Settlements, *ICLQ* 40 (1991), 492 *et seq.* For recent examples of such settlements by the United States with Albania, Cambodia and Vietnam see, *ILM* 34 (1995), 595, 600, and 685.

127 *Starrett Housing Corp. v. Islamic Republic of Iran*, *Iran-US CTR* 21 (1989-I) 112, at 201.

128 For example: *Phillips Petroleum Company of Iran v. The Government of the Islamic Republic of Iran*, *ibid.*, 79, at 122.

129 P. Malanczuk, International Business and New Rules of State Responsibility? – The Law Applied by the United Nations (Security Council) Compensation Commission for Claims against Iraq, in K.-H. Böckstiegel (ed.), *Perspectives of Air Law, Space Law and International Business Law for the Next Century*, 1996, 117–64.

130 See Christie, What Constitutes a Taking of Property under International Law?, *BYIL* 33 (1962), 307; Aldrich, *op. cit.*

131 On state contracts, see Chapter 3 above, 38–9.

One controversial problem is whether in the case of a 'going concern' (a business actually earning money) future expected profits are recoverable in addition to the current market value (after all, investors have taken risks to make profits). At least if the expropriation act was illegal under international law, there is a tendency to grant compensation also for lost profits.[128] To which extent the so-called 'discounted cash flow method', an accounting method calculating future profits and discounting certain amounts for costs and commercial risks, can be used in this connection, is another matter of dispute.[129]

Disguised expropriation

States often try to avoid unfavourable reactions from other states by carrying out expropriation in a disguised manner – for example, by placing a company under 'temporary' government control, which they then maintain indefinitely. Such subterfuges are seldom successful; any act which deprives a foreigner indefinitely of all benefit from his property is regarded by international law as an expropriation, even though a formal change of ownership may not have occurred. The position is less certain as regards acts which diminish the value of property but which do not deprive the owner of its use (for example, devaluation, exchange controls, restrictions on the remittance of profits, increases in taxation, and refusal to issue import licences, trading permits, or building permits). Such acts are permitted by international law, provided that they are not done for an improper motive. The easiest way of proving improper motives is to show that the acts in question discriminate against foreigners, or against a particular group of foreigners.[130]

Expropriation of contractual rights

So far we have been concerned only with expropriation of property, but there is no logical reason why the same principles should not apply to other forms of 'acquired rights', such as rights created by contracts between an alien and the defendant state.[131] However, such contracts are usually subject to the law of the defendant state, and it has been argued that the alien, by entering into a contract governed by the law of the defendant state, must take the risk of unfavourable amendments to that law, just as he takes the benefit of favourable amendments. This argument is fallacious; when an alien buys property in the defendant state, his title to the property is governed by the law of the defendant state, just as contracts made with the defendant state are governed by its own law, but few people would accept that the defendant state has an unlimited power to take away property rights; why, then, should it have an unlimited power to take away contractual rights? The idea that an alien voluntarily assumes the risk of unfavourable amendments to the law governing the contract has seldom been pushed to its logical conclusion, but it has exercised a limited influence on the law; breach of contract by a state does not engage the state's international responsibility unless it constitutes an abuse of *governmental* power. For instance, if a state makes a contract of sale and delivers goods of bad quality, that is not a breach of international law, because it is something which a private individual could have done. But if a state does not provide adequate remedies in its own courts for its breach of contract, or if it passes legislation annulling the contract, then it is abusing its governmental power and commits a breach of international law.

Historically, this branch of the law has been greatly influenced by the fact that most of the southern states of the United States had a bad record of default on loans. Other states were not slow to profit from this precedent, and as a result the rule grew up that states are not liable for contracts made by their political subdivisions (this is an exception to the general rule which makes the state liable for all acts of its political subdivisions).[132]

The right to development

The programme of a NIEO has been closely linked to the claim for recognition of a right to development[133] as a fundamental human right which is derived from the right to self-determination[134] and often interpreted in the sense of a legal obligation resting upon rich states to support poor states. Western states have opposed the recognition of a collective right to development, partly because of its undesired legal implications for financial transfers, partly because it is understood as being inconsistent with the Western concept of human rights.[135]

The right to development has been supported by the 1986 ILA Seoul Declaration[136] and in the same year the UN General Assembly adopted the Declaration on the Right of Development[137] with 146 votes in favour, but with the United States voting against it and seven other Western states abstaining (Denmark, Germany, Finland, Iceland, Israel, Japan and the UK). At the Rio Conference on Environment and Development in 1992, against the opposition of the United States, Canada and the European Community, developing countries managed to include the right to development in Principle 3 of the (non-binding) Rio Declaration. It is characteristic that the United States entered the following interpretative statement:

> The United States does not, by joining consensus on the Rio Declaration, change its long-standing opposition to the so-called right to development. Development is not a right. On the contrary, development is a goal we all hold, which depends for its realization in large part on the promotion and protection of the human rights set out in the Universal Declaration of Human Rights.[138]

Similarly, developing countries achieved a victory in trade-offs at the 1993 Vienna Human Rights Conference, the Declaration of which confirms that the right to development is a 'universal and inalienable right and an integral part of fundamental human rights'; but it also contains the caveat: '[w]hile development facilitates the enjoyment of all human rights, the lack of development may not be invoked to justify the abridgement of internationally recognized human rights.'[139]

The debate on the NIEO has currently lost much of its momentum with the collapse of the planned economies in socialist countries and the spread of market economy models throughout the world in the 1990s. However, as we shall see in the following chapter, the same problems have

132 See Randolph, Foreign Bondholders and Repudiated Debts of Southern States, *AJIL* 25 (1931), 63.
133 See P.J.I.M. de Waart/P. Peters/E. Denters (eds), *International Law and Development*, 1988; S.R. Chowdury/ E.M.G. Denters/P.J.I.M. de Waart (eds), *The Right to Development in International Law*, 1992; E.H. Riedel, Right to Development, in *Wolfrum UNLPP II*, 1103–10.
134 See Chapter 19 below, 326–40.
135 See Chapter 14 above, 209–11.
136 ILA Declaration 1986, *op. cit.*
137 UNGA Res. 41/128 of 4 December 1986.
138 J.D. Kovar, A Short Guide to the Rio Declaration, *CJIELP* 4 (1993), at 126.
139 Principle 10 of the 1993 Vienna Declaration.

140 K. Ginther/P.J.I.M. de Waart, Sustainable Development as a Matter of Good Governance: An Introductory View, in Ginther/Denters/de Waart (eds), *op. cit.*, 1, with reference to Boutros Boutros-Ghali, *An Agenda for Peace*, 1992, para. 59. See also Boutros-Ghali, *An Agenda for Development*, 1995.

reappeared in a new context, namely in the controversy between North and South on the protection of the global environment and its relationship to the concept of 'sustainable development'. A further new dimension has been added by the attempt to also link to this concept principles of 'good governance' (in the sense of good management), including

> sensible economic and social policies, democratic decision-making, adequate governmental transparency, financial accountability, creation of a market-friendly environment for development, measures to combat corruption, as well as respect for the rule of law and human rights.[140]

But at the moment this belongs more to the realm of the (possible) progressive development of international law than to the body of international law as it stands today.

16 Environment

Since the mid-1960s the obvious need to protect the deteriorating environment has led to environmental legislation in most countries of the world, to varying degrees and effect.[1] On the international level the United Nations Conference on the Human Environment held in Stockholm in 1972[2] became the starting point for the development of international environmental law as a separate and the youngest field of international law. Since the Stockholm Conference there has been a remarkable proliferation not only of universal policy statements, such as the World Charter for Nature, adopted by the UN General Assembly in 1982,[3] but also of international legal instruments in a broad variety of environmental areas.

The 1987 Brundtland *Report of the World Commission on Environment and Development*[4] emphasized the need for international cooperation and responsibility to activate common survival interests and to reduce the exhaustion of resources and the pollution of the environment. It also stressed the link between environment and development under the ambiguous concept of 'sustainable development'. The Commission defined sustainable development (in a rather ambiguous and abstract way) as 'development that meets the needs of the present without compromising the ability of future generations to meet their own needs'. The two key elements of the concept were identified as (1) 'the concept of "needs", in particular the essential needs of the world's poor, to which the overriding priority should be given', and (2) 'the idea of limitations imposed by the state of technology and social organization on the environment's ability to meet present and future needs'.[5] This process has culminated in the UN Conference on Environment and Development (UNCED) that was held in Rio de Janeiro in June 1992, twenty years after the Stockholm Conference.

Certainly, there were international legal developments concerning transboundary protection of the environment prior to the 1972 Stockholm Conference. But principles 21 and 22 in particular of the unanimously adopted Declaration are generally considered as the cornerstone of modern international environmental law. Principle 21 lays down the responsibility of all states 'to ensure that the activities within their jurisdiction and control do not cause damage to the environment of other States or areas beyond the limits of national jurisdiction', however, it also affirms the 'sovereign right of States to exploit their own resources pursuant to their own environmental policies' in accordance with the United Nations Charter and the principles of international law.[6] To make this principle operational in concrete terms, more specific rights and obligations had to be formulated. This was recognized in Principle 22 calling upon states 'to

1 See *Harris CMIL*, 242–9; R.-J. Dupuy (ed.), *The Future of the International Law of the Environment*, 1985; *Restatement (Third)*, Vol. 2, 99–143. A. Kiss/D. Shelton (eds), *International Environmental Law*, 1991, Supplement, 1994; W. Lang/H. Neuhold/K. Zemanek (eds), *Environmental Protection and International Law*, 1991; D.B. Magraw, *International Law and Pollution*, 1991; E. Brown-Weis (ed.), *Environmental Change and International Law*, 1992; P. Birnie/A.E. Boyle, *International Law and the Environment*, 1992; P. Sands (ed.), *Greening International Law*, 1993; M.A. Fitzmaurice, International Environmental Law as a Special Field, *NYIL* 25 (1994), 181–226; E.J. Urbani/C.P. Rubin (eds), *Transnational Environmental Law and its Impact on Corporate Behaviour*, 1994; H. Hohmann, *Precautionary Legal Duties and Principles of Modern International Environmental Law*, 1994; L. Gündling, Environment, International Protection, *EPIL* II (1995), 96–107; M. Kilian, Environmental Protection, in *Wolfrum UNLPP I*, 487–98; P. Sands/R. Tarasofsky/M. Weiss (eds), *Principles of International Environmental Law*, 1995; J. Kasto, *Modern International Law of the Environment*, 1995; V.P. Nanda, *International Environmental Law and Policy*, 1995. For collections of documents see B. Rüster/B. Simma, *International Protection of the Environment, Treaties and Related Documents*, 1975 *et seq.*; H. Hohmann (ed.), *Basic Documents on International Environmental Law*, 3rd edn 1992; P. Sands, *Principles of International Environmental Law*. Vol. II: Documents in International Environmental Law, 1995; W. Birnie/A. Boyle (eds) , *Basic Documents on International Law and the Environment*, 1995; W.E. Burhenne (ed.), *International Environmental Law: Multilateral Treaties*, 8 vols, 1996.
2 Stockholm Declaration on the Human Environment, Report of the United Nations Conference on the Human

Environment, UN Doc. A/Conf. 48/14/
Rev.1 (1972); *ILM* 11 (1972), 1416.
3 Resolution 37/7; Official Records of
the General Assembly, Thirty-Sixth
Session, Supplement No. 51 (A/36/51);
ILM 22 (1983), 455. See W.E.
Burhenne/W.A. Irwin, *The World Charter
for Nature*, 2nd edn 1986.
4 The World Commission on
Environment and Development, *Our
Common Future*, 1987. See also
*Environmental Protection and
Sustainable Development: Legal
Principles and Recommendations
adopted by the Experts Group on
Environmental Law of the World
Commission on Environment and
Development*, 1986; A. Hurrell/B.
Kingsbury, *The International Politics of
the Environment: Actors, Interests and
Institutions*, 1992; M.A.L. Miller, *The
Third World in Global Environmental
Politics*, 1995.
5 *Our Common Future, op. cit.*, at 43.
For a discussion see P. Malanczuk,
Sustainable Development: Some Critical
Thoughts in the Light of the Rio
Conference, in K. Ginther/E. Denters/
P.J.I.M. de Waart (eds), *Sustainable
Development and Good Governance*,
1995, 23–52; K. Hossain, Evolving
Principles of Sustainable Development,
ibid., 15–22; W. Lang (ed.), *Sustainable
Development and International Law*,
1995; P. Sands, International Law in the
Field of Sustainable Development, *BYIL*
65 (1994), 303–81; S. Lin/L.
Kurukulasuriya (eds), *UNEP's New Way
Forward: Environmental Law and
Sustainable Development*, 1995;
*Second Report of the ILA International
Committee on Legal Aspects of
Sustainable Development, Helsinki
Conference 1996*.
6 Principle 21, Stockholm Declaration,
op. cit., at 5.
7 Principle 22.
8 See G. Betlem, *Civil Liability for
Transfrontier Pollution*, 1993. On liability
and responsibility, see Chapter 17
below, 254–5.
9 J.J.A. Salmon, Marine Environment,
Protection and Preservation, *EPIL* 11
(1989), 200–7; J.H. Bates/C. Benson
(eds), *Marine Environmental Law*, 1993;
C.M. de la Rue (ed.), *Liability for
Damage to the Marine Environment*,
1993; D. Brubaker, *Marine Pollution and
International Law: Principles and
Practice*, 1993; J.J.A. Salmon,
International Watercourses, Pollution,
EPIL II (1995), 1388–92.
10 The 1982 Convention provides in
forty-six articles (Articles 192–237) for
the protection and preservation of the

develop further the international law regarding liability and compensation for the victims of pollution and other environmental damage caused by activities within the jurisdiction or control of such States to areas beyond their jurisdiction'.[7] But it is particularly in the area of their own liability (as distinct from the civil liability of private operators) over which states have proved highly reluctant to accept binding obligations.[8]

The scope and nature of international environmental law

International environmental law is primarily based upon treaties and other international legal instruments. As to the substantive areas, it is convenient to distinguish two phases in the development of international environmental law since Stockholm. The first phase introduced the United Nations Environment Programme (UNEP) and the Action Plan for the Human Environment which was followed by legal instruments dealing with water, air and soil pollution arising from industrial activities as well as from poverty.

With regard to the protection of the marine environment,[9] there is no comprehensive global treaty dealing with all relevant aspects. The 1982 Law of the Sea Convention[10] only provides for general principles in this area and for a new allocation of legislative and enforcement powers between the coastal states and the flag states. The global treaty regime thus rests upon the regulation of specific sources of sea pollution. There are several conventions dealing with oil pollution of the sea, such as the 1954 International Convention for the Prevention of Pollution of the Sea by Oil,[11] the 1969 International Convention on Civil Liability for Oil Pollution Damage,[12] the 1969 International Convention Relating to Intervention on the High Seas in Cases of Oil Pollution Casualties,[13] and the 1971 International Convention on the Establishment of an International Fund for Compensation for Oil Pollution Damage.[14] The hazardous experience of major oil pollution accidents led to the adoption in 1990 of a new Convention of the International Maritime Organization (IMO) on Oil Pollution, Preparedness, Response and Co-operation.[15]

Furthermore, the problem of the pollution of the sea by waste is covered by the 1972 Convention on the Prevention of Marine Pollution by Dumping of Wastes and Other Matter[16] and the 1973 International Convention for the Prevention of Pollution from Ships.[17] On the regional level, there are similar types of instrument aiming at the protection of the North Atlantic and the North Sea, including the 1972 Convention for the Prevention of Marine Pollution by Dumping from Ships and Aircraft,[18] the 1974 Convention on the Prevention of Marine Pollution from Land-Based Sources[19] and the 1992 Convention for the Protection of the Marine Environment of the North-East Atlantic.[20] But there are also more comprehensive treaties dealing with all sources of pollution, such as the 1976 Convention for the Protection of the Mediterranean Sea Against Pollution,[21] the 1974 Convention on the Protection of the Marine Environment of the Baltic Sea Area,[22] or the 1978 Kuwait Regional Convention for Co-operation on the Protection of the Marine Environment from Pollution.[23] Many (mostly regional) treaties are further concerned with the protection

of marine living resources.[24] However, such agreements have lost importance because of the emergence of the 200-mile exclusive economic zone
which grants coastal states jurisdiction in this respect.[25]

As far as rivers and lakes are concerned, there are also a number of
specific instruments, such as the 1992 Convention on the Protection and
Use of Transboundary Watercourses and International Lakes.[26] In Europe
one could mention the 1960 Convention on the Protection of Lake Constance Against Pollution,[27] the 1961 Protocol concerning the Constitution
of an International Commission for the Protection of the Moselle Against
Pollution,[28] the agreements between Belgium, France and the Netherlands
concerning the rivers Meuse and Scheldt,[29] and the international attempts
to mitigate the pollution of the Rhine, including the 1963 Agreement
concerning the International Commission for the Protection of the Rhine
Against Pollution,[30] the 1976 Convention on the Protection of the Rhine
Against Chemical Pollution,[31] the 1976 Convention Concerning the Protection of the Rhine Against Pollution by Chlorides,[32] and the 1987 Rhine
Action Programme.[33] A recent example outside of Europe is the agreement between Cambodia, Laos, Thailand and Vietnam on Cooperation
for the Sustainable Development of the Mekong River.[34] Furthermore, the
codification of international law in this area by the International Law
Commission[35] has made some progress with its 1994 Draft Articles on the
Law of the Non-Navigational Use of International Watercourses.[36]

In the field of air pollution only one multilateral treaty exists: the 1979
Geneva Convention on Long-Range Transboundary Air Pollution, to
which almost all European States and the United States and Canada
are parties.[37] The Convention has been amended by the 1984 Protocol
(concerning the long-term financing of the cooperative programme for
monitoring and evaluation of the long-range transmission of air pollution
in Europe),[38] the 1985 Protocol (concerning the reduction of sulphur emissions or their transboundary fluxes by at least 30 per cent),[39] the 1988
Protocol Concerning the Control of Emissions of Nitrogen Oxides or
Their Transboundary Fluxes, the 1991 Protocol on Volatile Organic Com-
pounds, and the 1994 Protocol on Further Reduction of Sulphur
Emissions.[40]

Another area where a number of international agreements have been
concluded is the protection of nature and the conservation of species.[41]
These include the 1971 Convention on Wetlands of International Importance, Especially as Waterfowl Habitat,[42] the 1972 Convention Concerning
the Protection of the World Cultural and Natural Heritage,[43] the 1973
Convention on International Trade in Endangered Species of Wild Fauna
and Flora,[44] the 1979 Convention on the Preservation of Migratory Species of Wild Animals,[45] and the 1979 Convention on the Conservation of
European Wildlife and Natural Habitats.[46] The concern about the hunting
of whales has also produced international instruments.[47]

Moreover, international transport and disposal of hazardous waste
has been regulated by treaties such as the 1989 Basel Convention on the
Control of Transboundary Movements of Hazardous Wastes and their
Disposal[48] and the 1991 OAU Bamako Convention on the Ban of the
Import into Africa and Management of Hazardous Wastes within Africa.[49]

marine environment. See W.v. Reenen,
Rules of Reference in the New
Convention on the Law of the Sea, in
Particular in Connection with the
Pollution of the Sea by Oil from Tankers,
NYIL 12 (1981), 3–44; B. Kwiatkowska,
Marine-Based Pollution in the Exclusive
Economic Zone: Reconciling Rights,
Freedoms and Responsibilities, *Hague
YIL* 1 (1988), 111; R.P.M. Lotilla, The
Efficacy of the Anti-Pollution Legislation
Provisions of the 1982 Law of the Sea
Convention: A View from South East
Asia, *ICLQ* 41 (1992), 137–51. See
Chapter 12 above, 173–5.
11 327 UNTS 3.
12 *ILM* 9 (1970), 45.
13 *Ibid.*, 25.
14 Cmnd. 7383. See R.B. Mitchell,
*International Oil Pollution at Sea:
Environmental Policy and Treaty
Compliance*, 1994; W. Chao, *Pollution
from the Carriage of Oil by Sea*, 1996.
15 *ILM* 30 (1991), 733.
16 *ILM* 11 (1972), 1294.
17 *ILM* 12 (1973), 1319. See also the
results of the 1996 IMO Conference on
hazardous and noxious substances and
limitation of liability, *ILM* 35 (1996),
1406.
18 *ILM* 11 (1972), 262.
19 *ILM* 14 (1975), 352.
20 *YIEL* 3 (1992), 759.
21 *ILM* 15 (1976), 290. See S.
Milenkovic, Mediterranean Pollution
Conventions, *EPIL* 9 (1986), 264–6;
22 *ILM* 13 (1974), 546. See M.
Fitzmaurice, *International Legal
Problems of the Environmental
Protection of the Baltic Sea*, 1992.
23 *ILM* 17 (1978), 511.
24 See B. Kwiatkowska, Conservation
of Living Resources of the High Seas,
EPIL I (1992), 761–3; R. Wolfrum,
Fisheries, International Regulation, *EPIL*
II (1995), 383–6 and Chapter 12 above,
175, 183–5.
25 See Chapter 12 above, 183–5.
26 *ILM* 31 (1992), 1313.
27 UN Doc. ST/LEG/SER.B/12. 438.
See J.A. Frowein, Lake Constance, *EPIL*
12 (1990), 216–19.
28 940 UNTS 211. See G. Nolte,
Moselle River, *EPIL* 12 (1990), 228–30.
29 *ILM* 34 (1995), 851.
30 994 UNTS 3.
31 *ILM* 16 (1977), 242.
32 *ILM* 16 (1977), 265.
33 See A. Rest, The Sandoz
Conflagration and the Rhine Pollution:
Liability Issues, *GYIL* 30 (1987), 160–
76; W.E. Haak, Experience of the
Netherlands Regarding the Case-Law of
the Chamber of Appeal of the Central
Commission for Navigation of the Rhine,

NYIL 19 (1988), 3–51; F. Meißner, Rhine River, *EPIL* 12 (1990), 310–6.

34 *ILM* 34 (1995), 864.

35 See Chapter 3 above, 61.

36 1994 ILC Report, UN GAOR, 49th Sess., Supp. No. 10. See A. Nollkaemper, *The Legal Regime for Transboundary Water Pollution: Between Discretion and Constraint*, 1993; E. Benvenisti, Collective Action in the Utilization of Shared Freshwater: The Challenge of International Water Resources, *AJIL* 90 (1996), 384–415.

37 *ILM* 18 (1979), 1442. See C. Flintermann/B. Kwiatkowska/J.G. Lammers (eds), *Transboundary Air Pollution*, 1986; A. Kiss, Air Pollution, *EPIL* I (1992), 72–4.

38 *ILM* 27 (1988), 701.

39 *Ibid.*, 707.

40 *ILM* 33 (1994), 1540.

41 See M.J. Forster, Plant Protection, International, *EPIL* 9 (1986), 303–5; P.H. Sand, Wildlife Protection, *ibid.*, 409–14; M.C. Maffie, Evolving Trends in the International Protection of Species, *GYIL* 36 (1993), 131–86.

42 996 UNTS 245.

43 *ILM* 11 (1972), 1358.

44 *ILM* 12 (1973), 1085. P. Matthews, Problems Related to the Convention on the International Trade in Endangered Species, *ICLQ* 45 (1996), 421–30.

45 *ILM* 19 (1980), 15.

46 Cmnd. 8738.

47 See D.D. Caron The International Whaling Commission and the North Atlantic Marine Mammal Commission: The Institutional Risks of Coercion in Consensual Structures, *AJIL* 89 (1995), 154 *et seq.*

48 *ILM* 28 (1989), 652. See G.J. Timagenis, Waste Disposal, EPIL 9 (1986), 401–6; M. Bothe, International Regulation of Transboundary Movement of Hazardous Waste, *GYIL* 33 (1990), 422; B. Kwiatkowska/A.H.A. Soons, Transboundary Movements of Hazardous Wastes and Their Disposal: Emerging Global and Regional Regulation, *Hague YIL* 5 (1992), 68–136; S.D. Murphy, Prospective Liability Regimes for the Transboundary Movement of Hazardous Wastes, *AJIL* 88 (1994), 24.

49 *ILM* 30 (1991), 775.

50 956 UNTS 252; *ILM* 2 (1963), 685.

51 *ILM* 2 (1963), 727.

52 974 UNTS 255.

53 See P. Sands, *Chernobyl: Law and Communication. Transboundary Nuclear Air Pollution – The Legal Materials*, 1988; P. Cameron/L. Hancher/W. Kühn, *Nuclear Energy Law after Chernobyl*, 1988; A.E. Boyle, Nuclear Energy and

Several treaties have addressed the issue of liability with regard to the peaceful use of nuclear energy. But they only laid down rules concerning the civil liability of operators, not the liability of states, like the 1960 and 1963 Conventions on Third Party Liability in the Field of Nuclear Energy,[50] the 1963 Vienna Convention on Civil Liability for Nuclear Damage,[51] and the 1971 Convention Relating to Civil Liability in the Field of Maritime Carriage of Nuclear Material.[52] These treaties were insufficient to deal with the Chernobyl catastrophe; new agreements were concluded only in the aftermath of the accident.[53] Still, as of 1996, the plant in the Ukraine continued to operate, for economic reasons.

Finally, there is also a special 1977 Convention on the Prohibition of Military or Any Other Hostile Use of Environmental Modification Techniques.[54] This issue moved to the forefront again in connection with the Second Gulf War when Iraq was accused of making detrimental use of the environment (burning of oil fields; oil pollution of the Gulf) as a weapon in armed conflict.[55] Claims arising out of these incidents will also be dealt with by the UN Compensation Commission in Geneva.[56]

The second phase added the concern for new issues, such as the protection of the ozone layer, which is being destroyed by the emission of chlorofluorocarbons (CFCs), which led to the Vienna Convention for the Protection of the Ozone Layer of 22 March 1985.[57] Other new problems, addressed finally at the Rio Conference,[58] include climate change due to global warming (the 'greenhouse effect'),[59] the preservation of biodiversity, and the problems of deforestation and desertification of particular concern in Africa.[60] In 1991 a Protocol on Environmental Protection to the Antarctic Treaty was adopted, which has four Annexes dealing with environmental impact assessment, conservation of flora and fauna, waste disposal and marine pollution.[61] Furthermore, in the context of the GATT/WTO negotiations the relationship between environmental protection and international trade regulation is recently receiving more attention.[62] The problem of 'space debris' and environmental hazards arising from outer space activities have already been mentioned.[63]

An inventory of actual treaty-making activities submitted in the preparatory process of UNCED registered more than one hundred relevant multilateral instruments in force.[64] This does not include the numerous instruments concerning shared water resources or natural risks or diseases. It also omits the entire body of European Community regulation.[65] More than half of the global and regional agreements are in the area of the protection of the marine environment and marine living resources. The second largest group deals with nature conservation and terrestrial resources and ecosystems, and the third most significant category addresses hazardous substances and processes. This still does not give a complete picture. A more comprehensive count arrives at 870 international legal instruments in which at least some provisions deal with the environment.[66]

Furthermore, in addition to treaties, the classical instruments of international law-making, there is a controversial category of so-called 'soft law' instruments, which are often regarded as being characteristic for international environmental diplomacy.[67] These instruments which may be in the form of a declaration, resolution or a set of guidelines or recommendations, such as the 1972 Stockholm Declaration, are not formally binding, but nevertheless have an important political-legal significance as a guide for political action and as a starting-point for the development of binding international environmental rules and principles, either in the form of a later treaty or in the form of customary international law. Moreover, 'there is an important margin of international technical regulations operating under agreements that are not environmental *per se* but the implementation of which increasingly requires a kind of "creeping" environmental standard-setting',[68] such as, for example, noise and air pollutant emission limits for aircraft engines or motor vehicle engines.

The method of treaty-making in environmental diplomacy may be described as a piecemeal approach which has failed to reach an integration of sectoral and cross-sectoral, regional and global policies.[69] In other words, there is no comprehensive legal regime protecting the environment or the 'biosphere' as a whole by international law and international organizations.[70] The new concept of 'ecological security'[71] has so far not been translated into a consistent and all-embracing normative framework; the interlinkages between the various treaty regimes are therefore not yet properly addressed. The nature of existing international environmental law has been described as an 'aggregate, rather than a system, of multiple environmental regimes'.[72] The effectiveness of many environmental treaties on the global level is also a problem.[73] An important step has been taken on the regional level by the Economic Commission for Europe (ECE) by adopting in 1991 the Convention on Environmental Impact Assessment in a Transboundary Context.[74]

In addition, the treaty-making process is rather slow. Normally it takes between two and twelve years for multilateral treaties to become effective; the average period appears to be about five years.[75] It must be said, however, that many environmental treaties seem to move faster, such as the Mediterranean Convention and the Ozone Layer Convention, which both became effective within only two years. The problem is that in the field of environmental protection, even such relatively short periods may be too long for an effective response to challenges requiring immediate action. Thus, in the case of the Montreal Protocol it soon became clear that the CFC reduction rates established in September 1987 were already outdated when the protocol entered into force. This necessitated a revision by a 'fast-track' procedure unknown to the treaty, the May 1989 Helsinki Declaration on the Protection of the Ozone Layer.[76]

Customary law and general principles

As in the area of space law[77] or in the field of international economic law,[78] customary international law dealing with the environment is at best rudimentary.[79] It traditionally relies on a few cases, the most important being the *Trail Smelter* arbitration between Canada and the United States, which was initiated in 1926 and finally concluded in 1941.[80] This decision is usually referred to for the basic legal proposition that no state may knowingly allow its territory to be used in a manner that would cause serious

International Law: An Environmental Perspective, *BYIL* 60 (1989), 257 *et seq.*; M.M. El Baradei/E.I. Nwogugu/J.M. Rames (eds), *The International Law of Nuclear Energy*, 2 Vols, 1993; M.T. Kamminga, The IAEA Convention on Nuclear Safety, *ICLQ* 44 (1995), 872–82; OECD, *Regulatory and Institutional Framework for Nuclear Activities*, 1995; Chernobyl: Ten Years After, *UN Chronicle* 33 (1996), 78–9.

54 *ILM* 16 (1977), 88.

55 See Chapter 20 below, 362.

56 See Chapter 22 below, 398–9.

57 *ILM* 26 (1987), 1550, as amended by the Montreal Protocol in 1990, *ILM* 30 (1991), 539, with further amendments in 1991 and 1992. See, e.g., R.E. Benedick, *Ozone Diplomacy: New Directions in Safeguarding the Planet*, 1990; V.P. Nanda, Stratospheric Ozone Depletion: A Challenge for International Environmental Law and Policy, *Mich. JIL* 10 (1989), 482; Environment: Ozone Layer, *UN Chronicle* 33 (1996), 73–4.

58 See text below, 247.

59 W. Lang, Auf der Suche nach einem wirksamen Klima-Regime, *AVR* 31 (1993), 13–21; see also W.R. Cline, *The Economics of Global Warming*, 1992.

60 See text below, 247–8.

61 *ILM* 30 (1991), 1460. See Chapter 10 above, 150.

62 See, for example, K. Andersen/R. Blackhurst (eds), *The Greening of World Trade Issues*, 1992; J. Schultz, The GATT/WTO Committee on Trade and the Environment – Toward Environmental Reform, *AJIL* 89 (1995), 423–39; H. Ward, Common But Differentiated Debates: Environment, Labour and the World Trade Organization, *ICLQ* 45 (1996), 592–632. See Chapter 15 above, 231–3.

63 See Chapter 13 above, 207.

64 See the revised list of agreements and instruments approved at the third session of the UNCED Preparatory Committee, in Decision I, Annex III, A/CONF.151/PC/94.

65 See A.C. Kiss/D. Shelton, *Manual of European Environmental Law*, 1993; P. Sands, *Principles of International Environmental Law*. Vol. III: Documents in European Community Environmental Law, 1995; S. Hollins/R. Macrory, *A Source Book of European Community Environmental Law*, 1995.

66 E. Weiss, Introductory Note, United Nations Conference on Environment and Development, *ILM* 31 (1992), 814.

67 See Chapter 3 above, 54–5.

68 P.H. Sand, International Law on the Agenda of the United Nations

Conference on Environment and Development: Towards Global Environmental Security?, *Nordic JIL* 60 (1991), 5, at 8.

69 P.H. Sand, *Lessons Learned in Global Environmental Governance*, 1990, 35; see further P. Malanczuk, Towards Global Environmental Legislation, in United Nations Office for Outer Space Affairs (ed.), *Proceedings of the UN/IAF Workshop on 'Organising Space Activities in Developing Countries: Resources and Mechanisms'* (Graz, 15–17 October 1993), 1994, 45–60.

70 O. Schachter, *International Law in Theory and Practice*, 1991, 362, with reference to the new concept of the 1972 Stockholm Conference.

71 See G. Handl, Environmental Security and Global Change: The Challenge to International Law, *YIEL* 1 (1990), 3–33.

72 Sand (1991), *op. cit.*, 33.

73 See P.H. Sand (ed.), *The Effectiveness of International Environmental Agreements – A Survey of Existing Legal Instruments*, 1992; M.E. O'Connell, Enforcing the New International Law of the Environment, *GYIL* 35 (1992), 293; L.E. Susskind, Environmental Diplomacy. Negotiating More Effective Global Agreements, 1994.

74 *ILM* 30 (1991), 800.

75 Sand (1990), *op. cit.*, 15 with reference to a 1971 UNITAR study and other literature.

76 Sand, *ibid.*, 15.

77 See Chapter 13 above, 201–7.

78 See Chapter 15 above, 223.

79 See W. Lang, Diplomacy and International Environmental Law-Making: Some Observations, *YIEL* 3 (1992), 108, who notes that today international environmental law is mostly treaty-based.

80 *Trail Smelter* case (1931–1941), *RIAA* III 1905. See K.J. Madders, Trail Smelter Arbitration, *EPIL* 2 (1981), 276–80.

81 *Affaire du Lac Lanoux* case, RIAA XII 281 (1963). See D. Rauschning, Lac Lanoux Arbitration, *EPIL* 2 (1981), 166–8.

82 *US v. Canada*, *ILM* 8 (1969), 118; G. Handl, Gut Dam Claims, *EPIL* II (1995), 653–6.

83 *ILM* 35 (1996), 809, at 821, para. 29. On the role of the ICJ in the development of international environmental law, see M. Fitzmaurice, Environmental Protection and the International Court of Justice, in V. Lowe/M. Fitzmaurice (eds), *Fifty Years of the International Court of Justice*,

physical injury to the environment of another state. It has been confirmed by other cases, such as the *Lac Lanoux* case[81] and the *Gut Dam* case.[82] In its 1996 *Advisory Opinion on the Legality of the Threat or Use of Nuclear Weapons*, the International Court of Justice confirmed for the first time in more general terms that the Court recognizes

> that the environment is not an abstraction but represents the living space, the quality of life and the very health of human beings, including generations unborn. The existence of the general obligation of states to ensure that activities within their jurisdiction and control respect the environment of other States or of areas beyond national control is now part of the corpus of international law relating to the environment.[83]

Although technically not legally binding,[84] this statement of the Court is likely to contribute in the future to the development of international environmental law in other cases.

There are also a number of general concepts and principles that have been applied or proposed to deal with transboundary harm, such as the *sic utere tuo ut alienum non laedas* principle ('use your own so as not to injure another'), the concept of 'abuse of rights', the principle of territorial integrity, the principle of 'good neighbourliness' (*bon voisinage*) and quite a few others.[85] The legal status of such principles and concepts, however, is not always secure and on their own they do not lend themselves easily to deciding between competing claims or, even less, to determining the scope, content and function of appropriate environmental regulation in an operational manner.

Since 1972 various non-official and official bodies have engaged in codifying and progressively developing international environmental law, including the Institut de Droit International, the International Law Association, the International Law Commission of the United Nations, the United Nations Environment Programme (UNEP)[86] and the International Union for the Conservation of Nature (IUCN). These efforts include the adoption of resolutions by the Institut de Droit International in 1979 on the pollution of rivers and lakes and in 1987 on transboundary air pollution, and by the International Law Association in 1982 on transfrontier pollution in general. The International Law Commission is still occupied with codifying law on environmental issues under various headings, such as the draft code of crimes against peace and humanity, the articles on non-navigational uses of international watercourses, the articles on international liability for injurious consequences arising out of acts not prohibited by international law, and its draft articles on state responsibility for internationally wrongful acts.[87] The UN General Assembly has included the future development of international environmental law in the programme of the United Nations Decade of International Law (1990–9) and taken note of the conclusions of the 1990 Sienna Forum on International Law of the Environment. The 1990–5 'system-wide medium-term environment programme' (SWMTEP) includes programme activities by the United Nations relating to environmental law and institutions. The work of UNEP in this area relies on the 1981 Montevideo

Programme for the Development and Periodic Review of Environmental Law.[88] While these texts generally require states to prevent, mitigate, repair or compensate for harm, as well as to notify others of transboundary risks, it is not quite settled to what extent these principles have actually become part of customary law.[89]

The United Nations Conference on Environment and Development

More than 170 countries and 103 heads of government attended the high-level United Nations Conference on Environment and Development (UNCED) which took place in Rio de Janeiro from 3–14 June 1992.[90] It was at that time the largest international conference ever, and a spectacular event with the presence of a large number of NGOs and other actors.[91] It has been noted that UNCED made its mark on the development of inter-national environmental law 'by formally anointing the concept of "sustain-able development" for legal use'.[92] While sustainable development was indeed at the heart of the Rio Conference, the conflict between North and South on its meaning was predominant. There were certainly also differ-ences between, for example, the United States and other industrialized countries, or between the African, Latin American and Asian states among themselves, or between the developing countries and the new states arising from the remains of the former Soviet Union. But the North–South con-flict was undoubtedly at the centre. Although the confrontation between North and South was on a lower level than some had expected, or was to some extent postponed, UNCED clearly manifested a trend towards fur-ther polarization which is reflected in 'a distinct new bipolar pattern of negotiating and decision-making procedures'.[93]

The 1989 UN General Assembly resolution which convened the Rio Conference had made it one of the objectives of UNCED 'to promote the further development of international environmental law, taking into account the Declaration of the United Nations Conference on the Human Environment, as well as the special needs and concerns of the developing countries, and to examine in this context the feasibility of elaborating general rights and obligations of States, as appropriate, in the field of environment, and taking into account relevant existing international legal instruments'.[94] The resolution also gave UNCED the mandate 'to assess the capacity of the United Nations system to assist in the prevention and settlement of disputes in the environmental sphere and to recommend measures in this field, while respecting existing bilateral and international agreements that provide for the settlement of disputes'.[95] The Conference finally adopted the Rio Declaration containing twenty-seven non-binding principles on environment and development from a global perspective.[96] It also passed the complex and equally non-binding Agenda 21, a com-prehensive blueprint of 800 pages designed to deal with the common environment and development problems of the next century. In addition, the Conventions on Climate Change and Biodiversity were adopted. With difficulties, parties managed to agree on a document with the illuminating title: 'A Non-legally binding Authoritative Statement of Principles for a Global Consensus on the Management, Conservation and Sustainable

1996, 293–315 and Chapter 18 below, 288.

84 See Chapter 18 below, 289.

85 See J. Lammers, *Pollution of International Waterways*, 1984, 556–80, who lists twenty-seven of such principles or concepts.

86 M. Kilian, UNEP, in *Wolfrum UNLPP II*, 1296–1303.

87 See Chapter 17 below, 254–6.

88 See G. Biggs, The Montevideo Environmental Law Programme, *AJIL* 87 (1993), 328–34.

89 Schachter, *op. cit.*, 364.

90 See D.H. Getches, Foreword: The Challenge of Rio, *CJIELP* 4 (1993), 1–19; M.F. Strong, Beyond Rio: Prospects and Portents, *ibid.*, 21–36; T.E. Wirth, The Road From Rio – Defining a New World Order, *ibid.*, 37–44; M.P.A. Kindall, Talking Past Each Other At The Summit, *ibid.*, 69–79; P.H. Sand, International Environmental Law after Rio, *EJIL* 4 (1993), 377 *et seq.*; U. Beyerlin, Rio-Konferenz 1992: Beginn einer neuen globalen Umweltrechtsordnung?, *ZaöRV* 54 (1994), 124–47; Malanczuk (1995), Sustainable Development, *op. cit.*; *idem*, Die Konferenz der Vereinten Nationen über Umwelt und Entwicklung (UNCED) und das internationale Umweltrecht, in *FS Bernhardt*, 985–1002.

91 At the Global Forum, NGOs negotiated more than thirty 'treaties'.

92 P.H. Sand, UNCED and the Development of International Environmental Law, *YIEL* 3 (1992), 17.

93 Sand (1992), *op. cit.*, 14 *et seq.*

94 UNGA Res. 44/228 of 22 December 1989.

95 *Ibid.*

96 For the Rio documents see *ILM* 31 (1992), 818 *et seq.* (except Agenda 21); N.A. Robinson (ed.), *Agenda 21 & UNCED Proceedings*, 1992; S. Johnson (ed.), *The Earth Summit: The United Nations Conference on Environment and Development (UNCED)*, 1992.

97 See the Convention to Combat Desertification in those Countries Experiencing Serious Drought and/or Desertification, Particularly in Africa, 17 June 1994, *ILM* 33 (1994), 1328; W.C. Burns, The International Convention to Combat Desertification: Drawing a Line in the Sand?, *Mich. JIL* 16 (1995), 831–82.

98 Text in *ILM* 31 (1992), 849. See *YIEL* 1 (1990), 101–4; 2 (1991), 111–15; 3 (1992), 228–31 (T. Goldman and S. Hajost as reporters); E.P. Barratt-Brown/S.A. Hajost/J.H. Sterne, Jr., A Forum for Action on Global Warming: The UN Framework Convention on Climate Change, *CJIELP* 4 (1993), 103–18; D. Bodansky, Managing Climate Change, *YIEL* 3 (1992), 60–74; M.J. LaLonde, The Role of Risk Analysis in the 1992 Framework Convention on Climate Change, *Mich. JIL* 15 (1994), 215–54.

99 *ASIL IELIGNewsl.* 3/2 (1993), 2.

100 *ASIL IELNews* 4/1 (1993), 2. See on the further development: S. Oberthür/H. Ott, First Conference of the Parties, *EPL* 25 (1995), 144–56.

101 *ILM* 30 (1991), 1735.

Development of all types of Forests'. The most contentious issues concerned the right to development, the demand to limit over-consumption and to increase forest cover in developed countries, and financial transfers. African countries succeeded in having UNCED adopt their proposal to negotiate a convention on desertification.[97]

The Convention on Climate Change

The Framework Convention on Climate Change was negotiated by the Intergovernmental Negotiating Committee, an independent body that had been established by the UN General Assembly.[98] It was signed by 154 states and the European Community and entered into force, after fifty ratifications, on 21 March 1994. As of 1995, more than 125 states had ratified the Convention. The general objective of the Convention is to stabilize atmospheric concentrations of all greenhouse gases, not only carbon dioxide. It sets forth a number of guiding principles relating to equity, 'common, but differentiated responsibilities' of States, precaution, the special needs and circumstances of developing countries, sustainable development, and international trade. The Convention goes further than the earlier framework Conventions such as the Montreal Protocol and the Long-Range Transboundary Air Pollution Convention. But, due to the resistance of the United States and the OPEC countries, it failed to establish definite quantitative restrictions on greenhouse gas emissions at any given level at a certain date in the future. Developed countries merely recognized the importance of the 'return . . . to earlier levels of anthropogenic emissions' by the year 2000. However, they agreed to stricter reporting requirements with the aim of returning individually or jointly to their 1990 levels of emissions. The European Community issued a statement that reaffirmed its objective of stabilizing carbon dioxide emissions by the year 2000 at 1990 levels in the Community as a whole. The United States was the first industrialized country (and second country overall after Mauritius) to ratify the Convention (on 7 October 1992),[99] but it was only in April 1993 that the United States declared that it would reduce emissions at 1990 levels by the year 2000.[100]

The Convention establishes a process by which parties, on the basis of national greenhouse inventories and regular national reports on policies and measures to limit emissions, can monitor and control effects on climate change. Developed countries agreed to fund the costs of developing country reports as well as other developing countries' projects approved by the Convention's financial mechanism which, on an interim basis, is the Global Environmental Facility (GEF)[101] of the World Bank, UNDP and UNEP. There are also general obligations with regard to scientific research, exchange of information, and education and training. The Convention further envisages the establishment of a subsidiary body to continue to provide scientific assessments and advice on advances in relevant technologies (Article 9). The dispute between North and South on the financial mechanism was carried on to the following meetings of the Intergovernmental Negotiating Committee. The first conference of the parties, which took place in Berlin in April 1995, failed to make significant progress, partly due to the blocking role played by oil-producing countries such as Saudi Arabia and Kuwait. It was agreed to negotiate on a protocol or other legal instrument to supplement the Framework Convention which might be adopted in 1997.[102]

The Biodiversity Convention

The Convention on Biological Diversity was prepared under the auspices of UNEP by an Intergovernmental Negotiating Committee and opened for signature in Rio.[103] As of June 1993, it was signed by 163 states. It entered into force on 29 December 1993 after thirty ratifications. The Convention aims at the conservation and sustainable use of biological diversity, the fair and equitable sharing of the benefits from its use, and the regulation of biotechnology. The parties failed to agree on the development of national lists of threatened species and areas of biological importance. The approach is rather to provide for national monitoring of and for national plans, programmes and measures for conserving biodiversity, supplemented by international reporting obligations.

Access to and transfer of technology 'shall be provided and/or facilitated under fair and favourable terms, including on concessional and preferential terms' – however, only 'where mutually agreed'. The transfer of patents shall be based upon 'terms which recognize and are consistent with the adequate and effective protection of intellectual property rights'.[104] Cooperation is required to ensure that intellectual property rights are 'supportive of and do not run counter to' the goals of the Convention. The Convention further deals with priority access of the source country to results and benefits arising from biotechnologies based upon its genetic resources on mutually agreed terms. Developed countries are obliged to provide 'new and additional financial resources' to fund the 'agreed full incremental costs' of developing countries to implement the Convention as agreed with the Convention's financial mechanism. The latter is put under the authority of the Convention's Conference of the Parties. On an interim basis the GEF will serve as the financial mechanism, provided it has been 'fully restructured'.

The only country that refused to sign the Biodiversity Convention at Rio was the United States, due to pressure from the biotechnology and pharmacology businesses interested in resources in tropical countries. The United States argued that in particular, the provisions on intellectual property, on the funding mechanism, and on biotechnology were 'seriously flawed'.[105] However, in June 1993 the United States signed the Convention, stating that it would formally address the question of intellectual property protection in a forthcoming interpretative document.[106] It also called upon other signatories to implement policies that do not restrict the development, commercialization and marketing of biotechnology products, and noted that the United States supports the use of creative economic incentives, such as the fair and equitable sharing of the benefits arising from the use of genetic resources, and would work to ensure that there will be full and fair consideration of the need for a protocol on biosafety, and that biosafety regulation must be scientifically based and analytically sound. The Convention was transmitted to the US Senate for advice and ratification on 30 November 1993.[107]

102 United Nations Framework Convention on Climate Change Conference of the Parties: Decisions Adopted by the First Session (Berlin, 28 March 28–7 April, 1995), Introductory Note by M. Carlson and A. Petsonk, *ILM* 34 (1995), 1671–1711.
103 Text of the Convention in *ILM* 31 (1992), 818. See M. Chandler, The Biodiversity Convention: Selected Issues of Interest to the International Lawyer, *CJIELP* 4 (1993), 141–75; R.L. Margulies, Protecting Biodiversity: Recognizing International Intellectual Property Resources, *Mich. JIL* 14 (1993), 322; M. Bowman/C. Redgwell (eds), *International Law and the Conservation of Biological Diversity*, 1995; F. McConnell, *The Biodiversity Convention. A Negotiating History*, 1996.
104 On the general international debate on intellectual property protection and the situation in North–South relations, see the differentiated analysis by J.v. Wijk/G. Junne, *Intellectual Property Protection of Advanced Technology – Changes in the Global Technology System: Implications and Options for Developing Countries*, The United Nations University, INTECH Working Paper No. 10, October 1993.
105 *ASIL IELIGNewsl.* 3/1 (1992), 2.
106 *ASIL IELNews* 4/1 (1993), 1.
107 *ASIL IELNews* 5/1 (1994), 2.

108 Text in *ILM* 31 (1992), 874. See F.K. Boon, The Rio Declaration and Its Influence on International Environmental Law, *Sing. JLS* (1992), 347–64; J.D. Kovar, A Short Guide to the Rio Declaration, *CJIELP* 4 (1993), 119–40; Malanczuk (1995), Sustainable Development, *op. cit.*

109 For an analysis of inter-generational and sustainable development standards emerging from Rio see M. Bothe/H. Hohmann, *YIEL* 3 (1993), 174 *et seq.* On the precautionary principle see Hohman, *op. cit.*, D. Freestone (ed.), *The Precautionary Principle and International Law*, 1995.

110 See Robinson (ed.), *op. cit.*

111 Bothe/Hohmann *op. cit.*, 177.

112 Agenda 21, Chapter 33, para. 20.

113 Introductory statement made by the Secretary-General of the Conference at the fourth session of the Preparatory Committee, UN Doc. A/CONF.151/PC/97/Add. 1 of 4 March 1992, 4.

114 See Chapter 15 above, 233–4.

The Rio Declaration and Agenda 21

The Rio Declaration, the counterpart to the 1972 Stockholm Declaration, was such a cumbersome compromise between North and South that the text considered at the final Preparatory Committee in April 1992 was not reopened for discussion at UNCED.[108] The twenty-seven principles contain references, *inter alia*, to common but differentiated responsibilities of states in view of their different contribution to global environmental degradation, the need to reduce and eliminate unsustainable patterns of production and consumption and of the promotion of appropriate demographic policies, the precautionary approach, the right to development, environmental impact assessments, the right of individuals to access to information held by public authorities, the avoidance of unilateral trade measures in response to environmental challenges outside their jurisdiction, and to the role of women and indigenous peoples.[109]

Agenda 21 constitutes a non-binding action plan on environment and development, divided into forty chapters covering sectoral issues such as the atmosphere, oceans, fresh water, and land resources, cross-sectoral issues such as poverty, demographics, and human health, means of implementation, including finances, transfer of technology as well as institutional and legal issues.[110] Major groups such as women, children, indigenous peoples and NGOs are also addressed. In spite of its comprehensive approach, Agenda 21 avoided many controversial issues such as population growth, consumption patterns and the international debt of developing countries. The most contentious issues, however, related to the crucial chapter on financial resources, in particular, on 'new and additional' financial resources sought by developing countries, partly in competition with the position of Central and Eastern European countries,[111] and on the appropriate funding mechanisms. The average annual costs for the period 1993–2000 of implementing Agenda 21 in the South, which do not include finances required for the UNEP Environment Fund and for funding environment-related conventions and protocols, were estimated to exceed US$600 billion. While the bulk of this amount is to be borne by the developing countries themselves, about US$125 billion annually would have to be provided on grant or concessional terms from the industrialized countries.[112]

The basis for these figures is obscure and they have been characterized as 'indicative' of orders of magnitude only because it was not possible to develop estimates in sufficient detail.[113] US$125 billion is less than 1 per cent of current levels of GNP of the principal donor countries, but it remains a substantial amount, in addition to Official Development Aid (ODA), with regard to which only few countries have managed to achieve the UNCTAD target of 0.7 per cent.[114] There was also no real expectation that more than an initial commitment of several billion US dollars per year to start Agenda 21 could be obtained in additional finance from the North, taking into consideration also the incapacity of many developing countries to absorb and effectively manage such large amounts of money as projected immediately. The financial issues remained unsettled by Agenda 21 and were linked to review on a regular basis to the institutional reform proposals set out in chapter 38 and the establishment of the Commission on Sustainable Development.

Conclusions

There are differing evaluations of the actual outcome of the Conference, ranging from disappointment to modestly positive reactions. The only two documents which were adopted at Rio as internationally legally binding instruments are the Climate Convention and the Biodiversity Convention. The non-binding Rio Declaration, the Forest Principles and Agenda 21 contain, with minor exceptions, only obligations of a political or moral nature.[115] In particular, the Forest Principles, which are termed 'non-legally binding', but 'authoritative', reflect the difficulties involved in achieving definite legal results in the controversy between North and South.

Principle 1 of the Rio Declaration, stating that human beings 'are at the centre of concerns for sustainable development' and 'entitled to a healthy and productive life in harmony with nature', Principle 3 on 'intergenerational equity', and Principle 4, proclaiming environmental protection to be an 'integral part of the development process', are clearly of a programmatic nature only.[116] The basis and precise meaning of 'intergenerational equity' as a possible legal concept has hardly been explored.[117] The language of other principles is such that they seem to reaffirm existing customary law. However, customary law in the field of transboundary international harm is of little assistance.[118] Principle 2 confirms the prohibition of transboundary environmental harm laid down in Principle 21 of the Stockholm Declaration which is now recognized as customary law reflecting the principle of limited territorial sovereignty and integrity, but only as far as 'substantial' transboundary harm is involved.[119] Furthermore, the mutual obligations of states concerning information and notification in Principles 18 and 19 of the Rio Declaration are procedural rules recognized in customary international law. With regard to public participation (Principle 10), the 'precautionary approach' (Principle 15), the 'polluter-pays principle' (Principle 16), and environmental impact assessment (Principle 17), there are strong doubts whether their status as principles of general international law is secured. These doubts are connected with the complicated issue of to what extent general customary law may be inferred from the development of rules in treaties.[120]

Moreover, although the Climate Convention and the Biodiversity Convention contain binding obligations, their normative scope is limited. The obligations under the Biodiversity Convention are often phrased in abstract wording and qualified by additions such as 'as far as possible'[121] or 'in accordance with its particular conditions'.[122] This is in line with general features of the law-making process in the field on the global protection of the environment. The two principal weaknesses of the Climate and Biodiversity Conventions at the moment are, first, that their normative objectives are not sufficiently global to establish a comprehensive international legal regime to protect the atmosphere and the living resources of the

115 See Beyerlin, *op. cit.*, 132–3.
116 *Ibid.*, 133.
117 For a discussion, see E.B. Weiss, *In Fairness to Future Generations: International Law, Common Patrimony, and Intergenerational Equity*, 1989; G.P. Supanich, The Legal Basis of Intergenerational Responsibility: An Alternative View – The Sense of Intergenerational Identity, *YIEL* 3 (1992), 94 *et seq.*
118 See Lang (1992), *op. cit.*, 108; Schachter, *op. cit.*, 364.
119 See Beyerlin, *op. cit.*, 126 and 133 with further references.
120 *Ibid.*, 134 with references.
121 Articles 5, 7, 8, 9, 11, 14, Biodiversity Convention.
122 Article 6.

123 See L.A. Kimball, Toward Global Environment: The Institutional Setting, *YIEL* 3 (1992), 19–42.

124 The International Court of Justice, however, has recently established a chamber for environmental matters; see Chapter 18 below, 288.

125 Eagerly Awaited Commission Established, *EPL* 23 (1993), 58–60; Commission on Sustainable Development – First Substantive Session, *ibid.*, 190–201.

126 See Chapter 21 below, 282–3.

127 Commission on Sustainable Development, Keynote Address by US Vice-President Al Gore, *EPL* 23 (1993), 183, at 184.

planet and, second, that they are only framework conventions requiring more specific regulation in the future to become effective.

Thus, the legal results of Rio are meagre in terms of substantive obligations. The important institutional aspects of clarifying the meaning of 'sustainable development' and arriving at effective solutions have recently been receiving more attention.[123] Far-reaching proposals of institutional reforms, such as the creation of a world environmental legislature, a council for 'ecological security', or an international environmental court,[124] were not seriously discussed at UNCED. The innovations are much more modest. Following the suggestions made in Chapter 38 of Agenda 21, the UN Commission on Sustainable Development was established in 1993.[125] The Commission is a 'functional commission' of the UN Economic and Social Council (ECOSOC)[126] and is composed of fifty-three state representatives who are elected for a term of three years according to a certain geographical distribution principle. The task of the Commission is to supervise the implementation of the Rio documents, especially Agenda 21, and to discuss further measures and the issues of financial resources and mechanisms.

The hope of achieving substantial commitments of the North to increase the flow of finances and technology to the developing countries has failed to materialize. Although much will still depend on the follow-up process to UNCED, the most persuasive evaluation of the results of Rio is that so far no crucial steps have been taken to save the global environment, nor has there been any significant move towards improving the development perspective of most countries in the South. In Rio the North succeeded in improving the framework for global environmental protection as desired by industrialized countries without making real concessions concerning economic development in the South. The bottom line is that, while Rio may have sent an important political signal, in substance it has failed to solve the dilemma of sustainable development and primarily has served to establish favourable negotiating positions for the future.

As regards international legal instruments, Agenda 21 focuses on four priorities: (1) review and assessment of relevant international law; (2) further development of implementation mechanisms and compliance measures; (3) effective participation by all countries in the international law-making process; and (4) the range and effectiveness of dispute resolution techniques. In the field of 'global environmental legislation' this describes in general terms the relevant programme of the newly established UN Commission on Sustainable Development. It is interesting to note that the Vice-President of the United States included the following words in his keynote address on the occasion of the establishment of the Commission on Sustainable Development:

> So I say this to citizens of developed nations: we have a disproportionate impact on the global environment. We have less than a quarter of the world's population – but we use three quarters of the world's raw materials and create three quarters of all solid waste. One way to put it is this: a child born in the United States will have 30 times more impact on the earth's environment during his or her lifetime than a child born in India. The affluent of the world have a responsibility to deal with their disproportionate impact.[127]

It is upon the success of the follow-up process of Rio in the difficult quest for a true integration of environment regulation and economic development policies[128] that the future of global environmental law-making will depend. Agenda 21 will be reviewed by a special session of the UN General Assembly in June 1997.[129] In the end, the contribution of international law as such to solve the global problems, however, can only be subsidiary.[130] Finances will remain the central issue in the decades to come. Institutional reform of the UN system is the other major aspect.

[128] See A.E. Boyle (ed.), *Environmental Regulation and Economic Growth*, 1995.

[129] See *UN Chronicle* 33 (1996), no. 2, 72.

[130] On new mechanisms to enforce international environmental standards see R. Wolfrum (ed.), *Enforcing Environmental Standards. Economic Mechanisms as Viable Means?*, 1996.

17 State responsibility

1 See *Harris CMIL*, 460–599; *Restatement (Third)*, Vol. 2, 184–229; R. Wolfrum, Internationally Wrongful Acts, *EPIL* II (1995), 1398–1403. See also I. Brownlie, *State Responsibility*, 1983, Part I; J. Quigley, Complicity in International Law: A New Direction in the Law of State Responsibility, *BYIL* 57 (1986), 77–132; K. Zemanek, Responsibility of States: General Principles, *EPIL* 10 (1987), 362–73; P.-M. Dupuy, The International Law of State Responsibility: Revolution or Evolution?, *Mich. JIL* (1989), 105; J. Wolf, Gibt es im Völkerrecht einen einheitlichen Schadensbegriff?, *ZaöRV* 49 (1989), 403; H. Fox, State Responsibility and Tort Proceedings Against a Foreign State in Municipal Courts, *NYIL* 20 (1989), 3–34; I. Brownlie, *Principles of Public International Law*, 4th edn 1990, 381–552; A. Reinisch, *State Responsibility for Debts*, 1995; P. Malanczuk, International Business and New Rules of State Responsibility? – The Law Applied by the United Nations (Security Council) Compensation Commission for Claims Against Iraq, in K.-H. Böckstiegel (ed.), *Perspectives of Air Law, Space Law and International Business Law for the Next Century*, 1996, 117–64.
2 On the concepts of reprisal and retortion see Chapter 1 above, 4 and text below, 271–2.
3 On the ILC in general see Chapter 3 above, 61.
4 M. Spinedi/B. Simma (eds), *United Nations Codification of State Responsibility*, 1987, Introduction; K. Zemanek/J. Salmon, *Responsabilité internationale*, 1987; S. Rosenne, *The International Law Commission's Draft Articles on State Responsibility*, 1991.

If a state violates a rule of customary international law or ignores an obligation of a treaty it has concluded, it commits a breach of international law and thereby a so-called 'internationally wrongful act'.[1] The law of state responsibility is concerned with the determination of whether there is a wrongful act for which the wrongdoing state is to be held responsible, what the legal consequences are (e.g. an obligation on the part of the wrong-doing state to restore the previous situation or to pay compensation), and how such international responsibility may be implemented (e.g. through countermeasures adopted by the victim state, such as reprisals or retortion).[2]

Sometimes the term 'responsibility' is used interchangeably with the term 'liability', but the use of terminology in this respect in the literature is by no means uniform. Often 'liability' simply means the obligation to pay compensation. But 'liability' may also refer to obligations of states arising from harmful consequences of hazardous activities which, as such, are not prohibited by international law, like operating a nuclear plant close to the border (a lawful activity) which by accident leads to damage in the form of radioactive contamination on the territory of a neighbouring state (a harmful consequence requiring compensation).

The work of the International Law Commission

The area of state responsibility has become the most ambitious and most difficult topic of the codification work of the International Law Commission (ILC).[3] As noted by the editors of a comprehensive study on the matter:

> While all the former and other current topics studied by the Commission deal with certain, defined 'primary' rules of international law, State responsibility, in a sense, embraces the entire 'other side of the medal', the totality of legal rules and consequences linked to the breach of any international obligation of the State. No other codification project goes so deeply into the 'roots', the theoretical and ideological foundations of international law.[4]

The current approach followed by the ILC in dealing with state responsibility has become rather abstract and complicated. Originally, the subject area had been more limited; the six reports submitted by the first Special Rapporteur, F.V. García Amador between 1956 and 1961 concentrated on state responsibility for injury to the person or property of aliens. This limited approach was then abandoned, partly because the topic was too controversial at the time. After a reconsideration of its approach in

1962 and 1963, the ILC decided not to restrict its study of the topic to a particular subject, such as responsibility for injuries to aliens, in order to include also the rules on state responsibility for the breach of fundamental principles of international law, such as the violation of obligations relating to international peace and security. Furthermore, it decided not to try to define and codify the 'primary' rules, the breach of which leads to international responsibility (which would have been impracticable because one would have to codify the norms of international law as a whole), but rather to focus on the 'secondary' rules of state responsibility as an abstract area of its own.[5] In 1975 the Commission adopted a general plan envisaging the structure of the draft articles to be as follows: Part 1 concerns the 'origin' of international responsibility; Part 2 concerns the 'content, form and degrees' of state responsibility; and Part 3 deals with the 'implementation' of responsibility and the settlement of disputes.

Moreover, the ILC later decided to proceed with a codification exercise on 'liability for injurious consequences arising out of acts not prohibited by international law'.[6] This project grew out of the growing international concern for transboundary environmental protection problems. The ILC decided to treat it separately from responsibility for internationally wrongful acts and in 1978 appointed R. Quentin-Baxter as Special Rapporteur, who was succeeded after his death in 1984 by Julio Barboza. The work on this topic has not made very much progress. The exact scope of application of the few draft articles so far agreed upon is unclear and commentators have quite rightly questioned the feasibility of distinguishing the whole area from the other project on responsibility for wrongful acts.[7]

The work of the Commission on state responsibility for internationally wrongful acts is much more important. On the basis of eight reports presented after 1969 by the new Special Rapporteur, Roberto Ago, in 1980 the ILC adopted in first reading (on a provisional basis) a comprehensive set of thirty-five draft articles dealing with the 'origin' of state responsibility as Part 1.[8]

Divided into five chapters, Part 1 is intended to give guidance as to which grounds and under which circumstances a state may be considered to have committed an internationally wrongful act. Chapter I (General Principles) defines some basic principles, such as that every internationally wrongful act entails responsibility on the part of the state committing it and that every international act consists of two elements, a subjective one and an objective one. Draft article 3 states:

> There is an internationally wrongful act of a State when:
> (a) conduct consisting of an action or omission is attributable to the State under international law; and
> (b) that conduct constitutes a breach of an international obligation of the State.

Chapter II (The 'Act of the State' under International Law) addresses the subjective element and determines the conditions under which particular conduct is to be considered as an act of the state. The objective element is dealt with in Chapter III (Breach of an International Obligation).

5 D. Alland/J. Combacau, 'Primary' and 'Secondary' Rules in the Law of State Responsibility: Categorizing International Obligations, *NYIL* 16 (1985), 81–109.

6 See M. Akehurst, International Liability for Injurious Consequences Arising Out of Acts not Prohibited by International Law, *NYIL* 16 (1985), 3–16; M.C.W. Pinto, Reflections on International Liability for Injurious Consequences Arising out of Acts Not Prohibited by International Law, *ibid.*, 17–48; G. Handl, Liability as an Obligation Established by a Primary Rule of International Law: Some Basic Reflections on the International Law Commission's Work, *ibid.*, 49–79; L.F.E. Goldie, Concepts of Strict and Absolute Liability and the Ranking of Liability in Terms of Relative Exposure to Risk, *ibid.*, 175–248; C. O'Keefe, Transboundary Pollution and the Strict Liability Issue: The Work of the International Law Commission on the Topic of International Liability for Injurious Consequences Arising Out of Acts Not Prohibited by International Law, *Denver JILP* 18 (1990), 145–208; S. Erichsen, Das Liability-Projekt der ILC, *ZaöRV* 52 (1991), 94–144; F. Francioni/T. Scovazzi, *International Responsibility for Environmental Harm*, 1991; A. Rest, Ecological Damage in Public International Law: International Environmental Liability in the Drafts of the UN International Law Commission and the UN/ECE Task Force, *EPL* 22 (1992), 31–41; P. Thomas, *Environmental Liability*, 1993; J. Barboza, International Liability for the Injurious Consequences of Acts Not Prohibited by International Law and Protection of the Environment, *RdC* 247 (1994-III), 291–406; S.D. Murphy, Prospective Liability Regimes for the Transboundary Movement of Hazardous Wastes, *AJIL* 88 (1994), 24; R. Lefeber, *Transboundary Environmental Interference and the Origin of State Liability*, 1996.

7 See A.E. Boyle, State Responsibility and International Liability for Injurious Consequences of Acts Not Prohibited by International Law: A Necessary Distinction?, *ICLQ* 39 (1990), 1–26; M.A. Fitzmaurice, International Environmental Law as a Special Field, *NYIL* 25 (1994), 181–226, at 203 *et seq.*

8 *ILCYb* 1980, Vol. 2, part 2, 30–4. Text in *Brownlie BDIL*, 426–37.

9 See S.P. Jagota, State Responsibility: Circumstances Precluding Wrongfulness, *NYIL* 16 (1985), 249–77; P. Malanczuk, Countermeasures and Self-Defence as Circumstances Precluding Wrongfulness in the International Law Commission's Draft Articles on State Responsibility, in Spinedi/Simma (eds), *op. cit.*, 197–286; A. Gattini, *Zufall and force majeure im System der Staatenverantwortlichkeit anhand der ILC Kodifikationsarbeit*, 1991.

10 For the draft articles 1 to 5 of Part 2 see 1985 ILC Report, UN Doc. A/40/10, 52–3.

11 S. Rosenstock, The Forty-Seventh Session of the International Law Commission, *AJIL* 90 (1996), 106. On the 1996 session, at which G. Arangio-Ruiz resigned, see B. Rudolf, *VN* 44 (1996), 226. The 1996 report was not available at the time of writing.

12 See Chapter 3 above, 58–60.

13 R.B. Lillich, *The Human Rights of Aliens in Contemporary International Law*, 1984; D.F. Vagts, Minimum Standard, *EPIL* 8 (1985), 382–5; S.S. Schwebel, The Treatment of Human Rights and of Aliens in the International Court of Justice, in: V. Lowe/M. Fitzmaurice (eds), *Fifty Years of the International Court of Justice*, 1996, 327–50.

14 See Chapter 15 above, 235–9.

15 See Chapter 14 above, 209–21.

16 R. Arnold, Aliens, *EPIL* I (1992), 102–7; K. Doehring, Aliens, Admission, *ibid.*, 107–9; Aliens, Expulsion and Deportation, *ibid.* 109–12; Aliens, Military Service, *ibid.*, 112–16; I. Seidl-Hoheveldern, Aliens Property, *ibid.*, 116–19.

17 See M. Akehurst, Jurisdiction in International Law, *BYIL* 46 (1972–3), 145–51 and Chapter 7 above, 109–10.

18 See text above, 255.

19 W.K. Geck, Diplomatic Protection, *EPIL* I (1992), 1045–67; R. Dolzer, Diplomatic Protection of Foreign Nationals, *ibid.*, 1067–70.

Chapter IV (Implication of a State in the Internationally Wrongful Act of Another State) is devoted to situations in which a state takes part in the commission of a wrongful act by another state and to cases in which responsibility is to be borne by a state other than the state that has committed the act. Finally, Chapter V (Circumstances Precluding Wrongfulness) lists a number of circumstances which may exceptionally result in precluding the wrongfulness of an act of a state which does not conform to an international obligation.[9] These circumstances include the consent of the injured state; legitimate countermeasures against a wrongful act; *force majeure* and fortuitous event; distress; necessity; and self-defence.

From 1980 onwards, the ILC concentrated on Part 2 of the draft articles dealing with the 'content, forms and degrees' of state responsibility, covering the legal consequences of an internationally wrongful act,[10] first on the basis of reports by the new Special Rapporteur Willem Riphagen, who was later succeeded by Gaetana Arangio-Ruiz. As of 1995, the ILC had finished much of its initial work (for submission to the General Assembly) concerning Part 2 and consideration had also been given to Part 3; both Parts were adopted by the ILC in first reading in 1996.[11] The notion of international 'crimes' of states (as addressed in draft article 19 in Part 1),[12] however, remains very controversial.

State responsibility and the treatment of aliens

Central aspects of the modern law of state responsibility have historically developed on the basis of cases concerning the unlawful treatment of aliens and the so-called international minimum standard.[13] This field is also the key to the understanding of the content of many of the ILC draft articles. The specific question of the expropriation of foreign property, which also belongs to this area, but has become somewhat separated due to the dispute between North and South on the 'New International Economic Order', has already been dealt with in Chapter 15 above;[14] thus the following is limited to the more general aspects.

As we saw in Chapter 14,[15] the modern rules concerning human rights (which prohibit the ill treatment of all individuals, regardless of their nationality) are of fairly recent origin. But for more than two hundred years international law has laid down a minimum international standard for the treatment of aliens (that is, nationals of other states).[16] States are not obliged to admit aliens to their territory, but, if they permit aliens to come, they must treat them in a civilized manner. *A fortiori*, a state is guilty of a breach of international law if it inflicts injury on aliens at a time when they are outside its territory (for example, if Utopia orders Utopian servicemen, stationed in Ruritania, to attack Ruritanian residents). Indeed, a state may not perform any governmental act whatsoever in the territory of another state, without the latter's consent.[17]

These obligations, in the terms of the ILC, belong to the category of primary rules.[18] To put it in technical terms, failure to comply with the minimum international standard 'engages the international responsibility' of the defendant state, and the national state of the injured alien may 'exercise its right of diplomatic protection',[19] that is, may make a claim, through diplomatic channels, against the other state, in order to obtain compensation or some other form of redress. Such claims are usually settled by negotiation; alternatively, if both parties agree, they may be dealt with by arbitration or judicial settlement.[20]

The defendant state's duties are owed not to the injured alien, but to the alien's national state.[21] The theory is that the claimant state itself suffers a loss when one of its nationals is injured. Consequently, the claimant state has complete liberty to refrain from making a claim or to abandon a claim; it may agree to settle the claim at a fraction of its true value; and it is under no duty to pay the compensation obtained to its national (although it usually does). In these respects, the injured individual is at the mercy of his/her national state. This aspect of diplomatic protection was clearly stated by the International Court of Justice in the *Barcelona Traction* case in which it held

> that, within the limits prescribed by international law, a State may exercise diplomatic protection by whatever means and to whatever extent it thinks fit, for it is its own right that the State is asserting. Should the natural or legal persons on whose behalf it is acting consider that their rights are not adequately protected, they have no remedy in international law. All they can do is resort to municipal law, if means are available, with a view to furthering their cause or obtaining redress....The State must be viewed as the sole judge to decide whether its protection will be granted, to what extent it is granted, and when it will cease. It retains in this respect a discretionary power the exercise of which may be determined by considerations of a political or other nature, unrelated to the particular case. Since the claim of the State is not identical with that of the individual or corporate person whose cause is espoused, the State enjoys complete freedom of action.[22]

However, international law does not entirely disregard the individual; the compensation obtained by the claimant state is usually calculated by reference to the loss suffered by the individual, not by reference to the loss suffered by the claimant state. But not always. For instance, in the *I'm Alone* case (1935),[23] the United States sank a British ship smuggling liquor into the United States. Although the arbitrators held that the sinking was illegal they awarded no damages for the loss of the ship, because it was owned by United States citizens and used for smuggling. But they ordered the United States to apologize and to pay US$25,000 to the United Kingdom as compensation for the insult to the British flag.

'Imputability'

A state is liable only for its own acts and omissions; and, in this context, the state is identified with its governmental apparatus, not with the population as a whole. If the police attack a foreigner, the state is liable; if private individuals attack a foreigner, the state is not liable.[24] The governmental apparatus of the state includes the legislature and the judiciary, as well as the executive; and it includes local authorities as well as central authorities.

The ILC draft articles on state responsibility make it clear that:

1   'conduct of any State organ having that status under the internal

20 On methods of dispute settlement see Chapter 18 below, 273–305.

21 See Chapter 6 above, 101–2.

22 *Barcelona Traction, Light and Power Company, Limited*, ICJ Rep. 1970, 3, at 44-5. On the case see also Chapter 3 above, 58–9.

23 RIAA III 1609.

24 G. Sperduti, Responsibility of States for Activities of Private Law Persons, *EPIL* 10 (1987), 373–50.

25 On the position taken by the ILC see M. Bedjaoui, Responsibility of States, Fault and Strict Liability, *EPIL* 10 (1987), 358–62; A. Gattini, La Notion de faute à la lumière du projet de convention de la Commission du Droit International sur la responsabilité internationale, *EJIL* 3 (1992), 253–84; for an interesting issue concerning the attribution of conduct see F. Kalshoven, State Responsibility for Warlike Acts of the Armed Forces, *ICLQ* 40 (1991), 827 *et seq.*
26 *RIAA* IV 110 (1926).
27 Cf. *Morton's* claim (1929), *RIAA* IV 428.

law of that State shall be considered as an act of the State concerned under international law, provided that organ was acting in that capacity in the case in question' (draft article 5);

2 '[t]he conduct of an organ of the State shall be considered as an act of that State under international law, whether that organ belongs to the constituent, legislative, executive, judicial or other power, whether its functions are of an international or an internal character, and whether it holds a superior or a subordinate position in the organization of the State' (draft article 6);

3 '[t]he conduct of an organ of a territorial governmental entity within a State shall also be considered as an act of that State under international law, provided that organ was acting in that capacity in the case in question' (draft article 7(1)); and that

4 '[t]he conduct of an organ of an entity which is not part of the formal structure of the State or of a territorial governmental entity, but which is empowered by the internal law of that State to exercise elements of governmental authority, shall also be considered as an act of the State under international law, provided that organ was acting in that capacity in the case in question' (draft article 7(2)).

A state is liable for the acts of its officials only if those acts are 'imputable' (that is, attributable) to the state. (The question of whether an act is attributable to a state must be distinguished from the issue of whether or not some form of fault on the part of the state needs to be established to engage its international responsibility, a matter which is controversial.[25]) The idea of 'imputability' creates problems when officials exceed or disobey their instructions. Obviously it would be unjust if a state could limit its liability simply by giving restrictive instructions to its officials (for example, if it could escape liability for road accidents merely by telling its chauffeurs to drive carefully); and the cases indicate that a state is liable for the acts of its officials, even when they exceed or disobey their instructions, provided that they are acting with *apparent* authority or that they are abusing *powers or facilities* placed at their disposal by the state. *Youmans* claim[26] is a striking example of the law's willingness to make the defendant state liable. In that case, Mexico sent troops to protect Americans from a mob; but, instead of protecting the Americans, the troops, led by a lieutenant, opened fire on them. Mexico was held liable, because the troops had been acting as an organized military unit, under the command of an officer. On the other hand, if the troops had been off duty, their acts would probably have been regarded merely as the acts of private individuals.[27]

The wording of ILC draft article 10 reflects this rule:

The conduct of an organ of a State, of a territorial governmental entity or of an entity empowered to exercise elements of governmental authority, such organ having acted in that capacity, shall be considered as an act of the State under international law even if, in the particular case, the organ exceeded its competence according to internal law or contravened instructions concerning its authority.

In principle, a state is not responsible for the acts of private individuals, unless they were in fact acting on behalf of that state or exercising elements of governmental authority in the absence of government officials and under circumstances which justified them in assuming such authority.[28] There are special rules concerning responsibility for acts of an insurrectional movement.[29] But the acts of private individuals may also be accompanied by some act or omission on the part of the state, for which the state is liable. Such act or omission may take one of six forms:

1   Encouraging individuals to attack foreigners.
2   Failing to take reasonable care ('due diligence') to prevent the individuals – for example, failing to provide police protection when a riot against foreigners is imminent.[30] For instance, early in 1969 the United Kingdom compensated South Africa for damage done to the South African embassy in London by demonstrators; the demonstration had been advertised several days in advance, and an attack on the South African embassy was foreseeable, even though the demonstrators' main target was Rhodesia House – and there was only one policeman on duty outside the embassy.[31] What constitutes 'reasonable care' will depend on the circumstances – foreigners who remain in remote areas of the countryside in times of unrest cannot expect the same police protection as foreigners in a peaceful capital city[32] – but special care must be taken to prevent injury to diplomats.[33]
3   Obvious failure to punish the individuals.[34]
4   Failure to provide the injured foreigner with an opportunity of obtaining compensation from the wrongdoers in the local courts. This is an example of what is called 'denial of justice'[35] – a term which is used in a bewildering variety of different meanings.
5   Obtaining some benefit from the individual's act – for example, keeping looted property.[36]
6   Express ratification of the individual's act – that is, expressly approving it and stating that that person was acting in the name of the state.[37]

The *Tehran Hostages* case is particularly illuminating in respect of the above. Following the overthrow of Shah Reza Pahlevi, a close ally of the United States, and the establishment of the Islamic Republic of Iran under the regime of Ayatollah Khomeini, on 4 November 1979, demonstrators attacked the American embassy in Tehran. Iranian security forces did not intervene, although they were called upon to do so. The embassy was invaded, its personnel and visitors were taken hostage and the archives were ransacked. Most of the hostages were kept for more than 14 months until 20 January 1981, an unprecedented event in the history of diplomatic relations. After an abortive military rescue attempt by the United States on 24–5 April 1980 (the helicopters encountered technical difficulties in the deserts of Iran), the matter was finally settled by an agreement (the 'Algiers Accords'), mediated by the Algerian Government, which led to the establishment in 1981 of the Iran–United States Claims Tribunal in

28 See ILC draft articles 8 and 11.
29 See ILC draft articles 14 and 15 and the *Tehran Hostages* case below. See also Chapter 8 above, 123, 126–7.
30 See H. Blomeyer-Bartestein, Due Diligence, *EPIL* I (1992), 1110–15; R. Mazzeschi, The Due Diligence Rule and the Nature of the International Responsibility of States, *GYIL* 35 (1992), 9.
31 *The Times*, 14 January 1969.
32 *Home Missionary Society* claim (1920), *RIAA* VI 42. This case concerned injuries caused by rebels, a topic which gives rise to special problems; see M. Akehurst, State Responsibility for the Wrongful Acts of Rebels – An Aspect of the Southern Rhodesian Problem, *BYIL* 43 (1968–9), 49.
33 See Chapter 8 above, 123–4.
34 J.L. Brierly, The Theory of Implied State Complicity in International Claims, *BYIL* 9 (1928), 42. Compare *Neer's* claim (1926), *RIAA* IV 60, with *Janes's* claim (1926), *RIAA* IV 82.
35 S. Verosta, Denial of Justice, *EPIL* I (1992), 1007–10.
36 *Mazzei's* claim (1903), *RIAA* X 525.
37 J.B. Moore, *A Digest of International Law*, Vol. 6, 1906, 989.

38 See Chapter 18 below, 296–8.

39 *Tehran Hostages* case , Order, *ICJ Rep.* 1979, 7–21; Judgment, *ICJ Rep.* 1980, 3–65; on the case see also Chapter 8 above, 123, 126–7.

40 See L.A.N.M. Barnhoorn, Diplomatic Law and Unilateral Remedies, *NYIL* 25 (1994), 39–81.

41 See text below, 270.

42 See Chapter 18 below, 296.

43 See Vagts, *op. cit.*

44 See F.V. García-Amador, Calvo Doctrine, Calvo Clause, *EPIL* I (1992), 521–3; W. Benedek, Drago-Porter Convention (1907), *ibid.*, 1102–3. See Chapter 2 above, 15.

45 For example, G. Roy, *AJIL* 55 (1961), 863.

The Hague to deal with some 4,000 outstanding claims between the two nations by arbitration.[38]

What matters here with regard to the issue of state responsibility is the view taken by the International Court of Justice to which the United States had taken resort (Iran refusing to participate in the proceedings).[39] The Court distinguished between Iran's responsibility for a first phase of events and for a second phase. In the first phase the Court regarded the militants as private individuals because it found no indication that they had any official status as 'agents' of the Iranian government. Thus, in this phase no direct responsibility on the part of Iran could be established. However, in this phase Iran was held responsible indirectly for the omission to protect the embassy. The direct responsibility of Iran was assumed for the second phase in view of public statements of Ayatollah Khomeini condoning the hostage-taking and in view of the decision of the Iranian government to maintain the situation from which it sought to benefit, and not to take steps against the militants. The Court dismissed the argument submitted by Iran in letters of December 1979 and March 1980 that the seizure of the embassy was a reaction to criminal interference by the United States in the affairs of Iran. Even if that were true, this would not have justified Iran's conduct, because diplomatic law itself provided the necessary means of defence against illegal activities of members of foreign diplomatic and consular missions (i.e. declaring them *persona non grata* and requiring them to leave the country).[40] The Court thus held Iran responsible and to be under an obligation to release the hostages, to restore the Embassy to the United States and to make reparation[41] to the United States, which was to be determined, if the parties failed to agree, in a further round of proceedings. The case was later terminated in accordance with the agreement reached between the parties in the Algiers Accords.[42]

Finally, there are special rules concerning the attribution of conduct of organs of international organizations and of a foreign state acting on the territory of another state (see ILC draft articles 12 and 13).

The minimum international standard

When someone resides or acquires property in a foreign country, he is deemed to accept the laws and customs of that country; his national state cannot base a claim on the fact that he would have been better treated in his home country. But the majority of states accept that the national state *can* claim if the foreign country's laws or behaviour fall below the minimum international standard.[43] During the nineteenth and early twentieth centuries, the United States and the Western European states upheld the idea of the minimum international standard, in opposition to the Latin American countries, which argued that a state's only duty was to treat foreigners in the same way as it treated its own nationals ('national standard').[44] In arbitrations between the two groups of countries the minimum international standard was usually applied.

History started repeating itself in the 1960s and 1970s, with certain lawyers from Third World countries arguing in favour of the national standard as opposed to the minimum international standard.[45] However, application of the national standard would simultaneously give the alien too much and too little. Carried to its logical extreme, it would mean that aliens could not be excluded from voting, from entering certain professions, or from enjoying welfare benefits – rights which states are not obliged to grant to aliens. Conversely, it would also mean that a state would be entitled to torture foreigners to death, provided that it also tortured its own nationals to death – a conclusion which would be repugnant to common sense and justice. If the minimum international standard appears to give aliens a privileged position, the answer is for states to treat their own nationals better, not for them to treat aliens worse; indeed, the whole human rights movement may be seen as an attempt to extend the minimum international standard from aliens to nationals, even though the detailed rules in declarations and conventions on human rights[46] sometimes differ considerably from those in the traditional minimum international standard.

What critics of the minimum international standard are really opposed to is not the *principle* of having such a standard, but the *content* of some of the rules which are alleged to form part of the standard. They might be reassured by reading the following quotation from the judgment in the *Neer* claim:

> The treatment of an alien, in order to constitute an international delinquency, should amount to an outrage, to bad faith, to wilful neglect of duty or to an insufficiency of governmental action so far short of international standards that every reasonable and impartial man would readily recognize its insufficiency.[47]

Some of the rules comprised in the minimum international standard are more widely accepted than others. For instance, few people would deny that a state's international responsibility will be engaged if an alien is unlawfully killed,[48] imprisoned,[49] or physically ill-treated,[50] or if his property is looted or damaged[51] – unless, of course, the state can rely on some circumstances justifying the act, such as the fact that it was necessary as a means of maintaining law and order (arrest and punishment of criminals, use of force to stop a riot, and so on). On the other hand, *excessive* severity in maintaining law and order will also fall below the minimum international standard (punishment without a fair trial, excessively long detention before trial, fatal injuries inflicted by policemen dispersing a peaceful demonstration, unduly severe punishment for a trivial offence, and so on).

There are also other ways in which the maladministration of justice can engage a state's responsibility – for instance, if the courts are corrupt, biased, or guilty of excessive delay, or if they follow an unfair procedure; these rules apply to civil proceedings brought by or against a foreigner, as well as to criminal proceedings.

In other areas the content of the minimum international standard is much more controversial. Deportation is an example.[52] Since 1914 most states have claimed wide powers of deportation. The United Kingdom recognizes that other states have a general right to deport United Kingdom citizens without stating reasons.[53] On the other hand, the United Kingdom has stated that the right to deport 'should not be abused by proceeding arbitrarily'[54] – a rather vague restriction on the right of

46 See Chapter 14 above, 208–21.
47 *RIAA* IV 60, 61–2.
48 *Youmans* claim, see text above, 258.
49 *Roberts* claim (1926), *RIAA* IV 77; *Tehran Hostages* case, *op. cit.*, at 42; J.C. Hsiung, *Law and Policy in China's Foreign Relations*, 1972, 186.
50 *Ibid.*
51 *R Zafiro* case (1925), *RIAA* VI 160; Hsiung, *op. cit.*
52 Doehring (1992), *op. cit.*
53 *BPIL* 1964, 210.
54 *Ibid.*, 1966, 115.

55 See M. Akehurst, The Uganda Asians, *NLJ*, 8 November 1973, 1021.

56 *Jack Rankin v. Islamic Republic of Iran*, Award 326-10913-2, para. 30.

57 The Tribunal thus followed Article 15 of the ILC's Draft Articles on State Responsibility.

58 *Alfred L. W. Short v. Islamic Republic of Iran*, Award 312-11135-3, paras. 33 et seq.

59 *Kenneth P. Yeager v. Islamic Republic of Iran*, Award 324-10199-1, para. 42.

60 H.W.A. Thirlway, Preliminary Objections, *EPIL* 1 (1981), 183–7. See also Chapter 18 below, 287.

deportation. It is often hard to prove that a deportation is arbitrary if no reasons are stated for it, but a statement of reasons given voluntarily by the deporting state may reveal that the deportation was arbitrary and therefore illegal, as was the case, for example, when the Asians were expelled from Uganda in 1972.[55]

The jurisprudence of the Iran–United States Claims Tribunal in The Hague in the so–called 'expulsion cases' is of particular interest in this connection. Several hundred American citizens had filed claims for compensation for damages from Iran, alleging that at the height of the revolution they had had to leave Iran due to acts which the government either initiated, supported or tolerated. Generally speaking, the Tribunal required proof in each individual case that the alien had been forced to leave because of a specific act that could be attributed to the state, and found that the contention that there was general 'anti-Americanism' was insufficient.[56] In principle, the Tribunal accepted the responsibility of a new revolutionary government, after it had brought the revolutionary situation under its control, even with regard to previous acts of the revolutionary movement which had led the government to power on the basis of the 'continuity existing between the new organization of the State and the organization of the revolutionary movement'.[57] In the case at issue, however, the Chamber was unable to determine that there had been an act of an 'agent of the revolutionary movement' which had forced the American claimant to leave the country. As a successor government, Iran was found not to be responsible for the conduct of mere 'supporters of a revolution', just as there is no state responsibility for acts of 'supporters of an existing government'.[58]

Under this standard the Tribunal arrived at a negative conclusion in the case of two Americans who had understandably left Iran during the Islamic Revolution in view of personal danger to them, but were unable to prove that specific enforcement measures had been taken against them which could be attributed to the state. On the other hand, the Tribunal granted compensation to another US citizen who, together with his wife, had been taken by Revolutionary Guards from his home to a hotel from which the claimant later, together with other Americans, had to depart from Iran.[59] In this case the Tribunal left it open whether the Revolutionary Guards might be seen as organs of the new government, because it found that, at any rate, there was also state responsibility for acts of persons acting *de facto* on behalf of the government in the sense of Article 8(b) of the ILC's Draft Articles.

Preliminary objections

When a case involving the treatment of aliens is brought before an international tribunal, it may be lost on a preliminary objection,[60] before the tribunal is able to deal with the substantive issue of whether there has been a violation of the minimum international standard. Although the term 'preliminary objection' is a term of judicial procedure, the rules giving rise to preliminary objections are so well established that they tend to be observed in diplomatic negotiations as well as in proceedings before international tribunals. The principal factors which can give rise to a preliminary objection are as follows: non-compliance with the rules concerning nationality of claims; failure to exhaust local remedies; waiver; unreasonable delay; improper behaviour by the injured alien.

Nationality of claims

A claim in respect of damage against another state will fail unless it can be proved that the injured individual is a national of the claimant state. This 'nationality of claims' rule is well established in customary international law.[61] In the *Panevezys-Saldutiskis Railway* case (concerning a claim for compensation for the expropriation of a railway company filed by Estonia against Lithuania in 1937), the Permanent Court of International Justice said that

> in taking up the case of one of its nationals . . . a State is in reality asserting its own right...This right is necessarily limited to intervention on behalf of its own nationals because, in the absence of a special agreement, it is the bond of nationality between the State and the individual which alone confers upon the State the right of diplomatic protection.[62]

This basic principle is clear, but the detailed rules flowing from the principle are not. This makes it imperative to say a few words on the concept of nationality first. Nationality may be defined as the status of belonging to a state for certain purposes of international law.[63] As a general rule, international law leaves it to each state to define who are its nationals, but the state's discretion can be limited by treaties, such as treaties for the elimination of statelessness. Even under customary law, a state's discretion is not totally unlimited; for instance, it is obvious that international law would not accept as valid a British law which imposed British nationality on all the inhabitants of France. Indeed, the modern tendency is for international law to be increasingly stringent in restricting the discretion of states in matters of nationality. In fact, the nationality laws of different states often have certain features in common.[64]

Thus, the commonest ways in which nationality may be acquired are as follows.

1   By birth. Some countries confer their nationality on children born on their territory (*ius soli* principle), others confer their nationality on children born of parents who are nationals (*ius sanguinis* principle); in some states nationality may be acquired in either way (subject to certain exceptions).

2   By marriage.

3   By adoption or legitimation.

4   By naturalization. Technically, this refers to the situation where a foreigner is given the nationality of another state upon his request, but the word is sometimes used in a wider sense to cover any change of nationality after birth (cf. below on 'involuntary naturalization'). The willingness of states to grant naturalization varies greatly from state to state; states like Switzerland, which wish to discourage foreigners from settling permanently, insist on a very long residence qualification, but in Israel any Jewish person (which in practice has

61 See A. Watts, Nationality of Claims: Some Relevant Concepts, in: V. Lowe/M. Fitzmaurice (eds), *Fifty Years of the International Court of Justice*, 1996, 424-39.

62 PCIJ, Series A/B, No. 76, at 16. See E.H. Riedel, Panevezys-Saldutiskis Railway Case, *EPIL* 2 (1981), 224-5.

63 P. Weis, *Nationality and Statelessness in International Law*, 2nd edn 1979; A. Randelzhofer, Nationality, *EPIL* 8 (1985), 416–24; R. Donner, *The Regulation of Nationality in International Law*, 2nd edn 1994; H.G. Schermers, The Bond between Man and State, in *FS Bernhardt*, 187–98; L. Henkin, 'Nationality' at the Turn of the Century, *ibid.*, 89–102. See also *Nationality Decrees in Tunis and Morocco Case*, PCIJ, series B, no. 4 (1923); W. Benedek, Nationality Decrees in Tunis and Morocco (Advisory Opinion), *EPIL* 2 (1981), 197–9. On nationality in the European Union after the Maastricht Treaty see S. Hall, *Nationality, Migration Rights and Citizenship of the Union*, 1995.

64 For different approaches see, for instance, R. Plender, British Commonwealth, Subjects and Nationality Rules, *EPIL* 8 (1985), 53–9; K.S. Sik (ed.), *Nationality and International Law in Asian Perspective*, 1990; R. Bernhardt, German Nationality, *EPIL* II (1995), 555–9; Brownlie (1990), *op. cit.*, 386 *et seq.*; T. M. Franck, Clan and Superclan: Loyalty, Identity and Community in Law and Practice, *AJIL* 90 (1996), 359–83.

65 See Chapter 11 above, 169.
66 K.M. Meesen, Option of Nationality, *EPIL* 8 (1985), 424–8. See also Chapter 11 above, 169.
67 F.L. Löhr, Passports, *EPIL* 8 (1985), 428–31.
68 H.v. Mangoldt, Stateless Persons, *EPIL* 8 (1985), 490–4; T. Jürgens, *Diplomatischer Schutz und Staatenlose*, 1987.

not been so easy to define) is entitled to apply for naturalization without needing to fulfil any residence or other qualification.

5   As a result of the transfer of territory from one state to another.[65]

The commonest ways in which nationality may be lost are as follows.

1   If a child becomes a dual national at birth, as a result of the cumulative applications of the *ius soli* and *ius sanguinis* principles by different states, he is sometimes allowed to renounce one of the nationalities upon attaining his majority.

2   Acquisition of a new nationality was often treated by the state of the old nationality as automatically entailing loss of the old nationality. Nowadays some states, including the United Kingdom, merely give such people the option of renouncing their old nationality; many loyal UK nationals resident abroad acquire foreign nationality solely for purposes of business convenience.

3   By deprivation. In the United Kingdom only naturalized citizens may be deprived of their nationality, and on very limited grounds. Other countries apply the concept of deprivation more widely; in particular, totalitarian states like Nazi Germany deprived vast numbers of people of their nationality on racial or political grounds.

4   As a result of the transfer of territory from one state to another.[66]

Because of the difference between nationality laws in different states, some people have dual or multiple nationality, while others are stateless. Dual or multiple nationality was regarded as undesirable at one time; hence the rule that acquisition of a new nationality automatically entailed loss of the old. The fact that that rule is being abandoned by many states reflects a realization that dual or multiple nationality is not as undesirable as people used to believe, and dual or multiple nationality is likely to become more common in the future as populations continue to become more mobile.

Statelessness used to be uncommon, but is becoming more frequent now as a result of legislation by totalitarian countries depriving people of their nationality on racial or political grounds (though it can, of course, arise in other ways also). It is a most unpleasant phenomenon. Being aliens wherever they go, stateless persons have no right of entry, no voting rights, are frequently excluded from many types of work and are often liable to deportation. States usually issue passports only to their own nationals,[67] and this makes it difficult for stateless people to travel when they want to. In recent years states have entered into treaties to reduce the hardship of statelessness (for example, by providing special travel documents for stateless persons), or to eliminate it altogether by altering their nationality laws.[68]

It is in the context of the nationality of claims that international law has gone farthest in limiting the discretion of states concerning the nationality of individuals. The traditional position concerning stateless persons is simple; no state may claim on their behalf. The law applied by the United Nations Compensation Commission for Claims Against Iraq, established by the UN Security Council after the defeat of Iraq's aggression against Kuwait, however, has explicitly abandoned this rule on humanitarian grounds.[69]

In the case of a person who is a dual national of two states, A and B, two problems arise. First, which state can claim against a third state, C? Second, can one of the national states claim against the other? As regards claims against third states, the most widely held view is that both states can claim,[70] although this view has not gone unchallenged.[71] As regards claims by one national state against the other, the orthodox view is that all such claims are inadmissible,[72] but there have been cases, particularly in recent years, which indicate that the state of the master nationality (that is, the state with which the individual has the closer ties) can protect the individual against the other national state (as will be discussed below).[73] The United Kingdom still accepts the orthodox rule.[74]

The orthodox rule applicable to dual nationals was that one national state could not protect the dual national against the other national state, and some Latin American states tried to abuse this rule by imposing their nationality on all persons in respect of whom a claim was likely to be brought. For instance, the Mexican Constitution used to impose Mexican naturalization on all foreigners who acquired land in Mexico or who became fathers of children born in Mexico. The United States protested against this rule in 1886, arguing that naturalization 'must be by a distinctly voluntary act', which it was not, under the Mexican Constitution. The United States contention was supported by several decisions of international arbitral tribunals, and in 1934 Mexico altered the relevant rules of its constitutional law. It was explained that henceforth becoming the father of illegitimate children born in Mexico was to be regarded as 'un accidente en la vida de los hombres' ('an accident in the life of mankind'), and not as evidence of permanent affection for the Mexican nation.

It was not until many years later that international law began to limit the power of states to turn themselves into claims agents by conferring their nationality on individuals who had no genuine link with them. The leading case is the *Nottebohm* case.[75] Nottebohm, a German national, owned land in Guatemala, and realized in 1939 that his German nationality would be an inconvenience to him if Guatemala entered the war on the Allied side. Therefore, in 1939 he went to stay for a few weeks with his brother in Liechtenstein and acquired Liechtenstein nationality, thereby automatically losing his German nationality under German law as it stood at that time; he then returned to Guatemala. When Guatemala later declared war on Germany, he was interned and his property confiscated. Liechtenstein brought a claim on his behalf against Guatemala before the International Court of Justice, but failed. The Court held that the right of protection arises only when there is a genuine link between the claimant state and its national, and that there was no genuine link between Nottebohm and Liechtenstein. The effect of the decision is not altogether certain; the Court did not say that Nottebohm's Liechtenstein nationality was invalid for all purposes, only that it gave Liechtenstein no right to protect Nottebohm against Guatemala.

It is significant that the *Nottebohm* case, like the Mexican law mentioned

69 See Malanczuk (1996), International Business, *op. cit.*, 135–8.

70 *Salem* case, *RIAA* II 1161.

71 *ILCYb* 2 (1958), 66–7. A report drawn up by a member of the Commission suggested that claims could be brought only by the state of the master nationality (that is, the state with which the individual had the closer ties).

72 *Reparation for Injuries* case, *ICJ Rep.* 1949, 174, 186 (*obiter*).

73 *Merge* case, *ILR* 22 (1955), 443; Iran-United States Claims Tribunal, *Decision in Case No. A/18, ILM* 23 (1984), 489. This is the rule followed by the United States, *AJIL* 74 (1980), 163.

74 *BYIL* 53 (1982), 492–3, and *BYIL* 54 (1983), 520–1.

75 *Liechtenstein v. Guatemala, ICJ Rep.* 1953, 111–25 (Jurisdiction), *ICJ Rep.* 1955, 4–65 (Judgment). See H.v. Mangoldt, Nottebohm Case, *EPIL* 2 (1981), 213–6.

76 See *Case No. A/18, op. cit.*; P.E. Mahoney, The Standing of Dual Nations Before the Iran-United States Claims Tribunal, *Virginia JIL* 24 (1984), 695; P. McGarvey-Rosendahl, A New Approach to Dual Nationality, *Houston JIL* 11 (1986), 305; D.J. Bederman, *Saghi v. Islamic Republic of Iran*, AWD 544-298-2, Iran-United States Claims Tribunal, January 22, 1993, *AJIL* 87 (1993), 447–52; Bederman, Nationality of Individual Claimants before the Iran-United States Claims Tribunal, *ICLQ* 42 (1993), 119 *et seq.*; Bederman, Historic Analogues of the UN Compensation Commission, in R.B. Lillich (ed.), *The United Nations Compensation Commission: Thirteenth Sokol Colloquium*, 1995, 257–310; D.S. Mathias, The Weighing of Evidence in a Dual National Case at the Iran-United States Claims Tribunal, *NYIL* 26 (1995), 171–89.

77 See A.A. Fatouros, National Legal Persons in International Law, *EPIL* 10 (1987), 299–306.

78 *Belgium v. Spain*, Judgment (Second Phase), *ICJ Rep.* 1970, 3–357, at 42.

79 *Ibid.*, 31–50. See F.A. Mann, The Protection of Shareholder's Interests in the Light of the Barcelona Traction Case, *AJIL* 67 (1973), 259–74.

above, was concerned with a change of nationality, or, more specifically, with naturalization. It is uncertain whether international law would apply the same tests to acquisition of nationality at birth, for instance, or upon marriage. It is possible to acquire the nationality of a country by virtue of being born there, without having any genuine link with that country; is such a nationality caught by the rule in the *Nottebohm* case? Maybe it would be better to think in terms not of genuine links but of what is acceptable under customary law. Thus it is perfectly normal to acquire nationality at birth under the *ius soli* principle, but the Mexican and Liechtenstein laws on naturalization were regarded as suspect by the relevant courts because they were not accepted under customary law.

The Iran–United States Claims Tribunal in The Hague was also confronted with politically highly sensitive dual national cases in which claimants seeking compensation from Iran had both American and Iranian nationality. The Tribunal decided on the lines of the *Nottebohm* case and other precedents that the 'dominant and effective nationality' of the claimant is decisive with regard to the admissibility of the claim; in other words, if the claim is raised against Iran, then the Tribunal has jurisdiction if the dominant and effective nationality of the dual national is American, based on factual criteria, such as residence, family connections, gravity of interests, participation in public life, etc.[76]

Claims may also be made on behalf of companies possessing the nationality of the claimant state.[77] For these purposes, a company is regarded as having the nationality of the state under the laws of which it is incorporated and in whose territory it has its registered office. As noted by the ICJ in the *Barcelona Traction* case (which concerned injuries allegedly inflicted by Spain on a Canadian company allegedly controlled by Belgian shareholders), even if the company operates in a foreign country and is controlled by foreign shareholders, the state whose nationality the company possesses still has a right to make claims on its behalf.[78] The Court thus distinguished the *Nottebohm* case (see above). If there is no 'genuine link' between the company and the state whose nationality the company possesses, it may be that the national state would have no right to make claims on the company's behalf. What the Court was really saying in the *Barcelona Traction* case was that the mere fact that a company operated abroad and was controlled by foreign shareholders did not, by itself, prevent the existence of a genuine link between the company and the state whose nationality it possessed.

As a rule, a state is not allowed to make claims on behalf of its nationals who have suffered losses as a result of injuries inflicted on foreign companies in which they own shares. The decision of the International Court of Justice in the *Barcelona Traction* case recognized one exception to this rule: when the company has gone into liquidation, the national state of the shareholders may make a claim in respect of the losses suffered by them as a result of injuries inflicted on the company.[79] In this case the claim failed because the company had not gone into liquidation. Where the injury is inflicted by the state whose nationality the company possesses, it may be that the national state of the shareholders is in a more favourable position as regards making claims. The ICJ left this point open in the *Barcelona*

Traction case,[80] and the *obiter dicta* of individual judges reached conflicting conclusions.[81] But even in these circumstances it is probably necessary to prove either that the company has gone into liquidation or that the injury in question has deprived it of so many of its assets that it can no longer operate effectively.[82]

In the *ELSI* case, decided by a Chamber of the ICJ, the United States filed a claim against Italy for compensation for the alleged expropriation of an Italian corporation wholly owned by a US corporation. Judge Oda argued in a separate opinion, citing extensively from the *Barcelona Traction* case, that the provisions of the 1948 Treaty of Friendship, Commerce and Navigation concluded between Italy and the United States (relied upon by the United States) were not intended to protect the rights of shareholders of companies organized under the law of another state.[83]

It is interesting to note that most of the 'large claims' (above US$250,000) brought before the Iran–United States Claims Tribunal involved claims of American companies against Iran, which often were huge enterprises with many thousands of shareholders, like the General Motors Corporation. These cases confronted the Tribunal with the question (in the light of what has been said above, one might think unnecessarily, but appropriate in view of the special provisions on the jurisdiction of the Tribunal) of how to assess whether the nationality of a multinational company was in practice truly (and not only formally) American, as required by the Claims Settlement Declaration that had established the Tribunal.[84] The Tribunal developed a rather complex set of criteria and accepted a presumption that a company was American if:

1 among a larger number of shareholders the majority had addresses in the United States; and
2 the company is able to submit the following 3 documents:

   (a) a state certificate on the incorporation and existence of the company in accordance with the law of the competent state of the United States;
   (b) copies of the relevant proxy statements which the company has submitted to the US Security and Exchange Commission at the occasion of annual meetings and contain information on the principal shareholders; and
   (c) a sworn statement by a company official on the percentage of the shareholders enjoying voting rights with addresses in the United States.[85]

Special problems arose with regard to 'controlled entities' (companies controlled either by Iran or the United States) in third states, which can be neglected here.

Exhaustion of local remedies

An injured individual (or company) must exhaust remedies in the courts of the defendant state before an international claim can be brought on his behalf.[86] Thus, ILC draft article 22 provides:

When the conduct of a State has created a situation not in conformity with the result required of it by an international obligation concerning the treatment to be

80 *ICJ Rep.* 1970, at 48.
81 *Ibid.*, 72–5, 191–2, 240–1, 257.
82 See M. Jones, Claims on Behalf of Nationals Who are Shareholders in Foreign Companies, *BYIL* 26 (1949), 225.
83 *Elettronica Sicula S.p.A. (ELSI)* case, *ICJ Rep.* 1989, 15–121; *ILM* 28 (1989), 1109. See also the Case Note by T.D. Gill, *AJIL* 84 (1996), 249–58; G. Schuster, Elettronica Sicula Case, *EPIL* II (1995), 55–8.
84 See Chapter 18 below, 296.
85 *Flexi-Van Leasing Inc. v. Islamic Republic of Iran*, Order of 15 December 1982; *General Motors Corporation v. Government of the Islamic Republic of Iran*, Order of 18 January 1983; confirmed by the Full Tribunal in *Islamic Republic of Iran v. United States of America*, DEC 45-A20-FT, *Iran-US CTR* 11 (1986-II), 271. See also C. Staker, Diplomatic Protection of Private Business Companies: Determining Corporate Personality for International Law Purposes, *BYIL* 61 (1990), 155 *et seq.*
86 K. Doehring, Local Remedies, Exhaustion of, *EPIL* 1 (1981), 136–40; C.F. Amerasinghe, *Local Remedies in International Law*, 1990; S. Schwebel, Arbitration and the Exhaustion of Local Remedies, in W.E. Ebke/J.J. Norton (eds), *Festschrift in Honor of Sir Joseph Gold*, 1990, 373; M.H. Adler, The Exhaustion of Local Remedies Rule After the International Court of Justice's Decision in *ELSI*, *ICLQ* 39 (1990), 641 *et seq.*; C.F. Asmeringhe, Arbitration and the Rule of Local Remedies, in *FS Bernhardt*, 665.

87 For example, *Brown's* claim (1923), *RIAA* VI 120.
88 *Greece v. UK*, *RIAA* XII 83, *ILR* 23 (1956), 306. See N. Wühler, Ambatielos Case, *EPIL* I (1992), 123–5.
89 *Switzerland v. USA*, *ICJ Rep.* 1959, 6, at 26–9. See L. Weber, Interhandel Case, *EPIL* II (1995), 1025–7.
90 *Op. cit.*, 42-4, 94.
91 A.M. Trebilcock, Waiver, *EPIL* 7 (1984), 533–6.

accorded to aliens, whether natural or juridical persons, but the obligation allows that this or an equivalent result may nevertheless be achieved by subsequent conduct of the State, there is a breach of the obligation only if the aliens concerned have exhausted the effective local remedies available to them without obtaining the treatment called for by the obligation or, where that is not possible, an equivalent treatment.

Many reasons have been suggested for this rule. The best is probably that it prevents friendly relations between states being threatened by a vast number of trivial disputes; it is a serious allegation to accuse a state of breaking international law. However, when the injury is inflicted directly on a state (for example, when its warships or its diplomats are attacked), there is probably no need to exhaust local remedies; the damage to friendly relations has already been done, and it is beneath the dignity of a state to be required to sue in the courts of another state.

Of course, local remedies do not need to be exhausted when it is clear in advance that the local courts will not provide redress for the injured individual.[87] But, apart from cases where local remedies are obviously futile, the rule is applied very strictly. For instance, in the *Ambatielos* case,[88] a Greek shipowner, Ambatielos, contracted to buy some ships from the British government and later accused the British government of breaking the contract. In the litigation which followed in the English High Court, Ambatielos failed to call an important witness and lost; his appeal was dismissed by the Court of Appeal. When Greece subsequently made a claim on his behalf, the arbitrators held that Ambatielos had failed to exhaust local remedies because he had failed to call a vital witness and because he had failed to appeal from the Court of Appeal to the House of Lords.

Similar conclusions may be drawn from the *Interhandel* case[89] where a Swiss company had its assets in the United States seized during the Second World War, on the grounds of its connection with the German company I. G. Farben. After nine years of unsuccessful litigation in US courts, the Swiss company was told by the State Department that its case in the US courts was hopeless. Switzerland started proceedings against the United States in the International Court of Justice; but, while the case was pending before the ICJ, the United States Supreme Court ordered a new trial of the Swiss company's action against the United States authorities. The International Court dismissed the Swiss government's claim on the grounds that local remedies had not been exhausted. It is sometimes said that local remedies need not be exhausted when they are excessively slow; one wonders what, if anything, the words 'excessively slow' mean after the *Interhandel* case. The judgment in the *ELSI* case is noteworthy because it confirmed that the rule of exhaustion of local remedies only requires the exhaustion of 'all reasonable' local remedies.[90]

Waiver

If a state has waived its claim, it cannot change its mind and put the claim forward again.[91] The claim belongs to the state, not to the injured individual; therefore waiver by the individual does not prevent the state pursuing the claim.[92]

At one time contracts between Latin American states and foreigners frequently contained a 'Calvo clause' (named after the Argentinean lawyer and statesman who invented it), in which the foreigner agreed in advance not to seek the diplomatic protection of his national state.[93] International tribunals generally disregarded such clauses, on the grounds that the right of diplomatic protection was a right which belonged to the state, not to the individual, and that the state was not bound by the individual's renunciation of rights which did not belong to him. For once, the individual's lack of rights works to his advantage.

States can also waive liability claims in advance with regard to certain situations in a treaty in order to enhance cooperation by minimizing the risk of being confronted with huge compensation demands. For example, Article 16 of the 1988 Agreement between the United States, member states of the European Space Agency, Japan and Canada on the Permanently Manned Civil Space Station lays down a 'cross-waiver of liability by the partner states and related entities in the interest of encouraging participation in the exploration, exploitation, and use of outer space through the Space Station.'[94]

Unreasonable delay and improper behaviour by the injured alien

A claim will fail if it is presented after an unreasonable delay by the claimant state.[95] Furthermore, it is sometimes said that a state cannot make a claim on behalf of an injured national if he suffered injury as a result of engaging in improper activities – or, as the graphic phrase puts it, 'if his hands are not clean'.[96] This is probably true, but only if the injury suffered by the national is roughly proportionate to the impropriety of his activities;[97] a state cannot, for instance, be allowed to put a foreign national to death for committing a parking offence. When it comes to severe punishment of foreign nationals for drug offences, for example, as can be seen from recent experience in some South-East Asian states (floggings in Singapore, and the imposition of the death penalty in Malaysia), the matter becomes more complicated.

Consequences of an internationally wrongful act

If it is established that a state has committed an internationally wrongful act, this leads to responsibility entailing certain legal consequences, which the ILC is attempting to codify in Part 2 of its draft articles on state responsibility dealing with 'content, forms and degrees of international responsibility'. Draft article 5 contains a definition of the term 'injured state' a right of which is infringed by the internationally wrongful act of another state. In the case of an international 'crime' in the sense of draft article 19[98] (as distinct from an ordinary 'delict'), the definition is extended to encompass not only the directly affected state but to include 'all other states'.[99] For example, if state A commits a mere 'delict' by confiscating property of a national of state B without offering compensation, only state B can react by raising an international claim in the appropriate forum or by

92 *Barcelona Traction* case, *ICJ Rep.* 1964, 22–3 (Preliminary Objections). See also Chapter 6 above, 102.

93 Geck, *op. cit.*; Dolzer, *op. cit.*. See also Chapter 2 above, 14–15.

94 Text in K.-H. Böckstiegel/M. Benkö (eds), *Space Law: Basic Legal Documents*, Vol. II, D.II.4.2. See also Chapter 13 above, 206.

95 *Centini's* claim (1903), *RIAA* X 552–5.

96 Cf. also draft article 6 *bis* of Part 2 of the ILC draft articles on state responsibility.

97 As in the *I'm Alone* case, *op. cit.*

98 See Chapter 3 above, 59–60.

99 See Part 2, draft article 5(3).

100 Part 2, draft article 6.
101 See R. Wolfrum, Reparation for Internationally Wrongful Acts, *EPIL* 10 (1987), 352–3. See also F.A. Mann, The Consequences of an International Wrong in International and National Law, *BYIL* 48 (1976–7), 1–6; G. White, Legal Consequences of Wrongful Acts in International Economic Law, *NYIL* 16 (1985), 137–73.
102 Part 2, draft article 6 *bis.*
103 Part 2, draft article 6 *bis* (2).
104 Part 2, draft article 6 *bis* (3).
105 S.D. Thomson, Restitution, *EPIL* 10 (1987), 375–8.
106 See Chapter 3, 57–8, on *ius cogens.*
107 Part 2, draft article 7.
108 E.H. Riedel, Damages, *EPIL* I (1992), 929–34. See also D.B. Southern, Restitution or Compensation: the Land Question in East Germany, *ICLQ* 42 (1993), 690–7.
109 See J.Y. Gotanda, Awarding Interest in International Arbitration, *AJIL* 90 (1996), 40–63.
110 Part 2, draft article 8. But see Chapter 15 above, 238.
111 E. Riedel, Satisfaction, *EPIL* 10 (1987), 383–4.
112 Part 2, draft article 10(2).

adopting countermeasures. Other states are not entitled to interfere, because their rights are not affected. On the other hand, if state A commits an international 'crime' by, for example, enslaving parts of the population of State B (slavery is considered to be a international crime, affecting the fundamental interests of the international community as a whole and thus the rights of all states), not only state B but all other states of the international community may be entitled to react, but this matter is controversial and has not yet been settled in the ILC.

The first legal consequence of international responsibility is that the wrongdoing state is obliged to cease the illegal conduct.[100] Moreover, as the ILC has put it, the injured state is entitled to claim 'full reparation,[101] in the form of restitution in kind, compensation, satisfaction and assurances and guarantees on non-repetition . . . either singly or in combination'.[102] However, account has to be taken of any negligence or wilful act or omission of the injured state as well as of a national of the state on the behalf of which a claim is made.[103] The wrongdoing state cannot defend itself by referring to its internal law to avoid providing full reparation.[104]

The rights to restitution in kind, compensation and satisfaction need some more explanation. Restitution in kind means that the wrongdoing state has to re-establish the situation that existed before the illegal act was committed,[105] provided that this

(a) is not materially impossible;

(b) would not involve breach of an obligation arising from a peremptory norm of general international law;[106]

(c) would not involve a burden out of all proportion to the benefit which the injured State would gain from obtaining restitution in kind instead of compensation; or

(d) would not seriously jeopardize the political independence or economic stability of the State which has committed the internationally wrongful act, whereas the injured State would not be similarly affected if it did not obtain restitution in kind.[107]

If restitution in kind is not available, compensation for the damage[108] caused by the act must be paid. Compensation covers any economically assessable damage suffered by the injured state and may include interest[109] and, under certain circumstances, also lost profits.[110]

Satisfaction[111] is a further remedy which is particularly (but not only) appropriate in cases where there is no material damage (so-called 'moral' damage) – for example, if one head of state is gravely insulted by another head of state. Satisfaction may take one or more of the following forms:

(a) an apology;

(b) nominal damages;

(c) in cases of gross infringement of the rights of the injured State, damages reflecting the gravity of the infringement;

(d) in cases where the internationally wrongful act arose from the serious misconduct of officials or from criminal conduct of officials or private parties, disciplinary action against, or punishment of, those responsible.[112]

However, the right to obtain satisfaction 'does not justify demands which would impair the dignity of the State which has committed the internationally wrongful act' (draft article 8(3)). 'Nominal damages' seems to mean that the wrongdoing state may be held to pay a symbolic amount (like US$1 or FF1) to satisfy the 'honour' of the injured state, which is rather atavistic in our times.

As a final form of reparation the ILC draft articles mention guarantees of non-repetition to be given by the wrongdoing state in article 10*bis*. While the notion of international 'crimes' of states (as addressed in draft article 19 in Part 1)[113] remained very controversial in the 1995 session of the ILC, some progress was made with regard to 'delicts' and the dispute settlement issues connected with countermeasures adopted by the victim state.[114]

Countermeasures and dispute settlement

The relevant draft articles concerning countermeasures so far dealt with by the ILC in Part 2 include article 11 (countermeasures by an injured state), article 12 (conditions relating to resort to countermeasures), article 13 (proportionality), and article 14 (prohibited countermeasures). The term 'countermeasures'[115] basically refers to acts of retaliation which are traditionally known as 'reprisals'.[116] If state A is injured by an internationally wrongful act for which state B is responsible, in principle, state A is justified in not complying with its legal obligations towards state B. Under certain conditions state A is allowed to take unilateral coercive countermeasures against state B that would otherwise be prohibited by international law. State A could, for example, suspend its treaty obligations towards state B. Alternatively, state A could seize the assets of state B available under the jurisdiction of state A in order to induce state B to discontinue the wrongful act and provide reparation. Such measures are a form of self-help and are characteristic of the decentralized international legal system, reflecting its horizontal nature.[117] Under certain conditions, even third states which are not directly affected by the illegal act of one state, may be entitled to react to a serious breach of international law if the obligation in question is an obligation *erga omnes*, in the protection of which all states have a legal interest.[118]

But there are certain legal limits to such countermeasures or acts of reprisal. The most important limit nowadays is the prohibition of armed reprisals (use of military force) because of the general prohibition of the use of force in Article 2(4) in the UN Charter (except, of course in self-defence against an armed attack).[119] Thus, if state A is responsible for dishonouring certain obligations under a bilateral trade agreement with state B, state B may not respond by a naval blockade of the harbours of state A. Furthermore, the countermeasure has to be proportionate to the initial wrongful act.[120] If state A imprisons a national of state B on false charges, state B is not allowed to react by expelling all nationals of state A and confiscating any property of state A it can lay its hands on. Furthermore, countermeasures which violate basic human rights or a peremptory norm of international law[121] are not admissible under international law. For

113 See Chapter 3 above, 58–60.

114 See R. Rosenstock, The Forty-Seventh Session of the International Law Commission, *AJIL* 90 (1996), 106.

115 E. Zoller, *Peacetime Unilateral Remedies. An Analysis of Countermeasures*, 1984; Malanczuk (1987), *op. cit.*, 197–286; O.Y. Elagab, *The Legality of Non-Forcible Counter-Measures in International Law*, 1988; L.-A. Sicilianos, *Les Réactions décentralisées à l'illicite – des contre-mesures à la légitime défense*, 1990; L.A.N.M. Barnhoorn, *op. cit.* See also the arbitration between France and the United States (1978) in the *Air Services Agreement* case, 18 *RIAA* 416; *Harris CMIL*, 11–7 and Chapter 1 above, 4.

116 P. Malanczuk, Zur Repressalie im Entwurf der International Law Commission zur Staatenverantwortlichkeit, *ZaöRV* 45 (1985), 293–323; K.J. Partsch, Reprisals, *EPIL* 9 (1986), 330–5; Partsch, Retorsion, *ibid.*, 335-7. On the distinction between reprisals and retorsion see also Chapter 1 above, 4.

117 See Chapter 1 above, 3.

118 See J. Charney, Third State Remedies in International Law, *Mich. JIL* 10 (1989), 57; J.A. Frowein, Reactions by Not Directly Affected States to Breaches of Public International Law, *RdC* 248 (1994-IV), 345–437, and Chapter 3 above, 58–60.

119 See Chapter 19 below, 309–18.

120 See the *Air Services Agreement* case, *op. cit*; J. Delbrück, Proportionality, *EPIL* 7 (1984), 396–400. See also Chapter 19 below, 316–17.

121 See Chapter 3 above, 57–8.

122 For a discussion see O. Schachter, Dispute Settlement and Countermeasures in the International Law Commission, *AJIL* 88 (1994), 471–7; Symposium: Counter-Measures and Dispute Settlement: The Current Debate within the ILC, *EJIL* 5 (1994), 20–119 (with contributions by G. Arangio-Ruiz, V.S. Vereshchetin, M. Bennouna, J. Crawford, C. Tomushat, D. Bowett, B. Simma and L. Condorelli).
123 On conciliation and arbitration see Chapter 18 below, 278–81, 293–5.
124 See the 1995 ILC Report, UN Doc. A/50/10 (1995), 192.
125 The 1996 report was not available at the time of writing.

example, state A cannot resort to the torture of citizens of state B as a retaliation in response to an internationally wrongful act committed by state B.

One of the problematic aspects of the approach adopted by the ILC is that it is attempting to make the use of unilateral countermeasures conditional upon the prior use of compulsory peaceful dispute settlement mechanisms.[122] The reason is to avoid a vicious circle of reprisals and counter-reprisals. However, this may not be very realistic and in effect, as the international legal system stands at the moment, they simply open avenues of abuse to the wrongdoing state and provide excuses for continuing with the violation of international law. On the other hand, where there is no neutral judge, there is also no neutral judgment and one should not overlook the fact that powerful states naturally prefer to make their own judgment on the legality or illegality of the conduct of other states, while weaker states mostly do not have many options left other than to comply with the demands of stronger states, if there is no third-party assessment of the real merits of the dispute.

With regard to dispute settlement, the approach so far accepted by the ILC provides for a formal conciliation process for disputes on the interpretation or application of the draft articles. If conciliation fails, arbitration is encouraged, as provided for in an annex to the articles (but the parties must agree to it).[123] The arbitral tribunal shall be given the authority to decide upon the basic dispute as well as upon the legality of the countermeasures. Furthermore, in order to induce states to accept arbitration, provision is made to offer a complete scheme also with respect to the challenge to the validity of an arbitral award on the grounds that the tribunal has exceeded its jurisdiction. Such a challenge is to be decided by the International Court of Justice.[124]

The ILC managed to complete its first reading of Parts 2 and 3 of the topic in 1996 and states may submit their comments by 1998.[125] It is doubtful whether in the end states will agree to be bound by the draft articles in the form of a multilateral treaty. Nevertheless, the draft articles and their useful extensive commentaries summarizing state practice have already become an important and frequent point of reference as evidence of international law. One needs to be careful, however, to distinguish what of the material is really the codification of existing international law and what is only 'progressive development', in the sense of proposals on what the law should be in the future.

18 Peaceful settlement of disputes between states

Disputes between states arising from claims and counter-claims concerning a matter of fact, law and policy are an inevitable part of international relations and have frequently led to armed conflict. The issue of dispute settlement between states[1] is the area which needs the most careful attention in order to understand the nature of international law properly, because it is the linchpin upon which the operation of all the other principles and rules rests, including the central area of state responsibility. Some more, deeper consideration of the matter is therefore required.

As noted in Chapter 2 above, the idea of peaceful settlement of disputes developed in international law during its 'classical' period, while there was no general prohibition on the use of force. The UN Charter[2] prohibits the use of force in Article 2(4) (with certain exceptions, to be discussed below in Chapter 19[3]) and requires all member states to 'settle their international disputes by peaceful means in such a manner that international peace and security, and justice, are not endangered' (Article 2(3)). However, the concrete obligations following from this provision are controversial and there is no agreement on the meaning of the term 'international dispute'.[4] Indeed, one of the prime purposes of the organization is described as being 'to bring about by peaceful means, and in conformity with the principles of justice and international law, adjustment or settlement of international disputes or situations which might lead to a breach of the peace' (Article 1(1)). Chapter VI of the UN Charter is completely devoted to this purpose, but, as stated in Article 33(1), it is limited to certain types of disputes, namely those 'the continuance of which is likely to endanger the maintenance of international peace and security'.

Article 33(1) of the UN Charter gives a list of the usual methods of the peaceful settlement of disputes between states in international law:

negotiation, enquiry, mediation, conciliation, arbitration, judicial settlement, resort to regional agencies or arrangements, or other peaceful means of their choice.[5]

These methods can be categorized into: (1) diplomatic means of dispute settlement, (2) legal (or judicial) means of dispute settlement, and (3) dispute settlement procedures among the member states of international organizations. Diplomatic means are negotiation, good offices, mediation, inquiry and conciliation. While negotiations only concern the parties to the dispute, in the case of the other aforementioned diplomatic means a third party is involved in the settlement in one way or another without, however, having the power to decide on the dispute with legally binding

1 See *Harris CMIL*, 908–69; *Restatement (Third)*, Vol. 2, 338–99; L.B. Sohn, Peaceful Settlement of Disputes, *EPIL* 1 (1981), 154–6; L.B. Sohn, The Future of Dispute Settlement, in R.St.J. Macdonald/D.M. Johnston (eds), *The Structure and Process of International Law*, 1983, 1121–46; I. Diaconu, Peaceful Settlement of Disputes between States: History and Prospects, *ibid.*, 1095–1120; R. Higgins, International Law and the Avoidance, Containment and Resolution of Disputes, *RdC* (1991-V), 230; J.G. Merrills, *International Dispute Settlement*, 2nd edn 1991, 1; E. Lauterpacht, *Aspects of the Administration of International Justice*, 1991; M. Brus *et al.* (eds), *The United Nations Decade of International Law: Reflections on International Dispute Settlement*, 1991; W.M. Reismann, *Systems of Control in International Adjudication and Arbitration: Breakdown and Repair*, 1992; J. Tacsan, *The Dynamics of International Law in Conflict Resolution*, 1992; P. Pazartzis, Les Engagements internationaux en matière de règlement pacifique des différends entre Etats, 1992; C. Chinkin, *Third Parties in International Law*, 1993; M. Brus, *Third Party Dispute Settlement in An Interdependent World*, 1995; K.-H. Böckstiegel, Internationale Streiterledigung vor neuen Herausforderungen, in *FS Bernhardt*, 671–86; I. Brownlie, The Peaceful Settlement of International Disputes in Practice, *Pace ILR* 7 (1995), 257–79; P. Malanczuk, 'Alternative Dispute Resolution' (ADR) in International Commercial Disputes: Lessons from Public International Law, in ICC Publishing S.A.R (ed.), *ADR – International Commercial Disputes: New Solutions?*, Special Dossier of the ICC International Institute of Business Law and Practice (forthcoming).
2 Text in *Brownlie BDIL*, 1.
3 See Chapter 19 below, 308–18.

4 See C. Tomuschat, Article 2(3), in *Simma CUNAC*, 97–106.

5 See C. Tomuschat, Article 33, *ibid.*, 505–14.

6 See Chapter 22 below, 385–430.

7 See K. Oellers-Frahm/N. Wühler (comps.), *Dispute Settlement in Public International Law: Texts and Materials*, 1984.

8 *The 95th Annual Report of the Administrative Council of the Permanent Court of Arbitration*, 1995, Annex 1; text of the 1899 Convention in UKTS 9 (1901) Cd. 798; 1907 Convention, UKTS 6 (1971) Cmnd. 4575. On the Hague Peace Conferences see Chapter 2 above, 22–3.

9 Text in 71 UNTS 101, revised by the United Nations in 1949, UNGA Res. 268A (III) of 28 April 1949. See F.v.d. Heydte, General Act for the Pacific Settlement of International Disputes (1928 and 1949), *EPIL* II (1995), 499–502; Heydte, Geneva Protocol for the Pacific Settlement of International Disputes (1924), *ibid.*, 529–31.

10 30 UNTS 55. See T.B. de Maekelt, Bogotá Pact (1948), *EPIL* I (1992), 415.

11 320 UNTS 243. See K. Ginther, European Convention for the Peaceful Settlement of Disputes, *EPIL* II (1995), 186.

12 *ILM* 3 (1964), 1116. See T. Maluwa, The Peaceful Settlement of Disputes Among African States, 1963–1983: Some Conceptual Issues and Practical Trends, *ICLQ* 38 (1989), 299–320.

13 *ILM* 32 (1993), 557. See also D. Bardonnet (ed.), *The Peaceful Settlement of International Disputes in Europe: Future Prospects*, 1991; K. Oellers-Frahm, The Mandatory Component in the CSCE Dispute Settlement System, in M. Janis (ed.), *International Courts for the Twenty-First Century*, 1992, 195–211.

14 UN Doc. A/47/558, 98. See J. Hilf, Der neue Konfliktregelungsmechanismus der OAU, *ZaöRV* 54 (1994), 1023–47.

15 D. Blumenwitz, Treaties of Friendship, Commerce and Navigation, *EPIL* 7 (1984), 484-90. See also Chapter 15 above, 237, on bilateral investment treaties.

16 See H. Fox, States and the Undertaking to Arbitrate, *ICLQ* 37 (1988), 1; N. Wühler, Arbitration Clause in Treaties, *EPIL* I (1992), 236; H.v. Mangoldt, Arbitration and Conciliation Treaties, *ibid.*, 230; K. Oellers-Frahm, Compromis, *ibid.*, 712.

17 On the doctrine of sovereignty see Chapter 2 above, 17–18.

effect. Legal means are arbitration and adjudication leading to a legally binding third party decision. This chapter focuses upon the diplomatic and legal methods of dispute settlement. The role of the United Nations in the settlement of inter-state conflicts will be dealt with separately in Chapter 22.[6]

States have concluded quite a number of general multilateral instruments aiming at the peaceful settlement of their quarrels.[7] The 1899 Hague Convention for the Pacific Settlement of International Disputes was revised by the Second Hague Peace Conference in 1907, and by 1996 eighty-two states were still bound by the 1899 or 1907 Convention.[8] The 1928 General Act for the Pacific Settlement of Disputes,[9] concluded under the auspices of the League of Nations, was accepted by only twenty-three states and was later denounced by Spain (1939), France, the United Kingdom and India (1974), and Turkey (1978). While the UN General Assembly approved a minor revision of the Act in 1949, only seven states adhered to it.

But there are also a number of regional instruments, including the 1948 American Treaty on Pacific Settlement (Bogotá Pact),[10] the 1957 European Convention for the Peaceful Settlement of Disputes,[11] the 1964 Protocol of the Commission of Mediation and Arbitration of the Organization of African Unity,[12] the 1992 Convention on Conciliation and Arbitration Convention Within the CSCE[13] and the 1993 OAU Mechanism for Conflict Prevention, Management and Resolution.[14] In addition to such general agreements on dispute settlement, there are many bilateral (especially the numerous treaties of friendship, commerce and navigation or on foreign investment)[15] and multilateral treaties which include specific dispute settlement clauses (so-called compromissory clauses)[16] relating to the interpretation and application of the treaty in question.

In the past, states have shown themselves very reluctant to limit their sovereignty in general terms by submitting *in abstracto* to binding third party settlement of their disputes, especially (but not only) the former socialist countries and most of the developing countries in Africa and Asia. After the Second World War, the predominant trend was to regard only minor conflicts and issues of a more technical nature to be suitable for binding dispute settlement, in view of the diversity of the international community and the absolutist version of the concept of sovereignty that prevailed.[17] It has been noted that even regional agreements on dispute settlement either are not ratified by a considerable number of the more important states in the region, if they provide for compulsory binding adjudication of 'legal' disputes and arbitration of 'non-legal' disputes, such as in Europe or America, or they remain on the level of voluntary dispute settlement, such as the 1964 OAU Protocol. Such general agreements on dispute settlement mechanisms have therefore remained weak and have mostly failed in practice.

In view of the fruitless efforts to replace the old general treaties by new ones and to find a universally acceptable solution, the tendency has been that states are more disposed to agree to third party decisions with regard to disputes concerning more specific matters.[18] The 1972 Outer Space

Liability Convention was in a way typical of a new form of compromissory clause acceptable to states. The claims commission it provides for is only a conciliation body unless the parties agree to accept its decision as a binding award.[19]

But even if states agree to a particular dispute settlement mechanism, this does not necessarily mean that they will actually use it in a given case or abide by a third party decision (although once they decide to accept the jurisdiction of a tribunal in a concrete case they usually do) and international law knows no effective general method to enforce the decisions of international courts and tribunals,[20] as is possible in the case of domestic courts in national legal systems.

The preferred methods of dispute settlement by states in practice are diplomatic methods which leave them as much as possible in control of the outcome of the process.

Diplomatic methods of dispute settlement

Negotiations

The vast majority of disputes between states are settled by direct diplomatic negotiations.[21] International law is not unique in this respect; the vast majority of disputes in any legal system are settled by negotiations.

A duty of states to enter into negotiations may be implied from the general obligation of states to settle their disputes peacefully according to Article 2(3) of the UN Charter and from the duty listed in the Friendly Relations Declaration of 1970 to select such 'means as may be appropriate to the circumstances and the nature of the dispute'.[22] As noted by the ICJ in the *North Sea Continental Shelf* cases, the parties to a dispute may even be under an 'obligation so to conduct themselves that the negotiations are meaningful'.[23] Specific obligations may arise under a treaty such as under Article 283 of the 1982 Law of the Sea Convention[24] which aims at keeping the disputing parties in contact and requires them to exchange views at any stage of the dispute and even thereafter to implement the final settlement or decision.[25]

But negotiation is not always a good method of settling international disputes. Neutral third parties seldom take part in negotiations, and this means that there is no impartial machinery for resolving disputed questions of fact. It also means that there is little to restrain a disputing state from putting forward extreme claims, especially where its bargaining power is very strong. States can also deny that a dispute exists and often demand that certain preconditions are fulfilled before entering into negotiations.

Dispute settlement clauses in treaties often provide for negotiation only as the first step of a dispute settlement procedure and allow for the submission of the quarrel to other means of peaceful settlement such as mediation, inquiry, conciliation, arbitration or adjudication, if the negotiations fail within a certain time-limit.

Good offices and mediation

Sometimes third states, or international organizations, or often even an eminent individual, may try to help the disputing states to reach

18 See K. Oellers-Frahm, Arbitration – A Promising Alternative of Dispute Settlement under the Law of the Sea Convention?, *ZaöRV* 55 (1995), 457–78, at 468 *et seq.*
19 See Chapter 13 above, 205–6.
20 On Article 94 of the UN Charter see below, 288–9.
21 C.-A. Fleischhauer, Negotiation, *EPIL* 1 (1981), 152–4.
22 Text of the Declaration in *Brownlie BDIL*, 36; see Chapter 2 above, 32.
23 *ICJ Rep.* 1969, 3, at 47. See also Chapter 12 above, 193.
24 See Chapter 12 above, 173–5.
25 On the dispute settlement system under the 1982 Convention see text below, 298–300.

26 R.L. Bindschedler, Good Offices, *EPIL* II (1995), 601–3; R.L. Bindschedler, Conciliation and Mediation, *EPIL* I (1992), 721–5; v. Mangoldt, *op. cit.*, 230–6.
27 R.L. Bindschedler, Permanent Neutrality of States, *EPIL* 4 (1982), 133; R.R. Probst, *'Good Offices' in the Light of Swiss International Practice and Experience*, 1989.
28 See E.A. Schwartz, International Conciliation and the ICC, *ICSID Rev.* 10 (1995), 98, at 100–1.
29 *Beagle Channel Arbitration*, *ILM* 17 (1978), 632. See Merrills (1991), *op. cit.*, Chapter 5; K. Lankosz, Beagle Channel, *EPIL* I (1992), 359; K. Oellers-Frahm, Beagle Channel Arbitration, *ibid.*, 363; G.R. Moncayo, La Médiation pontificale dans l'affaire du canal Beagle, *RdC* 242 (1993-V).
30 Text of the Algiers Accords in *ILM* 20 (1981), 223. See S.A. Riesenfeld, United States-Iran Agreement of January 19, 1981 (Hostages and Financial Arrangements), *EPIL* 8 (1985), 522. As to the *Tehran Hostages Case* see Chapters 8, 123, 126–7 and 17, 259–60 above; on the Iran-United States Claims Tribunal see text below, 296–8.
31 Such special rules are laid down, for example, in the World Intellectual Property Organization: Mediation, Arbitration, and Expedited Arbitration Rules, *ILM* 34 (1995), 559; J.A. Freedberg-Swartzburg, Facilities for the Arbitration of Intellectual Property Disputes, *Hague YIL* 8 (1995), 69–84.
32 See Chapter 2 above, 13.
33 See Chapter 5 above, 77.

agreement. Such help can take two forms: good offices and mediation.[26] A third party (as a 'go-between') is said to offer its good offices when it tries to persuade disputing states to enter into negotiations; it passes messages and suggestions back and forth and when the negotiations start, its functions are at an end. Switzerland, with its 'permanent neutrality',[27] for example, has often acted as a protecting power in times of war or peace, such as representing the United States in Cuba.

As compared with offering good offices, a mediator, on the other hand, is more active and actually takes part in the negotiations and may even suggest terms of settlement to the disputing states (which is often seen as a characteristic of conciliation). Under the Conciliation Rules of the International Chamber of Commerce (ICC) (which deal with commercial disputes and do not apply to inter-state disputes), however, the much discussed distinction between 'mediation' and 'conciliation' makes no practical difference, for the Rules leave it to the conciliator whether or not to make settlement proposals.[28] Obviously a mediator has to enjoy the confidence of both sides, and it is often difficult to find a mediator who fulfils this requirement. In the dispute between Argentina and Chile over the implementation of the *Beagle Channel* award,[29] both sides accepted Cardinal Antonio Samoré as a mediator, upon the proposal by the Pope. Good offices and mediation can be combined and are also not always easy to distinguish in practice. Such was the role of Algeria in 1980 in the diplomatic hostages dispute between Iran and the United States in which both sides were not speaking directly to each other. With the assistance of Algeria they concluded the Algiers Accords, leading to the establishment of the Iran–United States Claims Tribunal in The Hague in 1981.[30]

The consent of the parties to mediation is not necessarily required initially, but no effective assistance can be provided without it. General rules of procedure for the mediation of disputes[31] between states do not exist, unless there is a clear treaty basis for them. Mediation thus takes the form of flexible negotiations with the participation of a third party. A mediator can also provide financial support and other valuable assistance in the performance of the solution agreed upon. In the dispute between India and Pakistan on the waters of the Indus basin between 1951 and 1961 the World Bank mediated successfully by granting financial aid. Examples of successful mediations by states, usually by a great power, are the initiatives taken by Germany at the 1878 Berlin Congress,[32] by the USSR in 1966 in the conflict between India and Pakistan, and by the United States in the Arab–Israeli conflict in the 1978 Camp David peace negotiations between Israel and Egypt and in the recent agreements between Israel and the PLO.[33]

An old Chinese proverb says 'the go-between wears out a thousand sandals'. Mediation in conflicts between states is not easy and has its drawbacks also for the mediator, because taking an active role endangers the relations of the mediator with one or all of the disputing parties. A truly neutral stance is often not possible without favouring one side or the other, especially in armed conflicts. Third-party involvement in the settlement of international disputes has also frequently failed due to the lack of sufficient influence of the third party. Great powers have more chances of success due to their resources and weight, but, on the other hand, they tend to pursue their own interests at the same time. Small states or international organizations are less prone to such temptation, but they also have less leverage in persuading the parties to a dispute to reach a compromise. Mediation has most chances in the settlement of smaller issues or local conflicts, in stalemate situations where escalation threatens to occur, or when the dispute has in fact already been decided (i.e. by the military victory of one side) and the consequences have to be drawn.

Fact-finding and inquiry

'Fact-finding' and 'inquiry' as methods for establishing facts in international law can be used for a variety of purposes,[34] including the practice of decision-making of international organizations.[35] In the settlement of international disputes the two terms are more or less interchangeable. Many international disputes turn solely on disputed questions of fact, and an impartial inquiry is a good way of reducing the tension and the area of disagreement between the parties. After some negotiations, disputing states may sometimes agree to appoint an impartial body (mostly *ad hoc*, but sometimes also consisting of a permanent body established in advance by agreement for certain kinds of disputes) to carry out an inquiry; the object of the inquiry is to produce an impartial finding of disputed facts, and thus to prepare the way for a negotiated settlement. The parties are not obliged to accept the findings of the inquiry, but almost always do accept them.

The task of establishing the facts may also be combined with their legal evaluation and that of making recommendations for the settlement of disputes, which then makes a clear distinction between fact-finding/inquiry and conciliation and mediation not always possible, as in the case of the *Dogger Bank* incident.[36] In 1904, the Russian Baltic fleet, on its way to the Pacific to engage in the war with Japan, fired upon British fishing vessels operating around the Dogger Bank in the North Sea, alleging that it had been provoked by Japanese submarines. The parties appointed a commission of inquiry composed of senior naval officers from Great Britain, Russia, the United States, France and Austria, with the task not only of establishing what had actually happened (the facts), but also to make findings on the responsibility[37] and the degree of fault of those under the jurisdiction of both parties. On the basis of the report of the commission, Britain withdrew its insistence on the punishment of the Russian Admiral and Russia agreed to pay £65,000 in compensation.

Fact-finding is also mentioned in treaty instruments. The 1907 Hague Convention, for example, describes the task of a commission of inquiry as 'to facilitate a solution ... by means of an impartial and conscientious investigation' (Article 9) and limits its report 'to a statement of facts' which 'has in no way the character of an award' (Article 35). More recent instruments, however, also give 'fact-finding commissions' powers to evaluate the facts legally and to make recommendations, such as the 1977 Additional Protocol I to the 1949 Geneva Red Cross Conventions, or in the 1982 Law of the Sea Convention.[38]

34 R.B. Lillich (ed.), *Fact-Finding Before International Tribunals*, 1992; K.J. Partsch, Fact-Finding and Inquiry, *EPIL* II (1995), 343–5.

35 See the report of the UN Secretary-General on methods of fact-finding, UN Doc. A/6228, GAOR (XXI) of 22 April 1966, Annexes Vol. 2, Agenda item 87, 1–21.

36 See *Dogger Bank Inquiry* (1905), in J.B. Scott (ed.), *The Hague Court Reports*, 1916, 403–13; P. Schneider, Dogger Bank Incident, *EPIL* I (1992), 1090. For another famous case in which the commission of inquiry, chaired by Charles de Visscher, even went beyond its prescribed fact-finding task, but nevertheless found its findings accepted by the parties, see *Red Crusader Enquiry* (1962), *ILR* 35 (1967), 485–500; J. Polakiewicz, Red Crusader Incident, *EPIL* 11 (1989), 271.

37 See Chapter 17 above, 254–72.

38 Article 90, 1977 Protocol I, *ILM* 16 (1977), 1391; Article 5, Annex VII of the 1982 Convention, *ILM* 21 (1982), 1261. See E. Kussbach, The International Humanitarian Fact-Finding Commission, *ICLQ* 43 (1994), 174–84. On the 1949 Geneva Conventions see Chapter 20 below, 344.

39 UN Doc. A/6373 GOAR (XXI), Annexes, Vol. 2, Agenda item 87, 111–4; UN GA Res. 2329 (XXII) of 18 December 1967.

40 Partsch, *op. cit.*, at 345.

41 Article 1 of the Regulation on the Procedure of International Conciliation, *Ann. IDI* 49-II (1961), 385–91. For literature see Merrills (1991), *op. cit.*, 59.

42 See Chapter 2 above, 22–3.

43 See v. Mangoldt, *op. cit.*, at 232.

The question of whether fact-finding and inquiry should be pure and clearly separated from conciliation, as envisaged in the 1899 and 1907 Hague Conventions and the 1913/14 Bryan Treaties, has remained controversial. After intensive debate which took place from 1962 to 1967 the United Nations took the position that a combination of fact-finding and conciliation would be detrimental to a settlement[39] and rejected the proposal to create a permanent commission of inquiry available to states and organs of the UN and their Specialized Agencies. This would have avoided the necessity of having to reach an agreement in every individual case on the creation of the body, its terms of reference, composition and rules of procedure. General Assembly Resolution 2329 of 18 December 1967 merely requested the Secretary-General to prepare a register of experts on fact-finding. States found this less compromising of their sovereignty and also dismissed any obligation to proceed to fact-finding. The 1974 to 1977 Diplomatic Conference on Humanitarian Law had a similar result. As of 31 March 1991, the competence, for example, of the optional Fact-Finding Commission under Article 90(2) of the 1977 Additional Protocol I to the 1949 Geneva Conventions had been accepted by only twenty-one states. K.-J. Partsch concludes: 'The theory that genuine inquiries (restricted to fact-finding) do not meet with the reluctance of states to allow interference with their sovereignty to the same extent as inquiries combined with elements of conciliation has not been confirmed by international practice during the last eighty years.'[40] The role of bilateral fact-finding in preventing disputes or settling them finally has actually been rather modest. The few successful cases have mostly been limited to special areas such as maritime incidents, and they must be distinguished from 'fact-finding missions' of political organizations, such as the United Nations.

Conciliation

The Institut de droit international in 1961 defined conciliation as follows:

> A method for the settlement of international disputes of any nature according to which a Commission set up by the Parties, either on a permanent basis or an *ad hoc* basis to deal with a dispute, proceeds to the impartial examination of the dispute and attempts to define the terms of a settlement susceptible of being accepted by them or of affording the Parties, with a view to its settlement, such aid as they may have requested.[41]

The definition is generally accurate, but fails, however, to recognize that sole conciliators may also be appointed, although this is not the rule in practice.

The evolution of conciliation as a separate method of dispute settlement in international law can be traced back to the Bryan Treaties of 1913/14.[42] These treaties avoided the honour and vital interest clauses of earlier arbitration treaties and made allowance for the sensitivity of states by giving the permanent commissions to be established only the power to make non-binding decisions.[43] Following the German–Swiss Arbitration Treaty of 1921 and the model of a 1925 Treaty between France and Switzerland, there were hundreds of bilateral general arbitration and conciliation treaties which, *inter alia*, often provided that voluntary or compulsory conciliation should precede the arbitration or adjudication of all legal disputes, or even mentioned compulsory conciliation only.[44] Although some conciliation treaties were also accepted by the Soviet Union, the only global instrument providing for compulsory conciliation (and adjudication and arbitration) was the 1928 General Act for the Pacific Settlement of International Disputes. But it received only a few ratifications.

Since the Second World War the role of conciliation in bilateral treaties has diminished, although it has not completely vanished, especially in the practice of Switzerland, a major champion of conciliation. The picture presented by multilateral treaties is different, because the inclusion of conciliation, next to other forms of dispute settlement, has almost become a routine matter.

In conciliation proceedings between states, third parties cannot take the initiative on their own. Conciliators can be appointed on the basis of their official function, for example heads of state or the UN Secretary-General, or as individuals in their personal capacity. The general practice in establishing commissions is that the parties to the dispute nominate one or two of their own nationals and agree on a certain number of impartial and independent nationals of other states in order to provide a neutral majority.

Conciliation is also sometimes described as a combination of inquiry and mediation. The conciliator, who is appointed by agreement between the parties, investigates the facts of the dispute and suggests the terms of a settlement. But conciliation is more formal and less flexible than mediation; if a mediator's proposals are not accepted, he can go on formulating new proposals, whereas a conciliator usually only issues a single report. (However, the conciliator usually has discussions with each of the parties behind the scenes, with a view to finding an area of agreement between them, before issuing his report.) The parties are not obliged to accept the conciliator's terms of settlement (they are only recommendations); but, apart from that, conciliation often resembles arbitration, particularly when the dispute involves difficult points of law (and is not to be settled *ex aequo et bono*[45]); in order to make a good impression on the conciliator, states are forced to rephrase their case in more moderate language, as they would before an arbitrator. At least the arguments tend to become more reasonable.

Most conciliations were performed with commissions composed of several members, which is the normal arrangement under bilateral or multilateral treaties, but occasionally states may prefer a single conciliator, as in the case of the distribution of the assets of the former East African Community in 1977 when Kenya, Uganda and Tanzania, encouraged by the World Bank, requested the Swiss diplomat Dr Victor Umbricht to make proposals.[46] Other examples are the case of the appointment of the President of the International Monetary Fund in a complex matter concerning the financial consequences of a pre-war loan of Japan, or in a later similar case, the President of the World Bank.[47]

Although the practice of conciliation commissions reflects the same basic functions, namely to examine the dispute and make non-binding recommendations for a possible settlement, there are considerable

44 Merrills, 1991, *op. cit.*, at 60.

45 See Chapter 3 above, 55.

46 Merrills (1991), *op. cit.*, 65 *et seq.* See also N. Wühler, East African Community, *EPIL* II (1995), 1–3.

47 *Ibid.*, 69.

48 *Ibid.*, 67 *et seq.*
49 v. Mangoldt, *op. cit.*, 235.
50 See Merrills (1991), *op. cit.*, 70 *et seq.*
51 See, for example, I. Seidl-Hohenveldern, Conciliation Commissions Established Pursuant to Article 83 of the Peace Treaty with Italy of 1947, *EPIL* I (1992), 725–8.
52 Merrills (1991), *op. cit.*, 76 *et seq.*
53 v. Mangoldt, *op. cit.*, at 233.

differences of approach in essential matters, including the degree of the formality of the proceedings.[48] Often the procedures are kept highly flexible in the interest of being able to deal with the specific nature of a dispute.[49] Confidentiality of the proceedings, however, has been a key to success in dealing with governments. If the parties accept the proposals of a conciliation commission after the usual specification of some months for consideration, the commission drafts a *procès-verbal* which records the fact of conciliation and the agreed terms of settlement. If the proposal is not accepted, the work of the commission is at its end and there are no further obligations for the parties. Findings of fact or legal views of the commission are not to be used by the parties in subsequent arbitral or judicial proceedings, unless they agree.[50]

Mediation and conciliation have both advantages and disadvantages, as compared with the other methods of international dispute settlement. They are both more flexible than arbitration or adjudication, leaving more room for the wishes of the parties and for initiatives of the third party. 'Package deals' can be made more easily. Parties can avoid losing face and prestige by voluntarily accepting (or appearing to do so voluntarily) the proposal of a third party. They remain in control of the outcome. No legal precedent is created for the future. The third party does not have to give reasons and the proceedings can be conducted in secret. The whole matter thus tends to focus on the practical issues.

The disadvantages are also obvious. Conciliation and mediation procedures are difficult to start without the consent of the other side and require the goodwill of the opponent. The contribution to the development of the law is also much more reduced than in the case of arbitration or adjudication, but this is a more abstract systemic consideration. What matters for the parties is primarily the satisfactory settlement of the dispute as such, whether or not the compromise reflects the substantive law.

The practical significance of conciliation in international law depends on the area of study.[51] Generally speaking, it seems that conciliation is most desired where the dispute is a minor one and its central issues are of a legal nature, but the solution should reflect an equitable compromise in the eyes of the parties. It seems that in the seventy years of the modern history of conciliation, less than twenty cases have been heard, rather more than the number of inquiry cases, but still not an overwhelming number if one considers the hundreds of treaties providing for conciliation.[52] Of the thirteen conciliation cases referred to by Hans von Mangoldt, the author concludes:

> Nearly all of them involved legal questions, the majority of which were submitted under a general undertaking to conciliate. Eight of these were settled on the basis of the recommendations of the commission. This success may be due to the fact that in all but one case, failing conciliation, compulsory arbitration had been provided for.[53]

This seems to indicate that the existence of a default procedure leading to legally binding decisions in the next stage, if no result is achieved through non-binding conciliation, is conducive to a settlement. The relatively small number of cases reported, on the other hand, may find some explanation in the confidentiality of the proceedings. The general value that is still being attached to this method as such can be seen from the 1990 UN Draft Rules on Conciliation of Disputes Between States[54] and the 1992 CSCE Convention on Conciliation and Arbitration.[55] However, it has been in the context of the tragedy in former Yugoslavia where conciliation (and other) attempts by various parties and bodies have most visibly failed in recent times to settle an armed conflict fuelled by historically based hatred and nationalistic claims raised by politicians hungry for power.[56] One has to accept that in international affairs, problems often cannot be solved, because the positions of parties are simply irreconcilable.

Legal methods of dispute settlement

Should the above non-binding methods of dispute settlement remain fruitless, some treaties provide for arbitration and/or judicial means of settlement which both result in a third-party decision legally binding upon the parties. Both also require the consent of the parties. Adjudication (judicial settlement) is performed by a standing (permanent) court. The judges are already selected, the procedure is fixed and the law which the court has to apply is predetermined. Arbitration is much more flexible and will be dealt with later.

Adjudication

Among the few standing international courts and tribunals,[57] the International Court of Justice (ICJ) is certainly the most important one.[58] The following will therefore concentrate on the ICJ, or, as it is often, somewhat emphatically, also called, 'the World Court'.

The International Court of Justice

The ICJ and its predecessor the Permanent Court of International Justice (PCIJ) are often referred to together as 'the World Court'. The constituent treaty (or 'Statute') of the PCIJ was signed in 1920 and came into force in 1921.[59] The judges of the Court were not chosen by the parties to each dispute, but were elected by the League of Nations. It is unnecessary to describe the Court in detail, because it was dissolved at the same time as the League of Nations, in 1946; besides, it was very similar to the later ICJ. Although the ICJ is not the legal successor to the PCIJ, the continuity of the two courts is ensured in that cases that could be brought before the PCIJ under treaties still in force between parties to the ICJ Statute are now referred to the ICJ.[60] This also applies to declarations made under the optional clause (see below) of the previous Court.

The ICJ,[61] seated at the Peace Palace in The Hague, is one of the six principal organs of the United Nations, but it has a special position as an independent court and is not integrated into the hierarchical structure of the other five organs.[62] Its Statute, which closely resembles the Statute of the PCIJ, is annexed to the United Nations Charter, so that all members of the United Nations are automatically parties to the Statute.[63] However, in certain circumstances, states which are not members of the United

54 *ILM* 30 (1991), 231.

55 1992 CSCE Convention, *op. cit.*

56 See Chapter 22 below, 403–15.

57 H. Mosler, Judgments of International Courts and Tribunals, *EPIL* 1 (1981), 111–8; H. Steinberger, Judicial Settlement of International Disputes, *ibid.*, 120–33; H. Thirlway, Procedure of International Courts and Tribunals, *ibid.*, 183–7; C.D. Gray, *Judicial Remedies in International Law*, 1990; E. McWhinney, *Judicial Settlement of International Disputes*, 1991; G. Guillaume, *Les Formations restreintes des jurisdictions internationales*, 1992; M.W. Janis (ed.), *International Courts for the Twenty-First Century*, 1992; H. Thirlway, Evidence before International Courts and Tribunals, *EPIL* II (1995), 302–4; C. Tomuschat, International Courts and Tribunals, *ibid.*, 1108–15; M. Kazazi, *Burden of Proof and Related Issues: A Study on Evidence Before International Tribunals*, Studies and Materials on the Settlement of International Disputes, Vol. 1 (P. Malanczuk ed.), 1996. See also the literature above, 273.

58 On other courts see H. Hill, Central American Court of Justice, *EPIL* I (1992), 551–4; P. Nikken, Andean Common Market, Court of Justice, *ibid.*, 159–64; K.R. Simmonds, Central American Common Market, Arbitration Tribunal, *ibid.*, 550–1; T. Buergenthal, Inter-American Court of Human Rights, *EPIL* II (1995), 1008–11. See also P. Pescatore, Court of Justice of the European Communities, *EPIL* I (1992), 852–67; W.v.d. Meersch, European Court of Human Rights, *EPIL* II (1995), 201–17; G. Nolte/S. Oeter, European Commission and Court of Human Rights, Inter-State Applications, *ibid.*, 144–54. For the statute of the new Central American Court of Justice, see *ILM* 34 (1995), 921. On the European Court of Justice see also L.N. Brown/T. Kennedy, *The Court of Justice of the European Communities*, 1994; K.P.E. Lasok, *The European Court of Justice – Practice and Procedure*, 2nd edn 1994. On the Law of the Sea Tribunal see, text below, 238–300.

59 See Chapter 2 above, 24–5.

60 Article 37, ICJ Statute, text in *Brownlie BDIL*, 438.

61 G.C. Fitzmaurice, *The Law and Practice of the International Court of Justice*, 1986; H. Thirlway, The Law and Procedure of the International Court of Justice 1960–1989, *BYIL* 60 (1989), 1–158; Part Two, *BYIL* 61 (1990), 1–134; Part Three, *BYIL* 62 (1991), 1–76; Part Four, *BYIL* 63 (1992), 1–96; Part

Five, *BYIL* 64 (1993), 1–54; Part Six, *BYIL* 65 (1994), 1–102; E.J. de Aréchaga, The Work and the Jurisprudence of the International Court of Justice 1947–1986, *BYIL* 58 (1987), 1–38; R. Jennings, The Internal Judicial Practice of the International Court of Justice, *BYIL* 59 (1988), 31–48; S. Rosenne (ed.), *Documents on the International Court of Justice*, 1991; E. McWhinney, *Judicial Settlement of International Disputes. Jurisdiction, Justiciability and Judicial Law-Making in the Contemporary International Court*, 1991; R. Hofmann *et al.*, *World Court Digest*, Vol. 1 (1986–1990), 1993; S. Rosenne/T.D. Gill, *The World Court. What It Is and How It Works*, 5th edn 1994; H.-J. Schlochauer, International Court of Justice, *EPIL* II (1995), 1084–1107; G.Z. Capaldo, *A Repertory of the Decisions of the International Court of Justice (1947–1992)*, 1995; M. Schröder, ICJ, in *Wolfrum UNLPP I*, 673–85; A. Effinger/A. Witteveen, *The International Court of Justice 1946–1996*, 1996; V. Lowe/M. Fitzmaurice (eds), *Fifty Years of the International Court of Justice*, 1996.

62 On the delicate question of its relationship to the Security Council see text below, 292–3.

63 See Articles 92 and 93(1) UN Charter; H. Mosler, Article 92, in *Simma CUNAC*, 973–1001; Article 93, *ibid.*, 1001–3.

64 On UN membership see Chapter 21 below, 363–74.

65 See, for example, Elections to the International Court of Justice and the International Law Commission, *AJIL* 86 (1993), 173; Triennial Elections of Five Members of the International Court of Justice, *AJIL* 88 (1994), 178.

66 For a discussion of the problem see H. Mosler, 'Nationale' Richter in internationalen Gerichten, in *FS Bernhardt*, 713–31.

67 Article 34 ICJ Statute; F. Matscher, Standing before International Courts and Tribunals, *EPIL* 1 (1981), 191–6; J.I. Charney, Compromissory Clauses and the Jurisdiction of the International Court of Justice, *AJIL* 81 (1987), 855–87.

68 See R. Jennings, The International Court of Justice after Fifty Years, *AJIL* 89 (1995), 493–505, at 504–5. See also Chapter 6 above.

69 See Chapter 2 above, 27.

Nations may appear before the Court, and may even become parties to its Statute (Article 93(2) of the Charter). This has applied to Switzerland (1948), Liechtenstein (1950) and San Marino (1954). The two states which are currently not members of the UN but are parties to the Statute of the Court are Switzerland and Nauru.[64]

The Court has a double function: first, to settle legal disputes submitted to it by states in accordance with international law, and secondly, to give advisory opinions on legal questions referred to it by international organs and agencies duly authorized to do so.

Composition

The Court consists of fifteen judges; five are elected every three years to hold office for nine years. The election procedure is complicated, but can be summed up by saying that election requires an absolute majority of votes in both the Security Council and the General Assembly sitting independently of each other.[65] The Court may not include more than one judge of any nationality, but the composition of the bench should represent the main forms of civilization and the principal legal systems of the world. The recent practice has been to select four judges from West European states, one from the United States, two from South America, two from East European states and six from Africa and Asia. It should be noted that the five permanent members of the Security Council are always represented by a judge in the Court. In 1996 the Court consisted of judges from Algeria, the United States, Japan, France, Guyana, Sri Lanka, Madagascar, Hungary, China, Germany, Sierra Leone, Russia, Italy, the United Kingdom and Venezuela.

The judges are required to possess the qualifications required in their home countries for appointment to the highest judicial office, or must be jurists of recognized competence in international law. At least in theory, the members of the court are supposed not to represent their governments, but to act as independent magistrates.

If a state appearing before the Court does not have a judge of its own nationality at the Court, it may appoint an *ad hoc* judge for the particular case. The institution of the *ad hoc* judge is a survival of the traditional method of appointing arbitrators, and may be necessary to reassure litigants that the Court will not ignore their views; but it is hard to reconcile with the principle that judges are impartial and independent, and are not representatives of their national governments.[66]

Jurisdiction in contentious cases

Only states may be parties in contentious proceedings before the Court.[67] This restriction is antiquated because many areas of international law nowadays affect individuals, corporations and legal entities other than states and the application and interpretation of the law is thus left to municipal courts.[68] Jurisdiction in contentious proceedings is dependent on the consent of states; many of the smaller states represented at the San Francisco Conference in 1945[69] wanted to provide for compulsory jurisdiction in the Charter, but the opposition of the great powers prevented the adoption of any such provision.

The consent of a state to appear before the Court may take several forms. Article 36(1) of the Statute provides:

The jurisdiction of the Court comprises all cases which the parties refer to it and all matters specially provided for in the Charter of the United Nations or in treaties and conventions in force.

The words 'all cases which the parties refer to it' require some explanation. The word 'parties' is in the plural, and implies that all the parties to the dispute must agree that the case should be referred to the Court. Normally the parties refer the dispute to the Court jointly by concluding a special agreement, but there is no reason why each party should not make a separate reference at a separate time. The Court has held that a defendant state may accept the jurisdiction of the Court after proceedings have been instituted against it; such acceptance may take the form of an express statement, or it can be implied if the defendant state defends the case on the merits without challenging the jurisdiction of the Court.[70]

States can also agree in advance by treaty to confer jurisdiction on the Court; that is what Article 36(1) of the Statute means when it refers to 'matters specially provided for . . . in treaties'.[71] There are several hundred treaties in force which contain such a jurisdictional clause stipulating that if parties to the treaty disagree over its interpretation or application, one of them may refer the dispute to the Court. But the mention of 'matters specially provided for in the Charter of the United Nations' raises a problem. Article 36(3) of the Charter, dealing with the peaceful settlement of disputes, empowers the Security Council to recommend that the parties to a legal dispute should refer it to the Court, and in the *Corfu Channel* case the United Kingdom argued that such a recommendation, addressed to the United Kingdom and Albania, was sufficient to give the Court jurisdiction to hear a British complaint against Albania. The Court held that Albania had agreed to accept the Court's jurisdiction, and most of the judges therefore found it unnecessary to comment on the British argument about the effects of the Security Council resolution recommending Albania and the United Kingdom to go to the Court. But seven of the judges added a separate opinion in which they said that the British argument was wrong, since recommendations of the Security Council were not binding.[72] If the opinion of the seven judges is right, as it is generally accepted to be, one must conclude that there are no 'matters specially provided for in the Charter of the United Nations'. The explanation of this paradox is that Article 36(1) of the Statute of the Court was drafted at a time when it looked as if the Charter would provide for compulsory jurisdiction; the San Francisco Conference subsequently rejected proposals to provide for compulsory jurisdiction in the Charter, but forgot to delete the cross-reference in the Statute.

Furthermore, paragraphs 2 and 3 of Article 36 provide as follows:

2 The states parties to the present Statute may at any time declare that they recognize as compulsory *ipso facto* and without special agreement, in relation to any other state accepting the same obligation, the jurisdiction of the Court in all legal disputes . . .

70 *Corfu Channel* case (Preliminary Objection), *ICJ Rep.* 1948, 15–48, at 27–8; on the case see also R. Bernhardt, *EPIL* I (1992), 832–4 and Chapter 19 below, 310. See also *Haya de la Torre* case (Judgment), *ICJ Rep.* 1951, 71–84, at 78; on this case see K. Hailbronner, *EPIL* II (1995), 683–5 and Chapter 3 above, 41.

71 See S. Rosenne, The Qatar/Bahrain Case – What is A Treaty? A Framework Agreement and the Seising of the Court, *LJIL* 8 (1995), 161–82.

72 *ICJ Rep.* 1947–8, 15, 31–2.

73 R. Szafarz, *The Compulsory Jurisdiction of the International Court of Justice*, 1993.
74 *ICJYb* 1978/9, 56–86.
75 The Soviet decree of 10 February 1989 is published in *AJIL* 83 (1989), 457. See T. Schweisfurth, The Acceptance by the Soviet Union of the Compulsory Jurisdiction of the ICJ for Six Human Rights Conventions, *EJIL* 2 (1991), 110–17. See also G. Shinkaretskaya, A Changing Attitude Towards International Adjudication in the Soviet Union, *LJIL* 3 (1990), 59–66.
76 R. Szafarz, Poland Accepts the Optional Clause of the ICJ Statute, *AJIL* 85 (1991), 374–5.
77 *South West Africa* case, ICJ Advisory Opinions of 1950, 1955 and 1956: *ICJ. Rep.* 1950, 128–45; 1955, 67–123; 1956, 23–71; ICJ Judgments of 1962 and 1966: *ICJ. Rep.* 1962, 319–662; 1966, 6–505; ICJ Advisory Opinion of 1971, *ICJ Rep.* 1971, 16–345. See E. Klein, South West Africa/ Namibia (Advisory Opinions and Judgments), *EPIL* 2 (1981), 260–70. See Chapter 19 below, 328–9.
78 For example, in the *Elettronica Sicula S.p.A. (ELSI)* case (*US v. Italy*), *ICJ Rep.* 1989, 15–121; see Chapter 17 above, 267 or in cases brought against the United States by Iran concerning the Airbus incident and the destruction of oil platforms in the Gulf (still pending at the time of writing). The *Airbus* case was terminated on 22 February 1996 because the parties had reached a full and final settlement of the matter, see *ICJ Communiqué*, No. 96/6 of 23 February 1996; see also Chapter 13 above, 200.
79 *ICJ Reports* 1984, 392. See the US Department of State, Letter and Statement Concerning Termination of Acceptance of ICJ Compulsory Jurisdiction, 7 October 1985, *ILM* 24 (1985), 1742–5. See A. D'Amato, Modifying U.S. Acceptance of the Compulsory Jurisdiction of the World Court, *AJIL* 79 (1985), 385–405; A.C. Arend (ed.), *The United States and Compulsory Jurisdiction of the International Court of Justice*, 1986; M.N. Leich, The International Court of Justice. Termination of Acceptance of Compulsory Jurisdiction, *AJIL* 80 (1986), 163–5; K. Oellers-Frahm, Die 'obligatorische' Gerichtsbarkeit des Internationalen Gerichtshofs. Anmerkungen anläßlich der Zuständigkeitsentscheidung im Fall Nicaragua gegen USA, *ZaöRV* 47 (1987), 243; S. Oda, Reservations in the Declarations of Acceptance of the

3 The declarations referred to above may be made unconditionally or on condition of reciprocity on the part of several or certain states, or for a certain time.

This optional clause, as it is called, emerged as a compromise between the advocates and the opponents of compulsory jurisdiction.[73] At the end of 1978, forty-three member states of the UN (not even one-third of the states parties to the Statute at the time) had accepted the jurisdiction of the Court under the optional clause, including eleven West European and five South American countries, as well as Switzerland and Liechtenstein.[74] No Communist state ever accepted the compulsory jurisdiction of the Court. Since then there has been a modest increase in the number of declarations, amounting to fifty-nine as of 1 April 1996.

Gorbachev proposed in his speech before the UN General Assembly in December 1988 that all states should recognize the jurisdiction of the ICJ with regard to human rights treaties, and in 1989 the Soviet Union accepted the Court's jurisdiction under six human rights agreements.[75] Other former socialist states then also made a number of withdrawals of their reservations to the jurisdiction clauses of treaties of this type and the first former member of the Communist bloc in Eastern Europe to make a declaration under the optional clause was Poland, on 25 November 1990.[76] New declarations were notably also made by African states, which had long been discontented with the Court after its controversial handling of the *South West Africa* case.[77] (In a number of advisory opinions, judgments and orders stretching over decades starting in the 1950s, the Court had to deal with the problem of whether the mandate had survived the dissolution of the League of Nations, and what the legal consequences were for the rights and obligations of South Africa and the United Nations, with cases filed by Ethiopia and Liberia against South Africa concerning alleged violations of the mandatory obligations and with the international consequences flowing from the continued presence of South Africa in Namibia, after the mandate had been terminated by the UN.) On the other hand, the United States withdrew its declaration under the optional clause (but continued to participate in cases where it otherwise accepted the Court's jurisdiction)[78] in reaction to the Court's decision to accept jurisdiction in the *Nicaragua* case.[79] Appeals to reconsider the withdrawal have so far not been successful.[80] In addition, El Salvador and Israel were lost. It is notable that the only permanent member of the Security Council[81] that has made and maintained a declaration under Article 36(2) is the United Kingdom, although, as noted above, all five members always have a judge at the Court.

States which accept the jurisdiction of the Court under the optional clause do so, according to paragraph 2, only 'in relation to any other state accepting the same obligation'. This is known as the principle of reciprocity.[82] A state cannot enjoy the benefits of the optional clause unless it is prepared to accept the obligations of the optional clause. If state A has accepted the optional clause and state B has not, state A cannot be sued by state B. If the claimant state has accepted the optional clause subject to reservations, the defendant state can rely upon the claimant state's reservations by way of reciprocity. The provision in paragraph 3, which allows states to accept the optional clause 'on condition of reciprocity on the part of several or certain states', might appear to be redundant, in view of the words quoted from paragraph 2. But, according to the *travaux préparatoires*, paragraph 3 uses the word 'reciprocity' in a different sense; the effect of paragraph 3 is that a state may add a reservation to its acceptance of the optional clause, stating that its acceptance is not to come into force until states X and Y have also accepted the optional clause. Until states X and Y have accepted the optional clause, the state making such a reservation cannot be sued by any state. In fact, no reservations of this sort have been made.

Article 36(3) permits reservations relating to reciprocity and reservations relating to time.[83] In practice, reservations of many other types are also made and have always been accepted as valid. In particular, many states have made reservations permitting them to withdraw their acceptance without notice. Even if such a reservation has not been made, a state may withdraw its acceptance by giving reasonable notice.[84] If a state validly withdraws its acceptance, it prevents the Court trying future cases against it, but it does not deprive the Court of jurisdiction over cases which have already been started against it.[85] Many reservations concern disputes which fall 'essentially' or 'exclusively' within the state's domestic jurisdiction in order to exclude from the compulsory jurisdiction of the Court disputes which states view as affecting their vital interests.[86] For example, the Connally reservation of the United States to its declaration of 26 August 1946 excluded 'disputes with regard to matters which are essentially within the domestic jurisdiction of the United States of America as determined by the United States of America.'[87] Similarly, to take the example of a jurisdiction clause based on a treaty, when the United States became party to the Genocide Convention in 1986, it added a reservation to Article IX stating in plain terms that 'before any dispute to which the United States is a party may be submitted to the jurisdiction of the International Court of Justice under this article, the specific consent of the United States is required in each case'.[88]

Whether such 'automatic reservations', that is, reservations whose scope is to be determined by the reserving state unilaterally, are consistent with the Statute of the Court is a matter of debate.[89] In the *Norwegian Loans* case, the British judge, Sir Hersch Lauterpacht, said that such a reservation was invalid, because it was contrary to Article 36(6) of the Statute, which provides: 'In the event of a dispute as to whether the Court has jurisdiction, the matter shall be settled by the decision of the Court'; moreover, since the reservation could not be severed from the rest of the acceptance, the nullity of the reservation entailed the nullity of the whole acceptance.[90] However, most of the judges left Lauterpacht's argument open; they applied the reservation, since neither of the litigants had pleaded that it was invalid.[91] An ironic feature of the *Norwegian Loans* case was that the automatic reservation was contained in the acceptance filed by the claimant state, France, and was successfully invoked by the defendant state, Norway. This application of the principle of reciprocity, coupled with judicial criticisms of automatic reservations, led to the abandonment

Optional Clause and the Period of Validity of Those Declarations: The Effect of the Shultz Letter, *BYIL* 59 (1988), 1 *et seq.*; R. Ostrihansky, Compulsory Jurisdiction of the International Court of Justice in the Dispute between Nicaragua and the United States, *Hague YIL* 1 (1988), 3–15; T. Gill, *Litigation Strategy at the International Court. A Case Study of the Nicaragua v. United States Dispute*, 1989; D.W. Greig, Nicaragua and the United States: Confrontation Over the Jurisdiction of the International Court, *BYIL* 62 (1991), 119–282. On the *Nicaragua* case see also Chapters 3 above, 40 and 19 below, 319–22, 325.

80 A. D'Amato, The United States Should Accept, By A New Declaration, the General Compulsory Jurisdiction of the World Court, *AJIL* 80 (1986), 331–6; G.L. Scott /C.L. Carr, The ICJ and Compulsory Jurisdiction: The Case for Closing the Clause, *AJIL* 81 (1987), 57–76. On the ambivalent American attitude towards the Court generally see M. Pomerance, *The United States and the World Court as a 'Supreme Court of the Nations': Dreams, Illusions and Disillusion*, 1996.

81 See Chapter 21 below, 373–7.

82 See H.W.A. Thirlway, Reciprocity in the Jurisdiction of the International Court, *NYIL* 15 (1984), 97–138.

83 See generally S.A. Alexandrov, *Reservations in Unilateral Declarations Accepting the Compulsory Jurisdiction of the International Court of Justice*, 1995.

84 *Nicaragua* case, *ICJ Rep.* 1984, 392, at 420.

85 *Nottebohm* case, *ICJ Rep.* 1953, 111, 122–3. On this case see Chapter 17 above, 265–6.

86 See Chapter 2 above, 22.

87 R. Dolzer, Connally Reservation, *EPIL* I (1992), 755–68.

88 132 *Cong. Rec.* S1377 (daily edn 19 Feb. 1986). Ten states protested against this wording.

89 See the dissenting opinions of Judges Guerrero and Basdevant in the *Norwegian Loans* case, *ICJ Rep.* 1957, 9–100, at 68 and 75, and of Judge Lauterpacht in the *Interhandel* case, *ICJ Rep.* 1959, 6–125, at 104. See also on these cases E.K. Mertens, Norwegian Loans Case, *EPIL* 2 (1981), 210–11; L. Weber, Interhandel Case, *EPIL* II (1995), 1025–7; and Chapter 17 above, 268.

90 *ICJ Rep.* 1957, 9, 43–66.

91 *Ibid.*, 27.

92 Jennings, *op. cit.*, 495 with reference to the Portuguese Declaration of 19 December 1955.
93 See Chapter 12 above, 188.
94 Convention on Future Multilateral Cooperation in the Northwest Atlantic Fisheries (1978), *ILM* 34 (1995), 1452.
95 Jennings, *op. cit.*, 495.
96 *ICJ Communiqués*, 95/9 of 29 March 1995 and 95/12 of 2 May 1995. The case was still pending at the time of writing.
97 Jennings, *op. cit.*, 495. On the study by C.H.M. Waldock, Decline of the Optional Clause, see *BYIL* 32 (1955–6), 244. For a new assessment see J.G. Merrills, The Optional Clause Revisited, *BYIL* 64 (1993), 197.
98 *East Timor* case (*Portugal v. Australia*), judgment of 30 June 1995, *ICJ. Rep.* 1995, 90, *ILM* 34 (1995), 1581. See Chapter 3 above, 59 and Chapter 19 below, 327.
99 See Chapter 19 below, 329–30.
100 See P. Lawrence, East Timor, *EPIL* II (1995), 3–4. See also B.F. Fitzgerald, *Horta v. Commonwealth*: The Validity of the Timor Gap Treaty and its Domestic Implication, *ICLQ* 44 (1995), 643–50.
101 On the continental shelf, see Chapter 12 above, 131–3.
102 On *erga omnes* obligations see Chapter 3 above, 58–60 and on self-determination, see Chapter 19 below, 326–40.
103 *East Timor* case, *op. cit.*, judgment, paras. 29 and 37.

of such reservations by several states which had previously inserted them in their acceptances (for example, India, Pakistan and the United Kingdom). But automatic reservations were still retained, for example, by Liberia, Malawi, Mexico, the Philippines and the Sudan.

A now common reservation permits the exclusion, by notifying the UN Secretary-General, of 'any given category or categories of disputes'.[92] Moreover, following the fisheries incident with Spain in the North–West Atlantic,[93] in May 1994 Canada took the precaution of terminating its existing declaration and substituting it with one excluding 'disputes arising out of or concerning conservation and management measures taken by Canada with respect to vessels fishing in the NAFO Regulatory Area', as defined in the relevant Convention,[94] 'and the enforcement of such measures'. It also reserved the right by notification 'to add to, amend or withdraw' any reservations.[95] In the *Fisheries Jurisdiction* case which Spain brought against Canada before the Court on 28 March 1995, Canada contested the jurisdiction of the Court which Spain based on the declarations made by the two parties under Article 36(2).[96]

As Jennings has recently observed:

> The optional clause remains an underused and less than satisfactory method for augmenting the competence of the Court. It remains true, as it was when Waldock made his famous study of the optional clause, that despite the principle of reciprocity, states may well decide that there is some political advantage in remaining outside a system which permits states to join more or less on their own terms at an opportune moment. It would be difficult if not practically impossible to change the system, given the difficulties of amending the Statute of the Court.[97]

Once again, it must be stressed that the Court can only hear cases involving states with their consent. As can be seen from the recent decision of the ICJ in the *East Timor* case,[98] the requirement of consent is taken rather strictly and can lead to very unsatisfactory results. East Timor, once a colony of Portugal and still listed as one of the non-self-governing territories with the UN,[99] had been occupied by Indonesia in 1975 and was annexed as its twenty-seventh Province in 1976, a matter which was not accepted by the United Nations, which repeatedly confirmed the right of the people of East Timor to self-determination and independence, and called for Indonesia's withdrawal from the territory. East Timor is still on the annual agenda of the UN General Assembly, but the topic has not been addressed since 1982.[100] In 1991, Portugal, as the administering power of East Timor (according to Chapter XI of the UN Charter) filed an application against Australia with the ICJ for concluding with Indonesia in 1989 an agreement on the exploration and exploitation of the continental shelf[101] between Australia and East Timor. Portugal argued that this agreement and its implementation would not only violate East Timor's rights to self-determination over its natural resources, but also the rights of Portugal as the administering power with regard to its responsibilities towards the people of East Timor. Although the Court accepted the assertion by Portugal that the right of peoples to self-determination has an *erga omnes* character[102] and left no doubt that East Timor 'remains a self-governing territory and its people has the right to self-determination',[103] it dismissed the case because Indonesia as a substantially affected party had not consented to the jurisdiction of the Court in that case. It held

> that the *erga omnes* character of a norm and the rule of consent to jurisdiction are two different things. Whatever the nature of the obligations invoked, the Court could not rule on the lawfulness of the conduct of a State when its judgment would imply an evaluation of the lawfulness of the conduct of another State which is not a party to the case. Where this is so, the Court cannot act, even if the right in question is a right *erga omnes*.[104]

The Court noted that it was not *per se* prevented from adjudicating a case if a judgment might affect the legal interests of a state which is not a party to the proceedings.[105] But it found in this case that

> the effects of the judgment requested by Portugal would amount to a determination that Indonesia's entry into and continued presence in East Timor are unlawful and that, as a consequence, it does not have the treaty-making power in matters relating to the continental shelf resources of East Timor. Indonesia's rights and obligations would thus constitute the very subject matter of such a judgment made in the absence of that State's consent. Such a judgment would run directly counter to the 'well-established principle of international law embodied in the Court's Statute, namely that the Court can only exercise jurisdiction over a State with its consent'.[106]

This decision, carried by a majority of fourteen of the judges, met with criticism in dissenting opinions by Judge Weeramantry and by the *ad hoc* Judge Skubizewski, appointed by Portugal.[107] But legally speaking, under the Statute of the Court the majority view is correct and it shows that the dependence of the Court upon the consent principle curtails its capacity to act which in its results is often unfortunate with regard to the requirements of justice.[108]

Procedure

As laid down in its Statute and its Rules of Court, adopted in 1978, the procedure of the Court in contentious cases includes a written phase, in which the parties file and exchange pleadings, and an oral phase of public hearings at which the Court is addressed by agents and counsel of the parties.[109] English and French are the two official languages and everything written or said in one is translated into the other. Following the oral hearings, the Court deliberates in private and then delivers its judgment at a public sitting. The judgment is final and there is no appeal.

Before it can examine the merits of the case, the Court usually has to consider several preliminary objections.[110] Defendant states often plead, by way of a preliminary objection, that the Court lacks jurisdiction to try the case, but preliminary objections can take many other forms; for instance, if the claimant state is making a claim on behalf of one of its nationals, there may be preliminary objections based on the rules concerning nationality of claims[111] or exhaustion of local remedies.[112] Preliminary objections are usually dealt with separately in a preliminary judgment, but sometimes the Court 'joins them to the merits', that is, deals with them together with the merits in a single judgment.

104 *Ibid.*, para. 29.
105 *Certain Phosphate Lands in Nauru Case (Nauru v. Australia)*, *ICJ Rep.* 1992, 261–2. In this case the interests of the United Kingdom and New Zealand were also affected, but not seen as constituting the 'very subject matter of the judgment'.
106 Para. 34 with reference to the *Monetary Gold Removed from Rome* case (1943), *ICJ Rep.* 1954, 32. See N. Wühler, Monetary Gold Case, *EPIL* 2 (1981), 195–6.
107 Four other judges gave separate opinions, supporting the majority decision, but with different reasoning.
108 C.M. Chinkin, The East Timor Case (Portugal v. Australia), *ICLQ* 45 (1996), 712–24. See also A. Zimmermann, *ZaöRV* 55 (1995), 1051–76 and K. Oellers-Frahm, *VN* 44 (1996), 67–9. On some earlier considerations see Chinkin, East Timor Moves into the World Court, *EJIL* 4 (1993), 206–22; M.C. Maffei, The Case of East Timor before the International Court of Justice – Some Tentative Comments, *ibid.*, 223–38.
109 For a commentary see S. Rosenne, *Procedure in the International Court*, 1983. See also H.W.A. Thirlway, Procedural Law and the International Court of Justice, in Lowe/Fitzmaurice (eds), *op. cit.*, 389–405; R. Plender, Rules of Procedure in the International Court and the European Court, *EJIL* 2 (1991), 1–30.
110 See also Chapter 17 above, 262–3.
111 See A. Watts, Nationality of Claims: Some Relevant Concepts, in Lowe/Fitzmaurice (eds), *op. cit.*, 424–39. See also Chapter 17 above, 263–7.
112 See Chapter 17 above, 267–8.

113 R. Bernhardt (ed.), *Interim Measures Indicated by International Courts*, 1994; K. Oellers-Frahm, Interim Measures of Protection, *EPIL* II (1995), 1027–34; J.G. Merrills, Interim Measures of Protection in the Recent Jurisprudence of the ICJ, *ICLQ* 44 (1995), 90–146; S. Oda, Provisional Measures. The Practice of the International Court of Justice, in Lowe/ Fitzmaurice (eds), *op. cit.*, 541–56.
114 S.M. Schwebel, Ad hoc Chambers of the International Court of Justice, *AJIL* 81 (1987), 831–54; S. Oda, Further Thoughts on the Chambers Procedure of the International Court of Justice, *AJIL* 82 (1988), 556–62; R. Ostrihansky, Chambers of the International Court of Justice, *ICLQ* 37 (1988), 30–52; E. Valencia-Ospina, The Use of Chambers of the International Court of Justice, in Lowe/Fitzmaurice (eds), *op. cit.*, 503–27.
115 *ICJ Rep.* 1984, 246–390; K. Oellers-Frahm, Gulf of Maine Case, *EPIL* II (1995), 647–51.
116 *ICJ Rep.* 1986, 554 *et seq.*; K. Oellers-Frahm, Frontier Dispute Case (Burkina Faso/Mali), *EPIL* II (1995), 490–4.
117 *ELSI* case, *op. cit.*
118 *ICJ Rep.* 1990, 92.
119 K. Oellers-Frahm, Überlegungen anläßlich der Zulassung der Invervention Nicaraguas im Streit zwischen El Salvador und Honduras, *ZaöRV* 50 (1990), 795–811. For a general analysis of intervention under Articles 62 and 63 of the ICJ Statute see S. Rosenne, *Intervention in the International Court of Justice*, 1993. See also J.M. Ruda, Intervention before the International Court of Justice, in Lowe/Fitzmaurice (eds), *op. cit.*, 487–502.
120 See Jennings, *op. cit.*, 496.
121 *Ibid.*, 496.
122 *Certain Phosphate Lands in Nauru* (Nauru v. Australia) case, Preliminary Objections, *ICJ Rep.* 1992, 240, which was then settled by the payment of compensation by Australia, the UK and New Zealand; *Gabčíkovo-Nagymaros Project* (Hungary v. Slovakia) case, Order of December 20, *ICJ Rep.* 1994, 151. See also E. Honederkamp, The Danube: Damned or Dammed? The Dispute Between Hungary and Slovakia Concerning the Gabčíkovo-Nagymaros Project, *LJIL* 8 (1995), 287–310; M. Fitzmaurice, Environmental Protection and the International Court of Justice, in Lowe/Fitzmaurice (eds), *op. cit.*, 293–315. On the Advisory Opinion on the Legality of Nuclear Weapons, see

The Court can also be requested to take provisional measures under Article 41 of its Statute 'to preserve the respective rights of either party'.[113]

Ad hoc *chambers*

A new development since the ICJ changed its procedural Rules of Court in 1978 to try to 'attract more business' has been the use of *ad hoc* chambers under Article 26(2) of the Statute.[114] While normally the Court decides in its full composition of fifteen judges (sometimes sixteen or seventeen judges, if *ad hoc* judges are appointed by the parties), the use of chambers gives the parties influence as regards the number of judges to decide a case (Article 17(2) of the Rules of Court) and as regards the composition of the chamber. This enables them to have more confidence in the proceedings and their final outcome than submitting to the uncertainties of the full Court. The innovation has given rise to the criticism that the chamber procedure is not reconcilable with the judicial and independent nature of the Court, that the powers of the *ad hoc* chambers are too extensive, and that it has moved the Court into the direction of arbitration instead of adjudication.

Nevertheless, *ad hoc* chambers have been preferred by the parties in the *Gulf of Maine* case between Canada and the United States,[115] the *Frontier Dispute* case between Burkina Faso and Mali[116] (settled by five judges, two of them *ad hoc*), the *ELSI* case between the United States and Italy,[117] and the *Land, Island and Maritime Frontier Dispute between El Salvador and Honduras* case[118] (with Nicaragua intervening as a third party).[119] It is notable that in the first chamber case, the *Gulf of Maine* case, the ICJ was frankly told by Canada and the United States that if it was not in a position to provide a chamber with the membership the parties wished, they would resort to an *ad hoc* tribunal, for which the legal instruments of establishment had already been completed. While some judges of the Court took the view that such procedure was inappropriate, it is difficult to see why Canada and the United States had no right to express their preference and why the Court should have been thereby prejudiced. After all, it remained free to refuse to form the chamber,[120] but that, of course, would not have been conducive to the future business of the Court.

Another innovation, the Chamber of Summary Procedure, on the other hand, has never been activated, although it is appointed every year. The same has applied so far to a further invention in 1993, the establishment of a chamber for environmental disputes by the ICJ which is staffed by seven judges having a special interest in this field.[121] Instead, two large cases with an environmental focus went to the full Court.[122]

Enforcement of judgments

Judgments of the Court are binding (as are the judgments of all international courts and arbitral tribunals).[123] Article 94 of the United Nations Charter authorizes the Security Council to 'make recommendations or decide upon measures to be taken to give effect to the judgment', although these powers have not yet been used to enforce a judgment.[124] It should be noted that the only measures the Security Council may adopt in this respect are those under Chapter VI of the Charter, dealing with the settlement of disputes, and not the stronger measures under Chapter VII which require an immediate threat to the peace before sanctions can be adopted.[125] A request by Nicaragua to the Security Council to enforce the Court's decision in the *Nicaragua* case was vetoed by the United States.[126] But generally, the problem of enforcement is not as serious as one might imagine; if a state is willing to accept the jurisdiction of the Court in a specific case, it is usually willing to carry out the Court's judgment; the real difficulty lies in persuading a state to accept the Court's jurisdiction in the first place, or to stick to a commitment to do so made in advance, in the abstract.

Advisory opinions

In addition to its power to decide disputes between states (contentious jurisdiction), the Court also has a power to give advisory opinions (advisory jurisdiction).[127] Article 96 of the United Nations Charter provides:

1 The General Assembly or the Security Council may request the International Court of Justice to give an advisory opinion on any legal question.
2 Other organs of the United Nations and specialized agencies, which may at any time be so authorized by the General Assembly, may also request advisory opinions of the Court on legal questions arising within the scope of their activities.[128]

The advisory procedure of the Court is not open to states, but only to international organizations. At present, six organs of the United Nations and sixteen specialized agencies[129] are authorized to request advisory opinions of the Court. (The mandate of specialized agencies to submit requests for an advisory opinion is limited by their scope of activities as laid down in their constituent treaties.[130]) They must concern an abstract legal question and not a particular dispute, although often a specific dispute may be underlying the question put to the Court. When a request is filed, the Court invites states and organizations which might provide useful information with an opportunity of presenting written or oral statements. Otherwise the procedure is largely the same as in contentious proceedings.

Unlike judgments, advisory opinions are only consultative and not binding as such on the requesting bodies. (However, certain instruments can provide in advance that the advisory opinion shall be binding.) But they carry political weight and are complied with in most cases; some advisory opinions have significantly altered the course of the development of international law. *Inter alia*, the Court has given advisory opinions on the admission to UN membership,[131] the reparation for injuries suffered in the service of the United Nations,[132] the territorial status of South West Africa (Namibia)[133] and Western Sahara,[134] judgments rendered by international administrative tribunals,[135] the expenses of certain UN operations,[136] the applicability of the UN Headquarters Agreement,[137] the applicability of the Convention on the Privileges and Immunities of the UN,[138] and most recently, the legality of nuclear weapons.[139]

Chapters 3, 45, 50 and 16, 246 above and Chapter 20, 347–9 below.
123 Mosler (1981), *op. cit.*, 111–18. On the meaning of Article 59 of the ICJ Statute in this connection see Chapter 3 above, 51.
124 For a thorough discussion see A. Tanzi, Problems of Enforcement of Decisions of the International Court of Justice and the Law of the United Nations, *EJIL* 6 (1995), 539–72. See also H. Mosler, Article 94, in *Simma CUNAC*, 1005–6.
125 See Chapter 22 below, 387–90.
126 S/PV 2718 of 28 October 1986, 51 (UN Doc. S/18428). On the *Nicaragua* case see text above, 287 and Chapters 3, 40 and 19, 319–22, 325 below.
127 R. Ago, 'Binding' Advisory Opinions of the International Court of Justice, *AJIL* 85 (1991), 439–51; S.M. Schwebel, Was the Capacity to Request an Advisory Opinion Wider in the Permanent Court of International Justice than it is in the International Court of Justice?, *BYIL* 62 (1991), 77–118; H.W.A. Thirlway, Advisory Opinions of International Courts, *EPIL* I (1992), 38–43; R. Higgins, A Comment on the Current Health of Advisory Opinions, in Lowe/Fitzmaurice (eds), *op. cit.*, 567–84.
128 See H. Mosler, Article 96, in *Simma CUNAC*, 1008–17.
129 See Chapter 21 below, 382–4.
130 See, for example, the WHO case on the legality of nuclear weapons, Chapter 20 below, 347–9.
131 *Admission Case, ICJ Rep.* 1948, 57–119. See K. Herndl, Admission of a State to Membership in United Nations (Advisory Opinions), *EPIL* I (1992), 35–8.
132 *Reparation Case, ICJ Rep.* 1949, 174–220. See also E. Klein, Reparation for Injuries Suffered in Service of UN (Advisory Opinion), *EPIL* 2 (1981), 242–4. See Chapter 6 above, 93.
133 See text above, 284 and Chapter 19 below, 328–9.
134 *Western Sahara Case, ICJ Rep.* 1975, 12–176. See also K. Oellers-Frahm, Western Sahara (Advisory Opinion), *EPIL* 2 (1981), 291–3.
135 *Effect of Awards of Compensation Made by the United Nations Administrative Tribunal, ICJ Rep.* 1954, 47–97; *Judgments of the Administrative Tribunal of the ILO, ICJ Rep.* 1956, 77–168; *Application for Review of Judgment No. 158 of the UN, ICJ Rep.* 1973, 166–300; *Application for Review of Judgment No. 273 of the UN, ICJ Rep.* 1982, 325; *Application for Review of Judgment No. 333 of the UN, ICJ Rep.* 1987, 18. See further on these

cases L. Weber, M. Ruete, T. Bruha and
M. Marquardt in *EPIL* 2 (1981), at 29,
156, 157 and *EPIL* III (forthcoming). See
also C. Amerasinghe, Cases of the
International Court of Justice Relating to
Employment in International
Organizations, in Lowe/Fitzmaurice
(eds), *op. cit.*, 193–209. See also
Chapter 6 above, 103 and Chapter
21 below, 381.
136 *Advisory Opinion on Certain
Expenses of the UN, ICJ Rep.* 1962,
151. See also Chapter 22 below, 420.
137 *Applicability of the Obligation to
Arbitrate under Section 21 of the UN
Headquarters Agreement, ICJ
Rep.*1988, 12. See also Chapter 6
above, 105.
138 *ICJ Rep.* 1989, 177.
139 See Chapters 3, 45, 50 and 16,
246 above and Chapter 20, 347–9
below.
140 See Jennings, *op. cit.*, 503.
141 See the list in Schlochauer (1995),
op. cit., 1099–100.
142 See text above, 284.
143 Jennings, *op. cit.*, 493–4.
144 See the list by Oellers-Frahm,
Addendum to Schlochauer, *EPIL* II
(1995), 1105.
145 M.W. Janis, *An Introduction to
International Law*, 2nd edn 1993, 122
et seq.

Compared with the number of cases in contentious proceedings and with the respective work of the PCIJ, the advisory jurisdiction of the ICJ has been little used. The total number of advisory opinions of the ICJ in the period from 1948 to 1975 is only sixteen (as compared with the twenty-six opinions rendered by the PCIJ from 1922–35) and between 1980 and 1989 only five were issued, two of which concerned the appellate function of the Court *vis-à-vis* staff decisions of the UN Administrative Tribunal. Some explanation for this may be found in the fact that the organizations entitled to seek advisory opinions (within their area of competence) have their own staff of legal advisors, and that states have shown themselves reluctant to grant the UN Secretary-General the right to go to the Court.[140]

Evaluation of the Court

The case-load of the ICJ has been light in the past. Apart from the advisory opinions mentioned above, in the period up to the end of 1980 the Court delivered judgment in twenty-six disputes.[141] The decline of the utilization of the ICJ was particularly apparent in the 1970s, when many states had joined the UN as new members which preferred to avoid the judicial settlement of disputes. Moreover, in the words of a distinguished former President of the ICJ with reference to the *South West Africa* cases:[142] 'It is often supposed that the unpopularity of the Court's sterile Judgment of 1966, reached by the President's casting vote . . . was directly responsible for a falloff in the Court's work.'[143] From 1981 to 1991 the Court delivered another twelve decisions in contentious cases, still on average dealing with not more than one case a year.[144] If one counts everything together, from 1946 to 1990 the Court rendered fifty-two judgments in contentious cases, sixty substantive orders and twenty-one advisory opinions, which makes about three decisions on average per year.[145] In total since 1946 the court has now delivered some sixty judgments on disputes concerning, *inter alia*, land frontiers and maritime boundaries, territorial sovereignty, the use of force, non-interference in the internal affairs of a state, diplomatic relations, hostage-taking, the right of asylum, nationality, expropriation of foreign property and rights of passage.

This picture might have been very different if individuals and companies, increasingly affected by international regulation, had access to the Court, or, to take another reform proposal, if national courts could ask the ICJ for a preliminary ruling on issues of international law, as in the case of European Law under Article 177 of the European Community Treaty, permitting national courts to refer a matter to the European Court of Justice:

> Modelled upon German and Italian constitutional procedures, this form of process is known in French as the *renvoi préjudiciel* – reference before judgment, which more accurately describes what it involves. The purpose is to enable a national court, faced with a problem of Community law in a case pending before it, to obtain an authoritative ruling from the Court of Justice on the law to be applied. A national court or tribunal which, in the course of proceedings before it, encounters a question involving the interpretation of Community law or the validity of an act of a Community institution, can stay (sist) those proceedings and

refer that question to the Court of Justice. The ruling of the Court of Justice is transmitted back to, and is binding upon, the national court, which must apply it in disposing of the case.[146]

It is only since the end of the Cold War and the change in attitude towards adjudication in former socialist countries and changing perceptions in developing countries on the alleged Western bias of the Court, that a hitherto unknown situation has developed. There has been a marked change in the docket sheet of the Court from the beginning of the 1990s.[147] In March 1995, there were eleven cases pending before the ICJ.[148] This has raised questions on whether a reform of the rather cumbersome deliberation procedures is necessary, also considering that the Judges have no assistance from law clerks.[149]

Assessing the effectiveness of an institution such as the ICJ is always a matter of perspective and value-judgment.[150] It was to be expected that the official speeches given at the celebration of the fiftieth anniversary of the Court on 18 April 1996 at The Hague would be lofty ones, in line with the usual diplomatic courtesy at such occasions.[151] Writers, however, frequently scorn the Court because they see a lack of respect by states and, especially invoking cases of non-appearance[152] of defendant states before the ICJ, find that its decisions are often simply ignored.[153] Judges of the Court, perhaps quite naturally in their position, reject such sweeping contentions and are more optimistic with regard to the overall acceptance of the decisions of the Court by states.[154] At any rate, whatever the situation has been in the past, the recent development appears to be generally encouraging, if one takes the increase in the number of cases into account, as well as the fact that they are being brought from all parts of the world, including from developing countries which have previously, rightly or wrongly, criticized the ICJ for its Western-orientated composition and bias.

For poorer small countries there has also been some inhibition to use the Court, for simple reasons of lack of money. It is true that no fees are demanded by the ICJ because its administrative costs are financed out of the UN budget. But the costs of legal counsel, experts, secretarial assistance, travel and translation, as well as the costs of boundary demarcation in a territorial dispute, for example, are often immense. To facilitate access to the Court, in 1989 a UN Trust Fund to Assist States in the Settlement of Disputes through the International Court of Justice was created by the Secretary-General.[155] The Trust Fund is based on voluntary contributions which shows its weakness as an effective tool, considering the reluctance of states to pay their normal UN dues.[156] However, it was used to provide financial help in establishing the boundary in the dispute between Burkina Faso and Mali.

But the actual use of the Court is not in itself a sufficient criterion to understand its function in the international legal system in a realistic sense. Firstly, there are many ways to settle a dispute between states. Not all kinds of disputes between states are suitable for adjudication by the ICJ (although the distinction between 'political' and 'legal disputes', as part of the fiction that only 'legal' disputes are considered to be justiciable and

146 D.A.O. Edward/R.C. Lane, *European Community Law. An Introduction*, 2nd edn 1995, 40–1. See also E. Benvenisti, Judicial Misgivings Regarding the Application of International Law: An Analysis of Attitudes of National Courts, *EJIL* 4 (1993), 159–83.

147 H. Keith, The Peace Palace Heats Up: The World Court in Business Again?, *AJIL* 85 (1991), 646–54.

148 As of April 1996 there were still eight cases pending: *Maritime Delimitation and Territorial Questions (Qatar v. Bahrain)*; *Questions of Interpretation and Application of the 1971 Montreal Convention arising from the Aerial Incident at Lockerbie (Libya v. United Kingdom)* and *(Libya v. USA)*; *Oil Platforms (Iran v. USA)*; *Application of the Genocide Convention (Bosnia and Herzegowina v. Yugoslavia [Serbia and Montenegro])*; *Gabčíkovo-Nagymaros Project (Hungary v. Slovakia)*; *Land and Maritime Boundary between Cameroon and Nigeria (Cameroon v. Nigeria)*; and *Fisheries Jurisdiction (Spain v. Canada)*. On 29 May 1996, Botswana and Namibia submitted a dispute concerning the boundary around Kasikili/Seduda Island and the legal status of that island, see *ICJ Communiqué* No. 96/19 of 30 May 1996.

149 See the critical report of the Study Group established by the British Institute of International and Comparative Law (D.W. Bowett, J. Crawford, I. Sinclair, A.D. Watts), *The International Court of Justice. Efficiency of Procedures and Working Methods*, Supplement *ICLQ* 45 (1996).

150 See, for example, R. Falk, *Reviving the World Court*, 1986; S. Rosenne, The Role of the ICJ in Inter-State Relations Today, *RBDI* 20 (1987), 275–89; L.F. Damrosch (ed.), *The International Court of Justice at A Crossroads*, 1987; E. McWhinney, *The International Court of Justice and the Western Tradition of International Law*, 1987; J.P. Kelly, The ICJ: Crisis and Reformation, *Yale JIL* 12 (1987), 342–74; A. Bloed/P.v. Dijk (eds), *Forty Years International Court of Justice: Jurisdiction, Equity and Equality*, 1988; J.P. Kelly, The Changing Process of International Law and the Role of the World Court, *Mich. JIL* 11 (1989), 128–66; E. McWhinney, *Judicial Settlement of International Disputes. Jurisdiction, Justiciability and Judicial Law-Making in the Contemporary International Court*, 1991; E. Valencia-Ospina, The Role of the International Court of Justice in Fifty

Years of the United Nations, *Hague YIL* 8 (1995), 3–10; L. Condorelli, La Cour internationale de justice: 50 ans et (pour l'heure) pas une ride, *EJIL* 6 (1995), 388–400.

151 See *ICJ Communiqué* No. 96/15 of 19 April 1996.

152 H. Thirlway, *Non-Appearance Before the International Court of Justice*, 1985; J.B. Elkind, *Non-Appearance Before the International Court of Justice: Functional and Comparative Analysis*, 1986; J.B. Elkind, The Duty to Appear before the International Court of Justice, *ICLQ* 37 (1988), 674; S.A. Alexandrov, Non-Appearance before the ICJ, *Colum. JTL* 33 (1995), 41–72.

153 See the authors cited by Jennings, *op. cit.*, 494.

154 Jennings, *ibid.*; N. Singh, *The Role and Record of the International Court of Justice*, 1989; S. Oda, The ICJ – Retrospective and Prospects, *AsYIL* 3 (1993), 3–13; Oda, The International Court of Justice Viewed from the Bench (1976–1993), *RdC* 244 (1993-VII), 13–190; M. Shahabuddeen, The ICJ: The Integrity of an Idea, *CLB* 19 (1993), 738–53; St. M. Schwebel, The Performance and Prospects of the World Court, *Pace ILR* 6 (1994), 253–65; C.G. Weeramantry, The World Court: Its Conception, Constitution and Contribution, *Mont. LR* 20 (1994), 181–94; G. Guillaume, The Future of International Judicial Institutions, *ICLQ* 44 (1995), 848–62.

155 UN Doc. A/44/PV. 43, at 7–11 (1989). See P. Bekker, International Legal Aid in Practice: The ICJ Trust Fund, *AJIL* 87 (1993), 659–68. For details of the terms of reference, guidelines and rules of the Trust Fund see *ILM* 28 (1989), 1590.

156 See Chapter 21 below, 377–8.

157 I. Hussain, *Dissenting and Separate Opinions at the World Court*, 1984; L.V. Prott, Role, Consensus and Opinion Analysis at the International Court of Justice, *NYIL* 14 (1983), 75–105; F. Jhabvala, The Scope of Individual Opinions in the World Court, *NYIL* 16 (1985), 249–77.

158 K. Wellens, *Economic Conflicts and Disputes Before the World Court (1922–1995)*, Studies and Materials on the Settlement of International Disputes, Vol. 2 (P. Malanczuk ed.), 1996.

159 T.M. Franck, The 'Powers of Appreciation': Who Is the Ultimate Guardian of UN Legality?, *AJIL* 86 (1992), 519–23; E. McWhinney, The International Court as a Constitutional Court and the Blurring of the Arbitral/Judicial Processes, *LJIL* 6 (1993),

thereby admissible to judgment by the ICJ is almost impossible to draw clearly in practice), and sometimes it may appear better in international relations not to settle a dispute at all, at least for the time being, because of other political considerations. Especially where states see their vital interests involved, they will not submit easily to adjudication; and, in fact, this has never happened in history on a voluntary basis.

Secondly, the authority of the Court is established in those limited areas of international law where it had the opportunity to make decisions, although it must be added that the publication of (often very lengthy) 'dissenting' and 'separate opinions' of judges which are almost automatically added to the finding of the majority in each and every case tends to devalue the authority of the judgment in the eyes of the public.[157] Nevertheless, such opinions of individual judges are often more clearly and consistently formulated than the compromise text of the majority and can be an important stimulus for the development of the law on future occasions when the composition of the Court is different. The limits of the ability of the Court to adjudicate effectively in new areas of the law have not yet really been fully tested. One myth that has recently been destroyed by the study by Karel Wellens is that the ICJ, as a matter of principle, would lack the capacity to deal with disputes of an economic nature.[158]

It should be finally mentioned that recent applications submitted by Libya against the United States and the UK in connection with the Lockerbie incident and a case filed by Bosnia and Herzegovina against Yugoslavia (Serbia and Montenegro) have given rise to an interesting discussion of whether the Court can review decisions taken by the Security Council under Chapter VII of the UN Charter.[159] In the *Lockerbie* case the dispute submitted by Libya concerned the interpretation of a multilateral convention dealing with criminal jurisdiction and related rights of states to refuse to extradite their own nationals in connection with the measures adopted against Libya by the Security Council under the allegations of the UK and USA that Libya was responsible for terrorist activity in general and the bombing of Pan-Am flight 103 in particular.[160] The case filed by Bosnia Herzegovina was primarily motivated by the wish to have the legality of the mandatory arms embargo imposed against Bosnia reviewed by the Court. The first Application by Bosnia and Herzegovina requested provisional measures to stop the commission of horrific acts of violence, rape, torture, kidnapping, and extermination allegedly committed by Yugoslav forces against citizens of Bosnia and Herzegovina. The Application was made under Article IX of the Genocide Convention to which both sides were parties and the Court issued an Order on Provisional Measures on 8 April 1993 and Order of 16 April 1993.[161] The second Application by Bosnia and Herzegovina of 27 July 1993 in addition invoked the four 1949 Geneva Red Cross Conventions, the Hague Regulations of 1907 and the Nuremberg documents.[162] But as these instruments lack a jurisdiction clause, the Court did not accept them as *prima facie* sources of jurisdiction and only confirmed the previous Order.[163]

The history of the UN Charter reveals that the ICJ was not designed to be a constitutional court with the power to review the political decisions of the Security Council and it seems that the prevailing view is still that each organ of the United Nations has the autonomy to determine the scope of its own competence under the Charter.[164] However, this may change. Two issues must be distinguished in this connection. The first issue concerns the legal limits to the exercise by the Security Council of its broad powers. The second issue is whether there exists a procedure of judicial review of Security Council decisions which are challenged as being *ultra vires* of the Security Council's powers, and this is a different matter. The *Lockerbie* case and the case filed by Bosnia-Herzegovina may offer an opportunity to clarify this problem. In view of the recent unprecedented activism of the Security Council,[165] the recognition of a power of the ICJ to control the legality of Council decisions in one form or another may appear to be desirable because the international community certainly has an interest in the Security Council respecting the limits imposed on its political discretion by international law.[166] However, the matter is a complicated one in view of the current structure of the United Nations and would require more, deeper investigation, which is beyond the scope of this book.

Arbitration

The following is only concerned with the arbitration involving states under international law and disregards the area of international commercial arbitration between private parties,[167] although recent developments indicate that there is a process of cross-fertilization between public law and private law dispute resolution methods on the international level.[168] Arbitration is much more flexible than adjudication and gives the parties more choices as regards the seat of the tribunal, the appointment and selection of arbitrators and their qualifications, the procedure to be applied and regulating the power of the tribunal through formulating its terms of reference (the so-called *compromis*).[169] A further advantage is that arbitration proceedings can be kept confidential; there is then no 'washing of dirty linen in public'. The differences between arbitration and judicial settlement, however, are being blurred on the international level, as can be seen from the Chamber proceedings introduced at the International Court of Justice.[170]

A frequent pattern in arbitration treaties[171] is for each of the two parties to appoint an arbitrator; the two arbitrators thus appointed agree on the choice of the third arbitrator (or umpire); the arbitral tribunal consequently consists of three (or more) persons, who can decide by majority vote. Of course, the parties can also decide to refer the dispute to a single arbitrator, including to a foreign head of state or government (a practice which is now rare). In the nineteenth century there was a tendency for arbitrators appointed by the parties to regard themselves as representatives of the state which had appointed them, rather than as impartial dispensers of justice. Fortunately, such attitudes are now rare (or maybe more skilfully concealed).

Arbitration has been used for a long time by states to settle their disputes and it may be considered the most effective method, in view of the large number of cases and variety of types of disputes that have been settled in this way.[172] Inter-state arbitration had its heyday in the century following the Jay Treaty of 1794 between the United States and Britain,[173]

279–7; G.R. Watson, Constitutionalism, Judicial Review, and the World Court, *Harvard ILJ* 34 (1993), 1–45; E. McWhinney, The Inaugural Manfred Lachs Memorial Lecture – Manfred Lachs and the International Court of Justice as Emerging Constitutional Court of the United Nations, *LJIL* 8 (1995), 41–52; M. Bedjaoui, *The New World Order and the Security Council – Testing the Legality of Its Acts*, 1995; T.D. Gill, Some Legal and Political Limitations on the Power of the UN Security Council to Exercise Its Enforcement Powers under Chapter VII of the Charter, *NYIL* 26 (1995), 33–138; K. Roberts, Second-Guessing the Security Council: The International Court of Justice and Its Powers of Judicial Review, *Pace ILR* 7 (1995), 281–327; J.G. Gardam, Legal Restraints on Security Council Military Enforcement Action, *Mich. JIL* 17 (1996), 285–322; M. Koskenniemi, The Place of Law in Collective Security, *ibid.*, 455–90; J.E. Alverz, Judging the Security Council, *AJIL* 90 (1996), 1–39.
160 *Libya v. US* (Lockerbie), *ICJ Rep.* 1992, 114 (Provisional Measures) and 234 (Order); *Libya v. UK* (Lockerbie), *ibid.*, 3 (Provisional Measures) and 231 (Order). On the background see F. Beveridge, The Lockerbie Affair, *ICLQ* 41 (1992), 907 *et seq.*; V. Gowlland-Debbas, The Relationship between the International Court of Justice and the Security Council in the Light of the Lockerbie Case, *AJIL* 88 (1994), 643–77.
161 *ICJ Rep.* 1993, 3 and 29.
162 See Chapter 20 below, 344–5.
163 *ICJ Rep.* 1993, 325, at 341, para. 33. See R. Maison, Les Ordonnances de la CIJ dans l'affaire relative à l'application de la Convention sur la prévention et la répression du crime de génocide, *EJIL* 5 (1994), 423–39.
164 See Gill (1995), *op. cit.*, 116 *et seq.*; M. Herdegen, The 'Constitutionalization' of the UN Security System, *Vand. JTL* 27 (1994), 135–59.
165 See Chapter 22 below, 395–6.
166 See for interesting thoughts in this respect, K. Skubiszewski, The International Court of Justice and the Security Council, in Lowe/Fitzmaurice (eds), *op. cit.*, 606–29, 623–9.
167 With regard to the advantages of international arbitration in commercial disputes, see A. Redfern/M. Hunter, *Law and Practice of International Commercial Arbitration*, 2nd edn 1991; K.I. Vibute, Settlement of International Trade Disputes through Litigation and Arbitration: A Comparative Evaluation,

Arbitration 60 (1994), 125; W.L. Craig, Some Trends and Developments in the Laws and Practice of International Commercial Arbitration, *Texas ILJ* 30 (1995), 1; M. Hunter/A. Marriott/V.V. Veeder (eds), *The Internationalisation of Commercial Arbitration. The LCIA Centenary*, 1995; C. Bühring-Uhle, *Arbitration and Mediation in International Business*, 1996.

168 See, for example, J. Paulsson, Cross-Enrichment of Public and Private Law Dispute Resolution Mechanisms in the International Arena, *JIArb.* 9 (1992), 57–68; Malanczuk, 'Alternative Dispute Resolution', *op. cit.*

169 See text above, 282–3.

170 See text above, 288. But see G. Abi-Saab, The International Court as a World Court, in Lowe/Fitzmaurice (eds), *op. cit.*, 3–16.

171 v. Mangoldt, *op. cit.*, 230–6.

172 See Oellers-Frahm (1995), Arbitration, *op. cit.*, 457 *et seq.* See also N. Wühler, Mixed Arbitral Tribunals, *EPIL* 1 (1981), 142–6; S. Schwebel, *International Arbitration: Three Salient Problems*, 1987, 394–6; V. Coussirat-Coustère/P.M. Eisemann, *Repertory of International Arbitral Jurisprudence*, 3 vols, 1989-1990; A.H. Soons (ed.), *International Arbitration. Past and Prospects*, 1990; A.M. Stuyt, *Survey of International Arbitrations 1794–1989*, 1990; H.-J. Schlochauer, Arbitration, *EPIL* I (1992), 215–30; C. Gray/B. Kingsbury, Developments in Dispute Settlement: Inter-State Arbitration Since 1945, *BYIL* 63 (1992), 97; A.B. Boczek, *Historical Dictionary of International Tribunals*, 1994; R.B. Lillich/C.N. Brower (eds), *International Arbitration in the 21st Century: Towards 'Judicialization' and Uniformity?*, 1994.

173 See Chapter 2 above, 20.

174 Janis (1993), *op. cit.*, 111.

175 H.-J. Schlochauer, Permanent Court of Arbitration, *EPIL* 1 (1981), 157–63. See Chapter 2 above, 25.

176 See text above, 274.

177 See text below, 296–8.

178 Chapter 13 above, 201 n. 27.

179 See PCA Optional Rules for Arbitrating Disputes Between Two States, IB/doc/93/1, *ILM* 32 (1993), 572; PCA Optional Rules for Arbitrating Disputes Between Two Parties of which Only One is a State, IB/doc/94/1. See P.J.H. Jonkman, Introduction by the Secretary-General of the Permanent Court of Arbitration, *LJIL* 6 (1993), 199–201; J.L. Bleich, A New Direction for the PCA: The Work of the Expert Group, *ibid.*, 215–40; P.P. Sanders, Private Parties and the Permanent Court

under which 536 arbitral awards were issued between 1799 and 1804, followed by more than 200 other international tribunals established between 1795 and 1914, mostly, however, with the participation of either the United States or Britain.[174] Since then, public international arbitration has declined.

The Permanent Court of Arbitration (PCA), which was set up by the Hague Convention for the Pacific Settlement of International Disputes in 1899,[175] sponsored only twenty arbitrations between 1900 and 1932; since then it has been overshadowed by the Permanent Court of International Justice (PCIJ) and the International Court of Justice (ICJ), and has heard very few cases. The name of this 'Court' is misleading. Each state party to the Convention[176] may nominate four persons to serve on a panel of arbitrators, and disputing states may select arbitrators from this panel in the traditional way. In reality, therefore, the 1899 Convention did not create a court; it merely created the machinery for setting up arbitral tribunals. Also the composition of the 'Court' varies so much from case to case that it cannot develop any coherent case law.

Recent practice of the PCA has been limited to facilitating the establishment of other arbitration bodies with assistance provided by the Bureau of the PCA, such as in the case of the Iran–United States Claims Tribunal in The Hague,[177] or the arbitration between the United States and the United Kingdom on airport charges raised at Heathrow airport.[178] New reforms have been undertaken to attempt to find a niche for the PCA in the complex web of inter-state and commercial dispute settlement world of today. After some expert meetings, new 'optional' rules of procedure of the PCA have now been adopted, *inter alia*, enabling non-state parties, with the consent of the other side, to engage in arbitration with states. New rules on disputes involving international organizations are planned. In 1994 the PCA Administrative Council established a Financial Assistance Fund and a Steering Committee to make recommendations on whether to revise the 1899 and 1907 Conventions.[179]

The record of inter-state arbitration outside of the Permanent Court of Arbitration (which has in total only sponsored some twenty-two arbitrations since it was created in 1899, and only two since 1945) is of some 178 cases between 1900 and 1945, but since the Second World War there has been a clear decline, with only forty-three arbitrations between 1945 and 1990,[180] although the number of states being members of the United Nations has risen over this period from fifty-one to 185.

On the other hand, there is a clear recent tendency in international bilateral and multilateral treaty-making to provide for arbitration as the primary method of dispute settlement.[181] Even codification treaties drafted under the auspices of the United Nations, which in the earlier practice assigned disputes on interpretation or application to be decided by the International Court of Justice, now tend to accept clauses referring to arbitration instead. One reason for this trend is that recourse to the International Court of Justice has been impeded in the past for various reasons (see below), including the possibility of states to add far-reaching reservations to their declarations of the acceptance of the Court's jurisdiction,[182] reflecting the general reluctance of states to submit to compulsory adjudication by a standing court which is considered to have too much impact upon their sovereignty. The comparative advantages of arbitration in reaching a binding third-party decision, while at the same time assuring maximum control over the procedure by the states parties to the dispute, on the other hand, seem to be obvious. However, there is a considerable gap between theory and practice. Thus, Hans von Mangoldt concludes his survey as follows:

> It is difficult to explain the divergence between the elaborated systems of arbitration treaties and their practical result. Presumably, some reasons are: (a) The smaller the probability of a dispute arising between two States, the more they were prepared to engage in arbitration; if a dispute already existed, it was often exempted from the agreement; (b) States often respected the other party's unwillingness to submit to arbitration a dispute which it considered important, in order not to risk a termination of the general arbitration commitment as a whole; (c) it is argued that States may be more inclined to settle a dispute by negotiation if it would otherwise be possible for one of the parties to submit it unilaterally to arbitration; (d) politically sensitive disputes are not submitted to arbitration due to their political importance while politically unimportant disputes are not submitted either because they are too insignificant to pursue further or because they can be easily resolved even without the use of arbitrators.[183]

In a more recent analysis, K.-H. Böckstiegel arrives at the following conclusion:

> Dispute settlement by intergovernmental arbitration has a long history and has been subject to many changes in the course of this history. It has shared with adjudication by international courts the fate of being subjected to a general hesitation of states to submit to future binding third party dispute settlement. But in recent decades, states have shown to prefer international arbitration to the adjudication by international courts especially in view of the greater influence they have on the selection of arbitrators and the arbitral procedure in concrete cases. If one looks for trends, it may be said that bilateral arbitration has been more widely acceptable for limited fields of economic cooperation where the cooperation in the interest of all participating states can only be assured if disputes are not left open but brought to a final decision in due course.[184]

ICSID

The matter becomes more complicated if the arbitration involves a state and a foreign individual or company, often termed mixed international arbitration,[185] which in the past has often concerned the problem of so-called 'internationalized contracts' with a 'stabilization clause' aiming at protecting the foreign investor from changes in the national law of the host state.[186] An institutional solution to this difficult problem has been sought by the creation in 1965 of the International Center for the Settlement of Investment Disputes (ICSID) in Washington under the auspices of the World Bank.[187] Many bilateral investment treaties provide for recourse to this institution in cases of dispute.[188]

The primary purpose of ICSID is to promote foreign investment,

of Arbitration, *ibid.*, 289–96; Jonkmann, The Role of the Secretary-General of the Permanent Court of Arbitration Under the UNCITRAL Rules, *LJIL* 8 (1995), 185–92; B.E. Shifman, The Permanent Court of Arbitration: Recent Developments, *LJIL* 8 (1995), 193, and *ibid.*, 433–8. See also PCA: List of Current Proceedings, *LJIL* 9 (1996), 213–14.

180 Janis (1993), *op. cit.*, 117.

181 L.B. Sohn, The Role of Arbitration in Recent International and Multilateral Treaties, *Virginia JIL* 23 (1982/3), 171 *et seq.* and 172, n. 1. See also P. Peters, Dispute Settlement Arrangements in Investment Treaties, *NYIL* 22 (1991), 91–162. On bilateral investment treaties, see Chapter 15 above, 237. See further text below, 295–6 on the settlement of international trade disputes.

182 See text above, 285–6.

183 v. Mangoldt, *op. cit.*, at 233.

184 K-.H. Böckstiegel, Dispute Settlement by Intergovernmental Arbitration, in E.-U. Petersmann/G. Jaenicke (eds), *Adjudication of International Trade Disputes in International and National Economic Law*, 1992, 59, at 74.

185 See S. Toope, *Mixed International Arbitration*, 1990.

186 See Chapter 3 above, 38–9.

187 Text of the ICSID Convention in 575 UNTS 159. See A.S. El-Kosheri, ICSID Arbitration and Developing Countries, *ICSID Rev.* 8 (1993), 104–15; M. Hirsch, *The Arbitration Mechanism of the International Centre for the Settlement of Investment Disputes*, 1993; C.F. Amerasinghe, Investment Disputes, Convention and International Centre for the Settlement of, *EPIL* II (1995), 1447–51. See also Chapter 15 above, 228.

188 See Chapter 15 above, 237.

189 D.D. Caron, The Nature of the Iran–United States Claims Tribunal and the Evolving Structure of International Law, AJIL 84 (1990), 104–56; R. Khan, *The Iran–United States Claims Tribunal*, 1990; Chapter N. Brower, The Iran–United States Claims Tribunal, RdC 224 (1990-V), 123–396; J.A. Westberg, *International Transactions and Claims Involving Government Parties – Case Law of the Iran–United States Claims Tribunal*, 1991; A. Avanessian, *The Iran–United States Claims Tribunal in Action*, 1993; W. Mapp, *The Iran–United States Claims Tribunal: The First Ten Years 1981–1991*, 1993; G.H. Aldrich, *The Jurisprudence of the Iran–United States Claims Tribunal*, 1996.

190 *Iran–United States Claims Tribunal Reports* (since 1983).

191 R.B. Lillich (ed.), *The Iran–United States Claims Tribunal 1981–1983*, 1984.

192 Declaration of the Government of the Democratic and Popular Republic of Algeria (General Declaration); Declaration of the Government of the Democratic and Popular Republic of Algeria concerning the Settlement of Claims by the Government of the United States of America and the Government of the Islamic Republic of Iran (Claims Settlement Declaration); Undertakings of the Government of the United States of America and the Government of the Islamic Republic of Iran with respect to the Declaration of the Government of the Democratic and Popular Republic of Algeria (Undertakings), ILM 20 (1981), 224 et seq.

193 See Chapter 17 above, 259–60.

194 See Executive Order No. 12170 (14 November 1979), Federal Register 65729 (1979). Assets of Iran in all subsidiaries of American banks abroad were also frozen.

195 Case No. B1.

196 Para. 7 of the General Declaration.

197 See the Decision of the Full Tribunal in *Islamic Republic of Iran v. United States of America*, DEC 12-A1-FT (Issue I).

198 Claims Settlement Declaration, Article II (1).

199 Article II (2).

especially in developing countries, by offering a neutral method for settling disputes between states and private foreign investors. ICSID is based upon a multilateral treaty ratified by more than 100 states. The Centre may either conciliate or arbitrate disputes and has an annulment committee to review ICSID awards, the practice of which has given rise to some controversy. Municipal courts of member states have no power to control the validity of ICSID awards, but they can be directly used by both states and private parties to enforce such awards. However, not many cases have so far been filed with ICSID, and few have led to a decision.

The Iran–United States Claims Tribunal

The Iran–United States Claims Tribunal,[189] seated in The Hague has, in view of the large number of cases before it (more than 3,800 cases were filed), the financial amounts involved (total value in the vicinity of US$50 billion) and the wide range of issues of public international law and international commercial law addressed in its decisions, which are all published,[190] been described as the most significant body in the history of international arbitration.[191] The Tribunal was created by the Algiers Declarations[192] in 1981 as part of the solution to the Tehran hostages crisis[193] mediated by the Algerian Government: on 19 January 1981, the last day of office of President Carter, Iran released the fifty-two hostages held at the American embassy in Tehran, and the United States transferred about US$8 billion from the Iranian assets it had frozen[194] to trust accounts held by Algeria at the Bank of England. The Iran–United States Claims Tribunal was established to settle the numerous claims which each of the two state parties and its nationals had against the other state, ranging from a few thousand dollars in some cases to almost US$12 billion in the largest case (the *Foreign Military Sales* case brought by Iran against the United States).[195] As an unprecedented mechanism in inter-state claims settlement procedures, a special 'Security Account' holding US$1 billion was created at a subsidiary of the Dutch Central Bank (in the name of Algeria) to pay for awards rendered by the Tribunal against Iran, with the additional obligation for Iran to replenish the account, once it fell below US$500 million.[196] Iran repeatedly abided by this obligation, making use, *inter alia*, of the interest that accrued to the Security Account.[197]

The jurisdiction of the Tribunal to give final and binding decisions covers four areas:

1   claims of nationals of the United States against Iran and claims of nationals of Iran against the United States, and any counterclaim which arises out of the same contract, transaction or occurrence that constitutes the subject matter of that national's claim, if such claims and counterclaims are outstanding on the date of this Agreement, whether or not filed with any court, and arise out of debts, contracts (including transactions which are the subject of letters of credit or bank guarantees), expropriations or other measures affecting property rights;[198]

2   official claims of the United States and Iran against each other arising out of contractual arrangements between them for the purchase and sale of goods and services;[199]

3   disputes on whether the United States has met its obligations
    undertaken in connection with the return of the property of the
    family of the former Shah of Iran, Reza Pahlevi;[200] and
4   other disputes concerning the interpretation or application of the
    Algiers Accords.[201]

Matters that were expressly excluded from the Tribunal's jurisdiction
were claims related to the seizure of the American embassy in Tehran
and injury to US nationals or their property as a result of popular movements in the course of the Islamic Revolution which were not acts of the
Government of Iran; and claims arising out of contracts that specifically
provided for the sole jurisdiction of the Iranian courts.[202]

With regard to the substantive law to be applied, the Tribunal was given
a rather broad scope of discretion:

> The Tribunal shall decide all cases on the basis of respect for law, applying such
> choice of law rules and principles of commercial and international law as the
> Tribunal determines to be applicable, taking into account relevant usages of the
> trade, contract provisions and changed circumstances.[203]

The constitution of the Tribunal and its procedural rules were laid
down in the 'Tribunal Rules',[204] a specially adapted version of the UNCI-
TRAL Arbitration Rules which the United Nations had negotiated in
1976 as a model for conducting international commercial arbitration[205] and
now found the first larger (and successful) test in practice.[206] The Tribunal
consists of nine Members, three Iranians, three Americans and three from
third states. The President of the Tribunal is selected from the third-party
arbitrators. Most cases are decided by Chambers of threre arbitrators. The
'Full Tribunal' of all nine Members only decides on the international law
disputes between the parties and in some particularly important cases.

The Tribunal was created under unique circumstances, considering the
diverse ideological premises of the parties, their political and military
confrontation, and the volume of the economic interests at issue, and this
was often reflected in the difficulties of its operation in practice. The
Tribunal even had to interrupt its work for a longer period, following an
unprecedented event in the history of international arbitration when, in
1984, two Iranian arbitrators physically attacked a Swedish arbitrator.[207]
On the whole, however, in spite of the disruption of diplomatic relations
and the continuing confrontation between Iran and the United States
outside of the Tribunal, it was able, under some cumbersome security
arrangements and supported by a large staff of up to 100 persons, to
develop a professional working atmosphere leading to a large body of
decisions. Even in the autumn of 1987, by when Iran and the United
States were in direct military engagement with each other in the Gulf
during the war between Iraq and Iran,[208] the present author recalls taking
part in a large oral hearing in the Peace Palace in The Hague concerning
a claim by Iran for the delivery of military equipment held back by the
United States, with generals and other high-ranking military officers
in uniform represented on both sides, which the Tribunal managed to
conduct quietly.[209]

200 General Declaration, para. 16.
201 Para. 17.
202 Paras. 8 and 11.
203 Claims Settlement Declaration, Article V.
204 For the provisional and final text adopted in March 1982 and May 1983 see *Iran–US CTR* 2 (1983–I), 405, amended once in 1984, *Iran-US CTR* 7 (1984-III), 317.
205 *ILM* 15 (1976), 701 *et seq.*
206 J.J. van Hof, *Commentary on the UNCITRAL Arbitration Rules. The Application by the Iran–US Claims Tribunal*, 1991; S.A. Bakers/M.D. Davis, *The UNCITRAL Arbitration Rules in Practice – The Experience of the Iran-United States Claims Tribunal*, 1992; I. Dore, *The UNCITRAL Framework for Arbitration in Contemporary Perspective*, 1993; D.D. Caron/M. Pellonpää, *The UNCITRAL Arbitration Rules as Interpreted and Applied*, 1995.
207 The so-called 'Mangard incident'; see the Documents Arising From the Episode of 3 September 1984, *Iran-US CTR* 7 (1984-III), 281.
208 I.F. Dekker/H.H.G. Post, *The Gulf War of 1980–1988*, 1992.
209 The present author was legal assistant to the President of the Tribunal from 1986–9 and continued to work on the finalization of cases concerning the expropriation of American oil companies with Karl-Heinz Böckstiegel (also Chairman of Chamber One) until 1993.

210 See Chapter 22 below, 398–9.

211 *Iran–US Claims Tribunal Communiqué* No. 96/1 of 22 January 1996.

212 Of which 248 were 'Awards on Agreed Terms' or 'Partial Awards on Agreed terms' recording settlements by the parties.

213 Award on Agreed Terms No. 483-CLTDs/86/B38/B76/B77-FT, filed 22 June 1990.

214 R.B. Lillich, Lump Sum Agreements, *EPIL* 8 (1985), 367–72. See also Chapter 15 above, 237.

215 See *AJIL* 84 (1990), 891–5 for details.

216 Award No. 306-A15 (I:G)-FT.

217 Oellers-Frahm (1995), Arbitration, *op. cit.*, 458–78; T. Treves, The Law of the Sea Tribunal: Its Status and Scope of Jurisdiction after November 16, 1994, *ibid.*, 421. On the background see R. Bernhardt, Law of the Sea, Settlement of Disputes, *EPIL* 1 (1981), 133; A.O. Adede, *The System for Settlement of Disputes under the United Nations Convention on the Law of the Sea: A Drafting History and a Commentary*, 1987; G. Jaenicke, International Tribunal for the Law of the Sea, in *Wolfrum UNLPP II*, 797–804; S. Rosenne, Establishing the International Tribunal for the Law of the Sea, *AJIL* 89 (1995), 806–14; S. Oda, Dispute Settlement Prospects in the Law of the Sea, *ICLQ* 44 (1995), 683–712; J.I. Charney, The Implications of Expanding International Dispute Settlement Systems: The 1982 Convention on the Law of the Sea, *AJIL* 90 (1996), 69–75.

218 Noted by T. Eitel, Comment, *ZaöRV* 55 (1995), 452, at 456.

219 On the background see Merrills (1991), *op. cit.*, 153 *et seq.* with references.

The work of the Tribunal is now nearing its end. It has only a few cases left and some of the senior staff have already moved on to new tasks at the United Nations Compensation Commission for Claims Against Iraq in Geneva, a body which is not arbitral or judicial in nature, and which was imposed upon Iraq after the invasion of Kuwait.[210] Its success is demonstrated by the number of cases, most of which had been filed by US nationals and companies, that have so far been brought to a decision or a settlement and which cover the entire range of international commercial transactions and foreign investment. As of 31 December 1995,[211] it had issued 567 Awards[212] and 81 Interlocutory and Interim Awards, terminated 877 cases by Order or Decision, and filed 124 Decisions in 133 other cases. The total number of cases finalized was 3,892. However, it must be taken into account that more than 2,300 so-called 'small claims' of less than US$250,000 had been terminated by an Award on Agreed Terms in 1990[213] on the basis of a settlement agreement reached between the two governments, under which Iran accepted to pay the lump sum[214] of US$105 million.[215] The total amount awarded to US parties and paid out of the Security Account, as of the end of 1995, was US$2,091,696,325.96 plus the dollar equivalents of £303,196, DM 297,051 and Rials 97,132,598 (excluding interest). The total amount (excluding interest) awarded to Iran and Iranian parties (not payable out of the Security Account) was US$883,447,411.71 and the dollar equivalent of Rials 7,977,343. About US$500 million of this total amount was paid to Iran on the basis of a Tribunal award ordering the return of frozen Iranian assets held at the New York Federal Reserve Bank.[216]

The fact that the Tribunal still exists and has been able to function under such delicate circumstances is in itself a remarkable contribution in the history of international arbitration. The published decisions of the Tribunal, now approaching thirty volumes, constitute an invaluable collection of materials and jurisprudence on issues of public international law and international commercial law, which as a source for the development of the law will not be so easily surpassed in the future.

Settlement of disputes under the Law of the Sea Convention

The 1982 Law of the Sea Convention, in force since 16 November 1994, contains an elaborate system of dispute settlement, which must be considered as highly innovative because in most cases it will lead to a binding third-party decision in one form or another, with arbitration as the default procedure, if other mechanisms of dispute settlement fail.[217] The 1982 Convention and the Agreement for the Implementation of Part XI of the Convention adopted by the General Assembly on 28 July 1994 make the peaceful settlement of disputes an integrated part of the Convention. In fact nearly a quarter of the articles of the Convention are concerned with dispute settlement.[218] It should also be noted at the outset that the dispute settlement provisions of the Convention proved non-controversial among states,[219] as distinct from the parts dealing with the deep seabed mining regime.

The problem with earlier conventions, not only in the law of the sea, had been that procedures with binding decisions were either not applied (as in the case of the 1958 Fishing Convention providing for *ad hoc* commissions) or laid down in a separate protocol which was not ratified by all members to the Convention (the other three 1958 Law of the Sea Conventions or the 1961 Vienna Convention on Diplomatic Relations, the 1963 Convention on Consular Relations, the 1969 Convention on Special Missions, and others). The 1982 Law of the Sea Convention automatically makes each ratifying state at the same time a party to the dispute settlement provisions.

The system laid down in Part XV is rather flexible and may be briefly summarized as follows. As a starting point, states retain their basic freedom to select the method of dispute settlement in a given case (Article 280). They can choose other mechanisms than those provided for in Part XV of the Convention. But if this does not result in a settlement, the parties may return to the basic procedures of Section 1 of Part XV (Article 281). Article 282 gives priority to dispute settlement procedures the parties have agreed to in other general, regional or bilateral instruments leading to a binding decision, including the acceptance of the optional clause of the International Court of Justice.

If the methods under Section 1 fail to resolve the matter, Section 2 comes into operation which provides for compulsory procedures with binding decisions at the request of any party to the dispute. However, there are exceptions with regard to certain types of disputes which are excluded from this obligation (Section 3). The system in Section 2 gives the parties four different options of a compulsory settlement procedure which they may choose by a written declaration (Article 287):

1   the International Tribunal for the Law of the Sea in Hamburg;
2   the International Court of Justice;
3   an arbitral tribunal established in accordance with Annex VII to the Convention; or
4   a special arbitral tribunal for the settlement of disputes concerning fisheries, protection and preservation of the marine environment, marine scientific research, or navigation and pollution by vessels.

These courts and tribunals are competent with regard to all law of the sea matters submitted to them under the Convention, but also with regard to other rules of international law if they are not incompatible with the Convention. Decisions are binding as between the parties and at their request they can also be based on equity rather than on the law. However, there is no provision made for enforcement. If the parties by their declarations have chosen different procedures from the aforementioned menu, then the dispute is submitted to arbitration in accordance with Annex VII, defining the dispute settlement procedure which applies in any case where a settlement under Section 1 fails or where no other type of procedure has been accepted by both sides.

The dispute settlement system of the 1982 Law of the Sea Convention, which in the end provides for some form of binding third-party decision, also lays down the option of non-binding conciliation (Article 284). It is the only method specially mentioned in Section 1 of Part XV giving

220 See Treves, *op. cit.*, at 436 *et seq.*
221 Petersmann/Jaenicke (eds), *op. cit.*; R. Ostrihansky, Settlement of Interstate Trade Disputes – The Role of Law and Legal Procedures, *NYIL* 22 (1991), 163–216.
222 Text in *ILM* 27 (1988), 281. See J.-G. Castel, The Settlement of Disputes under the 1988 Canada-United States Free Trade Agreement, *AJIL* 83 (1989), 118–28.
223 North American Free Trade Agreement 1992, *ILM* 32 (1993), 289, 605. See J.A. Canela, *ASIL Proc.* 85 (1993), 6–10; G.N. Horlick/F.A. DeBusk, Dispute Resolution under NAFTA, *JIArb.* 10 (1993), 51–61; L.B. Sohn, An Abundance of Riches: GATT and NAFTA Provisions for the Settlement of Disputes, *US-Mexico LJ* 1 (1993), 3–17 and other contributions at 19–40; J.L. Siqueiros, NAFTA Institutional Arrangements and Dispute Settlement Procedures, *CWILJ* 23 (1992–3), 383–94; J.L. Miller, Prospects for Satisfactory Dispute Resolution of Private Commercial Disputes Under the NAFTA, *Pepp. LR* 21 (1994), 1313–89; K.L. Oelstom, A Treaty for the Future: The Dispute Settlement Mechanisms of the NAFTA, *LPIB* 25 (1994), 783–811; J.I. Garvey, Trade Law and Quality of Life – Dispute Resolution under the NAFTA Side Accords on Labor and the Environment, *AJIL* 89 (1995), 439–53.
224 Agreement Establishing the WTO, *ILM* 33 (1994), 1144, see primarily Annex 2: Understanding on Rules and Procedures Governing the Settlement of Disputes, at 1226; J.-G. Castel, The Uruguay Round and the Improvements to the GATT Dispute Settlement Rules and Procedures, *ICLQ* 38 (1989), 834–49; P.T.B. Kohona, Dispute Resolution under the WTO, *JWTL* 28 (1994), 23–47; J.L. Dunoff, Institutional Misfits: The GATT, The ICJ & Trade-Environment Disputes, *Mich. JIL* 15 (1994), 1043–128; M. Reisman/M. Wiedman, Contextual Imperatives of Dispute Mechanisms – Some Hypotheses and Their Application in the Uruguay Round and NAFTA, *JWTL* 29 (1995), 5; S.P. Croley/J.H. Jackson, WTO Dispute Procedures, Standard of Review, and Deference to National Governments, *AJIL* 90 (1996), 193–213; J.H. Bello, The WTO Dispute Settlement Understanding, *ibid.*, 416–18; A. Porges, The New Dispute Settlement: From the GATT to the WTO, *LJIL* 8 (1995), 115–34. See also Chapter 15 above, 231–3.

parties the basic freedom to select the means of dispute settlement. Conciliation is also expressly mentioned as an option with regard to deep seabed mining disputes (Article 285). Furthermore, in areas which are traditionally sensitive from the viewpoint of territorial sovereignty and military activities, or with regard to fishing and research (from the perspective of developing countries), states have shown themselves unwilling to accept binding third-party decisions. The 'optional exceptions' under Article 298 permit states to exempt certain types of disputes from the rules on compulsory jurisdiction. If no declaration is made to the contrary, then the disputes are covered by compulsory jurisdiction. Disputes that may be excluded are:

1   disputes 'concerning the interpretation or application of Articles 15, 74 and 83 relating to sea boundary delimitations';
2   disputes 'involving historic bays or titles';
3   disputes concerning military activities, including such activities by government ships and aircraft engaged in non-commercial service;
4   disputes on law enforcement activities concerning the exercise of sovereign rights or jurisdiction excluded from compulsory jurisdiction under Article 297 (2) and (3) (questions of marine scientific research and of fisheries); and
5   disputes in which the Security Council is exercising its functions under the UN Charter.

With regard to some of the disputes belonging to categories (1) and (2), conciliation is provided for as a method of dispute settlement at the request of one party.[220] Conciliation in these areas was thus the only avenue to secure general consensus on the acceptance of binding settlement procedures in general as an integral part of the Convention. It is obligatory for certain categories of disputes excluded under Section 3 of Part XV from adjudication or arbitration. Annex V sets out the procedure to be adopted in voluntary or mandatory conciliation under the Convention and the provisions largely correspond to those in other recent multilateral conventions.

Conclusions

Whether the 1982 Law of the Sea Convention will mark a new trend in international dispute settlement remains to be seen. The same applies to new developments in international trade agreements,[221] such as the 1988 Canada–US Free Trade Agreement,[222] the NAFTA[223] and GATT under the new umbrella of the WTO,[224] where new mechanisms have been introduced to overcome the inadequate aspects of pure conciliatory dispute settlement. But the reasons for these innovations are somewhat specific to the nature of international trade arrangements and also they differ in each case. NAFTA, for example, does not generally provide for binding dispute settlement procedures between the states parties but follows the model of GATT panel procedures. Moreover, it should be noted that many Asian members of GATT, for reasons of historical and cultural traditions, have shown themselves reluctant to use formal dispute settlement mechanisms and prefer non-litigious methods of dispute settlement, as witnessed by the recent APEC[225] agreement on a 'Voluntary Consultative Dispute Mediation Service'.[226] At any rate, the proliferation of different international courts and tribunals raises the problem of how to ensure consistency of the law, in view of the fact that there is no superior decision-making body which could ultimately unify conflicting decisions on international law.

Since the end of the Cold War there has been no lack of new ideas concerning the improvement of international dispute settlement. One of the main goals of the UN Decade of International Law (1990–9) proclaimed by the UN General Assembly, for example, is the promotion of methods for the peaceful settlement of disputes between states, including resort to the International Court of Justice.[227] In particular the non-aligned countries, recently supported by Russia,[228] have advanced the proposal to convene a Third Hague Peace Conference at the end of the decade (one hundred years after the First Hague Peace Conference) which may consider a new universal convention on the peaceful settlement of disputes.[229] Another new line of discussion was initiated by the submission in 1992 of the UN Secretary-General's 'Agenda for Peace', which apart from advocating the concept of 'preventive diplomacy', *inter alia*, urged greater reliance by states on the World Court for the peaceful adjudication of disputes.[230]

Experience shows, however, that the acceptance of international adjuca-tion by states cannot exactly be described as enthusiastic. Some of the reasons for the reluctance of states to accept the optional clause of the ICJ, for example, are fairly straightforward. For instance, a state which has just become independent may hesitate for a time before accepting unfamiliar commitments. Again, states may be reluctant to go to the ICJ because they prefer other tribunals which are smaller (and therefore cheaper and more expedient) or more specialized, and offer more chances of control over the outcome of the proceedings, as in the case of the Iran–United States Claims Tribunal.

But the reluctance of states to appear before the ICJ also has a more fundamental significance; it is symptomatic of a distrust which states feel for arbitration and judicial settlement in general. They are reluctant to appear before international courts either as plaintiffs or as defendants. (In the remainder of this chapter, the words 'court' and 'judge' are used to include arbitral tribunals as well as courts and judges in the strict sense.) Despite cynical views to the contrary, this reluctance is seldom caused by a desire to be able to break international law with impunity; still, it must be confessed that the absence of a competent court may sometimes have the effect of tempting a state to break international law. The rule that the jurisdiction of international courts is dependent on the consent of states is therefore a defect in international law. But it is not a fatal defect. Inter-national courts hardly existed before the nineteenth century, but inter-national law managed to work without them; even today, after the former communist states have changed their general opposition to international courts on principle, the actual mechanism of inducing states to follow international rules and principles does not in essence rest on adjudication.

225 On APEC see Chapter 15 above, 225.

226 Text in *ILM* 35 (1996), 1102.

227 GA Res. 44/23, 44 UN GAOR Supp. (No. 49), at 21, UN Doc. A/44/49 (1990).

228 See *AJIL* 90 (1996), 499.

229 See L.B. Sohn, Preparation of a New Treaty for the Settlement of International Disputes, *LJIL* 3 (1990), 51; see also C.M. Chinkin, The Peaceful Settlement of Disputes: New Grounds for Optimism?, in R.St.J. Macdonald (ed.), *Essays in Honour of Wang Tieya*, 1994, 165, at 167.

230 *ILM* 31(1992), 953. On 'preventive diplomacy' see B.G. Ramsharan, *The International Law and Practice of Early-Warning and Preventive Diplomacy*, 1991.

231 See Chapter 1 above, 5–7.

232 See T. M. Franck, *Fairness in International Law and Institutions*, 1995, 324 *et seq.*, with reference to the statistical analysis by E.B. Weiss, Judicial Independence and Impartiality: A Preliminary Inquiry, in Damrosch (ed.), *op. cit.*, 123.

233 See Chapter 2 above, 22.

Courts are probably an indispensable part of municipal legal systems, because fear of sanctions imposed by courts is one of the main reasons why people obey municipal law; international law is different, because states have other reasons for obeying international law, reasons which have no counterpart in municipal systems.[231] We must resist the temptation to condemn international law as deficient whenever it fails to resemble municipal law; international law and municipal law work in different ways, but that does not mean that one works less effectively than the other.

There are two reasons why it is instructive to consider the reasons which induce states to distrust international courts. First, such an examination will serve to refute the conclusion that distrust of international courts necessarily connotes disrespect for international law. Second, if an international lawyer is going to persuade states to overcome their distrust of international courts, he will need to have a very clear understanding of the fears felt by states before he can hope to show that those fears are exaggerated or unfounded.

The main reason why states are reluctant to accept the jurisdiction of an international court is because they believe that judicial decisions are often unpredictable. It is not that international law in general is uncertain; but, since most states have competent legal advisers and are fairly law-abiding, the fact that a dispute cannot be settled by negotiation often indicates that the relevant law or the facts of the case are uncertain. And it is these 'unpredictable' cases which are most likely to come before an international court.

States can also point to the prevalence of dissenting opinions as evidence of the unpredictability of judicial decisions; when several members of a court dissent from the judgment given by the majority, it is easy to argue that the case would have been decided the other way if the court had been differently constituted. If different judges are likely to reach different decisions, it may seem as if the outcome of litigation is sometimes a matter of pure chance.

Where the law is uncertain, a judge is likely to be influenced, consciously or unconsciously, by political considerations. This casts doubt on his impartiality; and states may be forgiven for thinking that political decisions should be taken by states and not by courts. The general allegation, however, that the judges of the ICJ would reflect the political biases present in the political organs of the UN has been shown to be empirically wrong.[232] Be that as it may, the element of unpredictability in judicial decisions (not unknown also in national ligitation) may be tolerable in minor cases, but not when important political issues are at stake. Arbitration treaties concluded in the early years of the twentieth century often contained clauses which excluded the obligation to arbitrate in cases affecting the honour or vital interests of the states concerned.[233] Before 1914, writers tried to explain these clauses by saying that 'political' disputes (which were defined in different ways by different writers) were, by their very nature, incapable of judicial settlement. This view is now discredited. But the fact that disputes affecting the vital interests of a state could in theory be decided by an international court does not alter the fact that states usually refuse to submit such disputes to international courts in practice.

An additional factor is that the effects of a court's decision are not limited to the facts of a particular case; it is also a precedent for future cases. Some states distrust the ICJ because they think that its decisions have changed the law too much. On similar grounds (albeit more with a view to the effects upon domestic law and national sovereignty), the UK is discontent with decisions rendered against Britain by the European Court of Justice in Luxembourg and the European Court of Human Rights in Strasbourg. Indeed, when a case turns on a point of law about which the parties honestly hold opposing views, the losing party will always feel that the court has changed the law. States create law for themselves through treaties and custom, and are jealous of rival sources,[234] such as judicial precedents; if changes in the law are needed, states prefer to retain the power of deciding for themselves what the new rules should be.

Conversely, other states distrust international courts because they think that international courts are too conservative. When a customary rule is changing, or a state has reasons to hope that the rule is about to change, a judgment reaffirming the old rule may, through its effect as a precedent, delay or prevent the change. It is significant that the rich states, which may be presumed to be satisfied with the *status quo*, are much readier to accept the Court's jurisdiction under the optional clause than the poor (and presumably dissatisfied) states. Besides, it is only recently that the number of Third World judges at the Court has begun to reflect the increased number of independent Third World states.

Although courts sometimes change the law indirectly, their main function is to apply the existing law; consequently, to expect a court to be able to settle an international dispute, when one side is demanding a change in the law, is rather like trying to settle a wage claim by telling the workers that wages are fixed by the contract of employment and that contracts can be altered only by mutual agreement. But the difference between claims for the application of the law and claims for changes in the law is not always clear. The law itself may be uncertain, and it is always bad tactics for a state to concede that its position is legally untenable; consequently, states often make claims in negotiations without indicating whether their claim is based on the existing law or whether it amounts to a demand for a change in the law. There is also the paradox caused by the element of *opinio iuris* in the formation of new rules of customary law;[235] because a new rule sometimes cannot become law until it is regarded as being already part of the law, claims for changes in the law are often disguised as claims for the application of the existing law. As a result, many cases which appear suitable for judicial settlement are in fact not so.

Finally, there are also a number of minor reasons for the reluctance of states to use international courts for the settlement of disputes. To start judicial proceedings against another state is sometimes regarded as an unfriendly act; states fear that they will lose face if the court's decision goes against them. Moreover, the reluctance of states to go to court produces a vicious circle, in the sense that the large number of preliminary objections raised by defendant states before international courts causes great complexity in the law and makes litigation very expensive and

234 See Chapter 3 above, 35–52.
235 See Chapter 3 above, 44–5.

236 For example, global settlements in cases of expropriation, see Chapter 15 above, 237.

time-consuming; and these consequences in turn intensify the reluctance of states to appear before international courts, either as plaintiff or as defendant.

What happens to disputes which states are unwilling to refer to international courts? Most of them are eventually settled by some political means of settlement, such as negotiation or mediation; indeed, the creation of international organizations like the United Nations has increased the chances of political settlement, by adding to the number of available means of political settlement. Very often the settlement takes the form of a compromise,[236] or of a 'package deal', in which one state makes concessions in one dispute in return for concessions by the other state in another, more or less unrelated, dispute.

Alternatively, the dispute can simply result in a stalemate; states are practically immortal and can afford to wait until a change in the law or in the balance of power enables them to negotiate a settlement on more favourable terms. Disputes over title to territory, in particular, can tend to drag on for centuries, because of the virtually indestructible character of territory; moreover, the complexity and uncertainty of the facts in most territorial disputes makes judicial decisions particularly unpredictable, and the strong emotional attachment felt by peoples for every inch of their territory, however useless the disputed territory may be, increases the unpopularity of international courts as a means of settling such disputes.

In the nineteenth century a strong state might take military action to compel a weak state to accept arbitration; nowadays, changes in the law and in popular attitudes concerning the use of force make such action unthinkable, and stalemate has replaced war as the main alternative to judicial settlement. However, the fact that many disputes lead to stalemate instead of being settled by a court results in an unnecessary prolongation of international tension. What is even more serious is that the absence of compulsory judicial settlement sometimes enables states to break international law with apparent impunity, saves them even from condemnation, and thus produces gross injustice (and cynicism about the effectiveness of international law).

How well founded are the reasons which induce states to distrust international courts? At one extreme, states are clearly right in thinking that a court cannot effectively settle a dispute which is concerned with demands for a change in the law. At the other extreme, the idea that litigation is an unfriendly act, and necessarily complex, expensive and time-consuming, is correct only because states have chosen to approach litigation in this spirit; if states accepted litigation as a normal and desirable means for settling disputes, and did not try to obstruct international courts, litigation would become a simple, quick, cheap and amicable process.

As for the central problem of judicial unpredictability, the fears of states are to some extent well founded, but only in certain cases; in other cases it is easy to predict the decision of the court. Similarly, as regards the related problem of vital interests, states sometimes have an exaggerated idea of what is vital; interests which states regarded as vital (and therefore non-justiciable) sixty years ago are now seen not to be vital after all, and there is no logical reason why this process of contraction should not continue.

Again, the fear of judicial precedents as a source of law is also probably exaggerated; in international law judicial precedents are merely persuasive, not binding, and in any case the effect of an unpopular precedent can always be eliminated by a treaty or by subsequent developments in customary law.

Finally, one or two suggestions can be made for overcoming the distrust which states feel for international courts. In the first place, if states do not want to submit certain categories of disputes to a court, they should try to define those categories precisely and accept the court's jurisdiction over all other categories of disputes; this would avoid the present situation, where reluctance to accept a court's jurisdiction over certain categories of disputes often results in a failure to accept the court's jurisdiction at all – or results in an acceptance coupled with vague and unnecessarily wide reservations. Second, more care should be exercised in selecting judges. The ideal international judge is someone who understands the political aspirations of different states, and who, if he is forced to make a political decision, will do so consciously and wisely, in an attempt to reach a solution which is acceptable to both parties. The judge who is loudest in professing his attachment to the letter of the law and his refusal to be swayed by political considerations often turns out to be basing his judgments on preconceived political ideas of which he is not even conscious. Judges of the latter type have been common in the past. But that is no reason for condemning international courts in general. The solution is to choose better judges in future.

19 International wars, civil wars and the right to self-determination: *ius ad bellum*

1 *Harris CMIL*, 817–73; D.W. Bowett, *Self-Defence in International Law*, 1958; I. Brownlie, *International Law and the Use of Force*, 1963; W. Meng, War, *EPIL* 4 (1982), 282–90; F. Kalshoven, War, Laws of, *ibid.*, 316–22; A. Randelzhofer, Use of Force, *ibid.*, 265–76; O. Schachter, The Right of States to Use Armed Force, *Mich. LR* 82 (1984), 1620; M. Reismann, Criteria for the Lawful Use of Force in International Law, *Yale JIL* 10 (1985), 279–85; C. Greenwood, The Concept of War in Modern International Law, *ICLQ* 36 (1986), 283–306; A. Cassese (ed.), *The Current Legal Regulation of the Use of Force*, 1986; D. Schindler/K. Hailbronner, Die Grenzen des völkerrechtlichen Gewaltverbots, *DGVR* 26 (1986), 11, 49; P. Malanczuk, Countermeasures and Self-Defence as Circumstances Precluding Wrongfulness in the International Law Commission's Draft Articles on State Responsibility, in M. Spinedi/B. Simma (eds), *United Nations Codification of State Responsibility*, 1987, 197–286; W.E. Butler (ed.), *The Non-Use of Force in International Law*, 1989; O. Schachter, *International Law in Theory and Practice*, 1991, Chapters VII and VIII; B. Asrat, *Prohibition of Force under the UN Charter – A Study of Article 2(4)*, 1991; L. Henkin *et al.*, *Right v. Might: International Law and the Use of Force*, 2nd edn 1991; L.F. Damrosch/D.J. Scheffer (eds), *Law and Force in the New International Order*, 1992; K.J. Partsch, Armed Conflict, *EPIL* I (1992), 249–53; Partsch, Armed Conflict, Fundamental Rules, *ibid.*, 253–6; T.D. Gill, The Forcible Protection, Affirmation and Exercise of Rights by States under Contemporary International Law, *NYIL* 23 (1992), 105–73; P. Malanczuk, *Humanitarian Intervention and the Legitimacy of the Use of Force*, 1993; Y. Onuma, *A Normative Approach to War*, 1993; A.C. Arend/R.J. Beck, *International Law and the Use of Force: Beyond the UN Charter Paradigm*,

Having dealt with the situation of normality, with the international law governing the peaceful relations between states, the book now turns to the situation of abnormality, to the rules governing the use of force and armed conflict.[1] The term 'laws of war' can have different meanings and refers to both the rules governing the resort to armed conflict (*ius ad bellum*) and the rules governing the actual conduct of armed conflict (*ius in bello*). It is reasonable to treat both areas separately, because of the recognized principle that *ius in bello* is applicable in cases of armed conflict whether the conflict is lawful or unlawful under *ius ad bellum*.[2]

The present chapter deals with the *ius ad bellum* and the rules governing the use of force in international wars, civil wars and in the exercise of the right of self-determination. The *ius in bello*, for which increasingly the term 'international humanitarian law applicable in armed conflicts' is being used, and individual criminal responsibility for violations of the laws of war will be dealt with separately in Chapter 20. Finally, the role of the United Nations in the maintenance of international peace and security and in dealing with armed conflicts will be taken up in Chapter 22, after describing the Charter and the organs of the United Nations in Chapter 21.

Lawful and unlawful wars: developments before 1945

For many centuries Western European attitudes towards the legality of war were dominated by the teachings of the Roman Catholic Church.[3] One of the first theologians to write on the subject was St Augustine (AD 354–430), who said:

> Just wars are usually defined as those which avenge injuries, when the nation or city against which warlike action is to be directed has neglected either to punish wrongs committed by its own citizens or to restore what has been unjustly taken by it. Further, that kind of war is undoubtedly just which God Himself ordains.

These ideas continued to be accepted for over 1,000 years. War was regarded as a means of obtaining reparation for a prior illegal act committed by the other side (the reparation sought had to be proportional to the seriousness of the illegality).[4] In addition, wars against unbelievers and heretics were sometimes (but not always) regarded as being commanded by God.

In the late sixteenth century the distinction between just and unjust wars began to break down. Theologians were particularly concerned with the state of man's conscience, and admitted that each side would be blameless if it genuinely believed that it was in the right, even though one of the sides might have been objectively in the wrong (this was known as the doctrine of probabilism). Moreover, the category of just wars (*bellum justum*) began to be dangerously extended. Although seventeenth century writers like Hugo Grotius made some attempt to re-establish traditional doctrines,[5] the eighteenth and nineteenth centuries produced an almost complete abandonment of the distinction between legal and illegal wars. Wars were said to be justified if they were fought for the defence of certain vital interests, but each state remained the sole judge of its vital interests, which were never defined with any attempt at precision.[6] Indeed, the whole doctrine of vital interests probably constituted, not a legal criterion of the legality of war, but a source for political justifications and excuses, to be used for propaganda purposes. The most realistic view of the customary law in the 'classical' period of international law, as it came to stand towards the end of the nineteenth century,[7] is that it placed no limits on the right of states to resort to war.

Some modern writers have suggested that a legal system which made no distinction between the legal and illegal use of force was not worthy of the name of law. Certainly this would be true of a system of municipal law which made no such distinction. Human beings are particularly vulnerable to physical attack; even the strongest man has to sleep sometimes, and, while he is asleep, anyone can kill him in a split second, with a fair chance of escaping detection. Consequently a law against murder is indispensable for any society composed of human beings. In the international society of states the position is different. States derive protection from the fact that they are few in number and are composed of territory and population. Because states are few in number, an attack on one state threatens the interests of the other states, which are therefore likely to come to its help. Similarly, the fact that states are composed of territory and population means that they cannot be overpowered instantaneously; until tanks and aircraft were invented, the time required for a hostile army to penetrate far into another state was usually long enough for the victim to mobilize resistance and to obtain help from its allies.

Alliances were, indeed, of crucial importance in the nineteenth century, the classic period of the balance of power.[8] Despite Alexander Pope's cynical comment – 'Now, Europe balanced, neither side prevails; For nothing's left in either of the scales' – the balance-of-power system was fairly successful in making wars rare. The expense, destructiveness and long duration of wars, and the risks of defeat, meant that wars were not worth fighting unless a state stood to gain a large amount of territory by going to war; but a state which seized too much territory threatened the whole of Europe because it upset the balance of power, and states were usually deterred from attempting to seize large areas of territory by the knowledge that such an attempt would unite the rest of Europe against them.

When studying comparative law,[9] one often comes across a topic which is regulated by law in one country and extra-legal factors in another. For instance, in Germany relations between trade unions and employers are

1993; Y. Dinstein, *War, Aggression, and Self-Defence*, 2nd edn 1994; G. Best, *War and Law Since 1945*, 1994; A. Randelzhofer, Article 2(4), in *Simma CUNAC*, 106–28; T. Bruha, Use of Force, Prohibition of, in *Wolfrum UNLPP II*, 1387–99.

2 See A. Roberts/R. Guelff (eds), *Documents on the Laws of War*, 2nd edn 1989, Introduction, 1; C. Greenwood, The Relationship between *ius ad bellum* and *ius in bello*, *RIS* (1983), 221–34.

3 See Chapter 2 above, 19–20.

4 On reparation see Chapter 17 above, 270–1.

5 H. Grotius, *De Jure Belli ac Pacis*, 1625. On Grotius see Chapter 2 above, 15–16.

6 On 'vital interests' see Chapter 2 above, 22.

7 See Chapter 2 above, 19–20.

8 See Chapter 2 above, 11–12.

9 See Chapter 1 above, 6.

10 See Chapter 2 above, 15. On arbitration, see Chapter 18 above, 293–5.
11 See Chapter 2 above, 22.
12 See H.-U. Scupin, Peace, Historical Movements Towards, *EPIL* 4 (1982), 78–86; L.B. Sohn, Peace, Proposals for the Preservation of, *ibid.*, 91–5.
13 See Chapter 2 above, 23–4.
14 Article 13(4), or with a unanimous report by the Council of the League of Nations, see Article 15(6).
15 Text of the Treaty in 94 LNTS 57 (1929). See Chapter 2 above, 24.

regulated by law, but in the United Kingdom, where the whole history of industrial relations is radically different, they are regulated in a more informal, extra-legal way, which (despite popular belief) is only slightly less successful, as a means of preserving industrial peace, than the German method of doing things. Similarly, in the nineteenth century, the prevention of violence, which in municipal societies was largely secured by rules of law, was achieved at the international level by extra-legal factors such as the balance of power.

Where necessary, the balance-of-power system could be supplemented by law (in the form of treaties), to deal with special cases. For instance, treaties of 1815 and 1839 guaranteed Switzerland and Belgium against attack. Later, the Latin American states persuaded several other states to sign the second Hague Convention of 1907, which prohibited the use of force to recover contract debts, unless the debtor state refused to go to arbitration or refused to carry out the arbitral award.[10] The third Hague Convention of 1907 required war to be preceded by a formal declaration of war or by an ultimatum containing a conditional declaration of war.[11]

The unprecedented suffering of the First World War caused a revolutionary change in attitudes towards war. Nowadays people (at least in Europe) are accustomed to regard war as an appalling evil. It is hard to realize that during the eighteenth and nineteenth centuries most people (except for a few pacifists)[12] regarded war in much the same way as they regarded a hard winter – uncomfortable, certainly, but part of the settled order of things, and providing excellent opportunities for exhilarating sport; even the wounded soldier did not regard war as wrong, any more than the skier with a broken leg regards skiing as wrong. All this changed after 1914, but the law took some time to catch up with public opinion. The Covenant of the League of Nations, signed in 1919, did not prohibit war altogether; instead, Article 12(1) provided:

> The Members of the League agree that, if there should arise between them any dispute likely to lead to a rupture, they will submit the matter either to arbitration or judicial settlement or to inquiry by the Council, and they agree in no case to resort to war until three months after the award by the arbitrators or the judicial decision, or the report by the Council.[13]

(The three-month period of delay was intended to allow time for passions to die down; if states had observed a three-month delay after the assassination of the Archduke Franz Ferdinand in 1914, it is possible that the First World War could have been averted.) In addition, members of the League agreed not to go to war with members complying with an arbitral award or judicial decision.[14]

During the 1920s various efforts were made to fill the 'gaps in the Covenant' – that is, to transform the Covenant's partial prohibition of war into a total prohibition of war. These efforts culminated in the General Treaty for the Renunciation of War (otherwise known as the Kellogg–Briand Pact, or the Pact of Paris), signed in 1928.[15] Almost all the states in the world became parties to this treaty, which provided:

The High Contracting Parties solemnly declare . . . that they condemn recourse to war for the solution of international controversies, and renounce it as an instrument of national policy in their relations with one another.

The High Contracting Parties agree that the settlement or solution of all disputes or conflicts of whatever nature or of whatever origin they may be, which may arise among them, shall never be sought except by pacific means.

But there is some dispute on whether the Kellogg-Briand Pact of 1928 already marks a general acceptance of the prohibition of the use of force in the absolute sense in which it was laid down in Article 2(4) of the UN Charter.

The prohibition of the use of force in the United Nations Charter

As has been explained in Chapter 2 above, a central feature of the modern international legal system in comparison with 'classical' international law is the normative attempt to control the use of force. Article 2(4) of the United Nations Charter provides:

All Members shall refrain in their international relations from the threat or use of force against the territorial integrity or political independence of any state, or in any other manner inconsistent with the Purposes of the United Nations.[16]

This rule is of universal validity; even the few states which are not members of the United Nations[17] are bound by it because it is also a rule of customary international law.[18]

Article 2(4) is well drafted, in so far as it talks of 'the threat or use of force', and not of 'war'. 'War' has a technical (but imprecise) sense in international law, and states often engage in hostilities while denying that they are technically in a state of war;[19] such hostilities can range from minor border incidents to extensive military operations, such as the Anglo-French attempt to occupy the area surrounding the Suez Canal in 1956.[20] The distinction between war and hostilities falling short of war may appear to be a very fine distinction, but it can have important consequences; for instance, war automatically terminates diplomatic relations and certain categories of treaties between the belligerent states,[21] but hostilities falling short of war do not; similarly, a technical state of war can have special effects in municipal law (for example, as regards trading with the enemy[22] and internment of enemy subjects).[23] Article 2(4) applies to all force, regardless of whether or not it constitutes a technical state of war.

On the other hand, Article 2(4) is badly drafted, in so far as it prohibits the threat[24] or use of force only 'against the territorial integrity or political independence of any state or in any other manner inconsistent with the Purposes of the United Nations'. This terminology opens up the possibility of arguing that force used for a wide variety of purposes (for example, to protect human rights,[25] or to enforce any type of legal right belonging to a state) is legal because it is not aimed 'against the territorial integrity or political independence of any state'. But the reference to territorial integrity or political independence should not distract our attention from the words 'or in any other manner inconsistent with the Purposes of the

16 For the text of the UN Charter see *Brownlie BDIL*, 1.

17 See Chapter 21 below, 369–73.

18 *Nicaragua v. USA*, *ICJ Rep.* 1986, 14, 98–101. See text below, 319–22.

19 See Meng (1982), *op. cit.*; K. Skubiszewski, Peace and War, *EPIL* 4 (1982), 74–8. See also W.M. Reisman/ J.E. Baker, *Regulating Covert Action: Practices, Contexts and Policies of Covert Coercion Abroad in International and American Law*, 1992.

20 See Chapter 2 above, 27–8.

21 J. Delbrück, War, Effect on Treaties, *EPIL* 4 (1982), 310–15. As to the effect of war on contracts see C. Steimel, *ibid.*, 303–10. See also Chapter 9 above, 145–6.

22 C.D. Wallace, Trading with the Enemy, *EPIL* 4 (1982), 245–9.

23 K.J. Madders, Internment, *EPIL* II (1995), 1403–14. See also J.M. Mössner, Enemies and Enemy Subjects, *ibid.*, 82–7; I. Seidl-Hohenveldern, Enemy Property, *ibid.*, 87–90.

24 See R. Sadurska, Threats of Force, *AJIL* 82 (1988), 239–68; Randelzhofer, Article 2(4), *op. cit.*, 118.

25 On the alleged unilateral right of humanitarian intervention by third states, see Chapter 14 above, 220–1. Collective humanitarian intervention authorized by the United Nations is discussed in Chapter 22 below, 393–407.

26 See also Randelzhofer, Article 2(4), *op. cit.*, 117–8. For the text of Article 1 of the UN Charter, see Chapter 21 below, 368.
27 *ICJ Rep.* 1949, 4, 35. See R. Bernhardt, Corfu Channel Case, *EPIL* I (1992), 831–4; Malanczuk (1987), *op. cit.*, 216 *et seq.* See also Chapter 18 above, 283.
28 See Chapter 12 above, 176–7.
29 See G. Hoog, Mines, *EPIL* 3 (1982), 283–5.
30 UNGA Res. 2625 (XXV) of 24 October 1970, text in *Brownlie BDIL*, 36. See Chapter 2 above, 32.

United Nations'. Although Article 1 of the Charter, which deals with the purposes of the United Nations, makes a passing reference to justice and international law, which could be used to support the argument that force used in the interests of justice and international law is not illegal, the overriding purpose mentioned in Article 1 is 'to maintain international peace and security' – which must surely indicate that any breach of international peace is automatically contrary to the purposes of the United Nations.[26]

This extensive interpretation of Article 2(4) is reinforced by an examination of other provisions of the Charter. The preamble says that 'the Peoples of the United Nations [are] determined to save succeeding generations from the scourge of war, which twice in our lifetime has brought untold sorrow to mankind'; and Article 2(3) obliges members to 'settle their international disputes by *peaceful* means in such a manner that *international peace and security*, and justice, are not endangered'.

The view that Article 2(4) should be broadly interpreted is also supported by the *Corfu Channel* case.[27] In that case, British warships had been struck by mines while exercising a right of innocent passage[28] in Albanian territorial waters, and the United Kingdom sent additional warships to sweep the minefield ('Operation Retail'). Minesweeping is not included in the right of innocent passage, but the United Kingdom argued that it had a right to intervene in order to make sure that the mines[29] were produced as evidence before an international tribunal. The International Court of Justice rejected this argument:

> The Court can only regard the alleged right of intervention as the manifestation of a policy of force, such as has, in the past, given rise to most serious abuses and such as cannot, whatever be the present defects in international organization, find a place in international law.

The Court went on to say:

> The United Kingdom Agent . . . has further classified 'Operation Retail' among methods of self-protection or self-help. The Court cannot accept this defence either. Between independent States, respect for territorial sovereignty is an essential foundation of international relations.

No doubt it may be galling for a strong state to be prohibited from using force against a weak state which infringes its legal rights; but the Charter is based on the belief that international law should not be enforced at the expense of international peace.

A confirmation of the broad normative scope of the prohibition of armed force in international relations may be found in the Friendly Relations Declaration, adopted by consensus by the UN General Assembly in 1970, which states:

> No State or group of States has the right to intervene, directly or indirectly, for any reason whatever, in the internal or external affairs of any other State. Consequently, armed intervention and all other forms of interference or attempted threats against the personality of the State or against its political, economic and cultural elements, are in violation of international law.[30]

But in legal literature the prohibition of the use of force and its limits in international law have remained the subject of a long-standing controversy,[31] inspired by the wide gap between official rhetoric and inconsistent actual practice of states in view of the numerous armed conflicts since 1945[32] and the ineffectiveness of the UN collective security system during the Cold War period,[33] which has given rise to the question whether the norm laid down in Article 2(4) can still be regarded as valid.[34] The prevailing view is that the Charter has enacted a comprehensive rule on the prohibition of the use of force, which has become recognized as *ius cogens*[35] and still admits only narrow exceptions to this prohibition. The recent decision by the International Court of Justice in the *Nicaragua* case has followed this direction and clarified some important aspects of relevant customary international law, which will be discussed in more detail below.[36]

It is submitted, therefore, that Article 2(4) should be interpreted as totally prohibiting the threat or use of force. However, there are other provisions of the Charter which contain exceptions to the principle, such as concerning military action taken or authorized by the United Nations or competent regional organizations, which will be dealt with in Chapter 22 below.[37]

Self-defence

Self-defence is another exception, although its extent is controversial. Article 51 of the Charter, which is the legal basis for alliances such as NATO and the Warsaw Pact[38] (dissolved after the break-up of the USSR), provides:

> Nothing in the present Charter shall impair the inherent right of individual or collective self-defence if an armed attack occurs against a Member of the United Nations, until the Security Council has taken the measures necessary to maintain international peace and security. Measures taken by Members in the exercise of this right of self-defence shall be immediately reported to the Security Council and shall not in any way affect the authority and responsibility of the Security Council under the present Charter to take at any time such action as it deems necessary in order to maintain or restore international peace and security.

There is disagreement about the circumstances in which the right of self-defence may be exercised.[39]

Preventive self-defence

The words 'if an armed attack occurs', interpreted literally, imply that the armed attack must have already occurred before force can be used in self-defence; there is no right of anticipatory self-defence against an imminent danger of attack. (It is true that the French text uses the words 'dans le cas ou un membre . . . est l'objet d'une agression armée', and a state can be the object of an attack before the attack occurs. But the Spanish text ('en caso de ataque armada') is closer to the English text.)

However, supporters of a right of anticipatory self-defence[40] claim that Article 51 does not limit the circumstances in which self-defence may be

31 See the literature cited above, 306–7. See also G. Arangio-Ruiz, Third Report on State Responsibility, International Law Commission, Forty-Third Session, UN Doc. A/CN.4/440/Add.1, 19 July 1991, 8.

32 For a list of the 160 wars fought in internal and international conflicts from 1945 to 1985, see U. Borchardt *et al.*, Die Kriege der Nachkriegszeit, *VN* (1986), 68; for the period 1985–92, see K.J. Gantzel/T. Schwinghammer/J. Siegelberg, *Kriege der Welt: Ein systematisches Register der kriegerischen Konflikte 1985 bis 1992*, 1992.

33 See Chapter 2 above, 26–8 and Chapter 22 below, 390–1.

34 See T.M. Franck, Who Killed Article 2(4)? Or: The Changing Norms Governing the Use of Force by States, *AJIL* 64 (1970), 809–37; L. Henkin, The Reports of the Death of Article 2(4) are Greatly Exaggerated, *AJIL* 65 (1971), 544–8; Malanczuk (1987), *op. cit.*, at 217 *et seq.*; Schachter (1991), *op. cit.*, at 129 *et seq.* As observed by E. Stein, The United Nations and the Enforcement of Peace, *Mich. JIL* 10 (1989), 304, at 314, it would be premature 'to suggest that the fundamental Charter principle prohibiting the use of force has become obsolete by inconsistent practice; but the precarious state of a system without a collective enforcement mechanism is self-evident.'

35 See, however, the critical remarks by G.A. Christenson, The World Court and Jus Cogens, *AJIL* 81 (1987) 93. On the concept of *ius cogens*, see Chapter 3 above, 57–8.

36 See text below, 319–22.

37 See Chapter 22 below, 387–90.

38 See Chapter 6 above, 95.

39 See B.-O. Bryde, Self-Defence, *EPIL* 4 (1982), 212–15; Malanczuk (1987), *op. cit.*; J. Mrazek, Prohibition of the Threat and Use of Force: Self-Defence and Self-Help in International Law, *CYIL* 27 (1989), 81–111, Dinstein, *op. cit.*; D.K. Linnan, Self-Defence, Necessity and UN Collective Security: United States and Other Views, *Duke JCIL* 1 (1991), 51–122; D.W. Greig, Self-Defence and the Security Council: What Does Article 51 Require?, *ICLQ* 40 (1991), 366–402; Randelzhofer, Article 51, in *Simma CUNAC*, 661–78; K.C. Kenny, Self-Defence, in *Wolfrum UNLPP II*, 1162–70; S.A. Alexandrov, *Self-Defense Against the Use of Force in International Law*, 1996 and the literature cited above.

40 For a discussion of these views, see Malanczuk (1987), *op. cit.*, 246–51.
41 For example, Bowett, *op. cit.*, Chapters 5, 6.
42 See text above, 307.
43 See Brownlie (1963), *op. cit.*, 250–7, 281–301; R. Higgins, *The Development of International Law through the Political Organs of the United Nations*, 1963, 216–21.
44 See Chapter 22 below, 388.
45 See G. Ress, Article 53, in *Simma CUNAC*, 722–52; Ress, Article 107, *ibid.*, 1152–62.
46 See Chapter 2 above, 27 and text below, 312–13.

exercised; they deny that the word 'if', as used in Article 51, means 'if and only if'. This argument sometimes takes the extreme form of saying that a state may use force in defence of a large range of interests, even when there is neither an actual armed attack nor an imminent danger of one.[41] This view, which is reminiscent of nineteenth-century ideas of vital interests,[42] is generally discredited.[43]

The difficulty about the approach of the authors supporting a right of preventive self-defence is that it is hard to imagine why the drafters of the Charter bothered to stipulate conditions for the exercise of the right of self-defence unless they intended those conditions to be exhaustive. Supporters of a right of anticipatory self-defence try to meet this objection in two ways. First, they argue that the conditions stated in Article 51 cannot be treated as exhaustive, otherwise the words 'if an armed attack occurs against a member' would have the absurd result of preventing members from protecting non-members against attack. In practice, members do claim a right to protect non-members against attack; one of the main purposes of NATO was to protect West Germany, although West Germany did not become a member of the United Nations until 1973. In 1945 it was expected that virtually all states in the world would soon become members of the United Nations, and therefore the failure of the Charter to mention attacks on non-members was probably due to an oversight. Second, the aforementioned authors point out that Article 51 describes self-defence as an 'inherent right', and they suggest that it would be inconsistent for a provision simultaneously to restrict a right and to recognize that right as inherent. This argument is less easy to refute and requires further consideration.

In evaluating whether anticipatory self-defence is incompatible with the Charter one should first note that Article 51 is an exception to Article 2(4), and it is a general rule of interpretation that exceptions to a principle should be interpreted restrictively, so as not to undermine the principle. Article 53 of the Charter provides that parties to regional arrangements[44] may take enforcement action against a 'renewal of aggressive policy' (a term which is much wider than 'aggression') on the part of former enemy states,[45] and one may argue that this provision would be unnecessary if Article 51 permitted anticipatory self-defence. (The 'enemy state clause' has become obsolete since all former enemy states have become members of the UN and it is likely to be removed in a future reform of the UN Charter.) It is also significant that the North Atlantic Treaty and similar treaties based on Article 51 provide only for defence against armed attacks, and not for defence against imminent dangers of armed attacks.

Furthermore, unlike many academic writers, the United States did not invoke a right of anticipatory self-defence in order to justify the 'quarantine' imposed on Cuba during the Cuban missiles crisis.[46] The United States realized that such an attitude would have created a precedent which the Soviet Union could have used against US missile sites in Europe; indeed, on the same reasoning, virtually every state in the world could have claimed to be threatened by a build-up of arms in a neighbouring state and could have resorted to preventive war. It is true that the facts of the Cuban missiles crisis are not a good example of the typical situation contemplated by supporters of the doctrine of anticipatory self-defence, because a communist attack was probably not imminent; but the question of whether an attack is imminent is inevitably a question of opinion and degree, and any rule founded on such a criterion is bound to be subjective and capable of abuse. To confine self-defence to cases where an armed attack has actually occurred, on the other hand, would have the merit of precision; the occurrence of an armed attack is a question of fact which is usually capable of objective verification.

From the practical point of view, the exclusion of a right of anticipatory self-defence deprives the 'innocent' state of the military advantage of striking the first blow (although the advantage of striking the first blow in hostilities between states is almost never as decisive as it can be in a fight between individuals). But the trouble about anticipatory self-defence is that a state can seldom be absolutely certain about the other side's intentions; in moments of crisis, there is seldom time to check information suggesting that an attack is imminent. Is a nuclear power entitled to destroy most of mankind simply because a radar system mistakes a flight of geese for enemy missiles? (Radar systems have actually made such mistakes in the past.) Fortunately, during the tensions of the Cold War, neither the United States nor the Soviet Union had to rely on anticipatory self-defence, since each had acquired a second-strike capacity (that is, a capacity to make a crippling nuclear counter-attack on the other side, even after suffering the effects of a previous all-out nuclear attack launched by the other side).[47]

Fear of creating a dangerous precedent is probably the reason why states seldom invoke anticipatory self-defence in practice. However, one clear example of a state invoking it occurred in 1981, when Israel bombed a nuclear reactor in Iraq.[48] Israel claimed that the reactor was going to be used to make atom bombs for use against Israel, and that Israel was therefore entitled to destroy the reactor as an act of anticipatory self-defence. The Security Council unanimously condemned Israel's action. The United States and the UK said that anticipatory self-defence was not justified on the facts, *inter alia*, because there was no evidence that the reactor had been going to be used for making atom bombs; they did not deal with the question whether Israel would have been entitled to use force in anticipatory self-defence if the reactor had constituted a real threat to Israel. A large number of states, from all parts of the world, said that anticipatory self-defence was always contrary to international law.[49] In the past, the United Kingdom has argued in favour of anticipatory self-defence,[50] but the Soviet Union has argued that it is illegal.[51] In 1986 the United States invoked anticipatory self-defence against acts of state-sponsored terrorism to justify the bombing of Libya.[52] When Egypt reinstituted its blockade of the Gulf of Aqaba in 1967,[53] Israel's attack and occupation of the Sinai was seen by many as a legitimate response.

State practice on the matter is thus rather inconclusive. But a unilateral use of force merely in view of some deployments of weapons or modernization of weapons systems in another country is certainly too dangerous to

47 On the legality of nuclear weapons, see Chapter 20 below, 346–50.

48 For a more detailed analysis of the case, see Malanczuk (1987), *op. cit.*, 245–51.

49 SC Res. 487, 19 June 1981, *UN Chronicle*, 1981, no. 8, 5–9, 61–74, at 68; *ILM* 20 (1981), 965–97.

50 *BPIL* 1963, 206.

51 B.A. Ramundo, *Peaceful Coexistence*, 1967, 129–33.

52 See text below, 316.

53 S. Less, Aqaba, Gulf of, *EPIL* I (1992), 197–202.

54 R.N. Gardner, Commentary on the Law of Self-Defense, in Damrosch/Scheffer (eds), *op. cit.*, 49–53, 51, citing M. McDougal.
55 See Malanczuk (1987), *op. cit.*, 246–51, 277–8; M. Akehurst has taken a different view; see the 6th edn of this book, at 262, arguing that anticipatory self-defence is incompatible with the Charter.
56 See W. Meng, The Caroline, *EPIL* I (1992), 537–8; O'Connell, *International Law*, Vol. 1, 2nd edn 1970, 316; Bowett, *op. cit.*, 58–9.
57 For a good discussion of the confusion between 'self-defence' and the concept of 'necessity' in this case, see Greig, *International Law*, 1970, 674–5.
58 Webster, *British and Foreign State Papers 1841–1842*, Vol. 30, 1858, 193.
59 O'Connell, *op. cit.*, 316. For a critical comment see Greig (1970), *op. cit.*, 666–7. On the Nuremberg and Tokyo trials, see Chapter 20 below, 354–5.
60 Greig, *ibid.*, 682.
61 *Ibid.*; see also A. Verdross/B. Simma, *Universelles Völkerrecht. Theorie und Praxis*, 3rd edn 1984, 288 *et seq.*
62 See Chapter 10 above, 145–58.
63 See Chapter 22 below, 384–7.

be regarded as generally admissible. However, can one realistically expect a state to 'be a sitting duck' and wait until 'the bombs are actually dropping on its soil'?[54] The present author[55] submits that, in the face of a manifestly imminent armed attack by another state, there is still a right to preventive self-defence under the Charter as a strictly limited exception, after all diplomatic means available under the circumstances have been exhausted, under the conditions of the famous *Caroline* case,[56] which is generally regarded as the classic illustration of the right to self-defence.[57]

During the rebellion in Canada in 1837, preparations for subversive action against the British authorities were made in United States territory. Although the Government of the United States took measures against the organization of armed forces upon its soil, there was no time to halt the activities of the steamer *Caroline*, which reinforced and supplied the rebels in Canada from ports in the United States. A British force from Canada crossed the border to the United States, seized the *Caroline* in the State of New York, set her on fire and cast the vessel adrift so that it fell to its destruction over Niagara Falls. Two citizens of the United States were killed during the attack on the steamer. American authorities arrested one of the British subjects involved in the action and charged him with murder and arson.

In the correspondence following Great Britain's protest, the conditions under which self-defence could be invoked to invade foreign territory were formulated by Daniel Webster in a manner that became to be treated as classic. There must be a 'necessity of self-defence, instant, overwhelming, leaving no choice of means, and no moment for deliberation' and the action taken must not be 'unreasonable or excessive', and it must be 'limited by that necessity and kept clearly within it'.[58] In many subsequent occasions the *Caroline* case was invoked and also employed by the Nuremberg Tribunal in handling the plea of self-defence raised to the charge of waging aggressive war.[59]

It seems hardly likely that the drafters of Article 51 of the UN Charter should have forgotten the lessons of recent history and to insist, as Greig puts it, 'that a state should wait for the aggressor's blow to fall before taking positive measures for its own protection'.[60] The Tokyo Tribunal, for example, decided that the Dutch declaration of war upon Japan in December 1941 was justified on the grounds of self-defence, although at that time Japan had not attacked Dutch territories in the Far East. It sufficed that Japan had made its war aims, including the seizure of those territories, known and which had been decided upon at the Imperial Conference of 5 November 1941.[61]

Self-defence and claims to territory

Self-defence cannot be invoked to settle disputes as to territory. It is unlawful to attack territory which is in the possession of another state, even though the state using force may consider that it has a better title to the territory[62] in question than the state in possession. Article 2(3) of the United Nations Charter requires member states to settle their disputes by peaceful means,[63] and this obligation applies as much to territorial disputes as to any other class of dispute. The General Assembly's

Friendly Relations Declaration of 1970 says that '[e]very State has the duty to refrain from the threat or use of force . . . as a means of solving international disputes, including territorial disputes'.[64]

When Argentina invaded the Falkland Islands in 1982,[65] the Security Council passed a resolution demanding an immediate withdrawal of all Argentinian forces from the islands;[66] this was an implied condemnation of Argentina's use of force. Jordan and Uganda voted for this resolution and said that Argentina's use of force was illegal, even though they thought that Argentina had a better title to the Falkland Islands than the United Kingdom.[67] A state in possession of territory is entitled to use force in self-defence against invasion by a rival claimant, even though the rival claimant may consider that it has a better title to the territory than the state in possession.[68] Both states that were attacked by Iraq on the basis of territorial claims in the two Gulf Wars (Iran in 1980 and Kuwait in 1990) were therefore entitled to self-defence, whatever the merits of Iraq's claims may have been.[69]

Self-defence against attacks on ships and aircraft

The attack which gives rise to the right of self-defence need not necessarily be directed against a state's territory.[70] Article 6 of the North Atlantic Treaty 1949 provides for collective self-defence against 'an armed attack on the territory of any of the parties in Europe or North America, . . . on the occupation forces of any party in Europe, on the islands under the jurisdiction of any party in the North Atlantic area . . . or on the vessels or aircraft in this area of any of the parties'. In the *Corfu Channel* case the International Court of Justice held that British warships, attacked while exercising a right of innocent passage in foreign territorial waters, were entitled to return fire.[71]

Armed protection of nationals abroad

Most states and most writers agree that attacks on a state's nationals resident abroad do not entitle the state to use force in order to defend its nationals without the consent of the foreign government (so-called 'military rescue operations', such as the Stanleyville operations in the Congo in 1964 by Belgium and the United States, the Israeli rescue mission at Entebbe in 1976, the abortive attempt of the United States to rescue the Tehran hostages in 1980).[72] The contrary view insists that an attack on nationals of a state abroad or the failure to provide the kind of protection to them, as required by international law, should be assimilated to the law of self-defence.[73]

In the case of Grenada one of the reasons presented by the United States to justify the invasion of the island was the alleged danger to American nationals.[74] Mr Robinson, then Legal Adviser of the Department of State, stated:

> Protection of nationals is a well-established, narrowly drawn ground for the use of force which has not been considered to conflict with the U.N. Charter. While the U.S. has not asserted that protection of nationals standing alone would constitute a sufficient basis for all the actions taken by the collective force, it is important to note that it did clearly justify the landing of U.S. military forces.[75]

64 Friendly Relations Declaration 1970, *op. cit.*
65 See also Chapter 10 above, 148.
66 SC Res. 502 (1982), 3 April 1982, text in *ILM* 21 (1982), 679. See *UN Chronicle*, 1982, no. 5, 5–10.
67 *Ibid.*, at 5–10.
68 Bowett, *op. cit.*, 34–6; Brownlie (1963), *op. cit.*, 382–3.
69 See Chapter 22 below, 396–9.
70 See Randelzhofer, Article 51, *op. cit.*, 670–1.
71 *ICJ Rep.* 1949, 4, 30–1. On the case, see text above, 310.
72 H. Bull (ed.), *Intervention in World Politics*, 1984, 99–118; N. Ronzitti, *Rescuing Nationals Abroad Through Military Coercion and Intervention on Grounds of Humanity*, 1985; Malanczuk (1987), *op. cit.*, 218–19; C. Warbrick, Protection of Nationals Abroad, *ICLQ* 37 (1988), 1002; R.J. Zedalis, Protection of Nationals Abroad: Is Consent the Basis of Legal Obligation?, *Texas ILJ* 25 (1990), 209–70; R.B. Lillich, Forcible Protection of Nationals Abroad: The Liberian 'Incident' of 1990, *GYIL* 35 (1992), 205; Randelzhofer, Article 2(4), *op. cit.*, 124–6; Randelzhofer, Article 51, *op. cit.*, 672. On the *Tehran Hostages* case, see Chapters 8, 123, 126–7 and 17, 259–60 above.
73 See, e.g., Gardner, *op. cit.*, at 52.
74 See also the statement by Ambassador Motley, Assistant Secretary for Inter-American Affairs, *Dept. State Bull.* 84 (1984), 70 *et seq.* For a legal evaluation of the Grenada action, cf. Dieguez, The Grenada Intervention: 'Illegal' in Form, Sound as Policy, *NYUJILP* 16 (1984), 1167–204; W.C. Gilmore, *The Grenada Intervention: Analysis and Documentation*, 1984, 65–7, 74; L.S. Doswald-Beck, The Legality of the U.S. Intervention in Grenada, *NILR* 31 (1984), 355–77; Joyner, Reflections of the Lawfulness of Invasion, *AJIL* 78 (1984), 131; Moore, Grenada and the International Double Standard, *ibid.*, 145; Vagts, International Law under Time Pressure: Grading the Grenada Take-Home Examination, *ibid.*, 169; L.K. Wheeler, The Grenada Invasion: Expanding the Scope of Humanitarian Intervention, *BCICLR* 8 (1985), 413; M.J. Levitan, The Law of Force and the Force of Law: Grenada, the Falklands, and Humanitarian Intervention, *Harvard ILJ* 27 (1986), 621; S. Davidson, *Grenada. A Study in Politics and the Limits of International Law*, 1987; R.J. Beck, *The Grenada Invasion. Politics, Law, and Foreign Policy Decisionmaking*, 1993.

75 *AJIL* 78 (1984), 664.

76 Bryde, *op. cit.*, 217; Beyerlin, Die israelische Befreiungsaktion von Entebbe in völkerrechtlicher Sicht, *ZaöRV* 37 (1977), 241.

77 See Beyerlin, *ibid.*, 240, Randelzhofer (1982), *op. cit.*, 273.

78 See Malanczuk (1987), *op. cit.*, 212 *et seq.*, 251–2. See Chapter 17 above, 271.

79 Principle 1, Res. 2625 (XXV), text in *Brownlie BDIL*, 39.

80 *Dept. State Bull.* (1986), 1–2 and 8.

81 See text above, 311–14.

82 *KCA* 1986, 34459.

83 See R.A. Friedländer, Terrorism, *EPIL* 9 (1986), 371–6; G. Gilbert, The 'Law' and 'Transnational Terrorism', *NYIL* 26 (1995), 3–32. See also Chapter 7 above, 112.

84 See the contributions by V.P. Nanda/ T.J. Farer/A. D'Amato, Agora: U.S. Forces in Panama: Defenders, Aggressors or Human Rights Activities?, *AJIL* 84 (1990), 494–524. On the *Noriega* case, see Chapter 7 above, 110.

85 W.M. Reisman, The Raid on Baghdad: Some Reflections on Its Lawfulness and Implications, *EJIL* 5 (1994), 120–33; L. Condorelli, Apropos de l'attaque américaine contre l'Iraq du 26 juin 1993: Lettre d'un professeur désemparé aux lecteurs du JEDI, *ibid.*, 134–44; D. Kritsiostis, The Legality of the 1993 US Missile Strike on Iraq and the Right to Self-Defence in International Law, *ICLQ* 45 (1996), 162–76. On the Gulf War (1990–1), see Chapter 22 below, 396–402.

86 *ILM* 35 (1996), 809, at 823, para. 46.

87 *Ibid.* See Chapter 20 below, 347–9.

88 *Nicaragua v. USA, ICJ Rep.* 1986, 14, at 94 and 122–3. See Malanczuk (1987), *op. cit.*, 253–5, 278, 280–2; *Ibid.*, 94; J.G. Gardam, Proportionality and the Use of Force in International Law, *AJIL* 87 (1993), 391–413; Randelzhofer, Article 51, *op. cit.*, 677.

On policy grounds such a development in international law recognizing the legality of the use of armed force in the aforementioned type of cases cannot be welcomed as it would privilege the powerful states enjoying the capability of undertaking such operations and as claims to protect nationals abroad could serve, as often in history, as a pretext for intervention.[76] Nevertheless, from a moral and political point of view, there are instances where the use of armed self-help is difficult to condemn. Rescue operations to protect a state's own nationals have found approval or understanding by other States under certain circumstances and have met a relative lack of condemnation by organs of the United Nations although they have not been approved as being lawful.[77]

Armed reprisals

Self-defence does not include a right of armed reprisal;[78] if terrorists enter one state from another, the first state may use force to arrest or expel the terrorists, but, having done so, it is not entitled to retaliate by attacking the other state. The Security Council has sometimes condemned Israel for carrying out armed reprisals against its neighbours and in 1970 the General Assembly declared that 'States have a duty to refrain from acts of reprisal involving the use of force'.[79] In April 1986 the United States bombed Libya, in response to a Libyan terrorist attack against United States soldiers in West Berlin, but the United States did not try to justify the bombing as a reprisal. Instead, President Reagan said that the bombing was justified under Article 51 of the United Nations Charter as a '*preemptive* action against [Libya's] terrorist installations' (emphasis added).[80] In other words, the bombing was an act of anticipatory self-defence[81] designed to prevent future acts of terrorism by Libya. The Foreign Ministers of the non-aligned countries condemned the bombing by the United States as an 'unprovoked act of aggression'.[82] The use of the word 'unprovoked' suggests that they did not believe that Libya was guilty of terrorism; on this interpretation, their statement cannot be regarded as dealing with the question whether the bombing by the United States would have been legally justified if Libya had been guilty of terrorism.[83] Other armed interventions such as the American invasion of Panama in 1989[84] or reprisals, such as the bombing of Baghdad by the United States on 26 June 1993, are equally legally suspect.[85]

In its *Advisory Opinion on the Legality of the Threat or Use of Nuclear Weapons* (1996), the ICJ did not examine the question of armed reprisals in times of peace. But it noted that such reprisals 'are considered to be unlawful'.[86] The Court also refrained from discussing the different issue of belligerent reprisals (during times of armed conflict); however, it did observe: 'in any case any right of recourse to such reprisals would, like self-defence, be governed *inter alia* by the principle of proportionality.'[87]

Immediacy and proportionality

Most important, force used in self-defence must be necessary, immediate and proportional to the seriousness of the armed attack.[88] This is a matter of common sense; otherwise a minor frontier incident could be made a pretext for starting an all-out war. The principle of immediacy requires that the act of self-defence must be taken immediately subsequent to the armed attack. The purpose of this requirement is to prevent abuse and military aggression under the pretext of self-defence long after hostilities have ceased. But the requirement of immediacy must take the individual circumstances into account. Therefore, in the Falkland Islands conflict in 1982, although almost a month passed before British forces were prepared to counterattack, in view of the geographical distance, Britain's response was immediate by ordering the Royal Navy to leave for the area of conflict.

The most important limitations on the right to self-defence are the traditional requirements of proportionality and necessity.[89] With regard to customary international law, in the *Nicaragua* case the ICJ stated that 'there is a specific rule whereby self-defence would warrant only measures which are proportional to the armed attack and necessary to respond to it, a rule well established in international law'.[90] The Court confirmed that this dual condition applies equally to Article 51 of the Charter, 'whatever the means of force employed', in its advisory opinion in the *Legality of Nuclear Weapons Case*.[91] The Court further held:

> The proportionality principle may thus not in itself exclude the use of nuclear weapons in self-defence in all circumstances. But at the same time, a use of force that is proportionate under the law of self-defence, must, in order to be lawful, also meet the requirements of the law applicable in armed conflict which comprise in particular the principles and rules of humanitarian law.[92]

The permissible use of force under Article 51 is restricted to the necessary minimum required to repulse an attack because retaliation and punitive measures are forbidden. It is not quite clear, however, whether proportionality must be measured with a view to the end (definitive repulsion of the attack or of the danger of its repetition, preservation or restoration of the *status quo ante*), with regard to the means employed in self-defence (necessary and proportional to the violation that gave rise to self-defence), or with respect to both. But, in essence, proportionality seems to refer to what is proportionate to repel the attack without requiring symmetry between the mode of the initial attack and the mode of response.[93] At any rate, Israel's seven-day bombing of South Lebanon in August 1993 in response to sporadic Hizbullah rocket attacks on northern Israel was clearly disproportionate. Further limits to self-defence are set by the laws of war.[94]

Collective self-defence

Finally, there is a controversy concerning the scope of collective self-defence.[95] Article 51 of the Charter speaks of 'individual or collective self-defence', and some have argued that a right of collective self-defence is merely a combination of individual rights of self-defence; states may exercise collectively a right which any of them might have exercised individually. The corollary, according to this view, is that no state may defend another state unless each state could have legally exercised a right of individual self-defence in the same circumstances; thus, Greece could not defend Peru against attack, because an attack on Peru does not affect the rights or interests of Greece.[96]

State practice lends no support to this view. Under the North Atlantic

89 See Chapters 1, 4, 3, 49 and 17, 271 above.
90 *Nicaragua* case, *op. cit.*, at 94, para. 176.
91 *ILM* 35 (1996), 809, at 822, para. 41.
92 *Ibid.*, para. 42.
93 See the Dissenting Opinion of Judge Higgins, *ibid.*, 934, para. 5, with reference to Ago. See also the Dissenting Opinion of Judge Schwebel, *ibid.*, 839.
94 See Chapter 20 below, 342–63.
95 See Malanczuk (1987), *ibid.*, 255–6, 279; J. Delbrück, Collective Self-Defence, EPIL I (1992), 656–9; Randelzhofer, Article 51, *op. cit.*, 675; Kenny, *op. cit.*, 1168–70.
96 Bowett, *op. cit.*, Chapter 10. For a discussion, see R. Mushkat, Who May Wage War? An Examination of an Old/New Question, *AUJILP* 2 (1987), 97–151, 146–50.

97 *ICJ Rep.* 1986, 14, 103–4, 105, 119–22. On the case, see text below, 319–22. For a different view requiring not an explicit request by the attacked state, but only its consent, see Randelzhofer, Article 51, *op. cit.*
98 See Chapter 22 below, 396–9.
99 R.A. Falk (ed.), *The International Law of Civil War*, 1971; D.E.T. Luard (ed.), *The International Regulation of Civil War*, 1972; T.J. Farer, The Regulation of Foreign Intervention in Civil Armed Conflict, *RdC* 142 (1974), 291; J.N. Moore (ed.), *Law and Civil War in the Modern World*, 1974; H.P. Gasser, International Non-International Armed Conflicts: Case Studies of Afghanistan, Kampuchea, and Lebanon, *AULR* 31 (1982), 911–26; A. Cassese, La Guerre civile et le droit international, *RGDIP* 90 (1986), 553–78; G. Klintworth, *Vietnam's Intervention in Cambodia in International Law*, 1989; M. Akehurst, Civil War, *EPIL* I (1992), 597–603; A. Tanca, *Foreign Armed Intervention in Internal Conflict*, 1993; H. McCoubbrey/N.D. White, *International Organizations and Civil Wars*, 1995.
100 C. Haverland, Secession, *EPIL* 10 (1987), 384–9.
101 See K.J. Partsch, Israel and the Arab States, *EPIL* II (1995), 1460–8; P. Malanczuk, Israel: Status, Territory and Occupied Territories, *ibid.*, 1468–508; A.L. Schild *et al.*, Conflicts, Middle East, in *Wolfrum UNLPP I*, 286–310.
102 See L. Doswald-Beck, The Legal Validity of Military Intervention by Invitation of the Government, *BYIL* 56 (1985), 189–252.
103 See text below.
104 On the role of insurgents as subjects of international law, see Chapter 6 above, 338–40.
105 See Chapter 5 above, 82–90.

Treaty and similar treaties, each party undertakes to defend every other party against attack, and this undertaking is not limited to circumstances where an attack on one party threatens the rights or interests of another party. According to the International Court of Justice in *Nicaragua v. USA*, one state may not defend another state unless that other state claims to be (and is) the victim of an armed attack and asks the first state to defend it.[97] Such requests for assistance were made by Kuwait and Saudi Arabia to the United States and its allies in August 1990 following the invasion and occupation of Kuwait by Iraq.[98]

Civil wars

A civil war can be defined as a war between two or more groups of inhabitants of the same states one of which may be the government.[99] A civil war may be fought for the control of the government of a state, or it may be caused by the desire of part of the population to secede[100] and form a new state. While these two types of civil war are the most common, other types also exist. For example, a rebelling group may simply try to force the government to make concessions (e.g. to grant regional autonomy). A civil war may even be fought between parties while the government remains neutral and ineffective (Lebanon 1975–6).

Most of the wars fought since 1945 have been civil wars; and even many of the international wars since 1945 have had their roots in civil wars (for instance, the conflict between the Arab states and Israel developed out of hostilities which had occurred between the Jewish and Arab communities in Palestine during the last years of the British mandate.[101]) In the modern world, states seldom try to enlarge their territory by sending their armies to overrun the territory of other states; instead, they increase their influence by encouraging factions sharing their own ideology to seize or retain power in other states. The existence of ideologies transcending national frontiers not only makes civil wars more frequent; it also increases the dangers of civil wars developing into international wars, because the rules of international law concerning participation in civil wars by foreign states are not as clear as the rules prohibiting international wars.[102] The rise of internal ethnic-nationalistic conflicts in many parts of the world after the end of the East-West conflict has made the topic even more prominent.[103]

The individuals who wish to set up a new government or a new state are often called insurgents,[104] and it is proposed to use that term in the present work; it has the merit of being less emotive than other words, such as 'rebels' or 'revolutionaries'. The party on the other side is often called the *de jure* government, or the *de jure* authorities, but in the present work it is proposed to use the more neutral expression 'established authorities'; the words '*de jure*' are misleading, because they introduce irrelevant overtones from the law of recognition,[105] and because they imply that international law is on the side of the established authorities – which is not wholly true.

The legality of civil wars

There is no rule in international law against civil wars. Article 2(4) of the United Nations Charter prohibits the use or threat of force in international relations only. It is possible that each side will regard the other side as traitors from the point of view of municipal law, but neither the insurgents nor the established authorities are guilty of any breach of international law. There may, however, be one exception to this principle. The use of force to frustrate the exercise of a legal right of self-determination is generally regarded as illegal nowadays, but it is uncertain whether such wars (wars of national liberation) should be classified as international wars or as civil wars. This will be discussed separately in more detail later.[106]

A more complicated issue is the lawfulness of intervention by other states in a civil war in another country. This chapter is concerned only with unilateral intervention by third states, not with intervention authorized by the United Nations, which is dealt with in Chapter 22 below.

Participation by other states: help for the insurgents

In international wars, the rules of neutrality assist in giving fairly clear guidance on which kind of assistance may be lawfully given to a belligerent state by a neutral state.[107] The rules governing foreign intervention in civil wars are less clear.[108] As a general rule, foreign states are forbidden to give help to the insurgents in a civil war. For instance, General Assembly resolution 2131 (XX) declares that

> no State shall organize, assist, foment, finance, incite or tolerate subversive, terrorist or armed activities directed towards the violent overthrow of the régime of another State, or interfere in civil strife in another State.[109]

The rule stated in this resolution has been repeated in later resolutions,[110] and was reaffirmed by the International Court of Justice in *Nicaragua v. USA*.[111] In the early 1980s, the United States adopted a counter-insurgency strategy against the establishment of the Sandinista regime in Nicaragua and the subsequent spread of revolutionary movements in neighbouring countries. The governments under pressure in Central America received massive American military aid. In addition, the United States established and financed an anti-government armed force in Nicaragua, known under the name of the 'contras'. Nicaragua took the United States to the International Court of Justice which, although the United States refused to accept the jurisdiction of the Court,[112] proceeded to a judgment on the merits against the United States which clarified a number of important legal issues.

The Court held that the United States had broken international law by aiding the contras, who were rebelling against the government of Nicaragua. It emphasized that participation in a civil war by 'organizing or encouraging the organization of irregular forces or armed bands . . . for incursion into the territory of another State' and by 'participating in acts of civil strife . . . in another State' was not only an act of illegal intervention in the domestic affairs of a foreign state, but also a violation of the principle of the prohibition of the use of force. While the Court clearly viewed the arming and training of the contras as having involved the threat or use of force, it was less explicit on the legal evaluation of other forms of assistance. Thus it considered that the mere supply of funds to the

106 See text below, 336–8.

107 See Chapter 20 below, 350–1.

108 T. Oppermann, Intervention, *EPIL* II (1995), 1436–9; Randelzhofer, Article 2(4), *op. cit.*, 116–7.

109 Res. 2131 (XX), 21 December 1965, *UNYb* 1965, 94; the resolution was passed by 109 votes to nil.

110 See, for instance, *Brownlie BDIL*, 42, and *ILM* 19 (1980), 534, para. 7.

111 *ICJ Rep.* 1986, 14, 101–2 and 106–8. For the Order on the discontinuance and removal of the case from the list of the Court see *ILM* 31 (1992), 103; *AJIL* 86 (1992), 173–4. On the dispute concerning this case, see D'Amato, Nicaragua and International Law: The 'Academic' and the Real, *AJIL* 79 (1985), 657; Kahn, From Nuremberg to The Hague: The United States Position in *Nicaragua v. United States* and the Development of International Law, *Yale JIL* 12 (1987), 1; M. Akehurst, Nicaragua *v.* United States of America, *Indian JIL* 27 (1987), 357; K. Highet, Evidence, the Court, and the Nicaragua Case, *AJIL* 81 (1987), 1; G.L. Scott/C.L. Carr, The ICJ and Compulsory Jurisdiction: The Case for Closing the Clause, *ibid.*, 57; and the Appraisals of the ICJ's Decision: *Nicaragua v. United States* (Merits) by various authors, *ibid.*, 77; T. Gill, *Litigation Strategy at the International Court, A Case Study of the Nicaragua v. United States Dispute*, 1989; S.M. Schwebel, Indirect Aggression in the International Court, in Damrosch/Scheffer, *op. cit.*, 298–303; C. Greenwood, The International Court of Justice and the Use of Force, in V. Lowe/M. Fitzmaurice (eds), *Fifty Years of the International Court of Justice*, 1996, 373–85; J. Crawford, Military Activities Against Nicaragua Case, *EPIL* III (forthcoming). See also Chapters 3, 40, 44 and 18, 284 above.

112 See Chapter 18 above, 284, 289.

113 *Nicaragua v. USA, op. cit.*, 119.
114 See Randelzhofer, Article 2(4), *op. cit.*, 115.
115 *Ibid.*, 83–6.
116 Such as H. Lauterpacht, Revolutionary Activities by Private Persons Against Foreign States, *AJIL* 22 (1928), 105, 126–7.
117 On state responsibility for acts of private individuals, see Chapter 17 above, 259–60.
118 *KCA* 1980, 30364, 30385.
119 See text below, 336–8.
120 *ICJ Rep.* 1986, 14, at 103–4, 105, 110–11, 118–23, 126–7.
121 See text above, 317–18.
122 The question of anticipatory self-defence (see text above, 311–14) was not pleaded by the parties and was therefore not discussed by the Court.

contras 'while undoubtedly an act of intervention in the internal affairs of Nicaragua . . . does not in itself amount to a use of force'.[113]

However, the Court failed to indicate any criteria explaining which kinds of acts of assistance and under which circumstances are to be considered a threat or use of force.[114] Thus, the specific scope of the prohibition of the indirect use of force under Article 2(4) of the Charter has still remained unclear with regard to assistance given by a foreign state to the 'private' use of force against another state.

The Court further held that Nicaragua was not liable for allowing weapons to be transported across Nicaraguan territory to insurgents in El Salvador, because Nicaragua had been unable to stop such transport.[115] The implication is that Nicaragua would have been under a duty to stop such transport if it had been able to do so. The Court's judgment does not make clear whether the weapons were being transported across Nicaraguan territory by private individuals or whether they were being transported by agents of another state; presumably the Court thought that this distinction made no difference to Nicaragua's legal position. The Court thus seems to have rejected the view expressed by some writers[116] that a state is not under any duty to prevent private individuals supplying weapons to foreign insurgents.[117]

An exception to the rule prohibiting assistance to insurgents probably exists when the established authorities are receiving foreign help. In these circumstances, states sympathetic to the insurgents often claim a right to help the insurgents, in order to counterbalance the help obtained by the established authorities from other states. For instance, after the Soviet intervention in Afghanistan at the end of 1979, Egypt started providing military training and weapons for the Muslim insurgents against the Soviet-backed government, and Saudi Arabia gave money to the insurgents.[118] This right of counter-intervention, as it is sometimes called, is often supported by the argument that counter-intervention is necessary to protect the independence of the country where the civil war is taking place, on the grounds that the established authorities have lost popular support and have become puppets controlled by their foreign supporters.

A more controversial exception to the prohibition against giving foreign help to the insurgents concerns wars of national liberation.[119]

Another possible exception to the prohibition against giving help to insurgents was discussed by the International Court of Justice in *Nicaragua v. USA*.[120] The United States admitted that it had been aiding the contras, but argued that such aid was justified as a form of collective self-defence[121] because Nicaragua had been supplying weapons to insurgents in El Salvador. The Court held that self-defence was justified only in response to an armed attack,[122] and said:

> an armed attack must be understood as including not merely action by regular armed forces across an international border, but also 'the sending by or on behalf of a State of armed bands, groups, irregulars or mercenaries, which carry out acts of armed force against another State of such gravity as to amount to' . . . an actual armed attack . . . 'or its substantial involvement therein'. This description, contained in Article 3, paragraph (g), of the Definition of Aggression annexed to

General Assembly resolution 3314 (XXIX), may be taken to reflect customary international law. The Court sees no reason to deny that, in customary law, the prohibition of armed attacks may apply to the sending by a State of armed bands to the territory of another State, if such an operation, because of its scale and effects, would have been classified as an armed attack rather than as a mere frontier incident had it been carried out by regular armed forces. But the Court does not believe that the concept of 'armed attack' includes . . . assistance to rebels in the form of the provision of weapons or logistical or other support.[123]

The Court's definition of armed attack was condemned as excessively narrow, in the dissenting opinions of Judge Schwebel (USA) and Judge Jennings (UK).[124] The Court did not clarify under which circumstances assistance given to rebel in the form of the supply of weapons or logistical support must be seen as so massive as to amount to an armed attack.[125] When is the point reached that an injured state may defend itself by the use of force against such indirect forms of intervention by a third state? In any case, the Court held that the government of Nicaragua was not responsible for the supply of weapons to the insurgents in El Salvador.[126] The United States also pleaded that Nicaragua had attacked Honduras and Costa Rica. The Court held that this did not justify United States support for the contras as a form of collective self-defence, because (among other reasons) Honduras and Costa Rica had not requested collective self-defence by the United States.[127]

The United States' plea of collective self-defence therefore failed on the facts of the case (because supplying weapons to insurgents in El Salvador did not constitute an armed attack), but would have succeeded if the facts had been different. If Nicaragua's help to insurgents in El Salvador had amounted to an armed attack (for instance, if Nicaragua had sent troops to help those insurgents), then El Salvador and the United States might have been entitled to help insurgents in Nicaragua, as a form of collective self-defence. To send troops to the territory of a state without the consent of the government of that state is invasion, which is listed in Article 3(a) of the General Assembly's Definition of Aggression as a form of aggression (and therefore as a form of armed attack).[128] Moreover, even though supplying weapons to insurgents does not constitute an armed attack, it is nevertheless illegal, and the injured state is therefore entitled to adopt proportionate countermeasures against the wrongdoing state; but such retaliation can be carried out only by the injured state, and not by third states, since the right of collective self-defence can be used only in response to an armed attack.[129]

The Court held:

While an armed attack would give rise to an entitlement to take collective self-defence, a use of force of a lesser degree of gravity cannot . . . produce any entitlement to collective counter-measures involving the use of force. The acts of which Nicaragua is accused . . . could only have justified proportionate counter-measures on the part of the State which had been the victim of these acts . . . They could not justify counter-measures taken by a third State . . . and particularly could not justify intervention involving the use of force.[130]

123 *ICJ Rep.* 1986, 14, 103–4.
124 *Ibid.*, 331–47, 348–50 and 543–4.
125 *Ibid.* See F.M. Higgenbotham, International Law, the Use of Force in Self-Defence, and the Southern African Conflict, *Colum. JTL* 25 (1987), 529–92, 548–50; T.D. Gill, The Law of Armed Attack in the Context of the Nicaragua Case, *Hague YIL* 1 (1988), 30–58; L.A. Sicilianos, L'Invocation de la légitime défense face aux activités d'entités non-étatiques, *Hague YIL* 2 (1989), 147–68, 153; Randelzhofer, Article 51, *op. cit.*, 674.
126 See text above, 320. On state responsibility see Chapter 17 above, 254–72.
127 *ICJ Rep.* 1986, at 103–4, 105 and 118–23.
128 Annex to UNGA Res. 3314 (XXIX); text in *AJIL* 69 (1975), 480. See T.W. Bennett, A Linguistic Perspective of the Definition of Aggression, *GYIL* 31 (1988), 48–69; B.B. Ferencz, Aggression, *EPIL* I (1992), 58–65.
129 *ICJ Rep.* 1986, 126–7.
130 *Ibid.*, 127.

131 J. Stone, *Conflict through Consensus*, 1977, 75, 183.
132 Such as the aforementioned article.
133 On states and governments, see Chapter 5 above, 75–90.
134 E.H. Riedel, Recognition of Belligerency, *EPIL* 4 (1982), 167–71; Riedel, Recognition of Insurgency, *ibid.*, 171–3.
135 See Chapter 20 below, 350–1.
136 P. Malanczuk, American Civil War, *EPIL* I (1992), 129–31.
137 See H. Lauterpacht, *Recognition in International Law*, 1947, 175–269; C. Rousseau, *Droit international public*, Vol. 3, 1977, 596–604.
138 See R. Jennings/A. Watts (eds), *Oppenheim's International Law*, I: Peace, 9th edn 1992, 435–9.
139 For examples, see Jennings/Watts, *ibid.*, 436–7.
140 See J.L. Hargrove, Intervention by Invitation and the Politics of the New World Order, in Damrosch/Scheffer (eds), *op. cit.*, 113; R. Mullerson, Intervention by Invitation, *ibid.*, 127–34; R.M. Gune-Wardene, Indo-Sri Lanka Accord: Intervention by Invitation or Forced Intervention?, *NCJILCR* 16 (1991), 211; Doswald-Beck, *op. cit.*, Tanca, *op. cit.*

What the decision did not clarify further, however, is what kind of 'proportionate counter-measures' may be taken by the state which is the victim of extensive assistance to insurgents by another state. The General Assembly's Definition of Aggression is also unclear on the following. The expression 'its substantial involvement therein' was a compromise between those states which thought that aggression was committed only by a state which sent armed bands to attack another state, and those states which thought that aggression also included supporting such bands or supporting violent civil strife in another state.[131] As often happens with compromise phrases, its meaning is not absolutely certain. 'Substantial involvement' would probably cover the case of a state which permits armed bands to use its territory as a base for launching attacks against another state (by analogy with Article 3(f) of the Definition of Aggression); it is uncertain whether it would cover the case of a state which supplies weapons to armed bands which launch attacks from the territory of another state against a third state. However, it is clear from the Court's judgment that Article 3(g) as a whole applies to insurgents only if they attack the government of their state from the territory of another state; if insurgents do not move across state boundaries, even the most substantial assistance to those insurgents is incapable of violating Article 3(g) (although it might violate other provisions of the Definition of Aggression).[132]

Participation by other states: help for the established authorities

The theory that help for the established authorities is legal

States have often argued that help given to the established authorities in a civil war is always legal. The assumption upon which this argument is based is that the government is the agent of the state,[133] and that therefore the government, until it is definitely overthrown, remains competent to invite foreign troops into the state's territory and to seek other forms of foreign help, whatever the effect which that help may have on the political future of the state.

Supporters of this 'rule' admit the existence of one exception to it; when the insurgents have been recognized as belligerents,[134] the rules of neutrality applicable to international wars[135] come into operation, and foreign help for the established authorities is no longer lawful. This exception is of no practical importance nowadays; recognition of belligerency occurred in some nineteenth-century civil wars, especially the US Civil War of 1861–5,[136] but has virtually never occurred in any civil war during the twentieth century.[137]

The argument of those supporting the intervention by invitation rule is that such intervention with the consent of the lawful government constitutes assistance which does not conflict with any interpretation of the principle of state sovereignty.[138] However, in the light of the abuses in the past of so-called 'invitations'[139] to intervene, the problem is how to establish what actually constitutes valid 'consent by the lawful government'.[140]

For example, in the cases of Soviet military intervention in Hungary (1956), Czechoslovakia (1968) and Afghanistan (1979), apart from invoking the need to counter foreign aggression or external interference, the USSR also maintained that it had been invited by the lawful government. In each of these cases the latter assertion was clearly a fabricated one.[141]

Similarly, the United States (in addition to relying on self-defence, the need to rescue American nationals, and decisions of the OAS) also invoked the alleged invitation from the lawful government to justify its military intervention in the Dominican Republic (1965) and in Grenada (1983).[142] In the case of the Dominican Republic, the majority of states did not accept the American justifications, but regarded the invasion as illegal interference in the internal affairs of the Dominican Republic.[143] In the case of Grenada (1983), the Legal Adviser of the US Department of State argued, *inter alia*:

> The lawful governmental authorities of a State may invite the assistance in the territory of military forces of other states or collective organizations in dealing with internal disorder as well as external threats.[144]

However, the legitimacy of the invitation by the Governor-General Sir Paul Scoon is open to a number of doubts; namely whether the invitation was actually made before or after the invasion, and whether the Governor-General (who had only ceremonial functions under the constitution) had the authority to extend such an invitation.[145]

The theory that help for the established authorities is illegal

The traditional view, that help for the established authorities is legal, is open to abuse; for instance, during the Spanish Civil War (1936–9),[146] Germany and Italy tried to legitimize their help to the nationalists (insurgents) by prematurely recognizing the nationalists as the *de jure* government of Spain. Even apart from such obvious instances of abuse, there may be situations where it is genuinely hard to say who are the established authorities and who are the insurgents. Thus, shortly after the Congo (now Zaire) became independent in 1960, the President (Kasavubu) and the Prime Minister (Lumumba) came into conflict with each other and each purported to dismiss the other.[147] Again, in Angola, rival nationalist movements formed two rival governments as soon as the country became independent in 1975. In such circumstances it is dangerously easy for foreign states to argue that their own protégés are the established authorities, and that the other side are the insurgents.

But the traditional view is also open to an even more fundamental objection. It is based on the idea that the government of a state is competent to act in the name of the state until it is overthrown. This idea is a fallacy; the competence of the government to act in the name of the state is the very thing which is called into question by the outbreak of a civil war. As Hall puts it:

> the fact that it has been necessary to call in foreign help is enough to show that the issue of the conflict would without it be uncertain, and consequently there is doubt as to which side would ultimately establish itself as the legal representative of the state.[148]

141 See Mullerson, *ibid.*, 128 *et seq.* also discussing other cases; M. Weller, Terminating Armed Intervention in Civil War: The Afghanistan Peace Accords of 1988, 1991 and 1993, *FYIL* 5 (1994), 505–689.
142 See text above, 315.
143 See Mullerson, *op. cit.*, 128–9 with references.
144 International Law and the United States Action in Grenada: A Report, *IA* 81 (1984), 331.
145 See text above, 315.
146 A.-M. de. Zayas, Spanish Civil War, *EPIL* 7 (1984), 434–8.
147 See B. Nolte, Conflicts, Congo, in *Wolfrum UNLPP I*, 225–32. See Chapter 22 below, 418–20.
148 A.P. Higgins (ed.), *Hall's International Law*, 8th edn 1924, 347.

149 On counter-intervention, see text below, 325.
150 *BPIL* 1963, 87.
151 See text above, 317–18.
152 See text above, 316–17.

Similarly, the outbreak of a secessionary revolt renders uncertain the status of the territory concerned and therefore suspends the right of the established authorities to seek foreign help in order to maintain their control over that territory.

The idea that foreign states should not intervene on either side in a civil war is a wise one, otherwise help given by some states to the established authorities runs the risk of provoking other states into helping the insurgents.[149] It was for this reason that many European states adopted a policy of non-intervention in the Spanish Civil War; the policy failed, but only because the fascist and communist dictatorships refused to abide by it. Non-intervention has received some support as a rule of law in subsequent state practice; in 1963 the United Kingdom stated before the Sixth Committee of the UN General Assembly that it

> considered that, if civil war broke out in a state and the insurgents did not receive outside help or support, it was unlawful for a foreign state to intervene, even on the invitation of the régime in power, to assist in maintaining law and order.[150]

But the practice of states is far from consistent. Only a few years after making the statement quoted in the previous paragraph, the British Government supplied arms to the Nigerian Government during the civil war in Nigeria (1967–70), while refusing to sell arms to the insurgents; the United Kingdom claimed that it was entitled to help the Nigerian Government because the insurgents had not been recognized as belligerents. However, help given by foreign states to a government during a civil war is usually rather limited unless the rebels have also received help from other states; states seldom send troops to help the government, and usually confine themselves to supplying arms. Uncertainty about the legal position may be one reason for this partial restraint, but fear of provoking counter-intervention by other states on behalf of the insurgents is probably a more potent motive.

Collective self-defence against subversion

The above United Kingdom statement of support for the rule of non-intervention was made subject to a condition: 'if . . . the insurgents did not receive outside help or support'. Virtually every state considers itself entitled to defend an ally against foreign subversion (subversion may consist of helping to start a revolt, or of helping a revolt which has already started).

Help against subversion can be regarded as a form of collective self-defence under Article 51 of the United Nations Charter.[151] Force used in self-defence must be proportionate to the other side's use of force,[152] so foreign help given to the established authorities must be proportionate to the foreign help given to the insurgents. This is particularly important in cases where an insurgent movement depends partly on internal support and partly on foreign help; in such cases foreign help to the established authorities must not exceed the foreign help to the insurgents. Moreover, disproportionately extensive help for the established authorities might be inexpedient in such circumstances, because it would probably provoke a massive increase in help for the insurgents from the other foreign state, and thus add to the dangers of the civil war escalating into an all-out international war. However, it must be confessed that there is something artificial in talking about proportionality in such circumstances, because it will probably be impossible to calculate exactly the amount of foreign help received by the insurgents.

Article 51 applies only if there has been an armed attack (or, more doubtfully, if there is an imminent threat of an armed attack). In *Nicaragua v. USA*, the International Court of Justice gave a narrow definition of armed attack; it does not include sending weapons to insurgents.[153] On the other hand, it is obvious that sending troops to help insurgents would amount to an armed attack.[154] Consequently, if one state sends troops to help insurgents, that is an armed attack, and other states are therefore entitled to send troops to help the established authorities; but if one state sends weapons to insurgents, that is not an armed attack, and other states are therefore not entitled to send weapons to the established authorities – this represents a serious gap in the law. (The only way to avoid this last conclusion is to argue that it is always lawful for a foreign state to supply weapons to the established authorities, whether or not the insurgents have received weapons from another foreign state.[155])

The point at issue in *Nicaragua v. USA* was whether Nicaragua's alleged assistance to insurgents in El Salvador justified United States assistance to insurgents in Nicaragua, not whether Nicaragua's alleged assistance to insurgents in El Salvador justified United States assistance to the government of El Salvador. But the Court's ruling that collective self-defence can be exercised only in response to an armed attack, and its restrictive definition of armed attack, are probably applicable by analogy to all forms of collective self-defence against subversion.

Anticipatory self-defence[156] is not usually invoked by states in the context of collective self-defence against subversion. Instead, states usually claim that their help to the established authorities is a response to prior foreign aid to the insurgents. For instance, the United States Government argued that its participation in the fighting in Vietnam between 1965 and 1973 was justified on the grounds that it was defending South Vietnam against subversion from North Vietnam, and that such subversion had started before the United States came to South Vietnam's defence. American critics of the US involvement argued that the insurgents in South Vietnam were an indigenous movement which received little or no support from North Vietnam, or that North Vietnam's aid to the insurgents in South Vietnam was a lawful counter-intervention,[157] provoked by prior US aid to the government of South Vietnam. There were also many controversies about the effects of the Geneva accords of 1954 concerning Vietnam.[158]

Conclusion

It seems to be generally agreed that a state may help the established authorities of another state against foreign subversion; as regards similar help to the established authorities against genuine insurgents, state practice is inconsistent. It is not that some states follow one practice and other states follow another practice; rather, each state follows one practice one year and

153 See text above, 319–21.
154 See text above, 321–2.
155 See text below, 326.
156 See text above, 311–14.
157 See text above, 322–3.
158 See R.A. Falk (ed.), *The Vietnam War and International Law*, 4 Vols, 1968–76. See also Chapter 2 above, 27.

159 See T. Farer, Intervention in Civil Wars: A Modest Proposal, *Colum. LR* (1967), 266.

160 See D. Thürer, Self-Determination, *EPIL* 8 (1985), 470–80; A. Cassese, *International Law in a Divided World*, 1986, 131 *et seq.*; J. Crawford (ed.), *The Rights of Peoples*, 1992; C. Tomuschat (ed.), *Modern Law of Self-Determination*, 1993; H. Hannum, Rethinking Self-Determination, *Virginia JIL* 34 (1993), 1–69; F.L. Kirgis, Jr., The Degrees of Self-Determination in the United Nations Era, *AJIL* 88 (1994), 304–10; M. Koskenniemi, National Self-Determination Today: Problems of Legal Theory and Practice, *ICLQ* 43 (1994), 241 *et seq.*; R. McCorquodale, Self-Determination: A Human Rights Approach, *ibid.*, 857–85; L.R. Beres, Self-Determination: The Ironies of Self-Determination under International Law, *Arizona JICL* 11 (1994), 1–26; A. Cassese, *Self-Determination of Peoples. A Legal Reappraisal*, 1995; P. Malanczuk, Minorities and Self-Determination in International Law, in N. Sybesma-Knol/J.V. Bellingen (eds), *Naar een nieuwe interpretatie van het Recht op Zelfbeschikking*, 1995, 169–93; K. Doehring, Self-Determination, in *Simma CUNAC*, 56–72; A. Cassese, The International Court of Justice and the Right of Peoples to Self-Determination, in Lowe/Fitzmaurice (eds), *op. cit.*, 351–63; J. Crawford, The General Assembly, the International Court of Justice and Self-Determination, *ibid.*, 585–605; K.-J. Partsch, Self-Determination, in *Wolfrum UNLPP II*, 1171–9; H. Hannum, Autonomy, Sovereignty, and Self-Determination: The Accommodation of Conflicting Rights, 1996.

161 See text below, 327–30.

162 R. Higgins, Postmodern Tribalism and the Right to Secession, Comments, in C. Brölmann/R. Lefeber/M. Zieck (eds), *Peoples and Minorities in International Law*, 1993, 29.

another practice another year. However, since 1945 there has been a tendency for states to try to justify their participation in foreign civil wars by saying that they are defending the established authorities against external subversion. This is certainly true of the United States' interventions in the Lebanon (1958), the Dominican Republic (1965) and Vietnam (1965–73), and of Cuba's intervention in the Ogaden (1977–8); even the Soviet Union made a half-hearted attempt to justify its invasions of Hungary (1956), Czechoslovakia (1968) and Afghanistan (1979) by arguing that it was defending those countries against Western subversion. The fact that such 'justifications' are often contrary to the facts is beside the point; the significant thing is the frequency with which the justifications are used (or abused) – it is almost as if states were implying that intervention in other circumstances would be illegal.

It is true that British and Soviet arms supplies to the Nigerian government during the Nigerian Civil War in the late 1960s indicate that foreign states are sometimes prepared to help the established authorities against genuine insurgents, as well as against external subversion; but the arms supplies to Nigeria differed from the interventions listed in the previous paragraph in one crucial respect – they did not involve the use of the troops of one state in the territory of another. It may be, therefore, that we are witnessing the emergence of a new rule of customary law, which will permit states to supply the established authorities with money and arms during every type of civil war, but which will forbid states to send troops to help the established authorities except when foreign subversion is occurring.[159]

Self-determination and the use of force

The principle of self-determination refers to the right of a people living in a territory to determine the political and legal status of that territory – for example, by setting up a state of their own or by choosing to become part of another state.[160] Before 1945 this right was conferred by a few treaties on the inhabitants of a few territories (for instance, the Treaty of Versailles 1919 provided for a plebiscite in Upper Silesia, to determine whether it should form part of Germany or of Poland); but there was probably no legal right of self-determination in the absence of such treaty provisions.

The 'principle of equal rights and self-determination of peoples' is explicitly mentioned in the UN Charter in Article 1(2), Article 55, and implicitly referred to in Articles 73 and 76(b), dealing with colonies and other dependent territories.[161] But these provisions are vague and it is doubtful whether they lend themselves to establishing specific rights and duties. The Charter leaves us ignorant on what is a 'people', entitled to self-determination, and it does not specify the legal consequences. It is also 'one of the great myths'[162] that the drafters of the Charter envisaged self-determination in the way it later evolved. Their concept of self-determination did not include the right of dependent peoples to be independent, or even to vote, but was linked to the equal rights of states (not individuals) in the sense of protecting the people of one state against interference by another state.

Since 1945, resolutions passed by the United Nations General Assembly have attributed a wider scope to the right of self-determination, and have brought about major changes in international law. The most important steps were the Declaration on the Granting of Independence to Colonial Countries and Peoples, adopted unanimously by the General Assembly in 1960,[163] and the two Human Rights Covenants: the International Covenant on Civil and Political Rights 1966, which entered into force in March 1976, and the International Covenant on Economic, Social and Cultural Rights 1966, which entered into force in January 1976.[164] The two Covenants have identical Articles 1:

1 All peoples have the right of self-determination. By virtue of that right they freely determine their political status and freely pursue their economic, social and cultural development.

2 . . .

3 The States Parties to the present Covenant, including those having responsibility for the administration of Non-Self-Governing and Trust Territories, shall promote the realization of the right of self-determination, and shall respect that right, in conformity with the provisions of the Charter of the United Nations.

The Friendly Relations Declaration of 1970[165] is perhaps the most authoritative document so far, stipulating that the principle of equal rights and self-determination of peoples includes the right of all peoples 'freely to determine, without external interference, their political status and to pursue their economic, social and cultural development' and the duty of every state 'to respect this right in accordance with the provisions of the Charter'. Methods of achieving self-determination mentioned are the creation of a sovereign and independent state, the free association or integration with another state, and the choice of any other political status freely accepted by the people. Self-determination is recognized by state practice as a basic principle of international law, to which even the status of *ius cogens* is attributed. Article 19 of the International Law Commission's Draft Articles on State Responsibility describes as an 'international crime', *inter alia*, 'a serious breach of an international obligation of essential importance for safeguarding the right of self-determination of peoples, such as that prohibiting the establishment or maintenance by force of colonial domination'.[166] As we have seen, in the *East Timor* case the ICJ described self-determination as an obligation *erga omnes* – however, without any further explanation.[167]

But what are the exact legal consequences of this principle? This question can be best clarified by first looking at the practice which emerged from the process of decolonization and then discussing the more recent developments relating to the status of suppressed minorities and other groups.

Mandated territories, trust territories and non-self-governing territories

Mandated territories

After the First World War, some of the Allies wanted to annex Germany's colonies and certain Arabic-speaking areas of the Turkish Empire;

163 Resolution 1514 (XV) of 14 December 1960, *UNYb* 1960, 49; Brownlie *BDIL*, 307.

164 Texts in *Brownlie BDIL*, 263 and 276. See Chapter 14 above, 215–16.

165 Friendly Relations Declaration 1970, *op. cit.*

166 Text in *Brownlie BDIL*, 431–2). See Chapter 3 above, 59–60.

167 *East Timor* case (*Portugal v. Australia*), *ICJ. Rep.* 1995, 90. See I.G.M. Scobie, Self-Determination Undetermined: the Case of East Timor, *LJIL* 9 (1996), 185–212. On the case see Chapters 3, 59 and 18, 286–7 above and text below, 332.

168 A. Whelan, Wilsonian Self-Determination and the Versailles Settlement, *ICLQ* 43 (1994), 99–115.
169 D. Rauschning, Mandates, *EPIL* 10 (1987), 288–95; F. Ermarcora, Mandates, in *Wolfrum UNLPP II*, 871–6.
170 *Namibia Case* (1971), *ICJ Rep.* 1971, 16, 28–32.
171 Articles 75–91 UN Charter. See U. Fastenrath, Articles 73 and 74, in *Simma CUNAC*, 923–31; D. Rauschning, Articles 75–85, *ibid.*, 933–62; R. Geiger, Articles 86–91, *ibid.*, 963–72; D. Rauschning, United Nations Trusteeship System, *EPIL* 5 (1983), 369–76; F. Ermarcora, Trusteeship/Trusteeship Council, in *Wolfrum UNLPP II*, 1259–66. On self-government of a former UN Trust Territory and the Covenant to Establish a Commonwealth of the Northern Mariana Islands-United States, see W.S. Fields, *United States v. Guerrero*, 4 F.3d 749, U.S. Court of Appeals, 9th Cir., September 1, 1993, reported in *AJIL* 88 (1994), 337. On US, UK, Spanish and French territories, see the articles by A.-M. de Zayas, H. Fox, C.C. Rodriguez Iglesias and M. Fromont, *EPIL* 12 (1990). See also E.W. Davies, *The Legal Status of British Dependent Territories – The West Indies and North Atlantic Region*, 1995.
172 A.-M. de Zayas, United States: Dependent Territories, *EPIL* 12 (1990), 388–97, at 390–1.
173 See P.-T. Stoll, Namibia, in *Wolfrum UNLPP II*, 904–12; D.S. Haase, Namibia Council, *ibid.*, 913–17.
174 *South West Africa* case, ICJ Advisory Opinions of 1950, 1955 and 1956: *ICJ Rep.* 1950, 128–45; 1955, 67–123; 1956, 23–71; ICJ Judgments of 1962 and 1966: *ICJ Rep.* 1962, 319–662; 1966, 6–505; ICJ Advisory Opinion of 1971, *ICJ Rep.* 1971, 16–345. See E. Klein, South West Africa / Namibia (Advisory Opinions and Judgments), *EPIL* 2 (1981), 260–70; Klein, Namibia, *EPIL* 12 (1990), 232–41. See also Chapter 18 above, 284.
175 *ICJ Rep.* 1950, 128.
176 *ICJ Rep.* 1955, 67, and 1956, 23.

but their plans were opposed by President Wilson, who wished to secure recognition for the ideal of self-determination.[168] Eventually a compromise was reached; each of the territories in question was to be administered by one of the Allies, under the supervision of the League of Nations. This was known as the mandate system.[169] Article 22 of the League of Nations Covenant implied that the peoples inhabiting the mandated territories would be allowed to exercise a right of self-determination at some time in the future, but it did not fix a date for the exercise of that right.[170]

Trust territories

The United Nations Charter provides for a trusteeship system, modelled on the League's mandate system.[171] In 1955 there were eleven trust territories, administered by seven different states. After Palau, the last entity of the Trust Territory of the Pacific Islands administrated by the United States,[172] had chosen free association with the United States in a plebiscite, in 1994 the UN Security Council terminated Palau's trusteeship status. The trusteeship system has completed its mission and now has no territories left. The most complicated case has been the question of South West Africa (Namibia).

South West Africa (Namibia)

Of the territories administered under the League of Nations mandate system, all but one became independent before or shortly after the dissolution of the League in 1946, or were placed under the United Nations trusteeship system. The exception was South West Africa (Namibia), a former German colony administered by South Africa.[173] The status of South West Africa has given rise to a prolonged dispute between South Africa and the United Nations, and to four advisory opinions and two judgments from the International Court of Justice.[174]

In its first advisory opinion, the Court said that South Africa was not obliged to place South West Africa under the trusteeship system. However, unless it did so, South Africa remained bound by the obligations contained in the mandate, and the General Assembly succeeded to the supervisory powers which the League had exercised under the mandate.[175] In two further advisory opinions the Court dealt with the procedure to be followed by the General Assembly when exercising its supervisory powers.[176]

These expressions of judicial opinion, being advisory opinions, were not binding, and South Africa refused to act in accordance with them, arguing that international supervision of its administration of South West Africa had lapsed when the League was dissolved in 1946. In 1960 Liberia and Ethiopia, two former members of the League, instituted contentious proceedings against South Africa before the International Court of Justice; they asked the Court to declare that South Africa had violated the mandate by introducing *apartheid* into South West Africa. If the Court had decided for Liberia and Ethiopia, its judgment, unlike the earlier advisory opinions, would have been binding upon South Africa; that is the big difference between advisory and contentious proceedings.

However, in 1966 the Court decided that South Africa's obligations under the mandate, in so far as they related to the treatment of the inhabitants of South West Africa, had been owed to the League, and not to individual members of the League; the Court therefore dismissed the cases brought by Ethiopia and Liberia, holding that Ethiopia and Liberia were not entitled to enforce rights which did not belong to them.[177]

The Court's judgment was severely criticized, particularly by African and Asian states, because the ground on which the Court decided the case was very similar to an argument which the Court had rejected in 1962, when it had handed down a preliminary judgment rejecting various pleas by South Africa that it had no jurisdiction to try the case.[178] As a result of changes in the composition of the Court, the judges who had been in a minority in 1962 found themselves in a majority in 1966, and proceeded to reverse the effect of the Court's earlier judgment.

Later in 1966 the General Assembly passed a resolution declaring, 'that South Africa has failed to fulfil its obligations in respect of the administration of the mandated territory . . . and has, in fact, disavowed the mandate', and deciding 'that the mandate . . . is therefore terminated, that South Africa has no . . . right to administer the territory and that henceforth South West Africa comes under the direct responsibility of the United Nations'.[179]

The International Court handed down a further advisory opinion in 1971,[180] in which it said that the General Assembly had succeeded to the League's supervisory powers[181] and had acted lawfully when terminating the mandate;[182] the Court also advised that South Africa was under a duty to withdraw from South West Africa (or Namibia, as it had been renamed by the General Assembly), and that other states were obliged, by a binding resolution passed by the Security Council, to refrain from any dealings with South Africa which were inconsistent with the termination of the mandate.[183]

In 1978 South Africa announced that it was willing in principle to allow elections to be held in Namibia under United Nations supervision, which would lead to independence for Namibia. However, South Africa failed to reach agreement with the United Nations and with the guerrilla movement in Namibia about safeguards to ensure that there would be no intimidation during the proposed elections, and for many years South Africa continued to administer Namibia in defiance of the United Nations.[184] In December 1988 a tripartite agreement, mediated by the United States, was concluded at the UN headquarters in New York between Angola, Cuba and South Africa which, after the withdrawal of Cuban troops from Angola, finally led to the independence of Namibia on the basis of UN-supervised elections by the UNTAG force, held in November 1989. Thereafter, the remaining South African forces left Namibia and in March 1990 the independence of Namibia was finally proclaimed.[185]

Non-self-governing territories[186]

Article 73 of the United Nations Charter provides:

> Members of the United Nations which have . . . responsibilities for the administration of territories whose peoples have not yet attained a full measure of self-government recognize the principle that the interests of the inhabitants of these territories are paramount, and accept as a sacred trust the obligation to

177 *ICJ Rep.* 1966, 6.

178 *ICJ Rep.* 1962, 319.

179 UNGA Res. 2145 (XXI) of 27 October 1966, *UNYb*, 1966, 606.

180 *ICJ Rep.* 1971, 16.

181 *Ibid.*, 27–45.

182 *Ibid.*, 45–50.

183 *Ibid.*, 51–8.

184 See M. Spicer, Namibia – Elusive Independence, *The World Today*, Oct. 1980, 406; R. Zacklin, The Problem of Namibia in International Law, *RdC* 171 (1981), 225.

185 See *Basic Facts About the United Nations*, 1995, 240–4; Stoll (1995), *op. cit.*, 908 *et seq.* See also E. Schmidt-Jortzig, The Constitution of Namibia: An Example of a State Emerging under Close Supervision and World Scrutiny, *GYIL* 34 (1991), 413–28.

186 J. Brink, Non-Self-Governing Territories, *EPIL* 10 (1987), 316–21.

187 See Fastenrath, *op. cit.*
188 *Basic Facts, op. cit.*, 234–40.
189 Resolution 1541 (XV) of 15 December 1960, *UNYb* 1960, 509.
190 See Chapter 10 above, 157.
191 Res. 1514 (XV), *op. cit.*

promote to the utmost . . . the well-being of the inhabitants of these territories, and, to this end:

(a) to ensure, with due respect for the culture of the peoples concerned, their political, economic, social, and educational advancement, their just treatment and their protection against abuses;

(b) to develop self-government, to take due account of the political aspirations of the peoples, and to assist them in the progressive development of their free political institutions, according to the particular circumstances of each territory and its peoples and their varying stages of advancement;

(c) to further international peace and security;

(d) to promote constructive measures of development . . . ; and

(e) to transmit regularly to the Secretary-General for information purposes, subject to such limitation as security and constitutional considerations may require . . . information . . . relating to economic, social, and educational conditions in the territories for which they are respectively responsible. [187]

Article 73 applies to colonies and to territories which resemble colonies. In total, seventy-two territories were enumerated as non-self-governing after 1946, most of which have since gained independence. As of 1994, there were only seventeen such territories left.[188]

According to Resolution 1541 (XV) of the General Assembly, there is a presumption that Article 73 applies to every territory 'which is geographically separate and is distinct ethnically and/or culturally from the country administering it'; this presumption is strengthened if the territory is in a position of 'subordination' to the administering power.[189] Thus the General Assembly considered that Article 73 applied to Portugal's territories in Africa, even though Portugal claimed that these territories were not colonies but overseas provinces of Portugal. On the other hand, the General Assembly has never regarded Northern Ireland as a non-self-governing territory;[190] Northern Ireland is geographically close to the rest of the United Kingdom, there is little cultural or ethnic difference between the population of Northern Ireland and the population of the rest of the United Kingdom, and Northern Ireland is not in a position of subordination to the United Kingdom, since it is represented in the United Kingdom Parliament.

Article 73 imposes fewer obligations than the provisions dealing with the trusteeship system; in particular, it does not provide for supervision by the United Nations. But in practice, and despite opposition from the colonial powers, the General Assembly has asserted considerable powers of supervision, by placing an extensive interpretation on the administering powers' duty to submit reports under Article 73(e). Anti-colonialist feeling increased in the General Assembly as more and more newly independent states joined the United Nations.

An important landmark in the anti-colonialist trend was Resolution 1514 (XV), passed by the General Assembly on 14 December 1960, by eighty-nine votes to nil, with nine abstentions.[191] This Resolution declares:

1   The subjection of peoples to alien subjugation and exploitation con-
    stitutes a denial of fundamental human rights, is contrary to the Charter
    of the United Nations and is an impediment to ... World peace and
    co-operation.

2   All peoples have the right to self-determination; by virtue of that right they
    freely determine their political status and freely pursue their economic, social
    and cultural development.

3   Inadequacy of political, economic, social or educational preparedness should
    never serve as a pretext for delaying independence.

4   All armed action or repressive measures of all kinds directed against depend-
    ent peoples shall cease in order to enable them to exercise peacefully and
    freely their right to complete independence, and the integrity of their national
    territory shall be respected.

5   Immediate steps shall be taken, in Trust and Non-Self-Governing Territories
    or all other territories which have not yet attained independence, to transfer
    all power to the peoples of those territories ... in accordance with their freely
    expressed will ... in order to enable them to enjoy complete independence
    and freedom.

6   Any attempt aimed at the partial or total disruption of the national unity and
    the territorial integrity of a country is incompatible with the purposes and
    principles of the Charter of the United Nations.

192 *ICJ Rep.* 1971, 16, 31; 1975, 12, 31–3, 121. See K. Oellers-Frahm, Western Sahara (Advisory Opinion), *EPIL* 2 (1981), 291–3; see also *Basic Facts*, 244–9. On Namibia, see above, 328–9.
193 Res. 1541 (XV), *op. cit.*
194 See J. Crawford, *The Creation of States in International Law*, 1979, 367–77.
195 *Western Sahara* case, *op. cit.*

To put it mildly, the Resolution is a bold interpretation of Article 73 of
the Charter. However, even the (mainly Western) states which had
abstained when the Resolution was adopted in 1960, had by 1970 come to
accept it as an accurate statement of modern international law, a view
which was echoed by the International Court of Justice in the *Namibia* and
Western Sahara cases.[192]

Self-determination normally leads to independence, but Resolution
1541 (XV) recognizes that the people of a non–self-governing territory
may choose integration with an independent state, or free association with
an independent state, as an alternative to independence.[193] 'Integration'
means that the territory becomes part of an independent state, as Alaska
and Hawaii did when they became part of the United States. 'Association'
means that the associated state has internal self-government, while the
independent state with which it is associated is responsible for foreign
affairs and defence. Resolution 1541 (XV) says that the people of each
non–self-governing territory should be allowed to choose freely between
independence, integration and association, but in practice the General
Assembly has shown a bias in favour of independence as opposed to other
forms of self-determination.[194]

In the case of very small territories (colonial enclaves) adjoining
another state, most members of the United Nations regard union with
the adjoining state as the appropriate method of decolonization, regardless of the wishes of the inhabitants, who are regarded as too few to
constitute a separate people. This approach is applied only to very small
territories. The General Assembly regarded Western Sahara and East
Timor as too large to be treated as colonial enclaves. It is true that
Morocco and Mauritania annexed Western Sahara[195] (a former Spanish

196 P.M. Lawrence, East Timor, *EPIL* II (1995), 3–4.

197 See generally Crawford (1979), *op. cit.*, 377–84; S. Oeter, Die Entwicklung der Westsahara-Frage unter besonderer Berücksichtigung der völkerrechtlichen Anerkennung, *ZaöRV* 46 (1986), 48 (see also Chapter 22); and see *UNYb* 1975 onwards, for discussions on Western Sahara and East Timor at the United Nations.

198 *Eastern Timor Case, op. cit.*

199 See T. Marauhn, Peacekeeping in a Critical Stage: The Operation in the Western Sahara, *IP* 2 (1995), 74–8; M. Niejahr, Conflicts, Western Sahara, in *Wolfrum UNLPP I*, 330–7.

200 See *FAZ*, 31 May 1996; *UN Chronicle* 33 (1996), no. 2, 54.

201 See Chapter 10, 148 and text, 315 above. For details of the relevant General Assembly resolutions, see *UNYb* 1965, 578–9; 1973, 713–14; *UN Chronicle*, 1983, no. 1, 4–5; 1984, no. 1, 17; 1986, no. 1, 8–10; *KCA* 1985, 33620, 34039.

202 See para. 5 of Res. 1514 (XV), and the *Namibia* case, *ICJ Rep.* 1971, 16, 31.

203 Text in *Brownlie BDIL*, 44.

colony) without the consent of the inhabitants, and that Indonesia annexed East Timor[196] (a former Portuguese colony) also without the consent of the inhabitants, but Morocco, Mauritania and Indonesia sought to justify their actions by pretending that the inhabitants had consented; the annexing states admitted that the inhabitants of Western Sahara and East Timor had a legal right to self-determination, and the dispute between them and their many critics at the United Nations was limited to the question of fact as to whether that right had been respected or violated.[197] In the case of *East Timor*,[198] the International Court confirmed the right of the people of East Timor to self-determination, but it dismissed the case for lack of jurisdiction.

In the case of the Western Sahara, it was planned to have a referendum to take place in 1992 to allow the people of the former Spanish colony to decide on their future.[199] However, in May 1996, the UN Security Council resolved to withdraw the UN MINURSO mission from the territory in view of obstruction by both Morocco and Polisario (the national liberation movement) against the determination of the lists of the persons entitled to vote.[200]

The General Assembly has never accepted the British argument that the inhabitants of the Falkland Islands are entitled to self-determination – perhaps because the 1,723 British settlers on the islands are too few to constitute a people. On the other hand, the General Assembly has never accepted the Argentinian argument that the Falkland Islands should be treated as a colonial enclave – probably because they are too large (4,700 square miles) and too far from Argentina (300 miles). Instead, the General Assembly has steered a middle course between the British and Argentinian positions; it has passed resolutions recommending the United Kingdom and Argentina to enter into negotiations to settle their dispute about sovereignty over the islands, and to terminate the colonial status of the islands. Argentina interprets termination of colonial status as meaning transfer of the islands to Argentina; but it could also be interpreted as including other options, such as independence, or integration or association with the United Kingdom.[201]

Double standards?

The legal right of self-determination clearly applies to non-self-governing territories, trust territories and mandated territories.[202] Whether it also applies to other territories is uncertain. On the one hand, paragraph 2 of Resolution 1514 (XV) says that all peoples have the right to self-determination; on the other hand, paragraph 6 of Resolution 1514 (XV) forbids secession (or maybe only foreign assistance to secessionary movements). In 1970 the General Assembly declared that the principle of self-determination did not authorize

> any action which would dismember . . . independent States conducting them-selves in compliance with the principle of . . . self-determination of peoples . . . and thus possessed of a government representing the whole people . . . without distinction as to race, creed or colour.[203]

This might perhaps be interpreted as implying that action to dismember an independent state is permitted if the government does not represent the whole people.

In practice, however, organs of the United Nations have shown little concern for self-determination in territories other than non-self-governing territories, trust territories and mandated territories. Many people in the West have accused the United Nations of applying double standards, but these double standards are inherent in the Charter; Article 73, dealing with non-self-governing territories, is far more specific than the vague general references to self-determination in Articles 1(2) and 55, which are so vague that it is doubtful whether they create any legal obligation at all.[204]

Many General Assembly resolutions stated that the inhabitants of South Africa were entitled to self-determination.[205] Since 1970 the General Assembly has frequently declared that the Palestinians are also entitled to self-determination;[206] none of these resolutions specifies the territories whose status is affected by self-determination for the Palestinians – self-determination for the Palestinians could be interpreted as limited to the West Bank and Gaza, which have been under Israeli military occupation since 1967 but are not legally part of Israel,[207] or it could be interpreted as implying the total replacement of Israel by a Palestinian state. With the agreements reached between Israel and the PLO following the historic event of the signing of the 'Declaration of Principles on Interim Self-Government' in Washington on 13 September 1993, the process has been now confined to the Gaza Strip, the Jericho area, and the West Bank, with a number of vexed questions concerning, *inter alia*, Jerusalem and the permanent status of the territories (whether independent statehood or only some form of autonomy) still to be resolved.[208]

The Palestinians and the inhabitants of South Africa (until the apartheid regime was abolished) are the only 'non-colonial' peoples whose right to self-determination has been expressly recognized by the General Assembly. Several states opposed the resolution dealing with the Palestinians and the inhabitants of South Africa, and some Western states explained their opposition by arguing that the right of self-determination did not apply outside the 'colonial' context. (But in 1980 the member states of the EEC recognized that the Palestinians were entitled to self-determination.[209]) Some Third World states try to rebut this point by arguing that South Africa and Israel were 'neo-colonialist'; most of the whites living in South Africa are the descendants of colonial settlers, and most of the Jews living in Israel when Israel became independent in 1948 had entered Palestine as immigrants while it was being administered by the United Kingdom under a League of Nations mandate. But, whatever the previous status of South Africa and Palestine may have been, South Africa and Israel became independent states, and it is illogical to treat them differently from other independent states. The General Assembly's extension of the right of self-determination to the Palestinians and the inhabitants of South Africa, coupled with its failure to extend that right to other 'non-colonial' peoples, has increased rather than reduced the problem of double standards.

204 For the text of Articles 1(2) and 55, see Brownlie, *BDIL* 3, 19.

205 See, for instance, GA Res. 2396 (XXIII), *UN Chronicle*, 1969 no. 1, 94; GA Res. 31/6 I, 1976 no. 11, 38–45, at 79.

206 See, for instance, GA Res. 2672 C (XXV), *UN Chronicle*, 1971 no. 1, 45–8, at 46; GA Res. 3236 (XXIX), 1974 no. 11, 36-74; GA Res. 33/23; 1978 no. 11, at 80; UNGA Res. 33/24, *ibid.*, at 81.

207 See Chapter 10 above, 153.

208 See Chapter 5 above, 77.

209 See *KCA* 1980, 30635.

210 See Chapter 5 above, 78–9.

211 Res. 3061 (XXVIII), 2 November 1973, *UNYb* 1973, 143–7, at 146.

212 E. Klein, South African Bantustan Policy, *EPIL* 10 (1987), 393–7. See Chapter 5 above, 85.

213 J. Delbrück, Apartheid, *EPIL* I (1992), 192–6.

214 See text above, 332–3.

215 Res. 34/93 G, *UN Chronicle*, January 1980, 26. See Crawford (1979), *op. cit.*, 103–6, 219–27.

216 Crawford, *ibid.*, 363–4.

217 *ICJ Rep.* 1960, 6–114, at 39. See L. Weber, Right of Passage over Indian Territory Case, *EPIL* 2 (1981), 244–6.

Consequences of violations of the right of self-determination

Violation of the right of self-determination creates a situation which has repercussions on many areas of international law. The effects of the interaction between the new rule of self-determination and various older rules of international law are often unclear, and the conclusions suggested below must be treated as tentative.

Creation of new states

Traditionally, secession was not regarded as creating a new state until the secessionary movement had established permanent control over the territory in question.[210] Has this rule been altered by the right of self-determination? Can a national liberation movement claim to be the government of a new state before it has established permanent control over the territory in question? The answer is probably no. It is true that the General Assembly passed a resolution recognizing Guinea-Bissau as an independent state in 1973, while it was still struggling for independence against Portugal, but many of the states which voted for this resolution argued that the national liberation movement already controlled most of the territory of Guinea-Bissau;[211] the resolution on Guinea-Bissau thus represents an application of the traditional test of control (even though the test was probably not applied as stringently as it usually is), and not the abandonment of the test of control in favour of some other criterion. In any case, the resolution on Guinea-Bissau is unique; no other national liberation movement has ever been recognized by the United Nations as the government of an independent state while it was still struggling for independence.

On the other hand, a state established in violation of the right of self-determination is probably a nullity in the eyes of international law. After 1976 South Africa purported to confer independence on a number of black states ('Bantustans')[212] established on South African territory in pursuance of the South African policy of apartheid.[213] The General Assembly regarded apartheid as a violation of the right of self-determination;[214] the creation of 'Bantustans' was equally illegal and invalid, according to the General Assembly, because it represented the implementation of apartheid. The General Assembly urged states not to recognize the Bantustans, and no state (except South Africa) in fact recognized any of them.[215]

Title to territory

A state administering a colony is under a legal duty to allow the inhabitants of that colony to exercise their right of self-determination. Does the state automatically lose sovereignty over the colony if it fails to carry out that duty? Opinions differ,[216] but in 1960 the International Court of Justice decided the *Right of Passage* case on the tacit assumption that this question should be answered in the negative.[217] It is submitted that that assumption is correct. Self-determination usually leads to independence, but, as we have just seen, peoples under colonial rule are not usually regarded as forming a new state until their struggle for independence has been successfully completed. The view that the colonial power no longer has sovereignty over its colony would mean that no state would have sovereignty over the territory in question while the inhabitants were still struggling for independence – a conclusion which would raise all kinds of practical and theoretical difficulties. These difficulties can be avoided if we accept that the colonial power retains sovereignty until the people have been allowed to exercise their right of self-determination. In the case of East Timor,[218] for example, Portugal is still formally regarded as the continuing administering power in spite of the military occupation of East Timor by Indonesia.

Self-determination does not affect boundaries between independent states. When a colony becomes independent, it succeeds to the boundaries established by the former colonial power, even though it may dislike those boundaries and even though those boundaries may artificially divide an ethnic group. The principle of automatic succession to boundaries overrides the principle of self-determination.[219] Thus, decolonization in Africa was based on the *uti possidetis* principle, borrowed from the experience of the former Spanish colonies in South and Central America.[220] Self-determination in this sense simply meant, in the words of Thomas Franck, that

> [p]eoples entitled to self-determination were defined as the inhabitants of a colony. The exercise of self-determination must occur, it was reasoned, within the colonial boundaries, which would remain sacrosanct, unless the people – as a whole – within those boundaries freely elected to change them by integrating with another state.[221]

The prevailing view in state practice under the UN Charter, as distinct from the pre-Charter situation, has been that self-determination is basically limited to the colonial context, that is to say, to the relationship between colonies in Africa, Asia and Latin America *vis-à-vis* the metropolitan powers. The 1960 UN General Assembly Resolution A/Res/1514 (XV) stipulated that self-determination was only available 'in respect to territory which is geographically separate and is distinct ethnically and/or culturally from the country administering it' in connection with a specific reference to 'the relationship between the metropolitan State and the territory concerned'.[222] Once independence was achieved in this context, the right of self-determination was considered to be consumed. This view was upheld to protect the territorial integrity of existing states and of the new states emerging from the decolonization process, as well as in the general interest of maintaining stability in the international system. It naturally also had the effect of securing the position of those groups which had assumed power in the new states against claims of self-determination by other groups within their territory, disregarding, for example, the arbitrary nature of the boundaries drawn by colonial powers in Africa. It must be noted, however, that this predominant view was not entirely unchallenged – for example, by Germany during its quest for reunification. Furthermore, Articles 1 of the two 1966 Human Rights Covenants went beyond the colonial context by indicating that self-determination is not restricted to the liberation of colonies and then the consummation of this right, but that it may be continuously exercised by 'all peoples'.[223] The problem is that the text fails to clarify the legal consequences of this right, although there is

218 See text above, 327, 332.
219 See Chapter 11 above, 162.
220 See Chapter 11 above, 162–3.
221 T.M. Franck, Postmodern Tribalism and the Right to Secession, in Brölmann/Lefeber/Zieck (eds), *op. cit.*, 3–27, at 9.
222 GA Res. A/Res/1514 (XV), *op. cit.*
223 See text above, 327.

224 See A.M. de Zayas, The International Judicial Protection of Peoples and Minorities, in Brölmann/Lefeber/Zieck (eds), *op. cit.*, 253–87; G. Alfredson/A.M. de Zayas, Minority Rights: Protection by the United Nations, *HRLJ* (1993), 1–9.

225 Thürer, *op. cit.*, 474.

226 See also Franck (1993), *op. cit.*, at 11 *et seq.*; R. Higgins, Postmodern Tribalism and the Right to Secession, Comments, in Brölmann/Lefeber/Zieck (eds), *op. cit.*, at 33.

227 K. Ginther, Liberation Movements, *EPIL* 3 (1982), 245–9; H.-J. Uibopuu, Wars of National Liberation, *EPIL* 4 (1982), 343–6; Malanczuk (1987), *op. cit.*; H.A. Wilson, *International Law and the Use of Force by National Liberation Movements*, 1988. See also Chapter 6 above, 104–5.

228 See Chapter 20 below, 352–3.

229 See text above, 318–19.

230 GA Res. 1514 (XV), *op. cit.*

some interesting practice of the Committee on Human Rights under the 1966 Covenant on Civil and Political Rights.[224]

The effect of linking self-determination to decolonization in this sense was to deny a general right to secession of groups within a state. State practice and cases, such as Tibet, Katanga and Biafra, confirm that customary international law does not recognize the general legality of secession as a consequence of the principle of self-determination.[225] The acceptance of such a general right would indeed conflict with fundamental principles structuring the current international system, such as sovereign equality, territorial integrity and political independence. On the other hand, while international law does not acknowledge a general right to secession, it is also generally agreed that it does not prohibit secession.[226] International law is neutral in this respect, and, in other words, follows reality and the principle of effectiveness.

The whole problem is connected with the complications with respect to the recognition of the legality of wars of national liberation and the lawfulness of military intervention of third states in support of such movements.

Wars of national liberation

If the people of a particular territory are regarded by international law as possessing a legal right of self-determination but the state administering that territory refuses to let them exercise that right, they may need to fight a war of national liberation in order to achieve self-determination in practice.[227]

Western states have always treated wars of national liberation as civil wars, but communist states and Third World states have regarded them as international wars; this difference of classification affects the application of the laws of war,[228] but for other purposes it has little practical importance.

There is general agreement that peoples who have a legal right to self-determination are entitled to fight a war of national liberation. Not even Western states dissent from this view, if only because there is no rule in international law against rebellion,[229] although they consider that General Assembly resolutions encouraging wars of national liberation are politically undesirable.

The use of force to prevent the exercise of self-determination is probably unlawful. Paragraph 4 of General Assembly Resolution 1514 (XV) states that 'all armed action or repressive measures of all kinds directed against dependent peoples shall cease in order to enable them to exercise . . . their right to complete independence'.[230] Even the Western states, after initial opposition in the early 1960s, have now accepted that there is a legal duty not to use force to frustrate the exercise of a legal right to self-determination. However, there is still disagreement between Western states and other states about the basis of this rule. Western states regard it as derived solely from the right of self-determination, and not from Article 2(4) of the United Nations Charter, because Article 2(4) prohibits the use of force in international relations only and Western states do not regard the use of force by a state against its own nationals (including its colonial subjects) as a use of force in international relations; most Third World states regard the rule as derived from Article 2(4) as well as from the right of self-determination.[231]

If a state is acting unlawfully when it uses force to prevent the exercise of a legal right of self-determination, it would seem to follow, as a matter of logic, that other states are acting equally unlawfully if they help that state in its struggle to frustrate self-determination.

There is still disagreement between Western states and other states as regards the legality or illegality of help given by foreign states to national liberation movements. Paragraph 10 of General Assembly Resolution 2105 (XX), passed on 20 December 1965 by seventy-four votes to six with twenty-seven abstentions,

> recognizes the legitimacy of the struggle by peoples under colonial rule to exercise their right to self-determination and independence and invites all states to provide material and moral assistance to the national liberation movements in colonial territories.[232]

But this view is not accepted by Western states, which abstained or voted against the resolution. Later resolutions[233] speak of the right of peoples struggling against colonial rule to receive 'support' from other states; but this formula is simply an attempt to paper over the disagreement between the communist and Third World states, which interpret 'support' to include material support and/or *matériel* (i.e. in the form of weapons), and the Western states, which think that support must be limited to moral and diplomatic support.[234]

The General Assembly considered that the right of self-determination applied not only to peoples under colonial rule, but also to the Palestinians and the inhabitants of South Africa when it was under the old regime of apartheid.[235] Despite Western opposition, the General Assembly has passed resolutions urging states to provide material assistance to the Palestinians and the inhabitants of South Africa in their armed struggle for self-determination.[236]

It is difficult to reconcile these resolutions with the general rule against giving help to insurgents in civil wars.[237] It is true that violation of the right of self-determination is a violation of international law. But breaches by a state of other rules of international law (for example, the rules protecting human rights)[238] are not treated as justifying help given to insurgents against that state, and there is no logical reason for treating violations of the right of self-determination differently from other breaches of international law.

Alternatively, if wars of national liberation are classified as international wars and not as civil wars, the General Assembly resolutions which urged states to help national liberation movements in colonial territories, in Palestine and South Africa, are hard to reconcile with the rules of international law concerning international wars. The use of force in international relations is normally prohibited by international law; there are some exceptions to this rule, but the only one which has any possible relevance to wars of national liberation is collective self-defence against armed attack.[239] This assumes that the rules of self-defence, which apply in the event of an armed attack against a state, can be extended by analogy to

231 See N. Ronzitti, Resort to Force in Wars of National Liberation, in *Current Problems of International Law,* Cassese (ed.), 1975, *op. cit.,* 319–53.

232 Res. 2105 (XX), *UNYb* 1965, 554–5.

233 For example, Article 7 of the General Assembly's definition of aggression, text in *AJIL* 69 (1975), 480.

234 *AJIL* 65 (1971), 730–3, 1977, 233–7.

235 See text above, 333.

236 See, for instance, GA Res. 3236 (XXIX), *UN Chronicle,* 1974 no. 11, 36–44; GA Res. 31/6 I, *ibid.,* 1976 no. 11, 38–45, at 79; GA Res. 33/24, *ibid.,* 1978 no. 11, 52–3, at 81; GA Res. 34/44 and 34/93 A-R, *ibid.,* 1980 no. 1, 24, 79.

237 See text above, 319–22.

238 On humanitarian intervention, see Chapter 14 above, 221.

239 See text above, 317–18, 324–5.

240 See Chapter 2 above, 12–14.
241 See Chapter 10, 151–2, 155–7 and text, 306–8 above.
242 See C.J.R. Dugard, The Organisation of African Unity and Colonialism: An Inquiry into the Plea of Self-Defence as a Justification for the Use of Force in the Eradication of Colonialism, *ICLQ* 16 (1967), 157–90.
243 B. Kingsbury, Self-Determination and 'Indigenous Peoples', *ASIL Proc.* 86 (1992), 383; S.J. Anaya, *The Rights of Indigenous Peoples and International Law in Historical and Contemporary Perspective*, Harvard Indian Law Symposium, 1990, 191–225; Human Rights – The Rights of Indigenous Peoples, *UNCHR Fact Sheet* 1990, no. 9; M.E. Turpel, Indigenous Peoples' Rights of Political Participation and Self-Determination: Recent International Legal Developments and the Continuing Struggle for Recognition, *Cornell ILJ* 25 (1992), 579–602; B.R. Howard, Human Rights and Indigenous People: On the Relevance of International Law for Indigenous Liberation, *GYIL* 35 (1992), 105; T.v. Boven, Human Rights and the Rights of Peoples, *EJIL* 6 (1995), 461–76.
244 See Chapter 6 above, 105–8.
245 See the literature cited above, 326.
246 See Chapter 11 above, 161, 165–7 and Chapter 22 below, 409–15.
247 Text in *Brownlie BDIL*, 287; C. Tomuschat, Protection of Minorities under Article 27 of the International Covenant on Civil and Political Rights, in R. Bernhardt *et al.* (eds), *Festschrift für Hermann Mosler*, 1983, 949–79.

an armed attack against a people who are not yet a state – an assumption which many lawyers in the West are unwilling to make. Foreign states seldom send their armed forces to help national liberation movements; instead, they usually confine themselves to providing weapons and military bases.

Accordingly, intervention by foreign states in wars of national liberation would be lawful only if it could be shown that the national liberation movement (or the people whom it claims to represent) was the victim of an armed attack. But wars of national liberation usually start with an armed attack by (not against) the national liberation movement, in order to overthrow the rule of the government which had previously been administering the territory peacefully. Some Third World writers and diplomats have tried to get round this objection by looking at the issue in a longer historical perspective and by arguing that the original acquisition of colonies by European states[240] involved the use of force and that colonialism therefore constitutes a form of permanent or continuing aggression. But not all colonies were acquired by conquest; some were acquired by cession from native rulers, or by other peaceful means. Even when colonies were acquired by conquest, the conquest was lawful under the rules of international law which existed at the time[241] and was completed a long time ago. It is absurd to suggest that a right of collective self-defence can be exercised today against an attack which was successfully and lawfully completed centuries ago; one might just as well argue that the United Kingdom can now reopen the hostilities with France in response to the Norman Conquest of 1066.[242]

New developments

The problems of minorities and of the special category of indigenous peoples,[243] which have been addressed in Chapter 6 above,[244] have led to a vivid discussion as to whether such groups have a right to self-determination or whether a new definition of self-determination is required to accommodate extreme situations.[245] The debate was reinforced by the minority problems arising in Yugoslavia and Eastern Europe after the break-up of the USSR.[246] Contemporary international law for the protection of minorities offers only a rather rudimentary framework built around the cornerstone of the general rules on non-discrimination in combination with Article 27 of the Covenant on Civil and Political Rights, which provides:

> In those States in which ethnic, religious or linguistic minorities exist, persons belonging to such minorities shall not be denied the right, in community with the other members of their group, to enjoy their culture, to profess and practise their own religion, or to use their own language.[247]

It implies that minorities, at least in principle, do not have a right to secession (in the sense of 'external' self-determination); they are restricted to a right of some form of autonomy within the given state structure (sometimes called 'internal' self-determination).

This conclusion is supported by the wording of Article 27 of the Political Covenant which does not grant minorities a right to secession, but only limited rights to 'enjoy their own culture, to profess and practise their own religion, or to use their own language'. Minorities are not, as such, recognized as legal subjects of international law.[248] Even the rights in Article 27 are formulated as individual rights, rights of the members belonging to a minority, and not as a collective right, although there is a tendency in the literature to move towards a group-orientated view.[249] The right of self-determination, in Article 1 of the Covenant, is reserved to 'peoples'. From the text, a systematic interpretation and the drafting history of this document, it is clear that, at least in the sense of the right to secession, self-determination is not a right of minorities in existing states, not even of ethnic ones with a relatively clear territorial basis within a state. This is confirmed by later pertinent instruments, including the Friendly Relations Declaration[250] and the 1992 UN Declaration on Minorities,[251] all of which, when granting certain rights, place emphasis on the preservation of the territorial integrity of States. Article 8(4) of the 1992 Declaration notes: 'Nothing in the present Declaration may be construed as permitting any activity contrary to the purposes and principles of the United Nations, including sovereign equality, territorial integrity and political independence of States.' The right to self-determination and to secession is not mentioned in the Declaration. International law also excludes a right of neighbouring 'mother countries' to intervene by force under the title or pretext of protecting sections of the population of other states with which they have a particular affiliation, as was, for example, invoked by Hitler in the case of the Sudeten Germans to begin the conquest of Czechoslovakia.

Again, neither the Covenant nor any other provision of international law prohibits minorities (as any other group in a state) from seeking secession. In principle, to put it crudely, from the viewpoint of international law, the armed struggle of a minority for independence is nothing more than a civil war, the outcome of which has to be awaited, except for those rules relevant to internal armed conflict and limits imposed by human rights standards.[252] Thus, other states are entitled to recognize the successful secession of a minority, unless it has come about by the military intervention of third parties. The case of Bangladesh (former East Pakistan) which declared its independence in March 1971 is a special one, because India's military intervention in October 1971 in the civil war and its armed conflict with Pakistan was caused, *inter alia*, by the tremendous burden caused by about ten million refugees (90 per cent of whom were Hindus) who had fled to India. It must also be seen against the background of the conflict between India and Pakistan over Kashmir. (Pakistan recognized the independence of Bangladesh in February 1974.[253])

In the literature, one finds a variety of proposals for an interpretation of the right of minorities to self-determination which go beyond these results. Some propositions are rather radical, trying to turn the fact that the world has recently seen an increasing number of victorious secessionist movements into a general right under international law, by advocating the need for a new interpretation of a 'post-colonial right of self-determination'.[254] Such proposals, however, are neither desirable, nor are they realistic. They are undesirable because the prospect of an infinite

248 See Chapter 6 above, 105–8.

249 See the survey given by Lerner, The Evolution of Minority Rights in International Law, in Brölmann/Lefeber/Zieck (eds), *op. cit.*, at 88 *et seq.*

250 UNGA Res. 2625 (XXV), *op. cit.*

251 UNGA Res. 47/135 of 18 December 1992, *ILM* 32 (1993), 911. See Chapter 6 above, 105.

252 See Chapter 20 below, 352–3.

253 See R. Geiger, Kashmir, *EPIL* 12 (1990), 195–200; A. Siehr, Conflicts, Indian Subcontinent, in *Wolfrum UNLPP* I, 243–54.

254 Noted by Franck (1993), *op. cit.*, at 12.

255 Similarly Higgins, Postmodern Tribalism and the Right to Secession, Comments, in Brölmann/Lefeber/Zieck (eds), *op. cit.*, at 35; E. Amitai, The Evils of Self-Determination, *FP* 89 (1992–3), 28 *et seq.*

256 S. Oeter, Selbstbestimmungsrecht im Wandel – Überlegungen zur Debatte um Selbstbestimmung, Sezessionsrecht und 'vorzeitige' Anerkennung, *ZaöRV* 52 (1992), 741–80, at 778.

257 Franck (1993), *op. cit.*, 13–14.

258 See T. Schweisfurth, *FAZ*, 20 January 1995, 13; M.R. Lucas, The War in Chechnya and the OSCE Code of Conduct, *HM* 6/2 (1995), 32–42.

259 See F.M. Hussein, *The Legal Concept of Self-Determination and the Kurdish Question*, 1985; P. Malanczuk, The Kurdish Crisis and Allied Intervention in the Aftermath of the Second Gulf War, *EJIL* 2 (1991), 114–32; O. Bring, Kurdistan and the Principle of Self-Determination, *GYIL* 35 (1992), 157–69; Malanczuk (1993), *op. cit.*, 17 *et seq.*; P. Akhavan, Lessons from Iraqi Kurdistan: Self-Determination and Humanitarian Intervention against Genocide, *NQHR* 1 (1993), 41–62; R. Falk, Problems and Prospects for the Kurdish Struggle for Self-Determination After the End of the Gulf and Cold Wars, *Mich. JIL* 15 (1994), 591–604. See also Chapter 22 below, 399–402.

260 See Chapter 10, 162–3 and text, 335 above.

cycle of the creation of numerous new states, many of which seem hardly viable in economic and political terms, would undermine the international order – in the absence of an unlikely world government – and strangle the existing international institutions. If we have 3,000 or more 'minorities', in- or excluding 'indigenous peoples', are we to support the idea of having as many entities claiming the right to become states and members of the United Nations and still expect the organization to function? In addition, in many cases the recognition of the right of secession of minorities would lead to new minorities then being submitted to the rule of the separatist government.[255] It is also not realistic because states are unlikely to agree to dig their own grave and accept a general entitlement of internal groups to secession as a legal principle threatening their territorial integrity.

But there are also more modest proposals focusing on certain extreme and exceptional situations. Some authors argue that, if internal conflict between a government and an ethnic group has escalated into genocidal actions, as a means of last resort, 'secession becomes a legitimate response which should be shielded by the international community'.[256]

A particularly interesting reasoning has been advanced by Thomas Franck, who finds that in circumstances in which

a minority within a sovereign state – especially if it occupies a discrete territory within that state – persistently and egregiously is denied political and social equality and the opportunity to retain its cultural identity . . . it is conceivable that international law will define such repression, prohibited by the Political Covenant, as coming within a somewhat stretched definition of colonialism. Such repression, even by an independent state not normally thought to be 'imperial' would then give rise to a right of 'decolonization'.[257]

It is submitted that these are only proposals *de lege ferenda*, which are not likely to succeed in practice. There is not much hope currently of fundamental changes in the international regime protecting minorities even on the regional European level in view of the resistance of important states to accept the most modest reform proposals. The source of this reluctance is, of course, the fear of destabilization and disintegration affecting the territorial integrity and sovereignty of states, if more far-reaching rights were granted to certain sections of the population. The experience of Russian intervention in Chechnya and the reaction of other states is particularly illuminating. Western states have limited themselves, so it seems, in the interest of not further destabilizing Yeltsin and the process of economic and political reform in Russia, to criticizing the disproportionality of the attacks on the civilian population, but have insisted that the matter is, in principle, within the domestic affairs of the Russian Federation.[258] Similarly, one could point to the fate of the Kurds.[259] Even in the case of Eritrea, which seceded from Ethiopia with the consent of the new government, after Colonel Menghistu had been overthrown, and on the basis of the recognition of the right to self-determination and secession in the new Constitution of Ethiopia, the reaction of other states in Africa was that of concern regarding an unfavourable precedent, in view of the principle of *uti posseditis*.[260]

The effectiveness of the modern rules against the use of force

261 See K.J. Partsch, Israel and the Arab States, *EPIL* II (1995), 1460–8.

For over fifty years since 1945 the world has been relatively free from international wars, despite the existence of acute political tensions which would almost certainly have led to war in previous ages. Such fighting as has occurred has mostly taken the form of civil wars, although there is always a danger that civil wars will escalate into international wars, as the war in Vietnam did in the 1960s. It would be foolish to suggest that international law is largely responsible for the infrequency of wars; the destructiveness of modern warfare is a much more potent factor. The popular revulsion against the destructiveness of modern war gave rise to rules of law against the use of force; but those rules have in turn served to augment popular revulsion against war (just as laws against homicide are simultaneously a consequence and a cause of popular revulsion against homicide).

The biggest defect in the modern rules is that they are often imprecise. Practice has done little to reduce this imprecision. Many states want to retain the possibility of using force in certain circumstances, but they know that an interpretation which allowed them to do so would also allow other states to use force against them; so they 'keep their options open' by failing to adopt a clear attitude towards the problem of interpretation. In moments of crisis a state will be tempted to exploit such uncertainties in the law; its sense of objectivity will be lost, and it may genuinely come to believe that a doubtful interpretation which suits its interests is well founded. In theory the organs of the United Nations ought to strengthen and clarify the rules by deciding whether they have been broken in particular cases. But sometimes the member states of the United Nations which consider that a particular state has acted legally are as numerous as those which consider that it has acted illegally, and in such cases the United Nations is unable to reach any decision (for instance, it was for this reason that the United Nations adopted a 'neutral' attitude to the fighting between Israel and its neighbours in 1967 and 1973[261]). Sometimes, moreover, a state may hope to escape censure at the United Nations if it uses force on a small scale (for example, the Indonesian 'confrontation' with Malaysia in 1963–6), or if it achieves a quick victory which presents the world with a *fait accompli* (for example, the Arab–Israeli Six-Day War in June 1967).

But although there are cases where the rules are unclear, and where the United Nations adopts ambiguous attitudes, there are also other cases where the law is perfectly clear; the rules may be blurred around the edges, but they have a hard core of certainty. And in cases of this second type the law exercises a real restraining influence on the actions of states.

20 Means of waging war and criminal responsibility: *ius in bello*

1 W. Meng, War, *EPIL* 4 (1982), 28; F. Kalshoven, War, Laws of, *ibid.*, 316–23; F. Kalshoven, *Constraints on the Waging of War*, 1987; F. de Mulinen, *Handbook on the Law of War for Armed Forces*, 1987; I. Detter DeLupis, *The Law of War*, 1988; D. Schindler/J. Toman (eds), *The Laws of Armed Conflicts: A Collection of Conventions, Resolutions and Other Documents*, 3rd edn 1988; A. Roberts/R. Guelff (eds), *Documents on the Laws of War*, 2nd edn 1989, 491–7; H. McCoubrey, *International Humanitarian Law*, 1990; A.J.M. Delissen/G.J. Tanja (eds), *Humanitarian Law of Armed Conflict: Challenges Ahead: Essays in Honour of Frits Kalshoven*, 1991; K.J. Partsch, Armed Conflict, *EPIL* I (1992), 249–53; Partsch, Armed Conflict, Fundamental Rules, *ibid.*, 253–6; F. Kalshoven, Prohibitions or Restrictions on the Methods and Means of Warfare (with comments by R. Lagoni and G.J.F.v. Hegelsom), in I.F. Dekker/H.H.G. Post (eds), *The Gulf War of 1980–1988*, 1992, 97 *et seq.*; H. McCoubrey/N.D. White, *International Law and Armed Conflict*, 1992; D.A. Wells, *The Laws of Land Warfare: A Guide to the U.S. Army Manuals*, 1992; E. Playfair (ed.), *International Law and the Administration of Occupied Territories*, 1992; J.G. Gardam, *Non-Combatant Immunity as a Norm of International Humanitarian Law*, 1993; E. Benevisti, *The International Law of Occupation*, 1993; L.C. Green, *The Contemporary Law of Armed Conflict*, 1993; D. Fleck (ed.), *The Handbook in Humanitarian Law in Armed Conflicts*, 1995; H.H.G. Post (ed.), *International Economic Law and Armed Conflict*, 1994; Y. Dinstein, *War, Aggression and Self-Defence*, 2nd edn 1994; M.S. McDougal/F.P. Feliciano, *The International Law of War: Transnational Coercion and World Public Order*, 1994; H.H.G. Post, Some Curiosities in the Sources of the Law of Armed Conflict Conceived in a General International Legal Perspective, *NYIL* 25

This chapter deals with the rules governing the actual conduct of hostilities, once an armed conflict has broken out (*ius in bello*).[1] For most purposes, this body of law can be treated as separate from the rules governing the resort to the use of armed force (*ius ad bellum*).[2] The basic reason is the consideration that, if it is not possible to fully prevent war (and history so far shows that it is indeed not possible), then at least warfare should be made subject to certain humanitarian restrictions in the interest of protecting, for example, prisoners, the wounded and the civilian population, or by prohibiting certain kinds of weapons.

There are a number of problems concerning the situations in which this body of law becomes applicable. On the one hand, although formal declarations of war are no longer a criterion because they have become uncommon,[3] still the distinction between a situation of 'war' or 'peace', between armed conflict and non-armed conflict, is not always easy to make. On the other hand, the rules pertaining to international armed conflict do not necessarily fully apply to non-international armed conflict, such as in the case of civil wars. The term 'international humanitarian law', which is frequently used to describe the area dealt with in this chapter, suggests that there is some synthesis between the laws of war and international human rights.[4] But that is far from being generally accepted, simply because it is quite unclear which of these human rights actually apply in times of war (which does not mean that human rights instruments are entirely irrelevant to situations of armed conflict and military occupation).

Finally, it should be noted that the legal issues of disarmament and arms control, including the problems of the demilitarization or neutralization of certain areas, are beyond the scope of the following.[5] They are not directly relevant to the actual conduct of armed conflict.

Lawful and unlawful means of waging war

The eighteenth and nineteenth centuries, which saw the abandonment of any attempt by international law to restrict the right of states to go to war, also saw the growth of rules regulating the way in which wars should be fought.[6] Nor was this a coincidence; in the days when the theory of the just war had been dominant, each side had usually considered that the other side's cause was unjust, and it had therefore tended to treat the other side as mere bandits, lacking any right to fair treatment.

To many people it seems a paradox that war, the ultimate breakdown in law and order, should be fought in accordance with rules of law; why should a nation fighting for survival allow its struggle to be impeded by legal restrictions? Part of the answer lies in the fact that nations did not regard themselves as fighting for survival in the eighteenth and nineteenth centuries. Wars were seldom fought for ideological reasons and tended not to rouse the same intensity of passion as twentieth century wars. In an age when governments interfered little with the lives of their subjects, a change of sovereignty over territory had little effect on the way of life of the inhabitants, who consequently tended to be philosophical about the prospect of defeat in war. In any case, the balance-of-power system[7] deterred the territorial aggrandizement of states and therefore limited the territorial changes which would otherwise have resulted from wars. The balance-of-power system also necessitated flexibility in political alignments and meant that a state's enemy today might be its ally tomorrow; this naturally had a restraining effect on the degree of brutality practised in wars, because states did not want to arouse undying bitterness among potential allies.

Even more important than these political considerations was the fact that the laws of war were designed mainly to prevent unnecessary suffering. 'Unnecessary suffering' meant suffering which would produce no military advantage, or a military advantage which was very small in comparison with the amount of suffering involved. However, there were a few exceptions to this general rule; for instance, it was and still is forbidden to torture prisoners in order to obtain information, although the military advantage could be enormous in certain cases. Violations of the laws of war were therefore rare, because the military advantage to be gained by breaking those laws was almost always outweighed by disadvantages such as reprisals, loss of neutral goodwill, and so on.

Wars in the eighteenth and nineteenth centuries were wars between armed forces, rather than wars between peoples. 'The destruction of the enemy's military force is the foundation-stone of all action in war,' wrote Clausewitz, the greatest military writer of the nineteenth century.[8] It was therefore easy for international law to protect civilians. But the protection was never absolute; for instance, an army besieging a town was entitled to hasten the fall of the town by preventing food from entering the town and by preventing civilian inhabitants from leaving. In other words, the army compelled the town to surrender by starving the civilian inhabitants. Moreover, Clausewitz explained that 'destruction of the enemy's military power' meant that 'the military power must be . . . reduced to such a state as not to be able to prosecute the war'; 'the aim of all action in war is to disarm the enemy'. Consequently, rules grew up to protect even members of the armed forces who were *hors de combat* – the sick and wounded, prisoners of war, and so on.[9] Although Clausewitz said that the laws of war were 'almost imperceptible and hardly worth mentioning', the reason for their imperceptibility was that they accorded so perfectly with the limits of military necessity:[10] 'if we find civilized nations do not put their prisoners to death, do not devastate towns and countries, this is because their intelligence . . . has taught them more effectual means of applying force than these rude acts of mere instinct.'

In the second half of the nineteenth century states began to issue manuals of military law, containing a restatement of the laws of war, for use by

(1994), 83–118; K.J. Partsch, Humanitarian Law and Armed Conflict, *EPIL* II (1995), 933–6; H. Risse, Humanitarian Law in Armed Conflicts, in *Wolfrum UNLPP I*, 638–45; A.P. Rogers, *Law on the Battlefield*, 1996.

2 See Chapter 19 above, 306.

3 See Chapter 19 above, 308.

4 K.J. Partsch, Human Rights and Humanitarian Law, *EPIL* II (1995), 910–12. On human rights, see Chapter 14 above, 209–21.

5 See C. Blacker/G. Duffy (eds), *International Arms Control, Issues and Agreements*, 1984; J.H. Barton, Disarmament, *EPIL* I (1992), 1072–6; J. Kolasa, *Disarmament and Arms Control Agreements – A Study on Procedural and Institutional Law*, 1995; J. Debrück, Arms Control, in *Wolfrum UNLPP I*, 39–47; T. Roeser, Arms, Trade in, *ibid.*, 49–54; O. Kimminich, Disarmament, *ibid.*, 407–17; W. Lang, Compliance with Disarmament Obligations, *ZaöRV* 55 (1995), 69–88.

6 See Chapter 2 above, 21–2.

7 See Chapter 2 above, 11.

8 C.P.G.v. Clausewitz, *Vom Kriege*, 1832–4.

9 A. Randelzhofer, Civilian Objects, *EPIL* I (1992), 603–6; A.-M. de Zayas, Civilian Population, Protection, *ibid.*, 606–11; Y. Dinstein, Prisoners of War, *EPIL* 4 (1982), 146–52; M. Bothe, Wounded, Sick and Shipwrecked, *ibid.*, 356–8. See also on the *Trial of Pakistani Prisoners of War Case*, ICJ *Rep.* 1973, 327 and 346, and K. Oellers-Frahm, *EPIL* 2 (1981), 280–1.

10 Y. Dinstein, Military Necessity, *EPIL* 3 (1982), 274–6.

11 See P. Malanczuk, American Civil War, EPIL I (1992), 129–31. For other examples, see Roberts/Guelff (eds), op. cit., 7.

12 AJIL 1 (1907) Supplement 89–90.

13 Texts of the Geneva Conventions of 1864 and 1906 in 129 CTS 361, 202 CTS 144; the 1907 Hague Conventions IV–XIII are reprinted in Roberts/Guelff (eds), op. cit., 43–119. See M. Bothe, Land Warfare, EPIL 3 (1982), 239–42; Y. Dinstein, Sea Warfare, EPIL 4 (1982), 201–12. See also Chapter 2 above, 21–2.

14 1930 London Naval Treaty, 112 LNTS 65; 1936 London Protocol, 173 LNTS 353, 353–7; AJIL 31 (1937) Supplement, 137–9. See also K. Zemanek, Submarine Warfare, EPIL 4 (1982), 233–5.

15 94 LNTS 65; AJIL 25 (1931) Supplement, 94–6. See E. Rauch, Biological Warfare, EPIL I (1992), 404–7; M. Bothe, Chemical Warfare, ibid., 566–9.

16 Texts in 249 UNTS 240, 249 UNTS 358.

17 ILM 11 (1972), 310.

18 ILM 16 (1977), 88. See M. Bothe, War and Environment, EPIL 4 (1982), 290–3.

19 Conference on Prohibitions or Restrictions on the Use of Certain Conventional Weapons, Final Act, ILM 19 (1980), 1523. See W.A. Soll, Weapons, Prohibited, EPIL 4 (1982), 352–4; M.A. Meyer (ed.), Armed Conflict and the New Law: Aspects of the 1977 Geneva Protocols and the 1981 Weapons Convention, 1989.

20 Text in ILM 35 (1996), 1206. See L. Doswald-Beck, New Protocol on Blinding Laser Weapons, IRRC 36 (1996), 272–99, and the report and documentation by P. Herby, ibid., 361 et seq.; K. Dörmann, The First Review Conference to the 1980 Convention on Prohibitions or Restrictions on the Use of Certain Conventional Weapons Which May Be Deemed to be Excessively Injurious or to Have Indiscriminate Effects – A Story of Failure?, HV 8 (1995), 203–11.

21 1929 Geneva Conventions I–II, 118 LNTS 303; 1949 Geneva Conventions I–IV, 75 UNTS 31, 75 UNTS 85, 75 UNTS 135 and 75 UNTS 287; 1977 Protocols I–II, 1125 UNTS 3 and 1125 UNTS 609. The four Geneva Conventions replaced three earlier humanitarian conventions of 1906 and 1929. See A. Schlögel, Geneva Red Cross Conventions and Protocols, EPIL II (1995), 531–4.

22 See T. Meron, The Continuing Role

their commanders in the field. A famous example is the Lieber Code. It was prepared by Dr Francis Lieber from Columbia University in 1863 as the 'Instructions for the Government of Armies of the United States in the Field'.[11] Such manuals led to greater respect for the laws of war, as well as more precision in their formulation. At the same time, the laws of war, which had hitherto been derived almost entirely from customary law, began to be codified and extended by treaties. The first agreement was the 1856 Paris Declaration Respecting Maritime Law.[12] The chief treaties were the Geneva Conventions of 1864 and 1906: the Convention for the Amelioration of the Condition of the Wounded in Armies in the Field and the Convention for the Amelioration of the Condition of the Wounded and Sick in Armies in the Field, the three Hague Conventions of 1899 (mainly on the law of land and maritime warfare), and the thirteen Hague Conventions of 1907, which dealt with most of the remaining aspects of the laws of war.[13] Although these treaties were of course binding only on the states which became parties to them, nearly all of them stated rules which either were already part of customary law or subsequently came to be accepted as new customary law.

Since the First World War further treaties on the laws of war have been concluded from time to time. The London Treaty of 1930 and the Protocol of 1936 sought to regulate the use of submarines;[14] the Geneva Protocol of 1925 prohibited the use of gas and bacteriological warfare;[15] a convention and a protocol was signed at The Hague in 1954 for the protection of cultural property (for example, works of art) in the event of armed conflict;[16] a convention of 1972 prohibited the use and possession of bacteriological (biological) and toxin weapons;[17] a convention of 1977 prohibited the military use of environmental modification techniques;[18] and a convention and three protocols were signed in 1980 to limit the use of cruel or indiscriminate non-nuclear weapons, such as incendiary weapons (for example, napalm), land-mines and booby-traps, particularly their use against civilians.[19] The First Review Conference of the 1980 Convention on Certain Conventional Weapons, held in 1995, adopted new protocols on blinding laser weapons and land-mines.[20] More important, however, are the two Geneva Conventions of 1929 for the protection of sick and wounded soldiers, of sick and wounded sailors and of prisoners of war, and the four Geneva Conventions of 1949 for the protection of sick and wounded soldiers, of sick and wounded sailors, of prisoners of war and of civilians, together with two protocols of 1977 which supplements the 1949 Conventions.[21] The scope of the Civilians' Convention is much less than its name implies; it is mainly concerned with protecting only two classes of civilians: those who find themselves in enemy territory at the outbreak of war, and those who inhabit territory which is overrun and occupied by the enemy during the war. But the Convention does contain some provisions which apply to all civilians, wherever they may be; for instance, it prohibits attacks on civilian hospitals. Articles 48–60 of the First Protocol of 1977 go much further in protecting civilians against attacks.

Ratification of such treaties by states varies considerably.[22] States have been reluctant to ratify conventions of the type formulated at The Hague. The 1980 Convention prohibiting the use of certain weapons, for example, has only fifty-seven parties (1995), and some of its protocols even less. The 1925 Geneva Protocol for the Prohibition of the Use in War of Asphyxiating, Poisonous or Other Gases, and of Bacteriological Methods of Warfare has 145 parties (1995). The recent Convention on the Prohibition of the Development, Production, Stockpiling and Use of Chemical Weapons and on Their Destruction, which will enter into force on 29 April 1997, 180 days after the deposit of the sixty-fifth instrument of ratification (by Hungary in 1996), has so far been signed by only 100 states.[23] Moreover, many types of weapons are still not regulated at all by treaties. The most positive result has so far been achieved in the case of the 1949 Geneva Conventions where ratification is now virtually universal (1996: 186 states).[24] In the case of the 1977 Additional Protocol I, however, far fewer states have decided to become parties (1996: 134 states).[25] With the accession of Cyprus on 18 March 1996 to the 1977 Additional Protocol II, the number of states party to the Protocol reached 135.[26] It is notable that only forty-seven states have so far made the declaration provided for under Article 90 of Protocol I recognizing the competence of an International Fact-Finding Commission to inquire into allegations made by other state parties of a violation of the Protocol.[27]

The codification of the laws of war in treaties did not diminish the continuing role of customary principles. This is expressed in the so-called 'Martens Clause' which was laid down in the Preamble to the 1899 Hague Convention II:

> Until a more complete code of the laws of war is issued, the high contracting Parties think it right to declare that in cases not included in the Regulations adopted by them, populations and belligerents remain under the protection and empire of the principles of international law, as they result from the usages established between civilised nations, from the laws of humanity and the requirements of the public conscience.[28]

The creation of new law by treaties has tended to lag far behind the development of military technology. For instance, until the First Protocol of 1977 there was no treaty dealing with the bombing of civilians. This would not have mattered much if the customary law on the subject had been clear, but it was not. State practice concerning the laws of war develops mainly during wartime, and therefore lacks continuity; major wars are infrequent, and nowadays technological changes occur so rapidly that each war differs radically from the previous war. It is also difficult to establish an *opinio iuris*,[29] because states seldom give legal reasons for what they do in wartime. Nor do war crimes trials do much to clarify the law.[30] For instance, not a single German was prosecuted after the Second World War for organizing mass bombing raids; it is understandable that the Allies were reluctant to prosecute Germans for doing what the Allies had also done on an even larger scale, but the result is that there is no judicial pronouncement on the legality of bombing.[31] Meanwhile, the Hague Conventions of 1899 and 1907 are still technically in force, but the fact that many of their provisions are manifestly inappropriate to modern conditions has often tempted states to break them.

of Custom in the Formation of International Humanitarian Law, *AJIL* 90 (1996), 238–49, 245 *et seq.*

23 1993 Chemical Weapons Convention, *ILM* 32 (1993), 800. The signatory states have established a Preparatory Commission in The Hague. See T. Taylor, The Chemical Weapons Convention and Prospects for Implementation, *ICLQ* 42 (1993), 912–19; D. Bardonnet (ed.), *The Convention on the Prohibition and Elimination of Chemical Weapons*, 1994; W. Krutzsch/R. Trapp, *A Commentary on the Chemical Weapons Convention*, 1994.

24 *IRRC* 36 (1996), no. 311, 255.

25 See G.H. Aldrich, Prospects for United States Ratification of Additional Protocol I to the 1949 Geneva Conventions, *AJIL* 85 (1991), 1–20; T. Meron, The Time Has Come for the United States to Ratify Geneva Protocol I, *AJIL* 88 (1994), 678–86; A.P. Rubin, Correspondence on United States's Ratification of Geneva Protocol I, *AJIL* 89 (1995), 363–5.

26 *IRRC* 36 (1996), no. 311, 247, 255.

27 *Ibid.*, 256–7. See also E. Kussbach, The International Humanitarian Fact-Finding Commission, *ICLQ* 43 (1994), 174–84. On fact-finding, see also Chapter 18 above, 277–8.

28 Cited in Roberts/Guelff (eds), *op. cit.*, 4. A common article in each of the 1949 Geneva Conventions draws upon the text of the Martens Clause: I (Article 63), II (Article 62), III (Article 142), IV (Article 158). See also Article 1 of the 1977 Additional Protocol I and the Preamble to Additional Protocol II. See further T. Meron, On Custom and the Antecedents of the Martens Clause in Medieval and Renaissance Ordinances of War, in *FS Bernhardt*, 173–7. On Martens, see V. Pustogarov, Fyodor Fyodorovich Martens (1845–1909) – A Humanist of Modern Times, *IRRC* 36 (1996), 300–14.

29 For a specific example of the problem, see E.J. Wallach, The Use of Crude Oil by an Occupying Belligerent State as a Munition de Guerre, *ICLQ* 41 (1992), 387–10. On the relevance of *opinio iuris* for the formation of customary law, see Chapter 3 above, 44–5. But see for this special area, Meron (1996), *op. cit.*

30 See text below, 353–61.

31 See T. Bruha, Bombardment, *EPIL* I (1992), 419–22.

32 GA Res. 1653 (XVI), 24 November 1961, *UNYb* 1961, 30–1. See also, for example, the later resolutions of the General Assembly on 'Non-Use of Force in International Relations and Permanent Prohibition of the Use of Nuclear Weapons', UNGA Res. 2936 (XXVII) of 29 November 1972; 'Non-Use of Nuclear Weapons and Prevention of Nuclear War', UNGA Res. 36/92 (I) of 9 December 1981. See further H. Blix, Area Bombardment: Rules and Reasons, *BYIL* 49 (1978), 31–69; D. Rauschning, Nuclear Warfare and Weapons, *EPIL* 4 (1982), 44–50; I. Pogany (ed.), *Nuclear Weapons and International Law*, 1987; N. Singh/E. McWhinney, *Nuclear Weapons and Contemporary International Law*, 2nd edn 1988; E.L. Meyrowitz, *The Prohibition of Nuclear Weapons: The Relevance of International Law*, 1990; W.R. Hearn, The International Legal Regime Regulating Nuclear Deterrence and Warfare, *BYIL* 61 (1990), 199 *et seq.*; Nuclear Weapons and the Right to Survival, Peace and Development, *Denver JILP* 19 (1990), no. 1 (Special Issue); B. Graefrath, Der aktuelle Stand der völkerrechtlichen Diskussion zur Legalität von Nuklearwaffeneinsätzen, *HV* 8 (1995), 124–7.

33 See text below, 351–2.

34 See Chapter 3 above, 52–4.

There are two further factors which have encouraged violations of the laws of war during the twentieth century. In the first place, the First and Second World Wars produced more bitter feelings than previous wars; they were fought for ideological reasons, and for virtually unlimited objectives. Belligerent states no longer sought to achieve a delicate adjustment to the balance of power, but adopted a policy of unconditional surrender, which naturally spurred on the other side to fight to the death. Second, economic and technological changes vastly increased the military advantage to be gained by breaking the laws of war. (There are exceptions, of course; for instance, killing prisoners of war still produces little military advantage, and the relevant rules of law therefore stand a good chance of surviving.) In particular, the distinction between the armed forces and civilians is largely illusory, now that the whole of a country's economy is geared to the war effort. Destruction of factories, and even the killing of factory workers, produces a military advantage which would have been inconceivable in earlier times; and the invention of the aircraft has given belligerent states the means to carry out such acts.

Nuclear weapons

In 1961 the United Nations General Assembly passed a resolution declaring that the use of nuclear weapons was illegal.[32] fifty-five states (consisting mainly of communist and Third World countries) voted in favour of the resolution, twenty states (consisting mainly of Western countries) voted against, and twenty-six states (consisting mainly of Latin American countries) abstained. The divergence between the positions of the communist and Western countries is explained by the fact that the Soviet superiority in conventional (that is, non-nuclear) forces in Europe was so great (before the withdrawal of the Red Army from Eastern Europe) that the Western countries would have been compelled to use nuclear weapons in order to defend themselves against an invasion of Western Europe by Soviet conventional forces; consequently, the Western countries argued that the use of nuclear weapons is not contrary to international law. The Soviet Union, on the other hand, was able to win Third World goodwill by subscribing to the view that the use of nuclear weapons is illegal, because it knew that it would not need to be the first state to use them; if Western countries had used them first, the Soviet Union would have been able to justify its own use of nuclear weapons by means of the doctrine of reprisals.[33]

A General Assembly resolution of this type is, at the most, merely evidence of customary law,[34] but the voting figures for this resolution show the absence of a generally accepted custom. The Western powers, at any rate, are probably entitled to claim that the resolution has no legal effect on them, since they have consistently repudiated the ideas stated in it.

Certain rules of international law might be extended by analogy to deal with nuclear weapons. For instance, Article 23(a) of the Hague Regulations 1907 declares that it is forbidden 'to employ poison or poisoned weapons', and the Geneva Gas Protocol 1925 prohibits 'the use in war of asphyxiating, poisonous or other gases, and of all analogous liquids, materials or devices'. It is arguable that the fall-out caused by nuclear weapons resembles poison, but the analogy is not close enough to be absolutely compelling; fall-out is only a side-effect of nuclear weapons, whereas poisoning is the main (if not the sole) effect of using poison gas.

Alternatively, nuclear weapons could be compared with the mass bombing raids of the Second World War; but there was no treaty prohibiting those raids, and it would be difficult to argue that they were contrary to customary law, in the light of the extensive use of them by both sides in the Second World War. If Articles 48–60 of the First Protocol of 1977 had been in force during the Second World War, they would have prohibited many of the bombing raids which occurred during that war. Article 48 of the 1977 Protocol I states as a basic rule:

> In order to ensure respect for and protection of the civilian population and civilian objects, the Parties to the conflict shall at all times distinguish between the civilian population and combatants and between civilian objects and military objectives and accordingly shall direct their operations only against military objectives.[35]

But the United States, when signing the First Protocol in 1977, placed on record its 'understanding . . . that the rules established by this Protocol were not intended to have any effect on and do not regulate or prohibit the use of nuclear weapons'.[36] Similar statements were made by the British and French governments.

There remains the underlying principle that acts of war should not cause unnecessary suffering, that is, suffering out of all proportion to the military advantage to be gained from those acts. Nuclear weapons cause enormous suffering, but they can also produce an enormous military advantage; if nuclear weapons had not been used against Japan in 1945, the war against Japan might have lasted at least another year.[37] It would therefore be unwise to conclude that the use of nuclear weapons is unlawful in all circumstances.

But, even if we accept that the use of nuclear weapons is sometimes lawful, this does not mean that the laws of war restricting the use of 'conventional' weapons are obsolete. To drop a nuclear bomb on a city may be lawful because the military advantage gained by destroying military installations, factories, means of communication, and so on, outweighs the suffering; but to drop a conventional bomb deliberately on a school or hospital in the same city would be illegal, because there would be no military advantage to outweigh the suffering. Thus, while the international community, including the nuclear powers, has not yet arrived at an explicit agreement concerning the use or non-use of nuclear weapons, this does not mean that the general principles and other customary rules of the laws of war which apply to the use of weapons and methods of warfare are irrelevant. In fact, the United States and the United Kingdom have at times confirmed that they are applicable.[38]

The issue of the legality of the use of nuclear weapons was brought before the International Court of Justice on the basis of two requests for an advisory opinion, one filed by the World Health Organization (WHO) on 3 September 1993, the other filed by the UN General Assembly on 6 January 1996. As it was doubtful whether the request on the question of legality of

35 See F.A.F.v.d. Heydte, Military Objectives, *EPIL* 3 (1982), 276–9.
36 *AJIL* 72 (1978), 407.
37 But see the recent discussion among historians, Chapter 2 above, 26.
38 See Roberts/Guelff (eds), *op. cit.*, 18–9.

39 The question set forth in the resolution (WHA 46.40), adopted by the WHO Assembly on 14 May 1993, was as follows: 'In view of the health and environmental effects, would the use of nuclear weapons by a State in war or other armed conflict be a breach of its obligations under international law including the WHO Constitution?'

40 UNGA Res. 49/75K. On the background and the procedural issues, see M. Lailach, The General Assembly's Request for an Advisory Opinion From the International Court of Justice on the Legality of the Threat or Use of Nuclear Weapons, *LJIL* 8 (1995), 401–29.

41 See text above, 345.

42 For the list of participants, see *ILM* 35 (1996), 816.

43 *ICJ Advisory Opinion on the Legality of the Threat or Use of Nuclear Weapons*, *ILM* 35 (1996), 809. Further Declarations and Separate Opinions of Judges are reproduced in *ILM* 35 (1996), 1343. On the case, see also Chapters 3, 42, 45, 50, 53–4 and 19, 317 above.

44 On the limited legal personality of international organizations, see Chapter 6 above, 91–3.

45 ICJ Advisory Opinion, *op. cit.*

the use by a state of nuclear weapons in armed conflict submitted by the WHO was within the mandate of the WHO,[39] it was supplemented by the request from the UN General Assembly which has the competence to ask the Court any kind of legal question. The request was embodied in General Assembly resolution 49/75K, adopted on 15 December 1994, in which the General Assembly decided, acting on the basis of Article 96(1) of the UN Charter, to ask the ICJ 'urgently to render its advisory opinion on the following question: "Is the threat or use of nuclear weapons in any circumstance permitted under international law?"'[40]

This case is interesting because combined pressure from NGOs and a majority of states managed to overcome the strong resistance of the great nuclear powers, in particular the United States, the UK and France, and to put the question to the Court. The International Court of Justice received a petition signed by more than one million persons declaring themselves against the legality of nuclear weapons with reference, *inter alia*, to the 'Martens Clause'.[41] During the public hearings in the Peace Palace in The Hague, which took place from 30 October to 15 November 1995, the majority of the twenty-one states and the WHO taking part expressed their opposition against the legality of these weapons. The Japanese delegation included the mayors of the cities of Hiroshima and Nagasaki.[42]

On 8 July 1996, the Court delivered its advisory opinions on both requests. The request made by the WHO was dismissed (by eleven votes to three)[43] with the reasoning that under the 'principle of speciality', which governs international organizations and limits their powers,[44] the WHO had no competence to deal with the *legality* of the use of nuclear weapons, even in view of their health and environmental effects.[45] With regard to the request filed by the General Assembly, different majorities emerged among the judges concerning different steps of the decision. The Court found that there is neither in customary nor conventional law 'any specific authorization of the threat or use of nuclear weapons' (unanimously), but also no 'comprehensive and universal prohibition' (by eleven votes to three). The Court further replied (unanimously) that '[a] threat or use of force by means of nuclear weapons that is contrary to Article 2, paragraph 4, of the United Nations Charter and that fails to meet all the requirements of Article 51, is unlawful' and that it 'should also be compatible with the requirements of the international law applicable in armed conflict, particularly those of the principles of international humanitarian law, as well as with specific obligations under treaties and other undertakings which expressly deal with nuclear weapons'. The most controversial finding (by seven votes to seven, by the President's casting vote) is rather mysterious:

> It follows from the above-mentioned requirements that the threat or use of nuclear weapons would generally be contrary to the rules of international law applicable in armed conflict, and in particular the principles and rules of humanitarian law.
>
> However, in view of the current state of international law, and of the elements of fact at its disposal, the Court cannot conclude definitely whether the threat or

use of nuclear weapons would be lawful or unlawful in an extreme circumstance of self-defence, in which the very survival of a State would be at stake.[46]

As noted by Judge Higgins in her Dissenting Opinion: 'the Court effectively pronounces a *non liquet* on the key issue on the grounds of uncertainty in the present state of the law, and of facts.'[47] The main holding is inconclusive and also the reasons give no answer to the question of when the use of nuclear weapons is actually to be considered legal or illegal. Instead, the Court (unanimously) agreed that there was an obligation to 'pursue in good faith and bring to a conclusion negotiations leading to nuclear disarmament in all its aspects under strict and effective international control'. Recently, the Treaty on the Non-Proliferation of Nuclear Weapons was prolonged for an indefinite period. While the treaty confirms the privileges of the five official nuclear powers, which are also the five permanent members of the UN Security Council, to keep their arsenals of nuclear weapons and excludes the possession of such weapons by other state parties, it also contains the obligation to conduct negotiations in good faith to discontinue the nuclear arms race and to achieve nuclear disarmament under international control.[48]

A related matter (but not an issue of the laws of war) is the legality of nuclear tests which are conducted in peacetime to ascertain whether nuclear weapons function effectively, what the results of their use are and to improve their development.[49] There are a number of limited bilateral and multilateral treaties which contain special provisions on this matter, and a comprehensive test ban has been laid down in a recent multilateral treaty.[50] The legal situation regarding the rights of third countries affected by such tests has not been authoritatively clarified, although it is clear that in the case of transfrontier damage caused by a testing state to the territory or population of another state there is international responsibility on the part of the testing state. When the ICJ was seised by cases brought in 1973 by Australia and New Zealand against France concerning its atmospheric nuclear tests in the Pacific,[51] the Court indicated certain provisional measures of protection against France in an order of 22 June 1973; but in its judgments of 20 December 1974 the Court held that it no longer had to render a decision because it found that France had meanwhile legally bound itself by a unilateral declaration[52] that it would discontinue atmospheric tests in the South Pacific.

Recent French underground nuclear tests in the South Pacific[53] again led to action before the Court. On 21 August 1995, New Zealand filed a request for an 'Examination of the Situation in Accordance with Paragraph 63 of the Court's Judgment of 20 December 1974 in the *Nuclear Tests (New Zealand v. France)* Case', accompanied by a request for the indication of provisional measures. Australia filed an application for permission to intervene on 23 August 1995, followed by similar applications[54] by Samoa, the Solomon Islands, the Marshall Islands and the Federated States of Micronesia. However, on 22 September 1995, only one month after the filing of New Zealand's request, the Court issued an Order deciding that the request did 'not fall within the provisions of the said paragraph 63 and must consequently be dismissed'.[55] The reasoning of the

46 *Ibid.*, at 831.

47 *Ibid.*, 934, para. 2. On *non liquet*, see Chapter 3 above, 50.

48 1968 Treaty on Non-Proliferation of Nuclear Weapons, *ILM* 7 (1968), 7; for the Final Document on the extension of the Treaty see *ILM* 34 (1995), 959. See also G. Bunn/R. Timerbaev/J. Leonard, *Nuclear Disarmament: How Much Have the Five Nuclear Powers Promised in the Non-Proliferation Treaty?*, 1994; G. Bunn, *Extending the Non-Proliferation Treaty: Legal Questions Faced by the Parties in 1995*, 1994; *The United Nations and Nuclear Non-Proliferation*, UN Blue Book Series, 1995; M. Rosenne, The Treaty on Non-Proliferation of Nuclear Weapons, *Justice–IAJLJ*, 1995, 15–8; M.v. Leeuwen (ed.), *The Future of the International Nuclear Non-Proliferation Regime*, 1995; E. El Baradei, Verifying Non-Proliferation Pledges: The Evolution and Future Direction of the IAEA Safeguards System, *LJIL* 8 (1995) 347–60.

49 See I.H.v. Arx, Nuclear Tests, *EPIL* 4 (1982), 41–4. See also N. Pelzer, Nuclear-Free Zones, *ibid.*, 38–41; P.G. Schrag, *Global Action: Nuclear Test Ban Diplomacy at the End of the Cold War*, 1992.

50 Opened for signature on 24 September 1996, *ILM* 35 (1996), 1439.

51 *Nuclear Tests Cases (Australia v. France)*, *ICJ Rep.* 1973, 99–133 (Interim Protection); *Nuclear Tests Cases (New Zealand v. France)*, *ICJ Rep.* 1973, 135–64 (Interim Protection). See also A. Berg, Nuclear Tests Cases (Australia *v.* France; New Zealand *v.* France), *EPIL* 2 (1981), 216–9; I. Scobbie, Discontinuance in the International Court: The Enigma of the *Nuclear Tests* Cases, *ICLQ* 41 (1992), 808 *et seq.*

52 *ICJ Rep.* 1974, 253–455 (*Australia v. France*); *ICJ Rep.* 1974, 457–528 (*New Zealand v. France*). See C.-A. Fleischhauer, Declaration, *EPIL* I (1992), 971–2. See also Chapter 9 above, 130.

53 See also the *Rainbow Warrior* case in Chapter 6 above, 98–9.

54 Under Articles 62 and 63 of the Statute of the ICJ. See Chapter 18 above, 288 n. 119.

55 *ICJ Rep.* 1995, 288, 307, para. 68. It should be noted that attempts to stop the French tests with reference to the Euratom-Treaty on the level of European Community Law equally failed. See M.C.R. Craven, New Zealand's Request for an Examination of the Situation in Accordance with Paragraph 63 of the

Court's Judgment of 20 December 1974 in the Nuclear Tests (*New Zealand v. France*), *ICLQ* 45 (1996), 725 *et seq.*
56 R.L. Bindschedler, Neutrality, Concept and General Rules, *EPIL* 4 (1982), 9–14; R.L. Bindschedler, Permanent Neutrality of States, *ibid.*, 133–8; E. Kussbach, Neutrality Laws, *ibid.*, 28–31; K.J. Madders, Neutrality in Air Warfare, *ibid.*, 14–16; K. Zemanek, Neutrality in Land Warfare, *ibid.*, 16–19; H. Miehsler, Permanent Neutrality and Economic Integration, *EPIL* 8 (1985), 431–4; S. Oeter, Ursprünge der Neutralität, *ZaöRV* 48 (1988), 447; S. Oeter, *Neutralität und Waffenhandel*, 1992; G.P. Politakis, Variations on a Myth: Neutrality and the Arms Trade, *GYIL* 35 (1992), 435; S.P. Subedi, Neutrality in a Changing World: European Neutral States and the European Community, *ICLQ* 42 (1993), 238 *et seq.*
57 See Chapter 19 above, 309–18.
58 See Chapter 22 below, 387–90. On the effect of Article 2(6) of the UN Charter on neutral non-member states, see W. Graf Vitzthum, Article 2(6), in *Simma CUNAC*, 652–3; see also B.-O. Bryde, Article 48, *ibid.*, 652–3.
59 See A. Gioia, Neutrality and Non-belligerency in Post (ed.), 1994, *op. cit.*, 51–110.
60 See Y. Dinstein, Neutrality in Sea Warfare, *EPIL* 4 (1982), 19–28; Dinstein, Sea Warfare, *ibid.*, 201–12; W. Rabus, Booty in Sea Warfare, *EPIL* I (1992), 434–7. See further M. Ronzitti (ed.), *The Law of Naval Warfare: a Collection of Agreements and Documents with Commentaries*, 1988; D. Fleck, Rules of Engagement for Maritime Forces and the Limitation of the Use of Force under the UN Charter, *GYIL* 31 (1988), 165–86; W.H.v. Heinegg (ed.), *Methods and Means of Combat in Naval Warfare*, 1992; H.S. Levie, *Mine Warfare at Sea*, 1992; N. Ronzitti, Le Droit humanitaire applicable aux conflits armés en mer, *RdC* 242 (1993–V), 13–196; L. Doswald-Beck, Vessels, Aircraft and Persons Entitled to Protection During Armed Conflict at Sea, *BYIL* 65 (1994), 211–302; L. Doswald-Beck (ed.), *San Remo Manual on International Law Applicable to Armed Conflicts at Sea*, 1995; W.H.v. Heinegg (ed.), *Visit, Search, Diversion and Capture, The Effect of the United Nations Charter on the Law of Naval Warfare*, 1995; Heinegg (ed.), *Regions of Operations of Naval Warfare*, 1995.
61 R. Lagoni, Merchant Ships, *EPIL* 11 (1989), 228–33; R.J. Grunawalt,

Court that the 1973 cases concerned atmospheric testing, while the present case concerned underground tests, confirms a recent tendency of the Court to interpret its jurisdiction rather narrowly.

The law of neutrality and economic uses of maritime warfare

In modern international law the traditional law of neutrality governing the legal status of a state which does not take part in a war between other states[56] has become complicated due to the rules on the use of force[57] and the collective security system laid down in the UN Charter.[58] Its state has been described as 'chaotic'.[59] One of the areas in which the traditional rules have retained much of their relative clarity concerns the economic uses of maritime warfare.

The sea has always been used for the transport of merchandise, and for centuries one of the main objects of naval warfare has been to cripple the enemy's economy.[60] Enemy merchant ships may be seized at sea; the rules of naval warfare are thus different from the rules of land warfare, which prohibit (or used to prohibit) the seizure of private enemy-owned property, subject to certain exceptions.[61] In addition, neutral merchant ships can be seized if they try to carry contraband[62] to the enemy, or if they try to run (that is, break through) a blockade.[63] (Neutral shipowners who carry contraband or who run a blockade are not acting illegally – nor is their national state acting illegally by permitting them to behave in this way – but they run the risk of confiscation if they are caught.)

In the eighteenth and nineteenth centuries goods were divided into three classes: absolute contraband, conditional contraband and free goods. Neutral ships carrying absolute contraband (that is, goods having an obvious military use, such as gunpowder) to an enemy country were always liable to seizure; neutral ships carrying free goods (for example, luxuries such as silk) to an enemy country were never liable to seizure; neutral ships carrying other goods (that is, conditional contraband, such as food or cloth) were liable to seizure if the goods were intended for the enemy government, but not if they were intended for private individuals in the enemy country. The distinctions between the three categories were never very precise, and belligerent states had a certain discretion in deciding what constituted absolute or conditional contraband. In the First and Second World Wars the whole economy of each of the belligerents was geared to the war effort, in a way unknown in previous wars, and consequently virtually all goods came to be listed as absolute contraband, even though they had been treated as conditional contraband or free goods in previous wars.

In the eighteenth and nineteenth centuries belligerent states were also entitled to blockade an enemy coastline, that is, to send warships to sail up and down near the enemy coastline in order to prevent other ships reaching or leaving enemy ports. Neutral ships which tried to run (that is, break through) a blockade were liable to seizure; but the right of seizure arose only if the blockade reached a certain degree of effectiveness. During the First World War German mines and submarines made it impossible for Allied warships to operate near the German coast; instead, the Allies instituted a 'long-distance blockade', stopping neutral vessels hundreds of miles from the German coast and seizing them if they were found to be carrying goods destined for Germany. Neutral states protested against this extension of the concept of blockade, and against the changes in the practice relating to contraband; but, after the entry of the United States into the war, neutral states were too few and weak to secure respect for their views.

Belligerent warships are entitled to stop and search neutral merchant ships (except in neutral territorial waters), to see whether they are carrying contraband or trying to run a blockade; if the search confirms the suspicion, the merchant ship is taken into port to be condemned as a 'lawful prize' by a Prize Court set up for this purpose by the captor state.[64] However, during the First and Second World Wars this practice was altered in several respects. In particular, it became more common to sink merchant ships instead of capturing them. Before 1914 there was controversy about the circumstances in which it was lawful to sink merchant ships, but on one point there was agreement; the warship had to rescue the crew of the sunk merchant ship. All this changed with the invention of the submarine.[65] The German policy of sinking merchant ships at sight, without rescuing their crews, provoked the United States into declaring war on Germany in 1917, but both sides adopted a similar policy in the Second World War. The Nuremberg Tribunal held that this policy was unlawful, but did not punish the German leaders for following it, because the Allies had done the same.[66]

Whether the experience of the attacks by Iran on neutral ships destined for Iraq in the First Gulf War (1980–8) and the reaction of the United States to reflag oil tankers of third countries in order to protect them has led to any different legal situation is open to doubt.[67] A recent study by Wolff Heintschel von Heinegg of the developments since 1945 concludes that the law of prize has not been extensively modified by the practice of states.[68] The current state of the law may be summarized as follows: belligerent states have broad discretion in determining whether vessels, aircraft and goods have 'enemy' character. In principle, all ships, whatever their nationality or function, are subject to visit, search and diversion beyond neutral territorial waters. Private enemy property, unless it enjoys special protection, may be captured and seized if it is found outside neutral jurisdiction. The right of capture and seizure does not apply to neutral vessels and goods, unless they contribute to the fighting or war sustaining efforts of the enemy. The law of prize applies in an international armed conflict irrespective of whether there is a 'state of war'. Prize measures, whether applied by the aggressor or the victim during ongoing hostilities, do not confer permanently valid legal titles over neutral private property.

Reprisals

Reprisals are one of the main means of forcing states to obey the laws of war – and indeed of forcing them to obey international law in general.[69] A reprisal is an act which would normally be illegal but which is rendered lawful by a prior illegal act committed by the state against which the reprisal is directed; it is a form of retaliation against the prior illegal act.

Targeting Enemy Merchant Shipping, 1993.
62 W. Meng, Contraband, *EPIL* I (1992), 809–12.
63 L. Weber, Blockade, *EPIL* I (1992), 408–12; Weber, Blockade, Pacific, *ibid.*, 412–15.
64 D.H.N. Johnson, Prize Law, *EPIL* 4 (1982), 154–9; J.H.W Verzijl/W.P. Heere/J.P.S. Offerhaus, *International Law in Historical Perspective. Part IX-C. The Law of Maritime Prize*, 1992; U. Scheuner, International Prize Court, *EPIL* II (1995), 106–8.
65 See Zemanek (1982), Submarine Warfare, *op. cit.*, 233-5.
66 13 AD 203 (1946), at 219–20.
67 For a discussion, see M. Jenkins, Air Attacks on Neutral Shipping in the Persian Gulf: The Legality of the Iraqi Exclusive Zone and Iranian Reprisals, *BCICLR* 8 (1985), 517–49; T.W. Costello, *Persian Gulf Tanker War and International Law*, 1987; M.H. Nordquist/M.G. Wachenfeld, Legal Aspects of Reflagging Kuwaiti Tankers and Laying of Mines in the Persian Gulf, *GYIL* 31 (1988), 138–64; R. Leckow, The Iran-Iraq Conflict in the Gulf: The Law of War Zones, *ICLQ* 37 (1988), 629; S. Davidson, United States Protection of Reflagged Kuwaiti Vessels in the Gulf War: The Legal Implications, *IJECL* 4 (1989), 173 *et seq.*; R. Wolfrum, Reflagging and Escort Operations in the Persian Gulf: An International Law Perspective, *Virginia JIL* 29 (1989), 387–99; F.U. Russo, Targeting Theory in the Law of Armed Conflict at Sea: The Merchant Vessel as Military Objective in the Tanker War, in Dekker/Post (eds), *op. cit.*, 153 *et seq.* (with comments by D. Fleck and T.D. Gill); M. Bothe, Neutrality at Sea, *ibid.*, 205 *et seq.* (with comments by C. Greenwood and A. Bos); A. Gioia/N. Ronzitti, The Law of Neutrality: Third States' Commercial Rights and Duties, *ibid.*, 221 *et seq.* (with comments by O. Bring); A. de Guttry/N. Ronzitti, *The Iran-Iraq War (1980–1988) and the Law of Naval Warfare*, 1993.
68 See W.H.V. Heinegg, The Current State of International Prize Law in Post (ed.), 1994, *op. cit.*, 5–31.
69 See F. Kalshoven, *Belligerent Reprisals*, 1971; F.J. Hampson, Belligerent Reprisals and the 1977 Protocols to the Geneva Conventions of 1949, *ICLQ* 37 (1988), 818 *et seq.*; C.J. Greenwood, The Twilight of the Law of Belligerent Reprisals, *NYIL* 20 (1989), 35 *et seq.*; F. Kalshoven, Belligerent Reprisals Revisited, *NYIL* 21 (1990),

43–80. On reprisals in peacetime, see Chapters 1, 4, and 17, 271–2 above.

70 See Chapters 1, 4 and 17, 271 above.

71 See Chapter 20 above, 318–26.

72 *Nicaragua v. US, ICJ Rep.* 1986, 14, 113–4. On the case, see Chapter 19 above, 319–22.

73 D.P. Forsythe, Legal Management of Internal War: The 1977 Protocol on Non-International Armed Conflict; *AJIL* 72 (1978), 272; D. Schindler, The Different Types of Armed Conflicts According to the Geneva Conventions and Protocols, *RdC* 163 (1979), 125; Y. Sandoz/C. Swinarski/B. Zimmermann (eds), *Commentaire des Protocoles additionnels*, 1986; R. Abi-Saab, *Droit humanitaire et conflits internes: origines er évolution de la réglementation internationale*, 1986; H.S. Levie, *The Law of Non-International Conflict, Protocol II to the 1949 Geneva Conventions*, 1987; T. Meron, *Human Rights in Internal Strife: Their International Protection*, 1987; C. Meindersma, Applicability of Humanitarian Law in International and Internal Armed Conflict, *Hague YIL* 7 (1994), 113–40.

74 On this latter point, see also *UNYb* 1973, 549–50, 552–3.

Reprisals may be used only when other means of redress (for example, protests and warnings) have failed.[70]

Reprisals have an undoubted deterrent effect; it was fear of reprisals which prevented gas being used during the Second World War. But reprisals often cause hardship for innocent persons, and consequently the four Geneva Conventions of 1949 forbid reprisals against the persons, buildings, vessels, equipment and property protected by those Conventions.

Rules governing the conduct of civil wars

Under customary international law, it was uncertain whether the laws of war protecting civilians, the sick and wounded, prisoners of war, and so on, applied to all civil wars regardless of recognition of belligerency. The appalling brutality of the Spanish civil war showed how unsatisfactory this position was, and Article 3 of each of the four Geneva Conventions of 1949 tried to remedy the situation by extending some of the more basic laws of war to civil wars.[71] In the *Nicaragua* case, the ICJ clarified that common Article 3 is more than a mere treaty provision. The Court viewed it as an expression of 'fundamental general principles of humanitarian law' which are legally valid independent of any treaty basis. Reflecting 'elementary considerations of humanity', Article 3 is thus a minimum yardstick forming also part of customary law.[72]

The Second Protocol to the 1949 Conventions, signed in 1977, goes further than Article 3 of the 1949 Conventions, by extending more (but not all) of the laws of war to civil wars.[73] Protocol II has a relatively high threshold of application; according to Article 1(1), it applies to armed conflicts

> which take place in the territory of a High Contracting Party between its armed forces and dissident armed forces or other organized armed groups which, under responsible command, exercise such control over a part of its territory as to enable them to carry out sustained and concerted military operations and to implement this Protocol.

Paragraph 2 continues:

> This Protocol shall not apply to situations of internal disturbances and tensions, such as riots, isolated and sporadic acts of violence and other acts of a similar nature, as not being armed conflicts.

Article 1(4) of the First Protocol to the 1949 Conventions, also signed in 1977, goes further still by classifying as international wars for the purposes of applying the rules contained in the First Protocol (and also perhaps, by implication, for the purposes of applying the laws of war in general):[74]

> armed conflicts in which peoples are fighting against colonial domination and alien occupation and against racist régimes in the exercise of their right of self-determination.

Article 3 has not worked well in practice, and it remains to be seen whether the 1977 Protocols will enjoy more success.[75] In a civil war each side tends to regard the other side as traitors, which does not create a favourable climate for the application of the laws of war. Moreover, civil wars are often fought by guerrillas or other irregular forces, which makes it difficult to distinguish between combatants and civilians.[76] Even when a civil war is 'internationalized' by the participation of foreign troops, experience in Vietnam between 1965 and 1973 indicates that the likelihood of compliance with the laws of war is not noticeably increased. However, fear of reprisals and fear of war crimes trials have sometimes secured a certain amount of compliance with Article 3. Desire to make a favourable impression on foreign public opinion has also often acted as a restraining influence.

A number of internal armed conflicts in the 1970s and 1980s which escalated following the intervention of third states (Cuba in Angola and Ethiopia; South Africa in Angola and Mozambique; Vietnam in Kampuchea; Syria and Israel in the Lebanon; the USSR in Afghanistan) have shown that common Article 3 and Article 1(4) of the Second Additional Protocol (which only reclassifies 'wars of national liberation' as 'international armed conflicts') are not sufficient.[77] Although there has been some debate on the 'internationalization' of civil wars by such intervention, state practice, in principle, viewed them still as purely internal conflicts. As we have seen in the recent conflicts in Bosnia, Rwanda, Afghanistan, Liberia and Chechnya, unfortunately, often not even the most elementary of these minimum standards are observed. Modern humanitarian law still needs to be adopted fully to internal situations of war.[78]

War crimes trials

War crimes trials are another means of forcing states to obey the laws of war.[79] For centuries, members of the armed forces and other persons who commit breaches (or, at any rate, serious breaches) of the laws of war have been liable to prosecution. Theoretically any state may try them (under the principle of universal jurisdiction),[80] but in practice jurisdiction is usually exercised by a state on the opposite side in the relevant war. There is obviously a danger that war crimes trials may sometimes degenerate into mere instruments of revenge, but abolition of a state's right to try enemy nationals for war crimes would mean that many guilty men would escape punishment. It is rare to find a state trying its own nationals for war crimes, although such trials do sometimes occur, and are usually used to create a favourable impression on neutral public opinion; for instance, in November 1968 Nigeria tried a Nigerian officer for shooting a Biafran prisoner, and executed him in front of British television cameras. One could also mention the Vietnam case of My Lai tried in the United States,[81] or the investigation into the tragedy caused by Israeli forces in the Palestinian refugee camps of Sabra and Shatila in the Lebanon.[82]

Defendants in war crimes trials often put forward the defence that they were carrying out the orders of a superior, but this defence rarely succeeds. The general view is that superior orders are not a defence, but that they

75 See E. Chadwick, *Self-Determination, Terrorism and the International Law of Armed Conflict*, 1995.

76 See M. Veuthey, *Guérilla et Droit Humanitaire*, 1983.

77 On wars on national liberation and liberation movements see Chapters 6, 104–5 and 19, 336–8 above. See also C. Koenig, *Der nationale Befreiungskrieg im modernen humanitären Völkerrecht*, 1988; S. Oeter, Terrorism and 'Wars of National Liberation' from a Law of War Perspective, *ZaöRV* 49 (1989), 445.

78 See A. Eide/A. Rosas/T. Meron, Combatting Lawlessness in Gray Zone Conflicts through Minimum Humanitarian Standards, *AJIL* 89 (1995), 215–23.

79 H.-H. Jescheck, War Crimes, *EPIL* 4 (1982), 294–8; D. Schindler, Crimes against the Law of Nations, *EPIL* I (1992), 875–7; H.-H. Jescheck, International Crimes, *EPIL* II (1995), 1119–23. See also D.A. Wells, *War Crimes and Laws of War*, 1984; A.P.V. Rogers, War Crimes Trials under the Royal Warrant: British Practice 1945–1949, *ICLQ* 39 (1990), 780 *et seq.*; F. Malekian, *International Criminal Law: The Legal and Critical Analysis of International Crimes*, 1994; *idem, The Monopolization of International Criminal Law in the UN*, 2nd edn 1995; Y. Dinstein (ed.), *War Crimes in International Law*, 1996.

80 See Chapter 7 above, 113–15.

81 *US v. Medina*, 20 USCMA 403, 43 CMR (1971), 243. See also the 1996 United States War Crimes Act with a definition of 'grave breach of the Geneva Conventions', *ILM* 35 (1996), 1539.

82 Final Report of the Commission of Inquiry into the Events at the Refugee Camps in Beirut, 7 February 1983, *ILM* 22 (1983), 473. See further, R. Maison, Les Premiers cas d'application des dispositions pénales des Conventions de Genève par les jurisdictions internes, *EJIL* 6 (1995), 260–73.

83 For a recent analysis, see J.W. Grayson, The Defence of Superior Orders in the International Criminal Court, *Nordic JIL* 64 (1995), 243–60. On the rules applied by the Yugoslavia Tribunal, see text below, 357.
84 E. Rauch, Espionage, *EPIL* II (1995), 114–6.
85 Trial of German Major War Criminals, 1946, Cmd. 6964, Misc. No. 12, at 65; 11 *Trials of War Criminals before the Nuremberg Military Tribunals under Control Council Law No. 10*, at 462, 533–35 (1948). See Q. Wright, The Law of the Nuremberg Trial, *AJIL* 41 (1947), 39–72; H.-H. Jescheck, Nuremberg Trials, *EPIL* 4 (1982), 50–5; B.V.A. Röling, Tokyo Trial, *ibid.*, 242–5; J.F. Willis, *Prologue to Nuremberg: The Politics and Diplomacy of Punishing War Criminals of the First World War*, 1982; *Le Procès de Nuremberg: Conséquences et actualisation. Centre de droit international de l'Institut de Sociologie de l'Université Libre de Bruxelles*, 1988; G. Ginsburg/V.N. Kudriavtsev (eds), *The Nuremberg Trial and International Law*, 1990; T. Taylor, *The Anatomy of the Nuremberg Trials*, 1992; B.V.A. Röling/A. Cassese, *The Tokyo Trial and Beyond*, 1993; G. Ginsburg, *Moscow's Road to Nuremberg: The Soviet Background to the Trial*, 1995; D. de Mildt, *In the Name of the People: Perpetrators of Genocide in the Reflection of their Post-War Prosecution in West Germany*, 1995.
86 Many acts are unlawful (for example, torts and breaches of contract in municipal law) without being crimes.
87 They are quoted in the Tribunal's judgment: *AJIL* 41 (1947), 172, 219–20.
88 B.B. Ferencz, Crimes Against Humanity, *EPIL* I (1992), 869–71; M.C. Bassiouni, *Crimes Against Humanity in International Criminal Law*, 1992. The 1968 UN Convention on the Non-Applicability of Statutory Limitations to War Crimes Against Humanity (text in *ILM* 8 (1969), 68) has been ratified only by 43 countries; see *ILM* 35 (1996), 1566.
89 See Chapter 14 above, 209.

may be taken into account to reduce the level of punishment imposed. A few cases, however, treat superior orders as a valid defence to minor charges.[83]

War criminals should be distinguished from 'unprivileged belligerents', such as spies.[84] Unprivileged belligerents are not entitled to be treated as prisoners of war, and may be shot upon capture, provided that their status as unprivileged belligerents is proved by a fair trial. But unprivileged belligerents, and the states which employ them, are not guilty of violating the laws of war; the state employing them is under no obligation to pay compensation for their activities, as it would have been if those activities had been contrary to international law. Similarly, a spy who returns to his own forces cannot subsequently be punished for spying; there is no similar rule of international law extinguishing a war criminal's liability.

The Nuremberg Tribunal, which (like the Tokyo Tribunal) was set up by an inter-Allied agreement at the end of the Second World War, tried the German leaders not only for war crimes, but also for crimes against peace and crimes against humanity.[85] Crimes against peace were defined in the Tribunal's Charter as 'planning, preparation, initiation or waging of a war of aggression, or a war in violation of international treaties'. This provision in the Tribunal's Charter was criticized by some people as retroactive legislation. Clearly a war of aggression was illegal under the Kellogg–Briand Pact, but there was nothing in the Kellogg–Briand Pact to indicate that aggression was a crime,[86] or that the Pact imposed obligations on individuals. However, a number of unratified treaties and League of Nations resolutions dating from the 1920s,[87] which can be regarded as evidence of customary law, did declare specifically that aggression was a crime. It should be noted that liability for crimes against peace falls only on the leaders of the state, and not on the ordinary soldiers who take part in a war of aggression. In this respect crimes against peace differ from war crimes (and from crimes against humanity).

As for the question of individual liability, pre-existing types of 'international crimes', such as war crimes, entailed individual liability, and it was therefore reasonable to apply the principle of individual liability by analogy to the new international crime of aggression.

The accusation about retroactive legislation is closer to the truth as regards crimes against humanity.[88] These were defined in the Tribunal's Charter as follows:

> murder, extermination, enslavement, deportation and other inhumane acts committed against any civilian population before or during the war, or persecutions on political, racial or religious grounds in execution of or in connection with any crime within the jurisdiction of the Tribunal, whether or not in violation of the domestic law of the country where perpetrated.

In some respects, crimes against humanity are wider than war crimes; they can be committed before a war as well as during a war, and they can be directed against 'any civilian population', including the wrongdoing state's own population. The prohibition of 'crimes against humanity' thus constituted an exception to the old rule that a state was entitled to treat its nationals as it pleased;[89] and it is fairly clear that this prohibition was not accepted as part of international law before 1945. However, the Tribunal restricted the scope of crimes against humanity by stressing the words 'in execution of or in connection with any crime within the jurisdiction of the Tribunal', and by interpreting the words 'any crime' to mean 'any other crime within the jurisdiction of the Tribunal' – that is, war crimes and crimes against peace. In other words, an act can constitute a crime against humanity only if it is 'in execution of or in connection with' a war crime or crime against peace. Thus, confiscation of Jewish property in Germany before the Second World War would have constituted a crime against humanity if the property had been used to finance a war of aggression, but not if it had been used to finance the Olympic Games. (But this restriction on the scope of crimes against humanity was not followed in some of the other post-war war crimes trials.)[90]

Whether certain provisions in the Charter of the Nuremberg Tribunal constituted retroactive legislation has remained a matter of dispute. Be that as it may, while it is true that retroactive legislation can lead to injustice in certain cases, anyone who thinks that justice demanded the acquittal of the men convicted at Nuremberg has a very peculiar idea of justice.[91] In any case, there can be no complaints about retroactive legislation in future cases; the judgment of the Nuremberg Tribunal constitutes a precedent for the future, and the principles laid down in the Charter and judgment of the Tribunal were later approved by the General Assembly (in 1946) and by the International Law Commission which was asked by the Assembly in 1947 to prepare a draft code relating to the Nuremberg principles.

However, in practice the Nuremberg and Tokyo Tribunals remained isolated precedents for the next five decades, in spite of many wars of aggression and atrocities, such as the genocide committed by the Khmer Rouge in Cambodia, which would have also called for the application of their principles. The projects of the International Law Commission[92] on a draft Code of Crimes against the Peace and Security of Mankind[93] and on a permanent international criminal court to deal with war crimes[94] failed to make progress until the events in former Yugoslavia and in Rwanda led to a historic turning point.

The International Criminal Tribunal for the Former Yugoslavia

The massive violence and brutality in the war that erupted in former Yugoslavia,[95] with an unprecedented scale in Europe since 1945 of mass killings and the implementation of policies of so-called 'ethnic cleansing', the existence of concentration camps and organized torture and rape,[96] caused the UN Security Council to decide to establish, by its resolution 827 of 25 May 1993, an *ad hoc* international criminal tribunal which would be required to 'try those persons responsible for serious breaches of international humanitarian law committed on the territory of Former Yugoslavia between 1 January 1991 and a date to be determined by the Council after peace has been restored'.[97] This decision was based upon Chapter VII of the UN Charter[98] and followed a report that the Council had requested from the UN Secretary-General.[99] The Statute of the Tribunal as proposed by the Secretary-General was approved without change.

90 See the *Eichmann* case (1961), *ILR*, Vol. 36, 5, 48–9. On the case, see also Chapter 7 above, 113.

91 See L. Mansfield, Crimes Against Humanity: Reflections on the Fiftieth Anniversary of Nuremberg and a Forgotten Legacy, *Nordic JIL* 64 (1995), 293–341.

92 See Chapter 3 above, 61.

93 See Ferencz (1992), *op. cit.*

94 B.B. Ferencz, International Criminal Court, *EPIL* II (1995), 1123–7.

95 See also Chapter 22 below, 409–15.

96 The Security Council had established a Commission of Experts to report on grave breaches of international humanitarian law in the Former Yugoslavia in October 1992, see SC Res. 780 of 6 October 1992, UN Doc. S/RES/780 (1992). See also T. Meron, The Case for War Crimes Trials in Yugoslavia, *FA* 72 (1993), 122; J. O'Brien, The International Tribunal for Violations of International Humanitarian Law in the Former Yugoslavia, *AJIL* 87 (1993), 639; P. Szasz, The Proposed War Crimes Tribunal for Yugoslavia, *NYUJIL* 25 (1993), 405; T. Meron, Rape as a Crime under International Humanitarian Law, *AJIL* 87 (1993), 424–8; S. Oeter, Kriegsverbrechen in den Konflikten um das Erbe Jugoslawiens, *ZaöRV* 53 (1993), 1–43; A. Stiglmayer (ed.), *Mass Rape: The War Against Women in Bosnia-Herzegovina*, 1994; T. Meron, War Crimes in Yugoslavia and the Development of International Law, *AJIL* 88 (1994), 78; C. Chinkin, Rape and Sexual Abuse of Women in International Law, *EJIL* 5 (1994), 326–41; D. Petrovic, Ethnic Cleansing – An Attempt at Methodology, *ibid.*; O. Gross, The Grave Breaches System and the Armed Conflict in the Former Yugoslavia, *Mich. JIL* 16 (1995), 783–830.

97 The decision of principle to establish the Tribunal was taken by SC Res. 808 of 22 February 1993 and SC Res. 827 of 25 May 1993, reprinted in *ILM* 32 (1993), 1203; the Security Council adopted the Statute of the Tribunal, UN Doc. S/25704 (1993), Annex, reprinted in *ILM* 32 (1993), 1192; the Rules of Procedure and Evidence adopted by the Tribunal on 11 February 1994, are reproduced in *ILM* 33 (1994), 484, with two amendments at 838 and 1620; for the most recent version of the Rules, see Doc. IT/32/Rev.8 (23 April 1996); for other Rules of the Tribunal, see *ILM* 33 (1994), at 1581 and 1590. See also K. Oellers-Frahm, Das Statut des Internationalen Strafgerichtshofs zur

Verfolgung von Kriegsverbrechen im ehemaligen Jugoslawien, *ZaöRV* 54 (1994), 416-45; M.C. Bassiouni, *Commentaries on the Statute and Rules Governing the International Criminal Tribunal for the Former Yugoslavia*, 1995; V. Morris/M.P. Scharf, *An Insider's Guide to the International Tribunal for the Former Yugoslavia: A Documentary History and Analysis*, 2 vols, 1995; K. Lescure/F. Trintignac, *International Justice for Former Yugoslavia: The Workings of the International Criminal Tribunal of The Hague*, 1996; M.C. Bassiouni/P. Manikas, *The Law of the International Criminal Tribunal for the Former Yugoslavia*, 1996.

98 See Chapter 22 below, 387–90, 425.

99 Report of the Secretary-General Pursuant to Paragraph 2 of Security Council Resolution 808 (1993), UN Doc. S/25704 (1993), reprinted in *ILM* 32 (1993), 1163. For an explanation of the report see D. Shraga/R. Zacklin, The International Criminal Tribunal for the Former Yugoslavia, *EJIL* 5 (1994), 360–80.

100 P.H. Kooijmans, The Judging of War Criminals: Individual Responsibility and Jurisdiction, *LJIL* 8 (1995), 443–8; G. Aldrich, Jurisdiction of the International Criminal Tribunal for the Former Yugoslavia, *AJIL* 90 (1996), 64–9.

101 Article 6, Statute of the Tribunal.

102 Article 8.

103 Alternative dates considered were 25 June 1991, the proclamation of independence by Croatia and Slovenia; 27 June 1991, the intervention of the Federal Army in Slovenia; and 3 July 1991, the first clashes between Serbian and Croatian militia; see Shraga/Zacklin, *op. cit.*, 362–3.

104 Articles 2–5 of the Statute.

105 As set out in the common articles 50/51/130/147, Geneva Conventions 1949, *op. cit.*

106 See Article 2 of the Statute.

107 See Shraga/Zacklin, *op. cit.*, 364.

108 Article 3 of the Statute.

109 Article 5.

110 Text in 78 UNTS 278. See Article 4 of the Statute.

Jurisdiction of the Tribunal

The jurisdiction of the Tribunal is limited both in territorial and temporal respects.[100] It does not extend beyond the territorial bounds of the former Yugoslavia.[101] Its temporal jurisdiction extends to the period beginning from 1 January 1991[102] to the date which the Security Council will eventually determine for the restoration of peace and security. The starting date was chosen as a neutral date in order not to prejudice the question of the international or internal nature of the conflict and in order to cover all crimes by whomsoever committed in the territory of former Yugoslavia in 1991.[103]

The subject-matter jurisdiction of the Tribunal is intended to be limited to those violations of international humanitarian law, the customary law nature of which is beyond any doubt and which have also customarily led to the criminal responsibility of the individual: grave breaches of the Geneva Conventions, violations of the laws or customs of war, the crime of genocide and crimes against humanity.[104] Thus, care was taken to avoid any criticism that the principle of *nullem crimen sine lege* is not respected with regard to the law to be applied.

The grave breaches of the four Geneva Conventions[105] include acts committed against persons or property protected under the Conventions, such as wilful killing; torture and inhuman treatment; wilfully causing great suffering or serious injury to body or health; extensive destruction or appropriation of property not justified by military necessity; compelling a prisoner of war or a civilian to serve in the forces of a hostile power; wilfully depriving a prisoner of war or a civilian of the rights of a fair and regular trial; unlawful deprivation or transfer or unlawful confinement of a civilian; and the taking of civilians as hostages.[106] The extended protection offered under Additional Protocol I was not included in the Tribunal's jurisdiction because of doubts concerning the customary law nature of a number of provisions of the Protocol.[107]

The list of war crimes under the jurisdiction of the Tribunal draws upon the 1907 Hague Convention on Land Warfare and the practice of the Nuremberg Tribunal. The list includes the use of poisonous weapons or weapons calculated to cause unnecessary suffering; the wanton destruction and devastation of cities not justified by military necessity; attack, or bombardment of undefended towns; the seizure of or destruction and damage to institutions dedicated to religion, charity, education, historic monuments or works of art or science; and the plunder of public or private property.[108] However, this list of crimes is not necessarily exhaustive because the Tribunal may determine that other war crimes may equally fall within its subject matter jurisdiction.

With regard to crimes against humanity, the Statute of the Tribunal also reflects the Nuremberg precedent.[109] It includes the crimes of murder, extermination, enslavement, deportation, imprisonment, torture, rape, persecution on political, racial and religious grounds and other inhumane acts, when committed in an armed conflict, whether international or national in character, and directed against any civilian population.

Genocide is a specific case of crimes against humanity and the Statute of the Tribunal draws upon Article II of the 1948 Genocide Convention.[110]

When committed with intent to destroy, in whole or in part, a national, ethnic, racial or religious group, genocide consists of any of the following acts: killing members of the group; causing serious bodily or mental harm to members of the group; deliberately inflicting on the group conditions of life calculated to bring about its physical destruction in whole or in part; imposing measures intended to prevent births within the group and forcibly transferring children of the group to another group. Such acts engage the individual criminal responsibility of those who commit the crime, independently of whether the home state has ratified the Genocide Convention, because the principles underlying the Convention are generally recognized as binding upon states 'even without any conventional obligation'.[111] Moreover, individual criminal responsibility can be accompanied by separate and independent responsibility of the state for the crime of genocide, if the conduct of the individual can be attributed to the state.[112] In the latter sense, Bosnia and Herzegovina instituted proceedings at the International Court of Justice against the Federal Republic of Yugoslavia concerning alleged violations of the Genocide Convention.[113]

The Tribunal has jurisdiction only over natural persons, excluding legal persons, organizations and states.[114] Any person accused of planning, instigating, ordering or committing a crime falling within the jurisdiction of the Tribunal can be held criminally responsible whether as a principal or as an accomplice.[115] Thus, the whole chain of command is included, from the top level of political decision-makers, down to officers, soldiers, militia or civilians. Those who ordered the commission of the crime, those who only knew of the crime (or could have known of it) but failed to prevent or repress it (when in a position and under a duty to do so), and those who actually committed the act, can all be held criminally responsible. Heads of State cannot plead their immunity[116] from prosecution. As in the case of the Nuremberg Tribunal, an accused also cannot defend himself by invoking obedience to superior orders, although this may be considered as a circumstance mitigating the punishment.[117]

The Tribunal has concurrent jurisdiction with national courts prosecuting persons for the same crimes, but its jurisdiction has been given primacy. It has the power to intervene at any stage of the national criminal proceedings and request that the national authorities or courts defer to the competence of the Tribunal.[118]

A number of provisions of the Statute deal with the principles of criminal procedure, such as due process of law and the rights of suspects and accused, and the various stages of the legal process.[119] One important point is that the possibility of conducting trials *in absentia* (as was allowed in the Nuremberg Trial) is excluded. Thus, an accused can only be tried in his presence in The Hague. The drafters of the Statute were primarily concerned about the detrimental effect that such 'show trials' would have upon the credibility of the Tribunal as an institution in cases in which states parties to the conflict would refuse to surrender an accused to the Tribunal.[120] Among the procedural provisions which have caused concern are those aiming at the protection of witnesses and victims, especially the use of witnesses who remain anonymous to the defence.[121] But in general they appear to be as fair as they can be under the circumstances. The

111 See the *Advisory Opinion of the International Court of Justice in Reservations to the Convention on the Prevention and Punishment of the Crime of Genocide, ICJ Rep.* 1951, 23. See E. Klein, Genocide Convention (Advisory Opinion), *EPIL* II (1995), 544–6.

112 See Chapter 17 above, 257–60.

113 Application of the Convention on the Prevention and Punishment of the Crime of Genocide *(Bosnia and Herzegovina v. Yugoslavia (Serbia and Montenegro)), ICJ Rep.* 1993, 3 and 325. See Chapter 18 above, 292.

114 Article 6 of the Statute. The Nuremberg and Tokyo Tribunals had the power to declare an organization to be criminal which entailed subsequent prosecution of its members by national courts.

115 Article 7.

116 On immunity in general, see Chapter 8 above, 118–29; on immunity of state representatives, see 119 n. 11.

117 Article 7(4) of the Statute.

118 Article 9. For details of the procedure and the obligations of states to cooperate under Article 29 of the Statute, see Shraga/Zacklin, *op. cit.*, 371 *et seq.*

119 Articles 18–28.

120 See Shraga/Zacklin, *op. cit.*, 376–7.

121 See M. Leigh, The Yugoslavia Tribunal: Use of Unnamed Witnesses Against Accused, *AJIL* 90 (1996), 235–8.

122 Article 63 of the Statute.
123 Article 24.
124 See L. Vierucci, The First Steps of the International Criminal Tribunal for the Former Yugoslavia, *EJIL* 6 (1995), 134–43; R. Kushen/K.J. Harris, Surrender of Fugitives by the United States to the war Crimes Tribunal for Yugoslavia and Rwanda, *AJIL* 90 (1996), 510–18.
125 *Indictment 1, ILM* 34 (1995), 996.
126 See *ICTY Bull.* No. 3 of 22.2.1996, 4.
127 Case IT-94-1-T, Decision on Jurisdiction (Aug. 10, 1995). On the appeal case see *Prosecutor v. Tadić*, Case No. IT-94-1-AR72, Appeal on Jurisdiction (2 October 1995), reprinted in *ILM* 35 (1996), 32. See further C. Meindersma, Violations of Common Article 3 of the Geneva Conventions as Violations of the Laws or Customs of War under Article 3 of the Statute of the International Criminal Tribunal for the Former Yugoslavia, *NILR* 42 (1995), 375–97; Meron (1996), *op. cit.*, 238–49; L.G. Maresca, The Prosecutor v. Tadić – The Appellate Decision of the ICTY and Internal Violations of Humanitarian Law as Internal Crimes, *LJIL* 9 (1996), 219–32; J.E. Alvarez, Nuremberg Revisited: The Tadić Case, *EJIL* 2 (1996), 245–64; C. Greenwood, International Humanitarian Law and the Tadić Case, *ibid.*, 265–83; R. Maison, La Décision de la Chambre de première instance no. 1 du Tribunal pénale international pour l'ex-Yougoslavie dans l'affaire Nikolić, *ibid.*, 284–98; C. Warbrick/P. Rowe, The International Criminal Tribunal for Yugoslavia: The Decision of the Appeals Chamber on the Interlocutory Appeal on Jurisdiction in the Tadić Case, *ICLQ* 45 (1996), 691–701.
128 See *ICTY Bull.* No. 4 of 15.3.1996, 3.
129 See R. Dixon, New Developments in the International Criminal Tribunal for the Former Yugoslavia: Prominent Leaders Indicted and Jurisdiction Established, *LJIL* 8 (1995), 449–61.
130 Especially to Articles 50–61, as amended in January 1996, see *ICTY Bull.* No.3 of 22.2.1996, 2–3.

accused also has a limited right of appeal (as distinct from the Nuremberg Tribunal, the decisions of which were final). The structure of the Tribunal provides for two Trial Chambers (three judges each) and a separate Appeals Chamber (five judges) to which both the Prosecutor and the defendant are entitled to resort against a judgment of the Tribunal on grounds of law or fact.[122] It is further remarkable that only prison sentences (to be pronounced in accordance with the general practice of the courts of former Yugoslavia) may be imposed; the death penalty is excluded – another difference to the Nuremberg and Tokyo Trials.[123]

The work of the Tribunal

It is too early to evaluate the work of the Tribunal which has just commenced.[124] The fact of its institution is a milestone in the development of international law and it is almost a miracle that it has actually started to operate. The Yugoslavia Tribunal held its first plenary session on 17 November 1993 in The Hague and started operating as a judicial body in November 1994 by issuing an indictment and warrants of arrest against Dragan Nikolić, a former commander of the Suscica camp in Bosnia-Herzegovina, and by issuing a request for deferral by Germany of the criminal proceedings being carried out in German courts in the case of the Serb Dusko Tadić accused of genocide on the basis of information provided by Muslim refugees.[125] As of February 1996, the eleven Judges, with Antonio Cassese from Italy as the President, and the Prosecutor, first Richard Goldstone from South Africa, succeeded by Louise Arbour from Canada, are supported by a staff of almost 300 persons of more than thirty-five nationalities.[126] It has commenced with the *Tadić* case and dismissed a defence motion challenging the jurisdiction of the Tribunal to try the accused currently before it.[127] As of March 1996, it had issued thirteen indictments naming fifty-three alleged war criminals.[128] These include first indictments issued (on 25 July 1995) against high-ranking political and military leaders, including Radovan Karadžić, the President of the Bosnian Serb Administration of Pale, Ratko Mladić, army commander of the Bosnian Serb Administration, and Milan Martić, the President of the former Croatian Serb Administration of Knin.[129]

But, as an old German proverb (dating from the Middle Ages and nothing to do with the Nuremberg Trial) says, 'the Nurembergers do not hang a man, unless they have him'. Is the Tribunal toothless, as many have said, including its own President? What if the defendants do not appear and if states parties to the conflict refuse to surrender their indicted leaders? The Tribunal answers by referring to its Rules of Procedure and Evidence.[130] These rules enable the Tribunal to issue an international arrest warrant against an indicted person and to inform the Security Council that there has been a lack or refusal of cooperation on the part of the authorities who were to serve the indictment on the accused. It is then up to the Security Council to decide on whether any enforcement measures should be taken. As far as the Tribunal is concerned, it matters that the non-appearance of the accused only prevents a trial (*in absentia*) temporarily until the warrant has been executed. In the view of the Tribunal, the accused will also suffer under the fact of being branded 'an international fugitive' and remain confined to an 'open-air prison' in the country sheltering him. Political changes in this country may also eventually lead to the loss of protection of the accused. Finally, accused leaders would be seriously affected in the exercise of their international and domestic responsibilities by being a 'wanted person'. At least the victims of the crimes would be able to testify to build up a historic record against the accused, preventing him from escaping international justice.[131]

Whether this really works, remains to be seen. One problem is to combine the requirements of justice with the requirements of peace. It is still difficult to envisage that peace negotiations in the region can lead to successful and lasting results if they have to be conducted with leaders who are at the same time indicted by the Tribunal and sought by international warrants, as long as they enjoy the political support of their people. The reluctance of the NATO's IFOR force in former Yugoslavia[132] to act as a police arm of the Tribunal and arrest suspects also bears witness to the existing difficulties, as did the refusal of the United States in June 1996 to adhere (at least for the time being) to the call of the President of the Tribunal to impose sanctions upon certain states in the region for refusing to cooperate with the Tribunal in accordance with their obligations under the 1995 Dayton/Paris Peace Agreement.[133] Furthermore, as a subsidiary body created by the Security Council, in theory, the Tribunal could also be abolished by the Security Council, although such a drastic measure is not likely to be taken in view of public opinion and the victims. However, there are other more subtle ways of restricting its impact, if necessary – for example, by reducing its financial resources.

It may not come as a surprise that from the Serbian point of view the Tribunal is accused of 'selective justice' (with reference to an alleged imbalance in the prosecution of Croation crimes) and being a 'political court' manipulated by Western powers.[134] As noted by one writer:

> The Hague International War Crimes Tribunal has serious procedural and related questions to answer: amongst others, those relating to the facts that, unlike any other court, it has no parliament to control it and to legislate about it, that it (more precisely, its Appeals Committee) is reviewing and considering appeals against its own decisions, that in its work it takes on legislative as well as judicial actions and tasks, etc. But the most important issue is that the Hague Tribunal must shed the influence of the major international players and must at least try to become more of a court of law, and less of an instrument of political vengeance.[135]

Other sceptical considerations are whether in the end the Tribunal will be limited to sentencing the 'small fish', while the 'big fish' who are ultimately responsible will manage to escape its nets. The experience with the Nuremberg Tribunal has also not been such that one would easily expect the Yugoslav Tribunal to be sufficiently effective to overcome the legacy of having being established to cover the failure of the international community to actually stop the war and the atrocities committed in Former Yugoslavia for more than five years.

A legal issue is whether the Security Council has the authority to

131 Ibid., 3.

132 See Chapter 22 below, 414.

133 Text in ILM 35 (1996), 89. For a summary of the obligations of the respective state parties to cooperate with the Tribunal see P.C. Szasz, The Protection of Human Rights Through the Dayton/Paris Peace Agreement on Bosnia, AJIL 90 (1996), 301–16, at 313–4.

134 See A. Fatić, The Need for a Politically Balanced Works of the Hague International War Crimes Tribunal, RIA, 1044 of 15 May 1996, 8–11.

135 Ibid., 10–11.

136 See Chapter 18 above, 281–305.

137 See Chapter 1 above, 3.

138 See Chapter 3 above, 58–60.

139 See K. Oellers-Frahm, Die Einsetzung des 'Internationalen Tribunals über Kriegsverbrechen im ehemaligen Jugoslawien' durch den Sicherheitsrat, in *FS Bernhardt*, 733–51.

140 See J.M. Sjöcrona, The International Criminal Tribunal for the Former Yugoslavia: Some Introductory Remarks From a Defence Point of View, *LJIL* 8 (1995), 463–74.

141 See also Chapter 22 below, 425–6.

142 For the Statute of the Rwanda Tribunal see SC Res. 995, Annex, of 8 November 1994, reprinted in *ILM* 33 (1994), 1602.

143 See T. Meron, International Criminalization of Internal Atrocities, *AJIL* 89 (1995), 554.

144 See the interview with Richard Goldstone, *UN Chronicle* 1996, no. 2, 35–8, at 36 and 38–40. See further R.S. Lee, The Rwanda Tribunal, *LJIL* 9 (1996), 37–62; P. Akhavan, The International Criminal Tribunal for Rwanda: The Politics and Pragmatics of Punishment, *AJIL* 90 (1996), 501–10.

145 See J. Crawford, The ILC's Draft Statute for an International Criminal Court, *AJIL* 88 (1994), 140–52; Crawford, The ILC Adopts a Statute for an International Criminal Court, *AJIL* 89 (1995), 404–16; S. Suikkari, Debate in the United Nations on the International Law Commission's Draft Statute for an International Criminal Court, *Nordic JIL* 64 (1995), 205–21. For the earlier discussion see M.C. Bassiouni, *A Draft International Criminal Code and Draft Statute for an International Criminal Tribunal*, 1987; B. Graefrath, Universal Criminal Jurisdiction and an International Criminal Court, *EJIL* 1 (1990), 67–88.

146 UNGA Res. 50/46 of 11 December 1995.

147 *UN Chronicle* 33 (1996), no. 1, 66; no. 2, 70.

establish such a judicial organ as a subsidiary organ with criminal jurisdiction over individuals under Chapter VII of the UN Charter. As we have seen in Chapter 18,[136] the establishment of any kind of international jurisdiction normally requires the consent of states in the decentralized international legal system.[137] One may perhaps be able to argue that in the case of such crimes to be investigated by the Tribunal, which have an *erga omnes* nature[138] and in view of the broad political discretion the Security Council enjoys under Chapter VII, the powers of the Council are sufficient to do so.[139] Still, there are doubts with regard to the contention that the Tribunal is an 'independent' body, while it is at the same time clearly a subsidiary organ of the Council.[140] There are also doubts whether the Security Council can 'delegate' functions, such as judicial ones, which it does not possess itself.[141] It is also clear that practical reasons prevailed in the decision to opt for a binding resolution under Chapter VII, rather than creating a Tribunal on the basis of a treaty concluded between states, simply because the latter process would have taken too long and, in view of the ongoing atrocities in former Yugoslavia and the lack of political will (or capacity) to intervene militarily, there was a widespread feeling of a strong need to do at least something.

The Rwanda Tribunal

Similarly, in November 1994 the Security Council decided to establish a Criminal Tribunal to deal with the crimes committed in the massacre in Rwanda.[142] Although the Rwanda Tribunal shares its appellate chamber and prosecutor's office with the Yugoslavia Tribunal, there are some differences regarding the respective jurisdiction of both Tribunals.[143] As of 1996, the Rwanda Tribunal had issued three indictments concerning ten people.[144]

Towards a permanent international criminal court?

It should also be mentioned that in the autumn of 1994 the International Law Commission submitted to the UN General Assembly a draft statute for a permanent international criminal court.[145] In December 1995 the General Assembly established a Preparatory Committee to draft an acceptable consolidated text of a convention for such a court which could then be considered to be adopted at an international conference.[146] The report of the Committee[147] is expected to be submitted in the autumn of 1996.

The establishment of a permanent international criminal court would indeed overcome the problems arising from the time and efforts required to create *ad hoc* tribunals on a case-by-case basis, as for Yugoslavia and Rwanda. It would also dispense with the inevitable selective application of justice under the *ad hoc* method by only addressing certain conflicts and not others. Finally, the creation of such a court on a treaty basis would remove any doubts as to the proper legal basis of the court under international law, as distinct from the constitution of *ad hoc* tribunals by Security Council resolutions. But the practical disadvantage is, of course, that the court will only be able to operate with respect to states which decide to join the convention. To what extent a universal consensus on its statute can be achieved, in view of the conservative force of the doctrine of state sovereignty, has to be awaited.

Possible future developments

Writers often assume that the erosion of the traditional laws of war, which took place during the First and Second World Wars, will continue in future wars.[148] In 1986 Antonio Cassese, the current President of the Yugoslavia Criminal Tribunal, remarked:

> [i]nternational legal control of warfare has kept pace with the developments in organized armed violence only to a limited extent. Major military Powers have not accepted sweeping restraints, with the consequence that this body of law is beset with deficiencies, loopholes, and ambiguity.[149]

It is possible, however, that the development of nuclear weapons will have the indirect and paradoxical effect of re-establishing some of the traditional rules which fell into decline during the two world wars. Different considerations apply to civil wars, or to wars which are 'semi-civil' and 'semi-international', like the war in Vietnam, and to internal conflicts of the type that has become virulent and dominant after the end of the Cold War.

Since 1945 fear of nuclear war has prevented nuclear powers from entering into even the most limited conflict with one another (apart from minor incidents on the Soviet-Chinese border), and it is likely that this state of affairs will continue, as long as there is sufficient nuclear balance. In future international wars, therefore, at least one of the two sides will probably not possess nuclear weapons. The corollary is that there are likely to be a large number of states, including one or more nuclear powers, which will be neutral in future wars, even though their sympathies may lie with one side or another. As a result, belligerent states will have to pay far more attention to neutral opinion than they did during the two world wars. Disregard of the rights of neutral shipping was by no means the only violation of the laws of war during the two world wars which was facilitated by the fact that neutrals were few and weak. If neutrals outnumber belligerents in future wars, the position will be very different. The parties involved in the wars in Nigeria and Vietnam in the late 1960s were very sensitive to allegations that they had committed atrocities, and this sensitivity shows the influence which sometimes can be exercised by public opinion in neutral countries. On the other hand, it is equally clear that public opinion as such had little impact on constraining the atrocities committed by the conflicting parties in situations such as in former Yugoslavia or Rwanda.

Even if nuclear powers become involved in 'conventional' hostilities with one another, the fear that the fighting may escalate into a nuclear war is likely to induce them to conduct the hostilities cautiously, on a limited scale and for limited objectives. In other words, the hostilities will bear more resemblance to the 'limited wars' of the eighteenth and nineteenth centuries than to the 'total war' of the two world wars; and it is not unreasonable to hope that respect for the laws of war, which characterized

148 See generally G.I.A.D. Draper, War, Laws of, Enforcement, *EPIL* 4 (1982), 323–6.
149 A. Cassese, *International Law in a Divided World*, 1986, 285.

150 M. Meijer/H. Fischer, Keeping Hope Alive – Do the Resolutions Fulfil the Expectations?, *HV* 1 (1995), 198.

151 M. Montani, Eine einzige Spur von Heuchelei – Wie das Völkerrecht den modernen Krieg humanisieren will und seine Inhumanität legalisiert, *HV* 8 (1995), 216–7. For a critical response to Montani, see M. Sassòli, Kriegsvölkerrecht: eine Heuchelei, die Inhumanität legalisiert, oder ein Minimum von Menschlichkeit für eine unmenschliche Situation?, *HV* 8 (1995), 218–20.

152 See R. Normand/C. Jochnick, The Legitimation of Violence: A Critical Analysis of the Gulf War, *Harvard ILJ* 35 (1994), 387–416 with extensive references.

153 See Chapter 1 above, 5. But for other aspects of the conflict concerning the conduct of Iraqi forces, see also W. Klein (ed.), *Human Rights in Times of Occupation: The Case of Kuwait*, 1995.

154 See Chapter 22 below, 396.

155 See UNEP Governing Council, 16th Session, Nairobi, 20–31 May 1991, Introductory Report of the Executive Director, Environmental Consequences of the Armed Conflict Between Iraq and Kuwait, UNEP/GC.16/4/Add.1, 10 May 1991; M. Bothe, The Protection of the Environment in Times of Armed Conflict, *GYIL* 34 (1991), 54–62; H.H. Almond, The Use of the Environment as an Instrument of War, *YIEL* 2 (1991), 455–68; G. Plant, *Environmental Protection and the Law of War: A 'Fifth Geneva' Convention on the Protection of the Environment in Time of Armed Conflict*, 1992; M.A. Ross, Environmental Warfare and the Persian Gulf War, *Dick. JIL* 10 (1992), 515–39; A. Roberts, Environmental Destruction in the Gulf War, *IRRC* 291 (1992), 538–53; R.C. Tarasofsky, Environmental Protection and Armed Conflict, *YIEL* 3 (1992), 217–21; K.M. Kelly, Declaring War on the Environment: The Failure of International Environmental Treaties during the Persian Gulf War, *AUJILP* 7 (1992), 921–50; A. Leibler, Deliberate Wartime Environmental Damage: New Challenge for International Law, *CWILJ* 23 (1992–3), 67–131; R.G. Tarasofsky, Legal Protection of the Environment during International Armed Conflict, *NYIL* 24 (1993), 17–79; F.P. Feliciano, Marine Pollution and Spoliation of Natural Resources as War Measures: A Note on Some International Law Problems in the Gulf War, in R.St.J. Macdonald (ed.), *Essays in Honour of Wang Tieya*, 1994, 285–310; H.-P.

the wars of the eighteenth and nineteenth centuries, will be revived in such hostilities. However, the experience of the vicious war between Iraq and Iran from 1980 to 1988, and of the other armed conflicts since 1990, is far from encouraging.

This raises the question of how 'legal' can a war be conducted at all? Can war really be 'humanized' by international rules? Or are we submitting ourselves to an illusion, considering that, after 1945, 22 million people died in more than 120 armed conflicts?[150] There are different views on this matter. Some authors argue that attempts to 'humanize' the use of force in wars by international rules have failed historically and that such rules have ultimately only contributed to the spread of armed conflict by providing war with a legal cloak.[151] Are we dealing only with cynical rhetorical language in the international documents on the laws of war? At the Hague Peace Conference of 1899, states agreed, in principle, to prohibit the use of long-range artillery against unfortified cities, but the German delegate added that his government understood the prohibition as not to prevent it from destroying buildings 'of military advantage'. The British delegation vetoed the prohibition of the use of dumdum ammunition with the argument that only these projectiles, causing terrible wounds, would be able to contain the 'wild people'.

Even the Second Gulf War conducted by the Allied forces against Iraq to repel its aggression against Kuwait, under the auspices of the United Nations, raises questions. The method of warfare was portrayed in the media as a 'high-tech' event with overwhelming forces deployed against Iraq using 'surgical' attacks against military targets; but apparently the fact is that, according to official statements of the US military, only 7 per cent of the bombs reached the programmed targets.[152] It is also questionable whether the almost complete destruction of the infrastructure and the energy system of Iraq, which caused the death of thousands of civilians after the war due to the lack of water and health care, was pursuing a legitimate military objective or only seeking to create conditions under which the Iraqi government could be put under political pressure.[153] Was this 'collateral damage' legally covered by military necessity, the principle of proportionality and the relevant Security Council resolution?[154]

Serious questions have arisen with regard to the use of oil as a weapon by Iraqi forces (the setting on fire of Kuwaiti oil wells and oil pollution of the Gulf) which has given impetus to a review of the law protecting the environment during armed conflict.[155] In a resolution adopted in 1992 on the Protection of the Environment in Times of Armed Conflict, the UN General Assembly stated that

> destruction of the environment, not justified by military necessity and carried out wantonly, is clearly contrary to existing international law.[156]

Similarly, in its 1996 *Advisory Opinion on the Legality of the Threat or Use of Nuclear Weapons*, the ICJ found that there is

> a general obligation to protect the natural environment against widespread, long-term and severe environmental damage; the prohibition of methods and means of warfare which are intended, or may be expected, to cause such

damage; and the prohibition of attacks against the natural environment by way of reprisals.[157]

However, this statement must be read in connection with the earlier reference by the Court to 'what is necessary and proportionate in the pursuit of legitimate military objectives and the requirement that states 'must take environmental considerations into account' when making such an assessment.[158] In the light of this wording, the problem lies legally in determining what is exactly covered by 'military necessity' or 'the pursuit of legitimate military objectives' in a given case, which would have to take the overall context of the armed conflict and the position and conduct of both sides into account. This area of the law still needs to be clarified in more detail.

Be that as it may, it would be wrong to conclude that international humanitarian law only serves to legitimize war. Its function is to provide minimum standards of humanity in a situation of inhumanity, although recent conflicts show that even the most elementary of these standards are often disregarded. The *ius in bello* certainly needs further development; but one has to take into account that such development requires the consent of states which make the law and shape it according to their interests, including military considerations concerning the preservation of effective means of warfare. Nevertheless, it is desirable that more states ratify the 1977 Additional Protocols, including the United States, and other humanitarian treaties. Also customary law on humanitarian law needs to be further developed to cover the gaps in situations where treaties are not applicable.[159] Another problem which has been receiving attention is the role of children and of child soldiers in armed conflicts.[160]

The main problem, however, is not so much the creation of new rules, but rather the application and enforcement of the existing body of humanitarian principles and rules. Only a few of the states parties to the 1949 Geneva Conventions have so far met their obligation to transform the Conventions into their national legal systems to ensure the punishment of war crimes and the misuse of the sign of the Red Cross.[161] It is also to be hoped that the development of effective international legal machinery to punish war crimes will succeed and may thus contribute to deter such serious violations of international law, wherever they may be contemplated.

Gasser, For Better Protection of the Natural Environment in Armed Conflict, *AJIL* 89 (1995), 637–43; W.D. Verwey, The Protection of the Environment in Times of Armed Conflict, *LJIL* 8 (1995), 7–40. See also Chapter 22 below, 398–9.

156 UNGA Res. 47/37 of 25 November 1992. See text above, 347–9.

157 *ILM* 35 (1996), 809, at 821, para. 31.

158 *Ibid.*, para. 30.

159 Meron (1996), *op. cit.*, 238–49. See also C. Greenwood, Customary Law Status of the 1977 Geneva Protocols, in Delissen/Tanja (eds), *op. cit.*, 93; G. Abi-Saab, The 1977 Additional Protocols and General International Law: Some Preliminary Reflections, *ibid.*, at 115.

160 G.H. Aldrich/T.A.v. Baarda, *Conference on the Rights of Children in Armed Conflict*, 1994; G.S. Goodwin-Gill/I. Cohn, *Child Soldiers: The Role of Children in Armed Conflict*, 1994.

161 M. Bothe *et al.* (eds), *National Implementation of International Humanitarian Law*, 1990; H. Fox/M.A. Meyer (eds), *Armed Conflict and the New Law. Effecting Compliance*, Vol. II, 1993. See for more details on the need to improve international humanitarian law the Resolutions of the 26th International Conference of the Red Cross and Red Crescent, *HV* 8 (1995), 224–9.

21 The Charter and the organs of the United Nations

1 See Chapter 2 above, 26–8. L.M. Goodrich/E.Hambro/A.P. Simons, *Charter of the United Nations: Commentary and Documents*, 3rd edn 1969; J.A. Frowein, United Nations, *EPIL* 5 (1983), 272–81; O. Schachter, United Nations Charter, *ibid.*, 287–93; J.-P. Cot/A. Pellet (eds), *La Charte des Nations Unies*, 2nd edn 1991; Y.Z. Blum, *Eroding the United Nations Charter*, 1993; A. Roberts/B. Kingsbury (eds), *United Nations, Divided World: The UN's Roles in International Relations*, 2nd edn 1993; P.R. Baehr/L. Gordenker, *United Nations in the 1990s*, 2nd edn 1994; E. Luard/D. Heater, *The United Nations: How It Works and What It Does*, 2nd edn 1994; B. Simma (ed.), *The Charter of the United Nations: A Commentary*, 1995; S.D. Bailey, *The United Nations: A Concise Political Guide*, 1995; R. Wolfrum (ed.), *United Nations: Law, Policies and Practice*, 2 vols, 1995; H.G. Schermers/N.M. Blokker, *International Institutional Law*, 3rd edn 1995; O. Schachter/C.C. Joyner (eds), *United Nations Legal Order*, 2 vols, 1995; C. Tomushat (ed.), *The United Nations at Age Fifty*, 1995; S.H. Mendlowitz/B.H. Weston (eds), *Preferred Futures for the United Nations*, 1995. The text of the UN Charter is reprinted in *Brownlie BDIL*, 1.
2 See Chapter 22 below, 395–6, 423–9.
3 See Chapter 22 below, 385–430.
4 See A. Roberts/B. Kingsbury, Introduction: The UN's Roles in International Society since 1945, in Roberts/Kingsbury (eds), *op. cit.*, 1–62.
5 See *Basic Facts About the United Nations*, 1995, 231–49. See also Chapters 2, 28 and 19, 326–38 above.
6 See T.J. Farer, The UN and Human Rights: At the End of the Beginning, in Roberts/Kingsbury (eds), *op. cit.*, 240–96; *Basic Facts, op. cit.*, 189–214. See also Chapter 14 above, 209–21.
7 See *Basic Facts, op. cit.*, 217–27; A. Grahl-Madsen, Refugees, United Nations High Commissioner, *EPIL* 5

As we have seen in Chapter 2 above,[1] the creation of the United Nations in 1945 was the second attempt at establishing a universal international organization with the main purpose of maintaining peace by a system of collective security. The emergence of differences between the Soviet Union and Western powers, and the Cold War, however, soon removed the basis for cooperation in the new organization between the founding members. The operation of the United Nations became even more complicated with the later admission of a large number of new states following the process of decolonization. It was only after the end of the Cold War that a new scenario of world order with a different role for the UN seemed to emerge, particularly in view of the firm international response to the aggression committed by Iraq against Kuwait in the Second Gulf War (1990–1), the unprecedented proliferation of various types of UN peacekeeping operations, and other forms of UN Security Council activism.[2] Meanwhile, a more sober view has come to prevail.

The following will deal with only certain aspects of the United Nations: the UN Charter and the problem of interpretation, membership and the main organs of the UN. The functions of the UN with regard to the peaceful settlement of disputes between states, the maintenance of peace and security and the problems of UN enforcement action and peacekeeping will be treated separately in Chapter 22 below.[3] It is important to note, however, that, while the prime task of the UN today is still in the field of international peace and security, the UN has many other important roles,[4] which are addressed in other parts of this book, such as with regard to decolonization,[5] human rights,[6] humanitarian assistance and assistance to refugees,[7] economic development and the relations between rich and poor states,[8] the protection of the environment,[9] and the development of international law.[10]

The United Nations Charter and the problem of interpretation

Like most international organizations, the United Nations was set up by a treaty:[11] the United Nations Charter. The Charter defines the purposes for which the United Nations was set up, and confers certain powers on it. If the United Nations acts for other purposes, or attempts to exercise other powers, it is acting illegally.

It is no exaggeration to say that the whole history of the United Nations has been a series of disputes about the correct interpretation of the Charter.[12] Language is inherently ambiguous, and there will often be disputes about the interpretation of rules of law which are expressed in words; laymen may be surprised by this fact, but lawyers take it for granted.[13] However, there are several reasons why the United Nations Charter has given rise to an abnormally large number of problems of interpretation. It was drafted mainly by politicians, with little assistance from lawyers; often it is ambiguous, or fails to make provision for a certain problem (either by accident, or because no genuine agreement could be reached by the parties on the point at issue); often it sets up machinery which has not worked well in practice, so that other machinery has had to be improvised to fill the gap.

There are five official texts, each of which is equally authentic: English, French, Spanish, Russian and Chinese.[14] These are the 'authentic' languages relevant for the interpretation of the Charter. They must be distinguished from the 'official' languages and the 'working' languages of the UN. Arabic was designated as one of the 'official' languages of the General Assembly in 1973, which has no effect on the interpretation of the Charter. Negotiations at the San Francisco Conference were in English and French, and the other three texts were later translations of the English and French texts; but, even if one looks only at the English and French texts, there are differences between the two. One of the objects of interpretation is to reconcile such differences, but reconciliation is not always easy.[15] It must also be remembered that neither English nor French was the native language of the majority of the delegates at San Francisco, so imprecise drafting was inevitable.

Various methods of interpretation are discussed below.[16] But it must not be imagined that such methods provide a simple answer to all problems of interpretation. Interpretation is an art, not a science. In a sense, there are no rules of interpretation, only presumptions; and the presumptions very often conflict with one another. The choice between conflicting presumptions is almost bound to be influenced by political factors, however hard one tries to exclude them. And it is this intermixture of political factors with legal factors which explains why states are reluctant to refer disputes about the interpretation of the United Nations Charter to the International Court of Justice.[17]

Literal interpretation

Literal interpretation may be described as a method of interpretation which looks exclusively at the words of a document, and which applies a number of different presumptions to determine the meaning of those words.[18] For instance, words are presumed to be used in their ordinary meaning, unless it is clear from the context that a technical meaning is intended, in which case the technical meaning is applied; the document must be read as a whole, and it will be presumed that the same word used in different parts of the document will have the same meaning; if possible, a particular provision should not be interpreted so as to conflict with another provision, or to make another provision redundant, or to lead to a manifest absurdity.

This is the method of interpretation used most frequently, for example, by English judges when interpreting Acts of Parliament and other documents, and it is also used by international lawyers to interpret treaties. But

(1983), 255–8; E. Jahn, Refugees, *EPIL* 8 (1985), 452–6; P. Macalister-Smith, United Nations Relief and Works Agency for Palestine Refugees in the Near East, *ibid.*, 519–22.

8 See K. Dadzie, The UN and the Problem of Economic Development, in Roberts/Kingsbury (eds), *op. cit.*, 297–326; *Basic Facts, op. cit.*, 133–85. See also Chapter 15 above, 233–5, 239–40.

9 See P. Birnie, The UN and the Environment, in Roberts/Kingsbury (eds), *op. cit.*, 327–83. See also Chapter 16 above, 240–53.

10 See N. Singh, The UN and the Development of International Law, in Roberts/Kingsbury (eds), *op. cit.*, 384–419; *Basic Facts, op. cit.*, 253–70.

11 See Chapters 6, 92–6 and 9, 130–46 above.

12 See R.St.J. Macdonald, The United Nations Charter: Constitution or Contract, in R.St.J. Macdonald/D.M. Johnston (eds), *The Structure and Process of International Law*, 1983, 889–912; C.F. Amerasinghe, Interpretation of Texts in Open International Organizations, *BYIL* 65 (1994), 175–210; G. Ress, The Interpretation of the Charter, in *Simma CUNAC*, 25–44.

13 For the rules of the interpretation of treaties see Articles 31–3 of the 1969 Vienna Convention on the Law of Treaties, reprinted in *Brownlie BDIL*, 388. On the law of treaties, see Chapter 9 above, 130–46.

14 Article 111 UN Charter. See M. Hilf, Article 111, in *Simma CUNAC*, 1196–1200.

15 Article 33, 1969 Vienna Convention. See M. Hilf, *Die Auslegung mehrsprachiger Verträge*, 1973; L.D.M. Nelson, The Drafting Committee of the Third United Nations Conference of the Law of the Sea: The Implications of Multilingual Texts, *BYIL* 57 (1986), 169–200; C.B. Kuner, The Interpretation of Multilingual Treaties: Comparison of Texts versus the Presumption of Similar Meaning, *ICLQ* 40 (1991), 953 *et seq.*

16 See B. Vitanyi, Treaty Interpretation in the Legal Theory of Grotius and its Influence on Modern Doctrine, *NYIL* 14 (1983), 41–67; E.S. Yambrusic, *Treaty Interpretation: Theory and Reality*, 1987; R. Bernhardt, Interpretation in International Law, *EPIL* II (1995), 1416–26.

17 See Chapter 18 above, 281–93, 300–5.

18 Article 31, 1969 Vienna Convention.

19 See Chapter 2 above, 26–8.
20 Article 32, 1969 Vienna Convention.
21 Article 31(3)(b).
22 See Chapter 6 above, 92–6.
23 See W. Karl, *Vertrag und spätere Praxis im Völkerrecht*, 1983.
24 H.G. Schermers, Voting Rules in International Conferences and Organizations, *EPIL* 5 (1983), 395–8; H.G. Schermers, Weighted Voting, *ibid.*, 398–9.

in international law it does not always provide a clear answer, because treaties are usually drafted in less precise and less technical language than Acts of Parliament; this is particularly true of the United Nations Charter. The Charter was drawn up mainly by politicians, and often recalls the deliberate vagueness of an election manifesto. Different parts of the Charter were drawn up by different committees at the San Francisco Conference in 1945,[19] and several amendments were made at the last minute; as a result, coordination between different provisions is sometimes poor.

Intention and *travaux préparatoires*

The intentions of the parties to a treaty may be discovered, not only by reading the treaty itself, but also by looking at the historical context in which the treaty was negotiated, and at the records of the negotiations themselves. Such records are called the *travaux préparatoires* (preparatory work), and are often used as a subsidiary means of interpretation in international law.[20]

But *travaux préparatoires* are used less for interpreting treaties setting up international organizations than for interpreting other kinds of treaty. Treaties setting up international organizations are intended to last longer than most other types of treaty, and recourse to *travaux préparatoires* would not always be appropriate in such circumstances, because it would mean looking at the (possibly distant) past, instead of looking at the present and the future; the intentions which states had in the 1940s may provide little guidance for solving the very different problems of the 1990s. Moreover, the fact that the majority of the members of the United Nations joined the United Nations after 1945 and were not represented at the San Francisco Conference makes it politically awkward to rely on the *travaux préparatoires* of the Charter.

Practice

The way in which states perform their obligations under a treaty can be evidence of what they originally intended when they drafted the treaty.[21] This is particularly true of treaties setting up international organizations,[22] because such treaties, by their very nature, are applied constantly over a number of years. In fact, one of the reasons why the United Nations Charter was loosely drafted was because the drafters wanted to leave room for flexibility in subsequent practice;[23] unfortunately, the lack of trust between the member states has not resulted in flexibility, but in constant disputes about interpretation.

When an organization is empowered to take decisions by majority vote,[24] it is inevitable that the practice supported by the majority of the member states will come to be regarded as the practice of the organization itself, and will be used as a means of interpreting the treaty setting up the organization, despite the fact that the practice in question is opposed by a minority of the member states. (Naturally, states forming the majority in an international organization tend to rely heavily on practice as a means of interpreting the constituent treaty, while states in a minority favour a strict, literal interpretation, with more reliance on *travaux préparatoires*.)

Moreover, with the passage of time, it becomes a fiction to regard practice merely as evidence of the parties' original intentions. Practice acquires a force of its own, and may actually develop in the opposite direction to the parties' original intentions.[25]

Practice may even develop in such a way as to run counter to the words of the treaty. Is such a practice illegal, or can it amend the treaty? There is little authority on this point, because the supporters of a particular practice usually defend it by saying that it is a mere interpretation of the treaty, not an amendment; but, if practice can terminate a treaty,[26] there is no logical reason why practice should not also be capable of amending a treaty. However, although the practice of the majority of member states can be used to interpret a treaty setting up an international organization, practice cannot be used to amend such a treaty unless it is unanimously accepted; all the parties must agree before a treaty can be amended.

The situation is different where the treaty itself provides for amendment by majority vote. For instance, Article 108 of the United Nations Charter provides that (express) amendments of the Charter

> shall come into force for all Members of the United Nations when they have been adopted by a vote of two thirds of the members of the General Assembly and ratified . . . by two thirds of the Members of the United Nations, including all the permanent members of the Security Council.[27]

If this provision is applied by analogy to amendments implied from practice, it would seem that practice can amend the United Nations Charter provided it is accepted by two-thirds of the members, including all the permanent members of the Security Council.

Effectiveness and implied powers

There is a presumption of interpretation in international law that a treaty should be interpreted so as to give full effect to its purposes. At first sight this presumption might seem to conflict with another presumption, that a treaty should be interpreted restrictively so as not to limit the sovereignty of states. In fact, however, the two presumptions are usually applied in different circumstances. The principle of restrictive interpretation is used most often to interpret treaties conferring jurisdiction on international tribunals, and treaties which place heavier burdens on one party than on the other party or parties (in such cases, restrictive interpretation seeks to minimize the inequality of the parties). Conversely, the principle of effectiveness[28] is used most often to interpret treaties placing identical burdens on all parties – such as treaties setting up international organizations.

The principle of effectiveness received a striking application in the *Reparation for Injuries* case, where the International Court of Justice advised that the United Nations possessed not only powers expressly conferred by the Charter, but also such implied powers as were necessary to enable it to achieve the purposes for which it was set up.[29]

However, it would be dangerous to regard the doctrine of implied powers as a solution to all problems of interpretation in international organizations. Most of the disputes about the interpretation of the United

25 For an example, see text below (domestic jurisdiction), 368–9.
26 See Chapter 9 above, 141–2.
27 See A. Tanzi, Notes on the 'Permanent Conference of Revision' of the United Nations Charter at the 50th Anniversary of the Organization, *Rivista di Diritto Internazionale* 1995, 723–37; M. Schöder, Amendment to and Review of the Charter, in *Wolfrum UNLPP I*, 20–6; W. Karl/B. Mützelberger, Article 108, in *Simma CUNAC*, 1163–78. On the discussion of the reform of the UN, see Chapter 22 below, 430.
28 On the different general meaning of the principle in international law, see Chapter 10 above, 153.
29 *ICJ Rep.* (1949), 174, at 180, 182; see Chapter 6 above, 92–4. See also G. Jaenicke, Article 7, in *Simma CUNAC*, 201–2; Ress, *op. cit.*, 42–3.

30 See R. Wolfrum, Article 1, in *Simma CUNAC*, 49–56; A. Randelzhofer, Purposes and Principles of the United Nations, in *Wolfrum UNLPP II*, 994–1002.
31 See Chapter 15 above, 233–5, 239–40.
32 See Chapter 19 above, 326–38.

Nations Charter have concerned powers which were clearly conferred expressly on the organization; the questions in dispute were: Which organ should exercise the power? And in accordance with what procedure? The doctrine of implied powers provides little help in answering such problems, because it is concerned with the powers of the organization as a whole, not with the internal distribution of powers within the organization.

The purposes of the United Nations

An international organization acts illegally if it acts for purposes other than those for which it was created (it is then said to act *ultra vires*, making the act in question legally void); and the purposes for which it was created must always be borne in mind when the constituent treaty of the organization is being interpreted. This makes it particularly important to ascertain the purposes of the United Nations, which are stated in Article 1 of the Charter as follows:

1 To maintain international peace and security, and to that end: to take effective collective measures for the prevention and removal of threats to the peace, and for the suppression of acts of aggression or other breaches of the peace, and to bring about by peaceful means, and in conformity with the principles of justice and international law, adjustment or settlement of international disputes or situations which might lead to a breach of the peace;

2 To develop friendly relations among nations based on respect for the principle of equal rights and self-determination of peoples, and to take other appropriate measures to strengthen universal peace;

3 To achieve international co-operation in solving international problems of an economic, social, cultural or humanitarian character, and in promoting and encouraging respect for human rights and for fundamental freedoms for all without distinction as to race, sex, language, or religion; and

4 To be a centre for harmonizing the actions of nations in the attainment of these common ends.

Obviously the purposes are defined in very wide terms.[30] Politicians in Western countries have sometimes been too ready to assume that the main or only purpose of the United Nations is to preserve international security; but Third World countries attach equal importance, if not greater importance, to 'solving international problems of an economic ... character'[31] and to securing 'respect of the principle of equal rights and self-determination of peoples' (or at least of peoples under colonial rule).[32]

Domestic jurisdiction

One provision of the Charter which is, or could have been, a serious limitation on the powers of the United Nations is Article 2(7), which provides:

Nothing contained in the present Charter shall authorize the United Nations to intervene in matters which are essentially within the domestic jurisdiction of any state or shall require the Members to submit such matters to settlement under the present Charter; but this principle shall not prejudice the application of enforcement measures under Chapter VII.

Article 2(7) has given rise to more controversy than any other provision in the Charter, but in practice its interpretation is still as uncertain as ever.[33] States which consider that Article 2(7) prohibits (or does not prohibit) the United Nations from taking a certain course of action in a particular case use all sorts of arguments to support their point of view, and the multiplicity of arguments used prevents the final decision from constituting an intelligible precedent.

The corresponding provision (Article 15(8)) of the Covenant of the League of Nations spoke of matters 'which by international law' were within a state's domestic jurisdiction. Domestic jurisdiction has a clear meaning in international law; it refers to those matters (for example, treatment by a state of its own nationals, until recently)[34] where a state's discretion is not limited by obligations imposed by international law. But the San Francisco Conference deliberately rejected the idea that 'domestic jurisdiction' in the Charter should be defined by reference to international law, on the grounds that international law was vague. There is some truth in this criticism, since the Charter itself contains a number of references to human rights,[35] self-determination,[36] and so on, which are so vague that it is difficult to say what, if any, legal obligations they impose.

In the practice of the United Nations, a number of different tests are applied in order to determine whether a matter falls within a state's domestic jurisdiction. Thus, a matter is unlikely to be regarded as within a state's domestic jurisdiction if it amounts to a breach of international law, an infringement of the interests of other states, a threat to international peace, or a gross violation of human rights,[37] or if it concerns progress towards self-determination in a colony.[38] Political factors influence the votes cast by states, which are not always consistent. But in general the practice is to interpret 'domestic jurisdiction' narrowly – the opposite of what was intended by the drafters of the Charter.

Article 2(7) states that the principle of non-intervention[39] in matters of domestic jurisdiction 'shall not prejudice the application of enforcement measures under Chapter VII'. Chapter VII is entitled: 'Action with respect to threats to the peace, breaches of the peace, and acts of aggression'.[40] According to the recent practice of the United Nations, the proviso at the end of Article 2(7) is unnecessary, because a threat to the peace, breach of the peace, or act of aggression is nowadays automatically treated as not constituting a matter of domestic jurisdiction.

Membership

The founding members of the United Nations were the states which were on the Allied side in the Second World War.[41] The admission of new members is governed by Article 4 of the Charter:

1   Membership in the United Nations is open to all other peace-loving states which accept the obligations contained in the present Charter, and, in the

33 See A. D'Amato, Domestic Jurisdiction, *EPIL* I (1992), 1090–6; F. Ermacora, Article 2(7), in *Simma CUNAC*, 139–54; G. Arangio-Ruiz, Le domaine réservé – L'Organisation internationale et le rapport entre droit international et droit interne, *RdC* 225 (1990-VI), 13–484; G. Arangio-Ruiz, The Plea of Domestic Jurisdiction Before the International Court of Justice: Substance or Procedure?, in V. Lowe/M. Fitzmaurice (eds), *Fifty Years of the International Court of Justice*, 1996, 440–64.

34 See Chapter 14 above, 209.

35 See Chapter 14 above, 211–12.

36 See Chapter 19 above, 326.

37 See Chapter 14 above, 214 and Chapter 22 below, 426–7.

38 See Chapter 19 above, 326–38 and Chapter 22 below, 393–5.

39 See M. Schröder, Non-Intervention, Principle of, *EPIL* 7 (1984), 358–61; P. Malanczuk, *Humanitarian Intervention and the Legitimacy of the Use of Force*, 1993, 12 *et seq.*; U. Beyerlin, Intervention, Prohibition of, in *Wolfrum UNLPP* II, 805–13.

40 On Chapter VII of the Charter, see Chapter 22 below, 387–90.

41 See Article 3 UN Charter and Chapter 2 above, 26–7.

42 This means that both the Security Council and the General Assembly must vote in favour of admission. See also K. Herndl, Admission of a State to Membership in United Nations (Advisory Opinions), *EPIL* I (1992), 35–8; H.-J. Schütz, Membership, in *Wolfrum UNLPP II*, 877–83; K. Ginther, Article 4, in *Simma CUNAC*, 158–75.

43 See Chapter 2 above, 28.

44 For an account of the admissions after 1990 see Ginther, *op. cit.*, 172–5. On the problem of the Russian Federation taking over the membership of the former USSR in the UN, including permanent membership in the Security Council, see Chapter 11 above, 166 and text below, 373.

45 See the overview in *VN* 43 (1995), 46–8; Roberts/Kingsbury (eds), *op. cit.*, Appendix C, 530.

46 SC Res. 963 (1994) of 29 November 1994.

47 See Chapter 19 above, 327–8.

48 J. Kokott, Micro-States, *EPIL* 10 (1987), 297–9; J. Rapaport/E. Muteba/ J.J. Therattil, *Small States and Territories – Status and Problems*, 1971; M.N. Gunter, What Happened to the United Nations Ministate Problem, *AJIL* 71 (1977), 110–24. See also Chapter 5 above, 76.

49 See Chapter 22 below, 387–90.

50 Article 5 of the UN Charter. See H.J. Schütz, Article 5, in *Simma CUNAC*, 175–85; L. Makarcyk, Legal Basis for Suspension and Expulsion of a State from an International Organization, *GYIL* 25 (1982), 476–89.

51 Article 6. See O. Kimminich, Article 6, in *Simma CUNAC*, 185–93.

52 See R. Suttner, Has South Africa Been Illegally Excluded from the United Nations General Assembly?, *CILSA* 17 (1984), 279–301; C.N. Patel, The Legal Aspects of State Expulsion from the United Nations: South Africa a Case in Point, *NULR* 3 (1982/3), 197–213.

53 See P. Malanczuk, Israel: Status, Territory and Occupied Territories, *EPIL* II (1995), 1468–1508, at 1488; M. Halberstam, Excluding Israel from the General Assembly by a Rejection of its Credentials, *AJIL* 78 (1984), 179–82. The UN General Assembly Resolution 3379 (XXX) of 10 November 1975, which equated Zionism with racism and racial discrimination, was revoked on 17 December 1991, albeit with only 111 votes in favour and twenty-five against, with thirteen abstentions, Malanczuk, *ibid.*, at 1501.

judgment of the Organization, are able and willing to carry out these obligations.

2   The admission of any such state to membership in the United Nations will be effected by a decision of the General Assembly upon the recommendation of the Security Council.[42]

At present (1996) there are 185 member states of the United Nations, of which only fifty-one were founding members. The growth in numbers is primarily attributable to decolonization in the 1960s[43] and the break-up of the Soviet Union and Yugoslavia.[44] Almost all independent states in the world are now members of the United Nations.[45] There are at present only a few non-member states, such as Kiribati, Nauru, Tonga, Tuvalu, the Vatican State, Taiwan and Switzerland (which seats many important UN bodies, but has never applied for UN membership – a referendum held in 1994 was negative). The members of the UN include micro-states with areas of less than 500 square miles and populations under 100,000, such as Andorra, Antigua and Barbuda, Grenada, St Kitts and Nevis, the Federated States of Micronesia and the Marshall Islands, Liechtenstein (admitted on 18 September 1990), San Marino (admitted on 2 March 1992), Monaco and Palau, which was admitted in November 1994[46] and constituted the last territory under the control of the UN trusteeship system.[47] Obviously, the equality in terms of membership of such micro-states with larger nations raises a number of problems which were reflected in the discussions in the United Nations up until 1971 on whether they could be admitted at all.[48] In the end, the principle of universality of membership of states, whether big or small, succeeded without solving the underlying issue of voting rights and by circumventing the question whether such states are actually, as required by Article 4 of the Charter, able to carry out its obligations. With the end of the trusteeship administration by the United States, Micronesia and the Marshall Islands entered into a compact of association with the United States under which the United States remains responsible for the defence of these two states. But this was not seen as a reason for denying that they were eligible for membership of the UN.

A member state against which enforcement action[49] is being taken may be suspended from exercising the rights of membership,[50] and a member state which has persistently violated the principles of the Charter may be expelled;[51] in each case the decision is taken by the General Assembly upon the recommendation of the Security Council. These provisions have never yet been applied, although many African and Asian states tried to expel South Africa during the period of apartheid,[52] and Arab states and Iran used to take regular initiatives to delegitimize gradually the presence of Israel in the United Nations by rejecting the credentials of the Israeli delegation in the General Assembly.[53] South Africa was only excluded from participating in the work of the General Assembly from 1974 until 1993 on the basis of a decision of the Credentials Committee of the General Assembly stating that the government of South Africa did not represent all its people. The legality of this finding is doubtful, considering that the legitimacy of the form of government, as such, is not a criterion for UN membership.[54] Expulsion, at any rate, is not necessarily an effective sanction; some people might interpret it as a confession on the part of the organization that it has failed to impose its will on the expelled member.

The Charter says nothing about withdrawal by member states; the omission is deliberate, because the insertion of a right of withdrawal in the Covenant of the League of Nations had encouraged many member states to withdraw, thereby seriously weakening the League.[55] But the San Francisco Conference in 1945 did recognize a right of withdrawal in exceptional circumstances, for example, 'if ... the organization was revealed to be unable to maintain peace or could do so only at the expense of law and justice', or if a member's

> rights and obligations as such were changed by Charter amendments in which it has not concurred and which it finds itself unable to accept, or if an amendment duly accepted by the necessary majority in the Assembly or in a general conference fails to secure the ratifications necessary to bring such amendment into effect.[56]

This statement of opinion forms part of the *travaux préparatoires* of the Charter, and may therefore be used to interpret the Charter.

The question of withdrawal has arisen only once in practice. In January 1965 Indonesia purported to withdraw, in protest against the election of Malaysia (part of whose territory was claimed by Indonesia) as a non-permanent member of the Security Council. Although the election of Malaysia could hardly be regarded as an 'exceptional circumstance' within the meaning of the San Francisco statement, the Indonesian withdrawal was apparently accepted as valid by the Secretariat at the time.[57] But in September 1966 Indonesia resumed participation in the United Nations. If its withdrawal had really been effective, Indonesia would have had to seek readmission under Article 4; instead, it simply resumed its seat, as if nothing had happened – which suggests that its withdrawal had been void. Logically, Indonesia should have had to pay all the arrears of its contributions as a member in respect of the period between January 1965 and September 1966, but, since it had derived no benefits from membership during that period, it was agreed that it should pay only 10 per cent of the arrears of its contributions.

The representation of China

The communists seized power in China at the end of 1949, but until 1971 China was represented at the United Nations by the nationalist government of Chiang Kai-shek based on Taiwan.[58] During that period one frequently heard people arguing that communist China should be 'admitted' to the United Nations; but, by treating the question as one of admission, they were unwittingly siding with the United States, which argued that communist China should not be 'admitted' because it did not fulfil the requirements of Article 4 – it was not peace-loving, it was not willing to carry out the obligations of the Charter, and so on.

The correct analysis is that states, not governments,[59] are members of the United Nations; the state of China is and always has been a member of

54 See also Chapter 5 above, 79.

55 See Chapter 2 above, 23–6.

56 Text in *United Nations Conference on International Organization: Documents*, Vol. 7, 328–9.

57 See Schwelb, *AJIL* 54 (1960), 661–72.

58 *Restatement (Third)*, Vol. 1, para. 202, Reporters' Notes, 76; R. Heuser, Taiwan, *EPIL* 12 (1990), 367–73; E.A. Danaher, The Representation of China in the United Nations, *Harvard ILJ* 13 (1972), 448–58; U. Fastenrath, Article 3, in *Simma CUNAC*, 197.

59 On the difference between states and governments, see Chapter 5 above, 75–90.

60 UNGA Res. 2758 (XXVI) of 25 October 1971. See also Schütz, Membership, op. cit, 881.
61 *FAZ* of 23 September 1994, 6.
62 See text below, 374–5.
63 See K.J. Partsch, Belgrads leerer Stuhl im Glaspalast. Das Einfrieren der UN-Mitgliedschaft Jugoslawiens durch Sicherheitsrat und Generalversammlung, *VN* 40 (1992), 181–8; Y.Z. Blum, UN Membership of the 'New' Yugoslavia: Continuity or Break?, *AJIL* 86 (1992), 830–3. See also the contributions on the 'UN Membership of the Former Yugoslavia', *AJIL* 87 (1993), 240–8 and Ginther, *op. cit.*, 174. See Chapters 5, 89–90 and 11, 167 above and Chapter 22 below, 409–15.
64 See Chapter 11 above, 167.

the United Nations; the question is, which government should represent it at the United Nations? Although Article 4 could perhaps be applied by analogy to questions of representation, it seems more logical to hold that a member state has a right to be represented by its effective government until that member state is suspended or expelled; any other solution would be out of keeping with the general principles governing the relationship between states and governments in international law. Although many states did not recognize the communist government of China until the 1970s, it is undeniable that that government had been the effective government of China since the end of 1949.

The distinction between admission and representation is important in other respects, too. If communist China had been admitted as a new member state, nationalist China (Taiwan) could have remained a member of the United Nations (and a permanent member of the Security Council) even after the admission of communist China. If, however, the question is treated as one of representation, the arrival of communist representatives must inevitably be accompanied by the departure of nationalist representatives from all the organs of the United Nations, because a state cannot be represented simultaneously by two rival governments in an international organization; and this is, in fact, what happened in 1971 when the General Assembly decided 'to restore all its rights to the People's Republic of China and to recognize the representatives of its government as the only legitimate representatives of China in the UN.'[60] In 1994, several UN member states made an attempt to restore the UN membership of Taiwan by instituting a committee on the question, which, however, failed.[61]

Moreover, questions concerning the admission of new members or the suspension or expulsion of existing members are treated as non-procedural questions, which means that the veto applies in the Security Council; questions concerning representation are treated as procedural questions, which means that the veto does not apply.[62]

The case of Yugoslavia

An indirect form of expulsion has been applied in the case of former Yugoslavia after 1991, following the independence of Bosnia-Herzegovina, Croatia, Macedonia and Slovenia.[63] With the exception of rump Yugoslavia (Serbia and Montenegro) all the new states seceding from the former federation applied for UN membership. They were admitted even though the armed conflict in Yugoslavia was continuing and the border issues were still unsettled. The early admission of Bosnia and Herzegovina on 20 May 1992 had the purpose of strengthening the position of a weak state against aggression. On the other hand, the admission of the former Yugoslav Republic of Macedonia met with difficulties because of Greek objections to the unqualified name 'Macedonia' adopted by the new state, which Greece viewed as a possible claim to its northern province with the same name. Greece also opposed the claim of the new state to use on its flag the star of Vergina (the emblem of the old Macedonian dynasty). Under a compromise the new state was admitted on 8 April 1993 under the condition that it would provisionally be called 'The Former Yugoslav Republic of Macedonia' until the differences with Greece were settled.[64]

The UN refused to allow the 'Federal Republic of Yugoslavia', represented by Serbia and Montenegro, to take the seat of the former Socialist Federal Republic of Yugoslavia, arguing that it was not the same legal entity because the former state of Yugoslavia had ceased to exist and there was no general recognition of the claim to continuity.[65] The Security Council and the General Assembly decided that the Federal Republic of Yugoslavia should apply for new membership and meanwhile refrain from taking part in the work of the Assembly,[66] although the state was allowed to continue to participate in some UN bodies.

The organs of the United Nations

There are six principal organs of the United Nations: the General Assembly, consisting of all the member states; the three Councils, which have more specialized functions and consist of a limited number of member states – the Security Council, the Economic and Social Council and the Trusteeship Council;[67] and two organs composed not of member states but of individuals – the Secretariat and the International Court of Justice.[68] There is also a vast number of subsidiary organs created by the principal organs.[69] The Security Council is the most important political organ.

The Security Council

The Security Council consists of fifteen member states.[70] Five are permanent members: China, France, the United Kingdom, the United States and Russia, which had informed the UN in 1991 that, with the support of the eleven members of the Commonwealth of Independent States arising from the remains of the former Soviet empire, it would continue the membership of the USSR in all UN organs.[71] This step taken by the Russian Federation is remarkable because it did not meet with any protest by a UN member state, although, strictly speaking, one could argue that in this matter an amendment of the Charter was necessary to change the composition of the Security Council.[72] The other ten members of the Security Council are non-permanent, elected for two years by the General Assembly. The number of non-permanent members was increased from six to ten on 1 January 1966, as a result of an amendment to the Charter; as the membership of the United Nations increased, it was considered that the membership of the Security Council should also be increased, in order to give more states an opportunity of sitting on the Security Council. The current practice is that five of the non-permanent places are filled by African and Asian states, two by Latin American states, one by an Eastern European state and two by Western European and other states (the 'other states' being principally the 'white' members of the Commonwealth – Canada, Australia and New Zealand).

Article 24(1) of the Charter provides:

In order to ensure prompt and effective action by the United Nations, its Members confer on the Security Council primary responsibility for the maintenance of international peace and security, and agree that in carrying out its duties under this responsibility the Security Council acts on their behalf.[73]

65 See Chapter 5 above, 167.

66 Res. 47/1 of 22 September 1992.

67 See Chapter 19 above, 326–32.

68 See Chapter 18 above, 281–93.

69 See G. Jaenicke, Article 7, in *Simma CUNAC*, 195–207.

70 E.J. de Aréchaga, United Nations Security Council, *EPIL* 5 (1983), 345–9; R. Geiger, Article 23, in *Simma CUNAC*, 393–6; T. Bruha, Security Council, in *Wolfrum UNLPP II*, 1147–61; K.C. Wellens (ed.), *Resolutions and Statements of the United Nations Security Council (1946–1992): A Thematic Guide*, 2nd edn 1993.

71 See Chapter 11 above, 166.

72 For a discussion see Y.Z. Blum, Russia Takes Over the Soviet Union's Seat at the United Nations, *EJIL* 3 (1992), 354–61. See Chapter 11 above, 166.

73 See J. Delbrück, Article 24, in *Simma CUNAC*, 397–407.

74 See Chapter 22 below, 386–7.

75 See Chapter 22 below, 387–90.

76 See Chapter 22 below, 416–25.

77 This does not apply to mere recommendations issued by the Council, see J. Delbrück, Article 25, in *Simma CUNAC*, 407–18.

78 Before the membership of the Security Council was increased in 1966, decisions were taken by an affirmative vote of seven members (instead of nine), 'including the concurring votes of the permanent members' in the case of non-procedural questions. See S.D. Bailey, *The Procedure of the UN Security Council*, 2nd edn 1988; Bruha, *op. cit.*, 1151–3; R. Wolfrum, Voting and Decision-Making, in *Wolfrum UNLPP II*, 1400–7; B. Simma/S. Brunner, Article 27, in *Simma CUNAC*, 430–69; M.C. Wood, Security Council Working Methods and Procedure: Recent Developments, *ICLQ* 45 (1996), 150–61.

79 F. Münch, Veto, *EPIL* 5 (1983), 389–92.

80 An important document in this respect is the Statement of the Four Sponsoring Powers on Voting Procedure in the Security Council, dated 7 June 1945, reprinted in *Brownlie BDIL*, 46.

The Security Council's principal functions consist of making recommendations for the peaceful settlement of disputes[74] and taking enforcement action to deal with threats to the peace, breaches of the peace and acts of aggression.[75] The Council also played an important role in the development of UN peacekeeping operations, an institution that was not foreseen in the Charter.[76]

Article 25 of the Charter provides:

> The members of the United Nations agree to accept and carry out the decisions of the Security Council in accordance with the present Charter.

The Security Council thus has a power to take binding decisions, which member states are under a legal obligation to obey.[77]

Voting procedure in the Security Council is regulated by Article 27 of the Charter:

> 1   Each member of the Security Council shall have one vote.
> 2   Decisions of the Security Council on procedural matters shall be made by an affirmative vote of nine members.
> 3   Decisions of the Security Council on all other matters shall be made by an affirmative vote of nine members including the concurring votes of the permanent members; provided that, in decisions under Chapter VI . . . a party to a dispute shall abstain from voting.[78]

The effect of Article 27(3) is that each permanent member of the Security Council has a 'veto'[79] on non-procedural questions. The veto does not apply to procedural questions. How does one decide whether or not a question is procedural? At the San Francisco Conference, the four powers which had convened the Conference (USA, USSR, UK and China) listed certain questions which would be regarded as procedural (for example, decisions under Articles 28–32 of the Charter, and questions relating to the agenda) and certain other questions which would be regarded as non-procedural (for example, recommendations for the peaceful settlement of disputes, and decisions to take enforcement action); in cases of doubt, which were expected to be rare, the preliminary question (that is, the question whether or not a particular question was procedural) would itself be a non-procedural question.[80] This led to the 'double veto'; a permanent member of the Security Council could veto any attempt to treat a question as procedural, and then proceed to veto any draft resolution dealing with that question. By means of the 'double veto', the Soviet Union sometimes tried to convert a number of questions, which were clearly listed as procedural in the four-power statement, into non-procedural questions. But the device of the presidential ruling can be used to prevent such abuse of the double veto. The post of president of the Security Council is held in turn by each member of the Security Council for a period of one month; if the president reacts to an attempted abuse of the double veto by ruling that the preliminary question is itself procedural, his ruling is final unless it is reversed by a (procedural) vote of the Security Council.

Each of the permanent members has used its veto on occasions, although the Soviet Union used it more frequently than the other permanent members of the Security Council. From 1945 to 1992 the actual use of the veto was as follows: Soviet Union 114; USA sixty-nine; United Kingdom thirty; France eighteen; China three.[81] While in the period from 1945 to 1990 there were a total of 279 vetos, since then the veto has been hardly used. This development is remarkable, considering that since the founding of the UN until 1990 there were only some 650 Security Council decisions, an average of less than eleven per annum, while between 1990 and 1993 there were about 250 resolutions, an average of more than sixty per year.[82] On 31 May 1990 the United States vetoed a resolution on the territories occupied by Israel and on 11 May 1993 Russia vetoed a resolution concerning the financing of the peacekeeping force in Cyprus. The significance of veto statistics, however, is limited because they do not include the 'hidden veto' (in the case of a sufficiently large number of abstentions), nor the 'unofficial veto' (preventing a motion from being put to a vote).[83]

The veto has often been criticized as a crippling limitation on the powers of the Security Council. It has in fact undermined the role of the Security Council in armed conflicts in which the permanent members were directly involved (e.g. Suez 1956, Hungary 1956, Vietnam 1946–75, and the war between China and Vietnam 1979) and prevented it from acting in many of the armed conflcits in which the permanent members were indirectly involved or had an interest. But the existence of the veto recognizes the realities of power politics; it is the price which must be paid for the unusually large powers conferred on the Security Council. Again, it must be stressed that it so happens that all the permanent members of the Security Council are nuclear powers; abolition of the veto would add little to the power of the United Nations, because it would still be virtually impossible for the United Nations to take enforcement action against a nuclear power.

In any case, some of the worst features of the veto have been softened in practice. A literal interpretation of Article 27(3) would produce the result that all permanent members would have to vote for a draft resolution in order for it to be passed; an abstention would constitute a veto.[84] But, since the first years of the United Nations, there has been a consistent practice of not treating abstentions as vetoes, and this practice was recognized as lawful by the International Court of Justice in the *Namibia* case.[85]

The effect of absence by a permanent member is less certain, because the problem has really arisen only once. In 1950 the Soviet Union boycotted the Security Council in protest against the Council's refusal to seat the communist representatives of China. In June 1950, when North Korea invaded South Korea, the absence of the Soviet Union enabled the Security Council to pass a resolution recommending member states to send forces to help South Korea.[86] The Soviet Union challenged the legality of the resolution on the grounds that it had been passed in the absence of the Soviet Union. It is debatable whether the practice which has developed in relation to abstentions by a permanent member can be applied by analogy to the absence of a permanent member; but the Soviet boycott was itself probably a violation of the Soviet Union's obligations under Article 28(1) of the Charter, which provides: 'The Security Council shall be so organized as to be able to function continuously. Each member of the

81 See Roberts/Kingsbury, Introduction, *op. cit.*, 10.

82 S.D. Murphy, The Security Council, Legitimacy, and the Concept of Collective Security After the Cold War, *Colum. JTL* 31 (1994), 201–88, at 207. See also A.W. Patil, *The UN Veto in World Affairs 1946–1990: A Complete Record and Case Histories of the Security Council's Veto*, 1992.

83 See Simma/Brunner, *op. cit.*, 466.

84 This conclusion is spelt out even more clearly in the French text: 'Les decisions du Conseil de Sécurité sur toutes autres questions sont prises par un vote affirmatif de neuf de ses membres dans lequel sont comprises les voix de tous les membres permanents.'

85 *ICJ Rep.* 1971, 16, 22. See Chapter 19 above, 328–9.

86 See Chapter 22 below, 391–2.

87 See T. Schweisfurth, Article 28, in *Simma CUNAC*, 469–80.

88 On this case see Chapter 18 above, 292–3.

89 See, for example, Roberst/ Kingsbury, *op. cit.*, 39 *et seq.*; M. Smith, Expanding Permanent Membership in the UN Security Council: Opening a Pandora's Box or Needed Change?, *Dick. JIL* 12 (1993), 173.

90 UN Doc. A/34/246 (1979). See Geiger, *op. cit.*, 396–7.

91 UN Doc. A/48/26 (1993).

92 See E. Kourula/T. Kanninen, Reforming the Security Council: The International Negotiation Process Within the Context of Calls to Amend the UN Charter to the New Realities of the Post-Cold War Era, *LJIL* 8 (1995), 337. For details on the positions taken by states, see D. Bills, International Human Rights and Humanitarian Intervention: The Ramifications of Reform of the United Nations' Security Council, *Texas ILJ* 31 (1996), 107–30.

93 See Chapter 18 above, 292–3 and Chapter 22 below, 425–9.

Security Council shall for this purpose be represented at all times at the seat of the Organization.'[87] On this reasoning, the absence of a permanent member ought not to prevent the Security Council from taking a decision; otherwise the illegal act of one state would bring the whole work of the Security Council to a halt. At any rate, the action taken by the Security Council in June 1950 has had one salutary effect: since then no permanent member has attempted to boycott the Security Council.

Article 27(3) of the Charter provides that in decisions under Chapter VI a party to a dispute shall abstain from voting. Chapter VI deals with the peaceful settlement of disputes – and also with the peaceful settlement of situations which might give rise to a dispute, and the distinction between disputes and situations is singularly imprecise. Moreover, it is often difficult to tell who is a party to a particular dispute; there are comparatively few states in the world, and many of them are linked together by alliances or other close ties, so that a dispute can affect the interests of many states to varying degrees. In the first few years of the United Nations, there were arguments about the difference between disputes and situations, about the definition of parties to a dispute and about the precise scope of Chapter VI. Since about 1950 such legalistic arguments have become rarer, and in many cases the obligation to abstain from voting has been simply ignored; states have frequently taken part in votes about disputes to which they were parties, and objections have seldom been made by other states. One recent example is the sanctions adopted by the Council against Libya for its alleged responsibility in the *Lockerbie* case, in which the United States, the UK and France took part in the voting.[88]

Recently, the composition of the Security Council, as well as its voting procedure, has come more fiercely under attack because the system does not reflect the changes in the international system since 1945.[89] The question of equitable representation and increase in the membership of the Security Council had already been raised by the non-aligned and developing countries in 1979.[90] But nothing came out of this initiative until after the end of the Cold War when Germany and Japan, followed by a number of other countries, expressed their interest in permanent membership. At the end of 1993, the General Assembly decided to establish an 'Open-ended Working Group on the Question of Equitable Representation on and Increase in the Membership of the Security Council'[91] to commence negotiations which, at the time of writing, are still continuing.[92] In view of the vested interests of the current permanent members which are not keen to renounce their privileges (and can veto any amendment or revision of the Charter they feel uncomfortable with) the process of reform is likely to be difficult. There is also no agreement on which state should represent which region, for example, in Africa or Latin America. Finally, there is the problem that, in the interest of the efficiency of the Council, there are political limits to making it too large, on the one hand, and to reducing the privileged position of the nuclear powers too much, on the other.

In part, this discussion is fomented by the perception that the enhanced role of the Security Council and its activism in the post-Cold War era raises broader constitutional issues relating to the use of the powers of the Council and the limits of these powers.[93] This concerns not only the lack of transparency of the decision-making by the P5 (the five permanent members) or P3 (the Western powers) which often hold meetings in secret, following which only the formal votes become part of the public record.[94] It also concerns the claim that the Security Council has now come under the effective control of the Western states, particularly with regard to action undertaken under the leadership of the United States.[95]

The General Assembly

The General Assembly[96] consists of all the member states of the United Nations. Some idea of the wide scope of the questions which it is competent to discuss may be obtained from examining the following provisions of the Charter:

The General Assembly may discuss any questions or any matters within the scope of the present Charter or relating to the powers and functions of any organs provided for in the present Charter, and . . . may make recommendations to the Members of the United Nations or to the Security Council or to both on any such questions or matters.[97]

. . .

The General Assembly may discuss any questions relating to the maintenance of international peace and security brought before it by any Member of the United Nations, or by the Security Council, or by a state which is not a Member of the United Nations . . . and . . . may make recommendations with regard to any such question to the state or states concerned or to the Security Council or to both . . .[98]

. . .

The General Assembly shall initiate studies and make recommendations for the purpose of:

(a) promoting international co-operation in the political field and encouraging the progressive development of international law and its codification;

(b) promoting international co-operation in the economic, social, cultural, educational and health fields, and assisting in the realization of human rights and fundamental freedoms for all . . .[99]

. . . the General Assembly may recommend measures for the peaceful adjustment of any situation . . . which it deems likely to impair the general welfare or friendly relations among nations.[100]

In addition to these general powers, the General Assembly has certain more specific powers. For instance, it receives and considers reports from all the other principal organs of the United Nations.[101] It approves the budget of the organization and fixes the amounts of the budgetary contributions which each member state must pay.[102] A member state which is in arrears in the payment of its financial contributions to the organization shall have no vote in the General Assembly if the amount of its arrears equals or exceeds the amount of the contributions due from it for the preceding two full years, although the General Assembly may waive this rule if it considers that failure to pay is caused by circumstances beyond the member state's control.[103]

94 See W.M. Reisman, The Constitutional Crisis in the United Nations, *AJIL* 87 (1993), 83–100, 85–6.

95 See Bills, *op. cit.*, 117–18, referring to such views, and Chapter 22 below, 395, 427–8.

96 S.F. Vallat, United Nations General Assembly, *EPIL* 5 (1983), 323–9; C. Tomuschat, General Assembly, in *Wolfrum UNLPP I*, 548–7; S. Magiera, Article 9, in *Simma CUNAC*, 217–26.

97 Article 10 UN Charter. See K. Hailbronner/E. Klein, Article 10, *ibid.*, 226–42.

98 Article 11(2). See K. Hailbronner/E. Klein, Article 11, *ibid.*, 242–53.

99 Article 13(1). See C.-A. Fleischhauer, Article 13, *ibid.*, 265–78. See also Chapters 3, 52–4 and 14, 211–15 above.

100 Article 14. See O. Kimminich, Article 14, *ibid.*, 279–87; J. Delbrück, Peaceful Change, in *Wolfrum UNLPP II*, 970–81.

101 Article 15. See R. Hilger, Article 15, in *Simma CUNAC*, 287–93.

102 Article 17. See R. Schmidt/W. Koschorreck, Article 17, in *Simma CUNAC*, 293–317; R. Wolfrum, Budget, in *Wolfrum UNLPP I*, 78–86.

103 Article 19. See C. Tomuschat, Article 19, in *Simma CUNAC*, 327–39.

104 See *The Independent Advisory Group on UN Financing: Financing an Effective United Nations*, 1993; W. Koschorreck, Financial Crisis, in *Wolfrum UNLPP I*, 523–31.
105 See Chapter 22 below, 423–5.
106 See for details A. Plaga, *VN 43* (1995), 30.
107 *VN* 43 (1995), 20–1.
108 See *UN Chronicle*, 1996, no. 2, 67.
109 See R. Wolfrum, Article 18, in *Simma CUNAC*, 317–27.
110 See Chapter 22 below, 385–7.
111 See Chapter 14 above, 211–15.
112 See Hailbronner/Klein, Articles 10 and 11, *op. cit.*, 231–42, 243–53.

The UN budget is indeed a chronic problem[104] which has been increased by the broader scope of activities after the Cold War, especially the increased peacekeeping activities around the globe,[105] which are not financed from the regular budget.[106] The basic principle of the UN budget system is the 'capacity to pay' (roughly related to the size of a member state's gross national product) which puts the burden on the largest economy, that of the United States. The United States originally had to pay almost 40 per cent of the UN budget, while Argentina and Brazil were asked for less than 2 per cent and India for a little more than 4 per cent. The contributions of the United States were subsequently gradually reduced to 25 per cent in 1972, although the actual capacity of the country to pay is above this level. In 1994, the UN adopted a new and more flexible, but also much more complicated system for 1995–2000. In effect, the United States will still pay the highest level of 25 per cent, while ninety-four member states (more than one half) contribute the minimum of 0.01 per cent each, a total of not even 1 per cent of the budget. Of the 185 member states fourteen pay more than 1 per cent and cater for more than 86 per cent of the regular budget (USA, Japan and Germany together close to 50 per cent).[107] As of 30 April 1996, the UN debt totalled US$2.8 billion – US$1.7 billion for peacekeeping and US$1.1 billion for the regular budget. More than half of the debt was owed by the United States (US$1.5 billion), over US$400 million by Russia and US$245 million by Ukraine.[108]

The voting procedure in the General Assembly is regulated by Article 18:

1   Each member of the General Assembly shall have one vote.
2   Decisions of the General Assembly on important questions shall be made by a two-thirds majority of the members present and voting. These questions shall include: recommendations with respect to the maintenance of international peace and security, the election of the non-permanent members of the Security Council, the election of members of the Economic and Social Council, the election of members of the Trusteeship Council in accordance with paragraph l(c) of Article 86, the admission of new members to the United Nations, the suspension of the rights and privileges of membership, the expulsion of Members, questions relating to the operation of the trusteeship system, and budgetary questions.
3   Decisions on other questions, including the determination of additional categories of questions to be decided by a two-thirds majority, shall be made by a majority of the members present and voting.[109]

On certain questions concerning the internal running of the United Nations, the General Assembly may take decisions which are binding on member states; budgetary resolutions are an obvious example. But, as regards other questions (for example, disputes between member states,[110] or questions of human rights),[111] the General Assembly has no power to take binding decisions, nor does it have any power to take enforcement action; it can only make recommendations.[112] In these respects its powers are much less than those of the Security Council, which explains why the veto exists in the Security Council but not in the General Assembly.

But, although General Assembly resolutions are not binding, they can have important legal effects.[113] They may be evidence of customary law, or of the correct interpretation of the United Nations Charter. A resolution condemning a state for breaking international law is a useful means of putting pressure on that state to reconsider its position. A resolution condemning state A for committing aggression against state B implies that it is lawful for other states to go to state B's defence, and may therefore encourage them to do so.

The drafters of the Charter took some care to prevent conflicts arising between the Security Council and the General Assembly. Article 12(1) provides:

> While the Security Council is exercising in respect of any dispute or situation the functions assigned to it in the present Charter, the General Assembly shall not make any recommendations with regard to that dispute or situation unless the Security Council so requests.[114]

Actually, Article 12(1) has turned out not to be a serious limitation for the General Assembly. Very often the Security Council has been unable to reach a decision on a question because of the veto, and in such cases the Security Council has adopted the practice of removing the question from its agenda (this decision is procedural, so the veto does not apply), in order to leave the General Assembly free to deal with the question.

In the early years of the United Nations, the Western powers were keen to emphasize the powers of the General Assembly, where they had a majority; despite Soviet objections, there was a shift of power from the Security Council to the General Assembly. The newly independent states of Africa and Asia became the largest group of states in the General Assembly, and acted as the chief supporters of an influential role for the General Assembly. By the same token the enthusiasm of the Western powers for the General Assembly declined. Communist countries came to realize the value of the General Assembly as a forum for propaganda and discussion, but neither the Soviet Union nor China was ever prepared to entrust real power to a body where it did not have a veto. When the Western powers dominated the General Assembly in the 1950s, they tried to develop it into a body which could take military action to preserve the peace of the world.[115] The African and Asian states, which dominate the General Assembly nowadays, never tried to use the General Assembly in this way; when there was still a balance between the superpowers they favoured the view that the Security Council is the most appropriate body for taking military action, and, in the past, they preferred to use their position in the General Assembly to try to obtain respect for their views on economic questions, colonialism and apartheid.[116] Now, in the post-Cold War era, the frequent practice of military intervention authorized by the Security Council under Chapter VII of the Charter[117] is viewed rather critically by many smaller states in the South and is one of the aspects underlying the demands for a reform of the Security Council. On the other hand, it is also the General Assembly which, in view of its overcrowded agenda, needs reform to improve its performance and effectiveness, but little progress has been made on the basis of recent (rather modest) proposals.[118]

113 See Chapter 3 above, 52–4.
114 See K. Hailbronner/E. Klein, Article 12, in Simma CUNAC, 253–64.
115 See Chapter 2 above, 28 and Chapter 22 below, 332–3.
116 See Chapters 2, 28–30 and 16, 233–5; 19, 326–38 above.
117 See Chapter 22 below, 395–416, 425–9.
118 See P. Wilenski, The Structure of the UN in the Post-Cold War Period, in Roberts/Kingsbury (eds), op. cit., 437, at 445–8; M. Bertrand, The Historical Development of Efforts to Reform the UN, ibid., 420–36; K. Dicke, Reform of the United Nations, in Wolfrum UNLPP II, 1012–24. See also Chapter 22 below, 430.

119 See B. Lindemann/D. Hesse-Kreindler, Secretariat, in *Wolfrum UNLPP II*, 1129–35; T. Meron, International Secretariat, *EPIL* II (1995), 1376–9; J. Lemoine, *The International Civil Servant – An Endangered Species*, 1995.

120 S.M. Schwebel, United Nations Secretary-General, *EPIL* 5 (1983), 341–5; J.E. Parber, Electing the UN Secretary-General after the Cold War, *Hastings LJ* 44 (1992), 161–84; H.v. Morr, Secretary-General, in *Wolfrum UNLPP II*, 1136–46.

121 See text above, 374.

122 Article 97. See W. Fiedler, Article 97, in *Simma CUNAC*, 1019–32.

123 Article 98. See Fiedler, Article 98, *ibid.*, 1033–44.

124 See Fiedler, *ibid.*, 1044–57.

125 See J.P. de Cuéllar, The Role of the UN Secretary-General, in Roberts/Kingsbury (eds), *op. cit.*, 125–42; R. Lavalle, The Inherent Powers of the UN Secretary-General in the Political Sphere: A Legal Analysis, *NILR* 37 (1990), 22–36; P. Szasz, The Role of the Secretary-General. Some Legal Aspects, *NYUJILP* 24 (1991), 161–98.

126 See T.M. Franck/G. Nolte, The Good Offices Function of the UN Secretary-General, in Roberts/Kingsbury (eds), *op. cit.*, 143–82; M.C. Bourloyanns, Fact-Finding by the Secretary-General of the United Nations, *NYUJILP* 22 (1990), 641–69; K. Skjelsbaek, The UN Secretary-General and the Mediation of International Disputes, *JPR* 28 (1991), 41–145; T.M. Franck, The Secretary-General's Role in Conflict Resolution: Past Present and Pure Conjecture, *EJIL* 6 (1995), 360–87.

127 de Cuéllar, *op. cit.*, 126.

The Secretariat

The UN Secretariat employs about 14,000 people, all of whom are located at UN Headquarters in New York and at other UN offices (such as in Geneva). In addition, there are about 17,000 people assigned to the secretariats of the various UN subsidiary organs.[119] The Secretariat is headed by the Secretary-General who is appointed by the General Assembly upon the recommendation of the Security Council.[120] This means that a candidate for the post of Secretary-General must secure the support both of the Security Council and of the General Assembly in order to be elected; the election is regarded as a non-procedural question,[121] and consequently the veto applies in the Security Council.

The Secretary-General is the chief administrative officer of the organization,[122] and performs such other functions as are entrusted to him by the General Assembly, the Security Council, the Economic and Social Council and the Trusteeship Council.[123] In addition, according to Article 99, he 'may bring to the attention of the Security Council any matter which in his opinion may threaten the maintenance of international peace and security'. Article 99 is important not only because of its actual terms, but also because of the light which it throws on the general nature of the Secretary-General's functions; he is not a mere servant of the political organs, but is expected to take political initiatives of his own. At any rate, that is the interpretation placed upon Article 99 by Western states; the Soviet Union, on the other hand, always tried to minimize the power of the Secretariat.[124] None of the great powers, however, have ever been interested in seeing a too independent Secretary-General.

In sum, the role of the UN Secretary-General is not merely an administrative one, but also a political one,[125] including the function of offering 'good offices' in the settlement of international conflicts.[126] The influence of the office of the Secretary-General also much depends on the person occupying it, the intellectual leadership the person can exercise, the willingness to take hard decisions without bending too much to the great powers, while at the same time not falling out of touch with the reality of power politics. As noted in a lecture at Oxford University in 1986 by a former UN Secretary-General, speaking from his own experience:

> Anyone who has the honour to be cast as Secretary-General has to avoid two extremes in playing his, or her, role. On one side is the Scylla of trying to inflate the role through too liberal a reading of the text: of succumbing, that is, to vanity and wishful thinking. On the other is the Charybdis of trying to limit the role to only those responsibilities which are explicitly conferred by the Charter and are impossible to escape: that is, succumbing to modesty, to the instinct of self-effacement, and to the desire to avoid controversy. There are, thus, temptations on both sides. Both are equally damaging to the vitality of the institution.[127]

Following the appointments of a Norwegian (Trygve Lie, 1946–53), a Swede (Dag Hammarskjöld, 1953–61), a Burmese (U Thant, 1961/2–71), an Austrian (Kurt Waldheim, 1972–81), and a Peruvian (Javier Pérez de Cuéllar, 1982–91), the UN selected Boutros Boutros-Ghali from Egypt in 1992 to give the opportunity for the African region to be represented. In June 1992 Boutros-Ghali published a much discussed report with the title 'Agenda for Peace' which contained proposals to member states on improving the capacity of the UN to deal with the new challenges, including concepts such as 'peace-making', 'peacekeeping', 'preventive diplomacy' and 'post-conflict peace-building'.[128] Some months before the November 1996 elections in the United States, however, the United States made it known that it would veto the reappointment of Boutros-Ghali (who was, *inter alia*, blamed (wrongly) for the death of American soldiers in the UN-sponsored intervention in Somalia)[129] for a second five-year period of office.

Article 100 provides:

1   In the performance of their duties the Secretary-General and the staff shall not seek or receive instructions from any government or from any other authority external to the Organization. They shall refrain from any action which might reflect on their position as international officials responsible only to the Organization.
2   Each Member of the United Nations undertakes to respect the exclusively international character of the responsibilities of the Secretary-General and the staff and not to seek to influence them in the discharge of their responsibilities.[130]

Article 100 has not always been observed; some states have tried to treat their nationals working in the Secretariat as if they were national agents or representatives. But the principles laid down in Article 100 are nevertheless indispensable if the Secretariat is to do its job properly. The staff of the Secretariat are appointed by the Secretary-General.[131] Recruitment for posts in the Secretariat, other than manual and clerical posts, is subject to complicated rules about national quotas, which favour the nationals of smaller countries; obviously a certain degree of cosmopolitanism is essential if the Secretariat is to be genuinely international and impartial, but the rules about national quotas have sometimes resulted in the appointment of poorly qualified candidates.

The terms of service of the staff are laid down mostly in Staff Regulations enacted by the General Assembly, and in Staff Rules issued by the Secretary-General under powers delegated to him by the Staff Regulations. Allegations by staff members that their terms of service have been infringed are heard by an Administrative Tribunal set up by the General Assembly; the Administrative Tribunal has applied a number of general principles of administrative law to fill gaps in the Staff Regulations and Rules.[132] The existence of the Tribunal is really in the long-term interests of the organization, because officials will not serve the organization loyally, or resist pressures from member states and other authorities outside the organization, unless they are given guarantees of fair treatment and security of tenure.

The Secretariat has been under increasing pressure (especially financial pressure from the United States due to the negative position

128 Agenda for Peace, reprinted in Roberts/Kinsbury (eds), *op. cit.*, 468 with an introductory note by Boutros Boutros-Ghali. See Chapter 22 below, 423–5.

129 See Chapter 22 below, 402–5. Boutros-Ghali was replaced by Kofi Annan from Ghana.

130 See C. Schreuer, Article 100, in *Simma CUNAC*, 1051–76.

131 See W. Göttelmann, Article 101, *ibid.*, 1077–1100.

132 See Chapters 6, 103 and 18, 289 above.

133 See Wilenski, *op. cit.*, 449 *et seq.*
134 See R. Wolfrum, Article 55 (a) and (b), in *Simma CUNAC*, 759–76 and Chapter 15 above, 222–40.
135 See K.-J. Partsch, *ibid.*, 776–93 and Chapter 14 above, 211–15.
136 See Chapter 14 above, 212–13.
137 See R. Wolfrum, Article 56, in *Simma CUNAC*, 793–5.
138 Article 60 UN Charter. See W. Meng, Article 60, *ibid.*, 821–5.
139 Article 61. See R. Lagoni, Article 61, *ibid.*, 827–34; J. Frederic/L. Kirgis, United Nations Economic and Social Council, *EPIL* 5 (1983), 310–14; R. Lagoni, ECOSOC, in *Wolfrum UNLPP I*, 461–9.
140 Article 67. See R. Lagoni, Article 67, in *Simma CUNAC*, 871–5.
141 Article 62. See Lagoni, Article 62, *ibid.*, 835–50.
142 Article 65. See P. Kunig, Article 65, *ibid.*, 865–7.
143 Article 66. See Kunig, Article 66, *ibid.*, 867–71.
144 Article 71. See R. Lagoni, Article 71, *ibid.*, 902–15.

towards the UN taken by Congress) since the 1980s to do something about disorganization and inefficiency.[133] This led to a 14 per cent cut-back in the number of staff. However, futher reforms are required, aiming at a rationalization of the bizarre structure of the Secretariat and at a more equitable and transparent method of recruiting senior officers. When Boutros-Ghali came into office in 1992 he took some steps in these directions, but the issue of the reform of the Secretariat is still a burning one.

The Economic and Social Council and the specialized agencies

Article 55 of the United Nations Charter provides:

> With a view to the creation of conditions of stability and well-being which are necessary for peaceful and friendly relations among nations based on respect for the principle of equal rights and self-determination of peoples, the United Nations shall promote:
>
> (a)   higher standards of living, full employment, and conditions of economic and social progress and development;
>
> (b)   solutions of international economic, social, health, and related problems; and international cultural and educational co-operation;[134] and
>
> (c)   universal respect for, and observance of, human rights and fundamental freedoms for all without distinction as to race, sex, language, or religion.[135]

Article 56 provides: 'All Members pledge themselves to take joint and separate action in co-operation with the Organization for the achievement of the purposes set forth in Article 55.' The extent to which Articles 55 and 56 create legal obligations for member states has already been discussed.[136] Futhermore, 'responsibility for the discharge of the functions[137] set forth in' Articles 55 and 56 is 'vested in the General Assembly and, under the authority of the General Assembly, in the Economic and Social Council'.[138]

The Economic and Social Council (ECOSOC) consists of fifty-four members of the United Nations; eighteen are elected each year by the General Assembly to serve for three years.[139] Decisions of the Council are taken by a majority of the members present and voting.[140] The Council may make or initiate studies and reports, make recommendations, prepare draft conventions and organize international conferences;[141] like the General Assembly, its terms of reference are wide, but its powers are limited, in the sense that it cannot take decisions which are binding on member states. It also assists the Security Council at the Security Council's request,[142] and performs such other functions as are assigned to it by the General Assembly; with the approval of the General Assembly, it may also perform services at the request of members of the United Nations or at the request of specialized agencies.[143]

The Economic and Social Council may arrange for consultation with non-governmental organizations which deal with matters within its competence.[144] Such arrangements have been made with hundreds of non-governmental organizations, giving them the right to send observers to the Council's meetings and (in some cases) to make written or oral statements to the Council.[145] So far, these arrangements have not produced very impressive results, but they do provide a useful channel of communication between the United Nations and public opinion.

One of the main functions of the Economic and Social Council is to coordinate the activities of the 'specialized agencies', which are defined as organizations 'established by intergovernmental agreement and having wide international responsibilities . . . in economic, social, cultural, educational, health and related fields'.[146] Such an organization becomes a specialized agency when it is 'brought into relationship with the United Nations'[147] by means of an agreement made by the agency with the Economic and Social Council and approved by the General Assembly.[148] The terms of the agreements vary from agency to agency, but certain features are common to most agreements. For instance, each of the two parties (the United Nations and the specialized agency in question) is usually given a right to send representatives (without voting rights) to meetings of certain organs in the other organization. Most of the specialized agencies agree to consider recommendations made by the General Assembly, and to transmit regular reports to the Economic and Social Council; many of them are given a right to request advisory opinions from the International Court of Justice on questions falling within their competence.[149] Provision is also usually made for the mutual exchange of information and documents, and for the enactment of similar Staff Regulations and Staff Rules by each of the organizations concerned.

The Economic and Social Council is empowered by Article 63(2) of the Charter to 'co-ordinate the activities of the specialized agencies through consultation with and recommendations to such agencies and through recommendations to the General Assembly and to the Members of the United Nations'. The General Assembly may 'examine the administrative budgets of . . . specialized agencies with a view to making recommendations to the agencies concerned'.[150] There is also an Administrative Committee on Co-ordination, composed of the Secretary-General of the United Nations and the administrative heads of the specialized agencies, which coordinates operations at the administrative level; but the coordination efforts have so far been of only limited success.

Various UN specialized agencies have already been mentioned in Chapter 6 above.[151] Currently there are sixteen such specialized agencies associated with the UN. They include the financial institutions of the World Bank Group (i.e. IMF, IBRD)[152] and the 'big four' (ILO, FAO, UNESCO and WHO).[153] Most of the specialized agencies have no power to take decisions binding on their members, but their constituent treaties often provide for interesting means of putting pressure on member states to act in a particular way. For instance, the ILO, UNESCO and WHO can draw up recommendations and draft conventions; member states are not obliged to accept the recommendations and draft conventions, but they must make periodic reports to the relevant organization about their law and practice in the fields covered by the recommendations and draft conventions in question, and in some cases they must state their reasons for not accepting

145 See Chapter 6 above, 96–100.
146 Article 57. See D.W. Bowett , *The Law of International Institutions*, 1982, 108 *et seq.*; E. Klein, United Nations, Specialized Agencies, *EPIL* 5 (1983), 349–69; D. Williams, *The Specialized Agencies and the United Nations*, 1987; I. Seidl-Hohenveldern, Specialized Agencies, in *Wolfrum UNLPP II*, 1202–8; W. Meng, Article 57, in *Simma CUNAC*, 796–816.
147 Article 57.
148 Article 63. See W. Meng, Article 63, in *Simma CUNAC*, 851–9.
149 See Chapters 18, 289–90 and 20, 347–9 above.
150 Article 17(3).
151 See Chapter 6 above, 94.
152 See Chapter 15 above, 223–8.
153 See Chapters 6, 94, 2, 24 and 15, 224 above.

them. On certain topics the WHO can adopt regulations, which are binding on every member state which does not 'opt out' of the regulations concerned. These are useful means of overcoming the inertia of states, and of inducing them to act together.

22 The United Nations and peace and security

After having discussed the interpretation of the UN Charter and the role of the main organs of the United Nations, we can now turn to the main functions of the organization in the field of the maintenance of peace and security. For the sake of convenience, these functions can be classified into three broad categories of activities: The first category concerns the political role of UN organs in the peaceful settlement of disputes, a matter mainly addressed in Chapter VI of the Charter entitled 'Pacific settlement of disputes'. The judicial role of the International Court of Justice, which is also one of the six principal organs of the UN (albeit an independent one which is not integrated into the structure of the other UN organs), and the general methods of international dispute settlement have already been discussed in Chapter 18 above.[1] The second category encompasses enforcement action which can be taken under Chapter VII dealing with 'Action with respect to threats to the peace, breaches of the peace, and acts of aggression'.[2] The third category, finally, deals with the peculiar institution of UN 'peacekeeping' operations which have no explicit legal basis in the Charter, but have developed in practice and are often described as being based upon 'Chapter VI and a half'.[3]

Pacific settlement of disputes under the United Nations Charter (Chapter VI)

Article 1(1) of the United Nations Charter states that it is one of the purposes of the United Nations

> to bring about by peaceful means, and in conformity with the principles of justice and international law, adjustment or settlement of international disputes or situations which might lead to a breach of the peace.[4]

Article 2(3) obliges member states to

> settle their disputes by peaceful means in such a manner that international peace and security, and justice, are not endangered.[5]

The two most important political organs of the United Nations for the peaceful settlement of disputes are the Security Council and the General Assembly. But, as noted above,[6] the UN Secretary-General also plays an important role in offering 'good offices' to conflict parties, a function which, to be effective, is often performed in secrecy.

A dispute may be brought before the Security Council:

1 See Chapter 18 above, 273–305.
2 See text below, 387–415.
3 See text below, 416–25.
4 See R. Wolfrum, Article 1, in *Simma CUNAC*, 49–56; Wolfrum, Peaceful Settlement of Disputes, in *Wolfrum UNLPP II*, 982–93; UN Handbook on the Peaceful Settlement of Disputes Between States, Annex to UN Doc. A/ 46/33 (1991), 23; S.R. Ratner, Image and Reality in the UN's Peaceful Settlement of Disputes, *EJIL* 6 (1995), 426–44 and the literature in Chapter 18 above, 273 n. 1.
5 See C. Tomuschat, Article 2(3), in *Simma CUNAC*, 97–106.
6 See Chapter 21 above, 380–1.

7 Art. 35(1) UN Charter. See T. Schweisfurth, Article 35, in *Simma CUNAC*, 527–34.
8 Article 35(2). See Schweisfurth, *ibid.*
9 Article 11(3) and also Articles 10 and 11(2). See K. Hailbronner/E. Klein, Articles 10 and 11, in *Simma CUNAC*, 226–53.
10 Article 99. See W. Fiedler, Article 99, *ibid.*, 1044–57.
11 See Chapter 21 above, 374.
12 *ICJ Rep.* 1971, paras. 114–16; see Chapter 19 above, 328–9. See P. Malanczuk, Countermeasures and Self-Defence as Circumstances Precluding Wrongfulness in the International Law Commission's Draft Articles on State Responsibility, in M. Spinedi/B. Simma (eds), *United Nations Codification of State Responsibility*, 1987, 197–286, at 237. But see R. Higgins, Peace and Security: Achievements and Failures, *EJIL* 6 (1995), 445–60, at 446, who notes (with reference to para. 105 of the Judgment) that the Court 'made the extremely important observation (which has implications for other chapters of the Charter as well) that resolutions may in any event have operative effect – that is to say, the findings of fact, or applications of law within an organ's own competence, are determinative.'
13 Article 36 of the Charter. See T. Stein/S. Richter, Article 36, in *Simma CUNAC*, 534–46.
14 As to decisions of the Security Council on measures to give effect to a judgment of the ICJ under Article 94 (2) of the Charter, see Chapter 18 above, 288–9.
15 See Malanczuk (1987), *op. cit.*, 237; J.A. Frowein, Article 39, in *Simma CUNAC*, 613.

1   by a member of the United Nations, whether or not it is a party to the dispute;[7]

2   by a state which is not a member of the United Nations, provided that it is a party to the dispute and 'accepts in advance, for the purposes of the dispute, the obligations of pacific settlement provided in the . . . Charter';[8]

3   by the General Assembly, which 'may call the attention of the Security Council to situations which are likely to endanger international peace and security';[9]

4   by the Secretary-General, who 'may bring to the attention of the Security Council any matter which in his opinion may threaten the maintenance of international peace and security'.[10]

However, a state, the General Assembly, or the Secretary-General can only request the Security Council to consider a dispute; it is for the Security Council to decide whether to accede to that request by placing the dispute on its agenda. Similarly, a dispute can be removed from the Security Council's agenda only by the Security Council, and not by the parties to the dispute; the wisdom of this practice was shown a few days after the Soviet invasion of Czechoslovakia in August 1968, when the Security Council refused to accept a request from Czechoslovakia (which was, of course, acting under Soviet pressure) to remove the question of the invasion from its agenda. Decisions concerning the agenda are procedural decisions, and therefore the veto does not apply.[11]

Chapter VI empowers the Security Council to make various types of recommendations for the peaceful settlement of disputes; the Security Council also has certain powers of investigation. According to the letter of the Charter, the circumstances in which the Security Council may recommend terms of settlement are different from the circumstances in which it may recommend procedures for settlement; but the circumstances in question are defined in very imprecise terms. In practice, the Security Council usually disregards these complexities and makes all sorts of recommendations, without citing any articles of the Charter, and without bothering about the tortuous and imprecise distinctions made in Chapter VI.

There has been some dispute in the literature on whether Security Council decisions taken under Chapter VI can be binding. The broader view which the International Court of Justice had expressed in its opinion in the *Namibia* case in 1970 failed to be established in practice. (The Court argued that a Security Council resolution not based on Chapter VII, but directly on Article 25 in Chapter V of the Charter, which states that UN Members 'agree to accept and carry out the decisions of the Security Council in accordance with the present Charter', could be binding.[12]) Recommendations made by the Security Council under Chapter VI therefore do not generally create legal obligations,[13] although they often exercise great political influence. The Council has authority to pass *binding* decisions only under Chapter VII.[14] The difficulty remains, however, that the Security Council has frequently refrained from clearly indicating upon which Articles of the Charter its decisions are based.[15] As regards voting procedure, recommendations under Chapter VI are non-procedural, so the veto applies.[16]

The General Assembly may also deal with disputes under Articles 10, 11(2), 12 and 14 of the Charter.[17] Any member state of the United Nations may ask the General Assembly to consider a dispute; and so may a non-member state, provided it is a party to the dispute in question and accepts in advance, for the purposes of that dispute, the obligations of pacific settlement contained in the Charter. The General Assembly may make recommendations and appoint fact-finding missions; states are under no legal obligation to comply with such recommendations or to cooperate with fact-finding missions,[18] although General Assembly recommendations often exercise great political influence.

The functions of the Security Council and the General Assembly in connection with the settlement of disputes represent a mixture of good offices, mediation, inquiry and conciliation.[19] But the Security Council and the General Assembly are not, and were never intended to be, judicial bodies. Although they take legal factors into account, they also take political factors into account, and political considerations often overshadow legal considerations in their deliberations. Moreover, members of the Security Council and the General Assembly are not always impartial; during the Cold War members of an alliance tended to support one another, and small neutralist states tried to avoid giving offence to the two superpowers. Experience has shown that if a dispute between two members of the same alliance is brought to the United Nations, enemies of the alliance may try to aggravate the dispute (instead of encouraging the parties to settle it), in the hope of disrupting the alliance. In view of these factors, the absence of a power to take binding decisions should be regarded as a necessary safeguard for member states, and not as a defect in the system.

Normally states take disputes to the United Nations in order to put political pressure on their opponents, by mobilizing world opinion against them. Sometimes, however, recourse to the United Nations may serve another purpose; a state which is under pressure from its own domestic opinion to take a 'strong line' against another state may try to satisfy domestic opinion by making fierce speeches at the United Nations, as a substitute for action of a more damaging character. In such cases, the United Nations acts as a safety valve, which enables states to 'let off steam'. But the frequency with which the United Nations is used for this purpose explains why states sometimes regard it as an unfriendly act to complain to the United Nations against another state.

Collective security and enforcement action (Chapter VII)

Based on the negative experience with the League of Nations,[20] the drafters of the Charter aimed to create a more advanced system of collective security for the enforcement of peace. Its pillars were to rest on the comprehensive prohibition of any force or threat of force in Article 2(4) of the Charter[21] and an elaborate system of economic, political and military enforcement measures against aggression in Chapter VII of the Charter.[22] The monopoly in enforcement power was made subject only to

16 On the veto see Chapter 21 above, 374–5.

17 See Chapter 21 above, 377–9.

18 See A. Berg, The 1991 Declaration on Fact-Finding by the United Nations, *EJIL* 4 (1994), 107–14.

19 See Chapter 18 above, 275–81. C. Murphy, The Conciliatory Responsibilities of the United Nations Security Council, *GYIL* 35 (1992), 190–204.

20 See Chapter 2 above, 25–6.

21 See Chapter 19 above, 309–11.

22 On Chapter VII (Articles 39–43) see Frowein, in *Simma CUNAC*, 605–39; B.O. Bryde, Articles 44–50, *ibid.*, 640–61; *Harris CMIL*, 874–907, 1010–17; O. Schachter, *International Law in Theory and Practice*, 1991, Chapter XVII; E. Stein, The United Nations and the Enforcement of Peace, *Mich. JIL* 10 (1989), 304–16; J. Delbrück, Collective Security, *EPIL* I (1992), 646–56; *idem*, Collective Measures, *ibid.*, 643–4; K. Doehring, Collective Security, in *Wolfrum UNLPP I*, 110–15; P. Malanczuk, *Humanitarian Intervention and the Legitimacy of the Use of Force*, 1993; H. Freudenschuß, Between Unilateralism and Collective Security: Authorizations of the Use of Force by the UN Security Council, *EJIL* 5 (1994), 492–531; Higgins (1995), *op. cit.*; Y. Kerbat, *La Référence au Chapitre VII de la Charte des Nations Unies dans les résolutions à caractère humanitaire du Conseil de sécurité*, 1995; Société Française pour le Droit International. Colloque de Rennes: *Le Chapitre VII de la Charte des Nations Unies*, 1995; J. Quigley, The 'Privatization' of Security Council Enforcement Action: A Threat to Unilateralism, *Mich. JIL* 17 (1996), 249–83; F.R. Tesón, Collective Humanitarian Intervention, ibid, 323–71; A.P. Mutharika, The Role of the United Nations Security Council in African Peace Management: Some Proposals, *ibid.*, 537–62; D. Bills, International Human Rights and Humanitarian Intervention: The Ramifications of Reform of the United Nations' Security Council, *Texas ILJ* 31 (1996), 107–30; R.E. Gordon, Humanitarian Intervention by the United Nations: Iraq, Somalia, and Haiti, *ibid.*, 43–56.

23 See Chapter 19 above, 311–26.
24 Article 53 has not worked well in practice, see the 6th edn of this book, 267–8. On Chapter VIII of the Charter which deals with 'Regional Arrangements' see further W. Hummer/ M. Schweitzer, Article 52, in *Simma CUNAC*, 679–722; G. Ress, Article 53, *ibid.*, 722–52; Hummer/Schweitzer, Article 54, *ibid.*, 752–7; S.v. Schorlemer, Blocs and Groups of States, in *Wolfrum UNLPP I*, 69–77; U. Beyerlin, Regional Arrangements, in *Wolfrum UNLPP II*, 1040–51. See also J. Wolf, Regional Arrangements and the UN Charter, *EPIL* 6 (1983), 289–95; J.A. Frowein, Legal Consequences for International Law Enforcement in Case of Security Council Inaction, in J. Delbrück (ed.), *The Future of International Law Enforcement*, 1993, 111–24; R. Wolfrum, Der Beitrag regionaler Abmachungen zur Friedenssicherung: Möglichkeit und Grenzen, *ZaöRV* 53 (1993), 603–7; G. Nolte, Restoring Peace by Regional Action: International Legal Aspects of the Liberian Conflict, *ZaöRV* 53 (1993), 603–37; M. Weller (ed.), *Regional Peacekeeping and International Enforcement: The Liberian Crisis*, 1994; J.A. Frowein, Zwangsmaßnahmen von Regionalorganisationen, in *FS Bernhardt*, 57–69. Recent proposals to give a central role to regional organizations in the area of military collective security overlook the fact that most regional organizations are not equipped for such tasks and are also often not sufficiently impartial, see Higgins (1995), *op. cit.*, 445–60, 450–2. On regional organizations, see Chapter 6 above, 94–5.
25 B.B. Ferencz, Aggression, *EPIL* I (1992), 58–65.
26 H. Neuhold, Peace, Threat to, *EPIL* 4 (1982), 100–2.
27 For the extension of the interpretation of these terms to situations of internal conflict in the practice of the Security Council, see text below, 426–7.
28 See Frowein, Article 39, in *Simma CUNAC*, 605–16.
29 M. Weller, Comments: The Use of Force and Collective Security, in I.F. Dekker/H.H.G. Post, *The Gulf War of 1980–1988*, 1992, 69, at 82, notes that it is not clear from the Charter and practice whether a determination as specified in Article 39 is required before Article 40 can come into operation. The position of Article 40 in Chapter VII, however, shows that it requires that Article 39 be applicable;

two exceptions: first, the unilateral or collective right of self-defence in Article 51[23] and, second, enforcement measures by regional organizations authorized by the Security Council under Article 53.[24]

The General Assembly was strengthened and accorded subsidiary functions in the maintenance of international peace. The Secretary-General was to play a stronger political role than his counterpart under the League system. It is helpful to first consider the general normative framework set out in the text of the Charter before looking at how Chapter VII has worked in actual practice.

Chapter VII is entitled: 'Action with respect to threats to the peace, breaches of the peace, and acts of aggression'.[25] The Charter does not try to define these terms (although it is fairly clear from the context that 'threats to the peace'[26] and 'breaches of the peace' were intended to refer to international peace);[27] instead, Article 39, the first Article in Chapter VII, provides:

> The Security Council shall determine the existence of any threat to the peace, breach of the peace, or act of aggression and shall make recommendations, or decide what measures shall be taken in accordance with Articles 41 and 42, to maintain or restore international peace and security.[28]

But the Council may also adopt provisional measures in accordance with Article 40[29] which provides:

> In order to prevent an aggravation of the situation, the Security Council may, before making the recommendations or deciding upon the measures provided for in Article 39, call upon the parties concerned to comply with such provisional measures as it deems necessary or desirable. Such provisional measures shall be without prejudice to the rights, claims, or position of the parties concerned. The Security Council shall duly take account of failure to comply with such provisional measures.[30]

The words 'call upon', used in Article 40, cause some problems of interpretation. They are often used in United Nations resolutions as a synonym for 'recommend',[31] but member states seem to agree that the words, when used in Article 40, mean 'order'; this interpretation is reinforced when Article 40 is read in conjunction with Article 25.[32] For instance, on 15 July 1948 the Security Council passed a ceasefire resolution calling upon the Arabs and Israelis to stop fighting, and this resolution was clearly understood to be mandatory – that is, it was an order which created a legal obligation to obey.[33] Naturally, such resolutions are not always followed, unless they are backed up by the threat of more severe measures, if the parties have not already decided, for political or military reasons, that they offer a welcome opportunity to lay down arms, while saving face.

In general, however, the Security Council has made sparing use of its powers under Article 40.[34] Most ceasefire resolutions are phrased as recommendations, not as orders. The reason is probably that members of the Security Council would feel morally obliged to take enforcement action against states which disobeyed an order, and they are reluctant to take enforcement action against states which are their own allies or *protégés*.

Even when phrased as recommendations, however, ceasefire resolutions have often succeeded in stopping the fighting; states are reluctant to continue fighting in defiance of the great powers and of world opinion generally.

Enforcement action *stricto sensu* (that is, action to deal with a threat to the peace, breach of the peace, or act of aggression) can take two forms; Article 41 provides for non-military enforcement action and Article 42 provides for military enforcement action.

Article 41 reads as follows:

> The Security Council may decide what measures not involving the use of armed force are to be employed to give effect to its decisions, and it may call upon the Members of the United Nations to apply such measures. These may include complete or partial interruption of economic relations and of rail, sea, air, postal, telegraphic, radio, and other means of communication, and the severance of diplomatic relations.

Decisions of the Security Council taken under Article 41 on measures not involving the use of armed force, such as to apply economic sanctions, are binding for the member states called upon.[35]

Article 42 provides:

> Should the Security Council consider that measures provided for in Article 41 would be inadequate or have proved to be inadequate, it may take such action by air, sea, or land forces as may be necessary to maintain or restore international peace and security. Such action may include demonstrations, blockade, and other operations by air, sea or land forces of Members of the United Nations.[36]

Article 42 must be read in conjunction with Article 43, which provides:

> All Members of the United Nations . . . undertake to make available to the Security Council, on its call and in accordance with a special agreement or agreements, armed forces, assistance, and facilities, including rights of passage, necessary for the purpose of maintaining international peace and security . . . The agreement or agreements shall be negotiated as soon as possible on the initiative of the Security Council. They shall be concluded between the Security Council and Members . . . [of the United Nations].

Member states have never made any of the special agreements envisaged in Article 43 and the Military Staff Committee established under Article 47 has remained a dead body which only holds regular ritual meetings.[37] The absence of special agreements with the Security Council in the sense of Article 43 does not preclude member states from placing troops *ad hoc* at the disposal of the Council. But the Security Council cannot order a state to take part in military enforcement action in the same way that it can order a state to take part in non-military enforcement action. This is so because a state is not obliged to take part in military operations under Article 42 unless it has concluded a 'special agreement' under Article 43.[38]

However, the Security Council can *authorize* a state to use force, even in circumstances where force would normally be illegal, if the conditions of

see Frowein, Article 40, in *Simma CUNAC*, at 618.

30 See Frowein, Article 40, *ibid.*, 617–21.

31 For instance, see text below, 390.

32 See Chapter 21 above, 374.

33 See text below, 391.

34 See text below, 419, 422.

35 J.A. Frowein, Article 41, in *Simma CUNAC*, 621–3; U. Beyerlin, Sanctions, in *Wolfrum UNLPP II*, 1111–28; J. Combacau, Sanctions, *EPIL* 9 (1986), 337–41; M.P. Doxey, *International Sanctions in Contemporary Perspective*, 1987; P. Weckel, Le Chapitre VII de la Charte et son application par le Conseil de Sécurité, *AFDI* 37 (1991), 165–202; E. Klein, Sanctions by International Organizations and Economic Communities, *AVR* 30 (1992), 101–13; R. Lapidoth, Some Reflections on the Law and Practice Concerning the Imposition of Sanctions by the Security Council, *ibid.*, 114–27.

36 See J.A. Frowein, Article 42, in *Simma CUNAC*, 628–36; see also text below, 389–90, 396–3.

37 See D.W. Bowett, International Military Force, *EPIL* 3 (1982), 221; R. Sommereyns, United Nations Forces, *EPIL* 4 (1982), 253; J.A. Frowein, Article 43, in *Simma CUNAC*, 636–40.

38 For the recent development of stand-by arrangements of member states with the UN to earmark national contingents for UN peacekeeping, see text below, 424–5.

39 See Frowein, Article 39, *op. cit.*, 614–6.

40 However, Frowein, *ibid.*, at 615, argues that action taken by member states against the target state pursuant to such a recommendation may nevertheless be justified, technically not by the recommendation, but by the presumption of legality created by the underlying legal opinion of the Security Council as the body of the United Nations responsible for securing international peace. He suggests that this could be possible under the condition that the Security Council has correctly assessed the legality of the conduct recommended to member states. But the question this view begs is who decides on whether the Council has done so.

41 Frowein, Article 42, *op. cit.*, 633; see also Frowein, Article 39, *op. cit.*, 613.

42 The Resolution seems to have been adopted under Chapter VI; see Beyerlin, Sanctions, *op. cit.*, 1115. See also text below, 393–5.

43 See Chapter 21 above, 374–5.

Articles 39 and 42 are met. Article 42 empowers the Security Council to use force in such circumstances, and therefore may be interpreted *a fortiori* as enabling the Security Council to authorize states to do the same. Such a decision of the Security Council can logically only be a *recommendation* to member states. It cannot bind member states to carry out a resolution to adopt military measures without their consent. However, it is binding upon the target state with the legal effect that it is barred from invoking self-defence under Article 51 of the Charter, taking resort to reprisals short of the use of force, or later claiming reparation in response to the use of force by the member states so authorized by the Council. Legally, the decision of the Security Council under Article 42 therefore has a double nature. With respect to the target state it is a binding decision, with regard to the authorized member states it is a recommendation which justifies in law the use of armed force otherwise prohibited by Article 2(4) of the Charter.

There is some dispute on the question of whether a mere recommendation adopted by the Security Council solely under Article 39 without direct reference to Articles 41 and 42 may include enforcement measures. The better view, in the light of the text and genesis of the Charter and the system of Chapter VII, is that such enforcement measures require a clear decision of the Council to apply Articles 41 or 42 and to determine which parties are placed under legal obligations.[39] As noted above, enforcement measures taken by the Council within its competence are binding upon the target state and prevent it from invoking other grounds of international law for the illegality of, for example, boycott measures. A mere recommendation under Article 39 by itself cannot have this effect.[40] In practice, however, the Security Council tends to refer only to Chapter VII as such and not to specific articles. Article 42, for example, has never been expressly invoked.[41] There are also resolutions of the Council which give no indication at all as to their legal basis. For example, in Resolution 569 (1985) of 26 July 1985, the Security Council requested member states to impose embargo measures on South Africa without having previously decided that there was a threat to international peace in the sense of Article 39.[42]

In examining the way Chapter VII has been applied in actual practice, the following will distinguish between the practice during the Cold War period and after the end of the Cold War because it marks an important turning point.

Practice under Chapter VII during the Cold War

During the Cold War the collective security system of the United Nations remained largely crippled, because the required continuing cooperation of the five major allied powers had evaporated soon after the Second World War was over. While the Soviet Union tended to view the UN as being controlled by inherently hostile powers, and made excessive use of its veto right,[43] in the early phase the United States, relying on its 'mechanical majority', favoured a normative approach based upon the Charter provisions. Eric Stein notes:

> It was United States diplomacy that championed the normative-institutional

approach to peace maintenance, particularly when it suited the American goals of the day. Without American support there seemed little strength behind the Charter claim of prohibition of force. With the 'normative retreat' by the United States, due as much to the changed constituency of the world community as to Soviet policy and to the emerging limits of American power, the United Nations' claim to the role of centralized peace enforcement lost any reality.[44]

During the Cold War the procedures for collective measures in Chapter VII were largely substituted by balance of power strategies implemented by the great powers outside the framework of the United Nations.[45] There was not much enforcement activity by the Security Council up to 1990. It was focusing on aspects of decolonization and did not affect any of the great powers or their close allies. Occasional attempts by the General Assembly to revitalize collective security remained fruitless.[46] From 1946 to 1986, there were only two determinations under Article 39 by the Security Council that there was a 'breach of the peace', in the case of Korea in 1950[47] and concerning the Falklands war in 1986.[48] In the same period the Council referred to 'aggression' only in the cases of Israel and South Africa and determined that there was a 'threat to international peace and security' in not more than seven instances.[49] From 1945 to 1990, there were only two cases in which the Security Council is considered to have authorized the use of force (apart from the use of self-defence to protect the mandate of peacekeeping operations conducted with the consent of the parties),[50] namely in the cases of Korea and Southern Rhodesia. Binding non-military sanctions were also only adopted twice, with the economic blockade of Southern Rhodesia (1966–79) and the arms embargo imposed upon South Africa in 1977. An attempt to apply Article 41 against Iran in January 1980, in order to compel Iran to release the United States diplomats being held as hostages in Tehran, was defeated by a Soviet veto.[51]

Thus, few of the more than seventy international wars that occurred until the end of the 1990s[52] led to a response under Chapter VII, and major conflicts in this period failed to be addressed by binding decisions of the Security Council. In the Cuban missile crisis of 1962,[53] involving a dangerous direct confrontation between the two great powers, the United States based its unilateral 'quarantine' action primarily on the authority of the Organization of American States.[54] The Vietnam War was kept outside of the Security Council and the General Assembly.[55] In the Arab-Israeli conflict, the Security Council repeatedly made threats to adopt sanctions under Chapter VII. But they remained empty threats and therefore lost all credibility.[56] The Council was unable to find a consensus on sanctions during the Tehran Hostages crisis of 1979–81.[57] The Soviet intervention in Afghanistan (1979–89) also never occupied the Security Council.[58] In the First Gulf War between Iraq and Iran (1980–8), one of the most vicious wars of modern times, it took seven years before the Security Council effectively responded.[59]

The United Nations force in Korea

When North Korea invaded South Korea ('the Republic of Korea') in June 1950, the Security Council, profiting from the absence of the Soviet

44 Stein, *op. cit.*, 312.
45 See N.D. White, *Keeping the Peace: The United Nations and the Maintenance of International Peace and Security*, 2nd rev. edn 1993.
46 For examples, see M. Koskenniemi, The Place of Law in Collective Security, *Mich. JIL* 17 (1996), 455–90, at 457; Beyerlin, Sanctions, *op. cit.*, 1113–14.
47 See text below, 391–2.
48 SC Res. 502 (1982) calling upon Argentina and the UK to cease their hostilities referred to a breach of the peace 'in the Falklands region'. See Chapters 10, 148 and 19, 315, 322 above.
49 See Koskenniemi, *op. cit.*, 458.
50 Such as in the Congo and in Cyprus, see text below, 412–20, 420–2.
51 SC draft resolution S/13735, 13 January 1980. See *UN Chronicle*, 1980, no. 2, 18–26. See also Chapter 17 above, 259–60.
52 See Chapter 19 above, 311.
53 See Chapter 2 above, 27.
54 See Chapter 6 above, 95.
55 See Chapter 2, 27 and Chapter 19, 325 above.
56 See text above, 388.
57 See Chapters 17, 259–60 and 19, 315 above.
58 See Chapter 19 above, 322–3.
59 See text below, 396–9.

60 See Chapter 21 above, 375–6.

61 SC Res. 83 (1950).

62 SC Res. 84 (1950). See D. Bindschedler-Robert, Korea, *EPIL* 12 (1990), 202–8; L. Gordenker, *The United Nations and the Peaceful Unification of Korea: The Politics of Field Operations 1947–1950*, 1959; D.B. Bowett, *United Nations Forces: A Legal Study of United Nations Practice*, 1964, 29–60; T.-H. Yoo, *The Korean War and the United Nations: A Legal and Diplomatic History*, 1965; M. Hastings, *The Korean War*, 1993; S. Brammer, Conflicts, Korea, in *Wolfrum UNLPP I*, 278–85; L. Fisher, The Korean War: On What Legal Basis Did Truman Act?, *AJIL* 89 (1995), 21–39.

63 See Chapter 19 above, 311.

64 See text above, 389–90.

65 See J. Delbrück, Article 24, in *Simma CUNAC*, 397–407.

66 *ICJ Rep.* 1962, 151, 162–3. See text below, 420–2.

67 UNGA Res. 377 (V), *UNYb* 1950, 193–5. See H. Reicher, The Uniting for Peace Resolution on the Thirtieth Anniversary of its Passage, *Colum. JTL* 20 (1981), 1–49; E. Stein/R.C. Morrissey, Uniting for Peace Resolution, *EPIL* 5 (1983), 379–82; B. Nolte, Uniting for Peace, in *Wolfrum UNLPP II*, 1341–8.

68 Article 28 UN Charter. See T. Schweisfurth, Article 28, in *Simma CUNAC*, 469–80.

69 Article 20. See G. Zieger *et al.*, Article 20, *ibid.*, 339–59.

70 Article 21. See M. Schaefer, Article 21, *ibid.*, 360–80.

representative,[60] passed a resolution recommending member states to 'furnish such assistance to the Republic of Korea as may be necessary to repel the armed attack and to restore international peace';[61] later it passed another resolution recommending them to place their forces in Korea under a unified command to be appointed by the United States.[62]

It is doubtful whether the forces in Korea constituted a United Nations force in any meaningful sense. They were always called a United Nations force, they were authorized by the Security Council to fly the United Nations flag and they were awarded United Nations medals by the General Assembly. But all the decisions concerning the operations of the forces were taken by the United States (sometimes after consulting the other states which had sent forces to Korea), and the Commander took his orders from the United States, not from the United Nations; the decision to dismiss the original Commander, General MacArthur, and to replace him by a new Commander, was taken unilaterally by the United States. Moreover, when the fighting ended and a conference met at Geneva in 1954 to try to reunify Korea, the 'Allied Side' at the conference did not consist of representatives of the United Nations, but of representatives of the individual states which had sent forces to Korea.

The states which sent forces to Korea might be regarded as exercising a right of collective self-defence under Article 51 of the Charter;[63] alternatively, they might be regarded as acting under an authorization conferred by the Security Council (if the Security Council can use force itself, it can *a fortiori* authorize member states to do the same).[64] But the forces were probably national forces, not United Nations forces.

The Uniting for Peace Resolution

The Security Council had been able to act in Korea because the Soviet Union had been boycotting the Security Council; it was unlikely that Soviet boycotts would recur in the future. After the outbreak of the Korean War, Western states therefore tried to strengthen the General Assembly, in order that it might be able to act when the Soviet veto prevented the Security Council from acting. Article 24 of the Charter gave the Security Council 'primary responsibility for the maintenance of international peace and security',[65] and it was argued that this did not preclude the General Assembly from exercising a secondary or residual responsibility – an argument which was approved by the International Court of Justice in the *Expenses* case.[66] On 3 November 1950 the General Assembly passed the Uniting for Peace Resolution, in order to increase its ability to exercise this secondary or residual responsibility.[67]

Unlike the Security Council, which is 'so organized as to be able to function continuously',[68] the General Assembly meets only 'in regular annual sessions and in such special sessions as occasion may require'.[69] Consequently, the General Assembly might find it difficult to deal with trouble which occurred when it was not in session. To remedy this defect, the Uniting for Peace Resolution streamlined the procedure for calling special sessions of the General Assembly. This was an exercise of the General Assembly's power to 'adopt its own rules of procedure';[70] even the communist countries, which challenged the legality of the resolution in

1950, have made use of this procedure when requesting special sessions of the General Assembly (for example, at the time of the Suez invasion in 1956).[71]

The Uniting for Peace Resolution states that, if the Security Council fails in its primary responsibility of maintaining international peace and security, the General Assembly shall consider the matter immediately with a view to making recommendations for collective measures, including the use of armed force where necessary; and it recommends members to maintain contingents in their armed forces which could be made available 'for service as a United Nations unit . . . upon recommendation by the Security Council or the General Assembly'. Needless to say, the communist countries opposed this part of the Resolution with special vehemence; and its legality is certainly open to doubt. Article 11(2) of the Charter says that 'any . . . question on which action is necessary shall be referred to the Security Council by the General Assembly', and it is fairly clear that this gives the Security Council a monopoly of 'action'.[72] In the *Expenses* case, the International Court of Justice interpreted 'action' to mean 'enforcement action', and said that the United Nations Emergency Force in the Middle East, created by the General Assembly in 1956, was not contrary to Article 11(2) because it was not designed to take enforcement action;[73] the Court clearly implied that the General Assembly would have acted illegally if it had set up a force designed to take enforcement action.

On the other hand, states have a right of collective self-defence under Article 51 of the Charter,[74] and there is nothing to prevent the General Assembly from recommending them to exercise this right in order to defend the victim of aggression; but in this case it is difficult to describe the forces of the states concerned as 'a United Nations unit'.

The Uniting for Peace Resolution was first invoked in 1956 in response to the military action taken by France, the United Kingdom and Israel following Egypt's seizure of the Suez Canal. The United States and the Soviet Union collaborated and succeeded in demanding the withdrawal of the foreign forces from Egypt.[75] However, the call of the General Assembly for a termination of the Soviet armed intervention in Hungary, which coincided with the Suez Canal crisis, found no response.

Rhodesia and South Africa

On 11 November 1965, the white population of the British colony of Rhodesia unilaterally declared Rhodesia independent, against the wishes of the United Kingdom and without reference to the Africans who formed 94 per cent of the population of Rhodesia.[76] The first resolution of the Security Council on Rhodesia, passed immediately after the declaration of independence, in effect merely recommended member states to suspend trade in certain commodities with Rhodesia.[77] On 9 April 1966, the Security Council passed a resolution authorizing the UK to search ships on the high seas to see whether they were carrying oil destined for Rhodesia.[78] On 16 December 1966, the Security Council decided that 'the present situation in . . . Rhodesia constitutes a threat to international peace', and ordered member states to suspend trade in certain commodities with Rhodesia.[79] The 'sanctions' were made mandatory. Indeed, the Rhodesia

71 See for other examples C. Tomuschat, General Assembly, in *Wolfrum UNLPP I*, 548–57, at 550; Nolte, Uniting for Peace, *op. cit.*, 1346–7.

72 See text above, 386.

73 *ICJ Rep.* 1962, 151, 165, 171–2. On this case, see text below, 420–2.

74 See Chapter 19 above, 311.

75 See Chapter 2 above, 27–8.

76 See J.E.S. Fawcett, Security Council Resolutions on Rhodesia, *BYIL* 41 (1965–6), 103; R. Higgins, International law, Rhodesia, and the UN, *The World Today* 23 (1967), 94; R. Zacklin, *The United Nations and Rhodesia*, 1974; H. Strack, *Sanctions: The Case of Rhodesia*, 1978; J. Nkala, *The United Nations, International Law and the Rhodesian Independence Crisis*, 1985; W. Morvay, Rhodesia/Zimbabwe, *EPIL* 12 (1990), 319–32; V. Gowlland-Debbas, *Collective Responses to Illegal Acts in International Law: United Nations Action in the Question of Southern Rhodesia*, 1990; P.-T. Stoll, Conflicts, Rhodesia/Zimbabwe, in *Wolfrum UNLPP I*, 311–16.

77 SC Res. 217 (1965), *AJIL* 60 (1966), 924; *ILM* 5 (1966), 167. Despite the use of the words 'call upon' in the resolution, it was not mandatory; see *BPIL* 1965, 101, 176–8.

78 SC Res. 221 (1966), *AJIL* 60 (1966), 925; *ILM* 5 (1966), 534.

79 SC Res. 232 (1966), *ILM* 6 (1967), 141. Subsequent resolutions, which were all based on Articles 39 and 41, reaffirmed these sanctions decisions; see, e.g., SC Res. 253 (1968) and SC Res. 277 (1970).

80 SC Res. 418 (1977), *UN Chronicle*, December 1977, 10. This made a voluntary arms embargo instituted by the Council in 1963 mandatory; J.C. Heunis, *United Nations versus South Africa*, 1986; T. Roeser, The Arms Embargo of the UN Security Council Against South Africa: Legal and Practical Aspects, *GYIL* 31 (1988), 574–94; L.B. Sohn, *Rights in Conflict: The United Nations and South Africa*, 1994; Beyerlin, Sanctions, *op. cit.*, 1116–17; P.-T. Stoll, Conflicts, South Africa, in *Wolfrum UNLPP I*, 317–29.
81 See *UN Chronicle*, 1980, no. 1, 13–6.
82 See *UN Chronicle*, 1994, no. 4, 4–14 for the end of apartheid and a chronology of UN involvement.
83 See text below, 426–7.
84 See Chapter 18 above, 292–3 and text below, 426–8.
85 See Chapter 5 above, 73–80.
86 See, for example, J. Delbrück, A Fresh Look at Humanitarian Intervention under the Authority of the United Nations, *Indiana LJ* (1992), 887–901, at 894; P. Fifoot, Functions and Powers, and Inventions: UN Action in Respect of Human Rights and Humanitarian Intervention, in N.S. Rodley (ed.), *To Loose the Bands of Wickedness – International Intervention in Defence of Human Rights*, 1992, 149–51, describes the determination of the Security Council in the case of Rhodesia that there was a threat to international peace and security as 'a legal fiction which enabled it to resort to Chapter VII in order to further the policy of the United Nations of self-determination for colonial peoples and the objective of ensuring the purposes of article 24 of the Universal Declaration of Human Rights that everyone has the right to take part in the government of his country' (at 151).
87 Frowein, Article 39, *op. cit.*, 612, observes that one has to take into consideration that the special situation in South Africa entailed the danger of armed conflicts with the neighbouring states and that, in the case of Rhodesia, the United Kingdom, as the state which was internationally responsible for the territory, had agreed to the measures.
88 See Fifoot, *op. cit.*, 151–3.

resolution of 1966 represents the first clear occasion on which the Security Council gave an order under Article 41. Apart from Rhodesia, during the Cold War, an order was issued under Article 41 on only one occasion: in 1977 the Security Council imposed a mandatory ban on exports of arms to South Africa.[80] The Security Council revoked its resolutions imposing sanctions on Rhodesia by Resolution 460 (1979), after the 'government' of Rhodesia had agreed to revoke the unilateral declaration of independence and to accept the principle of majority rule.[81] The Council lifted the embargo and other restrictions against South Africa on 25 May 1994 by Resolution 919 (1994), after South Africa's new (non-racial and democratic) constitution had entered into force.[82] On 23 June 1994, South Africa resumed its seat in the General Assembly.

Some right-wing politicians in the United Kingdom denied that the situation in Rhodesia constituted a threat to international peace; but Article 39 gives the Security Council a discretionary power to determine what constitutes a threat to the peace,[83] and member states cannot substitute their own opinion for that of the Security Council. Nor can it be said that the Security Council's decision was wholly unreasonable or an abuse of its discretionary power (in some systems of municipal law an administrative body's decisions are invalid if they are wholly unreasonable or an abuse of that body's discretionary power; but it is not certain whether a similar rule of international law applies to the Security Council[84]). The whole purpose of the unilateral declaration of independence in Rhodesia was to preserve the political and economic dominance of the whites (numbering 6 per cent of the population) over the Africans. There was obviously a risk that sooner or later the Rhodesian Africans would react violently against this state of affairs, and a risk that fighting between the Rhodesian Africans and the white regime might spill over into the territory of neighbouring states; indeed, both these risks became realities in the 1970s. If a situation is likely to lead to such results, it is not unreasonable to describe it as a threat to international peace.

Some people also criticized the Security Council action on Rhodesia on the grounds that Rhodesia was not a state,[85] and had not committed any breach of international law. (These two arguments were linked, because it was argued that Rhodesia could not have or break any obligations under international law unless it was a state.) But there is nothing in the Charter to suggest that a threat to the peace necessarily connotes action by a state or a breach of international law. Article 39 says that the Security Council's function is 'to maintain or restore international peace and security' – not to punish breaches of international law.

The cases of Southern Rhodesia and South Africa in which, *inter alia*, Article 41 was applied to impose boycott measures are often cited as evidence that internal conditions in a state, such as massive violations of human rights, could be viewed as by themselves creating a threat to the peace, meriting at least the imposition of collective economic sanctions under Chapter VII.[86] There are doubts, however, whether the special circumstances of the Rhodesian case admit this conclusion.[87] In the case of South Africa's regime of apartheid, the relevance of external factors for the Security Council's decision-making also raises some questions,[88] but it is, on the whole, an important precedent. At the same time, however, one could inquire into the significance of a 'colonial situation' in both cases and of the fact that the Security Council failed to adopt enforcement measures in quite a number of other obvious cases of gross violations of human rights during the Cold War, such as in Biafra (1967–70), Cambodia under the Pol Pot regime,[89] and many other situations.

It must also be noted that in the two aforementioned cases the Security Council did not adopt resolutions authorizing member states to use armed force generally within the territory of either Southern Rhodesia or South Africa. In the Rhodesian case the authorization by the Security Council, properly to be construed as an application of Article 42,[90] of Great Britain to use force against oil tankers with cargo for Southern Rhodesia destined for the harbour of Beira in Portuguese Mozambique,[91] was in fact, applied against a third state, the flag state Greece, under special circumstances.

Practice under Chapter VII after the end of the Cold War

With the break-up of the Soviet Union, the changing political conditions seemed to place the Security Council, now dominated by the Western powers under the leadership of the United States, into a new and central position with regard to the maintenance of international peace and security.[92] As noted by Rosalyn Higgins:

> Since the end of the Cold War there has been a marked decline in the unilateral use of force by the United States outside of the United Nations. Since the coincidence of its own objectives and those of the United Nations in the Iraq invasion of Kuwait, the advantage has been seen in the United States of making the United Nations the centre of foreign policy. The disappearance of the old, hostile Soviet Union has made the Security Council a more comfortable environment. There has been a substantial common interest in peace and security matters between the United States, France and the United Kingdom, with much common ground also with the Russian Federation. China remains uneasy, but does not feel strongly enough to veto.[93]

The new cooperation among the five permanent members of the Security Council had an early impact, bringing the First Gulf War between Iraq and Iran to an end in August 1988.[94] The withdrawal of Soviet forces from Afghanistan in 1988–9 was based upon a plan mediated by the UN Secretary-General.[95] In Africa, Cuban forces withdrew from Angola in 1989 and Namibia became independent in March 1990 on the basis of a resolution which the Security Council had adopted in 1978.[96] UN involvement in the solution of the conflicts in Central America became significant.[97] However, the two main developments which led to a challenge of the role of the United Nations emerged from the invasion of Kuwait by Iraq in August 1990, which was reversed by allied military action based upon Chapter VII in 1991, and from the spreading of massive violence in internal conflicts, mostly ethnically inspired, such as the tragedies in Yugoslavia, Somalia and Rwanda.

The new climate among the permanent members of the Security Council resulted in a much celebrated statement made in January 1992, after a

89 See A. Rapp/Chapter E. Philipp, Conflict, Cambodia/Kampuchea, in *Wolfrum UNLPP I*, 200–8.

90 Frowein, Article 39, *op. cit.*, 615–16; Article 42, *op. cit.*, 633–4, arguing that because of the special circumstances, the case should not be seen as a precedent for the 'recommendation' (under Article 39) of enforcement measures according to Article 42, but as a decision taken under Article 42 itself.

91 SC Res. 221 (1966), *op. cit.*

92 See, for example, P.B. Stephen/B.M. Klimenko (eds), *International Law and International Security: Military and Political Dimensions* (U.S.-Soviet Dialogue Series), 1991; B.B. Ferencz, *New Legal Foundations for Global Survival: Security Through the Security Council*, 1994; D.F. Vagts, Repealing the Cold War, *AJIL* 88 (1994), 506–11; W.M. Reismann, Haiti and the Validity of International Action, *AJIL* 89 (1995), 82–4.

93 Higgins (1995), *op. cit.*, at 449.

94 SC Res. 598 (1987). See Post/Dekker (eds), *op. cit.*; I.F. Dekker/H.H.G. Post, The Gulf War From the Point of View of International Law, *NYIL* 17 (1986), 75–105; E. David, La Guerre du golfe et le droit internationale, *RBDI* 20 (1987), 153–83; C. Gray, The British Position in Regard to the Gulf Conflict, *ICLQ* 37 (1988), 420, Part 2, *ICLQ* 40 (1991), 464; G. Eibach, Conflicts, Iran/Iraq, in *Wolfrum UNLPP I*, 255–60. See also the literature in Chapter 20 above, 351 n. 67.

95 See I. Jahn-Koch, Conflicts, Afghanistan, in *Wolfrum UNLPP I*, 176–88.

96 SC Res. 435 (1978).

97 See N. Bassenge, Conflicts, Central and South America, in *Wolfrum UNLPP I*, 209–24.

98 Note by the President of the Council, UN SCOR, 47th Session, 3046th meeting, UN Doc. S/23500 (1992), *ILM* 31 (1992), 759, at 761.
99 Koskenniemi, *op. cit.*, 458 with references.
100 SC Res. 660 (1990), *ILM* 29 (1990), 1323. See Agora: The Gulf Crisis in International and Foreign Relations Law, *AJIL* 85 (1991), 63 and 506; C. Greenwood, Iraq's Invasion of Kuwait: Some Legal Issues, *The World Today* (March 1991), 39; D. Raic, The Gulf Crisis and the United Nations, *LJIL* 4 (1991), 119; D.W. Greig, Self-Defence and the Security Council: What Does Article 51 Require?, *ICLQ* 40 (1991), 366; N. Schrijver, The United Nations and the Use of Force: Comparing the Korea and the Gulf Crises from a Legal Perspective, in P.J.v. Kieken/C.O. Pannenberg (eds), *Liber Akkerman, In- and Outlaws in War*, 1991, 255; L.C. Green, The Gulf War, the UN and the Law of Armed Conflict, *AVR* 28 (1991), 369; C. Dominicé, La Sécurité collective et la crise du Golfe, *EJIL* 2 (1991), 85; B. Conforti, Non-Coercive Sanctions in the United Nations Charter: Some Lessons from the Gulf War, *ibid.*, 110; *Entre les lignes: La guèrre du golfe et le droit international* (Seminar of the Law Faculty University of Brussels), 1991; C. Warbrick, The Invasion of Kuwait by Iraq, *ICLQ* 40 (1991), 482, Part II, 965; E. Lauterpacht *et al.* (eds), *The Kuwait Crisis: Basic Documents*, Vol. I, 1991; S. Sucharitkul, The Process of Peace-Making Following Operation 'Desert Storm', *AJPIL* 43 (1992), 1; R. Lavalle, The Law of the United Nations and the Use of Force, under the Relevant Security Council Resolutions of 1990 and 1991, to Resolve the Persian Gulf Crisis, *NYIL* 23 (1992), 3–65; K.H. Kaikobad, Self-Defence, Enforcement Action and the Gulf Wars, 1980–88 and 1990–91, *BYIL* 63 (1992), 299–366; J.N. Moore, *Crisis in the Gulf: Enforcing the Rule of Law*, Vol. 1, 1992; T. Eitel, The Escape and Parole of the Imprisoned God of War. An Overview of the Second Gulf War from the Perspective of International Law, *GYIL* 35 (1992), 170; P. Rowe (ed.), *The Gulf War 1990–1991 in International and English Law*, 1993; M. Weller (ed.), *Iraq and Kuwait: The Hostilities and Their Aftermath*, 1993; D. Campbell, *Politics Without Principle: Sovereignty, Ethics, and the Narratives of the Gulf War*, 1993; F. Malekian, *Condemning the Use of Force in the Gulf Crisis*, 1994; C. Gray, After the Ceasefire: Iraq, the Security Council and the Use of Force,

meeting in which the Council for the first time in its existence met at the level of Heads of State or Government. It emphasized that

> [t]he non-military sources of instability in the economic, social, humanitarian and ecological fields have become threats to peace and security.[98]

A hitherto unknown activism on the part of the Security Council developed in the short period from 1990 to 1995. Collective measures were taken under Chapter VII in eight instances, concerning Iraq, Liberia, former Yugoslavia, Somalia, Libya, Angola, Haiti and Rwanda, all of which entailed binding sanctions under Article 41.[99] In five cases the Council authorized the use of force (Iraq, Somalia, former Yugoslavia, Rwanda and Haiti). The latter five cases will be addressed in the following.

The invasion of Kuwait by Iraq

When Saddam Hussein invaded Kuwait on 2 August 1990 and declared it to be Iraq's seventeenth province, the Security Council responded immediately by condemning the act as a breach of the peace and of international security, and requiring Iraq's immediate and unconditional withdrawal.[100] Iraq did not abide by this requirement and subsequently the Security Council adopted more than thirty resolutions on the conflict and its consequences. *Inter alia*, it imposed an arms and trade embargo upon Iraq and Kuwait on 6 August 1990[101] and instituted a committee to supervise the implementation of the sanctions.[102] Following a naval blockade authorized on 25 August 1990,[103] on 28 November 1990 the Security Council finally adopted Resolution 678, in which the Council, '[a]cting under Chapter VII of the Charter', authorized

> Member States co-operating with the Government of Kuwait, unless Iraq on or before 15 January 1991 fully implements, as set forth in paragraph 1 above, the foregoing resolutions, to use all necessary means to uphold and implement resolution 660 (1990) and all subsequent relevant resolutions and to restore international peace and security in the area.[104]

Under the leadership of the United States the coalition forces launched 'Operation Desert Storm' on 16/17 January 1991 with airborne attacks against Iraqi targets in Iraq and Kuwait, followed by the main land offensive on 24 February. A suspension of hostilities came into effect on 28 February after the allied forces had occupied Kuwait and a part of southern Iraq.

There is no doubt that the wording in Resolution 678 'to use all necessary means' was an authorization to use armed force. But there are a number of other legal problems concerning the conduct of Operation Desert Storm which have given rise to some concern. One question is whether the Security Council may delegate its responsibility for military action under Article 42 and authorize states to employ force at their own discretion without retaining at least some form of control.[105] It is arguable that the Security Council was not exactly acting according to Chapter VII because Articles 46 and 47 imply that enforcement measures will be under the control of the Security Council and its Military Staff Committee.[106] However, it must be said that the UN is ill-equipped to effectively handle the complicated command and control functions involved in such complex military operations. Furthermore, it is also clear, as a matter of fact, that the United States would not have been prepared to accept anything other than American control over its forces and their cooperation with the allies. Without the leadership of the United States under these conditions, it is not likely that there would have been any UN-sponsored action at all, although there would still have been room for Allied support for Kuwait in the sense of collective self-defence under Article 51 of the Charter.[107] Nevertheless, the broad discretion left to the coalition forces has led to accusations that the Security Council was 'hijacked' by the United States.[108]

A second issue concerns the point whether the international community should not have waited longer to see whether the economic sanctions would lead to the desired result, before resorting to armed force and its consequences for the Iraqi civilian population.[109] In essence, this is a political question in which also a number of military considerations (*inter alia*, connected with the build-up of Allied forces in the region, their delicate presence in Saudi Arabia and climate conditions) have played an important role. There is also much doubt as to the general effectiveness of economic sanctions in view of past experience which indicates that they have more political and symbolic importance than real effect.[110] But there is also a legal point, namely whether, in the light of the wording of Article 42 of the Charter and its position after Article 41, the Security Council must first make a formal determination that the economic and other sanctions have been inadequate, before authorizing military measures.[111] It is submitted that such a requirement may be overstretching the matter; if the Security Council decides to adopt measures under Article 42, it implicitly says that other measures have been (or are) insufficient in its view and there is no reason to see what would be legally gained from the formal expression of this view, except that there may be more debate on the inadequacy of the sanctions because it is then a separate item to be formally decided.

A third problem that should be mentioned is related to Article 50 of the UN Charter which provides that in the case of enforcement measures adopted by the Security Council, any state (not only a UN member state)

which finds itself confronted with special economic problems arising from the carrying out of those measures shall have the right to consult the Security Council with regard to a solution of those problems.

A number of states tried to obtain compensation under this Article for damage which they or their companies incurred by adhering to the UN sanctions imposed upon Iraq. But these efforts remained fruitless. This may be a bad precedent for the future willingness of states to follow sanctions of the United Nations. Therefore, measures to address this problem have been proposed by the UN Secretary-General in his 'Agenda for Peace'.[112]

Harsh conditions were imposed upon Iraq in the monumental ceasefire Resolution 687 of 3 April 1991, which in UN parlance is referred to as the 'mother of all resolutions' because of its length and broad range of

BYIL 65 (1994), 135–74; J.A. Frowein, Gulf Conflict (1990/1991), *EPIL* II (1995), 643–7; *The United Nations and the Iraq-Kuwait Conflict 1990–1996*, UN Blue Book Series, Vol. IX, 1996.

101 SC Res. 661 (1990), *ILM* 29 (1990), 1325.

102 See P. Conlon, Lessons From Iraq: The Functions of the Iraq Sanctions Committee as a Source of Sanctions Implementation Authority and Practice, *Virginia JIL* 35 (1995), 633–68.

103 SC Res. 665 (1990), *ILM* 29 (1990), 1329.

104 SC Res. 678 (1990), *ibid.*, 1565.

105 See M. Bothe, The Legitimacy of the Use of Force to Protect the Rights of Peoples and Minorities, in C. Brölmann/ R. Lefeber/M. Zieck (eds), *Peoples and Minorities in International Law*, 1993, 289–99, at 296. His view is that peacekeeping by the Council is meant to be a real alternative to the unilateral use of force: 'It is, thus, not the role of the Security Council to just give its blessing to a unilateral use of force.' See further Schachter (1991), International Law, *op. cit.*, 396–9.

106 See, for example, B. Urquhart, The UN and International Security after the Cold War, in Roberts/Kingsbury (eds), *op. cit.*, 80, at 83.

107 See Chapter 19 above, 317–18. On the dispute on the relationship between Res. 678 and Articles 42 and 51 of the Charter see Frowein, Article 42, *op. cit.*, at 634–5.

108 See, for example, the critical article by B.H. Weston, Security Council Resolution 678 and Persian Gulf Decision-Making: Precarious Legitimacy, *AJIL* 85 (1991), 516–35.

109 See Chapter 1, 5 and Chapter 20, 362 above.

110 See L. Rosenzweig, United Nations Sanctions: Creating a More Effective Tool for the Enforcement of International Law, *AJPIL* 48 (1995), 161–95.

111 Urquhart, *op. cit.*, 84. See further D.L. Bethlehem (ed.), *The Kuwait Crisis: Sanctions and Their Economic Consequences*, 1991.

112 *Agenda for Peace*, United Nations, 1992, 24. The matter has also been raised by the former UN Legal Advisor and now Judge at the International Court of Justice, C.-A. Fleischhauer, Wirtschaftliche Zwangsmaßnahmen in Recht und Praxis der Weltorganisation, *VN* (1991), 41.

113 SC Res. 687 (1991), *ILM* 30 (1991), 84.

114 See T. Marauhn, The Implementation of Disarmament and Arms Control Obligations Imposed Upon Iraq by the Security Council, *ZaöRV* 52 (1992), 781–803; M. Weller/P. Hatfield (eds), *The Control and Monitoring of Iraqi Weaponry of Mass Destruction*, 1996.

115 See Chapter 10 above, 151.

116 Text in *ILM* 35 (1996), 1095; see also *UN Chronicle*, no. 2, 1996, 14–18. However, the implementation of this deal was suspended when later in September 1996 Iraqi forces intervened at the request of the Kurdish leader Barzani in the Kurdish civil war in the safety zone in northern Iraq, which caused the United States to retaliate unilaterally (except with the support of the UK) by destroying military targets in the south of Iraq.

117 For a highly critical evaluation as to the legality of the regime, see B. Graefrath, Iraq: Reparations and the Security Council, *ZaöRV* 55 (1995), 1–68. See also E.J. Garmise, The Iraqi Claims Process and the Ghost of Versailles, *NYULR* 67 (1992), 840–76; A.A. Levy, The Persian Gulf War Cease-Fire Agreement Compared with the Japanese Peace Treaty in Terms of Reparations and Reconstruction, *Dick. JIL* 10 (1992), 541–66. Generally, on war damages, see A. Steinkamm, *EPIL* 4 (1982), 298–301; V. Gowlland-Debbas, Security Council Enforcement Action and Issues of State Responsibility, *ICLQ* 43 (1994), 55–98.

118 SC Res. 674 (1990), para. 8.

119 SC Res. 686 (1991), para. 1(b).

120 SC Res. 687 (1991), *op. cit.*

121 SC Res. 692 (1991).

application.[113] The resolution requires Iraq, *inter alia*, to destroy or remove all weapons of mass destruction, including chemical and nuclear weapons, as well as missiles with a range of more than 150 kilometres (during the war with the coalition forces Iraq had sought relief and other popular Arab support by attacking Israel with Scud missiles, as it had been attacking Tehran with missiles in the First Gulf War). The respective disarmament of Iraq is supervised and enforced by the United Nations.[114] Other issues addressed by Resolution 687 concern the determination of the border between Iraq and Kuwait by the Iraq–Kuwait Boundary Commission,[115] the monitoring of the border by the UN Iraq–Kuwait Observation Mission, the coordination of the return of property to Kuwait, and the supervision of the continuing arms and trade embargo, including the prohibition of the export of oil, against Iraq by the Sanctions Committee of the UN Security Council. With the purpose of addressing the serious shortages of food supplies and medicine in Iraq, on 4 April 1995 the Security Council adopted Resolution 986 (1995) allowing, under certain conditions and strict control measures, states to import oil and oil products from Iraq amounting to the equivalent of US$1 billion every ninety days. Iraq refused to accept the conditions of this 'oil-for-food' deal because it saw its sovereignty as being impaired, until finally a memorandum of understanding was agreed upon between the UN Secretariat and the Government of Iraq in spring 1996.[116]

Another aspect which needs to be mentioned is the novelty of the reparations regime imposed upon Iraq by the Security Council, also acting under Chapter VII.[117] Already in October 1990, the Council had reminded Iraq that it was liable under international law for all damage caused to Kuwait, other states, companies and individuals arising as a consequence of the invasion of Kuwait.[118] After the defeat of Iraq, the Council demanded in a resolution adopted on 2 March 1991[119] that Iraq accepts its international liability 'in principle' as part of the cease-fire conditions. Paragraph 16 of Resolution 687 then confirmed (under Chapter VII):

> [t]hat Iraq, without prejudice to the debts and obligations of Iraq arising prior to 2 August 1990, which will be addressed through the normal mechanisms, is liable under international law for any direct loss, damage, including environmental damage and the depletion of natural resources, or injury to foreign Governments, nationals and corporations, as a result of Iraq's unlawful invasion and occupation of Kuwait.[120]

On the basis of this resolution the Security Council created a Compensation Fund and the United Nations Compensation Commission (UNCC), seated in Geneva, by a resolution adopted on 20 May 1991.[121] The UNCC is a subsidiary body of the Security Council and its main political organ, the Governing Council, mirrors the composition of the Security Council. Its task is to deal with the unprecedented amount of more than 2.6 million claims filed against Iraq from more than 100 countries, ranging from a mass of claims by persons who had to depart from Iraq or Kuwait or who suffered injury, corporate, property and business loss claims, various types of claims by governments and international organizations to the new field of claims for environmental damage caused by Iraq (accusing Iraq of using oil as a weapon polluting the Gulf and depleting or burning Kuwait's oil resources during the war) in the estimated total amount of US$160 billion. There are a number of legal questions concerning the establishment and mode of operation of this new body, which is not a form of arbitration or adjudication,[122] but a system of imposed administration of claims, often in a summary fashion, under which the defendant state (Iraq) has been deprived of any meaningful standing and is required to pay one-third of its annual oil revenues into the Fund when the embargo is lifted; but they are beyond the scope of this book.[123]

The Kurdish crisis

One of the great myths of the analysis of the events in the immediate aftermath of the Gulf War is that the Security Council also authorized Allied forces by Resolution 688 to militarily intervene in Iraq to protect the Kurds.[124] Therefore, the development deserves some closer attention. 'Operation Comfort', the allied intervention in 1991 to create 'safe havens', in northern Iraq for the vast numbers of Kurdish refugees which had fled to Turkey and Iran from the Iraqi Army and were suffering under appalling conditions, was conducted by more than 13,000 soldiers from various Western countries under the leadership of the United States, including Britain, France, the Netherlands, Spain, Italy and Australia.[125]

Security Council Resolution 688, adopted on 5 April 1991, has often been referred to as the 'legal basis' for the action (and also for later military strikes against Iraq) and the allies themselves have repeatedly described the intervention as being 'consistent' with that resolution. In the literature it has been interpreted as evidence that the Council may adopt measures under Chapter VII with regard to an internal situation if a massive violation of human rights amounts to a threat to or breach of the peace, in spite of the non-intervention principle in Article 2(7) of the Charter.[126] A closer analysis of the resolution, the discussion at the Security Council meeting and the factual context does not support these contentions.

Resolution 688, the draft of which was put on the agenda of the Security Council on 5 April 1991 by Belgium and France, joined by the United Kingdom and the United States as sponsors,[127] was accepted, with the least wide support of all the resolutions until then adopted by the Council in response to the invasion of Kuwait,[128] by ten votes in favour, three against (Cuba, Yemen, and Zimbabwe) and two members, including one permanent member, abstaining (China and India). The significance attributed to the issue is apparent from the fact that thirty-one states expressed their views at the meeting.

The operative part of the resolution begins by condemning 'the repression of the Iraqi civilian population in many parts of Iraq, including most recently in Kurdish populated areas, the consequences of which threaten international peace and security in the region' (paragraph 1). These 'consequences' are clearly identified in the preamble as 'a massive flow of refugees towards and across international frontiers' and as 'cross border incursions'.[129] Thus the resolution cannot be cited as a precedent for the

122 See Chapter 18 above, 281–98.

123 See P. Malanczuk, International Business and New Rules of State Responsibility? – The Law Applied by the United Nations (Security Council) Compensation Commission for Claims against Iraq, in K.-H. Böckstiegel (ed.), *Perspectives of Air Law, Space Law and International Business Law for the Next Century*, 1996, 117–64; R. Lillich (ed.), *The United Nations Compensation Commission*, 1995; R.J. Bettauer, The United Nations Compensation Commission – Developments Since October 1992, *AJIL* 89 (1995), 416–23. The documents concerning the settlement of claims against Iraq and UNCC Decisions 1–2 are in *ILM* 30 (1991), 1703; UNCC Decisions 3–13 and associated Report are reprinted in *ILM* 31 (1992), 1009; UNCC Decisions 14–23 and associated Panel Reports and Recommendations in *ILM* 34 (1995), 235; and UNCC Decisions 24, 30, 35 and associated Panel Reports in *ILM* 35 (1996), 939 (Introductory Notes by D.D. Caron).

124 See P. Malanczuk, The Kurdish Crisis and Allied Intervention in the Aftermath of the Second Gulf War, *EJIL* 2 (1991), 114–32; Malanczuk (1993), *op. cit.*, 20 *et seq.* Generally on the Kurdish problem see G. Chaliand, *The Kurdish Tragedy*, 1994; see also Chapter 19 above, 340.

125 An allied contingent of about 5,000 soldiers remained based in Turkey ('Operation Raised Hammer') until 10 October 1991 and the aircraft base of Incirlik thereafter continued to be used with the consent of Turkey, see Malanczuk (1991), *op. cit.*, at 122–3; L. Freedman/D. Boren, 'Safe Havens' for Kurds in Post-War Iraq, in Rodley (ed.), 1992, *op. cit.*, 43.

126 U. Heinz/C. Philip/R. Wolfrum, Zweiter Golfkrieg: Anwendungsfall von Kapitel VII der UN-Charta, *VN* 39 (1991), 121, at 125; Bothe (1993), *op. cit.*, 294–5 also considers Resolution 688 as an example of the Security Council's application of Chapter VII.

127 UN Security Council, Provisional Verbatim Record, S/PV 2982, 5 April 1991, at 3. The meeting was convened in response to requests from Turkey and France. Text of SC Res. 688 (1991) in *ILM* 30 (1991), 858.

128 See N.S. Rodley, Collective Intervention to Protect Human Rights and Civilian Populations, in Rodley (ed.), 1992, *op. cit.*, 29.

129 On the legal aspects of state responsibility for causing refugee flows, see R. Hofmann, Refugee-Generating

Policies and the Law of State Responsibility, *ZaöRV* 45 (1985) 694.

130 SC Res. 688 (1991), *op. cit.* However, as noted by Rodley (1992), Collective Intervention, *op. cit.*, at 31, it is true that there is also no reference to Chapter VI. This leads back to the difficulty that the Security Council often does not clearly indicate under which provision it is acting. The point is that, although in theory it can not be excluded that Resolution 688 may be based on Chapter VII, what matters is that no authorization of enforcement measures was made by the Security Council, or, as Rodley says himself, considered at the time when the resolution was adopted.

131 See also O. Schachter, United Nations Law in the Gulf Conflict, *AJIL* 85 (1991), 452, at 468.

132 SC Res. 688 (1991), *op. cit.*, at 859.

133 SC Res. 678, *op. cit.*, at 1565, para. 2.

134 SC Res. 794 of 3 December 1992, *UNYb* 1932, 209. See text below, 403–4.

135 See Malanczuk (1991), *op. cit.*, 119–20.

136 See also Rodley (1992), Collective Intervention, *op. cit.*, at 29; Schachter, *AJIL* 85 (1991), *op. cit.*, at 469 observes that 'the Security Council was not asked to authorize or endorse the protective measures in the safety zones, presumably because not all of the permanent members were prepared to support them. The absence of explicit Security Council endorsement, together with the basic Charter provision against intervention in matters essentially within domestic jurisdiction, was cited by dissenting UN members as grounds for condemning the use of troops in the safety zones as Charter violations of serious import. All states, it was argued, had reason to fear the effect of that precedent.'

proposition that the Security Council views massive, but purely internal human rights violations as such, without transboundary effects, as a direct threat to international peace and security. For cases with external effects of human rights violations, however, it is indeed an important precedent.

It is not a precedent, however, for the authorization of the use of force by the Security Council to protect human rights in such circumstances. Resolution 688 contains no reference to Chapter VII,[130] its wording does not mention any collective enforcement measures, and it did not expressly authorize or endorse the allied military intervention.[131] The resolution 'demands' that Iraq, 'as a contribution to removing the threat to international peace and security in the region', end the repression immediately, and expresses the hope for an 'open dialogue' to ensure 'that the human and political rights of all Iraqi citizens are respected' (paragraph 2). After requiring Iraq to allow immediate access by international humanitarian organizations (paragraph 3), the resolution requests the Secretary-General to pursue his humanitarian efforts in Iraq, to report forthwith (paragraph 4), and to 'use all the resources at his disposal, including those of the relevant United Nations agencies, to address urgently the critical needs of the refugees and displaced Iraqi population' (paragraph 5). The Security Council concluded by appealing to all Member States and all humanitarian organizations to contribute to the relief efforts (paragraph 6), demanding that Iraq cooperate with the Secretary-General (paragraph 7), and deciding 'to remain seized of the matter' (paragraph 8).[132] There is no language in Resolution 688 such as in the earlier Resolution 678 which authorized member states 'to use all necessary means' to repel the Iraqi aggression against Kuwait.[133] And there is also no comparable wording to the later Resolution 794 of 3 December 1992 on Somalia, in which the Council called upon 'all Member States which are in a position to do so to provide military forces' (paragraph 11), or 'to use all necessary means' to secure the humanitarian relief operations in Somalia (paragraph 10), or 'to use such measures as may be necessary' to enforce the earlier Resolution 733 (paragraph 16).[134] In fact, at the time of the adoption of Resolution 688, on 5 April 1991, the idea of military intervention to create such safety zones had not yet found the support of the United States.[135] While the plan found approval at the summit meeting of the European Communities on 8 April 1992, three days after the resolution, the reaction of the United States on the same day was that it had 'no position' on the question of Kurdish 'safe havens' and was unable to give the proposal 'specific endorsement'. It was only later that the United States clarified its position and, on 10 April 1991, demanded that Iraq cease all military activity on its territory north of the 36th parallel with the warning to Iraq that it would use force if there was any military interference in international relief efforts for the Kurds. The allied intervention itself started a week later, on 17 April 1991.

The statements made at the Security Council meeting reveal that nearly all states, even among those supporting the resolution, carefully balanced the right of the Security Council to deal with the matter with the principle of non-interference in the internal affairs of Iraq to avoid an unwelcome precedent for the future.[136] The wording of Resolution 688 is such to accommodate these concerns by giving room to their interpretation. While the resolution begins with a reference to duties and responsibilities of the Security Council for the maintenance of international peace and security, it immediately recalls Article 2(7) of the Charter. The preamble expresses grave concern on the part of the Council towards the Iraqi repression of the civilian population and notes that it was deeply disturbed 'by the magnitude of the human suffering involved', but it also reaffirms 'the commitment of all Member states to the sovereignty, territorial integrity and political independence of Iraq and of all States in the area'.

In practice, apart from humanitarian tasks assigned to the Secretary-General, Resolution 688 amounted to little more than a formal censure of Iraq. Otherwise it is most likely that it would have been vetoed by China. China explained its abstention, after expressing its concern with the situation in Iraq and the refugee influx into Turkey and Iran and the effects for these countries, by stating:

> However this is a question of great complexity, because the internal affairs of a country are also involved. According to paragraph 7 to Article 2 of the Charter, the Security Council should not consider or take action on questions concerning the internal affairs of any State. As for the international aspects involved in the question, we are of the view that they should be settled through the appropriate channels. We support the Secretary-General in rendering humanitarian assistance to the refugees through the relevant organizations.[137]

It is further of interest that the reaction of the UN Secretary-General to the 'safe havens' plan was to immediately raise the question whether enclaves for the Kurds could be imposed upon Iraq in disrespect of its sovereignty. On 17 April he expressed the view that any deployment of foreign troops in northern Iraq would require permission by Iraq.[138] Iraq denounced the allied action but it did not respond militarily. It continued to negotiate with both the United Nations Mission led by Erik Suy (Personal Representative of the UN Secretary-General) and with the UN Inter-Agency Mission led by Sadruddin Aga Khan (Executive Delegate of the UN Secretary-General for the UN Humanitarian Programme for Iraq, Kuwait and the Iraq/Iran and Iraq/Turkey Border Areas) on humanitarian relief. Agreements were concluded on 18 April and in May 1991.[139] Aga Khan and Iraq signed a Memorandum of Understanding concerning the role of the United Nations in providing humanitarian assistance in Iraq; based on discussions held on 17 and 18 May 1991 with the Iraqi Government, an annex to this Memorandum laid out the details of the deployment of about 500 'UN Guards' and their light armament. The deployment of these 'UN Guards' therefore rested on the consent of the Iraqi government.

The reaction of states from what used to be the 'Third World' to the allied intervention during the General Assembly debate in November 1991 on strengthening the UN ability to respond to human emergencies indicates that many saw in the rescue operation a fundamental breach of sovereignty with negative implications.[140] Erik Suy also views the allied intervention as unilateral action without authorization. He notes that the allied action was not condemned (which, one is tempted to add, as far as the Security Council is concerned, was not likely in view of the veto power

---

137 UN Doc. S/PV. 2982, 5 April 1991 (Provisional), 55–6.

138 See Malanczuk (1991), *op. cit.*, at 129.

139 *ILM* 30 (1991), 862 (annex, para. 6); see Malanczuk (1991), *op. cit.*, at 129–30.

140 See L. Minear, Humanitarian Intervention in a New World Order, Overseas Development Council, *Policy Focus* (1992), 1, at 2 *et seq.*

141 E. Suy, Commentaar: Humanitaire interventie – Tussen soevereiniteit en mensenrechten, *Transaktie* 21 (1992), at 319.

142 See *IHT*, 18 January 1992, 1 (a White House spokesman stated that the purpose of the attack against a 'nuclear installation' near Baghdad 'is to seek compliance with UN resolutions'); *NRC Handelsblad*, 18 January 1992, 1; European and Arab support for the US-led military action against Iraq began to waver on 19 January 1992; see *IHT*, 20 January 1992, 4; *NRC Handelsblad*, 19 January 1992, 1, 5; France did not participate in the action of attacking the outskirts of Baghdad on the grounds that it exceeded the framework of Security Council resolutions, as stated by the French Foreign Minister, *FAZ*, 21 January 1992, 1. Russia, in consultation with Arab states, requested the United States not to take further action without express authorization by the Security Council, *FAZ*, 20 January 1992, 1. A Russian Foreign Ministry statement accused Iraq of flouting UN resolutions, but also said: 'Our firm position is that reaction to the actions of Iraq must be proportionate and proceed from agreed decisions . . . The time is ripe to again review the situation in the UN Security Council', *IHT*, 19 January 1992, 1. See also Chapter 19 above, 316–17.

143 See Malanczuk (1993), *op. cit.*

144 This seems to be the view of R. Jennings/A. Watt (eds), *Oppenheim's International Law*, I: Peace, 9th edn 1992, 443, n. 18, stating that 'Iraq's attitude was ambivalent, formally protesting at the infringement of its sovereignty (e.g. UN Doc S/22459 of 8 April, S/22513 of 22 April and S/22531 of 25 April), but not resisting the action and in substance acquiescing'. Delbrück, A Fresh Look, *op. cit.*, at 985–6, presents the different argument that the Security Council 'clearly acquiesced in the temporary presence of American, British and French military forces in Northern Iraq . . . ' (at 986). On the legal concept of acquiescence, see Chapter 10 above, 154–5.

145 See the argument made by Schachter, *AJIL* 85 (1991), *op. cit.*, at 469.

146 See also Rodley (1992), Collective Intervention, *op. cit.*, at 33; Freedman/Boren, 'Safe Havens' for Kurds in Post-War Iraq, in Rodley (ed.), 1992, *op. cit.*, at 82; E. Suy, *Transaktie* 21 (1992), 317, at 319.

147 Malanczuk (1993), *op. cit.*, 24 *et seq.*; J. Clark, Debacle in Somalia, *FA*

of three of the Allies), and he also states that 'world opinion' supported the operation. But Suy arrives at the conclusion that it was illegal under international law and, as a single precedent, was not capable of creating a new customary norm.[141]

It is true that Resolution 688, invoked by the allies as justification, not only for the Kurdish action, but also, to justify the imposition of the no-fly zones over Iraq, and, at least partly in addition to the non-compliance by Iraq with UN resolutions among other reasons, to legalize military air strikes in and against Iraq in January 1992,[142] does not support such contentions. But the matter of the legality or illegality of the intervention to protect the Kurds is more complex. First, there is still the controversial issue of whether unilateral, unauthorized, humanitarian intervention may be still *de lege lata* admissible under exceptional circumstances.[143] Second, a more detailed analysis of the factual circumstances would have to inquire whether Iraq, in spite of its formal protest, may have later in fact acquiesced[144] in the rescue operation. Third, there is also the difficult question of whether the action, as a so-called 'follow-up measure', can be isolated from the general context of the Gulf War, including the previous authorization of enforcement action by the Council and/or the exercise of collective self-defence.[145] Nevertheless, the conclusion stands that Resolution 688 by itself did not provide the legal basis and as such is not a precedent for the Security Council practice of forcible humanitarian measures under Article 42.[146] The legal significance of the allied action as state practice, on the other hand, for the development of customary international law will become apparent only in a longer-term perspective, provided that it can find general acceptance as a precedent outside of the peculiar circumstances of the Gulf War.

Somalia

The case of Somalia, with the engagement of 37,000 foreign soldiers from more than twenty countries under the leadership of the United States in 1992, is a normative landmark of the genuine Security Council practice of humanitarian intervention which was based upon Chapter VII of the UN Charter.[147] At the same time it is an example of the failure of collective humanitarian intervention.

Somalia is unique among the sub-Saharan countries in that it is the only one which is composed of a single ethnic group. Nevertheless, the country, which in the last quarter of the nineteenth century had been divided under the rule of three colonial powers (Britain, France and Italy) has been torn apart by clan-based civil wars which led to the collapse of the government structure and made Somalia the prime example of the new phenomenon of 'failed states',[148] to a much higher degree than other states such as Liberia[149] and Rwanda.[150]

After independence, for twenty-one years Somalia had been ruled by President Siad Barre who attempted to overcome the clan structure on the basis of a combination of pan-Somali nationalism with a centralized Soviet model of socialism, although Barre himself was primarily basing his power on the Merihan clan and two other clans, the Ogadeni and Dolbahante. When Barre's regime fell in 1991, a power struggle and clan clashes in many parts of the country emerged. In the capital Mogadishu, factions supporting Interim President Ali Mahdi Mohamed, on the one hand, and General Mohamed Farah Aidid (Chairman of the United Somali Congress), on the other, engaged in heavy fighting. The county was torn apart by widespread death and destruction forcing hundreds of thousands of people to leave their homes. Almost five million people were suffering from hunger and disease; almost one million people fled to neighbouring countries. In May 1991, the north-western part of Somalia proclaimed its independence as the 'Somaliland Republic'.

The United Nations and a number of non-governmental organizations were engaged in humanitarian relief operations in Somalia and the UN Secretary-General, in cooperation with the Organization for African Unity (OAU), the League of Arab States (LAS) and the Organization of the Islamic Conference (OIC) made political efforts to restore peace.[151] On 23 January 1992, the Security Council imposed an arms embargo on Somalia and called upon all parties to discontinue hostilities.[152] Negotiations at the UN Headquarters involving the UN Secretary-General, the LAS, the OAU and the OIC led to an agreement on a cease-fire between interim President Ali Mahdi and General Aidid to be monitored by UN observers. Agreement was also reached on the protection of humanitarian relief convoys by UN security guards. In April 1992 the Security Council created the United Nations Operation in Somalia (UNOSOM) which resulted in the deployment of fifty UN military observers and about 500 UN security personnel.[153] The Security Council later decided to increase the security force up to 3,000 in view of the continuing fighting and attacks against humanitarian operations. But UNOSOM was not able to fulfil its mandate.

Following an offer made by the United States to lead a military operation to protect the delivery of humanitarian relief, on 3 December 1992, the Security Council unanimously adopted Resolution 794 under Chapter VII of the UN Charter and authorized the use of all necessary means to provide a secure environment for the relief operations. The circumstances, however, as expressed in Resolution 794 and by many states at the Council's meeting,[154] were special, as emphasized in the resolution, because of 'the unique character of the present situation in Somalia' with 'its deteriorating, complex and extraordinary nature, requiring an immediate and exceptional response'.[155] While there had been requests for help from Somalia to the UN, the fact that Somalia has no government and nothing akin to a structure of government must not be overlooked when evaluating the relevance of this precedent for the future.

It was the chaos of the endless civil war involving some fifteen different parties, mass starvation threatening millions, armed interference with humanitarian assistance, and the inability of the UN peacekeeping contingent with its limited mandate to make any difference that led the Council to determine 'that the magnitude of the human tragedy caused by the conflict in Somalia, further exacerbated by the obstacles being created to the distribution of humanitarian assistance, constitutes a threat to international peace and security'.[156] For the first time it is clearly stated in a Council resolution, without also invoking external 'consequences', that

72 (1993), 109; M.R. Hutchinson, Note, Restoring Hope: U.N. Security Council Resolutions for Somalia and an Expanded Doctrine of Humanitarian Intervention, *Harvard ILJ* 34 (1993), 624; and the literature cited above, 387 n. 22.

148 See I. Zartman (ed.), *Collapsed States: The Disintegration and Restoration of Legitimate Authority*, 1995.

149 See Nolte, *op. cit.*, 603–37; Weller (ed.), 1994, *op. cit.*

150 See text below, 405–7.

151 See *Basic Facts about the United Nations*, 1995, 50 *et seq.*

152 SC Res. 733 (1992), *op. cit.* This was in response to a request for an immediate Security Council meeting, to address the deteriorating security situation in Somalia, see Letter Dated 20 January 1992 From the Chargé d'Affaires A.I. of the Permanent Mission of Somalia to the United Nations Addressed to the President of the Security Council, UN SCOR, 47th Sess., UN Doc. S/23445 (1992).

153 SC Res. 751 (1992).

154 Provisional Verbatim Record of the Meeting on 3 December 1992, S/PV.3145, 3 December 1992.

155 SC Res. 794 (1992), *op. cit.*

156 Provisional Verbatim Record, *op. cit.*

157 *Ibid.*

158 *Ibid.* Res. 794 states merely that the Council welcomes 'the offer by a Member State described in the Secretary-General's letter to the Council of 29 November 1991 (S/24868) concerning the establishment of an operation to create such a secure environment' (para. 8).

159 See the document from the UN Department of Human Affairs, Review of the 100-Day Action Programme and Beyond: Key Issues for Somalia, 3 December 1992. The programme was launched in Geneva on 12 October 1992.

160 See Quigley, *op. cit.*, 267.

161 SC Res. 794 (1992), at 4.

internal aspects of a humanitarian problem, although in connection with armed interference with international humanitarian relief operations, threaten international peace and security and require military enforcement measures under Chapter VII.

A further point of interest is that the Security Council assumed responsibility for restoring 'peace, stability and law and order with a view to facilitating the process of a political settlement under the auspices of the United Nations' under the proviso, however, that the 'people of Somalia bear ultimate responsibility for national reconciliation and the reconstruction if their own country'.[157] It is known that the United States, the inaugurator of 'Operation Hope' and in military command of the operation in the first phase, but for political reasons only very indirectly referred to in the resolution because of the controversy regarding the extent to which the UN should be in control,[158] had views different to those of the Secretary-General on the issue of how far its intervention should go beyond terminating the fighting and securing the supply of relief. The text of the resolution, while guarding the principle of sovereignty by referring to the ultimate responsibility of the people of Somalia, raised the question of what exactly the long-term objectives of the UN were to be in the second phase of the operation, whether they were to include, for example, establishing a police force, law and order, and an administration, or reorganizing the educational system and the economy.[159]

It is further of interest to note that the reason why Resolution 794 was adopted unanimously (in contrast to the other resolutions authorizing the use of force in the cases of Rwanda, Haiti, etc.) was that it provided for mechanisms aiming at maintaining UN control over the operation.[160] The UN Secretary-General was to consult with the states taking part regarding their efforts and to arrange for 'the unified command and control of the forces involved'.[161] An *ad hoc* commission of members of the Security Council was to report to the Council on the conduct of operations by the participating states. Reports 'on a regular basis' were required from both the Secretary-General and the participating states.

In December 1992, the Unified Task Force (UNITAF) comprising military forces from twenty-four countries under the command of the United States was sent to Somalia and by March 1993, with about 37,000 soldiers, covered 40 per cent of the territory of the country. This resulted in a significant alleviation of the starvation conditions. On 26 March 1993, the Security Council decided to transform UNITAF into UNOSOM II and expanded its size and mandate. UNOSOM II was authorized under Chapter VII to use force to establish a secure environment in all of Somalia. It was also authorized to assist in rebuilding the economy and social and political institutions of the country. At a conference held in Addis Ababa in March 1993, the leaders of fifteen Somali political movements agreed on national reconciliation, disarmament and security, rehabilitation and reconstruction, restoration of property and settlement of disputes and on the creation of a transitional national council.

However, the agreement was only the prelude to further disaster. In June 1993, twenty-five Pakistani soldiers were killed by an attack upon UNOSOM II in Mogadishu. UNOSOM II became a party to the conflict and engaged in military operations in Mogadishu which led to casualties among the civilian population and UNOSOM forces. The United States deemed it necessary to defeat General Aidid and took military action against his forces, including a helicopter attack upon a command centre in Mogadishu which resulted in the death of fifty civilians.[162] The American approach was criticized by other states, especially by Italy, which requested the UN command to suspend combat operations in Mogadishu. The UN command responded by requesting Italy to replace the commander of its contingent, which Italy refused to do, with reference to its right to appoint the leader of its own forces. Thus, becoming a party to the conflict led to dissent among the member states and to an early withdrawal of forces.

After eighteen US soldiers were killed in October 1993, the United States finally announced that it would withdraw from Somalia by 31 March 1994. Belgium, France and Sweden also announced their withdrawal. The mandate of UNOSOM II was revised in February 1994 emphasizing its role in providing assistance to political reconciliation, reconstruction and stability. The Security Council also provided for a gradual reduction of UNOSOM forces and stated that its mission would be completed by March 1995. After further UN efforts in 1994 failed to make any progress in reconciliation between the Somali factions, the withdrawal of UNOSOM II was completed in March 1995. Neither the Somali factions nor the humanitarian agencies and NGOs requested an extension of UNOSOM's mandate.[163] The UN-sponsored collective intervention in Somalia thus ended in a débâcle, although it had been successful in distributing humanitarian aid.[164]

Rwanda

The case of Rwanda is an appalling human tragedy with mass killings arising from internal ethnic conflict which, as mentioned in Chapter 20 above,[165] has led to the establishment of an international criminal tribunal. Rwanda had been first colonized by Germany and was later transferred to Belgian colonial rule until it gained its independence in 1967. The country has a long history of ethnic clashes between the Hutu majority and the Tutsi minority, which reappeared in the form of a full-scale internal and cross-border conflict in October 1990 between the Hutu-controlled armed forces of the French-backed Government of Rwanda and the Tutsi-led Rwandese Patriotic Front (RPF) operating from Uganda and areas in the north of Rwanda.[166] In February 1993, hostilities recommenced in spite of a number of cease-fire agreements and disrupted peace negotiations between the parties sponsored by the OAU and Tanzania. At the request of Rwanda and Uganda, on 22 June 1993, the Security Council decided to establish the United Nations Observer Mission Uganda-Rwanda (UNOMUR) to help to prevent the military use of the border area. After the two civil war parties had signed a peace agreement in Arusha, Tanzania in August 1993, at their request the Security Council set up another international force, the United Nations Assistance Mission for Rwanda (UNAMIR), to assist in the implementation of the agreement on 5 October 1993.[167] Its mandate was to supervise the election and establishment of a new government by October 1995.

162 See Quigley, op. cit., 281.

163 Mutharika, op. cit., at 548.

164 See J. Clark, Debacle in Somalia: Failure of the Collective Response, in L.F. Damrosh (ed.), Enforcing Restraint: Collective Intervention in Internal Conflicts, 1993, 205. On the lack of clarity of the mandate of UNOSOM II which contributed to the undermining of the operation see R. Zacklin, Managing Peacekeeping from a Legal Perspective, in D. Warner (ed.), New Dimensions of Peacekeeping, 1995, 160.

165 See Chapter 20 above, 360.

166 See Basic Facts, op. cit., 46 et seq.; UN Chronicle, 1996, no. 2, 52–3.

167 SC Res. 872 (1993). For the background see M. Mubiala, L'Opération des Nations Unies pour les droits de l'homme au Rwanda, Hague YIL 8 (1995), 11–6; The United Nations and Rwanda, 1993–1996 (UN Blue Book Series), 1996.

168 See Tesón, *op. cit.*, 363.
169 SC Res. 912 (1994).
170 SC Res. 918 (1994).
171 SC Res. 929 (1994). See *UN Chronicle* 31 (1994), no. 4, 4–13.

There were difficulties in implementing the agreement, which exploded into a severe crisis after the Presidents of Rwanda and Burundi were killed by a missile attack on their aircraft on 6 April 1994 while returning from peace negotiations in Tanzania. Total chaos and massive ethnic violence with genocidal dimensions emerged throughout Rwanda in the weeks that followed. It was estimated that by September 1994 the pre-civil war population of 7.9 million in Rwanda had fallen to five million. Estimates of the number of people slaughtered ranged from several hundreds of thousands to one million, those of internally displaced persons from 800,000 to two million, and those of refugees fleeing to Zaire, Tanzania, Burundi and Uganda counted at more than two million.

The lightly armed 2,700 UNAMIR observer forces were not in a position to stop the killings, nor was this within its mandate. Belgium withdrew its 440 soldiers and the rest remained in their barracks after ten Belgian soldiers guarding the Prime Minister had been hacked to death when the Prime Minister was murdered.[168] On 21 April 1994, the Security Council decided to reduce the number of UNAMIR forces to 270 to prevent further UN casualties.[169] The mandate was changed to include working with the parties on a cease-fire agreement and in assisting in the resumption of relief operations.

At the beginning of May the Security Council, being aware that the massacres were continuing, commenced discussion on sending 5,500 African troops to Rwanda. On 17 May 1994, the Security Council determined that the situation in Rwanda constituted a threat to international peace and security and imposed an arms embargo against Rwanda.[170] It also authorized the enlargement of UNAMIR up to 5,500 soldiers and recognized the possible need for the force to use force against persons or groups threatening protected locations and populations. However, it had obtained no commitment from member states to supply such forces and a month later only Ethiopia had shown itself prepared to provide a fully equipped unit. It was only after France offered to intervene in Rwanda that on 22 June 1994, the Security Council adopted Resolution 929 and with reference to Chapter VII (by a vote of ten to nil with five abstentions) authorized France and other willing member states to use 'all necessary means' as a temporary multinational operation to protect the civilian population in Rwanda as a strictly humanitarian and impartial task without regard to the merits of the dispute between the Government of Rwanda and the RPF.[171] 'Opération Turquoise' established a safe protection zone in the south-west of Rwanda and was terminated on 21 August 1994, when the responsibilities in the zone were taken over by UNAMIR with units from Ethiopia, Ghana and Zimbabwe. UNAMIR's strength reached 4,270 in October 1994.The civil war in Rwanda was terminated by a unilateral cease-fire declared by the RPF on 18 July 1994 when it took control of Rwanda except for the protection zone.

The French-led intervention in Rwanda has most clearly shown the problem of self-interest of states authorized by the Security Council to take military action under Chapter VII. As one recent writer has observed:

> In Rwanda, France had a history of involvement that cast doubt on its good faith

in taking military action. France had backed the Hutu-led Rwandan government in its civil war against the Tutsi-led Rwanda Patriotic Front. France was alleged to favour the Hutus because they used French as their second language, while the Tutsis used English. France was criticized for failing to denounce major massacres of Tutsis by Hutus. French arms shipments to the Rwandan government continued as the massacres were underway. When the Rwanda resolution was adopted, the civil war still raged, and the Tutsi rebel force announced its objection to France's planned entry into Rwanda, vowing to attack French forces. Of all states in the world, France was probably the worst choice for intervention, but it was France that was willing to act.[172]

On the other hand, one has to take into account that, without self-interest, states are not likely to be willing to intervene militarily in distant countries and without such willingness the United Nations is powerless to act effectively on its own.

Haiti

Haiti is a special case in which the Security Council authorized the use of force under Chapter VII to implement a democratic election result without, however, explicitly determining that there was a threat to international peace and security.[173] Since 1957 Haiti had been ruled by the Duvalier family. After Jean-Claude Duvalier, the 'President for Life' had left the country in February 1986 and following the approval of a new constitution by referendum, in 1990 the Provisional Government of Haiti requested the UN to monitor the elections that were to be held. This led to the establishment of the UN Observer Group for the Verification of the Elections in Haiti (ONUVEH). The Reverend Jean-Bertrand Aristide was elected by 67 per cent of the vote and inaugurated President on 22 February 1991. On 30 September 1991, a military coup removed Aristide from office.

On the same day, the Security Council met at the request of Haiti's Ambassador to the United Nations. But it did not formally convene to address the coup because the majority, quite in accordance with international law, viewed the coup as an internal domestic matter which did not constitute a threat to the peace and thus bringing it within the ambit of the competence of the Council.[174] The Organization of American States (OAS), on the other hand, formally condemned the coup on 2 October 1991 and recommended its member states to adopt economic and diplomatic sanctions against Haiti. When one day later the Security Council assembled to listen to President Aristide, all members of the Council denounced the coup and expressed strong support for the position of the OAS, but no formal resolution on the coup was adopted because China and other non-aligned states were worried about increasing Security Council intervention into affairs which are traditionally considered to belong to the domestic jurisdiction of states under Article 2(7) of the UN Charter and are consequently not any business of the United Nations.[175]

However, on 16 June 1993 the Security Council finally, expressly referring to previous General Assembly and OAS resolutions and, acting under Chapter VII, imposed a mandatory embargo on the delivery of oil,

172 Quigley, *op. cit.*, 271–2. See also the analysis at 281–2.

173 See Agora: The 1994 U.S. Action in Haiti, *AJIL* 89 (1995), 58–87; O. Corton, La Résolution 940 du conseil de sécurite autorisant une intervention militaire en Haiti: L'emergence d'un principe de légitimité démocratique en droit international?, *EJIL* 6 (1995), 116–33; H.-J. Heintze, Völkerrecht und demokratische Staatsordnung. Zur Wiederherstellung der Demokratie in Haiti, *VRÜ* 29 (1996), 6–30; M. Weller/ A. MacLean (eds), *The Haiti Crisis in International Law*, 1996. On the subsequent development in Haiti see *UN Chronicle*, 1996, no. 2, 57. See also Chapter 2, 31 and the literature, 387 n. 22 above.

174 Tesón, *op. cit.*, at 355.

175 See UN SCOR, 46th Sess., 3011th Meeting, UN Doc. S/PV.3011 (1991).

176 SC Res. 841 (1993).
177 SC Res. 861 (1993).
178 SC Res. 867 (1993).
179 SC Res. 873 (1993).
180 SC Res. 875 (1993).
181 SC Res. 940 (1994).
182 Tesón, *op. cit.*, 355.
183 Provisional Verbatim Record, UN SCOR, 3413th meeting, UN Doc. S/PV.3412 (1994), at 12 (Mr Li Zhaoxing, China).

petroleum products, arms and police equipment to Haiti, and froze assets of the Haitian government and its military leaders.[176] An agreement was subsequently reached with the military junta, known as the Governors Island Agreement, in July 1993 that provided for the return to power of President Aristide. The UN economic sanctions were lifted on 27 August 1993.[177] The UN Mission in Haiti (UNMIH) was established to provide assistance in reforming the Haitian armed forces and to assist in creating a new police force.[178] The failure of the Junta to comply with its promises and violence preventing UNMIH troops from disembarking in Haiti, however, induced the Security Council to reimpose the economic sanctions on 13 October 1993.[179] In a further resolution adopted on 16 October 1993, the Council authorized member states to use armed force to enforce the sanctions.[180] In May 1994, the Council added a trade embargo to the sanctions, excepting only medical products and foodstuff.

On 31 July 1994, the Security Council adopted Resolution 940 which authorized member states 'to form a multinational force' and 'to use all necessary means to facilitate the departure from Haiti of the military leadership'.[181] The United States delivered an ultimatum to Haiti's military government on 15 September 1994 via an address to the American public by President Clinton on television. On 18 September 1994, mediation efforts by the former US President Jimmy Carter, Senator Sam Nunn and the former Chairman of the Joint Chiefs of Staff, General Colin Powell, persuaded the junta to agree to leave the country by 15 October 1994. The agreement was reached only some hours before a multinational force under American leadership was to invade Haiti. On 19 September 1994, 3,000 US soldiers arrived and within a few days the foreign forces reached the number of more than 20,000. President Aristide returned to power on 15 October 1994 and the United States officially handed over the mission to the United Nations on 31 March 1995. Of the 6,000 UNMIH troops, the task of which was to assist the government to maintain a secure and stable environment and to enable free and fair elections, about 2,400 were US soldiers.

The case of Haiti has been described as the most important precedent supporting the legitimacy of an international principle of democratic rule as well as of collective humanitarian intervention.[182] But under traditional international law it is a strange case because it has never previously been the practice to regard the overthrow of a democratic government by a military coup as a matter of international concern in terms of Chapter VII of the Charter. The United Nations and the United States never intervened against the establishment of military rule in most of the countries in South America after 1945. It is of no surprise that China abstained in the Security Council concerning the Haiti operation, arguing, *inter alia*, that

> [t]he practice of the Council's authorizing certain Member States to use force is even more disconcerting because this would obviously create a dangerous precedent.[183]

Because it happened in the Western Hemisphere, perhaps the Haiti case, mainly a US operation, is better understood as an application of the

Monroe Doctrine, which since its formulation by US President Monroe in 1823 has served as a political justification for frequent military intervention by the United States in Latin America,[184] this time under the umbrella of the United Nations.

Yugoslavia

The most complicated conflict the United Nations was confronted with after the end of the Cold War has been the tragedy in Yugoslavia.[185] The former Socialist Federal Republic of Yugoslavia was composed of six republics: Solvenia, Croatia, Serbia, Bosnia-Herzegovina, Montenegro and Macedonia, and the two autonomous regions of Kosovo and Vojvodina. After the collapse of communism, secessionist tendencies became stronger and hostilities commenced when in June 1991 Croatia and Slovenia declared their independence from Yugoslavia. The Serb-controlled Federal Government and the Yugoslav People's Army opposed the move and supported the Serbian militias in their struggle against the Croatian and Slovenian authorities. The armed conflict was aggravated when Bosnia-Herzegovina declared its independence in March 1992, an act supported by Bosnian Croats and Bosnian Muslims, but violently opposed by Bosnian Serbs.

The European Community and the CSCE were unable to resolve the Yugoslav crisis within the framework of the Conference on Yugoslavia, chaired by Lord Carrington, and had considerable difficulties in dealing with the complicated questions of recognition of the new states in former Yugoslavia.[186] As far as the UN Security Council is concerned, it remained inactive for three months, in spite of the massive scale of bloodshed. It was only on 25 September 1991 that the Council adopted Resolution 713 (unanimously) which expressed concern about the armed conflict in Yugoslavia and its consequences for neighbouring countries and stated that 'the continuation of this situation constitutes a threat to international peace and security'.[187] While this is a somewhat ambiguous reference to Article 39 of the Charter, the preamble of the resolution also declared that no territorial gains or changes within Yugoslavia brought about by force would be acceptable. In its operative part, Resolution 713 expressed support for the efforts of the European Community and the CSCE and invited the UN Secretary-General to offer his assistance. The Council called upon all parties to strictly observe the cease-fire arrangements and to settle their differences peacefully within the framework of the Conference on Yugoslavia. Moreover, the Council, invoking Chapter VII of the Charter, decided

> that all States shall, for the purposes of establishing peace and stability in Yugoslavia, immediately implement a general and complete embargo on all deliveries of weapons and military equipment to Yugoslavia until the Security Council decides otherwise following consultation between the Secretary-General and the Government of Yugoslavia.[188]

There are two interesting points to be made concerning this resolution. First, at this stage the majority of the delegations in the Council still viewed the conflict in Yugoslavia as an internal one, except for the aspect of

184 See P. Malanczuk, Monroe Doctrine, *EPIL* 7 (1984), 339–44.

185 See, for example, C.E. Philipp/W. Plesmann, Conflicts, Yugoslavia, in *Wolfrum UNLPP I*, 338–49; B. Bagwell, Yugoslavian Constitutional Questions: Self-Determination and Secession of Member Republics, *GJICL* 21 (1991), 489–54; M. Glenny, *The Fall of Yugoslavia: The Third Balkan War*, 1992; C.J. Gow/L. Freedman, Intervention in a Fragmenting State: The Case of Yugoslavia, in Rodley (ed.), 1992, *op. cit.*, 93; M. Weller, The International Response to the Dissolution of the Socialist Federal Republic of Yugoslavia, *AJIL* 86 (1992), 569; R. Higgins, The New United Nations and Former Yugoslavia, *IA* 69 (1993), 465–83; A.L. King, Bosnia-Herzegowina–Vance-Owen Agenda for a Peaceful Settlement: Did the UN Do Too Little, Too Late, to Support This Endeavour?, *Ga. JICL* 23 (1993), 347–75; A. D'Amato, Peace v. Accountability in Bosnia, *AJIL* 88 (1994), 500–6; M. Mercier, *Crimes sans châtiment: L'action humanitaire en ex-Yugoslavie 1991–1993*, 1994; *AJIL* 89 (1995), 92–4; P.C. Szasz, Peacekeeping in Operation: A Conflict Study of Bosnia, *Cornell ILJ* 28 (1995), 685–700; T. Varady, The Predicament of Peacekeeping in Bosnia, *ibid.*, 709; P. Akhavan/R. Howse (eds), *Yugoslavia, the Former and Future*, 1995; E. O'Ballance, *Civil War in Bosnia 1992–1994*, 1995; G.A. Moor, The Republic of Bosnia-Herzegovina and Article 51: Inherent Rights and Unmet Responsibilities, *Fordham ILJ* 18 (1995), 870; A.M. Weisburd, The Emptiness of Jus Cogens, as Illustrated by the War in Bosnia-Herzegovina, *Mich. JIL* 17 (1995), 1; S.L. Woodward, *Balkan Tragedy: Chaos and Dissolution After the Cold War*, 1995; V. Brunce, The Elusive Peace in the Former Yugoslavia, *Cornell ILJ* 28 (1995), 709–18; M. Weller, Peacekeeping and Peace-Enforcement in the Republic of Bosnia and Herzegovina, *ZaöRV* 56 (1996), 70–177.

186 See Chapter 5 above, 89–90.

187 SC Res. 713 (1991), *ILM* 31 (1992), 1431.

188 Para. 6, at 1432.

189 See Weller, The International Response, *op. cit.*, 580.

190 See Chapter 18 above, 292–3.

191 SC Res. 743 (1992), *ILM* 31 (1992), 1447.

192 For details on UNPROFOR see M. Bothe, Peacekeeping, in *Simma CUNAC*, 565–603, 584–5.

193 SC Res. 752 (1992), *ILM* 31 (1992), 1451.

194 SC Res. 757 (1992), *ibid.*, 1453.

195 *Basic Facts, op. cit.*, 115.

196 See J. Kramer, Bericht, *VN* 40 (1992), at 208.

197 SC Res. 764 of 13 July 1992, *ILM* 31 (1992), 1465, para. 10: '*Reaffirms* that all parties are bound to comply with the obligations under international humanitarian law and in particular the Geneva Conventions of 12 August 1949, and that persons who commit or order the commission of grave breaches of the Conventions are individually responsible in respect of such breaches' (at 1467).

its consequences for neighbouring states.[189] Second, the complete arms embargo was welcomed by the Yugoslav central government (which was present at the Council meeting, while Croatia and Slovenia were not invited) because it was in possession of the rich arsenals, including heavy weapons, of the Yugoslav People's Army. The maintenance of the undifferentiated arms embargo later led Bosnia-Herzegovina, the right to self-defence of which under Article 51 of the UN Charter was curtailed by the arms embargo, to bring a case against former Yugoslavia (Serbia and Montenegro) before the International Court of Justice, indirectly challenging the legality of the embargo.[190]

Soon after the adoption of Resolution 713, the UN Secretary-General appointed Cyrus Vance as his Personal Envoy for Yugoslavia to negotiate cease-fire agreements and explore the option of deploying UN peacekeeping forces. Cease-fire agreements, however, were frequently broken and it was only on 21 February 1992 that the Security Council decided that the conditions were present to establish a United Nations Protection Force (UNPROFOR) for immediate deployment.[191] The force was to consist of 13,870 military and police personnel, complemented by 519 civilians. UNPROFOR was deployed in four 'United Nations Protected Areas' in which Serbs were the majority or the substantial minority of the population and where ethnic clashes had led to armed conflict. The mandate of UNPROFOR was to supervise the withdrawal of the Yugoslav People's Army from the areas and to ensure their demilitarization and the protection of the population from armed attacks. The force was also to assist humanitarian agencies in their work and to facilitate the return of refugees to their homes.[192]

However, the situation in former Yugoslavia continued to deteriorate, particularly after the conflict in Bosnia and Herzegovina broke out in April 1992. When the Security Council responded on 15 May 1992 by adopting Resolution 752,[193] it did not consider peacekeeping measures because the traditionally required consent of the conflicting parties was absent. Resolution 752 called upon the parties fighting in Bosnia–Herzegovina to stop immediately and demanded that units of the Yugoslav People's Army and Croatian units be withdrawn. Because the 'Yugoslav' authorities failed to comply, on 30 May 1992, the Council adopted Resolution 757 and imposed comprehensive economic sanctions under Article 41 of the Charter and demanded that all parties permit the delivery of humanitarian aid to Sarajevo and other areas of Bosnia and Herzegovina.[194]

In mid-1992 widespread reports of 'ethnic cleansing' and mass sexual assault, mostly conducted by Bosnian Serb forces, were made public. The number of refugees had risen to more then 2.2 million.[195] Indeed, it took quite a while until the United Nations finally recognized the dimension of 'ethnic cleansing' in Bosnia.[196] Security Council Resolution 764 of 13 July 1992 still only briefly reaffirmed the obligations of all parties under international humanitarian law and indicated that individuals could be held responsible for violations.[197] On 4 August 1992, the President of the Security Council demanded that the International Committee of the Red Cross (ICRC) and other organizations must have immediate access to the camps holding Muslim prisoners and reminded all parties to the conflict of the obligations under humanitarian law, the violation of which would entail individual responsibility.[198] In Resolution 769 of 7 August 1992, the Council condemned 'the abuses committed against the civilian population, particularly on ethnic grounds', referred to in a report from the Secretary-General,[199] but no enforcement measures were envisaged.

In Resolution 770 of 13 August 1992, the Council recognized that 'the situation in Bosnia and Herzegovina constitutes a threat to international peace and security and that the provision of humanitarian assistance in Bosnia and Herzegovina is an important element in the Council's effort to restore international peace and security in the area'. It expressed its deep concern at 'reports of abuses against civilians imprisoned in camps, prisons and detention centres'. Making reference to Chapter VII, it reaffirmed its demand that all parties stop fighting and called upon states 'to take nationally or through regional agencies or arrangements all measures necessary to facilitate in coordination with the United Nations' the delivery of humanitarian assistance. It further demanded that 'unimpeded and continuous access to all camps, prisons and detention centres be granted immediately' to the ICRC and other organizations and 'that all detainees therein receive humane treatment, including adequate food, shelter and medical care'.[200] At the same meeting the Security Council adopted Resolution 771 which for the first time expressly condemned the practice of 'ethnic cleansing'. The preamble expressed

> grave alarm at continuing reports of widespread violations of international humanitarian law occurring within the territory of the former Yugoslavia and especially in Bosnia and Herzegovina including reports of mass forcible expulsion and deportation of civilians, imprisonment and abuse of hospitals and ambulances, impeding the delivery of food and medical supplies to the civilian population, and wanton devastation and destruction of property.[201]

The resolution repeated previous demands by the Council and requested information from states and relevant organizations relating to the violations of humanitarian law. Invoking Chapter VII, the Council decided that all parties and others concerned in the former Yugoslavia and all military forces in Bosnia and Herzegovina shall comply with the resolution, 'failing which the Council will need to take further measures under the Charter'.

Resolution 770 must be seen in connection with the discussion at the end of July and the beginning of August 1992 on launching a massive military relief operation for Bosnia-Herzegovina, not with UN 'blue helmets', but with national contingents of Western armies, for example within the NATO framework.[202] Resolution 770 may have been understood as an authorization of Western states to proceed with such plans, although the text limits the purpose of action by Member States to the facilitation of the delivery of humanitarian assistance. However, the idea vanished when the international conference on former Yugoslavia was convened in London on 26 August 1992. Action was restricted to supplementing UNPROFOR by 6,000 soldiers, deployed and financed separately, by six European states and the United States (without combat forces) and Canada at the

198 UN Doc. S/24378, 4 August 1992.
199 SC Res. 769 (1992), *ILM* 31 (1992), 1467, at 1468, para. 4. The report of the Secretary-General of 27 July 1992 (UN Doc. S/24353 and Add. 1) suggested to expand the mandate and strength of UNPROFOR.
200 SC Res. 770 of 13 August 1992, *ILM* 31 (1992), 1468.
201 SC Res. 771 of 13 August 1992, *ILM* 31 (1992), 1470.
202 Kramer, *op. cit.*, at 210 states that the deployment of 100,000 to 300,000 soldiers was seriously considered.

203 See Kramer, *ibid.*, On the expanding of the mandate and size of UNPROFOR see Res. 769 of 7 August 1992 (*ILM* 31 (1992), 1467), Res. 776 of 14 September 1992 (*ibid.*, 1472) and Res. 779 of 6 October 1992 (*ibid.*, 1474). The Security Council had decided by Res. 727 of 8 January 1992 (*ibid.*, 1437), Res. 743 of 21 February 1992 (*ibid.*, 1447) and Res. 749 of 7 April 1992 (*ibid.*, 1449) first to send fifty liaison officers and then to deploy 14,000 'blue helmets' in former Yugoslavia for a period of one year.
204 J.B. Steinberg, International Involvement in the Yugoslavia Conflict, in L.F. Damrosch (ed.), *Enforcing Restraint: Collective Intervention in Armed Conflict*, 1993, 27, 44.
205 SC Res. 781 of 9 October 1992, *ILM* 31 (1992), 1477; SC Res. 786 of 10 November 1992, *ibid.*, 1479. While China abstained in the vote on the first of these resolutions, the second was adopted unanimously with China maintaining its reservation as to any future authorization of the use of force to implement the ban on military flights in the airspace of Bosnia and Herzegovina, see Provisional Verbatim Record of the Security Council Meeting on 9 October 1992, S/PV.3122, 9 October 1992 at 7, and of the Meeting on 10 November 1992, S/PV.3133, 11 November 1992 at 8.
206 SC Res. 780 (1992), *ILM* 31 (1992), 1476.
207 Kramer, *op. cit.*, at 208.
208 UN Doc. S/24744, 30 October 1992.
209 Human Rights Commission resolution 1992/S-1/1.
210 Kramer, *op. cit.*, at 209 with reference to S/24516-A/47/418, 3 September 1992; S/24766-A/47/635, 6 November 1992; and S/24809-A/47/666, 17 November 1992.
211 SC Res. 787 (1992), 16 November 1992; *ILM* 31 (1992), 1481. It was adopted by thirteen votes to nil, with China and Zimbabwe abstaining.
212 SC Res. 798 (1992), quotations from provisional text UN Doc. S/24977, 17 December 1992.

beginning of November 1992 (UNPROFOR II) to ensure the delivery of humanitarian supplies.[203] The success of this force was limited because of the military opposition of Bosian Serb militias.[204] The Security Council also instituted a 'no-fly zone' in October 1992, banning all military flights over Bosnia and Herzegovina.[205]

On 6 October 1992, the Council took the unusual step of creating an impartial Commission of Experts to investigate the allegations concerning the violation of international humanitarian law.[206] The five members of the commission, chaired by Professor Frits Kalshoven, were appointed by the Secretary-General on 23 October 1992.[207] Following the attacks by Serbian militia in Bosnia and Herzegovina on civilians fleeing from the city of Jajce, on 30 October 1992, the President of the Security Council condemned these attacks, and reaffirmed that those who committed or ordered serious violations of humanitarian law were individually responsible, and advised to inform the Commission of Experts of such violations.[208] In addition, the Human Rights Commission in Geneva met for the first time in its history for a special meeting on 14 August 1992 to adopt a resolution by consensus which condemned the policy of 'ethnic cleansing'.[209] The former Polish Prime Minister Mazowiecki was then appointed as special rapporteur for Yugoslavia, and he submitted reports confirming serious human rights abuses.[210]

In Resolution 787 of 16 November 1992, concerning the enforcement of the economic sanctions imposed on Serbia and Montenegro, the Council again also addressed the massive and systematic breaches of human rights and humanitarian law in former Yugoslavia, declared that annexation of territory by force and the practice of 'ethnic cleansing' were illegal and that all persons expelled must be permitted to return to their homes in peace. While the Council authorized states under Chapters VII and VIII of the Charter to take the necessary measures which were appropriate under the circumstances to control the cargo and destination of ships and to ensure respect for Resolutions 713 (1992) and 757 (1992), no measures were adopted in response to the continuing violation of human rights. The Council merely requested the Secretary-General, in cooperation with other bodies, to examine the possibility and requirements to promote the idea of safety zones for humanitarian purposes.[211] Based on reports of 'the massive, organized and systematic detention and rape of women, in Bosnia and Herzegovina', on 17 December 1992, the Council adopted Resolution 798, which had been introduced by Belgium, France and Britain, and demanded that all the detention camps and camps for women be immediately closed, condemned 'these acts of unspeakable brutality' and supported the dispatch of the delegation from the European Communities to investigate the facts. It further decided to 'remain actively seized of the matter'.[212]

On 18 December 1992, the General Assembly passed a strongly worded resolution on the 'ethnic cleansing' and the detention camps, on the violation of the territorial sovereignty of Bosnia and Herzegovina by Serbia and Montenegro, and urged the Security Council to consider, by 15 January 1993 at the latest, authorizing member states under Chapter VII 'to use all necessary means' in cooperation with Bosnia to repel Serbian and Montenegrin forces, to exempt Bosnia from the arms embargo and to consider additional measures, such as establishing an *ad hoc* international war crimes tribunal.[213] It must be noted, that while there were no votes against this resolution, fifty-seven states abstained.

The developments in the following years of war in former Yugoslavia included unsuccessful diplomatic efforts to end the conflict, such as the Vance-Owen plan, the establishment by the Security Council of an International Criminal Tribunal with jurisdiction to prosecute crimes committed in the armed conflict in former Yugoslavia,[214] and the authorization of member states by the Security Council in Resolution 816 in 1993, with reference to Resolution 770 of 1992, to take

> all necessary measures in the airspace of the Republic of Bosnia and Herzegovina, in the event of further violations, to ensure compliance with the ban on flights.[215]

China abstained in the vote on this resolution and later Russia protested against the use of the Bosnia resolutions of the Security Council by the United States and NATO to justify air strikes around Sarajevo against Bosnian Serb emplacements, apparently because Russia viewed their true objective as being to open an arms supply route to Sarajevo for the Bosnian government, rather than to protect the delivery of humanitarian aid.[216] On 6 May 1993, Security Council Resolution 824 declared Sarajevo, Tuzla, Žepa, Gorazde and Bihac safe areas, after Srebrenica and its surroundings had already been declared safe areas by Resolution 819 of 16 April 1993.[217] Between April 1994 and February 1995 NATO airplanes conducted nine limited attacks against Serbian targets on the ground. In March 1995, the Security Council decided on the replacement of UNPROFOR by three separate but interlinked peacekeeping operations in Bosnia-Herzegovina (UNPROFOR), Croatia (UNCRO) and Macedonia[218] (UNPREDEP).

After the Mladić army and Bosnian Serbian militias had conquered Srebrenica (11 July 1995) and Žepa (25 July 1995), two of the enclaves vanished which had made agreement on borders in a future peace settlement rather difficult. Moreover, the Krajina campaign of the Croatian President Tudjmann (4 to 7 August 1995) ended with considerable territorial gain by the allied Croats and Muslims in West Bosnia. Thus, the previously agreed formula of a settlement envisaging 51 per cent for the Muslims and Croats and 49 per cent for the Serbs was now almost reflecting the reality of the control of territory by the parties. These conditions led to a new American peace initiative with the mission led by Richard Holbrooke who took up negotiations with the parties on 15 August 1995. The Serbs were offered two new important concessions. First, they obtained the option of establishing an independent state. Second, the long-term possibility of a close connection, or even unification, with the Serbian Republic was offered under conditions similar to those which had been granted to the Muslims and Croats one year earlier. On 29 August 1995, the Serbian leaders Karadžič (Republic of Serbia) and Milošević (Bosnian Serbs) agreed to accept peace negotiations on this basis.

213 UN Doc. A/47/L.47/Rev.1, 17 December 1992, adopted as Resolution 47/121.

214 See Chapter 20 above, 355–60.

215 Sc Res. 816, 31 March 1993, *UNYb* 1993, 463, at 464.

216 Quigley, *op. cit.*, 280.

217 SC Res. 819 (1993), *UNYb* 1993, 452; SC Res. 824 (1993), *ibid.*, 455.

218 On the dispute between Macedonia and Greece, see Chapters 5, 90 and 11, 167 above.

219 See Chapter 19 above, 311–18.
220 See R. Mutz, Legenden auf dem Balkan, *Der Spiegel* 27/1996, 114–6.
221 The texts of the General Framework Agreement for Peace in Bosnia and Herzegovina and the Dayton Agreement on Implementing the Federation of Bosnia and Herzegovina are in *ILM* 35 (1996), 75 *et seq.*, 170 *et seq.* The text of the Conclusions of the London Meeting (12 December 1995) of the Peace Implementation Conference for the Bosnian General Framework Agreement is in *ILM* 35 (1996), 223. See also *UN Chronicle*, 1996, no. 1, 25 *et seq.*, 35 *et seq.* For the International Conference on the former Yugoslavia Documentation on the Arbitration Commission under the UN/EC (Geneva) Conference: Terms of Reference, Reconstitution of the Arbitration Commission, and Rules of Procedure, see *ILM* 32 (1993), 1572. See further P. Gaeta, The Dayton Agreements and International Law, *EJIL* 2 (1996), 147–63; N. Figà-Talamanca, The Role of NATO in the Peace Agreement for Bosnia and Herzegovina, *ibid.*, 164–75; S. Yee, The New Constitution of Bosnia and Herzegovina, *ibid.*, 176–93; E. Andersen, The Role of Asylum States in Promoting Safe and Peaceful Repatriation under the Dayton Agreements, *ibid.*, 193–206; J. Sloan, The Dayton Peace Agreement: Human Rights Guarantees and Their Implementation, *ibid.*, 207–25; J.R.W.D. Jones, The Implications of the Peace Agreement for the International Criminal Tribunal for the Former Yugoslavia, *ibid.*, 226–4; B. Ramcharan, The Bosnian Peace Accord, *LJIL* 9 (1996), 131–40.
222 SC Res. 1031 (1995), *ILM* 35 (1996), 251.
223 SC Res. 1035 (1995), *ibid.*, 256.
224 SC Res. 1021 (1995) and 1022 (1995), *ibid.*, 257 and 259. On the further development and problems of implementing the agreement, see *UN Chronicle* 33 (1996), no. 2, 24–34. Noting that elections took place in Bosnia on 14 September 1996, SC Res. 1074 (1996) of 1 October 1996 lifted the sanctions on the Federal Republic of Yugoslavia; *ILM* 35 (1996), 1561.

One day earlier, on 28 August 1995, thirty-eight persons were killed in the Muslim part of Sarajevo by artillery fire, for which Serbian forces were held responsible. This provided a cause for the launching of the NATO operation 'Deliberate Force' on 30 August 1995 which lasted until 14 September 1995 and which included heavy bombardment of troops, weapons, military installations and production sites, as well as of civilian traffic routes, intersections and bridges. Thus, the action is difficult to qualify as an act of self-defence[219] and because it included targets comprehensively in the whole part of Bosnia-Herzegovina controlled by Serbian forces, it went beyond the UN mandate concerning the protection of the safety zones.

It is important to note that the NATO decision to take retaliatory measures against the Serbs had already been taken at the end of July 1995, following the war crimes committed against the civilian population when Srebrenica and Žepa fell to the Serbs. Operation 'Deliberate Force' was an American idea, reluctantly accepted by NATO allies, and de facto it was also largely a US enterprise. Although eight NATO states participated in the operation, two-thirds of the 3,500 air strikes were conducted by aircraft of the US Air Force and US Navy. It is a myth that NATO ended the war in the former Yugoslavia by military action.[220] The basic agreement of the Serbian leadership to negotiate a peace settlement had already been made prior to Operation 'Deliberate Force', the implementation of which was more likely to endanger the success of the Holbrooke mission. On 5 October 1995, the Bosnian parties to the conflict finally agreed on a cease-fire which came into effect five days later and led to a significant improvement of the situation.

A decisive break of the deadlock was then achieved with the General Framework Agreement for Peace in Bosnia and Herzegovina that was initialled on 21 November 1995 at a US Air Force base near Dayton, Ohio, and signed in Paris on 14 December 1995.[221] The agreement is a treaty between three of the five successor states to former Yugoslavia, the Bosnia and Herzegovina Republic, the Federal Republic of Yugoslavia and the Republic of Croatia and was witnessed by the five members of a 'Contact Group' (USA, Russia, France, Germany and Britain) which had been formed in May 1994 to facilitate the final stage of negotiations, and by the European Union. In accordance with the terms of the peace agreement, on 15 December 1995, the Security Council authorized the deployment of a 60,000-strong multinational military implementation force (IFOR),[222] composed of NATO and non-NATO forces, to replace UNPROFOR as of 20 December 1995 and to ensure compliance with the Dayton/Paris Agreement. A UN civilian police force in Bosnia-Herzegovina, the International Police Task Force (IPTF), was established by the Security Council on 21 December 1995.[223] In view of the developments the Security Council had already on 22 November 1995 lifted the arms embargo imposed by Resolution 713 of 25 September 1991 (Russia abstaining) and indefinitely suspended the economic sanctions against the Federal Republic of Yugoslavia (Serbia and Montenegro).[224]

How can one explain the reluctance of the Security Council to (apart from the air strikes) back up by military sanctions its decisions taken under

Chapter VII following the initial Resolution 713 of 25 September 1991 in the case of Yugoslavia? Since the London conference in summer 1992 a series of agreements had been signed and broken by the parties, while in fact the practice of ethnic cleansing, rape, and the deterioration of the situation of the civilian population continued also during the subsequent negotiations in Geneva.

It appears that states with the power to do so were for a variety of reasons reluctant to intervene militarily in Yugoslavia, especially with ground troops. First of all, there were different interests of states, as can be seen from the sympathetic attitude of Russia towards Serbia and the Greek position on the Macedonian question, which conflicted with the view of other members of the European Communities. There was also no clear or common Western policy on what the future order in the Balkans should be. Furthermore, it seemed difficult to clearly define limited objectives of military intervention with troops and their requirements. Special technical difficulties for effective military operation in the area, the prospect of having to face at least one well-equipped, trained and determined enemy army, and the risks involved for the lives of their soldiers, including those of the national contingents of the UN peacekeeping forces already in place, were other more specific considerations. There was also the fear of becoming entangled in a complex guerrilla war with eventual long-term commitments as to military presence in the area. Thus, the calculation may have been that it was better, by maintaining pressure with sanctions and by involving the parties in the negotiating process, to at least try to reduce the suffering and to contain the conflict, until the warring parties had exhausted themselves. The long-term effect of the perceived inaction of Western powers and the UN in view of the fate of Bosnian Muslims on the relationship to the Muslim world, however, remains an open question.

In a complicated scenario such as the war in Yugoslavia, political choices are not easy to make, perhaps even on the limited question of lifting the undifferentiated arms embargo that was imposed on all parties. The United States appeared to view the problem in Yugoslavia as a primarily European responsibility and to consider American vital interests[225] only to be affected should the war have spread to other areas of the Balkans, threatening to engage Greece and Turkey. It was only at a late stage that the United States decided to engage its air forces to retaliate massively against the Serbs and to exercise pressure to complete a peace settlement. European institutions and states were unable to respond militarily to a major conflict in their own region without American leadership. There were some statements from the French government on whether France might be prepared to use military force unilaterally to liberate civilians from prison camps in Bosnia which, however, remained rather confusing.[226] Other European states were not willing to go along with Dutch demands for stronger action. The experience has clearly demonstrated the need for strengthening the common elements of the foreign and defence policy of the member states of the European Union, of the upgrading of the Western European Union (WEU) and of improving other aspects of regional security in Europe.

225 On this point see C.J.P. Terry, The Criteria for Intervention: An Evaluation of U.S. Military Policy in U.N. Operations, *Texas ILJ* 31 (1996), 101–5.

226 *IHT*, 11 January 1993, 1; 13 January 1993, 2.

227 See D.W. Bowett, *United Nations Forces*, 1964; R. Higgins, *United Nations Peacekeeping 1946–1967, Documents and Commentary*, Vols 1–3 (1969–80); E. Suy, United Nations Peacekeeping System, *EPIL* 4 (1982), 258; I. Pogany, The Evaluation of United Nations Peace-Keeping Operations, *BYIL*, 57 (1986), 357–70; UNITAR, *The United Nations and the Maintenance of International Peace and Security*, 1987; R.C.R. Siekmann, *Basic Documents on United Nations and Related Peace-Keeping Forces*, 2nd edn 1989; Siekmann, *National Contingents in United Nations Peace-Keeping Forces*, 1991; Y. Hirose, *Peace-Keeping Operations of the United Nations*, 1992; R. Connaughton, Military Intervention and UN Peacekeeping, in Rodley (ed.), 1992, *op. cit.*, 165; P.F. Diehl, *International Peacekeeping*, 1993; Bothe, Peacekeeping, *op. cit.*, 565–603; K. Rudolf, Peace-Keeping Forces, in *Wolfrum UNLPP II*, 957–69; D. Warner (ed.), *New Dimensions of Peacekeeping*, 1995; M. Bothe/R.C.R. Siekmann (eds), *International Peacekeeping*, Vols 1–3, 1994–6; R.S. Lee, United Nations Peacekeeping: Development and Prospects, *Cornell ILJ* 28 (1995), 619–30; R. Wedgwood, The Evolution of United Nations Peacekeeping, *ibid.*, 631–44. See also the literature cited below, 423–5.

228 See S.R. Ratner, *The New UN Peacekeeping: Building Peace in Lands of Conflict After the Cold War*, 1995.

229 See text above, 392–3.

230 See text below, 417–18.

231 See text above, 389.

232 *Expenses* case, *ICJ Rep.* 1962, 151, 166, 171–2, 177. See text below, 419, 420.

233 *Ibid.*, 167.

UN peacekeeping

UN peacekeeping operations[227] have traditionally been clearly distinguished from 'enforcement action' authorized by the UN Security Council under Chapter VII, because they have always been based upon the consent of the conflicting parties to the deployment of peacekeeping troops and military observers under the auspices of the UN. The distinction between UN 'enforcement action' and 'peacekeeping' has increasingly become blurred, due to new kinds of operations (often labelled 'second generation peacekeeping' or 'mixed peacekeeping' which may include some enforcement elements). Indeed, the terminology concerning UN peacekeeping has recently become rather confusing. For the sake of convenience, it is useful to distinguish in the following simply between the 'old' peacekeeping during the Cold War and the 'new' peacekeeping after the Cold War. In practice, both forms continue to exist alongside each other.[228]

The 'old' peacekeeping during the Cold War

After 1945 Chapter VII of the Charter, which contemplated action by the Security Council, did not work well in practice, and states sometimes (especially during the 1950s) turned to the General Assembly and the Secretariat to fill the gap. The Soviet Union always used to oppose this trend, and after 1960 power swung back to the Security Council.[229] In the 1950s the General Assembly claimed the power to create a United Nations peacekeeping force, and actually exercised this power in 1956.[230] From 1960 onwards all United Nations peacekeeping forces have been created by the Security Council, and no serious attempt has been made to get the General Assembly to create another such United Nations force; the question whether the General Assembly has the legal power to create a United Nations peacekeeping force is no longer of much political importance, although it is still worth examining because it throws light on wider legal issues.

As noted above, no agreements have been concluded under Article 43 of the Charter.[231] This has not prevented the United Nations from assembling forces by other means. Such forces were, for instance, sent to the Middle East in 1956 and to the Congo in 1960. The Soviet Union argued that these two forces were illegal, because they had not been set up in accordance with Article 43. The International Court of Justice replied that the forces in question were not designed to take enforcement action, and that Article 43 applied only to forces designed to take enforcement action; consequently, failure to comply with the procedure of Article 43 did not invalidate the creation of the forces.[232]

It seems, however, that the International Court did not intend to imply that failure to comply with the procedure of Article 43 would have invalidated the creation of a force designed to take enforcement action.[233] When Article 42 says that 'action by . . . [United Nations] forces . . . may include . . . operations by . . . forces of Members of the United Nations', it clearly implies that there is more than one way in which United Nations forces may be recruited.

The purpose of Article 43 was to *facilitate* action by the Security Council; it would be wholly alien to that purpose to argue that the absence of agreements under Article 43 should prevent action by the Security Council. In other words, Article 43 provides a procedure by which the Security Council *may* act, but it does not prevent the Security Council from choosing an alternative procedure.

The first United Nations Emergency Force in the Middle East (UNEF)

At the end of October 1956 Israel, France and the United Kingdom attacked Egypt. But within a few days the states concerned agreed to a ceasefire, and on 5 November 1956 the General Assembly set up a United Nations Emergency Force (UNEF) 'to secure and supervise the cessation of hostilities'.[234] Later, when Israel, France and the United Kingdom had withdrawn their troops, UNEF was sent to patrol the Israeli–Egyptian armistice line, in order to encourage 'the scrupulous maintenance of the armistice agreement of 1949'.[235]

The Force consisted of contingents of national armies, made available under agreements between the contributing states and the Secretary-General. The General Assembly appointed the Commander of the Force, and authorized the Secretary-General to enact regulations setting out the rights and duties of soldiers serving in it. The Force was paid by the United Nations, and it took its orders solely from the General Assembly and the Secretary-General. Consequently, although certain questions such as promotion were still dealt with by the contributing states, the Force was a United Nations force in a much more real sense than the forces in Korea.

The Force was founded very largely on the principle of consent. No state was obliged to provide a contingent unless it consented to do so. The Force could not enter the territory of any state without that state's consent; thus it operated solely on Egyptian territory and not on Israeli territory, because Israel, unlike Egypt, did not consent to its presence.

The Force was authorized to fight in order to defend itself, but it was not expected to resist large-scale invasions across the armistice line; indeed, the fact that it never numbered more than 6,000 men would have made such a role impracticable. Its function was to patrol the armistice line and to report troop movements taking place near the line; it was also used to arrest individuals trespassing near the armistice line and hand them over to the Egyptian police. For over ten years, until it was withdrawn at the request of Egypt in 1967, its presence helped to create a peaceful atmosphere in which there were very few guerrilla raids across the armistice line.

The legal basis for the creation of the Force was uncertain. The communist countries, which abstained in the vote setting up the Force, said that the use of any type of United Nations force constituted enforcement action, which could be taken only by the Security Council. In the *Expenses* case, the International Court of Justice said that the operations of UNEF did not constitute enforcement action because they were not directed against any state without that state's consent.[236] But it is one thing to show that there is no provision in the Charter forbidding the creation of the Force; it is quite another thing to find a provision authorizing its creation. The International Court suggested that the force might have been based

234 GA Res. A/3276 of 4 November 1956, *UNYb* 1956, 36. See Higgins, *op. cit.*, Vol. 2, 221 *et seq.*

235 *Ibid.*, 61.

236 *ICJ Rep.* 1962, at 171–2. See also text below, 420. Most commentators have described UNEF as a 'peacekeeping force'. The concept of peacekeeping forces, and the distinction between peacekeeping and enforcement action, are not mentioned in the Charter, but as noted at the beginning of this chapter, have been developed by practice.

237 *Ibid.,* 172. For the text of these Articles, see Chapter 21 above, 377.

238 *Effect of Awards of Compensation made by the UN Administrative Tribunal, ICJ Pleadings, Oral Arguments, Documents* 1954, 295–301.

239 See B. Nolte, Conflicts, Congo, in Wolfrum *UNLPP I,* 225–32; D.W. Bowett, *United Nations Forces: A Legal Study of United Nations Practice,* 1964, 153–254; G. Abi-Saab, *The United Nations Operations in the Congo 1960– 1964,* 1978.

240 SC Res. 4383 (1960), *UNYb* 1960, 97.

241 *Ibid.*

242 See Chapter 21 above, 374.

243 SC Res. 4424 (1960), *UNYb* 1960, 98.

either on Article 11 or on Article 14 of the Charter.[237] The trouble with these Articles is that they merely empower the General Assembly to recommend measures to be taken by somebody else; they do not empower it to take measures. But the practice of the General Assembly suggests that the fact that the General Assembly can only make recommendations does not prevent it from setting up subsidiary bodies to carry out those recommendations, provided that the consent of the states concerned is obtained.[238]

The United Nations Force in the Congo (ONUC)

On 30 June 1960 Belgium granted independence to the Belgian Congo.[239] Little had been done to prepare the Congo (subsequently renamed Zaire) for independence, and almost immediately the Congolese army mutinied and began attacking Europeans resident in the Congo. Belgium, which had retained military bases in the Congo, deployed troops to protect the Europeans, and the Congolese government appealed to the United Nations for military assistance against 'Belgian aggression'. On 14 July 1960 the Security Council authorized the Secretary-General to provide the Congo with military assistance;[240] the Secretary-General had announced in advance that he would interpret this resolution as authorizing him to create a force modelled on UNEF, and the action which he took to set up the force was approved unanimously by the Security Council eight days later.[241] Despite the circumstances in which the force was set up, it was not intended to take military action against Belgian troops; its function was to help the Congolese government to maintain law and order, and thus to create a situation in which the Europeans in the Congo would not need protection by the Belgian army. The force was modelled on UNEF, but a number of differences soon began to appear.

In the first place, the Security Council was prevented by the veto from giving clear instructions to the Secretary-General, and consequently the Secretary-General had to take all sorts of decisions which, in the case of UNEF, had been taken by the General Assembly (for example, appointing the Commander of the force).

Second, although the force was intended to operate with the consent of the Congolese government, this principle became difficult to observe when the Congolese government disintegrated into warring factions. Another departure from the principle of consent can be seen in the Security Council resolution passed on 9 August 1960, which referred to earlier resolutions on the Congo and reminded member states that they were under a legal obligation, by virtue of Article 25 of the Charter,[242] 'to accept and carry out the decisions of the Security Council'.[243] One of the earlier decisions referred to in the resolution of 9 August 1960 was the resolution of 22 July 1960, which *inter alia* requested 'all states to refrain from any action which might . . . impede the restoration of law and order . . . and also to refrain from any action which might undermine the territorial integrity and political independence . . . of the Congo'. This request, which was transformed into an order by the resolution of 9 August 1960, was ignored by certain Western financial interests, which assisted the secessionist activities of Moise Tshombe in Katanga, and by the Soviet

Union, which supported the Prime Minister, Patrice Lumumba, in his struggle against President Kasavubu.

Third, although the force was originally intended to fight only in order to defend itself, it was subsequently authorized to fight in other circumstances as well – in order to prevent civil war, and in order to expel foreign mercenaries. In the end the force found itself engaged in extensive military operations against the secessionist movement in Katanga.

The legal basis for the creation of the force is obscure and controversial. The Soviet Union argued that the creation of the force was illegal for a number of reasons, including the fact that the force was virtually under the control of the Secretary-General, instead of being under the control of the Security Council, as it ought to have been. But there is no reason why the Security Council should not delegate its powers to the Secretary-General under Article 98 of the Charter, which provides that 'the Secretary-General . . . shall perform such . . . functions as are entrusted to him by' the Security Council. In any case, the Soviet position is hard to reconcile with the fact that the Soviet Union had voted for the resolutions creating the force.

In the *Expenses* case the International Court of Justice said that the operations of the force did not constitute enforcement action.[244] This statement by the Court is rather surprising, considering the scale of the military operations in Katanga. However, commentators have generally described the operations of the force as 'peacekeeping action', as opposed to 'enforcement action'. But one of the resolutions concerning the force was phrased in mandatory terms;[245] several commentators suggested that the creation of the force constituted 'provisional measures' within the meaning of Article 40, and this view received some support from the United Nations Secretariat. Although Article 40 appears in Chapter VII, it would seem that 'provisional measures' under Article 40 do not constitute 'enforcement action'; otherwise, a state which had been called upon to comply with provisional measures could be suspended from exercising the rights and privileges of membership under Article 5,[246] which would be incompatible with the principle, laid down in Article 40, that 'provisional measures shall be without prejudice to the rights . . . of the parties concerned'.[247]

Reliance on Article 40 implies that the situation in the Congo must have amounted to (at least) a threat to international peace.[248] Although the original resolutions concerning the Congo contained no express finding to that effect by the Security Council, it is obvious that the danger of civil war in the Congo was a threat to international peace in the same way that the danger of civil war in Rhodesia was a threat to international peace.[249] The preamble to the Security Council's later resolution S/4722 of 21 February 1961 recited that the Security Council was 'deeply concerned at . . . the danger of widespread civil war and bloodshed in the Congo and the threat to international peace and security'.[250] Indeed, the situation in the Congo was much more serious, because there was a risk of the Soviet Union and the United States taking sides in the civil war. The United Nations action did not entirely succeed in averting that risk, but, if it had not been for the United Nations action, the two superpowers might have found themselves

244 *ICJ Rep.* 1962, at 177.
245 See text above, 418.
246 see Chapter 21 above, 369–71.
247 For the text of Article 40, see text above, 388.
248 See text above, 388.
249 See text above, 393–5.
250 *UNYb* 1961, 104.

251 *ICJ Rep.* 1962, 151. See M. Bothe, Certain Expenses of the United Nations (Advisory Opinion), *EPIL* I (1992), 557–60.
252 See Chapter 18 above, 289–90.
253 See Chapter 21 above, 377.

dragged against their will into a war of Vietnamese proportions in the Congo. Each superpower was therefore probably glad that the United Nations filled the vacuum in the Congo and thus prevented the Congo falling under the control of the other.

The Expenses *case*

When the United Nations forces in the Middle East and the Congo were set up, the General Assembly decided that member states were under a legal duty to pay for the forces. However, the forces were not financed out of the ordinary budget, but out of separate accounts (one for each force); and a different scale of contributions was used, which reduced the size of the contributions payable by the poorest member states. These facts led some states to argue that the expenses of the forces were so different from the ordinary expenses of the United Nations that member states were under no obligation to pay for the forces. The communist countries also argued that there was no duty to pay for the forces because the forces had been created illegally. Soon it became clear that the United Nations was facing a major financial crisis, and shortage of money forced the United Nations to reduce the force in the Congo in 1963 and to withdraw it altogether in 1964.

Consequently the General Assembly asked the International Court of Justice to advise whether the expenses of the two forces were indeed expenses of the United Nations within the meaning of Article 17(2) of the Charter, which provides that 'the expenses of the organization shall be borne by the members as apportioned by the General Assembly'. On 20 July 1962 the Court answered this question in the affirmative, by nine votes to five.[251] The question put to the Court was not directly concerned with the legality of the creation of the forces, and the Court's brief remarks about the legality of their creation were somewhat inconclusive; it limited itself to saying that the creation of the forces was probably legal, and to rejecting various arguments against their legality, but it did not say precisely which provisions of the Charter constituted the legal justification for their creation.

The Court's opinion, being an advisory opinion,[252] was not binding, and, although some of the states which had previously defaulted began to pay after the Court had delivered its opinion, the Soviet bloc and France remained adamant in their refusal to pay. The United States and its allies threatened to invoke Article 19 of the Charter, which deprives a defaulting state of its right to vote in the General Assembly 'if the amount of its arrears equals or exceeds the amount of the contributions due from it for the preceding two full years'.[253] The Soviet Union retorted by threatening to leave the organization if it was deprived if its vote in the General Assembly. Eventually, in August 1965, the United States and its allies gave way and agreed not to invoke Article 19; in return, the Soviet Union promised to make a voluntary contribution towards the expenses of the two forces.

The United Nations Force in Cyprus (UNFICYP)

When Cyprus became independent in 1960, it had a complicated constitution designed to protect the interests of the Turkish-speaking minority;

in a 1960 Treaty of Guarantee Cyprus agreed not to alter the basic provisions of the constitution, and gave each of the other parties to the treaty (Greece, Turkey and the United Kingdom) a right to take unilateral 'action' (a word which was probably deliberately ambiguous) in order to uphold the constitution.[254] In 1963 President Makarios of Cyprus declared that the constitution was unworkable and would be altered. This led to fighting between the Greek and Turkish communities in Cyprus, and British troops arrived, with the consent of all the interested parties, to keep the peace between the two communities. Keeping the peace turned out to be a harder task than the British had expected, and so the British asked the United Nations to send a peacekeeping force to the island.

There was clearly a danger that war between Greece and Turkey could develop out of clashes between the Greek and Turkish communities in Cyprus. The Security Council therefore decided unanimously on 4 March 1964 to set up a United Nations force for the purpose of preventing a recurrence of fighting between the two communities in Cyprus.[255]

The force was largely modelled on UNEF, but with some significant differences. First, it was financed by voluntary contributions. Second, as in the case of the force in the Congo, the composition and the size of the force were to be decided by the Secretary-General, and the Commander was to be appointed by him. On the other hand, a certain distrust of the Secretary-General was shown by the fact that the force was set up for only three months; since then the Secretary-General has had to ask the Security Council to prolong the existence of the force for successive periods of three or six months.

The Secretary-General instructed the force to be impartial and to fight only in order to defend itself. These restrictions have not limited the usefulness of the force as much as one might have expected. The force patrols territory separating areas held by the rival communities, and escorts people from one community across areas held by the other community; if it is fired upon when carrying out these functions, it has the right to return fire in self-defence. It also investigates and reports outbreaks of fighting, and tries to persuade the parties to cease fire when such outbreaks occur. However, it was not intended to impose a political settlement on the parties, who have still not yet reached agreement about the constitutional future of Cyprus. Nor was it intended to take part in large-scale hostilities, and consequently it did not attempt to resist the invasion of northern Cyprus by Turkey in 1974.[256]

As usual, the resolution setting up the force does not specify the Articles of the Charter justifying its creation. Some commentators have suggested that it is based on Chapter VI of the Charter (peaceful settlement of disputes)[257] rather than on Chapter VII (enforcement action). The preamble to the resolution setting up the force says that 'the present situation with regard to Cyprus is likely to threaten international peace and security', which echoes the language of Chapter VI ('dispute or situation ... likely to endanger the maintenance of international peace and security'), rather than the language of Chapter VII (Chapter VII applies only when there is already an actual threat to the peace,

254 See T. Oppermann, Cyprus, *EPIL* I (1992), 923–6; E. Michos-Ederer, Conflicts, Cyprus, in *Wolfrum UNLPP I*, 233–42; Z.M. Necatigil, *The Cyprus Question and the Turkish Position in International Law*, 1989; S. Muller/W. Mijs (eds), *The Cyprus Question and the Turkish Position in International Law*, 2nd edn 1993.

255 SC Res. 186 (1964), *UNYb* 1964, 165.

256 For further information about the functions of the force, see A.J.R. Carrion, The United Nations Force in Cyprus: An Uncertain Case of Peace-Keeping, in A. Cassese (ed.), *United Nations Peace-Keeping*, 1978, 158–60, 163–9. On subsequent developments see Michos-Ederer, *op. cit.*, 237; Bothe, Peacekeeping, *op. cit.*, 578.

257 See text above, 385–7.

258 See text above, 417–18.

259 *ILM* 12 (1973), 1528–30, 1537–40; *ILM* 14 (1975), 1450 *et seq.*; on the first United Nations Emergency Force, cf. text above, 417–18.

260 SC Res. 350 of 31 May 1974, *UN Chronicle*, June 1974, 26–8, at 26. See I.S. Pogany, *The Security Council and the Arab-Israeli Conflict*, 1984

261 SC Res. 425 and 426 of 19 March 1978, *UN Chronicle*, April 1978, 5–22; SC Res. S/12611, *ibid.*, 75–6. See I. Pogany, *The Arab League and Peacekeeping in the Lebanon*, 1987.

262 Cf. text above, 388, 419. This view is strengthened by the fact that para. 6 of SC Res. 521 of 19 September 1982 'insists that all concerned must permit UN . . . forces established by the Security Council in Lebanon to be deployed and to discharge their mandates and . . . calls attention to the obligations on all member States under Article 25 of the Charter to accept and carry out the decisions of the Council in accordance with the Charter' (text in *ILM* 21 (1982), 1169).

263 Cf. text above, 385–7.

264 On the right of peacekeeping units to use force in self-defence see Bothe, Peacekeeping, *op. cit.*, 589 *et seq.*

breach of the peace, or act of aggression). Unlike Chapter VII, the relevant provisions of Chapter VI do not authorize the Security Council to address orders to states, but that does not matter in the present context, because the resolution setting up the force in Cyprus was not phrased in mandatory terms. A more serious limitation to Chapter VI is that, interpreted literally, it does not authorize the Security Council to do anything; it merely empowers the Security Council to recommend states to do certain things. But, if the General Assembly could set up UNEF on the basis of Articles 11 or 14,[258] there is no reason why the Security Council should not set up a similar force on the basis of Chapter VI.

New forces in the Middle East

Further fighting broke out between Egypt and Israel in October 1973. The Security Council called for a ceasefire and set up a second United Nations Emergency Force (UNEF II) to supervise the ceasefire. Later, Egypt and Israel entered into two disengagement agreements, which provided that UNEF II should occupy a buffer zone between the Egyptian and Israeli forces, and should carry out periodic inspections to ensure that Egypt and Israel were complying with the terms of the disengagement agreements which limited the forces which each state was allowed to keep in the areas adjacent to the buffer zone.[259]

In May 1974 Israel entered into a disengagement agreement with Syria, under which Israel withdrew from some of the Syrian territory which it had occupied in 1967 and 1973, and the Security Council set up a Disengagement Observer Force (UNDOF), which performs the same type of functions as UNEF II performed under the disengagement agreements between Egypt and Israel.[260] But UNDOF consists of only about 1,050 men, compared with 7,000 in UNEF II.

In March 1978 Israel invaded Lebanon, as a reprisal against raids by Palestinian terrorists from Lebanon against Israel. The Security Council called on Israel to withdraw its forces from Lebanon, and decided 'to establish a United Nations Interim Force for Southern Lebanon (UNIFIL) for the purpose of confirming the withdrawal of Israeli forces, restoring international peace and security and assisting the government of Lebanon in ensuring the return of its effective authority in the area'.[261] Despite the presence of UNIFIL, fighting has continued in southern Lebanon between right-wing Lebanese Christians (armed and paid by Israel) and their Palestinian or Shiite opponents; each of these rival factions has attacked UNIFIL from time to time.

UNEF II, UNDOF and UNIFIL have many things in common. They were created by the Security Council, but the relevant resolutions and debates do not indicate which provisions of the Charter provided the legal basis for the Forces. One possibility is that the Forces were based on Article 40 of the Charter,[262] another possibility is that they were based on Chapter VI.[263] However, it is clear that all three of these Forces were intended to be peacekeeping forces; they were authorized to fight only in order to defend themselves,[264] and therefore UNIFIL did not try to resist Israel's second invasion of Lebanon in 1982. Each of the Forces was created originally for six months, and since then their mandates have been renewed by the Security Council for successive periods varying between three and twelve months; when the mandate of UNEF II expired for the last time in July 1979, it was not renewed because the Soviet Union had threatened to veto any attempt to renew it.[265] The Secretary-General appointed the Commander of each Force, with the consent of the Security Council, and selected contingents (from states willing to provide them) in consultation with the Security Council. The General Assembly decided that members of the United Nations were under a legal obligation to pay for the Forces, but the contributions which members were required to pay were based, not on the scale used for the ordinary budget, but on a special scale, which increased by more than 15 per cent the proportion which the permanent members of the Security Council were required to pay, and reduced by 80 or 90 per cent the proportion which the developing countries were required to pay; however, some states have refused to pay their contributions.[266] China, which had been one of the states refusing to pay contributions, announced at the end of 1981 that it would pay contributions for the Forces.[267]

New forms of peacekeeping after the Cold War

The 'old' forms of UN peacekeeping during the Cold War were aimed at avoiding further violence by trying to freeze the conflict, for example by observing a cease-fire line on the basis of a military mandate.[268] The UN presence in the field with military and civilian personnel focuses upon monitoring the implementation of agreements of cease-fires or the separation of forces, to help to promote a settlement of the conflict and/or to secure the delivery of humanitarian aid. Such operations always require the consent of the host state[269] and normally also of the other conflicting parties involved and they must be conducted in an impartial manner without favouring one side or the other.[270] The operation may consist of unarmed officers or of peacekeeping troops provided by UN member states, or of a combination of both, financed by the international community. Armed force may normally be used by UN peacekeeping forces only in self-defence.

In the first forty years of the existence of the UN, thirteen peacekeeping operations were launched; apart from the ones discussed above there were also missions concerning the conflict between India and Pakistan (UNMOGIP 1949; UNIPOM 1965–6), in West New Guinea (UNSF 1962–3), Yemen (UNYOM 1963–4), and the Dominican Republic (DOMREP 1965–6). After the end of the Cold War, between 1988 and 1994 alone, twenty-one new peacekeeping operations were undertaken by the UN, including conflict areas such as Afghanistan and Pakistan (UNGOMAP 1988–90), Iran and Iraq (UNIIMOG 1988–91), Iraq–Kuwait (UNIKOM 1991–), Angola (UNAVEM 1989–91; UNAVEM II 1991–5; UNAVEM III 1995–), Namibia (UNTAG 1989–90), Central America (ONUCA 1989–92), El Salvador (ONUSAL 1991–5), Cambodia (UNAMIC 1991–2; UNTAC 1992–3), Somalia (UNOSOM 1992–3; UNOSOM II 1993–5), Mozambique (ONUMOZ 1992–4), Uganda-Rwanda (UNOMUR, 1993–4), the Aouzou Strip (UNASOG 1994),

265 *IR* (May 1981), 1044–7.
266 See GA Res. 3101(XXVIII) of 11 December 1973 on UNEF operations, *UN Chronicle*, January 1974, 72–4; GA Res. S-8/2 on UNIFIL, 21 April 1978, *ibid.*, May 1978, 5–17, 44–8; GA Res. 33/14 on UNIFIL, *ibid.*, December 1978, 59–60; GA Res. 33/13 B, C, D, E and on UNEF and UNDOF, *ibid.*, January 1979, 73–4; GA Res. 34/9 and 34/166 on UNIFIL, GA Res. 34/7 A-D on UNEF and UNDOF, *ibid.* March 1980, 84–6.
267 GA Res. 36/116 A and B of 10 December 1981, *UNYb* 1981, 1298–300; *UN Chronicle* 19 (1982), no. 2, 61–2; *The Economist*, 5 December 1981, 52. On the development of the financing of peacekeeping see Bothe, Peacekeeping, *op. cit.*, 594 *et seq.*
268 N.J. Prill, Observers, *EPIL* 4 (1982), 60–2.
269 See Bothe, Peacekeeping, *op. cit.*, 597 *et seq.*
270 S. Vohra, Impartiality in United Nations Peace-Keeping, *LJIL* 9 (1996), 63–86.

271 See Ratner, *op. cit.*, 22.

272 See Chapter 11 above, 163.

273 *Basic Facts, op. cit.*, 28; G.S. Goodwin-Gill, *Free and Fair Elections: International Law and Practice*, 1994; W.M. Reisman, Preparing to Wage Peace: Toward the Creation of an International Peacemaking Command and Staff College, *AJIL* 88 (1994), 76; N.T. Vu, The Holding of Free and Fair Elections in Cambodia: The Achievement of the United Nations' Impossible Mission, *Mich. JIL* 16 (1995), 1177 *et seq.*

274 See Ramcharan, *op. cit.*

275 Boutros Boutros-Ghali, Empowering the United Nations, *FA* 3 (1992) at 93–4, noting, however, that although the operation would be deployed without the express consent of the parties, its basis would be a cease-fire agreement previously reached between them. See also his 'Agenda for Peace' suggesting 'peace-enforcement units', *ILM* 31 (1992) 956, at 966, para. 4; D. Leurdijk, *A UN Rapid Deployment Brigade*, 1995.

276 C. Tomuschat, Die Zukunft der Vereinten Nationen, *EA* 2 (1992), 42, at 46 *et seq.* See also E.G. Primosch, The Roles of United Nations Civilian Police (UNCIVPOL) within United Nations Peacekeeping Operations, *ICLQ* 43 (1994), 425.

277 *UN Chronicle*, 1996, no. 1, 39. See further L.J. Sise, Illusions of a Standing United Nations Force, *Cornell ILJ* 28 (1995), 645–8; D.J. Scheffer, United Nations Peace Operations and Prospects for a Standby Force, *ibid.*, 649–60; A. Morrison, The Theoretical and Practical Feasibility of a United Nations Force, *ibid.* 661–73; S. Telhami, Is a Standing United Nations Army Possible? Or Desirable?, *ibid.*, 673–84.

Western Sahara (MINURSO 1991–), Yugoslavia (see above), Georgia (UNOMIG 1993–), Liberia (UNOMIL 1993–), Haiti (see above), Rwanda (see above), and Tadjikistan (UNMOT 1994–).

The nature of recent peacekeeping operations has also changed. They still rest upon the consent of the parties, but often their purpose is to implement a settlement that has already been negotiated, as in the recent case of the peace agreement concerning Yugoslavia. Thus they are often part of an attempt to implement an agreed political solution of a conflict.[271] The mandate is still often predominantly military, but it may include a range of civilian tasks. Certain operations have focused upon the protection of civilians and the delivery of humanitarian aid. Such new forms of peacekeeping are much more complex. More actors are involved (guerrilla movements, regional organizations, NGOs and domestic parties) and the UN often has to play conflicting roles as executor, mediator and guarantor.

A special new task has developed with regard to election monitoring. Since the engagement of UNTAG in 1989 in Namibia where the UN monitored the whole electoral process, governments have requested such UN assistance in Nicaragua and Haiti (1990), Angola (1992), Cambodia (1993), El Salvador, South Africa and Mozambique (1994). The UN has also monitored the referendum in Eritrea (1993) on independence from Ethiopia.[272] An Electoral Assistance Division, which was created in 1992 within the UN Department of Peacekeeping Operations, has provided technical assistance in election issues to fifty-five states.[273]

Moreover, in recent years, emphasis has been laid on the concept of conflict prevention, because of the experience that once there is armed conflict between or within states, it is very difficult to restore peace, in particular, for the UN. 'Early warning' and 'preventive diplomacy', focusing on the internal situations of states (which is a problem because of the principle of state sovereignty) have become magic catchwords.[274] There are some new proposals by the UN Secretary-General which clearly go beyond traditional UN peacekeeping. They envisage not only more effective military protection of humanitarian operations against armed interference, but also the creation of UN 'ceasefire enforcement units' to be deployed without the express consent of the parties to a domestic conflict to enforce by military means the respect for a ceasefire agreement the parties have signed, but fail to honour.[275] Furthermore, there are attempts in recent UN practice which, in the sense of 'peacemaking' place much more influence on establishing or re-establishing governmental structures and law and order in a state.[276]

A new development has been to try to establish a 'rapid reaction capacity' of the UN in peacekeeping operations by inviting member states to make 'stand-by arrangements' with the United Nations (which are not to be confused with the special arrangements envisaged in Article 43 of the Charter concerning collective security measures) to make contingents of national troops and equipment available for peacekeeping operations. However, as of 31 October 1995, only forty-seven member states had made such a commitment, involving a total of 55,000 personnel.[277] Under the stand-by arrangements member states also retain their discretion whether or not to cooperate on a case-by-case basis. It is illustrative of the lack of true enthusiasm of member states to note that when in May 1994 the Security Council decided to enlarge the UNAMIR force in Rwanda,[278] not one of the nineteen states which at that time had made such stand-by arrangements agreed to contribute.

The demands of the new peacekeeping have overstretched the capacity of the United Nations both in quantitative and qualitative terms. This is quite apparent from the financial crisis of UN-peacekeeping showing that member states expect the UN to respond to the many conflicts in the world while at the same time they refuse to pay the financial contributions they owe to the organization.[279] The experience in Somalia, Rwanda and Yugoslavia, in view of the dangers involved for the safety of UN and associated personnel, has also led to the drafting of a special treaty in 1994.[280] But there is a more fundamental conceptual problem regarding the new forms of peacekeeping, peace making, peace-building and peace enforcement and humanitarian assistance. The approach suggested by the UN Secretary-General, in essence, abandons the requirement for clear prior agreements by the parties in the conflict to UN involvement.[281] Experience has shown that this creates a dangerous situation with regard to the operation of UN forces on the ground both with regard to the security of UN personnel as well as with respect to the effectiveness of the undertaking. 'Mixed peacekeeping' trying to incorporate enforcement elements confuses the different legal basis and functions of enforcement action, on the one hand, and peacekeeping, on the other. The two forms of UN action should remain clearly differentiated.[282]

Conclusion

After the end of the Cold War, it seemed that the Security Council was now able to make full use of its powers under Chapter VII, not only to repel external aggression, but also to pursue quite different goals, such as to intervene militarily in internal conflicts for humanitarian reasons and even to enforce democracy. As we have seen, the use of powers by the Security Council under Chapter VII has in fact gone much further than that, ranging from the determination of borders (Iraq–Kuwait),[283] the imposition of a disarmament scheme backed by comprehensive controls and sanctions against a state (Iraq),[284] and the creation of 'subsidiary bodies' of the Security Council to assess and administer claims for war damages (UN Compensation Commission for Claims Against Iraq),[285] to the prosecution of individuals for crimes (Yugoslavia and Rwanda Tribunals)[286] and the ordering of sanctions against a state for refusing to extradite persons accused of state-sponsored terrorism (concerning Libya in the *Lockerbie* case).[287] Furthermore, following the assassination attempt on the life of the Egyptian President Hosni Mubarak on 26 June 1995 at a conference in Addis Ababa, Ethiopia, acting under Chapter VII, the Security Council (Russia and China abstaining) adopted Resolution 1054 (1996) against Sudan, which was accused of supporting terrorism. Sudan's failure to extradite to Ethiopia three suspects wanted in connection with the assassination attempt[288] was found to constitute a 'threat to international

278 See text above, 405–7.
279 See Chapter 21 above, 378.
280 UNGA Res. 49/59 of 9 December 1994. See M.-C. Bourloyannis-Vrailas, The Convention on the Safety of United Nations and Associated Personnel, *ICLQ* 44 (1995), 560–90; E.T. Bloom, Protecting Peacekeepers: The Convention on the Safety of United Nations and Associated Personnel, *AJIL* 89 (1995), 621–30.
281 See Higgins (1995), *op. cit.*, 445–60, 450.
282 *Ibid.*, 459–60.
283 See Chapter 10 above, 151.
284 See text above, 396–8.
285 See text above, 398–9.
286 See Chapter 20 above, 355–60.
287 See Chapter 18 above, 292, 293.
288 See the earlier Resolution 1044 (1996) of 31 January 1996.

289 See also UN *Chronicle*, 1996, no. 2, 55.

290 See Chapters 2, 23–6 and 19, 308 above.

291 The attempted definition of aggression by the United Nations General Assembly, adopted in 1974, has not brought more clarification, see Chapter 19 above, 320–2. At any rate, such subsequent attempts at definition do not have the same legal status as the Charter itself.

292 See, for example, the argument by Tesón, *op. cit.*, at 338 *et seq.*

293 On this point see Chapter 18 above, 292–3.

peace'. If Sudan failed to comply by 'one minute after midnight Eastern Standard Time on 10 May 1996', member states would be required to reduce the number and level of staff at Sudanese diplomatic missions and to restrict the movement within their territories of remaining Sudanese staff and entry into and transit through their territories of officials and members of the Sudanese Government and armed forces. In addition, international and regional organizations were called upon not to convene any conferences in Sudan.[289]

It has become clear from the above analysis that the Security Council enjoys wide discretion in deciding when to apply collective measures under Chapter VII of the UN Charter to preserve peace and security. In other words, a threat to the peace in the sense of Article 39 seems to be whatever the Security Council says is a threat to the peace, which is a political decision and, as a matter of principle, not easily subject to legal evaluation. This may seem startling, but it demonstrates political reality. The Covenant of the League of Nations obliged member states to apply sanctions against a member state which had resorted to war in violation of its obligations under the Covenant, but every member state was left to itself to decide whether another member state had resorted to war in violation of its obligations under the Covenant; and naturally different states reached different conclusions.[290] Article 39 of the United Nations Charter was intended to prevent a repetition of that state of affairs. The omission of definitions from the Charter is equally realistic; there is a danger that definitions of aggression will merely leave loopholes which will be exploited by future aggressors.[291]

However, especially with regard to the use of force under Chapter VII, this does not necessarily mean that the authority of the Security Council is unlimited and open to its complete political discretion.[292] The Security Council is also bound by the Charter and has to act within the law. It is therefore also subject to legal criticism for acting beyond its competence or violating well-established principles of international law. An entirely different question is whether a decision taken by the Security Council is procedurally subject to a formal legal review by another body, such as the International Court of Justice.[293]

Under Chapter VII the Security Council is empowered to adopt enforcement measures only if it determines that there is a threat to the peace, breach of the peace or an act of aggression. This refers to *international* peace and security. Apart from the special case in which Article 39 might be applied to the oppression of a 'people' exercising its right of self-determination, the question has emerged whether internal conflicts and the domestic gross violation of human rights can be considered as constituting at least a threat to international peace or affecting international security, or whether there must be at least some relevant external aspect with transboundary effect for the right to impose enforcement measures, in particular authorizing the use of force under Article 42.

Indeed, we have seen that there is a tendency in the practice of the Security Council to relate internal conflicts and especially human rights violations to international peace and security. The analysis of the practice of the Security Council shows that its authority to authorize the use of force under Chapter VII is not limited to cases of military aggression, or military threats to international peace and security. To intervene by force in a human emergency within a member state, whether or not there are external effects, can be brought within the scope of Chapter VII, if the circumstances are such as in Somalia or Rwanda and the government structure in the member state has collapsed. If there are transboundary effects of a human emergency, such as a large exodus of refugees, or other external aspects which threaten international peace and security and are determined as such under Article 39 by the Security Council, the case for applying forceful collective measures would seem even stronger. But as Resolution 688 (1991)[294] in the case of the Kurdish crisis shows, this conclusion is difficult to draw in cases where a government exists even if it is responsible for the problem. The case is evidence for the link between massive human rights violations to international peace and security in general, but not for the specific application of force under Chapter VII. The case of Yugoslavia has only delivered an example of a rather limited, and largely ineffective, authorization of the use of force by the Security Council to protect humanitarian relief operations.

While the effectiveness that had been apparently regained by the Council in the post-Cold War phase was originally hailed by many, some even euphorically expecting the dawn of a 'New World Order', recently more sober conclusions have come to the forefront,[295] although there are still a number of authors who welcome the development as a chance to argue that the establishment of internal freedom, democracy and respect for human rights (in the Western sense) are 'the only morally defensible foundation of international law'.[296] The question is to what extent the collective security system as envisaged by the drafters of the Charter has really been revitalized, or whether this practice is actually something different, namely the use of the umbrella of the UN by Western powers, foremost among which is the United States, for operations conducted under their own command and control and for interests of their own.

Thus, questions have been raised, in particular, with regard to the Council's 'notorious selectiveness'.[297] Professor Matti Koskenniemi from Finland, for example, has asked:

> Why Libya, but not Israel? Why the Council's passitivity during most of the eight-year Iran-Iraq war? Why has the Council's reaction in Africa been markedly less vigorous and effective than in the Gulf? Why the discrepancy between the Council's forceful attack on Iraq (an Islamic country) and its timidity to defend the Muslims of Bosnia-Herzegovina? The choice of targets, as well as the manner of reacting, has certainly not been automatic. The argument is made that the Council has not reflected the collective interests of United Nations members as a whole, but only the special interests and factual predominance of the United States and its Western allies within the Council.[298]

Of course, the Security Council is not under a legal duty to act in each and every case. But such questions have been reinforced by the experience in various UN operations led by the United States that the role of the United Nations is in effect reduced to authorizing the use of

---

[294] See text above, 399–402.

[295] See the analysis by F.L. Kirgis, The Security Council's First Fifty Years, *AJIL* 89 (1995), 506–39.

[296] Tesón, *op. cit.*, 371. On human rights see Chapter 14 above. See further S.D. Bailey, *The UN Security Council and Human Rights*, 1995; N.M. Blokker/M. Kleibor, The Internationalization of Domestic Conflict: The Role of the UN Security Council, *LJIL* 9 (1996), 7–36.

[297] See Koskenniemi, *op. cit.*, 460; O. Russbach, *ONU contre ONU: Le Droit international confisqué*, 1994.

[298] Koskenniemi, *ibid.*, 460–1.

299 Quigley, *op. cit.*, 248–83, at 282–3.
300 See text above, 396.
301 Weston, *op. cit.*, 523–4.
302 See Chapter 21 above, 376–7, 379.
303 See Chapter 1 above, 3.
304 See Chapter 2 above, 25.

force, and thereby providing legitimacy to the action (and for claims to assistance and financial support from the international community), without having much say in, or meaningful control of, what happens on the ground. In a critical analysis of the use of the authorization technique used by the Council after the Cold War, Professor John Quigley concludes:

> Member states, and particularly the major powers, have not been willing to subordinate their actions to the organization and have insisted on retaining the free hand that the authorization technique affords. These states have, in effect, blackmailed the United Nations into accepting authorization. Their implicit message to the organization has been that it either accept authorization or stand by idly in the face of threats to the peace. If the Security Council succumbs to such blackmail, perhaps the fault lies less with the Council itself than with the states that pressure it . . . The Western powers, enjoying predominance in the Security Council, are in a position to secure the adoption of resolutions giving themselves a free hand to use military force.[299]

It is indeed illuminating to read what Professor Burns H. Weston has noted regarding the circumstances under which Resolution 678, authorizing the use of force against Iraq,[300] was adopted:

> To ensure the votes of the Latin American and African delegations (Colombia, the Côte d'Ivoire, Ethiopia, Zaire), the United States is said to have promised long-sought financial help and attention. To win reliable Soviet support, the United States, according to news accounts, agreed to help keep Estonia, Latvia, and Lithuania out of the November 1990 Paris summit conference, and it additionally pledged to persuade Kuwait and Saudi Arabia to provide Moscow, as they ultimately did, with the hard currency that Moscow desperately needs to catch up on overdue payments to commercial creditors. And, it is reported, to secure a 'voluntary' Chinese abstention in lieu of a threatened Chinese veto, the United States, disregarding a then-current crackdown on political dissidents, consented to lift trade sanctions in place since the Tiananmen Square massacre of pro-democracy protesters, to support a $114.3 million loan to China from the World Bank, and to grant a long-sought Washington visit by the Chinese Foreign Minister, since realized, and the resumption of normal diplomatic intercourse between the two countries. Not to be overlooked either is the 'reward' reportedly communicated to Yemen as a result of its opposition and negative vote: a cutoff of Washington's $70 million in annual aid.[301]

Such observations reflect reality and they tend to reinforce the argument that the structure and method of decision-making of the UN Security Council needs reform.[302] But one should perhaps not jump too easily to conclusions. The international legal system is decentralized,[303] composed of very unequal states in factual terms, and the interests of great powers simply cannot be discarded in any system of 'collective security', a concept which is in itself, for the same reasons, a dubious one, if it is associated on a too high level of abstraction with so-called 'communal interests'.[304] Such interests do exist among states, but they exist on different levels of intensity, depending on the degree of reciprocity involved. This degree is rather different in the fields of, for example, immunities accorded to diplomatic staff or in airline agreements, than in the much more vital and sensitive area of national and international security.

But that is only one side of the coin. The other side of the coin is that no state can be expected to act outside the limits of its national self-interest, as defined by its government. This can be clearly seen from the recent guidelines adopted by the United States stipulating the specific conditions, taking into account primarily the national interest, under which American forces may be committed to intervention in foreign countries, whether or not under the auspices of the UN.[305] Military intervention inevitably has human, financial and political costs, and elected governments cannot easily disregard their impact on the electorate, no matter how urgent an intervention to stop ongoing atrocities in a distant country may seem from an international and domestic moral or political perspective. Once dead bodies of soldiers start arriving back home, the media will make sure that the politicians will have to answer as to why the soldiers were sent there in the first place. If the national interest to intervene, however, is considered to be overriding, as in the case of the intervention of Western powers to repel the invasion and occupation of Kuwait by Iraq to protect the stability of the Middle East and its oil production, then such matters become secondary. It is not legal considerations, but rather material, political and strategic interests which primarily, if not often exclusively, govern such situations.

Many people, especially in Western countries, feel that the United Nations has achieved very little. Unfortunately, such people often have very exaggerated ideas about what the United Nations set out to achieve; they tend to imagine that the United Nations was intended to be a sort of embryonic world government. On the other hand, some politicians, especially when elections are pending, seem to see an advantage in overstating the actual power of the UN. For example, an article published in *Foreign Affairs* in 1996 (before the elections in America) by Senator Jesse Helms, the Chairman of the US Senate Committee on Foreign Relations, accused the UN of having usurped power from its member states and of threatening American interests, with the conclusion that '[t]he time has come for the United States to deliver an ultimatum: Either the United Nations reforms, quickly and dramatically, or the United States will end its participation.'[306] It is true that the provisions of the United Nations Charter concerning enforcement action give the United Nations one or two of the powers of a world government, and it is also true that those provisions have not worked well. But taking enforcement action is only one of the functions of the United Nations. The United Nations has had far more success in performing its other functions: economic and social cooperation, peaceful settlement of disputes, decolonization and the development of international law. These other functions have one thing in common: they involve cooperation by states, and not coercion by the United Nations. Indeed, experience shows that the United Nations achieves most when it works with the consent of states, rather than when it tries to work without their consent; United Nations peacekeeping forces, for instance, which operate with the consent of the states concerned, have been more successful than the United Nations' attempts to take enforcement action.

305 See Terry, *op. cit.*, 101–5; R.N. Haass, *Intervention: The Use of American Military Force in the Post-Cold War World*, 1994.
306 J. Helms, Saving the U.N. A Challenge to the Next Secretary-General, *FA* 75 (1996), 1–7, at 7.

307 On the current discussion in the UN see C.L. Willson, Changing the Charter: The United Nations Prepares for the Twenty-First Century, *AJIL* 90 (1996), 115–26. See also M. Bertrand, *The Third Generation World Organisation*, 1989; J.P. Renninger (ed.), *The Future Role of the United Nations in an Interdependent World*, 1989; J.W. Müller, *The Reform of the United Nations*, 2 vols, 1992; B. Urquhart, The United Nations: From Peace-Keeping to a Collective System?, *Adelphi Papers* 1992, no. 265, 18–29; E. Childers/B. Urquhart, *Renewing the United Nations System*, 1994; K.P. Sakensa, *Reforming the United Nations: The Challenge of Relevance*, 1993; W. Gordon, *The United Nations at the Crossroads of Reform*, 1994; A. Roberts/B. Kingsbury, *Presiding Over a Divided World: Changing UN Roles, 1945–1993*, 1994; T.G. Weiss/D.P. Forsythe/R.A. Coate, *The United Nations and Changing World Politics*, 1994; S. Hoffmann, Thoughts on the UN at Fifty, *EJIL* 6 (1995), 317–24; M. Koskenniemi, The Police in the Temple – Order, Justice and the UN: A Dialectical View, *ibid.*, 325–48; M. Bertrand, The UN as an Organization. A Critique of its Functioning, *ibid.*, 349–59; *The United Nations in its Second Half-Century*. A Report of the Independent Working Group on the Future of the United Nations, 1995; South Centre, *Whither the United Nations? A View from the South. Contribution to an Economic Agenda for the Non-Aligned Movement*, 1995; D.M. Snider/S.J.D. Schwartstein (eds), *The United Nations at Fifty: Sovereignty, Peacekeeping and Human Rights*, 1995; R. Righter, *Rosemary, Utopia Lost: The United Nations and World Order*, 1995; D. Bourantonis/J. Wiener (eds), *The United Nations in the New World Order: The World Organization at Fifty*, 1995. See also Chapter 21 above, 376–7, 379, 381–2.

Obviously, states would cooperate with one another to some extent even if there were no United Nations. But the existence of the United Nations increases the readiness of states to cooperate with one another; debates and votes at the United Nations exert political influence, which often induces the minority to act in accordance with the wishes of the majority. For instance, the colonial powers would probably not have granted independence to their colonies so quickly, or on such a wide scale, if it had not been for the political influence exerted by and through the United Nations.

In the final analysis, the effectiveness of the United Nations depends on the willingness of member states to cooperate, and no amount of changes in the structure of the United Nations[307] will guarantee its effectiveness unless member states are willing to cooperate with the United Nations and with one another. To a large extent, the United Nations is a mirror of the world in which we live, and there cannot be a perfect United Nations in an imperfect world.

Table of cases

Table of treaties, declarations and other documents

Index